The PUBLIC RECORDS of the COLONY of CONNECTICUT

PRIOR TO THE UNION WITH NEW HAVEN COLONY, MAY 1665

TRANSCRIBED AND PUBLISHED (IN ACCORDANCE WITH A RESOLUTION OF THE GENERAL ASSEMBLY,) UNDER THE SUPERVISION OF THE SECRETARY OF STATE,

WITH OCCASIONAL NOTES, AND AN APPENDIX

VOLUME 1

J. Hammond Trumbull

COR. SEC. CONN. HIST. SOCIETY; COR. MEMB. N. YORK HIST. SOCIETY, ETC.

HERITAGE BOOKS
2011

HERITAGE BOOKS
AN IMPRINT OF HERITAGE BOOKS, INC.

Books, CDs, and more—Worldwide

For our listing of thousands of titles see our website
at
www.HeritageBooks.com

A Facsimile Reprint
Published 2011 by
HERITAGE BOOKS, INC.
Publishing Division
100 Railroad Ave. #104
Westminster, Maryland 21157

Originally published 1850

At a General Assembly of the State of Connecticut, holden at Hartford, in said State, on the first Wednesday of May, in the year of our Lord, one thousand eight hundred and forty-nine:

Resolved, That the Secretary of State be authorized to purchase for the use of the State, two hundred and fifty copies of a publication of the Public Records of the Colony of Connecticut, prior to the union with New Haven colony, under the Charter of 1662. *Provided*, that such publication shall be made with the approval, and under the supervision of the Secretary, and shall be authenticated by his official certificate as a true and literal copy of the original record; *and provided also*, that the expense of the same shall not exceed two dollars per copy; and that the literal copy of the original record, above specified, be deposited with the Secretary of State, for the use of the State.

Resolved, That the copies so purchased be distributed by the Secretary, as follows: on copy to the town clerk of each town in this State, to be preserved in his office, for the use of the town; one copy to the Governor and to each of the State Officers of this State; one copy to the Governor of each of the several states and territories, of the United States; one copy to the library of Congress; and the remainder of said two hundred and fifty copies, to be deposited in the office of the Secretary of State, subject to the disposal of the General Assembly.

— Publisher's Notice —
In reprints such as this, it is often not possible to remove blemishes from the original. We feel the contents of this book warrant its reissue despite these blemishes and hope you will agree and read it with pleasure.

International Standard Book Numbers
Paperbound: 978-1-55613-669-6
Clothbound: 978-0-7884-8622-7

PREFACE.

The early annals of a State require no formal introduction to the descendants of its founders. If the transcriber have well accomplished the task which a love of the olden time impelled him to undertake, and which the liberality of the Legislature supplied, in part, the means of prosecuting, no doubt can exist as to the favorable reception of the volume now presented to the citizens of Connecticut. The value which may attach to it must, of course, mainly depend upon the degree of confidence entertained in its accuracy as a 'true, full and literal copy of the original Record.' The professions or assurances of the transcriber, could do little to impart such confidence; nor could they give additional weight to the certificate of official authentication, or to such *internal* evidence of reliability as, it is hoped, a careful perusal of the volume may supply.

A notice of the condition and arrangement of the original records, and of the plan adopted by the transcriber in the construction of this work, may not, however, be deemed inappropriate.

The *first* volume of the Colony Records is in three parts, originally bound in as many separate volumes. The first of these consists of the records of the General and Particular Courts, commencing with the session held at Newtown, (Hartford,) April 26th, 1636, (by the magistrates commissioned by Massachusetts, to 'govern the people at Connecticut,'*) and closing with the December session of the Court of Magistrates, 1649. Next following, (separated by a few blank pages from the Court Records,) are the records of Wills

---

* The commission "to severall persons, to govern the people at Connecticutt for the space of a year [then] next coming," was granted by the General Court of Massachusetts, March 3d, 1635(6,)—after consultation with John Winthrop, then lately "appointed governor by certain noble personages and men of quality, interested in the said River, which are yet in England." The commissioners named were Roger Ludlow Esq., William Pincheon Esq., John Steele, William Swaine, Henry Smith, William Phelps, William Westwood and Andrew Ward. See the commission, at length, in Hazard's State Papers, Vol. 1, p. 321.

PREFACE.

and Inventories. The remainder of the volume contains Grants and Conveyances of Lands, by towns and individuals, some of which are of as recent date as 1702; the greater part, however, having been transcribed from the several town records, between 1662 and 1690. These have not been included in the present publication, the proposed limits of which would not admit of their insertion, and the omission being regarded of the less importance, as copies of most of them are to be found elsewhere, and as the interest which attaches to them is mainly local or personal. Six pages of recognizances and bonds for prosecution, of various years, entered at the beginning of the volume, preceding the first page of the Court records, have likewise been omitted, in publication.

The *second* volume contains the records of the General Court from February, 1650, to October, 1669;—and at the other end of the book, separately paged, is recorded the Code of 1650, with such additional orders 'of general concernment,' as were, from time to time, passed by the General Court.

The second volume of the records of the Particular Court, or Court of Magistrates, comprising a period of about thirteen years, (from January, 1650, to June, 1663,) and including the Probate Records, long since disappeared from the Secretary's Office, and is supposed to be irrecoverably lost. The third volume, commencing June, 1663, and containing, at one end, such Wills and Inventories as were brought for record between that date and Sept. 1677, was, some years since, rebound, and lettered, "PROBATE RECORDS, VOL. III.—COUNTY COURT."

In transcribing the first volume for the press, occasional changes of its arrangement have been deemed advisable, for the purpose of facilitating reference, and to preserve chronological sequence. Thus, the Constitution of 1639, has been transposed from the end of the volume, to its proper place, preceding the record of the April Court :* the wills and inventories recorded prior to 1644, have been brought together, at the end of the Court Records, and placed with others subsequently recorded :† the records of such sessions of the Court as were entered by the Secretary after others of subsequent date, have been restored to their proper order. These, with other similar changes, have been made with less hesitation, from the fact that the paging of the original has been carefully retained, at the side of each printed page.

---

* Pages 20–26. † See note, on page 442.

PREFACE.

The names of magistrates and deputies, and of jurors in the several courts, are, in the original, recorded on the margins of the pages. To retain this arrangement, in the printed copy, would have been, on many accounts, inconvenient. The names of the members of the court have therefore been placed, in double columns, at the commencement of each session.

While the orthography of the original has been preserved throughout, it has not seemed necessary to adhere as closely to the anomalous *punctuation*, or the use of *capital letters*, practised by the early recorders. To have done so would have increased the difficulties of perusal and materially detracted from the interest of the volume to the general reader. Yet the liberty taken in these particulars has been cautiously used, and in all cases where the sense of the original could be affected by the change of position or interpolation of a comma or period, the record has been printed precisely as originally punctuated.

The more common abbreviations employed in the work, require no explanation. Nor will it be necessary to inform those who are at all conversant with old manuscripts, that a single m or n, with a circumflex or dash above it, (m̃ or ñ) was frequently substituted for the *double* consonant;—or that the same mark placed above a *vowel* indicated the omission of the consonant, (usually m or n,) immediately following; (as *frō* for *from*, *tiō* for *tion*, at the end of a word.)

Where portions of the original are wholly or in part obliterated, the missing words (when obviously indicated by the context,) have been supplied by the transcriber. Such words are, in all cases, included *in brackets*. If the word to be supplied has seemed at all *doubtful*, or if the record could possibly have admitted of a different reading, the portion in brackets has been *italicized* or is followed by a mark of interrogation. In a few instances, where a slip of the recorder's pen has occasioned an evident error in the original, the correction has been suggested in a foot note, or indicated by an italicized word, placed in brackets, with an interrogation mark.

In two instances only, slight changes have, for obvious reasons, been made in the language of the record. In one case, (on page 55,) a few words, (in brackets,) have been substituted, as of less exceptionable phraseology than the original : in the other, (on page 157,) the omission of a line is indicated by a note at the foot of the page.

Such extracts from the Records of the United Colonies as have been occasionally introduced in the notes and appendix, have been made from the manuscript (cotemporary) copy preserved in the Secretary's Office. Numerous errors, especially in dates and names, occur in the copy of these records published in the second volume of Hazard's State Papers,—to which publication, however, it has in some cases been found convenient to refer, by page.

When the publication of this volume was first proposed by the transcriber, and at the time of securing a legislative appropriation for its encouragement, an accurate copy of the original was all that was contemplated. In the course of publication, however, the liberty has been taken of introducing an occasional note, explanatory or illustrative of the text,—and a number of interesting historical documents, not previously published, have been included in an Appendix. Two Indexes, of names and subjects, have also been prepared, which, if less copious and complete than the antiquarian or genealogist could wish, it is hoped may in some degree facilitate their researches, and aid the general reader to refer to the contents of the volume. Fac-similes of the autographs of members of the first Court of Election under the Constitution of 1639, and of Magistrates chosen at the Union of the Colonies, in 1665, have been prepared with all possible care and accuracy, from originals collected in part from early files in the State Department, and in part from the town records of Hartford, Wethersfield and Windsor. Fac-similes of portions of the original records, in the hand writing of each of the secretaries* who held office prior to the Union, have also been introduced. These additions, and the consequent increase of the cost of publication, will account for the advance upon the original subscription price, at which the remainder of the edition is offered to non-subscribers.

However imperfectly the task of the transcriber may have been accomplished, it is hoped that succeeding Legislatures may not thereby be deterred from lending their aid to the prosecution of a work, already too long delayed, of which this volume is to be regarded only as the commencement ;—that of giving to the public, in

---

* A reference (upon the fac-simile, facing page 9,) to John Steel, as 'Secretary' of the colony, from 1636 to 1639, may require a word of explanation,—as his appointment to that office is no where mentioned in the record. A comparison of the first pages of the Colony Records with the early records of Hartford and Farmington, during the period Mr. Steel was recorder of those towns, leaves no doubt of the identity of the hand writing. The chirography of Mr. S. was somewhat *peculiar* (as may be seen by inspection of the fac-simile of an unusually legible specimen of it,) and cannot well be mistaken. The first four, part of the fifth, and the tenth pages of the first volume are in this hand. Pages six to nine, inclusive, are in a different, and far more legible hand,—possibly that of Mr. Clement Chaplin, whom Dr. Trumbull concludes (in Hist. of Conn., 1. 95,) to have been "the first secretary." There are, however, upon all of these pages, occasional interlineations and additions, in the hand writing of Mr. Steel.

PREFACE.

a permanent form, and thus securing the preservation of all the early records of the Colony, prior to 1700,—together with such cotemporary documents of historical value or interest, as are preserved in the State Department. These latter constitute a large portion, indeed, almost all that yet remains to us, of the documentary history of the colony for the first half century succeeding its settlement. Of comparatively few of them are copies, even in manuscript, extant,— and the loss or injury of the originals would therefore be utterly irreparable. And yet, whatever precautions may be taken to ensure their preservation, by placing them beyond the reach of ordinary accident, no care can enable them much longer to withstand the ravages of time. As the ink fades and the paper crumbles, the work of transcribing not only becomes more difficult, but leads to less accurate and reliable results. Whatever is to be done to perpetuate these early annals of our state and memorials of its founders, should be done soon.

J. H. T.

Hartford, March 1st, 1850.

CONTENTS.

	PAGE
Records of the General and Particular Courts, from April, 1636, to December, 1649, [from Vol. I., pp. 1-209.]	1
Records of the General Court, from Feb., 1650, to May, 1665, [from Vol. II., pp. 1-205.]	204
Record of Wills and Inventories, 1640 to 1649,—[from Vol. I.]	442
Code of Laws, established by the General Court, May, 1650,	509
Certificate of the Secretary of State,	554

Appendix:

No. I. Letter from Sir Wm. Boswell, relating to encroachments of the Dutch, ... 565

No. II. The articles of combination with Southampton, (L. I.) 566

No. III. Respecting the agreement with Mr. Fenwick, . 568

No. IV. The claims of Massachusetts to the Pequot country, 570

No. V. Letter from Connecticut to Easthampton, . . 572

No. VI. Respecting the settlement of accounts with Capt. John Cullick, ... 573

No. VII. Abstract of the will of George Fenwick, . . . 574

No. VIII. Letter to the Comm'rs of the U. Colonies, complaining of affronts received from the Narragansetts, . 576

No. IX. Letters from Mr. William Goodwin, respecting Gov. Hopkins' Legacy, ... 578

No. X. Instructions to Gov. Winthrop, agent for procuring the Charter; Address to the King; and Letter to the Earl of Manchester, ... 579

No. XI. Petition of Mrs. Elizabeth Cullick, to the General Court, 1663, ... 585

No. XII. List of documents relating to the Union with New Haven, ... 586

Index of Names, ... 591
General Index, ... 597

COLONIAL RECORDS.

[VOLUME I.]

[1] A CORTE HOLDEN ATT NEWTON 26 APR. 1636.

Roger Ludlowe Esqr.,   Mr. Westwood,
Mr. Steele,   Mr. Warde.
Mr. Phelpes,

It was now complayned y^t Henry Stiles or some of the ser-[vants] had traded a peece wth the Indians for Corne. It is ordered y^t [the] saide Henry Stiles shall, betweene & the next Cort, regaine [the] saide peece from the saide Indians in a faire & legall waye, or els this Corte will take it into further consideracõn.

It is ordered y^t from henceforth none y^t are wthin the Jurisdic[tion] of this Cort, shall trade wth the natiues or Indians any peece or pistoll or gunn or powder or shott, vnder such heavie penalty as vppon such misdemeanor the Corte shall thinke meete.

Constables sworne, for Dorchester, Newtowne & Watertowne, for this next yeere and vntill newe be chosen, are Henry Walcott for Dorchester, Samuell Wakemã for Newtowne & Daniell Finch for Watertowne.

Whereas there be divers strange Swine in the seu^{r}all plantacõns y^t their owners are not knowen & yet doe & are likelie to Comitt many trespasses. It is therefore ordered y^t the saide plantacõns shall forthwth take notice of them & their markes, & giue speedy notice amonge the plantacõns both of them & their m^{r}kes & if in a fortenight noe owners come forth then the saide plantacõns or plantacõn where such Swine are, may appraise them att a value & sell them & take the money to some publicke vse of the saide plantacōn, vnlesse their doe w^{th}in one whole yeere after app^r a true owner & then the money it was sould for is to be restored, p^riuded alwaies y^t when the owner app^r before the money or Swine be redeliu^red there be deducted such Somēs & Chardges & trespasses as haue beene comitted & expended in & aboute him or them.

It is likewise ordered if any Swine stray from oute their owne Plantacōn into another they shalbe subiect [to] the orders y^t are there made concerninge Swine.

Whereas there was a dismission granted by the C[hurch] of Waterton in the Masachusetts, dated 29th of Ma[ ] last to Andrewe Warde, Jo: Sherman, Jo: Stickland, Rob'te Coo, Rob'te Reynold & Jonas Weede, wth intent to forme a newe in a Ch: Coveññte in this River of Conectecott, the saide p^rties haue soe accordingly done wth the publicke allowance of the rest of the members of the saide Churches, as by certificate nowe p^rduced app^{rs}. It is therefore in this p^rsent Cort ratified & confirmed, they p^rmissing shortlie publicquely to renewe the [said] Coveññte vppon notice to the rest of the Churches.

A Corte held att Dorchester, June 7th, 1636.

  Mr. Ludlowe, Mr. Westwood,
  Mr. Steele,   Mr. Warde.
  Mr. Phelpes,

Whereas, the last Corte Henry Stiles was ordered to regaine [a] peece he had traded wth the Indians wch doth not app^r that he hath done, It is ordered that a warr^t shalbe directed to him to p^rforme the same by the next Cort & and then p^rsonally to app^r [&] answere his neglect.

It is ordered y^t there shalbe a sufficient Watch maynte[ined] in every towne & y^t the Constable of each Towne shall d[uly] warne the same & see y^t the inhabitants or residents doe seu^rally in their Turne observe the same accordinge as [the] Inhabitants doe agree, wch said watch shall begin & end w^n the Courte or magistrates shall thinke meete.

It is ordered y^t Samuell Wakeman & Geo: Hubberd shall [survey] the breadth of the plantacōn of Dorchester howe farre [it] shall extend aboue Mr. Stiles & shall certifie vnto the [next] Corte their pʳceedinges herein to th' end it may be then confirmed, and yᵗ they shall haue from the saide Towne satisfaccōn for their paines. And the saide Samuell Wake[man] shall doe the like for Watertowne in their bredth toward [the] mouth of the River & have the like satisfaccōn. And this done wᵗʰout faile before the next Corte vppon peine [of] 40ᵗⁱᵉ shillinges of each heade yᵗ shall faile therein.

It is ordered that every souldier in each plantacōn shall haue in his howse in a readines before th' end of August next twoe pounde of powder, & yᵗ they shall shew it to the Constable whenever he shall call them vnto it vppon the penalty of X*s.* for every failure wᶜʰ is presentlie to be le[vied] by the saide Constable wᵗʰout [resistance] as alsoe 20 bul[letts] of leade in the like readines vppon the same penalty and in the same manner to be levied.]

---

[2]   A Corte held att Watertowne 1º 7ᵇʳ, 1636.
   Roger Ludlowe Esqʳ., Mr. Wm. Phelps,
   Mr. Jo: Steele,   Mr. Wm. Westwoode,
   Mr. Wm. Swaine,   Mr. Andr: Warde.

It is ordered yᵗ the order concerninge Powder & Bulletts, of the 7ᵗʰ of June last be nowe pʳsentlie published in the seuʳall plantacōns & yᵗ there be respite given vntill th'end of this instant moneth & then to be putt in execucōn wᵗʰout faile.

Whereas there was tendered to vs an Inventory of the estate of Mr. Jo: Oldā wᶜʰ seemed to bee somewhat vncerteinely valued, wee therefore thinke meete to, & soe it is ordered, that Mr. Jo: Plum̄ & Rich: Gildersleeue togeather wᵗʰ the Constable shall survey the saide Inventory and pʳfect the same before the next Corte & then to deliuʳ it into the Corte.

It is ordered yᵗ Thurston Rayner as he hath hitherto done soe shall continue to looke to & pʳserue the Corne of Mr. Oldā & shall inn* the same in a seasonable tyme & shall bringe an Accompt the next Cort what quantitie there is of it as alsoe of his labor & then the Cort will out of the same allott vnto him soe many bushells as shalbe reasonable for his paines &

---

*Inn; to house, to put under cover. *Webster.*

labor. And in the meane if he hath vse of some for his owne spendinge to take some wch shalbe then deducted out of what wilbe due to him. And then the Cort will give finall order concerninge the same.

It is ordered y^t every plantacõn shall traine once in every moneth, & if vppon complainte of their military officer it app^r that there bee divers very vnskilfull the sayde plantacõn may appointe the officer to traine oftener the saide vnskillfull. And y^t the saide military officer take veiwe of their seu^rall Armes whether they be seruiceable or noe. And for default of every souldiers absent the absent to paye 5s. for every tyme w^thout lawfull excuse w^thin 2 dayes after tendered to the Com^rs or one of them in the saide plantacõn. And for any default in Armes vppon warnings to them by the saide officer to amend the same & a tyme sett & if not then amended by the tyme appointed, 1s. every tyme. And where Armes are wholly wantinge to be bounde over to answere it at the next Corte.

Whereas it app^red by a wrytinge vnder hand of Mr. Oldā that twoe of the mares y^t are nowe seized vppon by Daniell Finch Constable of Watertowne, as Mr. Oldames goodes, are the goodes of Mr. Tho: Allen. And therefore it is ordered that the said mares shalbe deliu^red to the saide Mr. Allen into his owne possession or his assignes.

It is ordered by consent of S^rieant Seely pl^t against the inhabitants of the Towne of Watertowne def^ts, y^t a Jurer shalbe w^thdrawen, and y^t the def^ts doe vndertake to p^rduce an order wherein they will make it app^r y^t it was ordered y^t if the inhabitants of the saide Towne did not remoue wth their Families to Conectecott by th' end of this instant moneth or els there was noe p^rpriety due to them in the devident of the landes of the saide Towne & y^t the hand or the consent of the saide Willm̄ Bassum is herevnto. And if the saide order be not p^rduced here to the Corte by the 2^d Cort after this the Inhabitants are to pay the pl^te damages.

The first of November, 1636.

S^rieant Seely pl^te.
Inhabitants of Watertowne def^ts.
The Jury finde for the pl^te that hee is to have as an adven-

turer & as a man that was in the Condicõn that Bassam vnder whom he claymed was in.

 Guilford, June 16: 1665.*
 This is to certify unto all whom it may concerne, that vpon his certaine knowledge, by the advice of the Court, Wethersfeild men gaue so much unto Sowheag as was to his sattisfaction for all their plantations lyeing on both sides the great Riuer, wth the Islands, viz. six miles in bredth on both sides the Riuer, & six miles deep from the River westward, and three miles deep from the Riuer eastward. Thus testifyeth George Hubbard.   By me George Hubbard.
 Taken upon oath Before me Willm Leete;
 This is a true coppy of the originell being examined & compared therewith this 18 of May, 1667, p^r me
John Allyn: Secret'y.

---

[3]   A Corte held att Newe Towne 8^{br} 4to, 1636.

   Mr. Ludlowe,   Mr. Phelpes,
   Mr. Swaine,   Mr. Westwoode,
   Mr. Steele,   Mr. Warde.

It is ordered that a Warrant be directed to Daniell Finch to sumõn Rich: Gildersleeue to app^r the next Corte or other meetinge of the Com^{rs} to bringe in an Inventory of Mr. Oldames estate wch was sometyme in his handes as alsoe to sumõn any other to app^r that hath in his handes or canne declare where any of th' estate of the saide Mr. Oldā is y^t is not as yet revealed.

 A Corte held att Newe Towne 1o Novemb^r, 1636.

   Mr. Ludlowe,   Mr. Phelps,
   Mr. Pyncheon,   Mr. Westwoode,
   Mr. Swaine,   Mr. Warde.
   Mr. Steele,

 It is ordered that S^{r}ieant Seely shall betweene this & the next Corte consider of such noates & Inventories as haue come to his handes or knowledge concerninge the estate of

---

* This certificate, is inserted at the foot of the 2d Page of the original, in the hand writing of Mr. Allyn.

Mr. Oldam & then deliuer them into the Corte vppon oath & in the meane to p^rduce any noate or Inventory to Mr. Swayne & Mr. Warde that he hath or cann come by y^t may make for the furtherance of the discouery of the estate of the saide Mr Oldā, to th' end the Cort may then p^rceede in y^t business as they shall see cause.

It is ordered y^t S^rieant Stickland is to haue for 7 days seruice to the Rivers mouth, aboute Cattle of Mr. Michell & the lo : or their Agents, 21s. The rest y^t went in the same seruice 14s. a peece, every Plantacõn to defray the chardge of their owne men for the p^rsent & y^t the constables shall make a rate to that purpose.

It is ordered that Mr. Clement Chaplin shall take into his Custody the goodes of Mr. Oldam deceased, according to an Inventory in Corte & in the Custody of Daniell Finch & he the saide Mr. Chaplin is to be responsiue for them as the Corte shall thinke meete, & if the saide Mr. Chaplin thinke meete he may sell them or any of them.

It is ordered y^t Jo : Reeues is to retorne to his M^r, Mr. Stiles whoe hath his Indenture & the saide Mr Stiles is to pay Willm̄ Quicke 15s. for his passage, if not the C[orte] will take order in the same as they shall see meete.

A Corte at New Towne 27 Decr. 1636.

Mr. Ludlowe,   Mr. Westwoode,
Mr. Swaine,   Mr. Phelps,
Mr. Steele,   Mr. Warde.

It is ordered y^t Daniell Finch shall haue for sixe dayes imploym^t about Mr. Oldames estate & a Corte 13s.—6.

It is ordered y^t Mr. Clement Chaplin shall diligentlie inquire after any the goodes of Mr. Oldam deceased & if there bee any p^rson or p^rsons y^t he can finde y^t hath or hadd any of the saide goodes in his handes & will not deliu^r the same nor an Inventory of them he may sum̄on him or them to app^r the next Corte to answere the same.

It is ordered y^t all the Creditors of Mr. Oldā in the River of Conectecott bringe in their debts before the next Corte or e[ls] he shall not be deemed as a Crediter in th' estate that is now extant.

21 Febr. 1636.

Mr. Ludlowe,   Mr Phelps,
Mr. Steele,   Mr. Westwoode,
Mr. Swaine,

Whereas it was ordered y^t Samuel Wakeman, Geo: Hubbert, & Anncient Stoughton were to consider of the boundes of Dorchester towarde the Falls & of Watertowne towards the mouth of the River; The saide Samuell Wakeman & [Geo:] Hubberd thinkes meete y^t the plantaĉon of Dorchester shall extend towards the Falls, on the same side the plantaĉon standes, to a Brooke called Kittle Brooke & soe over the greate River vppon the same line that Newe Towne & Dorchester doth betweene them. And soe it is ordered by the Corte.

It is ordered that the plantaĉon nowe called Newtowne shal be called & named by the name of Harteford Towne, likewise the plantaĉon now called Watertowne shalbe called & named Wythersfeild.

Samuell Wakeman & Ancient Stoughton doe thinke meete that the boundes of Wythersfeild shalbe extended toward the Rivers mouth in the same side it standes in to a Tree sixe miles downeward from the boundes between them & Harteford [marked wth] N: F: & to [runn in an east] & west line, [& over] the great River, the saide Wythersfeild to begin att [4] the mouth of Pewter pott Brooke & there to runn due east into the Countrey 3 miles & downeward sixe miles in breadth, wch is ordered accordingly.*

It is ordered y^t the plantaĉon called Dorchester shalbee called Windsor.

The boundes betweene Weathersfeild & Harteford are agreed on the side wherein they stand to be att a Tree m^{r}ked N: F: & to wch the Pale of the saide Harteford is fixed, to goe into the

---

* The words in brackets, (now illegible in the original Record) are here supplied from a certified copy of this and the next preceding order, made in 1708. Towns & Lands, Vol. iv. Doc. No. 1.

Countrey due east & on the other side of the greate River from Pewter pott Brook att the lower side of Hocannō due east into the Countrey, wch is nowe ordered accordingly.

The boundes betweene Harteford & Windsor is agreed to be att the vpper end of the greate meadowe of the saide Harteford toward Windsor att the Pale that is nowe there sett vpp by the saide Harteford wch is abuttinge vppon the great River vppon a due east line & into the Countrey from the saide Pale vppon a due west line as paralell to the saide east line as farr as they have now paled & afterward the boundes to goe into the Countrey vppon the same west line. But it is to be soe much shorter towards Windsor as the place where the Girte that comes alonge att th' end of the saide meadowe & falls into the saide greate River is shorter then their Pale & over the saide greate *Riuer the saide Plantacōn of Windsor is to come to the Riveretts mouth that falls into the saide greate River of Conectecott and there the saide Harteford is to runn due east into the Countrey, wch is ordered accordingly.

It is ordered y^t noe yonge man y^t is neither maried nor hath any servaunte, & be noe publicke officer, shall keepe howse by himself, w^thout consent of the Towne where he liues first had, vnder paine of 20s. p^r weeke.

It is ordered y^t noe M^r of a Family shall giue habitacōn or interteinment to any yonge man to soiourne in his family, but by the allowance of the inhabitants of the saide Towne where he dwelles vnder the like penalty of 20s. p^r weeke. These 2 last orders to take effect the first of Aprill next.

Att a Cort att Harteford, M^rch 28th, 1637.

Mr. Ludlowe,	Mr. Steele,
Mr. Welles,	Mr. Phelps,
Mr. Swaine,	Mr. Warde.

It is ordered y^t Mr. Frances Stiles shall teach Geo. Chapple, Tho: Coop^r & Tho: Barber his servaunts in the trade of a Carpenter accordinge to his p^rmise for there s^rvice of their

---

* [In margin] The Riuerett on the other side by the Indians is called Podanke.

The 16th day of May 1637 There was delivered att Egerton
that there hath bene sold Egerton of Brawne of my servant for Egenorth
nosuly my horses go may horses out of 2 of 3 flight of one Barreston
30 nBoat for horses 8 : midow(n) out of Barreton on 9 42 m: nd or
may on 3 m : Boxford of the dor and 18 : nidsom(n) of the of horse fenne for
Hoghtrs Goo by the foot 3 Bushett mount on militarey: of Comones of
the romonts of the Bo to 978 my henry
the gurnering the fourth four the Earby Ands 14 ormenn in the
land or n : nine for
the monors soul Brow Zalbs h h good forers for 30 days tenne
a mile or or might bows to only 304 gallons of browngs water
the gallons of Beant

John Steel (Secretary, 1636-1639.)

terme behinde 4 dayes in a weeke onelie to sawe & slitt their owne worke that they are to frame themselves wth their owne hands togeather wth himself or some other M^r workmen, the tyme to begin for the p^rformance of this order 14 dayes hence w^thout faile.

It is ordered y^t every Juryman shall haue sixe pence for every acc̃on that is given to them vppon evidence, to bee paide by him the Acc̃on goes against.

THE FIRST DAY OF MAY, 1637, GEN^rALL CORTE ATT HARTEFORD.

 Mr. Ludlowe, Mr. Wells, Mr. Swaine, Mr. Steele, Mr. Phelps, Mr. Warde.

 Comittees.—Mr. Whytinge, Mr. Webster, Mr. Willm̃s, Mr. Hull, Mr. Chaplin, Mr. Talcott, Mr. Hosford, Mr. Mychell, Mr. Sherman.

It is ordered that there shalbe an offensiue warr ag^t the Pequoitt, and that there shalbe 90 men levied out of the 3 Plantac̃ons, Harteford, Weathersfeild & Windsor (vizt) out of Harteford 42, Windsor 30, Weathersfeild 18 : vnder the Com̃ande of Captaine Jo: Mason & in Case of death or sicknes vnder the Com̃and of Rob'te Seely Leift, & the'ldest S^rieant or military officer survivinge, if both these miscary.

It is ordered that Harteford shall send 14 Armour in this designe, Windsor 6.

It is ordered that there shalbe 1^hh of good beare for the Captaine & M^r & sick men, if there be only 3 or 4 gallons of stronge water, 2 gallons of sacke.

It is ordered that Windsor shall p^ruide 60 bushells of Corne, Harteford 84 bushells, Weathersfeild 36 bushells, of this each plantac̃on to bake in biskett the on half if by any meanes they cann, the rest in grounde meale. Weathersfeild tenn bushells to bee allowed vppon Accompt.

Harteford is to p^ruide 3 firkins of suett, 2 firkins of Butter, wth y^t att Rivers mouth, 4 bushells of Oatemeale, 2 bushells of Pease, 500 of fish, 2 bushells of salt; Weathersfeild 1 bushell of Indian Beanes; Windsor 50 peeces of Porke, 30^lb of Rice, 4 Cheeses.

It is ordered that every souldier shall cary wth him 1^{lb} pouder, 4^{lb} of shott, 20 bulletts; 1 barell of Powder from the Riuers mouth, [a light] Gunn if they cann.

[It is ordered] y^t Mr. Pincheons shallopp shalbe taken to be imployed [in this desi]gne.

---

[5] June 2^d, 1637. A General Corte att Harteford.

It is ordered y^t there shalbe sent forth 30 men out of the seu^{r}all plantac̃ons in this River of Conectecott to sett downe in the Pequoitt Countrey & River in place convenient to maynteine o^r right y^t God by Conquest hath given to vs, & Leiftenn^t Seely shall haue the Comande of them. The men are to be raised 14 out of Harteford, tenn out of Windsor, 6 out of Wytheresfeild.

It is ordered y^t 60 bushells of Corne shal be p^{r}uided for the designe aboues^d, Windsor 20, Harteford 28, Wythersfeild 12, 1^{hh} of Pease, 2 bushells of Oatemeale, 150 pounde of Beefe, 80^{lb} of Butter, (vizt) Windsor 30, Wythersfeild 30, Harteford 20, fish.

---

26 June, 1637, Harteford Gen^{r}all Corte.

It is ordered that 10 men more shalbe levied out of the plantac̃ons aforesaide to goe in the designe ag^t the Pequoitts as an adition to the form^r 30, (vizt) 5 out of Harteford, Windsor 3, Weathersfeild 2.

It is ordered y^t Mr. Haine & Mr. Ludlowe shall goe to the mouth of the River to treate & Conclude wth o^r frendes of the Bay either to joine wth their forces in p^{r}secutinge o^r designe against o^r enemies or if they see cause by aduise to interprise any Acc̃on accordinge to the force we haue. And to parle wth the bay aboute o^r settinge downe in the Pequoitt Countrey.

It is ordered y^t there shalbe 1 hogg p^{r}vided att Wythersfeild for the designe in hande, wch is conceiued to be Nathaniell Footes, 20^{lb} of Butter, half C of Cheese; Harteford 20^{lb} of Butter, half hundred of Cheese; Windsor 1 Ram goate, 20^{lb} of Butter, half C of Cheese, 1 gallon of stronge Water; Harteford 1 C of beefe from Mr. Whittinge, Windsor 3 bushells of mault, 2 from Wythersfeild, Mr. Wells 2.

HARTEFORD. GENERALL CORT, TUESDAY, Nov: 14th, 1637.

Mr. Haines, Mr. Ludlowe, Mr. Wells, Mr. Phelps, Mr. Swaine, Mr. Mychell, Mr. Hull, Mr. Whytinge, Capt : Mason, Mr. Warde, Goodman Smith, Goodmā Bacon.

It is ordered that every common souldier that went in the late designe against o^r enemies the Pequoites shall have 1s. 3d. p^r day for theire service at sixe dayes to the weeke, the Sergants 20d, p^r day, the Leiftenant 20s. p^r weeke, the Captn 40s. p^r weeke, any man that was publiquely imployed in the said service and dyet themselves shall have 2s. p^r day ; and that the saide payment shalbe for a moneth although in strictnes there was but three weekes and 3 dayes due ; such as did returne from the Forte and never went in the seruice to bee allowed but for 12 dayes.

It is ordered that the pay in the second designe shalbe the same with the former, and the tyme a month as abouesayde.

HARTEFORD.   9º FEBR. 1637.

Mr. Haynes, Mr. Ludlowe, Mr. Wells, Mr. Plum, Mr. Mychell, Capt : Mason, p^{r}sent.

Whereas vppon serious Consideracõn wee conceiue that the plantacõns in this River wilbe in some want of Indian Corne, And on the same Consideracõn wee conceiue if every man may be at liberty to trucke with the Indians vppon the River where the supply of Corne in all likeliwood is to bee had to furnish o^r necessities, the market of Corne amonge the Indians may be greatly advanced to the preiudice of these plantacõns, wee therefore thinke meete and doe soe order that noe man in this River nor Agawam shall goe vpp River amonge the Indians or at home at theire houses to trade for Corne or make any Contract or bargaine amonge them for corne either privately or publiquely vppon the paine of 5s. for every bushell that hee or they shall soe tr[ade] or contract for ; this order to endure vntill the next Generall Courte and vn[till] the Courte take other order to the contrary, and at the saide generall Courte there wilbe a setled order in the thing.

It is ordered that there shalbe a prticular Courte on the first Tuesday of M[ay] at Harteford, and that then Mr. Oldā businesses and John Jesopps are to be handled, therefore the severall Creditors are then to come and make their claime.

It is ordered that Mr. Clement Chaplin shalbe Treasurer for this next yeare to Collect and gather such Rates as are now to [6] be levied in the seve[rall] ‖ plantacōns, and that there shalbe vnder Collectors to whom the said Mr. Treasurer may direct his Warrants in every plantacōn, and that the said Treasurer may giue order to the said Collectors to pay the severall bills of theire plantacōns and give it in Accompte to the said Mr. Treasurer, and after the bills be paide to returne in the rest to the said Mr. Treasurer: the collectors are, for Harteford Willm̄ Wadsworth, Windsor Henry Wolcott the elder, and Andrew Warde for Wethersfeild and John Bur for Agawam.

It is ordered there shalbe forthwith a levey of sixe hundred and twenty poundes to be levied for to defray the charges of the late designes of warr that is already past, Aggawam 86l. 16s, Windsor 158l. 2s, Harteford 251l. 2s, Wethersfeild 124l. The payment to be made either in monney, in Wampum at fower a penny, or in good and marchantable beaver at 9s. p^r pounde.

It is ordered that there shalbe generall notice giuen in all the plantacōns that if there be any Arm^r, gones, swordes, belts, Bandilers, kittles, pottes, tooles, or any thinges els that belonges to the commonwealth, that were lost, landed or leafte in any plantacōns, they are to be delivered into the handes of the saide Constables of the said townes, and the said Constables to bring them to the next Courte at Harteford, and if after the said notice there be any thinges found in any mans house or custody, it concerning the said Commonwealth, they shalbe subiect to the sensure of the Courte for their*   tenure or concealing.

It is ordered y^t the generall Courte now in being shalbe dissolved and there is noe more attendance of the members thereof to be expected except they be newly chosen in the next generall Courte.

---

*This blank in the original.

8to die Mrtii, 1637.

A Genrall Cort houlden att Harteford.

Mr. Haines, Mr. Ludlowe, Mr. Pincheon, Mr. Welles, Mr. Plum, Mr. Phelpes, Mr. Mychell, Mr. Smith.

Committees: Capt: Mason, Mr. Hopkins, Mr. Steele, Mr. Talkott, Mr. Webster, Mr. Hull, Mr. Ford, Tho: Marshall, Adr: Warde, Geo: Hubberd, Jo: Gibbes. Thurston Raynr absent.

Thurston Raynor being chosen a Committee for the Towne of Wethersfeild being now absent is fined 1s, to be forthwith paide.

Whereas Mr. Pincheon was questioned aboute imprisoning an Indian at Aggawam, whipping an Indian and freeing of him, the Courte is willing to passe over Mr. Plumms failings against an Indian.

It is ordered with the consent of Mr. Pincheon that the saide Mr. Pyncheon will deliver att Harteford goods Marchantable Indian Corne att 5s. pr bushell as farr as 500 bushells will goe at, if hee can save by that, for the residue hee is to have 5s. 2d. pr bushell, provided also that that proporcon that Windsor is to have shalbe landed there at Mr. Ludlowes, for that proporcon that Wethersfeild is to have they are to fetch it att Harteford. In consideracon whereof the is a restrainte of any to goe vpp the River to trade with the Indians for Corne; as alsoe if any Indians bring downe any Corne to vs wee are not to exceede 4s. pr bushell; as alsoe in case of necessity that any family or familyes doe complaine of present necessities they are to repaire to 3 magistrates which may advise them for the supply, although it be to the dispensing with this order; prouided alsoe that if the said Mr. Pincheon bee inforced to raise the price with the Indians of sixe sixes of Wampom a pecke then the plantacons are to increase the pay of 5s. pr bushell, if he can abate any thing hee will sett of soe much of 5s. pr bushell. The payment to be made in wampom at 3 a penny or marchantable beaver at Xs. pounde.

9o die. It is ordered that whosoever doth disorderly speake privately during the sitting of Courte with his Neibour or twoe or 3 togeather, shall presently pay 1s, if the Courte soe thinke meete.

[7] It is ordered that Captaine Mason, Mr. Allen, Mr. Warde, shall go to Agawam and treate with the Indians of Waronocke concerning the tribute towards the charges of o^r warres, to the value of one Fatham of Wampom a man. Nawattocke a fatham and a quarter, Pacomtuckett one fatham and a quarter.

It is ordered y^t Mr. Ludlowe, Mr. Hopkins, Mr. Michaell shall have power to deale with Elias Parkman aboute his vessell to goe to the Narragansett to trade for Corne and they are likewise to take vpp such commodities as may freight the saide vessell to the end aforesaide, and doe therein what they shall see meete that may tend for the publique good in that way, and that the plantacõns shall beare the chardge of the saide Freight and have the proceede of the Corne and trade according to the proporcõn of the last publique rate to the warrs, as alsoe of what comes from Agawam.

It is ordered that noe Commissioners or other person shall binde, imprison or restraine, correct or whipp any Indian or Indians whatsoever in his owne case or in the case of any other, nor giue them any menacing or threatning speeches, exc[ept] it be in case any Indian or Indians shall assault or affront theire person or persons, or shall finde them either wasting, killing or spoiling any of theire goodes or estate, and he or they shall finde them soe doeing, and in that case if they refuse to come before a magistrate they may force them to goe and binde them if they refuse. But if any iniurie or trespasse be offered or done by any Indian or indians or their dogges, he or they are to complaine to some magistrate or magistrates, provided alwaies that any twoe magistrats togeather may vppon any speciall occasion send for any Indian or Indians to come before them and if they see cause to restraine or imprison him or them and in case of refusall or contumacy or other extraordinary misdemeanor or occasion, to send force to apprehend or take him or them if they see cause.

It is ordered that there shalbe fiftie Costlets provided in the plantacõns, vid. Harteford 21 Costlets, Windsor 12, Weathersfeild 10, Agawam 7, which are to bee provided within 6 monthes at farthrest. And the saide Costlets are to be veiwed by the military officer that is provided for that purpose, and if he disallowe them as insufficient they are to pᵣuide better. And alsoe yᵗ the saide Townes are to giue in the names of such as are to finde the saide Cosletts, att the next generall Courte, and then such as shall faile to provide by the day aforsaide shall forthwith pay 10s. and five shillings a moneth vntill he hath supplied them; and it shall alsoe be lawfull for the saide military officer to call for the saide costeletts to viewe whether they [be] in repaire or noe.

It is ordered that Captaine Mason shalbe a publique military officer of the plantacõns of Conecticot, and shall traine the military men thereof in each plantacõns according to the dayes appointed, and shall have 40*l*. pᵣ annum, to be paid oute of the Treasury quarterly, the pay to begine from the day of the date hereof. This order to stand in force for a yeere and vntill the generall Courte take other order to the contrary.

It is alsoe ordered that the saide Captaine Mason shall have liberty to traine the saide military men in every plantacõn tenn dayes in every yeere, soe as it be not in June or July, giving a weekes warning before hand and whosoever yᵗ is allowed a souldier and faile to come at the time appointed by the saide publique officer to pay for his defaulte 3s. for yᵗ time, and if it be vsuall for the second offence 5s, and if not amended the saide delinquent is to bee bounde to answere it att the next Courte.

Itm̃, it is ordered that all pᵣsons shall beare Armes that are aboue the age of sixteene yeeres except they doe tender a sufficient excuse [to] the Corte & the Cort allowe the same. The Comʳˢ & Church officers for the present to bee exempted, as [8] alsoe for the tyme∥ to come after they have beene a Comissioner or Comʳˢ or Church officer to bee likewise for all tymes afterward exempted for bearing Armes, Watchinges & Wardinges.

It is ordered that there shalbe a magaceⁿ of powder and shott in every plantacõn that the supply of oʳ military men if occasion serve, videlicet, Hartefᵈ twoe barrels, Windsor 1 barrell of powder, 300 weighte of leade, Weathersfeild 1 barrell of powder, 300 of leade, Aggawam halfe a barrell of powder, 150 of leade; and every military man is to have continually in his house in a readines halfe a pounde of goode powder, 2ˡᵇ of bullets sutable to his peece, one pounde of match if his peece be a match locke, and whosoever failes of his halfe pounde of powder and 2ᵗᵇ of [*bulletts*] and match to pay Vs. for every tyme yᵗ is wanting; the plantacõns or plantacõn for not providing the saide magacen of powder and lead within this 3 monethes to pay 2ᵗᵇ forty shillings, and tenn shillings for every moneth vntill it bee pʳvided.

It is ordered that there shalbe a measure of each plantacõn brought to Harteford on the next perticular Courte and then there wilbe a setled Course for an measure in each plantacõn.

The generall Courte is appointed on the 22ᵗʰ of this instant moneth, the pʳticular the day after it.

It is ordered that all orders formerly made concerning military discipline vntill the orders of this Courte shalbe voide.

---

* Whereas, It was ordered octo die [Martii] last that there should be a restrainte of tradinge for Corne in regarde of some † with Mr. Pincheon to supply the plantacõns, vppon consideracõn of Mr. Pincheons that hee is somwhat fearefull of supplying the plantacõns, and whereas there is a Clause in case of necessitie 3 magistrates may dispence with the order, It is therefore ordered that Mr Ludlowe and Captaine Mason or either of them, taking likewise such with them as shalbe meete, shall trade to supply theire owne necessities and the necessities of some other that are in wante.

It is ordered that in the setting forth Elias, that Mr. Phelps, Mr. Whiting and Mr. Mychell is to agitate that busines for the Comõnwealth.

Vppon the complainte of Aramamett and the Indians cohabiting with him, aboute Leiftenant Holmes denying the planting of the old grounde planted the last yeere aboute Plymouth house, It was ordered that they should plante the old ground they planted the last yeer for this yeere onely, and they are to sett theire wigwams in the olde grounde and not withoute.

---

* The date or caption of this Session of the Court is omitted in the original Record. No break occurs, (except a slight one between the line commencing " Whereas," &c. and the preceding paragraph,) from the commencement of the proceedings of the March Session, on page [6.]

† A blank in the original.

OF CONNECTICUT. 17

5to Apr, 1638. A GENrALL CORT AT HARTEFORD.

Mr. Haines, Mr. Ludlowe, Mr. Pincheon, Mr. Wells, Mr. Plum, Mr. Phelps, Mr. Smith, Mr. Michell,

Comittees; Mr. Hull, Mr. Webster, Mr. Talkott, Mr. Moxā, Mr. Burr, Mr. Steele, Mr. Hopkins, [Capt:] Mason, [Mr.] Ward, [*Thurston*] Rayner, [*Tho:*] Ford, [*Tho: Mars*]hall, [Geo: Hubberd.]

Captaine Mason, Thomas Ford, Thomas Marshall, Thurston Rayner, George Hubberte, are fined 1s. a peece for failing att the hower appointed which 7 of the Clocke.

It is ordered that there shalbe sixe sent to Warranocke Indians to declare unto them that wee have a desire to speake with them, to knowe the reasons why they saide they are affraide of vs, and if they will not come to vs willingly then to compell them to come by violence, and they may leave 2 of the English as pleadges in the meane time and to trade with them for Corne if they can.

[9] It is ordered that Captaine Mason, Thomas Stanton, Jeremy Adams, John Gibbes, Searieante Stares and Thomas Merricke, and if Thomas Merricke be gone to Aggawam then Captaine Mason to take another whom he please, shall goe in the saide service; and if hee see cause to leave hostages hee may; if hee see cause to goe to Aggawam he may.

It is thought meete that the Costlets that were in the last service shalbe made good to the Commonwealth and made as serviceable as before, and that Richard Lord shall take such Costlets into his Custody as are in the meeting house of Harteford and make them vpp, and when they bee fitted vpp the saide Lord is to bring in his noate and the Courte to appointe one to veiw ye same, and when they are certified to bee in good kelter there must be speedy course taken by ye Courte for the speedy payment of the said Lord.

It is ordered that there shalbe a warant directed to ye severall Collectors of each plantacõns to make theire retornes to the Treasurer within these 25 dayes or els to answere theire contempte att the next particular Courte.

Whereas there is a desire of or neibours of Harteford that there may be a publique highway for Carte and horse vppon the

vpland betweene the said Harteford and Windsor as may be
convenient, it is therefore thought meete that Henry Wolcott
the younger and Mr. Stephen Terr[e] and Willm̃ Westwood
and Nathaniell Warde shall consider of a fitting and convenient high way to bee marked and sett oute, and bridges made
over the swampes, and then itt being confirmed by the Courte,
the inhabitants of Harteford may with making a comely and
decent Stile for foote and fence vpp ye vpper end of the meadow; this to be done by Mun[day] seavennights vppon penalty
of 10s. every defaulte.

It is ordered that with the consent of Mr. Pincheon, that the
said Mr. Pincheon shall within these 18 dayes pay Mr. Whiting 40l. by sending downe as much Corne as the saide 40l. comes
to, or els to pay him the saide Mr. Whiting in marchantable
beaver att 9s. pr pounde provided that if in the Bay the saide
Mr. Whiting cann put it away att higher rate the saide Mr.
Pincheon to have the benefitt of it, if it be put away at losse
the saide Mr. Pincheon to stand to it, and the saide Mr. Pincheon may write to his frends to see that the saide Mr. Whiting doth his best for the saide Mr. Pincheons advantage.

It is ordered that the Indian Corne that is brought into the
plantacõns for the supply of theire necessitis, either by agreement with Mr. Pincheon or any other way of a generall trade,
shall goe att 5s. 6d. in money, in wampum att 3 a penny, 6s. pr
bushell, or if in beaver according to the order att 9s. pr pounde,
yett this is not any way to infringe the bargaine formerly made
with Mr. Pincheon for soe much Corne as he bringes in.

It is ordered that these men followinge shall receive the
Corne aforesaide for the plantacõns according to their proporcõn
agreed on, and shall keepe one exact account of what every
man hath att the rates aforesaid; the men appointed for this
service are Henry Wolcott ye younger for Windsor, Edwarde
Stibben and Thomas Scott for Harteford, For Wethersfeilde
Mr. Plum. It is alsoe ordered yt such as are in want of Corne
or like to betwene this and harv[est] must give in theire names
and wants to ye parties aforesaide of the severall plantacõns,
and they are to retorne it in ye next particular Courte, provided yt the receivers of Corne aforesaid are not to deliver any
Corne without the present payment formerly mencõned.

It is ordered that Thomas Staunton shall haue for the seruice hee hath done for the Countrey already past, tenn poundes.

[10] It is ordered that Thomas Staunton shalbe a publicke officer for to attend the Corte vppon all occasions, either Generall or p^rticuler, as alsoe any meetinge of the Magistrates to interprett betweene them and the Indians, as also is to haue for it 10l. p^r Anñm.

It is ordered y^t Captaine Mason & Jeremy Adames shal goe on Thursday next, accordinge to o^r p^rmise to trade wth the Indians for Corne and to settle a Trade between vs and them aboute Corne.

It is ordered that the order of the 9th of March last be againe renewed.

It is ordered where any Company of Indians doe sett downe neere any English plantacõns that they shall declare whoe is their Sachem or Cheife & that the saide Cheife or Sachem shall paye to the saide English such trespasses as shalbe cõmitted by any Indian in the saide plantacõn adioyninge, either by spoilinge or killinge of Cattle or Swine either wth Trappes, dogges or arrowes & they are not to pleade that it was done by Strangers vnlesse they cann p^rduce the p^rty and deliu^r him or his goodes into the Custody of th' English; and they shall paye the double if it were voluntarily done.

Whereas there was some complainte made against Mr. Willm̃ Pincheon of Agawam for that as was conceiued & vppon p^rfe app^red he was not soe carefull to p^rmote the publicque good in the trade of Corne as hee was bounde to doe, It is ordered the saide Mr. Pincheon shall wth all convenient speede pay as a fine for his soe failinge 40^tie bushells of Indian Corne for the publicque & the saide Corne to be deliu^red to the Treasurer to be disposed of as shalbe thought meete.

Whereas vppon full debate & hearinge the matters of Iniuries & difference betweene Soheage, an Indian the Sachem of Pyquaagg nowe called Wythersfeild, & th' English Inhabitants thereof, and It app^res to the Cort that there hath beene divers Iniuryes offered by some of the saide English inhabitants to the said Soheage, as alsoe the saide Soheage & his men haue likewise comitted divers outrages & wronges against the saide English, yet because as was conceiued the first breach was on the saide English p^rte, All former wronges whatsoeuer are remitted on both sides and the saide Soheage is againe receiued in Amytie to the saide English, & Mr. Stone, Mr. Goodwin & Tho: Staunton are desired to goe to the saide Soheage & to treate wth him accordinge to the best of their discretion & to compose matters betweene the saide English and the saide Soheage, and vppon their reporte there shalbe som setled course in the thinge.

It is ordered there shalbe 1s. p^r skin of beaver to be paide to the publicqu^e out of the Trade of beaver, to be paide into the Treasury every half yeere: this order to stand for an yeere & vntill the Cort take other order to the Contrary.

It is ordered that none shall trade in this River wth the Indians for beau^r but those that are hereafter named (vizt) For Agawam Mr. Pyncheon, for Windsor Mr. Ludlowe, Mr. Hull; for Harteford Mr. Whytinge, Tho: Staunton; Wythersfeild Geo: Hubberd & Rich: Lawes; and if any trade for beauer other then are fornamed they shall forfeit 5s. p^r pounde to be paide p^r eu^ry pounde they soe trade.

[*Pages* 12-22, *blank:* these pages were probably designed for the insertion of the Constitution, Oaths, &c., which were subsequently recorded on pp. 215-227 of the original as now paged.]

[220] Forasmuch as it hath pleased the Allmighty God by the wise disposition of his diuyne p^ruidence so to Order and dispose of things that we the Inhabitants and Residents of Windsor, Harteford and Wethersfield are now cohabiting and dwelling in and vppon the River of Conectecotte and the Lands thereunto adioyneing; And well knowing where a people are gath-

ered togather the word of God requires that to mayntayne the peace and vnion of such a people there should be an orderly and decent Gouerment established according to God, to order and dispose of the affayres of the people at all seasons as occation shall require ; doe therefore assotiate and conioyne our selues to be as one Publike State or Comonwelth ; and doe, for our selues and our Successors and such as shall be adioyned to vs att any tyme hereafter, enter into Combination and Confederation togather, to mayntayne and p^rsearue the liberty and purity of the gospell of our Lord Jesus wch we now p^rfesse, as also the disciplyne of the Churches, wch according to the truth of the said gospell is now practised amongst vs ; As also in o^r Ciuell Affaires to be guided and gouerned according to such Lawes, Rules, Orders and decrees as shall be made, ordered & decreed, as followeth :—

1. It is Ordered, sentenced and decreed, that there shall be yerely two generall Assemblies or Courts, the on the second thursday in Aprill, the other the second thursday in September, following; the first shall be called the Courte of Election, wherein shall be yerely Chosen frõ tyme to tyme soe many Magestrats and other publike Officers as shall be found requisitte : Whereof one to be chosen Gouernour for the yeare ensueing and vntill another be chosen, and noe other Magestrate to be chosen for more then one yeare ; p^ruided allwayes there be sixe chosen besids the Gouernour ; wch being chosen and sworne according to an Oath recorded for that purpose shall haue power to administer iustice according to the Lawes here established, and for want thereof according to the rule of the word of God ; wch choise shall be made by all that are admitted freemen and haue taken the Oath of Fidellity, and doe cohabitte wthin this Jurisdiction, (hauing beene admitted Inhabitants by the maior p^rt of the Towne wherein they liue,*) or the mayor p^rte of such as shall be then p^rsent.

[222] 2. It is Ordered, sentensed and decreed, that the Election of the aforesaid Magestrats shall be on this manner : euery p^rson p^rsent and quallified for choyse shall bring in (to the p^rsons deputed to receaue thē) one single pap^r wth the name of him written in yt whom he desires to haue Gouernour, and he

---

* This clause has been interlined in a different hand writing and at a more recent period.

that hath the greatest nūber of papers shall be Gouernor for that yeare. And the rest of the Magestrats or publike Officers to be chosen in this manner: The Secretary for the tyme being shall first read the names of all that are to be put to choise and then shall seuerally nominate them distinctly, and euery one that would haue the p^rson nominated to be chosen shall bring in one single paper written vppon, and he that would not haue him chosen shall bring in a blanke: and euery one that hath more written papers then blanks shall be a Magestrat for that yeare; wch papers shall be receaued and told by one or more that shall be then chosen by the court and sworne to be faythfull therein; but in case there should not be sixe chosen as aforesaid, besids the Gouernor, out of those wch are nominated, then he or they wch haue the most written pap^rs shall be a Magestrate or Magestrats for the ensueing yeare, to make vp the foresaid nūber.

3. It is Ordered, sentenced and decreed, that the Secretary shall not nominate any p^rson, nor shall any p^rson be chosen newly into the Magestracy wch was not p^rpownded in some Generall Courte before, to be nominated the next Election; and to that end yt shall be lawfull for ech of the Townes aforesaid by their deputyes to nominate any two whō they conceaue fitte to be put to Election; and the Courte may ad so many more as they iudge requisitt.

4. It is Ordered, sentenced and decreed that noe p^rson be chosen Gouernor aboue once in two yeares, and that the Gouernor be alwayes a mēber of some approved congregation, and formerly of the Magestracy w^thin this Jurisdiction; and all the Magestrats Freemen of this Comonwelth: and that no Magestrate or other publike officer shall execute any p^rte of his or their Office before they are seuerally sworne, wch shall be done in the face of the Courte if they be p^rsent, and in case of absence by some deputed for that purpose.

[224] 5. It is Ordered, sentenced and decreed, that to the aforesaid Courte of Election the seu^rall Townes shall send their deputyes, and when the Elections are ended they may p^rceed in any publike searuice as at other Courts. Also the other Generall Courte in September shall be for makeing of lawes, and

any other publike occation, w[ch] conserns the good of the Com̄onwelth.

6. It is Ordered, sentenced and decreed, that the Gou[r]nor shall, ether by himselfe or by the secretary, send out sum̄ons to the Constables of eu[r] Towne for the cauleing of these two standing Courts, on month at lest before their seu[r]all tymes: And also if the Gou[r]nor and the gretest p[r]te of the Magestrats see cause vppon any spetiall occation to call a generall Courte, they may giue order to the secretary soe to doe w[th]in fowerteene dayes warneing: and if vrgent necessity so require, vppon a shorter notice, giueing sufficient grownds for yt to the deputyes when they meete, or els be questioned for the same; And if the Gou[r]nor and Mayor p[r]te of Magestrats shall ether neglect or refuse to call the two Generall standing Courts or ether of thē, as also at other tymes when the occations of the Com̄onwelth require, the Freemen thereof, or the Mayor p[r]te of them, shall petition to them soe to doe: if then yt be ether denyed or neglected the said Freemen or the Mayor p[r]te of them shall haue power to giue order to the Constables of the seuerall Townes to doe the same, and so may meete togather, and chuse to themselues a Moderator, and may p[r]ceed to do any Acte of power, w[ch] any other Generall Courte may.

7. It is Ordered, sentenced and decreed that after there are warrants giuen out for any of the said Generall Courts, the Constable or Constables of ech Towne shall forthw[th] give notice distinctly to the inhabitants of the same, in some Publike Assembly or by goeing or sending frō howse to howse, that at a place and tyme by him or them lymited and sett, they meet and assemble thē selues togather to elect and chuse certen deputyes to be att the Generall Courte then following to agitate the afayres of the com̄onwelth; w[ch] said Deputyes shall be chosen by all that are admitted Inhabitants in the seu[r]all Townes and haue taken the oath of fidellity; p[r]uided that non be chosen a Deputy for any Generall Courte w[ch] is not a Freeman of this Com̄onwelth.

[226] The foresaid deputyes shall be chosen in manner following: euery p[r]son that is p[r]sent and quallified as before exp[r]ssed, shall bring the names of such, written in seu[r]rall papers. as they desire to haue chosen for that Imployment, and these 3

or 4, more or lesse, being the nūber agreed on to be chosen for that tyme, that haue greatest nūber of papers written for the shall be deputyes for that Courte; whose names shall be endorsed on the backe side of the warrant and returned into the Courte, wth the Constable or Constables hand vnto the same.

8. It is Ordered, sentenced and decreed, that Wyndsor, Hartford and Wethersfield shall haue power, ech Towne, to send fower of their freemen as their deputyes to euery Generall Courte; and whatsoeuer other Townes shall be hereafter added to this Jurisdiction, they shall send so many deputyes as the Courte shall judge meete, a resonable p^rportion to the nūber of Freemen that are in the said Townes being to be attended therein; wch deputyes shall have the power of the whole Towne to giue their voats and alowance to all such lawes and orders as may be for the publike good, and unto wch the said Townes are to be bownd.

9. It is ordered and decreed, that the deputyes thus chosen shall haue power and liberty to appoynt a tyme and a place of meeting togather before any Generall Courte to aduise and consult of all such things as may concerne the good of the publike, as also to examine their owne Elections, whether according to the order, and if they or the gretest p^rte of them find any election to be illegall they may seclud such for p^rsent frō their meeting, and returne the same and their resons to the Courte; and if y^t proue true, the Courte may fyne the p^rty or p^rtyes so intruding and the Towne, if they see cause, and giue out a warrant to goe to a newe election in a legall way, ether in p^rte or in whole. Also the said deputyes shall haue power to fyne any that shall be disorderly at their meetings, or for not coming in due tyme or place according to appoyntment; and they may returne the said fynes into the Courte if y^t be refused to be paid, and the Tresurer to take notice of y^t, and to estreete or levy the same as he doth other fynes.

10. It is Ordered, sentenced and decreed, that euery Generall Courte, except such as through neglecte of the Gou^rnor and the greatest p^rte of Magestrats the Freemen themselues doe call, shall consist of the Gouernor, or some one chosen to moderate the Court, and 4 other Magestrats at lest, wth the mayor p^rte of the deputyes of the seuerall Townes legally chosen;

and in case the Freemen or mayor p^rte of the, through neglect or refusall of the Gouernor and mayor p^rte of the magestrats, shall call a Courte, y^t shall consist of the mayor p^rte of Freemen that are p^rsent or their deputyes, wth a Moderator chosen by the: In wch said Generall Courts shall consist the supreme power of the Comonwelth, and they only shall haue power to make lawes or repeale the, to graunt leuyes, to admitt of Freemen, dispose of lands vndisposed of, to seuerall Townes or p^rsons, and also shall haue power to call ether Courte or Magestrate or any other p^rson whatsoeuer into question for any misdemeanour, and may for just causes displace or deale otherwise according to the nature of the offence; and also may deale in any other matter that concerns the good of this comon welth, excepte election of Magestrats, wch shall be done by the whole boddy of Freemen.

[227] In wch Courte the Gouernour or Moderator shall haue power to order the Courte to giue liberty of spech, and silence vnceasonable and disorderly speakeings, to put all things to voate, and in case the voate be equall to haue the casting voice. But non of these Courts shall be adiorned or dissolued w^thout the consent of the maior p^rte of the Court.

11. It is ordered, sentenced and decreed, that when any Generall Courte vppon the occations of the Comonwelth haue agreed vppon any sume or somes of mony to be leuyed vppon the seuerall Townes w^thin this Jurisdiction, that a Comittee be chosen to sett out and appoynt w^t shall be the p^rportion of euery Towne to pay of the said leuy, p^rvided the Comittees be made vp of an equall nūber out of each Towne.

14th January, 1638, the 11 Orders abouesaid are voted.

---

[216] The Oath of the Gou^rnor, for the [p^rsent.]

I N. W. being now chosen to be Gou^rnor w^thin this Jurisdiction, for the yeare ensueing, and vntil a new be chosen, doe sweare by the greate and dreadfull name of the everliueing God, to p^rmote the publicke good and peace of the same, according to the best of my skill; as also will mayntayne all lawfull priuiledges of this Comonwealth; as also that all wholsome lawes that are or shall be made by lawfull authority here established, be duly executed; and will further the execution of Justice according to the rule of Gods word; so helpe me God, in the name of the Lo: Jesus Christ.

The Oath of a Magestrate, for the p^rsent.

I, N. W. being chosen a Magestrate w^thin this Jurisdiction for the yeare ensueing, doe sweare by the great and dreadfull name of the euerliueing God, to p^rmote the publike good and peace of the same, according to the best of my skill, and that I will mayntayne all the lawfull priuiledges thereof according to my vnderstanding, as also assist in the execution of all such wholsome lawes as are made or shall be made by lawfull authority heare established, and will further the execution of Justice for the tyme aforesaid according to the righteous rule of Gods word; so helpe me God, etc.

[215]   ### The Oath of a Constable.

I, A. B., of W, doe sweare by the greate and dreadfull name of the euerliueing God, that for the yeare ensueing, and vntill a new be chosen, I will faythfully execute the office and place of a Constable, for and w^thin the said plantac̃on of W: and the lymitts thereof, and that I will endeuor to p^rsearue the publike peace of the said place, and Com̃onwealth, and will doe my best endeauor to see all watches and wairds executed, and to obey and execute all lawfull com̃aunds or warrants that com frõ any Magestrat or Magestrats or Courte, so helpe me God, in the Lo: Jesus Christ.

---

[11] Ja: 14th 1638. It is Ordered that the tresurer shall deliuer noe mony out of his hands to any p^rson w^thout the hands of two Magistrats if the som̃ be above 20s.; if it be vnder then the tresurer is to accept of the hand of on; but if it be for the payment of some bylls to be alowed, wch are referred to some Com̃ittes to consider of whether alowed or not, That such bylls as they alowe & sett there hands vnto the Tresurer shall accept & give satisfactñ.

Jo: Haynes: (Governor.)

Ro: Ludlowe (Depy. Governor.)

Geo: Wyllys
Edwa: Hopkins
Tho: Welles
John Webster
William Phelps
} (Magistrates.)

(Deputies.)

John Steel   Henry Woolcott.
John Pratt   Thomas Stoughton
William Spencer   Thomas Ford
Edw. Stebbin.   James Boosey
William Westwood George Hubbard

John Mason   Tho: Stanton

[23] [April 11th, 1639.

At a Generall Meeting of the Freemen] for the Election of Magistrates, according [to the]orders.

Jnº. Haynes Esqʳ., was chosen Governoʳ for the y[eare ensueing] and vntill a new be chosen.

Mr. Roger Ludlowe, Deputy.

Mr. George Willis, Mr. Edward Hopkins, Mr. Thomas Wells, Mr. Jnº. Webster, Mr. Wm. Phelps, were chosen to assist in the Magis[tracy] for the yeare ensueing, and all tooke the oathes app[ointed] for them.

Mr. Edward Hopkins was chosen Secretary and [Mr. Thomas] Wells Tres'r. for the yeare ensueing.*

Committees: Mr. Jno. Steele, Mr. Spencer, Jno. Pratt, Edw: Stebbing, [Mr.] Gaylard, [Henry] Woolcott, [Mr. S]toughton, [Mr.] Foard, Thurston Rayner, James Boosy, George Hubbard, Ric: Crabb.

Elty Pomry of Windsor complayned that he had [a mare] taken away by the Pequatts, wᶜʰ after the warrs [   ] was killed by the Naanticke Indians; he desir[ed] therefore the helpe of the Court to be releeved [and that] some order may be taken with them for restitucõn. [The] Courte tooke the same into serious consideracõn and [thinke] it according to their duty and good reason to pʳtect [the] persons and estates of all the members of the Com̃[onwealth] soe farr as lyeth in their power in a way of Just[ice,] and accordingly pʳmised as opportunity shall be off[ered] to deale with those Indians about it.

The like was desired by Mr. Ludlow in regard of [   ] of his, and the like pʳmise made to him.

The Court in regard of the state of the present ty[me] and the many occasions that ly vppon men, thought f[itte to] referr the pʳticulars hereafter mentioned to a Co[mittee,] vizt. the

---

* Pages 23-26 of the original are more mutilated and defaced than any other portion of the Volume. Thus far, on page [23] the words in brackets have been supplied from a copy made in 1743, and attested by George Willys, Secretary, which is printed with the Proceedings in the Mason case, p. 148.

Treaty with Vncus concerning the land [   ] by him and other Indians between Hartford and W[indsor,] as also with Pequannocke Indians, who are now co[   ] to answere any letters sent from o^r neighbo^{rs} of Q[*uinnipiac*] and to ripen orders formerly in agitacōn against [the] next meeting of the Court : They are also des[*ired to*] putt Mr. Goodwin in mind of finishing the treaty [   ] of the Towne of Wethersfeeld with Seq[*uassen*] concerning the land beyond the River : and [the] Governo^r, Mr. Deputy, Mr. Willis, Mr. Hopkins, Mr. [   ] Mr. Steele & Mr. Spencer were intreated to attend [the said] services.

It is ordered that the watch be renewed in each [Towne, and] begin the second day of the next weeke.

The Court was adiorned till the third T[hursday in[   ]

[24] [Two or three lines are torn from the top of this page, which contains the record of a Particular Court.]

Jno. Edmunds, Aaron Starke and Jno. Williams were censured for vncleane practises as foll^s. Jno. Williams [*Edmunds?*] to be whipt att a Carts[tail] vppon a lecture day at Hartford. Jno. Williams to stand vppon the pillory from the ringing of the first bell to the end of the lecture, then to be whipt at a Carts [tail,] and to be whipt in like manner att Windsore within 8 dayes following. Aaron Starke to stand vppon the pillory and be whipt as Williams, and to haue the letter R burnt vppon his cheeke, and in regard of the wrong done to Mary Holt to pay her parents 10*l.* and in defect of such to the Comōnwealth, and when both are fit for that condition, to marry her.

It is the mind of the Court that Mr. Ludlow and Mr. Phelps see some publique punishment inflicted vppon the girle for concealing it soe long.

Mr. Williams brings his action of trespasse aganst Matthew Allen for 74 Rod of Corne destroyed through defect of his fence : Thomas Moore for 10 Rod,
  Mr. Woolcott for 60 Rod,
  Ann Marshall for 2 Rod,
  George Phelpes for 8 Rod,
  Jno. Porter for 70.

The Jury find for the pl^{fs}, to pay for 224 rod of Corne spoyled, three pounds; for keeping of the ground 20 dayes, 30s; Costs 10s.

[*In margin,*]
[Mr.   ] foreman, [Mr. S]kinner, [Mr.] Steele,
[Mr.] Smith, [Mr.] Moore, [Mr.] Weed, [Jeffe]ry Ferris,
[R]obins, [S]cott, [Pan]try, [S]tanley,
[   ] Birchard.

Thomas Bull informed the Court that a muskett with 2 letters I W was taken vp att Pequannocke in pursuit of the Pequatts, wch was conceaved to be Jno. Woods who was killed att the Rivers mouth. It was ordered for the present [that] the muskett should be delivered to Jno. Woods freinds vntill other appeare.

August the first, 1639.

Jno. Bennett & Mary Holt were both censured to be whipt for vncleane practises, and the girles M^r is inioyned to send her out of this Jurisdiction before the last of the next month.

These following were censured & fined for vnseasonable and imoderate drinking att the pinnace.

Thomas Cornewell, 30s.	Samuell Kittwell, 10s.
Jno. Latimer, 15s.	Thomas Vpson, 20s.
Mathew Beckwith, 10s.	

Jno. Moody had an attachment graunted vppon the g[oods of Thomas] Gaines, in the hands of Mr. Stoughton, for a debt [of 5^{lb} weight of Tobacco.]

[25]   A Generall Court att Hartford, the 8th of Aug. 1639.

Jno. Haynes Esqr. Govr.
Roger Ludlow, Dep'ty.
   Mr. Willis, Mr. Wells, Mr. Webster, Mr. Hopkins, Mr. Phelpes.
   Comittees. Mr. Talcott, Mr. Spencer, [Jn]o. Pratt, Mr. Hull, Mr. Porter, Mr. Tappin, Mr. Ward, Geo. Hubbard, James Boosy, Mr. Hill, Mr. Stoughton.

The Constables of Hartford were fined 2s. 6d. for not returning their warrants according to order, being much favoured in regard it was the first tyme and one of them sicke.

Mr. Wells, Mr. Hill and Mr. Ward were intreated to auditt the last Tres'rs acc°.

The order of the 9° March, 1637, concerning powder and shott is renewed, and yf it be not provided by the severall Townes within 6 weeks, the penalty to be taken without any mitigaĉon.

Whereas there was an order of the 18th of Febr. 1638, for surveying the armor and other military provitions in each Towne once a quarter, wch hath hitherto beene too much neglected, for the execution hereof Mr. Spencer was now chosen for Hartford, Mr. Hill for Windsor and James Boosy for Wethersfeeld, and they are to begin before the last of this month: And in case any of these persons before chosen be negligent in this great trust coṁitted to him, he shall pay 20s. for every default; and they are to make returne of such wch they find defective, the nex P^rticular Court after each tyme of their view, and during the tyme of this service they are freed from watching, warding and trayning.

It is ordered that all the military men shall be trayned att least 6 dayes in the yeare; the tymes are to be chosen att the discretion of the Capt., only the monthes of May, June and July are excepted vnles it be vppon spetiall occation.

The Tresurers acc° being audited, the Country was found indebted to him 16l. 10s. 6d.

Mr. Governo^r, Mr. Deputy and Mr. Wells, or any two of them, are intreated to goe to the Rivers mouth to consult with Mr. Fenwicke about a treaty of combinaĉon wch is desi[red] againe to be on foott with the Bay.

The occations of the Coṁonwealth being taken into consideraĉon, it was thought fitt and ordred that a Rate of 100L. be made in these plantaĉons, and Mr. Talcott, Mr. Hull and Mr. Tapping are intreated to p^rportion it vppon the several plantaĉons, to be payd in, the one halfe within [one] month and the other within 3 monthes.

The Court is adiorned till the 15 of this month.

[26] August the 15º, 1639.

A Meeting of the Generall Court, wch was Adiourned untill this day.

Mr. Deputy declared that he with Mr. Wells and Mr. Hooker had repayred to Mr. Fennicke according to the direction of the Court, whom they found every wayes sutable to their minds, and in p^rticular for the present agitaĉon with the Bay he is willing the State here should p^rceed to a mutuall agreement for an offenciue and defenciue warr and all other offices of loue, but desires that matters of Bounds may be respitted vntill he vnderstand further the minds of the rest that are equally interested with him in the patent of the River. Vppon consideraĉon hereof, Mr. Governo^r was intreated to write an answere to Mr. Winthropp that the Court is very ready and willing to entertaine a firme combinaĉon for a defenciue and offenciue warr, and all other mutuall offices of loue and friendshipp, according to the propositions formerly agreed, wch are the desires also of Mr. Fennicke with whom they haue consulted in the case. But the matter of bounds he desires may be a little respited vntill he haue opportunity to intimate his owne apprehensions, or some others who have equall interest with himselfe arriue in these Coasts, whom he hopes to see the next spring.

M^r. Tres^r. had order to call in for all the fines due to the Cuntrey, and for such monyes as are due from the traders for Bevar.

The manifold insolencyes that haue beene offered of late by the Indians, putt the Court in mind of that wch hath beene too long neglected, vizt, the execution of justice vppon the former murtherers of the English, and it was vppon serious consideraĉon and debate thought necessary and accordingly determined, that some speedy course be taken herein, and for effecting hereof it was concluded that 100 men be levyed and sent downe to Mattabesecke, where severall guilty persons reside and haue beene harbored by Soheage, notwithstanding all meanes by way of persuation haue beene formerly used to him for surrendring them vpp into o^r handes; and it is thought fit that these counsells be imparted to o^r friends att Quinnipi-

[ocke] that p^rvition may be made for the safety of the new plantacõns, and vppon their ioynt consent to p^rceede or desist.

The 100*l*. rate was layd vppon the severall Townes in this p^rportion;

Hartford,	43*l*.	00	00
Windsore,	28	06	8
Wethersfeild,	28	13	4
	100	00	0

The Courte was adiorned to the 26 of this month.

[27]   August the 26°, 1639.

Mr. Webster informed the Court that according to the determinacõn of the last meeting, Mr. Deputy, Mr. Willis and himselfe acquainted o^r freinds of Quinnipiocke with their purposes concerning the murtherers, and desired the concurrence of their apprehensions therein, who fully approving of the thing yett intimated their thoughts somewhat to differ from o^rs in the present execution of it, in regard of some new plantacõns that are now beginning and some inconvenience wch may fall vppon these parts of the Cuntrey by a noise of a new warr, wch may hinder the coming of shipps the next yeare.

Whereas divers of the Pequatts who were given to Vncus and Antinemo haue planted againe part of the land wch was conquered by us contrary to o^r agreement with them, It was thought fitt and ordered, that 40 men be p^rportioned out of the severall plantacõns and imediately sent away to gather the Corne there planted by them.

The men are p^rportioned for the severall Townes thus,

Windsor,	13
Hartford,	17
Wethersfield,	10
	40

It was referred to Mr. Governo^r, Mr. Willis, Mr. Phelps, Capt. Mason and Mr. Ward, to agitate this businesse and bring it to an issue with what speed may be, and they haue power to presse 20 armes, 2 shallopps and 2 Canowes, for this service.

It was concluded that there be a publique day of thanksgiving in these plantacons vppon the 18th of the next month.

This Court is dissolved.

Sept. the 5th, 1639.

Jno. Haynes Esqr. Govr.

Mr. Hopkins, Mr. Wells, Mr. Phelps, Mr. Webster.

Richard Lyman complayneth against Sequassen for burning vpp his hedge wch, before Mr. Governor, formerly he prmised to satisfy for, but yett hath not done it. Sequassen appeared and prmised to pay within 4 dayes, or elce an attachment to be graunted.

Edward Hopkins compt. in behalfe of Mr. Jno. Woodcocke, against Fr. Stiles, for breach of Covenants, in 500l.

Mr. Stiles desires respite till the next Court in regard of witnes in the Bay : Graunted.

Jno. Moody contra   Blachford, for a fowling peece he bought and should have payd for it 40s. pr bill of. The Jury find for the pl. 41 damages, costs 6s.

Ric. Lord against Thomas Allen for 40s. debt. Mr. Allen appeared not. Mr. Spencer witnessed that he borrowed 40s. in the Bay, of Ric. Lord and prmised to repay it here. 2s. 6d. graunted for costs and an attachment vppon his goodes.

Fr. Stiles contra Jno. Woodcocke in an action of debt for 2 hhds malt & a hhd of meale.

[28] Samuel Ireland was fined 10s. for contempt of ye Court in not appearing vppon a warrant served vppon him. Vppon his submission he payd 5s. & was acquitted.

Thomas Gridley of Windsore was complayned of for refusing to watch, strong suspition of drunkennes, contempteous words against the orders of Court, quarrelling and striking Mr. Stiles his man : he was censured to be whipt att Hartford and bound to his good behavior. He entred a recognizance of 10l. for his good behaviour.

October the 3ᵈ, 1639.

Mr. Haynes, Mr. Ludlow, Mr. Willis, Mr. Wells, Mr. Webster, Mr. Phelpes, Mr. Hopkins.

Edwa. Hopkins contra Fr. Stiles, in behalfe of Jno. Woodcocke, in an accōn for breach of Covenants. Covenants pᵣduced. The Jury find that the deft. hath in his hands 80l. and 150l. for the purchase of the house, and for not taking in 400 acres of ground according to Bargaine, that Mr. Stiles should take the house backe againe and repay backe the 230l. with 70l. damages: costs 10s.*

It is ordered that the souldiers for the last exploit shall be payd for 9 dayes, att 2s. pʳ day, the mony to be payd to the Constable of every Towne and he to deduct the cost of the provisions he pressed for them.

Sept. the 10ᵗʰ, 1639.   A Generall Court.

Jno. Haynes, Esqr.

Mr. Willis, Mr. Hopkins, Mr. Wells, Mr. Webster, Mr. Phelps.

Comittees: Mr. Steele, Mr. Talcott, Mr. Spencer, Jno. Pratt, Mr. Gaylord, Capt. Mason, Mr. Hill, Mr. Hull, Mr. Tapping, Mr. Ward, James Boosy, George Hubbard.

The Constables of Windsor were fined 5s. for not returning the warrant of the Comittees that were chosen for that Towne.

Mr. Deputy was fined 5s. for being absent.

Mr. Hopkins, Mr. Wells, Mr. Steele and Mr. Spencer were intreated to ripen some orders that were left vnfinished the former Court, as about pʳvition of settling of lands, testaments of the deceased, and recording spetiall passages of Pʳvidence.

The Court was adiorned vntill the second thursday in the next month, vnlesse spetiall occations occurr to call it sooner.

---

* An imperfect record of this trial and verdict is made at the bottom of page [25.]

[29] Octob{r} the 10th, 1639. A Session of the Generall Court.

Mr. Deputy informed the Court that he hath vnderstood since his returne, offence hath beene taken att some of his p{r}ceedings in his late jorney to Pequannocke, and the parts thereabouts: he therefore desired to make knowne what had beene done by * him therein, w{ch} was this; Att his coming downe to Quinnipiocke the hand of the Lord was vppon him in taking away some of his Cattle, w{ch} prevented him in some of his purposes there for selling some of them: Afterwards att his coming to Pequannocke he found cause to alter his former thoughts of wintering his Cattle there, and vnderstanding that the beginnings of a Plantaçon beyond that was not caryed on according to the agrement made with those who were interessed in ordering the same, and that by some things w{ch} appeared to him, his apprehensions were that some others intended to take vp the sayd place, who had not acquainted this Court with their purposes therein, w{ch} might preiudiciall to this Comon wealth, and knowing himselfe to be one of those to whom the disposal of that plantaçon was comitted, he adventured to drive his Cattle thither, make provision for them there,† and submitts himselfe to the Court to judge whether he hath transgressed the Comission or nott.

The Court taking the premises into consideraçon, did vnanimously conceaue that his p{r}ceedings could not be warranted by the Comission, nor can he be excused of neglect of his duty, that he had not given notice to these plantaçons of what he did, notwithstanding his allegations of the inconveniences w{ch} otherwise might have accrued; yett that the thing may fully appeare as it is, and matters ordered in a comely mañer, It is conceaued fitt that a Comittee be chosen to repaire thither and take a view of the aforesayd occations, and yf in their judgments both persons & things settled by him be soe as comfortably be confirmed, they may remayne as they are, or otherwise altered att their discretions; and they are to report things how they find them, to the next Generall Court, that then a full issue may

---

* [Margin] "Mr. Ludlow his Apology for taking vp Vncoa;"
† [Margin] "and to sett out himselfe and some others house lotts to build on there."

be given to the matter in hand, as things shall then appeare; and Mr. Governo__r__ and Mr. Wells were intreated to attend this service, and they are desired to conferr with the planters att * Pequannocke, to give them the oath of fidelity, make such free as they see fitt, order them to send one or two deputyes to the two Generall Courts in September and Aprill, and for deciding of differences & controversies vnder 40s. among them, to p__r__pound to them & give them power to choose 7 men from among themselues, with liberty of appeale to the Court here; as also to assigne S__r__ieant Nicholls for the present to trayne the men and exercise them in military discipline; and they are farther desired to speake with Mr. Prudden, and that Plan[tacõn] that the difference betweene them and Pequannocke plantacõn may be peaceably decided, and to this end that indifferent men may be chosen to iudge who have most right to the places in controversy and most nead of them, and accordingly determined as shall be most agreeable to equity and reason.

[30]   It is ordered that Mr. Willis, Mr. Webst__r__ and Mr. Spencer shall review all former orders and lawes and record such of them as they conceave to be necessary for publique concernement, and deliver them into the Secretaryes hands to be published to the severall Townes, and all other orders that they see cause to omitt to be suspended vntill the Court take further order.

Mr. Fenwicke, Mr. Whiting, Mr. Hill and Mr. Ward are nominated by the Court to be presented to the vote of the Cuntrey for magistratts att the Court in Aprill next, p__r__vided Mr. Fenwicke and Mr. Whiting shall be freemen by that tyme.

The Townes of Hartford, Windsore and Wethersfield, or any other of the Townes within this jurisdiction, shall each of them haue power to dispose of their owne lands vndisposed of, and all other comõdityes arysing out of their owne lymitts bounded out by the Court, the libertyes of the great River excepted, as also to choose their owne officers, and make such orders as may be for the well ordering of their owne Townes, being not repugnant to any law here established, as also to impose penaltyes for the breach of the same, and to estreat and levy the same, and for non-payment to distrayne, and yf there

---

* [In margin] "Gou'r & Mr. Wells sent to P__e__q."

be noe personall estate, to sue to the Court to sell his or their house or land, for making satisfaction. Also each of the aforesayd Townes shall haue power by a generall consent once every yeare to choose out 3, 5 or 7 of their cheefe Inhabitants, whereof one to be chosen moderator, who having taken an oath prouided in that case, shall haue a casting voice in case they be equall; wch sayd p^rsons shall meett once in every 2 monthes & being mett together, or the maior part of them, whereof the moderato^r to be one, they shall haue power to heare, end and determine all controversies, eyther trespasses or debts not exceeding 40s. provided both partyes live in the same Towne; also any two of them or the moderato^r may graunt out sumons to the party or partyes to come to their meetings to answere the actions; also to administer oath to any witnesses for the clearing of the cause, and to giue judgment and execution against the party offending. But yf eyther party be grieved att the sentence, he shall haue liberty to appeale to a higher Court, p^rvided it be before iudgment and execution be graunted. But yf it fall out there be noe ground for the appeale, the Court to confirme the iudgment and giue good costs, and fine or punish the p^rty appealing.

The Townes aforesayd shall each of them p^rvide a Ledger Booke, with an Index or alphabett vnto the same: Also shall choose one who shall be a Towne Clerke or Register, who shall before the Generall Court in Aprill next, record every man's house and land already graunted and measured out to him, with the bounds & quantity of the same, and whosoever shall neglect 3 monthes after notice given to bring into the sayd Towne [31] Clerke ‖ or Register a note of his house and land, with the bounds and quantity of the same, by the nearest estimaĉon, shall forfeit 10s. and soe 10s. a month for every month he shall soe neglect. The like to be done for all land hereafter graunted and measured to any;* and all bargaines or morgages of land whatsoever shall be accounted of noe value vntill they be recorded, for wch entry the Register shall receaue 6d. for every parcell, delivering every owner a coppy of the same vnder his hand, whereof 4d. shall be for himselfe and 2d. for the Secretary of the Court. And the sayd Register shall, every Generall

---

* [In margin;] " Heere insert so much ye printed booke fol: 24 : from A : to B :"

Court, in Aprill and September, deliver into the same a transcript fayrely written of all such graunts, bargaines or ingagements recorded by him in the Towne Booke, and the Secretary of the Court shall record it in a booke fayrely written p^rvided for that purpose, and shall preserue the coppy brought in vnder the hand of the Towne Clerke. Also the sayd Towne Clerke shall haue for every serch of a parcell 1d. and for every coppy of a parcell ij$d$; and a coppy of the same vnder the hands of the sayd Register or Towne Clerke and two of the men chosen to governe the Towne, shall be a sufficient evidence to all that haue the same.

After the death and decease of any person possessed of any estate, be it more or lesse, and who maketh a will in writing or by word of mouth, those men wch are appointed to order the affayres of the Towne where any such person deceaseth, shall within one month after the same, at furthest, cause a true Inventory to be taken of the sayd estate in writing, as also take a coppy of the sayd will or testament and enter it into a booke or keepe the coppy in safe custody, as also enter the names vppon record of the Children and Legatees of the Testator or deceased p^rson, and the sayd orderers of the affayres of the Towne are to see every such will and Inventory to be exhibited into the publique Court, within one quarter of a yeare, where the same is to be registered; and the sayd orderers of the affayres of the Towne shall doe their indeauour in seeing that the estate of the Testator be not wasted nor spoyled, but improved for the best advantage of the Children or Legatees of the Testator, according to the mind of the Testator, for their and euery of their use, by their and every of their allowance and approbacõn. But when any p^rson dyeth intestate, the sayd orderers of the affayres of the Townes shall cause an Inventory to be taken, and then the publique Court may graunt the administracõn of the goodes and Chattells to the next of kin, jointly or severally, and divide the estate to wiefe (yf any be,) children or kindred, as in equity they shall see see meet; and yf noe kindred be found, the Court to administer for the publique good of the Comõn, p^rvided there be an Inventory registered, that yf any of the kindred in future tyme appeare they may haue justice and equity done vnto them; and all charges that the publique Court or the orderers of the affayres of the Townes are att about the trust comitted to them, eyther for writing or otherwise, it is to be payd out of the estate.

Within 20 dayes after the end of this Court, the Secretary shall provide a coppy of all the penall lawes or orders standing in force, and all other that are of generall concernement for [32] the ‖ governement of the Comonwealth, and shall giue direction to the Constables of every Towne to publish the same within 4 dayes more, att some publique meeting in their severall Townes, and then shall cause the sayd lawes and orders to be written into a booke in their severall Townes, and kept for the use of the Towne, and soe for future tyme for all lawes or orders that are made as aforesayd, each session of the Generall Courts; and once every yeare the Constables, in their severall Townes, shall read or cause to be read in some publique meeting all such lawes as then stand in force and are not repealed ; and the Secretary of the Court shall haue 12$d.$ for the coppy of the orders of each session of every generall Court, from each of the Townes.

Also, the Secretary of the Court shall have xij$d.$ for every action that is entred, to be payd by him that enters the action, and he that is cast in the suit to allow it in costs.

Whatsoever member of the generall Court shall reveale any secrett wch the Court inioynes to be kept secrett, or shall make knowne to any p^{r}son what any one member of the Court speaks concerning any p^{r}son or businesse that may come into agitacõn in the Court, shall forfeit for every such fault ten pounds, and be otherwise dealt withall, at the discretion of the Court. And the Secretary is to read this order att the beginning of every generall Court.

For the better keeping in mind of those passages of Gods p^{r}vidence wch haue beene remarkable since o^r first undertaking these plantacõns, Mr. Deputy, Capt. Mason, Mr. Stone, Mr. Goodwine, Mr. Chapleyn, and George Hubberd, are desired to take the pains severally in their severall Townes and then ioyntly together, to gather vp the same, and deliver them into the generall Court in Aprill next, and yf it be iudged then fitt, they may be recorded ; and for future tymes whatsoever remarkable passages shall be, yf they be publique, the sayd partyes are desired to deliver in the same to the generall Court. But yf any p^rticular p^rson desires to bring in any thing, he shall bring it vnder the handes of two of the aforementioned p^rtyes that it is true, and then present it to the generall Court, that yf it be there iudged requisite it may be recorded; provided that any generall Court for the future may alter any of the partyes beforementioned or add to them as they shall iudge meet.

The Court was dissolved.

---

[33]   Novemb^r the 7th, 1639.   A P^rticular Court.

Jno. Haynes Esqr., Mr. Wells, Mr. Webster, Mr. Phelps.

Richard Gildersley contra Jacob Waterhouse, in an action of debt. Jury find for pl^f. 14*l*. 18*s*. 9*d*.   Costs & damages 6*s*.

Jacob Waterhouse contra Ric. Gildersleeue, in an action of debt. The Jury find for the pl^f.

For a hogg,	2*l*.	0*s*.	0*d*.
Damages,	1.	17.	4.
Costs of suite,	0.	6.	0.
	3.	17.	4.

The Court adviseth vpon informacon given that the levying of Mr. Michell his fine be forborne vntill the next Generall Cou^t.

The Court admitteth the relict of Jno. Brundish of Wethersfield dec.ased to be Administratrix for the use of her and her children.*

Decr. the 5th, 1639.   A P^rticular Court.

Jno. Haynes Esqr., Roger Ludlow, Mr. Hopkins, Mr. Willis, Mr. Wells, Mr. Webster, Mr. Phelps.

Richard Westcoat contra Jno. Plum, in an action of trespasse, to the value of 10*l*. The Jury find for the pl^f. 6 Bushells of Corne: costs of suit 12*s*.

---

* An Inventory of the estate of John Brundish is recorded at page [70]

January. the 16th 1639

At generall Court.

Mr Governor enformed the Court that he at motion of rollinge from together on this bench was on the misgovernment of ministers, it avayringe to Lowes to Cause an sparinge of menistery. A serious Consideringe, and that on the notinge at that ended in all matters of generall concernment as a messare from Agawam and Mr Ludlow Letters to Mr Hoocker and Mr Stones from Agawam, By so many [illegible]. Sundry [illegible] in the Courte.

Edwa: Hopkins
(Secretary, 1639–1640.)

Jno. Plum contra Wm. Westcoat in an action of the case, not p^rforming the trust of a Cowkeeper, to his damage of 20*l*. The Jury find for the Deft.; costs 12*s*.

JANUARY THE 2^d, 1639.   A P^rTICULAR COURT.

Wm. Clarke, servant to Jno. Crow, was fined 40*s*. for misdemeano^r in drinking, and corporall punishment was remitted vppon his p^rmise of his care for the future to avoyd such occations.

Execution was granted to Richard Westcoat.

It was thought fitt and ordered that Frauncis Norton and Thomas Coleman shall haue power to call before them such as Mr. Plum shall suggest to them, to be (as he conceaues) joint offenders in the damage layd vppon his swine in the case of Ric. Westcoat, eyther in regard of any other Cattle that were knowne to be in the sayd Corne, or weaknesse of fence, or neglects in keeping shutt any gate or gates into the sayd Corne, and yf they can with the consent of the partyes, to divide the sayd damages layd vppon Mr. Plum. But yf they agree not, to returne their opinions concerning the same into the Court.

[34]   JANUARY THE 16th, 1639.   A GENERALL COURT.

Jno. Haynes Esqr., Roger Ludlow Esqr., Mr. Willis, Mr. Hopkins, Mr. Webster, Mr. Welles, Mr. Phelpes.

Comittees.   Mr. Steele, Mr. Spencer, Mr. Talcott, Jno. Pratt, Mr. Hill, Mr. Hull, Mr. Gaylord, Mr. Stoughton, Mr. Ward, Thurston Rayner, James Boosy, Ric. Crabb.

Mr. Governo^r informed the Court that the occation of calling them together att this tyme was att the importunity of o^r neighbo^{rs} of Wethersfeeld, who desired to haue some answere to their request concerning Vncoa, and therevppon he related that himselfe with Mr. Wells, according to the order of Court, went thither, and tooke a view of what had been done by Mr. Ludlow there, and vppon due consideracon of the same they haue thought fitt, vppon Mr. Ludlowes assenting to the tearmes propounded by them, to confirme the same.

It is ordered both for the satisfaction of those of Hartford & Windsore, who formerly mooved the Court for some inlargement of accommodaĉon, and also for o^r neighbo^{rs} of Wethersfeeld who desire a plantaĉon there, that Mr. Phelps, Mr. Hill, Thomas Scott, W^m. Gibons, Robert Rose and James Boosy, shall as soone as with any conveniency may be, view those parts by Vnxus Sepus wch may be suitable for those purposes and make report of their doings to the Court wch is adiorned for that end to the 20th of Feb^r. att 10 of the clocke in the morning.

F<small>EBR. THE</small> 20th, 1639. A <small>SESSION OF THE</small> G<small>ENERALL</small> C<small>OURTE.</small>

Mr. Hull moved the Court in behalfe of Thomas Foard of Windsore, that in regard the workemen are much taken vp and imployed in making a bridge and meeting house with them, and his worke hendred of impaling in the ground wch was graunted him by the Court for a hogg parke, that there may be graunted him a yeare longer tyme for the fencing it in; wch was vppon the reasons aforesayd condiscended to.

O^r neighbo^{rs} of Wethersfeeld, in regard the weather hath not hitherto suited for the viewing of Vnxus Sepos, and that a Generall Court ere long will fall in course, intimated their willingness to deferr the issue of the busines vntill then; onely it was conceaued fitt and ordered accordingly, that Mr. Wells, Capt. Mason and George Hubberd be added to the former Coĩmittee, who are with their view to vnderstand the desires of o^r neighbo^{rs} of Wethersfeeld, and to consider of such bounds as they iudge fitt for them, and to returne their opinions to the Court.

Mr. Deputy was intreated to consider of some orders concerning an inquiry into the death of any that happen eyther accidentally or by violence, and for disposing the estate of persons that dy intestate, and for ye power of the magistrate in inflicting corporall punishment, and present it to the next Court, as also what course may be best taken with any that shall buy or possesse lands within this Jurisdiction, that the publique good may be best promoted.

The Court was dissolved.

[35]   FEBR. THE 6th, 1639.   A P^{r}TICULAR COURT.

Jno. Haynes Esqr.
Roger Ludlow Esqr., Mr. Willis, Mr. Hopkins, Mr. Welles, Mr. Webster, Mr. Phelpes.

Jno. Porter was sworne a Constable for Windsore, Nathaniell Eli for Hartford, Robert Rose for Wethersfeeld, for the yeare ensueing.

Whereas there was graunted the first of August last an execution to Roger Williams and others of Windsore, vppon the goodes of Mr. Mathew Allen, for 5l. damages and costs, in a tryall of 12 men, wch execution was served by the officer of the Court and goodes or Cattell sold for p^{r}formance of the same, and the remainder offered by the sayd officer to Mr. Allen, wch he refused. The officer now brought fower pounds six shillings into the Court, wch was delivered into the hands of Mr. Tres^r. vntill further orders.

Mr. Oldams estate being examined the account of it as it stands in this Jurisdiction is as followeth:

Estate of Mr. Oldam deceased is debtor,

	£. s. d.		
To Mathew Marvine,	1. 6. 8.		
To Richard Lord,	5. 5. 0.		
To W^m. Lewis,	9. 12. 3.	Pr Contra is Credit$_r$,	
To Edward Mason,	3. 3. 0.	By Lieftenant Seely,	£28. 15. 2.
To Jeffery Ferris,	3. 15. 0.	By Jno. Chapman,	£ 4. 15. 0.
To Henry Browning,	11. 0. 0.	By Ric. Lawes,	£ 6. 4. 11.
To Thomas Staunton,	03. 5. 0.	By Mr. Chapleyne,	£89. 15. 2.
To Thomas Scott,	00. 18. 0.	By Thomas Allen,	£ 6. 16. 6.
To Mr. Chapleyn,	146. 18. 0.		
To Mr. Pincheon,	022. 19. 9.		£136. 6. 9.
To Andrew Warner,	009. 19. 0.		
To Edwa. Stebbing,	002. 13. 4.		
To Mr. Talcott,	021. 6. 3.	Jan. the 6o, 1640.	
To Mr. Jno. Haynes,	002. 0. 0.	Wm Lewis abated out of his debt on the other side 2l. 16s., wch he was to allow for a hogg he bought of Mr. Oldam.	
To Mathew Allen,	020. 15. 0.		
To Lieftenant Seely,	010. 13. 0.		
To Edward Hopkins, & Mr. Mathew Craddocke,	229. 00 0.		
	0504. 09. 3.		

It was thought fit and ordered that this Acc^o be sent to the Bay, and yf a iust acc^o be also returned from thence in a reasonable tyme, an equal division may be made of the whole; yf not, the estate here shall be divided among the Creditors here.

Frauncis Norton and Thomas Coleman deliuered into the Court their apprehensions touching the case betweene Mr. Plum and Ric. Westcoatt, wch being taken into full considera̅con by the Court, It was ordered that the iudgment by the jury shall stand, and execution to be graunted to Westcoatt; but it is thought fitt that Jeffery Ferris shall allow Mr. Plum two bushells of Corne, towards the damages layd vppon his swine, in regard his fence is found to be insufficient, and his Cowes were p^rved to be in Westcoatts corne, and Mr. Chester is to allow Mr. Plum̅ one bushell of Corne, in regard his bore was found to be in the sayd Corne as well as Mr. Plum̅s.

[36] And it was further ordered that Jeffery Ferris, in regard he challenged the partyes interested by the Court for searching out the sayd businesse, not to be indifferent men, and denyed to attend them according to the order of Court, shall pay as a fine to the Cuntrey 20s.; and in regard he was one occation of much charge to Mr. Plum̅ in bringing many witnesses this day, vppon his suggestion to the Court that they would not speake that that in the face of the Court wch they did before the Com̅issioners, wch was found otherwise, he was adiudged to pay 10s. to Mr. Plum towards his charges; and Richard Westcoat, for misleading Jno. Whitmore, was fined 10s. to the Cuntrey.

March the 5th, 1639.   A P^rticular Court.

Jno. Haynes Esqr. Governo^r.
Roger Ludlow Esqr. Dep'ty.
Mr. Hopkins, Mr. Wells, Mr. Webster, Mr. Phelpes.

This present day there was returned into the Court by Mr. Gaylard, one of the overseers, a Coppy of the estate of the children of Thomas Newbery deceased, dated the 10th of Febr. 1639, subscribed by Mr. Ludlow, Mr. Phelpes, Mr. Huett, Mr. Hill, George Hull and Wm. Hosford.

Whereas a difference hath arisen betweene Mr. Smith and some others of Wethersfeeld, about the measure of some ground, wᶜʰ being long debated it was thought fitt that it be referred to some indifferent men to issue, and Mr. Wells and Mr. Webster are intreated by the Court, in the first and fittest season to goe downe to Wethersfeeld, and to settle the same as in equity and justice they shall see fitt, that peace and truth may be continued. But it was iudged very equall and reasonable, in regard Mr. Smith in setting vp his posts pʳceeded in a legall and iust way, that he be not putt to the charge of taking vp and setting downe his posts againe : the rule that Mr. Wells and Mr. Webster are to goe by is one of the other 3 ranges of meadow, and they may call whom they thinke meet in Weathersfeeld to assist in the busines.

Whereas there was an attachment graunted to Ric. Lord vppon the goodes of Thomas Allen, for 42s. 6d. debt and costs, the attachment was served and 6 cushions, 3 Barstable ruggs, 6 paire of Childrens shues, one paire of Boots, and an ould Cloakebagg were put into the hands of Thomas Staunton vntill the action be tryed, and further order taken therein.

Mr. Deputy returned a recognisance into Court wherein James Northam was bound by him for his appearance this day. But he came nott.

[37]   Aprill the 2ᵈ, 1640.   A Pʳticular Court.
  Jno. Haynes Esqʳ. Govʳ.
  Mr. Willis, Mr. Welles, Mr. Webster, Mr. Phelpes, Mr. Hopkins.

Mary Brunson, now the wiefe of Nicolas Disborough, Jno. Olmested, Jonathan Rudd and Jno. Peerce were corrected for wanton dalliance and selfe pollution.

This day Rachel Brundish of Weathersfield presented an Inventory of her husbands estate,* wᶜʰ amounted (all debts being payd) to 90l. 5s. 4d. and the house and land was rated at 130l. And it was thought fitt and ordered that the relict of the sayd Jno. Brundish shall haue to her owne use the 90l. 5. 4.; and the land with the house to be for the childrens portions, vizt. 30l. to the sonne and 25l. a peece to each of the 4 daughters to be

---

* Recorded at page [70.]

payd into the Court for their use when each of them come to the age of sixteene yeares and in the meane tyme the widow to haue the use of the land for bringing vp the children.

It was also ordered that yf the sayd Rachell doe thinke fitt to sell the house and land, she may haue liberty soe to doe, provided before she make any sale thereof she giue suffitient security into ye Court for the payment of the childrens portions att the tymes prefixed, and for the due education of them; and having soe done, she may make her best advantage of the sayd house and landes, provided also that yf any one or more of the children depart this life before they come to the age of 16 yeares, his or their portion is to be divided equally among those that survive.

---

[39]   April the IX.th. 1640.   The Court of Election.

Mr. Hopkins Esqr. Gouer^r.
Mr. Haynes, Deputy,
Mr. Wyllis,
Mr. Ludlow, *absent* — These elected Magestrats.
Mr. Welles,
Mr. Phelps,
Mr. Webster,

Deputyes: Mr. Steele, Mr. Talcott, Mr. Spenser, Ed: Stebbing, Willm. Gaylard, Tho: Ford, Mr. Stoughton, Mr. Hull, Thurston Rayner, James Boosy, George Hubberd, Rich: Crabbe.

These were made Free:—

These inhabitants of Wyndsor: Mr. Ephra: Huytte, Mr. Arther Willm̃s, Michaell Tray, Richard Parsons, Tho: More, John More, Tho: Dyblie, Henry Clarke, Willm̃: Gylbert, Tho: Bassette, Elias Parkmã.

Hartford: Daniell Garrette, Robert Wade, Tho: Seldon. Mr. Parke at Wethersfyeld.

It is Ordered that the Gouernor shall giue Mr. Ludloe his Oath, for the place of Magestracy.

It is Ordered that yf any Indean be discouered by the Watch in the night wthin any of the Plantations of this Jurisdiction, or be found by the ward in the day breakeing open any house or offering any desp^rate assaulte, wch may indaynger the life of any p^rson, it shall be lawfull for the watch or ward in such case to shutte any such Indean or Indeans, if he or they shall not subiect thēselues to the watch or ward. And that Tho: Steynton shall, w^thin fowerteene dayes, giue notice of this Order to all the Chiefe Indeans who haue ordinary recourse to these Plantations.

It is Ordered that the Towne of Wyndsor shall haue liberty, vntill the Generall Courte in September next, to bring in the Records of their lands.

It is Ordered that Mr. Haynes, Mr. Ludloe & Mr. Welles shall setle the diuision of the bounds betwixt Paquanocke & Uncowaye, by the 24th day of June next, according to their former Comīssion: And also that they tender the Oath of Fidellity to the Inhabitants of the said Townes, and make such free as they shall aproue of.

Aprill the Xth. 1640.

Forasmuch as many stubborne & refractory Persons are often taken w^thin these libertyes, and no meet place yet p^rpared for the detayneing & keepeing of such to their due & deserued punishement, It is therefore Ordered that there shall be a house of Correction built, of 24 foote long & 16 or 18 foote broad, wth a Celler, ether of wood or stonne, according as Mr. Talcotte, Ed: Stebing, Tho: Ford and James Boosy shall thinke meete, who are chosen by the Courte to lette out the worke, appoynt out the place & to order and directe whatsoeuer occations and businesses that may fall out for the compleate finishing the said house, wch is to be done by the next Courte, in September.

Forasmuch as many Persons intangle thmselues by rashe & inconsiderat Contracts for their future joyneing in Maridge Couenant, to the great troble and greife of thēselues and their frynds; for the avoyding whereof, It is Ordered, That whosoeuer intend to joyne themselues in Maridge Couenant shall cause that their purpose of Contracte to be published in some publike place & att some publike meeting in the seuerall

Townes where such persons dwell, at the lest, eight dayes before they enter into such Contracte, whereby they ingadge [41] thēselues ech to other; and that || they shall forbeare to joyne in Maridge Couenant at lest eight dayes after the said Contracte. And also the Magestrate who solemnizeth Mariedge betwixt any, shall cause a record to be entered in Courte of the day & yere thereof.

It is Ordered, that Mr. Moody of Hartford, and Ensigne Stoughton of Wyndsor, shall be p^{r}ferred Liuetenants, and Mr. Rocester of Wyndsor shall be p^{r}ferred Ensigne, for the severall bands in the said Townes.

It is Ordered, that the Liuetenants & Ensignes shall be freed frō watching & warding, and the Seargeant frō warding and halfe their watch.

Aprill XI. 1640.

It is Ordered, there shall be a Rate of a hundred pownd leuyed vppon the Country, wch is to be p^{r}portioned by Mr. Talcott, Mr. Stoughton & James Boosy;—who haue p^{r}portioned the said Rate as followeth:

Imp^{rs}. Hartford,	43l.	0.	0.
Wyndsor,	28.	10.	0.
Wethersfyeld,	28.	10.	0.
Sum̄	100l.		

Mr. Steele is returned Recordor for the Towne of Hartford, and hath brought into the Courte 114 coppyes of the severall p^{r}cells of land belonging to & conserneing 114 p^{r}sons.

Mr. Rocester is returned Recordor for the Towne of Wyndsor.

Mr. Michell is returned Recordor for the Towne of Wethersfyeld, but he is found vncapable of the place, lying vnder censure of the Courte, and he and the Towne who chose him to that place are to haue notice to apeare at the next adiournement of the Courte. They are to haue liberty to bring in the Records of their lands vntill the Generall Courte in September nexte.

The Courte adioyrned vntill the 2^d Thursday in June, 1640.

[42]   The Pʳticuler Courte May the vii^{th}, 1640.
  Mr. Ed: Hopkins Esqr. Gou^r.
  Mr. Haynes, Deputy.
     Mr. Wyllis, Mr. Welles, Mr. Phelps, Mr. Webster.

George Abbott of Wyndsor, searuant to*
he is adiudged to pay fiue pownd fyne for selling a pystoll & powder to the Indeans, and to be bound to his good behauior. He is to be disposed of by the Courte for further searvice, to his Master or some other as they shall judge meete, for his paying the said fyne.

Simon Hoyette and his family are to be freed frō watch & ward vntill there be further Order taken by the Courte.

Andrew Bacon and John Barnard haue returned into the Courte a Inventory of the goods of Tho: Johnson decessed, to the some of 11*l*. 5*s*. 10*d*.

At the request of Mr. Phelps, in the behalfe of Mr. Rocester, an attachment is graunted for the Constable of Wyndsor to distreyne & take into his custody 20 bush^s. of Corne, of James Nortons of Quinipwucke, and that to keepe vntill the said James shall appeare at the Courte at Hartford and there answere what shall be laid to his chardge.

Mr. John Shareman of Wethersfyeld is to be freed frō watching vntill the Courte take further Order.

John Hopkins of Hartford is also freed frō watching vntill further Order be taken by the Courte.

Whereas there was an Agreement betwixt the Inhabitants of Wethersfyeld and Liuetenant Seely that the differences betwixt them in sute for Lands, should be referred to Arbitriment by partyes betwixt them agreed vppon, vizt. Mr. Hooker & Mr. Welles, and in case they two should differ, they were to chuse a third, for the issuing thereof, who did accordingly make choyce of Mr. Webster, the Court also consenting thereunto, It is now the Appʳhension of the Courte that the foresaid partyes shall stand to the award as yt is deliuered in by the said Mr. Webster, vizt. That the said Inhabitants of Wethersfyeld shall pay to the said Liuetenant, 150 bush^s of Corne, and this the Court adiudgeth to be paid by ech mans proportion through't the

---

* This blank occurs in the original.

whole Meadowes. The said Liuetenant is also to be alowed 20s. for his chardges and delay of payment.

[43]   THE PʳTICULER COURT. JUNE 4th, 1640.

Mr. Ed: Hopkins Esqʳ. Gouʳ.
Mr. Haynes,
   Mr. Wyllis, Mr. Welles, Mr. Phelps, Mr. Webster.

Ed: Veare of Wethersfyeld is fined Xs. for cursing & swereing, and also he is to sitt in the stocks at Wethersfyeld, two howers the next Trayneing day.

Williā. Hill of Hartford, for buying a stolen peece of Mr. Plums man, and brekeing open the Coblers Hogshed & Packe, for boath these mysdemenors hes fyned fower pownds to the Country.

Nicholas Olmsteed for his laciuious caridge & fowle mysdemenors at sundry tymes wᵗʰ Mary Brunson is adiudged to pay twenty pownd fyne to the Country, and to stand vppon the Pillery at Hartford the next lecture day dureing the time of the lecture. He is to be sett on, a lytle before the begining & to stay thereon a litle after the end.

The foresaid Nicholas Olmsteed acknowledgeth hymself to be bound in a Recognizance of xxxl. to the Country, to repaire the foresaid next lecture day by nyne of the clocke to the Constable of Hartford, to submitt to the said judgment of the Courte.

[44]   A GENERALL COURTE.   JUNE XIth, 1640.   HARTFORD.

Mr. Ed: Hopkins Esqʳ. Gouʳ.
Mr. Haynes, Deputy.
   Mr. Wyllis, Mr. Welles, Mr. Phelps, Mr. Webster.

Deputyes :—Mr. Steele, Mr. Talcott, Ed: Stebing, Willm̄ Gaylard, Mr. Stoughton, Mr. Hull, Thurston Raynor, James Boosy, Richard Crabbe.

It is Ordered, that if any deputy shall be absent vppon such occation as the Gouerno{r} for the tyme being shall approue of, or by the P{r}uidence of God shall decease this life, w{th}in the adioyrnement of any Courte, that yt shall be at the liberty of the Gou{r} to send forth a warrent in such case, for supply thereof, vppon resonable warneing.

It is Ordered, that the highway betwixt Hartford & Wyndsor, as yt was laste sette forth vppon the vpland, shall be made sufficiently passable, by ech Towne what lyeth w{th}in their owne bownds, w{th}in the space of on month, and there shall be liberty graunted to vse the highway through the meadowes vntill the said vpland highway be so sufficiently mended, for horse and drifte, as yt shall be aproued of by Mr. Plum, James Boosy, Henry Wolcotte & Tho: Scotte, and then the highway through the medowe to cease.

Richard Gyldersly was conuented before the Courte for casteing out p{r}nitious speeches, tending to the detriment & dishonnor of this Com̃onwelth, and was fyned to pay to the Country forty shillings, and was bownd to his good behauior, in a Recognizance of 20*l*. to apeare at the next Generall Courte, to the w{ch} he submitted himselfe.

Whereas the Dutch Catle are impounded for trespassing the Englishmens Corne, It is the iudgment of the Courte that the Dutchmen shall be made acquainted w{th} the trespasse, and satisfaction demaunded, the w{ch} if they refuse to pay, the Cattell are to be kepte in the pownd three dayes, and then to be prysed & sold, and the trespasse to be satisfied, togather w{th} the chardge of impounding, keepeing & tending the said Catle dureing their custody.

Yf Mr. Michell shall giue satisfaction to Mr. Chaplin in some publike meeting, as p{r}te of his censure, by acknowledging his fault, in such forme and manner as he hath related to this Courte, It is referred to the p{r}ticuler Courte to continue or take off his former censure as they shall see cause.

The said Mr. Michell, for vndertaking the office of Towne Clarke or Recordor, notw{th}standing his vncapablenes of such office by censure of Courte, he is fyned to pay to the Country twenty Nobles.

That p{r}te of the Towne of Wethersfyeld who chose the said

Mr. Michill to office, notw^th^standing the censure of Courte, are fyned to the Country five pownds.

Its desired that Mr. Gouernor & Mr. Deputy should returne an answer to the laste letter sent frō the Dutch Gouernor.

Mr. Gouernor, Mr. Deputy & Mr. Wyllis are desired to treate wth the Ilandors & Vncuus, conserneing the Mohegins kylling the Indean wth a peece, and to put yt to issue, if they can, or returne yt agayne to the Courte.

Forasmuch as our lenity & gentlenes toward Indeans hath made thē growe bold & insolent, to enter into Englishemens howses, and vnadvisedly handle sowrds & peeces and other instruments, many times to the hazard of the lymbs of liues of Englishe or Indeans, and also to steale diuers goods out of such howses where they resorte; for the p^r^uenting of such mischeifs, yt is Ordered, that whatsoeu^r^ Indean shall hereafter medle wth or handle any Englishemans weapens of any sorte, ether in their howses or in the fyelds, they shall forfeit for euery such default halfe a fadom of wampū; and if any hurt or ‖ iniury [45] shall therevppon followe, to any p^r^sons life or lymbe (though accidentall) they shall pay life for life, lymbe for lymbe, wound for wound, and shall pay for the healeing such wounds & other damages; and for any thing that they steale, to pay double, and suffer such further punishement as the Magestrats shall adiudge thē. The Constable of any Towne may attach and areste any Indean that shall transgresse in any such kynd before mentioned, and bring thē before some Magestrate, who may execute the penalty of this Order vppon offendors in any kynd excepte life or lymbe; and any p^r^son that seeth such defaults may p^r^secute & shall haue halfe the forfeiture.

June the 15th, 1640. The Order concerneing Artificers & laborers for wages, is renewed dureing the pleasure of the Courte.

The p^r^ticuler Courte is to conclude the conditions for the planting of Tunxis.

And also to p^r^secute the murtherers as they shall see cause. vppon consultation wth the Bay and o^r^ neighbor Plantations aboute the sea coste.

It is Ordered, that the Magestrats shall send for the Tribuit of the Indeans aboute Cuphege, Vncoway & there aboute.

It is Ordered, that in all appropriated ground, the owners thereof shall bound every p^rticular p^rcell wth sufficient mere-stones, and so to p^rsearve & keepe them.

It is Ordered, that Mr. Ludlowe, Mr. Hopkins & Mr. Blakman shall survey & divyde and sett out the bownds betwixt the Plantations of Cuphege & Vncoway, p^rvided if they cannot accord, Mr. Welles at his next coming to those p^rts shall issue yt.

It is Ordered, that what p^rson or p^rsons wthin this jurisdiction shall, after September, 1641, drinke any other Tobacco but such such as is or shalbe planted wthin these libertyes, shall forfeit for every pownd so spent fiue shillings, except they haue license frõ the Courte.

Whereas by an Order the 14th of January, 1640, none is to be chosen a Magestrate but such as are p^rpounded in some generall Courte before, yet notwthstanding, as Cuphege & Vncoway are somewhat farre distant frõ this Courte, and there is a necessity of the dispensation of justice in those Townes, therefore in the meane & vntill the next Generall Courte of Election, yt it thought meet & so ordered, that Mr. Williã Hopkins of Cuphege be a Comĩssion^r to joyne wth Mr. Ludlow in all Executions in their p^rticuler Courte or otherwise, & is now sworne to that purpose.

[46] Whereas by an Order the seaventh of December last, the difference betweene Mr. Allen & Wyndsor conserneing land purchased of Plymõth, was, by consent, referred to Mr. Haynes, Mr. Ludlowe, Mr. Hopkins, & Mr. Phelps, to end the same, & what is agreed on by thẽ is to be yelded vnto on boath sides ; according to wch Order & reference we who are mentioned in the saide Order haue seriously weighed all such arguments as haue bine tendred vnto vs on both syds, and we cannot see but Mr. Allen ought to be subiecte, for the said land & purchase, to the lawes & Orders and Jurisdiction of this Comõnwelth, and by a necessary consequence, subject to that Plantation of Wyndsor, wherein the said land lies, & to all such resonable & lawfull Orders as are agreed there for the publike good of the same, and in equall p^rportion to beare his share in all rates there, soe as while he or his successors liue elsewhere then he or they are to pay only according to his p^rportion of land there, & p^rfitte & benefitts thence ariseing, and such stocke as is resident or vsually imployed in & thereuppon. And o^r judgment for the

p^rsent is, that the said Mr. Allen nor his successors should not be rated in any other place for that land and estate he hath there, as afores'd. It is intended that Mr. Allen haue notice giuen him, in conuenient tyme, of all such orders as doe or may concerne him, and that the orders, be such as ly w^thin his compasse & power to accomplishe & p^rforme in a resonable way.

Dated the 4th of Ja: 1638, and subscribed by

Jo: Haynes,
Ro: Ludlowe,
Ed: Hopkins,
Will' Phelps.

An Oath for Paqua' and the Plantations there.

I 𝔄. 𝔅. being by the P^ruidence of God an inhabitant w^thin the Jurisdiction of Conectecotte, doe acknowledge myselfe to be subject to the gou^rment thereof, and doe sweare by the great and dreadfull name of the eu^rliueing God to be true and faythfull vnto the same, and doe submitt boath my p^rson & estate thereunto, according to all the holsome lawes & orders that ether are or hereafter shall be there made by lawfull authority: And that I will nether plott nor practice any euell agaynst the same, nor consent to any that shall so doe, but will tymely discou^r the same to lawfull authority established there; and that I will mayntayne, as in duty I am bownd, the honor of the same & of the lawfull Magestrats thereof, promoteing the publike good thereof, whilst I shall so continue an Inhabitant there, and whensou^r I shall give my vote, suffrage or p^rxy, being cauled thereunto, touching any matter wch conserns this Comonwelth, I will giue yt as in my conscience may conduce to the best good of the same, w^thout respect of p^rson or favor of any man; so helpe me God in the Lo: Jesus Christ.

[48]   July the 2^d, 1640. The P^rticuler Courte.
    Samuell Smith pl^t ag^t Andrewe Waird.
    Richard Coker pl^t ag^t John Cable.
    Richard Lord pl^t ag^t Tho: Robinson.

Ed: Hopkins Esquire, Gou^r.

Mr. Haynes, Mr. Wyllis, Mr. Welles, Mr. Phelps, Mr. Webster.

The Jury :—Williā Whiting, Gent. Ju^r., Robert Parke, John Edwards, Robert Abbott, John Notte, Bray Rocester, Richard Whithead, John Byssyll, Walter Fyler, Williā Wodsworth, Richard Lord, Gregory Wynterton, Ju^r.

John Haynes, Esquire, pl^t ag^t John Cockerryll defend^t in an action of debt of xiij *l*. The Jury find for the plan^t. The defend^t is to pay damages xiij *l*. and costs of sute viij *s*. The Courte graunts the pl execution ag^t the body or goods of the defend^t for the foresaid damages and Costs.

M^r. Mytchel hath this day returned into Court his acknowledgement to Mr. Chaplin, and for that, wth other considerations, for former extraordinary chardges wch he hath formerly borne for publike seruice at the Forte, the Court hath remitted his former censure.

Nicholas Senthion, for not apeareing to witnesse agaynst Aron Starke, is fyned to pay fiue pownd to the Country.

John Porter, one of the Constables of Wyndsor, is to keepe the said Aron Starke wth locke and chaine and hold him to hard labour & course dyet vntill he be cauled to bring him forth vppon the next somons.

The said Aron being accused of [bestiality, confessed that he had committed the crime.]

John Euens, for his contempte ag^t the Townsmen, is fyned x*s*.

Andrewe Bacon and John Barnard an appoynted to sell the goods of the Cobler* deceased, formerly taken by Inventory given into Courte by the said partyes.

It is Ordered, that whosoeuer enters any action in the Court, the Plan^t. shall pay the costs of Court, though the action be not tryed, and the Jury to haue their p^rts.

George Wolcott acknowledge himselfe to be bownd in a Recognizance of ten pownd that his brother Henry Wolcott shall p^rsecut an action of the case & bring it to tryall ag^t

---

* Thomas Johnson. See account of sales, p. [75].

Church of Hartford, for impownding the hoggs of Henry Wolcott his father, and will subiect to the issue thereof as y^t shall be adiudged the next Court holden at Hartford.

Thos : Welles.

[49]   Henry Wolcotte pl^t agaynst   Church defend^t, in in an action of the case, wherein the said Henry complaynes ag^t the said   Church for takeing into his custody & deteyneing thirty swyne of Henry Wolcotts the elder, father to the said Henry, to the damage of

Williā Whiting Gent^m. pl^t. ag^t. Jasp^r Rowlins defend^t. in an action of debt 20s. debt.

Leonard Chester pl^{te}. ag^t John Edwards, Nathaniell Foote, defend^t in an action of trespas, for brech of order, to the damage of 4 l.

Saqueston testifies in Court that he neu^r sould any grownd to the Dutch, nether was at any tyme conquered by the Pequoyts, nor paid any trybuit to thē. And when he sometymes liued at Mattanag and hard by his fryends that liued here, that he and his men came & fought wth thē.

Whereas there was an Order of Court made for the vewing of the hie waie leading frō Hartford to Wyndsor, amongst others, there was appoynted James Boosy and John Plum, who haue, according to direction of Court, vewed the same; and that p^{rte} wch was shewed vs by Tho : Scott, wch lyeth betweene Hartford Towne and the lyne wch deuid betweene yt and Wyndsor, we find to be mended sufficiently, so as men may both ryde and goe one foote, and make drifte of Cattle, comfortablie : but that parte in Wyndsor bound was nothing done when wee vewed yt, wch was about the seauententh of July, 1640.

The Coppy.   Jo : Plum, Ja : Boosy.

---

[50]   September the 4th, 1640.

Henry Packs (?) his Wyll.

It is my Will to bestow vppon the Church the Clocke that Brother Thorneton had bought, to Mr. Wichfyeld my best Coate and whoight (?) Cappe, to Mr.   my best dublets.

Ed: Masons Inuentory.

A true Inuentory of the goods and Chattells of Edward Mason of Wethersfyeld, late deceased, vizt.

	£	s	d
Impr^s The Cloathes of the said Edward,	4	0	0
Itē, in Halle, brasse, Pewter etc.	7	16	0
Itē, in the parlour, a fetherbed, wth chests, lynens and other things,	13	0	0
Itē, in the Celler,	2	0	0
Itē, Englishe Corne, wth Indean Old and New,	41	0	0
Itē, in the Chamber, a fetherbedde wth others,	9	10	0
Itē, twenty sixe borrowe hoggs, stores & sowes,	31	0	0
Itē, 3 Ewes, one Ewe kydd, 2 weathers,	8	0	0
Itē, Tooles & all other Implyments belonging to the trade of the said Edward.	4	15	0

Valued p^r Som̄ totalis 121. 1. 00
  Williā Swayne,
  George Hubberd,
    Test Leo: Chester.

---

[51]   OATH FOR THE JURY.

You shall swere that you 𝔄. 𝔅. shall duly try the cause or causes now giuen you in chardge, betweene the pl^t & def^t or pl^{ts} & defend^{ts}, according to yor euidence giuen in Courte, and accordingly a true verdict giue; yor owne counsell & yor fellowes you shall duly keepe; you shall speake nothing to any one, of the busines & matters in hand, but amongst yo^{r}selues, nor shall you suffer any to speake vnto you about the same, but in Court: when you are agreed of any verdicte you shall keep yt secret till you deliuer yt vp in Court: so helpe you God.

SEPTEMBER THE Xth, 1640.

It is Ordered, that Ed: Hopkins Esqr. now Gouernour, shall haue the benefitte and liberty of free trade at Waranocoe & att any place thereabout, vppe the Riuer, and all other to be restreyned for the terme of seauen yeres, and the land to be purchased for the Com̄onwelth.

[56] THE GENERALL COURT, FEBRUARY THE viij^th, 1640.
Edward Hopkins Esqr, Gour^r.
John Heynes Esqr, Dep^ty.
Mr. Wyllis, Mr. Welles, Mr. Phelps, Mr. Webster.
Deputyes :—Mr. Steele, Mr. Talcott, John Pratt, Ed : Stebbing, Samuell Smith, George Hubbert, James Boosy, Richard Crabb, Captain Mason, Mr. Hill, Mr. Hull, Will' Gaylord.

Forasmuch as Sequin hath so long delayed in making satisfaction for the mare that was killed by his Indeans, the Court thinks meet that a p^rmptory answer be required of him, and in case full satisfaction be not therevppon giuen, that p^rsent intelligence shall be giuen to Quinipiouck & o^r neighbour Plantations, that we shall accoumpte of him as o^r enimy, in regard of that affornt & many other insolent caridges of his, and shall speedily right o^rselues of him. The Gouernour & Mr. Deputy are desired by the Court to agitate & issue the whole busines.

Forasmuch as the Court, takeing into consideration the p^rsent condition of these Plantations, doe find a great expence yerely to be laid out to fetch in supply frō other p^rts in such comodityes as are of necessary vse, and not knowing how this Comōnwelth can be long supported vnlesse some staple Comōdity be raysed amongst o^rselues wch may in some sort answer and defray the chardge,—haue therefore thought requisite that all incouridgement be giuen for the full imployment of men & cattle for the improuement of such ground as the Country affords for English grayne where yt may be raysed wth lest chardge ; for the speedy furthering thereof liberty is graunted to all such persons w^thin these Plantations as stand disposed to imploy theselues or their estats in husbandry as aforesaid, to find out any sutable grownd w^thin these libertyes yet vnpossest, where the said Englishe grayne may be soonest raysed, and haue graunted to ech Teeme a hundred acres of plowing grownd and twenty acres of meadow, p^rvided they improue twenty acres the first yere, wch is to be accoumpted frō the date of these p^rsents, & eighty acres the second yeare, and the whole hundred the third yeare. And for the orderly p^rceeding therein, the Court hath desiered the W^{orll} Edward Hopkins Esqr. Gou^r, Mr. Deputy & Mr. Willis to appoynt and sett forth the forme and order how ech mans p^rportion shall be laid out, togather wth a competent quantity of vpland to the same, and to alowe to the owner of ech Teeme a competent lott for a workman wch may be helpfull to manadge the busines and carry on the worke; as also to admit inhabitants (if any place so found out shall be iudged meete for a plantatiō) and to sett out their bownds; and those p^rsons who first giue in their names to the Comittee, to vndertake the worke and attend to haue their diuisions sett forth, shall be first searued in order as they com, next after the Comittee haue made choyce for thēselues: But if any p^rson so vndertakeing the manadgeing of a hundred acres, or a lesse p^rportion, vppon the terms before mentioned, shall neglect to p^rforme the conditions before specified, or be vnable to accomplish the same, the Court hath researued power to dispossesse him or thē of the grownd, giueing such resonable satisfaction for the chardge bestowed thereuppon as the said Court shall judge meete. And if any p^rson or p^rsons tendreing thēselues to vndertake the manadgeing of 100 acres as aforesaid shall be iudged by the Comittee vnable or vnmeet for the worke, not likely to p^rforme the conditions in so great a quantity, they may ether refuse to admitt such or alowe a lesser p^rportion to them.

It is also Ordered, that what stocke shall be remoued to any such place, shall be levied to the Towne frō whence yt came, as if yt were resident there; And the chardge disbursed for makeing wayes or any comon benefitt to such place, shall be paid by the land wthin the said liberty, as yt shall be taken vppe [57] and possest. ǁ But when such Place shall becom a Plantation & be at chardge to mayntayne Officers wthin thēselues, then other considerations may be had by the Courte.

Whereas yt is thought necessary for the comfortable support of these plantations, that a trade of Cotten wooll be sett vppon and attempted, for the furthering whereof yt hath pleased the Gouerno^r, that now is, to vndertake the furnisheing and setting forth a vessell, wth convenient speed, to those parts where the said comodity is to be had yf yt proue phesable: In consideration whereof, as also frō the considerations in the former order specified, It is ordered by the Authority aforesaid, that vppon the Returne of the said vessell, the Plantations by p^rportion shall take offe the said Cotten, at such valuable consideration as yt may be afforded, according as chardge shall aryse and acreue thereuppon; the pay for the said Cotten wooll to be made in Englishe Corne or Pype-staues as the Country shall afford: The p^rportions to be diuiyded and laid vppon the seuerall Townes are according to the diuision of the last Country Rate.

And for the better p^rsearuing of Tymber, that the Country may haue p^rvisions of Pypestaues for the furthering the said trade of Cotten wooll, It is Ordered that no Tymber shall be felled frō w^thout the bownds of these Plantations, w^thout lycence frō the p^rticuler Courte, nor any Pipestaues to be sould out of the Riuer w^thout alowance frō the said Courte, nor transported into foraigne p^rts vntill they be vewed (by such Cōmittee as the said Court shall appoynt) and app^rued by such to be vendable, boath for the goodnes of the Tymber, and due p^rportion & size thereof.

The p^rticuler Court also is desiered to take order for the veweing of Pequot Country and disposeing of the Tymber there, as also to settle Inhabitants in those p^rts yf they see cause, so far as yt may be acted w^thout chardge to the Country.

For the p^ruenting of differenses that may arise betwixt the Plantations frō trespasses by Cattle wch are ofte necessitated, by reson of their bordering on ag^t another, It is Ordered, that Nathaniell Waird, Andrewe Warner, Mr. Plum, Robert Rose, Mr. Porter & Tho: Ford, shall take into their serious considerations how the grownd belonging to the seuerall Plantations may be best imp^rued, so as to sute ech others conuenience, whereby their Corne may be p^rserued and their Cattle keepte wth lest chardge of fencing or herding, as may most conduce to the cōmon good, and deliuer in their app^rhentions to the next Generall Court.

Whereas yt is obsearued that many skins and felts of Cowes & goats, through want of p^ruident p^rsearueing and seasonable bringing forth to dressing, suffer great losse, It is Ordered, that whatsoeu^r skins are or shall be in any mans hands w^thin these libertyes shall be carefully p^rsearued and seasonably brought in to such as improue thē, vnder such penalty as the Court shall inflict vppon the neglect thereof, and that care be taken in fleeing the skins, the neglect whereof occasioneth great losse.

[58] Whereas yt is obserued as experience hath made appeare, that much grownd wthin these libertyes may be well improued in hempe & flaxe, and that we myght in tyme haue supply of lynnen cloath amongst o^{r}selues, and for the more speedy p^{r}curing of hempseed, It is Ordered, that euery p^{r}ticuler family wthin these Plantations, shall p^{r}cure & plant this p^{r}sent yeare at lest on spoonefull of Englishe hempseed, in some frutfull soyle, at lest a foote distant betwixt eu^r seed, and the same so planted shall p^{r}searue and keepe in husbanly manner for supply of seed for another yeare.

It is also Ordered, that the second yeare, euery family that keeps a Teeme, though not aboue two or three drafte Cattle, shall sowe the second yeare at lest on rood of hempe or flaxe, and eu^r p^{r}son that keeps any Cattle, namely, cowes, heifers or steers, shall sowe 20 p^{r}ches, & eu^r family, though he keepe no Cattle, shall sowe tenn p^{r}ches, and ech p^{r}ticuler of the foresaid families shall in husbandly sorte p^{r}searue & tend their seuerall p^{r}portions, or in default thereof are to vndergoe the censure of the Courte.

It is further Ordered, that eu^r p^{r}ticuler family wthin these plantations shall also p^{r}vide this p^{r}sent yeere, at lest halfe a pownd of hemp or flaxe.

It is Ordered, that Country Rates yet behind vnpayd, shall be accepted by Mr. Tresurer in marchandable Indean Corne at three shillings the bush[1]:

It is also Ordered, that whatsoeu^r debts shall be made wthin the libertyes of these Plantations, after the publishing of this Order, ether by labour of men or cattle or contract for comodityes, yt shall be lawfull for the buyer or hierer to pay it in marchantable Indean corne at three shillings fower pence the bush[1]:

It is Ordered, that the late Order conserneing Wampū at sixe a penny shalbe dissolued, and the former of fower a penny and two pence to be paid in the shilling shall be established.

The Order for the regulating of worke and wages is dissolued.

It is ordered that Mr. Heynes, Mr. Wells and Captain Mason shall goe downe to Paquanucke, to settle the bownds betwixt them and the Plantations on boath sids them, according as they judge equall, as also to heare and determin the difference betwixt the inhabitants of Cuphege amongst theselues. They also, wth Mr. Ludlow, are to require the Tribuit of the Indeans about those p^rts, that is behind vnpaid, due by articles formerly agreed vppon, as also to inquire out the p^rticuler Indeans that are vnder ingadgement, wth the lymitts of the grownd formerly belonging to them, and vppon refusall to p^rceed wth the as they shall see cause.

Mr. Williā Whiting of Hartford & Frances Styles of Windsor are admitted freemen.

Mr. Whiting & Mr. Allen of Hartford and Mr. Hill of Windsor are nominated to stand in election for magistrats the next Courte.

Vppon the heareing of Mr. Robert Saltingstons petition, the Court hath graunted that the Gouernour, Mr. Deputy, Mr. Willis & Mr. Welles shall heare and determin the p^rticulers therein mentioned, p^rvided the Towne of Windsor consent thereunto, vnto wch reference the s^d Mr. Saltingston hath agreed.

Arther Smiths sallery is to cesse after three months frō this p^rsent tyme.

It is Ordered, that the deputyes wh^ch searue at any Generall Court shall be freed frō watch, ward & trayneing, vntill the next Court following that wherein they searued.

Mr. Webster and Mr. Phelps are desiered to consult wth the Elders of boath Plantations to p^rpare instructions ag^t the next Court for the punisheing of the sin of lying wch begins to be practised by many p^rsons in this Comonwelth.

---

[73]   THE OATH OF A FREEMAN.

I, 𝔄. 𝔅. being by the P^ruidence of God an Inhabitant w^thin the Jurisdiction of Conectecott, doe acknowledge myselfe to be subiecte to the Gouerment thereof, and doe sweare by the great and fearefull name of the euerliueing God, to be true and faythfull vnto the same, and doe submitt boath my p^rson and estate thereunto, according to all the holsome lawes and orders that there are, or hereafter shall be there made, and established by lawfull authority, and that I will nether plott nor practice any euell ag^t the same, nor consent to any that shall so doe, but will tymely discouer the same to lawfull authority there established; and that I will, as I am in duty bownd, mayntayne the honner of the same and of the lawfull magestratts thereof, p^rmoting the publike good of yt, whilst I shall soe continue an Inhabitant there; and whensoeu^r I shall giue my voate or suffrage touching any matter wch conserns this Comon welth being cauled thereunto, will give yt as in my conscience I shall judge, may conduce to the best good of the same, w^thout respect of p^rsons or favor of any man. Soe helpe me God in o^r Lord Jesus Christe.

Aprill the xth, 1640.

April the 10th, 1640.

Its the aprehensions of the Courte that by the meadow vndeuided wth apportion of vpland, mentioned in the agreement betwixt the 34 men & the Towne & Church in Wethersfield, is vnderstood all the meadowing w^thin the bownds of Wethersfield on this side the Riuer yet vndeuided, wth apportion of vpland on this side & the other side the Riuer; And that the said 34 men haue an equall right or p^rportion vnto the resdue of the vpland vndevided, wth the Church and the resdue of the Towne, ether in comon wth the or in any other kynd, according as yt shall be Ordered by the three men chosen on ech side, or in case they differ, by the the said sixe men and a seventh man taken into the, according to the agreement before the Assembly, p^ruided this hinders not the nyne men frō acting according to the agreement by the Counsell in deuisions that are in hand.

There is 15 acres for Mr. Deynton and a frynd of his, to be sett out by the foresaid sixe men, wth two howse lotts and p^rportion of vpland thereunto belonging.

[74]   THE GENER{ll} COURT.   APRILL THE ix{th}, 1641.
   John Heynes Esq{r}. Gouer{r}.
   George Willis Esq{r}. Deputy.
   Magistr{s}:—Ed: Hopkins Esq{r}, Rodger Ludlow Esq{r}, *absent;* Mr. Will: Hopkins, *absent;* Mr. Phelps, Mr. Webster, Mr. Whiting, *Tresurer,* Mr. Welles, *Secretary.*
   Deputyes:—Mr. Steele, Mr. Taylcoate, Ed: Stebbing, Capten Mason, Mr. Hull, Mr. Gaylor, George Hubberd, Samuell Smith, Richard Crab, James Boosy; John Pratt, *absent;* Tho: Ford, *absent.*

For the better p{r}searuing of Corne and meadow on the east side of the Greate River, yt is Ordered, that there shall no hoggs or swyne of any sorte be put ouer thither or keepte there at any tyme after the publishing this Order, w{th}in the tearme of on yeare, and all those that are now at this p{r}sent on that side, are to be remoued thence w{th}in on weeke after the publisheing hereof, vnder the penalty of fiue shillings vppon euery hogge for euery weeke that any such remayne there.

Notw{th}standing the late Order conserneing the restraynt of excesse in apparrell, yet diuers p{r}sons of seuerall ranks are obsearued still to exceede therein: It is therefore Ordered that the Constables of euery Towne w{th}in these libertyes, shall obsearue and take notice of any p{r}ticuler p{r}son or p{r}sons w{th}in their seuerall lymitts, and all such as they judge to exceede their condition and ranks therein, they shall p{r}sent and warne to appeare at the p{r}ticuler Courte; as also the said Constables are to p{r}sent to the said Courte all such p{r}sons who sell their comoditƴes at excessive rats; And the said Courte hath power to censure any disorder in the p{r}ticulers before mentioned.

Whereas yt was Ordered that euery family should plant a spoonefull of hempe seed, at a foote distant euery seed: vppon complaint that the said hempseed cannot be p{r}cured, It's Ordered, that such p{r}sons who haue aboue the quantyty of a spoonefull, and deny to sell to others that are vnprouided, they shall plant so many spoonefulls themselues, according to the said Order, as they deny to sell to others that want and desire to buy yt of thē at a resonable rate.

Vppon Mr. Wyntrops motion to the Courte for Fyshers Iland, It is the mynd of the Courte, that so farre as yt hinders

Notwithstanding the late Order concerning the Inhabitants
of Pequett in Approwess, yet divers Persons of Seabrooke
have obtained will to receive them / It is therefore
Ordered that the Constables of every Towne within these
liberties shall observe and take notice of any persons
that are p[er]sons w[i]thin their severall lymitts, and at the first
shall Judge to exhibit their names and at the next
shire, then they shall and warne to appeare at
the Perticuler Court[y]

Tho: Welles

(Secretary, 1640–1648.)

not the publike good of the Country, ether for fortifieing for defence, or setting vppe a trade of fisheing or salt & such like, he shall haue liberty to p^rceed therein.

Its Ordered, that the Plantations shall alow tenn pownd to the Gouernour and others that vndertake wth him to send sixe men to abyde in Mohegin country for to plant corne, neere Vncoas, for the incouridgement of his men to stay wth him, the wch sixe men are to remayne in the said Parts to the end of their haruest.

Rich: Gyldersly his fyne of 40s. is to be forborne vntill the Generall Court in September.

[76] A GENERALL COURTE THE vii^th OF JUNE, 1641.

Forasmuch as the Court haueing lately declared their appr^-hensions to the Country conserneing the excesse in wages amongst all sorts of Artifficers and workemen, hopeing thereby men would haue bine a law vnto theselues, but finding litle reformation therein, The said Court hath therefore Ordered, that sufficient able Carpenters, Plow writs, Wheelewrits, Masons, Joyners, Smithes and Coopers, shall not take aboue 20d. for a dayes worke frō the xth of March to the xi^th of October, nor aboue 18d. a day for the other p^rte of the yeare, and to worke xi howers in the day the sumer tyme, besids that wch is spent in eateing or sleeping, and ix howers in the wynter: also, mowers, for the tyme of mowing shall not take aboue xxd. for a dayes worke.

It is Ordered, also, that all other Artificers, or handicrofts men and cheife laborers shall not take aboue xviijd. a day for the first halfe yeare as aforesaid, and not aboue 14d. p^r day for the other p^rte of the yeare; and w^tsoeuer worke is lett or taken by the great or p^rsell, by any workemen, laborers or artificers w^tsoeu^r, shall be valued by the p^rportion aforesaid.

Also, Sawyers shall not take aboue 4s. 2d. for slitt worke or three inch planke, nor aboue 3s. 6d. for boards, by the hundred. Also, boards shall not be sold for aboue 5s. vid. the hundred.

It is also Ordered, that fower of the better sorte of Oxen or Horsses, wth the tacklin, shall not be valued at aboue 4s. xd.

the day, frõ the xith of March to the xith of October, and to worke frõ the xith of March to the xith of May vj howers, and frõ the xith of May to the xith of October viiij howers, except they be imployed in breakeing vp of vpland grownd, for wch worke they are alowed 4s. xd. though they worke but vj howers: also the said cattle shall not be alowed aboue 4s. p^r day frõ the xith of October to the xith of March, and to worke sixe howers, and so for a greter or lesser nũber of Cattle according to the said p^rportion.

And yts Ordered, that if any p^rson ether directly or indirectly, shall giue or take any greter wages for the worke ether of men or cattle then the pryses before mentioned, shall abyde the censure of the Court.

[78]   SEPTEMBER THE 2^d, 1641.

    John Haynes Esqr. Gouer^r.
    George Willis Esqr. Deputy,
    Ed: Hopkins Esqr, Tho: Welles, Mr. Phelps, Mr. Webster.
    The Jury.—Mr. Plum, *Jur.* Tho: Stolton, Henry Clarke, John Byssell, Henry Wollcott, Robert Parks, Robert Rose, Robert Abbott, John Talcott, Will: Lewis, John Clarke, Andrew Bacon ; *Jur.*

Mathew Allen pl^t ag^t John Coggen def^t, in an action of slaunder, to the damage of a thousand pownds   The Jury find for the pl^t damages 20*l.* Costs vij*s*.   Mr. Hill hath vndertake to satisfie the 20*l.* for Mr. Allen, when the Court shall require yt.

Tho: Munson pl^t ag^t John Hall defend^t, in an acⁿ of defamation.   The Jury find for the pl^t damages 20*s*. Costs, vij*s*.

Frances Styles pl^t ag^t Ed: Hopkins Esqr. defend^t, in an action of the Case.   The Jury find for the pl^t damages xvj*l.* x*s.* Costs, vij*s.*

Samuell Gardner for his affront of the watch is fyned x*s*, and is to acknowledge his fault the next trayneing day.

Robert Saltingston gent. plan^t ag^t Edward Hopkins Esqr. defend^t, as an assigne to Mr. John Woodcoke, in an action of the case, to the damage of 200*l.*

For the 4th action of Math: Allen Pl^t ag^t John Coggen def^d, the Jury find for the pl^t damages xx*l*. Costs, vij*s*.

Mr. Hill of Wyndsor vndertaks to satisfie Mr. Allen the 20*l*. for Mr. Coggen when the Courte shall appoynt yt.

For the 5th acⁿ of John Coggen pl^t ag^t Math: Allen def^d, the Jury find for the defen^d. Costs vij*s*. Mr. Coggen denyed to appeare to his action wⁿ the Jury was cauled to giue in their verdicte, aleadging he hath not his full testimony.

[79] Mr. Robert Saltingston hath an attachment graunted ag^t Mr. Edward Hopkins, whereby he hath attached halfe the Myll standing by the New Bridge.

---

[80] A GENERALL COURT HELD THE IXth OF SEP: 1641.

John Haynes Esqr. Gou^r.
George Willis Esqr. Deputy.
Ed: Hopkins Esqr, Mr. Welles, Mr. Phelps, Mr. Webster.
Deputyes:—Mr. Steele, Mr. Talcott, Ed: Stebbing, John Pratt, Capten Mason, Mr. Hill, Mr. Hull, Mr. Clarke, Mr. Swayne, Nath: Foote, Robert Rose, Samuell Smith, John Burr, John Sticklin.

The Order for the restreyneing of the felling of Tymber is repeled, p^ruided that no Tymber be falen wthin three myles of the mouth of Matabezeke river, nor at vnseasonable tymes, vizt. fr̄o the beginning of Aprill to the end of Septēber, and that it be improued into pipestaues or some other marchantable com̄odity wthin on month after the felling thereof, or carted togather; and that the Tymber so improued shall not be transported fr̄o the Riuer but for dischardge of debts or fetching in some necessary p^rvisions.

It is Ordered, that the size of Pipestaues shall be 4 foote 4 inches in length, halfe an inch at lest in thicknes, besids the sappe: they are to be 4 inches in bredth, if vnder to goe for halfe staues, and non are to goe if vnder 3 in bredth. And there shall be appoynted in every Towne wthin these libertyes, one experienced man to vew & obsearue all such staues as aforesaid, and ech p^rcell by him approued of shall be sealed, who shall be sworne to that searuice. And all such p^rsells so approued & sealed, shall passe to the Marchant at 5*l.* the thousand, to be deliuered at the Riuers mouth, at wch place the Country hath vndertook to p^rvid for Mr. Hopkins, by the begining of June next, 70000, vizt. Wethersfield 30000, Wyndsor, 20000, Hartford 20000, if Mr. Hopkins can p^ruid shipping and aford to giue that price.

Mr. Hopkins is desiered by the Courte, if he see an op^rtunity, to arbitrate or issue the difference betwixt the Dutch and vs, as occation and op^rtunity shall be offered when he is in Ingland.*

Mr. Fowler, Mr. Astwood & Mr. Tappe of Mylford are desired by the Courte as neighbours (if they please to take such paynes,) to settle the bownds betwixt Paquanucke and Vncoway, as they shall iudge meete, or vppon their suruey thereof to report their app^rhensions to the seuerall Townes, vppon wch if they shall not accord and consent thereunto, the Court will thereuppon issue the same.

Mr. Gouern^r and Mr. Whiting are desiered to take the late Tresurer's accoumpte.

Mr. Willis and Mr. Hopkins are desiered, if they haue an op^rtunity, to further the league of Vnity wth the Bay.

The Gouernour, Mr. Phelps and Capten Mason are desiered to treat wth Mr. Phenicke, conserneing liberty for making salt in Long Iland and takeing fishe, who haue power also to contract wth whō they can p^rcure for effecting the same.

For the p^ruenting and avoyding that fowle and grosse sin of lying, yt is Ordered, that when any p^rson or p^rsons shall be accused and proued guilty of that vice, yt shall be lawfull for the p^rticular Courte to adiudge and censure any such p^rty, ether by fyne or bodily correction according as they shall judge the nature of the fault to require ; this to hold to the next Court.

[81] It is Ordered, that whosoeu^r trads for any Indean planted Corne, after the publisheing this Order, shall pay to the Country 4*d.* for euery bush: p^ruided they buy it not for to supply their owne necessity.

The Secretary is appoynted to giue to Mr. Hopkins, vnder his hand, the nūber of the bush: of Corne p^rsented to the Courte by the Plantacõns.

---

* See a letter from Sir Wm. Boswell, English ambassador at the Hague, in relation to the encroachments of the Dutch—in Appendix, No. 1.

[82] A General Court held the ix[th] of Nouēber, 1641.

John Heynes Esqr. Gouern[r].
George Willis Esqr.
Mr. Welles, Mr. Phelps, Mr. Webster, Mr. Whiting.
[*Deputies :*]—Mr. Steele, Mr. Talcoat, Ed: Stebing, John Prat, Mr. Plum, Mr. Swayne, Samuell Smith, Nath: Foote, Capten Mason, Mr. Hill, Mr. Hull, Will' Gaylard.

Whereas by reson of the great scarcity of mony, execution being taken of seuerall p[r]sons goods, that haue bine sowld at very cheap rats to the extreame damage of the debtor, It is therefore Ordered, that whatsoeuer execution shall be graunted vppon any debts made after the publisheing this Order, the Creditor shall make choyse of one p[r]ty, the debtor of a second, and the Court of a third, who shall pryse the goods so taken vppon execution as aforesaid and deliuer thē to the Creditor.

The former Order conserneing the payment of debts to be made by Indean Corne is repealed.

It is Ordered that Mr. Welles, Mr. Steele, Mr. Plum and James Boosy shall runne the lyne west into the Country betwixt Hartford and Wethersfield, to begin at the great Riuer against the marked tree.

The Country Rate of   *graunted the last Court may be paid in Old Indean Corne at 3s. the bush[l] new at 2s. vi*d*, Inglishe wheat at 4s.

Its Ordered, that 160 bush[l] of Corne shall be sent in by the Country to the Gouernour, to be levied vppon the Townes by the p[r]portion of the last rate.

The Cort is adioyrned to the first Wensday in January, to meet at the Gouernours howse after the Lecture.

---

[84]   Dec[r]. the ix[th], 1641.   The P[r]ticuler Court.

John Heynes Esq[r]. Gou[r].
George Willis Esq[r]. Dep[ty].
Mr. Whiting, Mr. Webster, Mr. Welles.
The Jury.—Andrew Bacon, *Jur:* Tymothy Standly,

---

* This blank occurs in the original.

Tho: Scott, Tho: Osmore, James Boosy, George Hubberd, Tho: Coleman, Henry Woolcott, John Porter, Tho: Ford, Joshua Carter, Williā Rescue; *Jur.*

Frances Styles pl^t ag^t Robert Saltingston, gent., defen^t, in an action of the Case to the damage of 70*l*. The Jury find for the pl^t damages 51*l*. Costs vij*s*.

Robert Saltingston, gent., pl^t ag^t Frances Styles defen^t, in an action of the Case to the damage of 800*l*. The Jury find for the defen^t. Costs x*s*.

Frances Styles pl^t ag^t Robert Saltingston, gent., defen^t, in an Action of debte to the damage of 100*l*. The Jury find for the pl^t, eighty one pownd twelue shillings damages according to the award, and the double costs of the Court.

Robert Saltingston gent. pl^t ag^t Frances Stiles defen^t, in a second action of the Case to the damage of 500*l*.

Robert Saltingston gent. pl^t ag^t Frances Stiles defen^t, in a third action of the Case, to the damage of 50*l*.

The Jury is to be warned for Thursday com fortnight.

---

[86]   JANUARY THE 5th, 1641.

John Heynes Esqr. Gou^r.
George Willis, Esqr. Dep.
  Mr. Welles, Mr. Phelps, Mr. Webster, Mr. Whiting.
  [*Deputyes:*]—Mr. Steele, Mr. Tailcoate, Ed: Stebbing, Jo: Pratt, Mr. Plume, Mr. Swayne, Sam̃: Smith, Nath: Foote, Capten Mason, Mr. Hill, Mr. Hull, Will' Gaylard.

Mr. Huits Petition for the Iland at the Falls, is graunted.

Its Ordered, that Capten Mason shall haue 500 acres of grownd, for him and his heires, about Pequoyt Country, and the dispose of 500 more to such souldears as joyned wth him in the searuice when they conquered the Indeans there.

The Court adiorned to the 19th of this month. . . . To the 26th. . . . To the first Wensday in March.

The Courte desiereth Mr. Whiting, Capten Mason, Mr. Plum̃ and Henry Clarke to take course for the p^{r}cureing some peeces of Ordnance from Piscataq' or elsewhere; the frayght is to be at the chardge of the Country. And also to take order for erecting some fortifications where they thinke meete for searuice, and to doe therein as they shall see cause.

Yf The Towne of Windsor p'uid a Ferry Boate to attend the River, they are to be alowed 3d. for a single Passenger and two pence a person w^n they carry more then one att a frayght, and twelue pence for a horse.

---

[88]   THE GENERALL COURTE FOR ELECTION OF MAGISTRATS, THE SECOND THURSDAY IN APRILL, 1642.

George Willis Esqr, Gou^r.
Roger Ludlow Esqr, Dep.
Magestrats: John Haynes Esqr, Mr. Phelps, Mr. Webster, Capten Mason, Mr. Welles, Mr. Whiting: *these p^{r}sent.* Ed: Hopkins Esqr, Will' Hopkins: *absent.*
Deputyes: Mr. Steele, Mr. Taylcoate, Mr. Westwood, Andrew Bacon, Mr. Hill, Mr. Hull, Will' Gaylard, Henry Clarke, Mr. Plum, Mr. Swayne, George Hubberd, James Boosy, Phillip Groues.

Its the app^{r}hension of the Generall Courte that the p^{r}ticuler Courte should not be inioyned to be keepte aboue once in a quarter of a yeare.

It is ordered, that the p^{r}ticuler Courte shall haue liberty to dispose of ten thousand acres of grownd in Pequoyt Country, as yt lyeth togather, wth lest p^{r}iudice to others that may hereafter succeed the͂, for the further planting the Country.

Its Ordered, that the Gou^{r}nor and Mr. Heynes shall haue liberty to dispose of the ground vppon that p^{r}te of Tunxis River cauled Mossocowe, to such inhabitants of Wyndsor as they shall see cause.

It is Ordered, that there shall be an Artillary Yard, where the Company shall haue liberty to exercise their Arms once a month, and chuse their Officers according to the course of Artillary men, and there shall be 300 acres of grownd alowed thereunto for their incouridgement therein, in some conuenient place, where yt may be found for the benefitt and vse of the Company successively.

It is Ordered, that there shall be a restraynt for any p^r^son w^th^in this Jurisdiction frō trading wth Indeans in Long Island, vntill the Courte in September com twelue month, only Tho: Steynton and Richard Lord haue liberty to goe one vyadge, for the putting offe the smale comodityes they haue p^r^uided for that end, and to gather in their old debts.

Tho: Ford is to enioy the 200 acres of grownd formerly graunted to him, and his neglect of improueing yt, w^th^in the tyme formerly lymited, is remitted.

The Courte adioyrned to the last Wensday in this month.

The Courte adiorned to the xi^th^ of May.

May the xi^th^, 1642.

Its Ordered, that the magestrats, or the gretest p^r^te of them, shall haue liberty to agitate the busines betwixt vs and the Dutch, and if they thinke meete to treate wth the Gouernor conserneing the same.

It is graunted, that Wyndsor lyne shall run vppon Mr. Saltingstall his land, neere the falls, according to their other lotts, p^r^uided yt p^r^ue not aboue a poynt and halfe towrd the north, and w^t^ preiudice Mr. Saltingstall shall susteyne thereby, the Country shall make good.

And whereas the foresaid grownd formerly graunted to Mr. Saltingstall, was to haue bine impaled w^th^in three yeares after the graunt, he is now released of that ingadgement, and the land confirmed to him. He, the s^d^ Mr. Saltingstall doth p^r^mise to lend the Country two peeces of Ordnance, Sakers or Minions, and if he require thē before the Country can spare thē, he is to pay for the frayght.

[89] It is ordered, that no man w^th^in these libertyes shall refuse marchantable Indean Corne at the rate of 2s. vid. the bush^l^. for any contracte made for the labour of men or cattell or comodityes sold after the publisheing this Order.

The Courte is adioyrned to the last Wensday of July, excepte the Gou^r^ see cause to call it before.

<blockquote>
May the 2d. The Court hath appoynted that Mr. Hill shall satisfie Mr. Coggens debte of 20l. to Mr. Allen, w^th^in a month after the date hereof, according to his p^r^mise, vppon the verdicte of the Jury vppon the sute of the action of slaunder.
</blockquote>

July 25th, 1642. The Court is adioyrned for a fortnight.
August the 9th. The Courts dissolued.

A Generall Courte, August the 26th, 1642.
Roger Ludlow Esqr, Deputy.
Jo: Heynes Esqr, Mr. Welles, Mr. Phelps, Capten Mason.
[*Deputyes:*] Mr. Steele, Mr. Talcote, Mr. Westwood, Andrew Bacon, Mr. Hill, Mr. Hull, Mr. Clark, Will'. Gaylord, Mr. Swayne, Mr. Parke, George Hubbert, Robert Rose.

It is Ordered, that there shall be a letter writt frō the Courte to the Bay to further the prsecution of the Indeans, to pruent their mischeuos plotte in their late Combination.*

It is Ordered, that the Clarke of the band in euery Towne wthin these libertyes, shall haue an Oath giuen him by the Gournour or some Magistrate, to vewe the arms in their seurall Plantations, and make returne of such as are defectiue or want the quantity of powder or bullitts according to Order of Courte, and also of such as are absent at tymes of Trayneing.

It is Ordered, that the Inhabitants wthin these libertyes shall not suffer any Indean or Indeans to com into their howses, only the Magistrats may admitte of a Sachem, if he com not wth aboue two men.

It is Ordered, that there shall be a gard of 40 men to com compleate in their Arms to the meeting euery Sabbath and lecture day, in euery Towne wthin these libertyes vppon the Riuer.

---

* "The letters and other intelligence" from Connecticut, relating to the alleged designs of Miantonimo "to draw the Indians into a confederation" against the English, were laid before the General Court of Massachusetts, at its session in September. Information of the plot had been communicated to Mr. Ludlow, then residing at Uncowa, (now Fairfield) by one of the neighboring Sachems, about the 20th of August. See, in Mass. Hist. Coll. 3d Ser., iii. 161, "A true relation of a conspiracy of Maantanemo, the greate Sachem of the Naragancetts, Soheage or Sequin, the Sachem of Matabeseck, and Sasawin or Sequassen, the Sachem of Sicaogg, for destruction of the English and generally throughout New England, as it hath beene discovered by a Sachem living neere Mr. Ludlowe, as also of another Indian of Long Island to Mr. Eaton of New Haven, and of another Indian in the River of Conectecott."

Septem̃ 5th, 1842. The Courte manifest their willingnes, according to theire abillityes, to further the imployment of the Shipcarpenter & Roper motioned by Mr. Whiting.

The Court agree to take an Oath to keepe secret what they shall determine and conclud to conceale, as followeth :—

There shall be a Com̃itte chosen to make p^rparation ag^t [*] and the murtherers, (this to be kept secret,) and to defeat the Plott of the Indeans meeting about Tunxis.

[90] The Gou^r, Mr. Heynes, the Capten and the rest of the Magestrats, are chosen for a Com̃itte to agitate the businesses before mentioned.

Septem̃ the 8th, 1642.

George Willis Esqr, Go^r.

Jo: Heynes Esqr, Mr. Welles, Mr. Phelps, Capten Mason. [*Deputyes :*] Mr. Parke, Mr. Swayne, Mr. Clarke, Wm. Gaylord, Andrew Bacon, Mr. Talcot, Mr. Westwood.

Forasmuch as the Indeans growe insolent and combyne thẽselues togather, being suspected to p^rpare for warr, It is Ordered, that no Smith w^thin these libertyes shall doe any worke for thẽ, nor any p^rson w^thin these libertyes shall trade any Instrument or matter made of iron or steele wth thẽ, nor deliuer any that are allreddy made, w^thout lycense frõ two Magistrats, nor buy any of their venison vntill further liberty be graunted.

It is Ordered, that eu^ry Towne w^thin these libertyes, p^ruide w^thin fowerteene dayes, twenty halfe Pickes, of ten foote in length at lest in the wood.

Andrewe Bacon is joyned wth the Capten and Mr. Clarke, to p^rpare caridges for the peeces that cam frõ Piscataq'.

It is Ordered, that for the secureing of the Plantations there shall be two wards men at lest, in eu^ry seuerall Towne w^thin these libertyes, to giue notice of any sudden daynger that may com vppon the Plantations, and to execute the Order for keepeing out Indeans ; And also that there remayne w^thin euery Towne a competent nũber of men dayly, for the defence thereof, vizt. Hartford 40, Wyndsor, 30, Wethersfield 20.

---

* Blank in the original. The order doubtless refers to Sowheag or Sequin, who had been charged with secreting the murderers of the English.

Its agreed that Wyndsor shall take offe the worth of 90l. in Cotten Wooll, frō Mr. Hopkins; Wethersfield, the worth of 110l.; Hartford 200l.; wth liberty to the Plantations to p^{r}portion yt according to their former Rats, if Wyndsor and Wethersfield shall wthin on month desire yt.

The Courte is adioyrned for a month, vnless the Gou^r see cause to caull yt sooner.

Sep^t. the 17th, 1642.

Its Ordered, that the Clarke of the Band in euery Plantation wthin these Libertyes, shall giue in to the deputyes of their seu^{r}all Townes, an exacte list of all the Trayne men frō 16 yeares to 60 : and the deputyes to deliu^r the same to the Comītte who haue power to levy the said Townes for the p^{r}secution of the warre.

Sept. 29th, 1642.

The Courte aduiseth that a letter be returned to the Dutch in answer to their letter brought by Mr. Whiteing. Mr. Heynes, Mr. Hopkins and Mr. Whiteing are desiered to write yt, as also to write to Mr. Dudlie and Mr. Bellinghā conserneing what the Dutch Gouernor reporteth that they haue wrote to him about o^r differences etc.

That the Country may be better enabled to kill yearely some Beves for supply of Leather, It is Ordered, that no Calues shall be killed wthin these Plantations, wthout the approbation of two men wthin ech Towne, by the Court to be appoynted for that searuice, vppon forfeture of ten shillings to the Country. For Hartford, Wm. Butler, George Steele; Wyndsor, John Bissell, John Portor; for Wethersfield, Leo: Chester, Rich: Trotte.

[49] Vppon a bill exibited by Mr. Tailcoate, there appeareth due to Mr. Eldridge, 4. 4. 6.

October the 4th, 1642.

Its ordered, there shall be 90 Coats p^{r}vided wthin these Plant^{ns}, wthin tenn dayes, basted wth cotten wooll and made defensiue ag^t Indean arrowes; Hartford 40, Wyndsor 30, Wethersfield 20.

The Courts adiorned for a month, vnles the Gou^r see cause to call yt soooner.

The P^{r}tic^r Court, 14th of Octob^r, 1642.

George Willis Go^r, Esqr.

Jo: Heynes Esqr, Ed: Hopkins Esqr, Mr. Phelps, Mr. Webster, Mr. Whiting, Mr. Welles.

Jury : Mr. Cullicke, Tho: Osmore, Gregory Wilterton, Will' Pantry, Tymothy Standly, John Clarke, Frances Styles, John Byssell, Roger Willm̃s, John More, Nath: Dickinson, John Trott.

The ac^n of Seargeant Fyler pl^t. in the behalfe of the Towne of Wyndsor ag^t Mat: Allen, def^t, in an ac. of the Case. The said Math: Allen is to pay costs for non apparance viij$s$. vi$d$. The Court following, Seargeant Fyler was adiudged to pay the said costs, haueing made a referance before the sute.

The sute of Ephraim Huit pl. ag^t Tho: Steynton, is wthdrawn by consent.

Bray Rocester pl. ag^t Wyddow Hudgison, Executrixe to Will' Hudgison, defen^t, in an action of debt to the damage of 16l.

Whereas many sutes com into the Court ag^t Tho: Marshfield, and he is wthdrawen and non soluit, The Court hath appoynted Henry Woolcott & Tho: Ford to take into their chardge or custody all the estate, goods & chattells of the said Tho: Marshfields, as they shall be able to discou^r yt, and to dispose of yt to the best aduantage for the vse of the creditors, and the same to accoumpt to the Court w^n they shall be therevnto cauled.

Mr. Eldridge pl. ag^t Tho: Marshfield def^t, in an ac. of debt to the damage of 12l.

Henry Woolcott pl. ag^t Tho: Marshfield def^t, in an ac. of the case to the damage of 40l.

In the ac. of Richard Trott and Samuell Smith ag^t John Plum def^t, the Jury find for the pl^s. Damages 15s. Costs viij$s$. ij$d$. *Execution graunted.*

[92] CAPITALL LAWES ESTABLISHED BY THE GENERALL COURT, THE FIRST OF DECEMBER, 1642,

1. Yf any man after legall conuiction shall haue or worship any other God but the Lord God, he shall be put to death. Deu: 13. 6, & 17. 2: Ex: 22. 20.

2. Yf any man or woman be a witch (that is) hath or consulteth wth a familliar spirit, they shall be put to death. Ex: 22. 18: Lev: 20. 27: Deu: 18. 10, 11.

3. Yf any p^rson shall blaspheme the name of God the Father, Son or Holy Goste, wth direct, expres, p^rsumptuous, or highhanded blasphemy, or shall curse God in the like manner, he shall be put to death. Leu: 24. 15, 16.

4. Yf any p^rson shall comitt any willfull murther, wch is manslaughter comitted vppon mallice, hatred or cruelty, not in a mans necessary and iust defence, nor by mere casualty against his will, he shall be put to death. Ex: 21. 12, 13, 14: Num: 35. 30, 31.

5. Yf any person shall slay another through guile, ether by poysonings or other such divillishe practice, he shall be put to death. Ex: 21. 14.

6. Yf any man or woman shall ly wth any beast or bruit creature, by carnall copulation, they shall surely be put to death, and the beast shall be slayne and buried. Leu: 20. 15, 16.

7. Yf any man lye wth mankynd as he lyeth wth a woman both of them haue comitted abomination, they both shall surely be put to death. Leu: 20. 13.

8. Yf any p^rson comitteth adultery wth a married or espoused wife, the adulterer and the adulteres shall surely be put to death. Le: 20. 10, & 18. 20: Deu: 22. 23, 24.

9. Yf any man shall forcebly and w^thout consent rauishe any mayd or woman that is lawfully maried or contracted, he shall be put to death. Deu: 22. 25.

10. Yf any man stealeth a man or mankind, he shall be put to death. Ex: 21. 16.

11. Yf any man rise vp by false witnesse, wittingly and of purpose to take away any mans life, he shall be putt to death. Deu: 19. 16, 18, 19.

12. If any man shall conspire or attempte any inuasion, insurrection or rebellion against the Comon welth, he shall be put to death.

And whereas frequent experience giues in sad euidence of seuerall other wayes of vncleanes and lasiuious caridges practised among vs, whereunto, in regard of the variety of Circūstances, p^rticular and expresse lawes and orders cannot suddenly be suted; This Court cannot but looke vppon evells in that kind as very p^rnitious and distructiue to the welfare of the Comon weale, and doe judge that seuere and sharpe punishement should be inflicted vppon such delinquents, and as they doe approue of what hath bine alreddy done by the p^rticuler Court, as agreeing wth the generall power formerly graunted, so they do hereby confirme the same power to the p^rticuler Court who may proceed ether by fyne, comitting to the howse of correction or other corporall punishement, according to their discretion, desiering such seasonable, exemplary executions may be done vppon offondors in that kynd, that others may heare and feare.

Forasmuch as incorigiblenes is also adiudged to be a sin of death, but noe lawe yet amongst vs established for the execution thereof; For the p^ruenting that great evell, It is Ordered, that whatsoeuer Child or searuant w^thin these libertyes, shall be conuicted of any stubborne or rebellious caridge against their parents or gouernors, wch is a forerunner of the forementioned evell, the Gouernor or any two Magestrats haue liberty and power frō this Court, to comit such p^rson or p^rsons to the howse of correction, and there to remayne vnder hard labour and seuere punishement, so long as the Court or the mayor parte of the Magestrats shall judge meet.

[93] Whereas diuers p^rsons dep^rte from amongst vs, and take vp their abode wth the Indeans in a p^rphane course of life, For the p^ruenting whereof, Yt is Ordered, that whatsoeuer p^rson or p^rsons that now inhabiteth or shall inhabite w^thin this Jurisdiction, and shall dep^rte frō vs and sette or joyne wth the Indeans, that they shall suffer three yeares imprisonment at lest, in the howse of correction, and vndergoe such further censure by fyne or corporall punishement as the p^rticuler Court shall judge meet to inflict in such case.

For the better furnisheing the Riuer wth Cordage towards the rigging of Shipps, It is Ordered, that what hempseed any p^rson hath w^thin these libertyes, that they shall ether sowe yt themselves, or sell yt to some others w^thin the Riuer that may sowe the same.

The late Rate graunted, of 50*l*. is to be made vp a 100*l*. and to be p^rportioned vppon the three Townes according to the former Rate, wch may be paid in sumer Wheat at 4*s*. 4*d*. the bush¹, Rye at 3*s*. vi*d*, Pease at 3*s*. vi*d*, Indean at 2*s*. viij*d*, p^ruided yt be Marchantable Corne, and the Constables of ech Towne are Ordered to receaue no other but at such vnder Rate as they shall esteeme yt at, or in wampū at 6 a penny.

The former Order of Indean at 2*s*. vi*d*. the bush¹ is repealed, and the seu^rall sorts of Corne before mentioned are made payable, vppon the pryses herein specified, for any labour or hyer of men or cattle, hereafter to be done.

The size of Pipestaues is to be 4 foote vi inches in length, the breadth and thicknes according to the former Order.

It is Ordered, that noe man w^thin this Jurisdiction shall directly or indirectly amend, repaire, or cause to be amended or repaired, any gun, smale or greate, belonging to any Indean, nor shall endeuor the same, nor shall sell or giue to any Indean, directly or indirectly, any such gun or gunpowder, or shott, or lead, or mould, or millitary weapons, or armor, nor shall make any arrowe heads, vppon payne of ten pownd fyne for euery offence at lest, nor sell nor barter any guns, powder, bullitts or lead, wherby this Order might be evaded, to any p^rson inhabiting out of this Jurisdiction, w^thout lycence of this or the p^rticuler Court, or som two Magistrats, vppon payne of ten pownd for every gun, fiue pownd for eu^ry pownd of powder, 40*s*. for euery pownd of bullitts or lead, and so p^rportionably for any greater or lesser quantity.

Mr. Whiteing & Capten Mason are desiered to take Order to demaund the Tribuit due frō Long Iland and the Indeans vppon the mayne, and w^t they can receaue may be accoumpted towards that wch is due to the frō the Country. Mr. Whiteing is contente to accepte of the Corne at Mohegen, and to dischardge the prises of the two cloathes, p^ruided he be abated by the Country for so much of yt as was sould & not traded for Corne; and if any cloath be lefte, yts at his dispose.

The Gou^r, Mr. Heynes, Mr. Hopkins, Mr. Whiting, Capten Mason, Mr. Chester, Mr. Hill and Mr. Trott are desiered to take the accoumpt of what the seuerall Townes will disburse toward the building of a Shippe, (and if they find yt phesable,) they haue power to agree wth workemen to carry on the worke and to take ingadgements of the Country to p^{r}forme what they vndertake, and to doe all things requisit for the full accomplisheing of the worke.

The Gou^r, Mr. Heynes, Mr. Hopkins, Mr. Welles & Mr. Phelps are desiered to consider wth the Elders, conserneing the the synns of Curseing father or mother, Incorigiblenes, Rauishement, Contempt of Ordinances, Lying, and Brech of p^{r}mise, and to make some lawes ag^t the & p^{r}sent the to the next Generall Courte.

---

[91]   Decē. 18 : 1642.

It is Ordered that no man wthin this Jurisdictñ shall, directly or indirectly, amend, repaire, or cause to be amended or repaired, any gun smale or greate, belonging to any Indean, nor shall indeavor the same, nor shall sell nor giue to any Indean, directly nor indirectly, any such gun, or any gunpowder or shott or lead or shott mould, or any millitary wepons, armor or arrowe heads, nor sell nor barter any such, vppon payne of ten pownd fyne for euery offence att lest, and the Court shall haue power to encrese the fine or to impose corporall punishement where a fyne cannot be had, at their discretion.

Whereas yt appeares that notwthstanding the former lawes made ag^t selling guns & powder to Indeans, they are yet supplyed by indirect meanes, It is thereof Ordered, that if any p^{r}son, after publicatñ of this Order, shall sell, barter or transporte any guns, powder, bullitts or lead, to any p^{r}son inhabiting out of this Jurisdic^n wthout lycense of this Court, or frō some two Magistrats, he shall forfeit for eu^{r}y gun ten pownd, for euery pownd of gun powder 5l. & for eu^{r}y pownd of bullitts or lead 40s. & so p^{r}portionably for any greater or lesser quantity.

[94] The Prticr Court, the 27th of January, 1642.
George Willis Esqr, Gour.
Jo: Heynes Esqr Ed: Hop: Esqr, Mr. Phelps, Mr. Webster, Mr. Whiting, Cap: Mason, Mr. Welles.
*The Jury.**

It is Ordered, that the prtr Court shall be held the first Thursday in these seurall months; March, June, Sep., Decēbr.

The will and Inuentory of Richard Lyman decessed is brought into the Court. John Moody maks Oath that yt is the last will of the said Rich: and also the noate then brought in is the note of the Widdow Lyman decesed. The seuerall prtyes prsent at the prsenting the said will, agree that John Lyman, if he liue, will be 22 yere ould in Septē. 1645, Robert Lyman 22 in Septē. 1651.

The Prticr Court, the 2d of March, 1642.
The Jury:—Bray Rocester, Nath: Waird, Jo: Barnard, Ed: Sebbing, John Demon, Jo: Olester, Will' Palmer, John Stedder, Tho: Stoughtn, Tho: Dewye, Joseph Lumis, Walter Fyler.

In the Ac. of Henry Woolcott pl. agt Tho: Spenser defent, the Jury find for the pl. damages vid. & Costs of Court.

In the ac. of Math: Beckwytt pl. agt Math: Allen deft, the Jury find for the pl. damages viijs. & chardges of Court. Executn graunted.

In the ac. of Elias Putmā pl. agt Ed: Vere deft, the Jury find for the pl. damages xviijs. & Costs of Court.

Tho: Hurlbut for exacting and incouridging others to take excessiue Rats for worke and ware, is adiudged to pay to the Country 40s.

Tho: Ford is to giue notice to the Wyddow Hudgison to answer Mr. Rocester his sute, the first Thursday in Aprill next, at wch tyme though he should rec. no answer, he is to answer to the sute himselfe.

---

* The names of the jurors are not recorded.

The creditors of Tho: Marshfield are to repaire to the Court to haue their sute tryed, the first Thursday in June.

Will' Rescue is to take into his Custody James Hullett, Tho: Gybbert, Lidea Blisse & George Gybbs, and to keepe thē in giues* & giue thē course dyet, hard worke, sharpe correction.

The ac. of Josp^r Raulding pl. ag^t Tho: Hurlbut is wthdrawen by consent, and the chardges of the Court to be paid betwixt thē.

John Tynker pl. as assigne to Henry Webb, ag^t Tho: Marshfield def^t, in an ac. of the Case to the damage of 7*l*.

In the ac. of Ed: Elmor pl. ag^t Tho: Bailis def^t, the Jury find for the pl. damages 35*s*. and Costs of Court.

---

[96] MARCH THE 27th, 1643.

George Willis Esqr, Gou^r.

Jo: Heines Esqr, Ed: Hopkins Esqr, Mr. Webster, Mr. Welles, Mr. Phelps, Capten Mason.

[*Deputyes:*]—Mr. Steele, Mr. Tailcoat, Mr. Westwood, Andr: Bacon, Mr. Swaine, Mr. Plum, Mr. Chaplin, Robert Rose, Mr. Hill, Mr. Hull, Will' Gailard, Henry Clarke.

Mr. Heines and Mr. Hopkins are desiered to goe into the Bay to p^{r}secute the combination betwixt thē and vs and New Hauen, wth full power if they haue op^{r}tunity to conclud the same, and in case that should fayle, they are desiered to treat and conclud of a Vnion wth them, researueing the priuilidges we haue in o^r fundamentall lawes.

The Court consenteth that the former answer shall be returned to the p^{r}positions made by the Lords, the p^{r}ticulers at p^{r}sent not coming to vewe, and if yt please Mr. Fenwicke to joyne wth the Plantations, it shall not infring any of his priuilidges wch belong to him.

The Court graunteth Mr. Heynes, a thousand acres of land about Pequoit country, p^{r}uided it be vewed that it hinder not a plantation.

---

* gyves.

That p^{r}te of the Order concerneing recording of bargens and morgages of land (made the 11 of October,) was now by generall consent ordered & agreed to be in these words, That noe bargaine or morgage of land whatsoeuer shall be of any value vntill the same be recorded.

It is Ordered, that Frances Stiles, for his forceble resistance of the Officer of the Court vppon the execution of his office, is fyned to pay to the Country fifty pownd.

Mr. Plum & Mr. Swaine are nominated to stand in election for Magestrats.

Its the judgment of the Courte that the Dutchmens hoggs should be liable to the same orders as the Towne hoggs, where they trespasse.

The decons of Wyndsor are appoynted to supply the searuice that the decons of Roxberry were to p^{r}forme, conserneing the distribution of the seuerall portions of Mr. Stoughtons children, and his wiues, if the said decons of Roxberry refuse to doe yt.

---

[99] APRILL ye 6th, (1643.) THE P^{t}TICULER COURT.

George Willis Esqr, Governour.

Mr. Whiting, Mr. Phelps, Captaine Mason, Mr. Webster.

The Jury :—Jo: White, W^m. Gibbings, Mr. Alcocke, Jo : Porter, Tho : Thornton, Walter Filer, Benedict Afford, Leo : Chester, Jo: Edwards, Tho: Trott (?) Jo: Elsey, Nat : Ely.

Lisley Bratfield pl^t in an actio^n of trespas ag^t Tho : Coleman defend : damages 5l.

Bray Rocester pl^t in an action of debt against Tho : Ford, attur[*ney*] to Widow Huchinson, defend : vpon a Bill of 240£. But forasmuch as Tho: Ford before this Court could not rec[*eiue*] instruction, y^e tryall is defer$d$ till next Court.

Jo: Stoder pl^t in an act^n of trespas against Jo : Plum͂, defend^t, damage xxs. The action betwene Jo: Stoder & Jo: Plum͂ is by consent wthdrawen, & referred fully to be issued by Jo: White & W^m. Gibbings. Y^e charges of y^e Court is equally to be payd betwene y^e p^{r}t[yes.]

An attachm^t graunted to Rob'te Parke for fiue pownds ten shillings two pence, in y^e hands of Anthony Wilson of Vncawa.

In y^e action betwene Lisley Bratfield pl^t, & Tho : Coleman defend : y^e Jury doe find for pl^t, 2l. xs. damage, & y^e cost of y^e Court & for witnesses xiij$s$.

Aron Starke is ajudged to be whiped at Winsor to morrow, & then to serve Capten Mason during y^e pleasure of y^e Court.

James Hallet is to returne frō y^e Correction house to his master *Barclet, who is to keepe him to hard labor & course dyet, during y^e pleasure of y^e Court, p^{r}vided that Barclet is first to remove his daughter frō his family before the sayd James enter therein.†

[102] THE COURT OF ELECTION HELD THE 13th OF APRILL, 1643.

John Heynes Esqr, Gou^r.

Ed : Hopkins Esq. Deputy.

George Willis Esqr, Roger Ludlowe Esqr, Mr. Webster, Mr. Whiting, *Tres^r*., Mr. Welles, *Sec^r*., Capten Mason, Mr. Woolcott, Mr. Swaine.

[*Deputyes* :] Mr. Steele, Mr. Talcoat, Mr. Westwood, Andrewe Bacon, Mr. Chaplin, Rob'te Rose, John Robins, John Edwards, Mr. Hull, Will' Gaylard, Mr. Stoughton, Mr. Rocester, Henry Gray.

Whereas, in regard of the diu^{r}sity of mens judgements amongst Jurors, yt falls out diu^{r}s tymes that no verdict is giuen in, or else wth great difficulty ; Wherefore yt is thought meet and so Ordered, that the Jurors would wth all dilligence attend the issue and evidence of the Cause before thē, to wch they are sworne, and if in that case they cannot agree after all reasons disputed, but some remayne vnsatisfied, their reasons are to be tendered to the Court, and to be answered, and then they are

---

* Blank in the original.

† The record of this session is not in the handwriting of the Secretary, Mr. Welles, who, (as will be seen by referring to the names of the Magistrates,) was not present.

to consult togather agayne, and if as yet any cannot bring their judgments to joyne wth their fellowes in a joynt verdict, the greater p^rte shall giue yt in by their voate, and yt shall be deemed to all intents and purposes a sufficient and full verdict, vppon wch judgement may be entered and execution and other p^rceedings to be had therein, as though they had all agreed; p^ruided also, that if yt fall out the case be so difficult that the Jury are equally diuided sixe [to] sixe, the Jurors are to tender yt to the Court, wth their reasons, and a spetiall verdict is to be drawen thereuppon; and then the Court are to appoynt a tyme to argue the same, and the voate or greater nūber of Magistrats are to carry the same, and judgement to be entered thereuppon, and execution and other p^rceedings as in case of a verdict by a Jury.

Whereas, we find by experience that there followes great inconueniences in regard diuers are suddenly cauled to answer sutes in the P^rticuler Court, w^thout tymely notice, and so many tymes the most harmeles are soonest overtaken, For the p^ruention whereof, It is Ordered, that frō henceforth all p^rsses* that yssue forth shall be returnable one full weeke before euery p^rticuler Court, at wch tyme the pl^te or pl^ts shall, is or are to bring in their plea or declaration to the Secretary, where the defen^t or defendants are to repaire and take a coppy, and w^thin three dayes to deliuer in his or their answer or answers, that men may be p^rpared to come to judgment; and if yt fall out the pl^t or pl^ts fayle of putting in his or their declaration or declarations according as aforesaid, the sute to surcesse and the defend^t or defend^ts not bownd to p^rceed w^thout a new sumōns, and if the def^t or defen^te fayle on his or their p^rts according to the true intent of this Order, the pl^t or pl^ts may p^rceed vppon his or their declaration or declarations, and the def^t or defend^ts ar likewise subiect to a fyne of the Court for any misdemeanor therein. These Orders to stand vntill the next generall Court.

The Clarkes of ech Towne that are appoynted to size the waights and measures are Ordered to bring in the standards of boath frō the seuerall Townes to the next p^rticuler Court, there to be compared togather and made equall. John Banks is re-

---

* processes.

turned Clarke to size the waights and measures for Wyndsor, & Fraunces Norton for Wethersfield.

[103]   It is Ordered, that one or two of the Magistrats shall be sent to Stratford and Vncoway, to joyne wth Mr. Ludlowe for the execution of Justice, twice this yeare, vizt. the last Thursday in Aprill and the last in September.

Capten Mason and Mr. Welles are appoynted for the last in Aprill.

It is Ordered, that euery Towne vppon the Riuer shall p^{r}uide one man in ech Towne to doe execution vppon delinquents, by whipping or other correction as they shall be thereunto cauled by Order frō the Magistrats.

It is Ordered, that good Rialls of $\frac{8}{9}$ and Reix Dollers shall passe betwixt man & man att fiue shillings a peece, in all payments, the debts being made after the publisheing of this Order.

It is Ordered, that Mr. Ludlowe shall be moderator the next p^{r}ticuler Court, if he be p^{r}sent, or in his absence and the absence of the Gou^r. & Deputy, the eldest Magistrat, p^{r}uided the Court consist of fiue Magistrats wth the Moderator.

The Go^r, the Deputy, Mr. Willis, Mr. Ludlow, Capten Mason, Mr. Webster, Mr. Whiting and Mr. Rocester are desiered to debate wth Mr. Huit conserneing Mr. Styles his petition and other offensiue cariedges, and if they receaue not satisfaction to returne their report to the next Generall Court. They may also take such other helpe as they shall see cause.

The opinion of the Cōmittee to whō the consideration of the petition of our neighbours of Wethersfield was cōmitted, was now returned to the Court, and for p^{r}sent aproued of, and ordered that one coppy thereof be sent to Mr. Smith and another be giuen to the mēbers of the Court for the Towne, and the said Cōmittee are desiered by the Court to receaue Mr. Smiths answer, and in case they find him vnsatisfied in the aduise giuen, they are desiered to take such an indifferent course that the true state of the question may be p^{r}pownded, and the aduise of Elders here and elsewhere taken vppon the same, that accordingly an issue may be put thereto.

The Court is adioyrned vntill the first Wendsday in July.

The Coppy of the opinion of the Comittee vppon the Petition of those of Wethersfield.

The Petition of those of Wethersfield hath bine taken into sadde and serious consideration, and we doe find the distance & differences to be exceeding great, and some of the such as will necessarily require publique examinatiō and censure, so that till then we cannot expresse or judgments conserneing prticulers: We find also that many of those who put vp their names for remoueall were not induced thereunto by any dislike, or ingadgement they haue in the prsent quarrells, but for want of lotts and other considerations : Yet vppon the vew of the generall, conceaueing yt will be disaduantagious to the publique & vncomfortable if not distructiue to themselues that so many as are interested in the prsent differences should remoue, and vppon other considerations, we are of opinion that the best way for recouering and prsearueing the publique peace is that Mr. Smith lay downe his place, if yt may be done according to God.

---

[104] THE PRTICULER COURT, THE FIRST OF JUNE, 1643.

Roger Ludlowe Esqr, Moderator.
George Willis Esqr, Mr. Webster, Mr. Whiteing, Mr. Welles, Capten Mason, Mr. Swaine, Mr. Woolcotte.
[*The Jury :*]—Mr. Parke, Mr. Stoughton, John Bissell, Henry Woolcotte, Aron Cooke, Roger Willm̄s, Nath: Foote, John Westoll, Tho: Standly, Joseph Maggott, George Steele, Tho: Scotte.

In the ac. of Will' Gailard, as Attorny for Nath. Patten, plt, against Tho: Marshfield, defent, the Jury find for the plt, damages, 20*l*.

In the ac. of Math: Allen, as Attorny for Tho: Allen, plt, agt Tho: Marshfield deft, the Jury find for the plt, damages, 2*l*. 16*s*.

In the ac. of Mr. Woolcott, as Attorny for Henry Webb plt, agt Tho: Marshfield deft, the Jury find for the plt, damages, 5*l*. 7*s*.

In the ac. of Henry Woolcott pl^t ag^t Tho: Marshfield def^t, the Jury find for the pl^t, damages, 19s.

In the ac. of Mr. Woolcott, for Mr. Branker pl^t, ag^t Tho: Marshfield defen^t, the Jury find for the pl^t, damages, 15s.

In the ac. of Will' Hill, for Lawrance Ellison pl^t, ag^t Tho: Marshfield def^t, the Jury find for the pl^t, damages, 4*l*.

In the ac. of Mr. Will' Whiting pl^t, against Tho: Marshfield def^t, the Jury find for the pl^t, damages, xxvi*l*.

In the ac. of debt vppon a bill of exchainge, by Mr. Will' Whiting pl^t, ag^t Tho: Marshfield def^t, the Jury find for the pl^t, damages, 20*l*. 10s.

In the ac. of Will' Torrey pl^t, ag^t Tho: Marshefield defen^t, the Jury find for the pl^t, damages, 182*l*. vis. 9*d*.

In the ac. of Richard Trott pl^t, ag^t Tho: Marshfield defen^t, the Jury find for the pl^t, damages, xvi*l*. 13s. vi*d*.

In the ac. of Bray Rocester pl^t, ag^t Wyddow Hudgison def^t, as executrixe to Will' Hudgison deceased; Tho: Ford appeareing to the sute, the Jury find for the pl^t, damages, 23*l*. The Court graunteth execution to the pl^t vppon the goods of the defen^t.

[105] Willm Turrey pl^t, ag^t Nath: Willet & Elizabeth Willet def^ts, in an ac. of debt.

John Robins pl^t, ag^t Richard Belden & Nath: Woodroofe defen^ts, in an ac. of the Case.

Will' Whiting——

---

[106]   June the 15th, 1643.   [A P^rticuler Court.]

John Heynes Esqr, Gou^r.

Ed: Hopkins Esqr, Dep.

George Willis Esqr, Mr. Welles, Mr. Webster, Mr. Whiting, Capten Mason, Mr. Swayne, Mr. Woolcott.

The Jury :—Mr. Chester, Rich: Webb, Rich: Goodman, Will' Gybbins, Rich: Butler, Tho: Ford, John Porter, John Drake, Robert Howard, Nath: Dickinson, Josias Churchill, John Demon, (Mr. Trotte.)

In the ac. of Battery and Trespasse of Tho: Waynewright pl^t, ag^t his Master, Mr. Henry Smith def^t, the Jury find for the defen^t Costs of the Court.

In the ac. of Henry Woolcotte pl^t, as Attorny to John Witchfield, ag^t Tho: Marshfield def^t, the Jury find for the pl^t, dam̃: 30s.

In the ac. of Henry Woolcott pl^t, as Attorny to John Brocke, ag^t Tho: Marshfield def^t, the Jury find for the pl^t, dam̃: xi*l*.

In the ac. of Nath: Willet & Elizabeth Willett pl^t, ag^t Tho: Marshfield def^t, the Jury find for the pl^t, dam̃ages, 14*l*. 11s. 2d.

In the ac. of Will' Palmer pl^t, ag^t Tho: Marshfield def^t, the Jury find for the pl^t, dam̃ages, viii*l*. 3s. 4.

In the ac. of Henry Woolcot pl^t, ag^t Tho: Marshfield def^t, the Jury find for the pl^t, dam̃ages, 4*l*. 3s. 4d.

In the ac. of Tho: Ford pl^t, ag^t Tho: Marshfield def^t, the Jury find for the pl^t, dam̃ages, 4*l*. 13s. 10d.

In the ac. of Henry Woolcott & Nath: Willet pl^t, ag^t Tho: Marshfield def^t, the Jury find for the pl^t, dam̃ages, vii*l*.

Mr. Eldridge pl^t, ag^t Tho: Marshfield in an ac. of debt to the dam̃age of 13*l*.

Benedict Aluer pl^t, ag^t Tho: Marshfield def^t, in an ac. of * to the dam̃age of 10*l*.

Will' Hubbert pl^t, ag^t Tho: Marshfield def^t, in an ac. of the Case to the dam̃age of 12*l*.

Mr. Woolcott pl^t, ag^t Tho: Marshfield in an ac. of the Case to the dam̃age of 39*l*. 15s.

Mr. Whiteing pl^t, as Attorny to Henry Bartlemewe, ag^t Tho: Marshfield def^t, in an ac. of the Case to the dam̃age of 40*l*.

Tho: Ford pl^t, as assigne Edward Smith, ag^t Tho: Marshfield defen^t, in an ac. of debt to the dam̃age of 30*l*. 13s. 4d.

---

[107]   JUNE THE 16th, 1643.

Henry Woolcott & Tho: Ford are Ordered to bring vnto the Gouernour a p^rticuler of the Estate of Tho: Marshfield, as yt consists in land, goods or debts, and that they doe yt wthin on weeke; & Mr. Whiting, Mr. Hull and Will' Gaylard are to

---

* Blank in the original.

price the pʳticulers, and to make an equall diuision thereof amongst the creditors, and that pʳportion wᶜʰ is to be sequestred for debts oweing by the sᵈ Marshfield and yet vnproued, are to be lefte wᵗʰ Henry Woolcott, who must accoumpt for the same. And the creditors are to be accoumptable for to returne such a pʳportion of what they shall receaue as shall appeare to belong to such Creditors frō old Ingland as may challing and make pʳufe of any just debts frō the said Marshfield, pʳuided they appeare wᵗʰin 14 months; to wᶜʰ the Creditors consent.

---

[108]   JULY THE 5ᵗʰ, 1643.

   John Heynes Esqʳ, Gouʳ.

   Ed: Hopkins, Esqʳ, Dep:

      Roger Ludlowe Esqʳ, George Willis Esq, Mr. Webster, Mr. Welles, Mr. Whiting, Mr. Swayne.

      [*Deputyes :*]—Mr. Taylcott, Andrew Bacon, Mr. Chapline, Robert Rose, John Edwards, John Robins, Mr. Rocester.

Those of Wethersfield who conceaue thēselues to be vnder some wronge in caring of Church and Towne occations, they are ordered to gather vp the pʳticuler greiuences or wrongs and pʳsent them wᵗʰ their names to the Gouʳ & Deputy, wᵗʰin three weekes, who are desiered to send a coppy thereof to Mr. Smith, who is to returne his answer wᵗʰin three weeks, that the differences may be ripened agᵗ the Court in Septēber, and a finall end put thereunto.

Mr. Hopkins is desiered to pʳforme the searuice to be one*

---

* At the first meeting of the Commissioners of the United Colonies, in September following, "an order from the Generall Court of Connectacutt was presented and read, dated at Hartford, the fifth of July last, by which it appears *George Fenwicke Esq.* and Mr. Edward Hopkins were chosen Commissioners for that Jurisdiction." (Rec. of U. Colonies.)

  The name of Mr. Fenwick does not appear in the record of the General Court;—but the appointment of Mr Hopkins as "*one* of the Committee" seems to imply the recognition of Mr. F. as his associate. The latter represented the 'Lords and gentlemen,' his fellow proprietors under the Earl of Warwick's Patent; as whose agent he maintained the Fort and plantation at Saybrook and claimed the jurisdiction of the lands upon the Connecticut. The agreement between Mr. F. and the General Court, by which Saybrook was ceded to Connecticut was not executed until December, 1644.

of the Comittee for this Riuer, to goe to the Bay to agitate the businesses of the Combination, according to the agreement betwixt the vnited Colonyes, the first Thursday in Septem., if his shippe occations be then ouer, otherwise the Gou^r is desiered to supply the place, and to treate and conclude touching appeales in such Cases as shall be by the Comission^{rs} judged necessary.

Whereas there hath bine great neglect by the plant[ations] in not p^{r}uiding powder according to order of Court, It is now Ordered, that if the seuerall Townes shall not p^{r}uide their seu^{r}all quantityes, according to former Order, by the Court in Septē., all the former forfetures shall be leuyed vppon thē wthout delay.

It is Ordered, that there shall be liberty for a Markett to be held att Hartford weekely, euery Wensday, for all manner of comodityes that shall be brought in, and for cattell, or any marchandise w^{h}soeuer.

Mr. Webster and Mr. Whiting are desiered by the Court to answer the petition conserneing the makeing pitch and tarre.

It is Ordered, that Mr. Huit and Mr. Styles shall be cauled to the next generall Courte, to answer for their miscaridge in their petition formerly giuen into Courte.

It is Ordered, that ech Towne chuse two surueyors yerely, to looke to the highwayes, who shall haue liberty to call out euery Teeme & p^{r}son fitt for labour, in their course, one day euery yeare, to mend the said highwayes wherein they are to haue a spetiall regard to those Comon wayes wch are betwixt Towne and Towne. The chardge hereof is lefte to the p^{r}ticuler Townes for thē p^{r}sent, to be ordered according to their owne rules, & in case any surueyor shall not attend the said searuice by cauleing out the teemes & p^{r}sons aforesaid, where need is, he shall forfeit 5s. for euery offence.

[109] It is Ordered, there shall be a Grand Jury of 12 p^{r}sons warned to appeare eu^r Court yerely in Septēber, or as many & oft as the Gouerno^r or Courte shall thinke meet, to make p^{r}sentment of the breches of any lawes or orders, or any other misdemeanors they know of in the Jurisdiction.

Mr. Chaplin shall haue a coppy of the creditors & debtors to Mr. Oldoms estate, and is to inquire of the debtors to whō they haue paid & to make returne to the next p^{r}ticuler Court.

The Tresurer is to haue a noate to take vppe the Fynes.

Whereas, the p^rsp^rity and well being of Com̃on weles doth much depend vppon the well gouerment and ordering of p^rticuler Familyes, wch in an ordinary way cannot be expected where the rules of God are neglected in laying the foundation of a family state ; For the p^ruention therefore of such evells and inconueniences, wch by experience are found not only to be creepeing in but practised by some in that kynd, It is Ordered, that no p^rson whatsoeuer, male or female, not being at his or her owne dispose, or that remayneth vnder the gouerment of parents, masters or gardians or such like, shall ether make, or giue entertaynement to any motion or sute in way of mariedge, wthout the knowledge and consent of those they stand in such relation to, vnder the seuere censure of the Courte, in case of delinquency not attending this order ; nor shall any third p^rson or p^rsons intermedle in makeing any motion to any such wthout the knowledge and consent of those vnder whose gouerment they are, vnder the same penalty.

Mathew Allen pl^t, ag^t Rich: Fellowes def^t, in an ac. of the Case, to the dam̃age of 20s. The said Mathewe Allen acknowledgeth himselfe to be bownd to the Cuntry in a Recognizance of 10l. to p^rsent the said Rich : Fellowes, the next Court.

---

[110]   September the 4th, 1643.   [A P^rticuler Courte.]
John Heynes Esqr, Gou^r.
Mr. Welles, Mr. Webster, Mr. W. Swayne, Mr. Woolcott.
[The Jury :]   Tho: Ford, Will' Wodsworth, Nath : Richards, John Hopkins, Arther Smith, John More, Will' Heiton, Josua Carter, Samuell Smith, Tho : Wright, Samuell Hale, Andrew Longdon.

In the ac. of Math : Allen pl^t, ag^t Rich : Fellowes defen^t, the Jury find for the def^t, chardges of Court & viiid. for powndage.

In the ac. of Math : Allen pl^t, ag^t Nich: & Will' Clarke def^{ts}, the Jury find for the pl^t, dam̃ages 3l. 3s. 4d. & costs of Court vijs.

The ac. of Math : Allen pl^t, ag^t Tho : Olcott is forborne vntill the next Court.

In the ac. of John Robins pl^t, ag^t Tho: Holibut defen^t, the Jury find for the pl^t, damages 25s. & costs of Court.

Tho: Ford pl't, as assigne to Edward Smith, ag^t Tho: Marshfield def^t, in an ac. of debt to the damage of 30l. 13s. 4d.

Roger Ludlowe Esqr, pl^t, ag^t Will' Whiting def^t.

SEPTĒBER THE 14th, 1643. A GENERALL COURTE.

John Heynes Esqr, Gou^r.

Mr. Webster, Mr. Welles, Capten Mason, Mr. Swayne, Mr. Woolcott.

Mr. Steele, Mr. Taylcote, Mr. Westwood, Andrew Bacon, Mr. Hill, Mr. Stoughton, Mr. Hull, Will' Gaylard, Mr. Chapline, Mr. Robins.

The Courte is adiorned for a month.

---

[112]   SEPTĒBER THE 15th, 1643.

Jo; Heynes Esqr, Gou^r.

Ed: Hopkins Esqr, Deputy.

George Willis Esqr, Mr. Webster, Mr. Welles, Mr. Whiting, Capten Mason, Mr. Swayne, Mr. Woolcott.

[*Deputyes:*] Mr. Steele, Mr. Talcott, Mr. Westwood, Andrew Bacon, Mr. Hill, Mr. Hull, Mr. Stoughton, Will' Gaylard, Mr. Chaplin, Mr. Robins, James Boosy, Samuell Smith.

The Grand Jury. Mr. Phelps, *Jur;* Williā Pantry, Richard Webb, John Pratt, Nath: Waird, John White, Mr. Trott, Mr. Parke, Mr. Chester, Nath: Foote, Nath: Dickinson, Tho: Ford, Mr. Clarke, Mr. Porter, Mr. Terry; *Jur.*

The Court adioyrned for a month.

OCTOBER THE 12th, 1643.

John Sadler was to be warned to the next Generall Court.

Whereas Mr. Hopkins, Mr. Willis & Mr. Whiting have p^rmised to vse their best endeauors to p^ruide fower barrells of powder, It is Ordered, that Wyndsor shall take offe two barrells,

Hartford one barrell and Wethersfield one, yf yt may be had, & to make the best pay the Country afords to sute the occations of the p^rtyes that p^ruide yt.

It is ordered, that Wyndsor shall haue for the p^rsent 30*l.* of powder out of the Comon stocke, wch they are to restore so soone as they can p^ruide.

It is Ordered, that Mr. Talcott and Andrewe Bacon are to take a record of the debts of the Country oweing in Hartford, Mr. Woolcott & Mr. Hill for Wyndsor, James Boosy for Wethersfield.

Mr. Whiteing and Capten Mason are to examine whether the Country or some p^rticuler p^rson are to dischardge the debt due to Roger Anadowne.

Mr. Hopkins, Mr. Whiteing and Capten Mason are to p^rsse eight souldiers wth sufficient arms and p^ruisions to be sent to Mohegen to defend Vncas,* and to doe such seruice in building or otherwise as shall be thought meet, and there to remayne as the said comittee shall see cause.

It is ordered, that the Gou^rnor or deputy, or any two Magistrats, vppon any sudden occation or eminent daynger may presse men and munition for a defensiue warre or to garde & defend the Country in their necessary occations or passage frō Towne to Towne. Also, the deputyes in the seu^rall Townes are desiered to call their p^rticuler Townes togather, to take Order w^thin thēselues to be in a posture of defence vppon an alarū, that the seu^rull souldears may know to what quarter to resorte and where to stand vppon their p^rsent defence.

Richard Lord† for his miscariedge in draweing his sowrd and vseing thretening speeches in contending wth Tho: Stanton† about tradeing for indean corne, is fyned to pay to the Country fiue† pownd.

---

* The Commissioners of the United Colonies (who were at this time in session, at Boston,) having decided upon delivering up Miantonimo to be murdered by his captor, Uncas, ("that so execution may be done according to justice and prudence,") were apprehensive that the Narragansetts, or some of the neighboring tribes, allied with or tributary to the Narragansett Sachem, would seek to revenge his death. They therefore directed that measures should be taken to pro. vide for the defence of the Colonies, and "that Hartford furnish Vncas with a competent strength of English to defend him against any present fury or assault of the Narragansetts or any other." (*Records of U. Colonies.*)

† The names of Richard Lord and Tho. Stanton, and the word 'fiue,' have been partially obliterated, by drawing a pen across them, at a date evidently long subsequent to that of the record.

It is Ordered that there shall be a rate of forty pownd leuied, to be paid to Mr. Fenwicke, to be laid out for the repaireing the Fort.

For the avoyding of many differences and quarrells that may arise by takeing vppe debts of Indeans, It is Ordered, that whosoeuer, after the publisheing this Order, shall sell for day, or trust any Indean or Indeans wth goods or comoditye, shall forfeit to the Country the double some or value of what they do betrust them wthall ; and that no man shall trade wth them at or about their wygwams, but in their vessells or Pynnaces or att their owne howses, vnder the penalty of 20s. ech tyme.

To p^{r}uent or wthstand such sudden assaults as may be made by Indeans vppon the Sabboth or lecture dayes, It is Ordered, that one p^{r}son in euery seuerall howse wherein is any souldear or souldears, shall bring a muskett, pystoll or some peece, wth powder and shott to ech meeting, excepte some on Magistrate dispense wth any on, and appoynt some other to supply his roome.

Jacob Waterhowse doth acknowledge himselfe bownd in a recognizance of Fifty pownd, to attend the next Court to answer for his mysdemeanor towards the Indeans.

The Court is adioyrned vntill Thursday next.

---

[113]   A P^{r}ticuler Court, held the ixth of No: 1643.

John Heynes Esqr, Gou^r.

Ed: Hopkins Esqr, Dep.

Roger Ludlowe Esqr, George Willis, Mr. Webster, Mr. Welles, Mr. Whiteing, Capten Mason, Mr. Woolcott, Mr. Swayne.

The Jury.   Mr. Tailcott, Tho: Osmore, Ed: Stebbing, John Barnard, Arther Williams, Mathewe Sension, Tho: Dewey, Tho: Orton, Tho: Vffoote, Samuel Hales, Richard Parke, John Demon.

In the action of Nathaniell Dickinson pl^t, ag^t John Robins defen^t, the Jury find for the deft. Costs of Court vijs,

In the ac. of Nathaniell Eldredge pl^t, ag^t Tho: Marshfield, the Jury find for the pl^t, the debt and costs of Court, x*l*.

In the ac. of Tho: Ford pl^t, as assigne to Ed: Smith, ag^t Tho: Marshfield def^t, the Jury find for the pl^t, the debt & costs of Court. The debt, 30l. 13s. 4d.

In the ac. of Math: Allen pl^t ag^t, Tho: Olcocke def^t, the Jury find for the pl^t, damages six pownd, fiue shillings, and costs of Court.

In the action of Roger Ludlowe Esqr pl^t, against Williā Whiteing gent. defen^t, the Jury find for the pl^t, damages thirty-nyne pownd, and costs vij$s$.

Willi' Lewes his fyne is to be paid at these seu^{r}all tymes, vizt. 5l. the 20th of March, and 5l. the 20th of Septēber, and the other xl. three months after.

[114]   No: xth, 1643. A GENERALL COURT.

John Heynes Esqr, Gou^r.

Ed: Hopkins Esqr, Dep.

 Roger Ludlowe Esqr, George Willis Esqr, Mr. Webster, Mr. Whiting, Mr. Welles, Capten Mason, Mr. Swayne, Mr. Woolcott.

 Deputyes: Mr. Steele, Mr. Talcoate, Mr. Westwood, Andrewe Bacon, Mr. Hill, Mr. Hull, Mr. Stoughton Will' Gaylard, Mr. Chaplin, Mr. Robins, Samuell Smith, James Boosy.

Whereas in the fundamentall Order* yt is said (that such who haue taken the Oath of fidellity and are admitted inhabitants) shall be alowed as quallified for chuseing of Deputyes, The Court declares their judgement, that such only shall be counted admitted inhabitants, who are admitted by a generall voate of the mayor p^{r}te of the Towne that receaueth them.

Whereas yt is obsearued that the late Order for on in a Family to bring his Arms to the meeting house euery Sabboth and lecture day, hath not bine attended by diuers p^{r}sons; It is now Ordered, that whosoeuer hereafter shall at any tyime neglecte the same, shall forfeit xij$d$. for euery neglect, whereof vi$d$. to the p^{r}ty that shall informe and vi$d$. to the Country.

---

* See page 23. [Or. 224.]

It is Ordered that all the souldears in the severall Townes w^{th}in this Jurisdiction shall be trayned sixe dayes yerely* as they shall be appoynted by the Capten or other officer, Viz^t. one day in the first weeke of these seuerall months here mentioned, March, Aprill, May, Septēber, October & Nouēber; and if the day appoynted p^rue vnseasonable, the Officer is to appoynt the next fayer day. The hower tō begin is eight of the clocke. And whosoeuer shall be absent any of the said dayes after the hower lymited, or shall not continue the whole tyme shall forfeit 2s. vid. for euery default, excepte such as are lycensed vnder the hands of two magistrats. The Clarkes of the seuerall bands are to distreyne the delinquents w^{th}in 14 dayes after the forfeture, and to take vid. for thēselues, the remaynder to be for the mayntenance of drums, cullers & such like; and if any of the said Clarks shall omit to distreine any delinquent for the said terme of 14 dayes, shall forfeit to the Country the double some. The Capten and officers shall haue liberty to relesse such as they approue for expert souldears for halfe a day, at any time. Mr. Ludlowe is desiered to call forth the souldears of the Towns vppon the sea cost, to see thē exercise as aforesaid, vntill there be some fitt officers p^ruided.

Mr. Chaplyn, for diuulgeing and setting his hand to a writing cauled a declaration, tending to the defamation of Mr. Smith, is fyned to pay to the Country xi*l*.

Frances Norton, for setting his hand to the said writeing, is fyned 5*l*.

John Goodridge also, for setting his hand to the said writeing is fyned 40s.

Mr. Plum, for p^rferring a rowle of diuers greuinces ag^t Mr. Smith & fayleing of proufe in the p^rsecutiō thereof, is fyned x*l*.

Robert Rose for joyneing wth Mr. Plum therein is fyned 40s.

Its concluded that a writeing shall be p^rpared and openly read in the seuerall Townes, for the clereing Mr. Smith, and an Order made of ten pownd fyne for whosoeuer shall be conuicted vnder two witnesses to diuulge any the said greiuences to his defamation.

The Court is adiurned vntill Wensdey com seuennight.

---

* "It is iudged meet by the Commissioners that there be trayneings at least sixe tymes eu^rie yeare in each Plantacon w^{th}in this confederacon." (Rec. of U. Colonies, Sept. 1643.)

Mr. Webster and Mr. Welles are to take vppe of the Traders for Indean corn, the forfetures due to the Country.

WENSDAY THE   *DAY OF No: 1643.

Its Ordered, that there shall be a Rate of 150l. levied vppon the three Towns, wch is to be p^rportioned by Mr. Taylcott and Andrewe Bacon, Mr. Hill, Willā. Gaylard, Mr. Chaplin and James Boosy.

The Gouernor and Deputy are desiered to examine the Tresurers accoumpt and to assigne the bylls for the Country debts, what shall be alowed.

Its Ordered that the plantations shall keepe a day of humiliation vppon Wensday com three weeks.

Mr. Branker is freed frō watching & warding.

[115] Whereas many clamors haue bine raysed & spred through seu^rall p^rts of the Country, of some indirect p^rceedings of Mr. Smith of Wethersfield, both in Church administrations & in acting in the ciuell occations of the Towne, whereby the peace of the Comon welth was disturbed, wch gaue occation to the Court to giue liberty to all who had any iust greiuences in ether kynd ag^t him to p^rduce them in publique, and to apoynt a tyme for hereing and determining the same, wch accordingly was attended by seuerall in that Towne, and many complaints made, wherein Mr. Smith was accused and judged by thē to lye vnder much guilt. But vppon a full heareing of all that was aleadged by any in mayntenance of their accusations, It was found that most of their accusations were mistaks, wherein Mr. Smith was much wronged, both by false reports and vniust surmises. It was therefore, by vnanimos consent of the whole Court, Ordered, for p^ruention of the further spreading of the said reports wch tend so much to the p^riudice of the publique peace and th' aparent wrong of Mr. Smith, That whosoeuer w^thin this jurisdiction shall hereafter be conuicted by the testimony of two witnesses, to continue or renewe any of the former complaints (most of the said greiuences haueing bine also formerly hard by the magistrats and elders,) wherein he hath

---

* Blank in the original.

bine clered by this Court, shall forfeit to the Country ten pownd for euery such offence.

JANUARY 3ᵈ, 1643.

The Courte takeing the state of oʳ natiue Country into consideration haue Ordered, that there shall be monthly a day of humiliation keept through the Plantations, according to the course of oʳ neighbours at New hauen, and to begin vppō Wensday the xᵗʰ of this month.

Mr. Fenwicke is pʳpownded to stand in election for a Magistrate, the Court in Aprill.

The Gouʳ & Deputy are desiered to returne an answer to the request of the Ilanders, signified by their letter pʳsented to the Court.

Gyles Whiteing is dismissed frō trayneing & is content to pay 12ᵈ. euery trayneing day, to the Clarke of the land, towards the maynetenaunce of drums & cullers.

The Court is adiorned for sixe weekes.

[116] FEB. 14ᵗʰ, 1643.

John Heynes Esqʳ, Gouʳ.
Ed: Hopkins Esqʳ, Dep.
George Willis Esqʳ, Mr. Webster, Mr. Whiteing, Mr. Welles, Capten Mason, Mr. Woolcott, Mr. Swayne.
[*Deputyes* :] Mr. Steele, Mr. Talcott, Mr. Westwood, Andrewe Bacon, Mr. Hill, Mr. Hull, Mr. Gaylard, Mr. Stoughton, Mr. Chaplin, Mr. Robins, Samuell Smith, James Boosy.

Nath: & Elizabeth Willet plᵗˢ, agᵗ Benedict Alueret defenᵗ, in an ac. of debt to the damage of 12*l*.

Math: Allen plᵗ, agᵗ Tho: Steynton defenᵗ, in an ac. of the Case.

All pʳsons that can bring in sufficient proufe that they are aboue 60 yeares of age, are freed frō watching.

Whereas yt is obsearued that many differences arise frō the inequallity of measures that are vsed amongst vs, for the pʳuenting whereof, It is Ordered, that the Clarks in the seuerall

Townes wch are appoynted for the fixeing the said measuers shall once in euery yeare appoynt a certen day and place & giue notice to the Inhabitans to bring in their measures to them to be tryed and compared wth the standard; and they shall haue 3d. for the first fitting and sealeing ech measuer, and 2d. for euery tryall and sealeing, p^ruided that non be sealed but of seasoned wood; and it shall not be lawfull for any p^rson w^thin these libertyes to sell by any other measure but such as are sealed, and whosoeuer shall fayle to bring in his measure to the said Clarke at the tyme & place appoynted shall forfeit 12d. for euery default, wch forfetures shall be gathered by the said Clarks, and they shall haue 4d. in the shilling to theselues; and if vppon tryall any measure be found to little they shall cutte out the seale. They are also to size & seale all yards and wayghts.

Forasmuch as many laborers and workemen complayne that they are forced to put offe their Corne wch they receaue for their worke to seuerall Chapmen, for comodityes, at a cheper rate then they take yt att, For the p^ruenting whereof, It is now Ordered, that whosoeuer w^thin these libertyes shall sell any Comodityes or make any bargaine to be paid in Corne, after the publisheing this Order, shall take the said Corne att the Country rate.

[117] Whereas many complaynts are brought into the Court by reason of diu^rs abuses that fall out by seuerall p^rsons that sell Wyne and strong water, as well in vessells on the Riuer as also in seuerall howses, for the p^ruenting whereof yt is now Ordered, that no p^rson or p^rsons, after the publisheing this Order, shall nether sell Wyne nor strong water in any place w^thin these libertyes, w^thout license fro the p^rticuler Court or any two magistrates.

Whereas the Condition of these seuerall Plantations in these beginnings wherein we are, is such that necessity constraynes to improue much of the grownds belonging to the seuerall Townes in a comon way, and yt is obsearued that the publique & generall good, wch ought to be attended in all such improuements, receaues much p^riudice through waint of a prudent ordering and disposeing of those seuerall Comon lands to such wayes of improuement as are most p^rp^r to the, and may best aduance the publique good, It is therefore Ordered, that ech Towne shall before the sitting of the next Court, chuse frō among thēselues seaven able and discreet men, who by this Order haue power giuen thē, and are required to take the comōn lands belonging to ech of the seu^{r}all Townes respectiuely, into serious and sadde consideratiō, and after a through disgesting of their owne thoughts, sett downe vnder their hands in what way the said lands may in their judgement be best improued for the comōn good. And whatsoeu^r is so decreed & determined by the said 7 men in ech Towne, or any fiue of thē, conserneing the way of improuement of any such lands, shall be attended by all such p^{r}sons that haue any p^{r}priety or interest in any lands that shall be so iudged by the said Comīttee.

And whereas also, much damīage hath risen not only frō the vnrulynes of some kynd of Cattell but also frō the weaknesse & insufficiency of many fences, whereby much variance and difference hath followed, wch if not p^{r}uented for the future may be very p^{r}iudiciall to the publique peace ; It is therefore likewise Ordered, that the said 7 men soe chosen, or at lest 5 of thē, shall sett downe what fences are to be made in any Comōn grownds, and after they are made to cause the same to be vewed, and to sett such fynes as they iudge meet vppon any as shall neglect or not duly attend their Order therein. And when fences are made and judged sufficient by thē, whatsoeu^r damīage is done by hoggs or any other cattle shall be paid by the owners of the said cattle, wthout any gaynesaying or releife by Repleivy or otherwise. And the seu^{r}all Townes shall haue liberty once euery yeare to alter any 3 of the former 7, and to make choyse of others in their roome : It being p^{r}uided that any p^{r}ticuler man or men shall haue liberty to inclose any of their p^{r}ticuler grownds, and improue thē according to their owne discrētiō by mutuall agreement, notwthstanding this Order.

---

[118]   [A P^{r}ticuler Courte.*]
    John Heynes Esqr, Gou^r.
    Ed : Hopkins Esqr, Dep.

---

* The date is not given.

George Willis Esq\\r, Mr. Webster, Mr. Whiting, Mr. Welles, Capten Mason, Mr. Woolcott.

The Jury :—Ed: Stebbin, John Edwards, John Stadder, John Cattell, John Wastoll, John Byssell, Water Fyler, John More, Henry Woolcott, Will' Wadsworth, Andrew Bacon, Will' Gybbins.

Henry Woolcott pl. ag\\t Bray Rocester def\\t, in an ac. of the Case, to the damage of 5*l*.

John Dymon pl. ag\\t Tho: Gunne def\\t, in an ac. of trespasse for Fals Imprisonment.

John Dymon pl. ag\\t Edward Presson def\\t, in an ac. of the Case to the damage of vij*l*.

Ed: Presson pl. ag\\t Will' Perwidge def\\t, in an ac. of the Case to the damage of x*l*.

Tho: Steynton pl. ag\\t Tho: Crump def\\t, in an ac. of Slaunder.

Jaruis Mudgge

Nath: & Eliz: Willet pl. ag\\t Benedict Alueret def\\t, in an ac. of debt to the damage of 12*l*.

Math: Allen pl. ag\\t Tho: Steynton def\\t, in an ac. of the Case, 28*s*. damage.

Mr. Will' Whiteing pl. ag\\t Tho: Bassett defen\\t, in an ac. of the Case to the damage of v*l*. 10*s*.

Mr. Will' Whiting pl. against Dauid Wilton def\\t, in an ac. of the Case to the damage of ix*l*.

In the ac. of Math: Allen pl. ag\\t Tho: Steynton def\\t, the Jury find for the pl. damages 28*s*. & Costs of Court. *Execution graunted.*

In the ac. of Willia Whiteing pl. ag\\t Tho: Basset def\\t, the Jury find for the pl. damages 5*l*. and Costs of Court.

In the ac. of Nath: & Eliz: Willet pl. ag\\t Benedict Alueret def\\t, the Jury find for the pl. damages 5*l*. & 2*d*. and Costs of Court.

Tho: Hurlbut his fyne is respited, vppon Peter Bassakers tryall to make nayles w\\th less losse and at as cheape a rate, then he is to duble the fyne, otherwise to be quit.

The Jury find that John Ewe, by misaduenture, was the cause of the death of Tho : Scott.

The said John Ewe is fyned to pay fiue pownd to the Country and ten pownd to the Wyddowe Scotte.

---

[119]   THE COURT OF ELECTION, APRILL, 1644.

Edward Hopkins Esqr, Gou^r.

John Heynes Esqr, Dep.

George Fenwicke Esqr, George Willis Esqr, Roger Ludlowe Esqr, Mr. Webster, Mr. Whiting Tres^r., Mr. Welles Sec., Capten Mason, Mr. Woolcott, Mr. Swayne.

Mr. Steele, Mr. Talcoat, Mr. Westwood, Andrew Bacon, Mr. Trott, James Boosy, Nath : Foote, Sa: Smith, Mr. Hill, Mr. Hull, Mr. Gaylard, Tho: Ford.

Vppon the petition of Benedict Alfford for reliefe ag^t the verdict giuen in by the Jury at the sute of Nath: Willet pl. It is Ordered, that judg^t shall be respited till the Court put an issue thereto.

Its the app^{r}hension of the Court that the damages & Costs of Court mentioned in the petition of Benedict Alford, that yt shall be layd vppon Marshfields estate, by the p^{r}portion of other creditors, and what that falls short shall be borne by the said Benedict & Mr. Woolcott & Nath: Willet by equall p^{r}portions.

The Courts adioyrned to the second Thursday in May.

MAY THE IXth, 1644.

The Court is adioyrned vntill Munday, the third of June, eight of the clocke, vnder the penalty of 2s. vi$d$. eu^r default.

JUNE THE 3, 1644.

Whereas many strayngers & passengers that vppon occation haue recourse to these Townes, and are streightened for waint of entertainment, It is now Ordered, that these seuerall Townes shall p^{r}uide amongst theselues in ech Towne one sufficient inhabitant to keepe an Ordinary, for p^{r}uisiō and lodgeing in some comfortable manner, that such passengers or strayngers may know where to resorte; and such inhabitants as by the seuerall Townes shall be chosen for the said searuice shall be p^rsented to two Magistrats, that they may be judged meet for that imployment, and this to be effected by the severall Townes w^thin one month, under the penalty of 40s. a month, ech month ether Towne shall neglect yt.

Whereas many differences arise about dresseing and measureing of Corne, betwixt the buyer and seller, It is now ordered, that the sealer of the measures in eu^ry Towne shall keep a standard whereunto the buyer may resort; and the said measurer hath power, and is appoynted by the Court to determine and issue the differences that may arise both in respect of the measur and also the dresseing & cleanes of the grayne. The mesurer to be paid by the guilty p^rty.

[120] The Court adiorned to the last July, (x a clock) vnles the Gou^r see cause to call yt sooner.

Its Ordered that the two Peeces that came frō Piscataq' shall be purchased for the vse of the Country; the Gouernour and Deputy are desiered to contract wth the owners for thē.

Whereas by reson of the badnes and rottennes of much yarne and other defects that fall out in the ordering of yt, both lynnen and woollen, many weauers are discouridged to goe on in their trade, It is therefore Ordered, that two experienced men shall be chosen in ech Towne who shall haue power to judge and determine the price or rate that any weauer in the said Towne shall receaue by the yard for such yarne, who shall vewe and make tryall thereof, vppon complaynt made vnto thē; and whereas they are many tymes much hindred by seekeing for their pay, they are now to retayne their worke in their custody vntill they receaue their pay for yt. Joseph Magott & George Graues are chosen for Hartford, Will' Gaylard & Eldweed Pomry for Wyndsor.

The Gouer^r and Mr. Fenwicke are desiered and chosen by the Court to be Comīssioners for this Jurisdiction, to agitate such businesses as shall fall out to be attended in behalfe of the Combinatiō, the next meeting in September and for the yeare following.

Mr. Steele, Andrewe Bacon & James Boosy are to order &

appoynt some conuenient howse in Hartford, for the comly and sutable meeteing of the Comissioners in September next, wherein they may agitate the affaires of the Combination.

Whereas many stubborne, refrectary and discontented searuants and app^rntices w^thdrawe themselues frō their masters searuices, to improue their tyme to their owne aduantage; for the p^ruenting whereof, It is Ordered, that whatsoeuer searuant or apprentice shall heareafter offend in that kynd, before their couenants or terme of searuice are expiered, shall searue their said Masters, as they shall be app^rhended or retayned the treble terme, or threefold tyme of their absence in such kynd.

For the p^ruenting of differences that may arise in makeing or setting downe of Fences, as well in meadowe as vpland, It is Ordered, that in the setting posts and rayles or hedges, in the meadowes and homelotts, there shall be a liberty for ether p^rty of 12 inches frō the diuident lyne, for breakeing of the grownd to sett the posts, or for the laying on the hedge, but the staks and posts are to be sett in the diuiding lyne; and in vpland there is alowed a liberty of fower foote for a ditch, frō the diuiding lyne, for ether of the bordering p^rtyes where the p^rportiō of fence belongs vnto thē.

[121] The Gou^r is desiered to returne an answere to the Towns of Stratford and Vncocoaue, of Mr. Ludlowe his letter conserneing his p^rpositions made to the Court about the manner of Rateing & his chardges for Country imployment.

It is Ordered, that whosoeuer arests or retaynes any mans goods by way of Attachment or Repliuy, shall put in good security to prosecute the sute w^thin conuenient tyme, and to pay what damages shall arise vppon his neglect or not makeing good his action, and shall pay xij$d$. for the attachment or repliuy & vi$d$. for his recognizance or bond.

Also, no Magistrate shall graunte any warrant conserneing p^rsonall actions, but the demaunder thereof shall pay 4d. for yt.

Also, there shall be 2s. vi$d$. payd for the Recording euery Will and Inuentory that is vnder the somē of 40l. and iij$s$. 4d. if aboue 40l.

It is Ordered, that the Towne Clarkes or Registers in the seuerall Townes within this Jurisdiction, shall ech of them keepe a record of the day of mariedge of euery p^rson hereafter maried w^th^in theire libertyes, and of the day of the birth of euery child hereafter borne, to whō the parent of the child shall w^th^in three dayes after the birth of his child certifie the day of the childs birth, and to whō euery man that shall be maried shall w^th^in three dayes after his mariedge certifie his mariedge day, vnder the penalty of 5*s*. euery default. The said Register is to receaue vi*d*. for recording the day of mariedge & ii*d*. for recording the birth of the child.

It is Ordered, that no Inhabitant w^th^in these libertyes shall suffer any Indean or Indeans to com into their howses, except the Magistrats or Traders, who may admitte of a Sachem if he com not wth aboue 4 men; Only Vncus who hath bine a fryend to the Englishe may com wth 20 and his brother wth 10.

The Order of the 8th of Septēber, 1642, conserneing trading wth Indeans, is repealed.

Whereas Mr. Mathew Allen hath presented seuerall petic̃ons to this Court for releefe against the Church of Hartford, in regard of his censure of excommunicac̃on, wherein he affirmes he hath beene wronged by the sayd Church; It was the iudgment of the Court that the sayd Allyn by his petic̃ons and expressions in Court concerning the sayd businesse, hath layd an accusation vppon the Church of Hartford, and that he ought to bring into the Court the p^r^ticulars of his accusation, that the Church of Hartford may giue answere thereunto.

[122]   June the vi^th^, 1644.

    Ed: Hopkins Esqr.
    Jo: Heynes Esqr, Dep.
        George Willis Esqr, Mr. Webster, Mr. Whiting, Mr. Welles, Capten Mason, Mr. Woolcott.
    The Jury.—Nath: Waird, Jo: White, Wm. Pantry, Rich: Gudman, Mr. Olister, Mr. Chester, Jo: Demon, Tho: Tracy, Roger Williās, Walter Fyler, John Taylor, Tho: Boscom.

Clement Chaplin pl. againste Henry Smith and Samuell Smith def^ts^, in an action of the Case. The pl. appeareth not.

Math: Allen plan^t, against Will' Lewis def^t, in an ac. of the Case, to the damage of 14l.

Will' Whiting pl. ag^t Dauid Wilton def^t, in an action of the Case, to the damage of xl.

George Steele pl. ag^t John Carrington def^t, in an action of the Case.

Nath: Willet pl. ag^t Will' Edwards deft, in an ac. of debt.

Will' Perwydge pl. ag^t Math: Allen def^t, in an ac. of the Case.

Robert Howard pl. as attorny to Ed: Welles ag^t Will' Edwards, def^t, in an ac. of debt.

Will' Edwards pl.

Daniell Frost

1. Will' Lewis pl. ag^t Mathew Allen def^t, in an ac of the Case.

Tho: Osmore pl. ag^t John Plum def^t.

2. Will'. Lewis pl. ag^t Math: Allen def^t, in a 2^d action of the Case.

Mr. Woolcot pl. ag^t Tho: Marshefield def^t, in an ac. of the Case to the damage of 43l. *Execution graunted.*

In the ac. of Clement Chaplin pl. ag^t Henry Smith & Samuell Smith def^{ts}, the Jury find for the def^{ts}, costs of the Courts. One witnesse.

In the ac. of Mathew Allen pl. ag^t Wm. Lewis defen^t, the Jury find for the pl. that the def^t is to pay rent according to his bargen wth Will' Cornewell, as he was to pay, for the p^{r}portion of land he holds, for the terme of three yeres & a halfe paste, and 20s. 4d. costs.

In the action of Will' Whiteing pl. ag^t Dauid Wilton def^t, the Jury find for the pl. the def^t is to returne the steere, and costs of Court 8s. vi$d$.

In the ac. of Will' Perwydge pl. ag^t Math: Allen def^t, Mr. Styles and Will' Pantry are the Arbitrators chosen to value the worke according to their last agreement; & w^n Wm. Perwydge hath giuen security to p^{r}form the bargen, Math: Allen is to satisfie for the worke as the Arbitrators shall award.

[123] In the ac. of Robert Howard pl. ag^t Wm. Edwards def^t, the Jury find for the def^t, xi$s$. vi$d$. Costs.

In the ac. of Tho: Osmore pl. ag^t John Plum def^t, the Jury find for the pl. fiue pownd fiue shillings damages & costs of Court.

The actions of Will' Lewis pl. ag^t Math: Allen def^t, are referred to arbitriment of John White & John Taylor.

In the ac. of Henry Woolcott pl. against Tho: Marshefield def^t, the Jury find for the pl. 25*l*. xs. damages & costs of Court.

John Pratt is freed frō watching, according to the p^rmise of the Generall Court.

John Styles is fyned, 2s. vi*d*. John Sadler is fyned, 5s.

Tho: Watts, for trayneing wth a peece chardged, is fyned 20s. Peter Blachfield is fyned 5s.

Vppon the further euidence that Tho: Steynton hath brought into the Court conserneing a late sute p^resented ag^t him by Math: Allen pl., execution is respited vntill the next Court.

The p^rticuler Court is to be held the first Thursday in August

Benedictus Aluerd acknowledgeth himselfe bound in a recognizance of x*l*. to the Country, p^ruided if in conuenient tyme he p^rsecute the sute vppon an attach^t he hath taken ag^t the goods of John Cooke or answer such damages as may vppon his neglect or not makeing good the action, then this to be voyd.

Tho: Welles.

The 7 men who haue power to Order Fences and sett penaltyes, haue the like power to graunt execution vppon the forfeture thereof.

July the 4th, 1644.

Mr. Hill is desiered to assist the Gou^r and Deputy to audicte the Tresurers accoumpte.

There is a Rate of 100*l*. graunted to be leuied vppon the three Townes.

---

[124]   August the first, 1644.

Ed: Hopkins Esqr, Gou^r.

Mr. Webster, Mr. Whiting, Mr. Welles, Mr. Woolcott.

The Jury.—Mr. Parke, Mr. Cullicke, Jo: Barnard, Will: Gybbins, Rich: Lord, Mr. Chester, Frances Norton, Sa: Smith, John Byssell, Rob: Wynchell, Tho: Buckland, Tho: Ford; *Jur.*

John Demon pl. ag^t Ed: Preston, in an actiō of the Case, 20 bush^l of Ry & 10s. damages.

Ephrā Huit pl. ag^t Walter Fyler def^t, in the behalfe of the Towne of Wyndsor, in an ac. of the Case.

Richard Mylls pl. ag^t Willī Combstocke & John Sadler def^{ts}, in an ac. of Slaunder to the damage of 200*l*.

Rich: Mills pl. ag^t James Norton def^t, in an ac. of debte to the damage of 20*l*.

Mr. Wm. Whiting pl. ag^t James Whatly def^t, in an ac. of the Case to the damage of 4*l*.

James Whatly pl. ag^t Tho: Osmore def^t, in an ac. of the Case.

James Whatly pl. ag^t Tho: Ketling def^t, in an ac. of Slaunder to the damage of 5*l*.

In the ac. of John Robins pl. ag^t Nath: Foote def^t, the Jury find for the def^t costs of Court.

In the ac. of John Robins pl. ag^t Rich: Beldon def^t, the Jury find for the pl. damages 5*l*. according to the Arbitribers, leaueing the former damages to be issued by the Arbitrators, and costs of Court.

In the ac. of Nath: Foote pl. ag^t Robert Rose def^t, the Jury find for the pl. damages xii*d*. and costs of Court.

In the ac. of John Demon pl. ag^t Ed: Preston def^t, the Jury find for the pl. 20 bush. of Ry & 10s. damages & costs of Court.

In the ac. of Mr. Whiteing pl. ag^t James Whately def^t, the Jury find for the pl. damages 3*l*. 16s. country pay, or 3*l*. mony, and costs of Court.

In the ac. of Ephrā Huit pl. ag^t Walter Fyler def^t, the Jury find for the pl. the land he sued for & costs of Court.

[125] In the action of James Whatly pl. ag^t Tho: Ketling defen^t, the Jury find for the pl. 13s. 4d. damages and costs of Court. *Execution graunted.*

[126]   Sept. the   * 1644.

Edward Hopkins Esqr, Gou^r.
Jo: Heynes, Esqr, Dep.
George Willis Esqr, Mr. Webster, Mr. Welles, Mr. Woolcott.

The Jury.—Nath: Foote, Nath: Dickinson, Tho: Vffoote, John Elson, Rich: Webb, Will' Rescue, Tho: Osmor, Rich: Butler, Joseph Loomes, Franc: Styles, Tho: Dewe, Tho: Orton ; *Jur.*

Nath: Wylled plan^t ag^t Will' Edwards def^t, in an action of debt.

James Whatly pl. ag^t John Lattimore def^t, in an ac. of Slaunder.

James Whatly pl. ag^t Tho: Osmor deft, in an ac. of the Case.

James Whately pl. ag^t Richard Harris def^t, in an ac. of slaunder.

Will' Perwidge pl.

Math: Beckwith & Tho: Hungerford pl. ag^t Will' Edwards def^t, in an ac. of slaunder.

Tho: Steynton pl. ag^t Math: Allen def^t, in an actiō of the Case.

John Lattimor to pay 5s. damages to James Wakely.

Rich: Mylls to pay 5s. damages to James Northū.

The Inuentory of John Cattell was brought into the Court & by Will' Gybbins & his wyddowe to administer.

James Hallet, for his thefte, is adiudged to restore fowerfold for what shall be proued before Capten Mason & Mr. Woolcott, and to be branden in the hand, the next Trayneing day at Wyndsor.

In the ac. of James Whatly pl. ag^t Richard Harrison, the Jury find for the pl. vi$d$. damages & costs of sute.

In the ac. of Math: Beckwith & Tho: Hungerford pl. ag^t Will' Edwards def^t, the Jury find for the pl. damages 20s. & costs of Court.

---

* Blank in the original.

[128]   SEPTEMBER THE 12th, 1644.

John Heynes Esqr, Dep. Gou^r.
George Willis Esqr, Mr. Webster, Mr. Whiteing, Mr. Welles, Mr. Woolcott, Capten Mason.
Deputyes :—Mr. Steele, Mr. Talcoate, Mr. Westwood, Mr. Cullicke, Mr. Hill, Mr. Hull, Mr. Gaylard, Henry Clarke, Mr. Trott, Mr. Olyster, James Boosy, Samuell Smith.

The Court is adioyrned to the 25th of this month, after the lecture.

Mathew Maruen pl. ag^t Peter Bassaker.

THE P^rTICULER COURT, THE 24th OF OCTOBER, 1644.

Ed: Hopkins Esqr, Gou^r.
Jo: Heynes Esqr, Dep.
George Willis Esqr, Mr. Webster, Mr. Welles.
The Jury.—Henry Woolcott, Jo: More, Dauid Wilton, Tho: Gunne, Richard Wascote, Joseph Magott, Will' Lewes, Tymothy Standly, Tho: Coleman, Will' Palmer, Jo: Stadder, Jo: Wastall.

In the action of James Whatly pl. ag^t Tho: Osmore defen^t, the Jury find for the pl. damages 4*l.* 12*s.* and costs of Court. *Execution graunted.*

THE GENERALL COURT, THE 25th OF OCTOBER, 1644.

Whereas, Mr. Mathew Allen of Hartford formerly p^rsented a petition to the Court, wherein he chardged the Church of Hartford to doe him wrong, the wch he was to haue p^rued in Court, but hath neglected to make yt appeare, It is now Ordered, that he shall haue a coppy of the answer formerly giuen to the petition now sent to him, and be required to bring in his answer thereunto & giue yt in Court the 27th of Nouēber, and also answer his former contempt.

It is agreed that the p^rpositions concerneing the mayntenaunce of mynisters, made by the Comissioners of the Vnited

Collonies, shall stand as an Order for this Jurisdiction, to be executed accordingly where there shall be cause.*

[129] The p^{r}positions conserneing the mayntenaunce of scollers at Cambridge, made by the said Comissio^{rs} is confirmed, and It is Ordered that 2 men shalbe appoynted in euery Towne wthin this Jurisdiction, who shall demaund what euery family will giue, and the same to be gathered and brought into some roome, in March; and this to continue yearely as yt shalbe considered by the Comissio^{rs}.† The p^{r}sons to demand what will be giuen are

For Hartford, Nathaniell Waird and Ed: Stebbing.
(to gather yt, Rich: Fellowes, Tho: Woodford.)
For Wyndsor, Will' Gaylard, Henry Clarke.
For Wethersfield, Mr. Trott, Mr. Wells.
For Stratford, Will' Judson, Jo: Hurd.
For Vncowaue, Jehue Burre, Ephraim Wheeler.
For Southampton,‡ Mr. More, & Robert Band.

---

* "Whereas the most considerable p^{r}sons in these colonyes came into these parts of America that they might inioye Christ in his ordinances, wthout disturbance; And whereas among many other precious mercyes, the ordinances are & haue beene dispensed among us wth much purity & power, The Commissioners tooke it into serious consideracon, how some due mayntenance according to God might be p^{r}uided & setled, both for the present and future, for the encouradgment of the Ministers whoe labour therein, & concluded to p^{r}pound & commend it to each Gen^{r}all Court, that those that are taught in the word in the seu^{r}all Plantacons be called together, that eu^{r}ie man voluntarily set downe what he is willing to alowe to that end & vse; and if any man refuse to pay a meet p^{r}portion, that then he be rated by authority in some iust & equall way; and if after this any man withhould or delay due paym^t the ciuill power to be exercised as in other iust debts." [Records of U. Colonies, Sept. 5, 1644.]

† This "proposition of a gen^{r}all contribution for the mayntenance of poore schollers at the Colledge at Cambridge" was presented to the Commissioners, at their meeting in September, 1644, by the Rev. Mr. Shepard,—" and fully approved by them, & agreed to be commended to the seu^{r}all gen^{r}all Courts as a matter worthy of due consideracon & enterteinm^t for the aduancement of learning, wch we hope will be chearfully embraced." Mr. Shepard, after requesting the Commissioners to consider "some way of comfortable mayntenance for that Schoole of the Prophets wch now is," suggests that "If therefore it were commended by you, & left to the freedome of eu^{r}ie family wch is able & willing to giue, throughout the Plantacons, to give yearly but the fourth part of a bushell of corne or something equivalent thereunto,—and for this end, if eu^{r}ie Minister were desired to stirre up the hearts of the people once in the fittest season of ye yeare, to be freely enlarged therein, & one or two faithfull men appointed in each Towne, to receaue & seasonably to send in what shall be thus giuen by them,—It is conceaued that as noe man could feele any grievance hereby, soe it would be a blessed meanes of comfortable p^{r}vision for the dyet of dyuers such students as may stand in neede of some support, & be thought meet & worthy to be contynued a fit season therein." [Rec. of U. Col., Sept 1644.]

‡ Southampton had been received under the Jurisdiction of Connecticut, not long previous to this time, with the approval of the Commissioners of the U. Colonies. See copy of the Articles of Combination, in Appendix, No. II.

OF CONNECTICUT.   113

The p^rpositions of the Com̃issio^rs concerneing a generall Indean trade (except corne, fishe and venison) is also approued and setled by the Court, vppon the terms therein p^rpounded, if other Jurisdictions doe the like.

Also, the said Com̃issioners Order concerneing verdicts is approued.*

The Gouernour, Deputy, Capten Mason, Mr. Steele, Mr. Gaylard & James Boosy are desiered to treat wth Mr. Fenwicke concerneing the setling of the Rivers mouth, to know vppon what terms we stand wth him in that respecte, and also to consider what they thinke meet to be done for matter of Fortificatiõ there, and to take the first op^rtunity they can for the issueing of yt, and to determine and conclud wth him as they shall judge meete.

It is Ordered, that all p^rsons hereafter com̃itted vppon delinquency shall beare the chardges the Country shall be att in the p^rsecutiõ of thẽ.

Its Ordered, there shalbe a publike day of thanksgiueing through this Jurisdiction, vppon Wensday com fortnight.

Its Ordered, that all Collectors and gatherers of Rates, shall appoynt a day & place and giue resonable warneing to the Inhabitants to bring in their p^rportions, vppon wch every man so warned shall duely attend to bring in his rate, or vppon neglecte thereof shall forfeit 2*d*. in the shilling for what he falls shorte, and the said Collector shall haue authority hereby to distreyne the delinquents, or be accoumptable thẽselues for the rates & penaltyes so neglected by thẽ.

There is a Rate of 10*l*. to be added to the former of 140*l*.

[130] Whereas yt is obsearued that the Dutch and French doe sell and trade to the Indeans, guns, pistolls and warlike instruments, It is now Ordered,† that no p^rson w^thin these libertyes

---

* " There being a question p^rpounded of what esteeme & force a verdict or sentence of any one Court w^thin the Colonyes, ought to be of in the Court of another Jurisdiction, The Commissioners well weighing the same, thought fit to commend it to the seu^rall Gen^rall Courts, that auery such verdict or sentence may have a due respect in any other Court through the Colonyes, where occasion may be to make use of it, & that it be accounted good euidence for the Plaintife, vntill eyther better evidence or some other iust cause appeare to alter or make the same voyd; & that in such case, the issuing of the cause in question be respited for some convenient tyme, that the Court may be advised with, where the verdict or sentence first passed." [Rec. of U. Col.]

† " And it is commended to the serious consideracon of the seu^rall jurisdictions, whether it be not expedient & necessary to p^rhibit the selling of the aforesayd ammunicon either to

shall at any tyme hereafter sell nēther gun nor pistoll nor any Instrument of warre, nether to Dutch nor French men, vnder the penalty of forfeting twenty for one, and suffering such further corporall punishement as the Court shall inflicte.

A GENERALL COURT, NOUEB^r THE 15th, 1644.

Edward Hopkins Esqr, Go^r.

Jo: Heynes Esqr, Dep.

George Willis Esqr, Mr. Webster, Mr. Whiteing, Mr. Welles, Capten Mason, Mr. Woolcotte.

Mr. Steele, Mr. Talcote, Mr. Westwood, Mr. Cullicke, Mr. Trotte, Mr. Oyllister, Samuell Smith, James Boosy, Mr. Hill, Mr. Hull, Mr. Gaylard, Mr. Clarke.

Richard Lyman hath the like liberty, wth John Tynker and his p^{r}tners, for the making pitch and tarre, p^{r}uided they gather not their wood wthin halfe a myle one of another, and that whatsoeuer wood is or shall be gathered for that vse be imp^{r}ued wthin three months after the gathering.

A P^{r}TICULER COURT THE FIRST THURSDAY IN DECĒBER.

Ed: Hopkins Esqr, Go^r.

Jo: Heynes Esqr, Dep.

Mr. Webster, Mr. Whiting, Capten Mason, Mr. Welles, Mr. Woolcotte.

The Jury:—John Porter, Walter Filer, Aron Cooke, Math: Sention, Nath: Dickenson, Jo: Demon, Will: Smith, Jo: Notte, Will: Pantry, Ed: Stebbin, Jo: White, Jo: Watson.

Tho: Steynton pl^t, against Math: Allen def^t.

Rich: Mylls pl^t, ag^t Will' Comstocke def^t.

Mathew Allen plantife, ag^t Tho: Hollibut def^t.

Will' Hill pl^t, ag^t Peter Bassaker def^t.

French or Dutch, or to any other that doe comonly trade the same wth Indians." [Records of U. Col., Sept. 1644.]

Henry Densloe pl. ag^t Jaruis Mudge def^t, in an ac. of Slaunder.

Math: Allen pl. ag^t Peter Bassaker defen^t.

[131] An executiō to be graunted ag^t Tho: Osmore, at Ja: Whatly his sute, Jo: Barnard, 3l. 6s. 8d.

Will' Edwards pl. ag^t Peter Bassaker def^t, in an ac. of debt to the damage of 3l.

In the actiō of slaunder by Henry Densloe pl. ag^t Jaruis Mudgge def^t, the Jury find for the def^t costs of Court.

Mr. Trott & Nath: Dickinson vndertake that Carrington shall appeare w^n the Court or the Gou^r shall call for him.

Mr. Ollister & Jo: Edwards vndertake that Robert Bedle shall appeare at the Court at Hartford, uppon Thursday next.

Dec. the xith, 1644.

Mr. Heynes & Mr. Willis are desiered to consider of the estate of Nath: Foote deceased, and to take in what helpe they please frō any of the neighbours to aduise how yt may be disposed of and to report their app^{r}hensions to the next Court.

Mr. Webster & Mr. Whiteing & Mr. Woolcot are desiered to see an equall deuision made of Marshfields estate to the seuerall creditors.

Tho: Walston is fyned 20s. for inuegling the affections of Mr. Alcocks mayde.

Dauid Wilton and Daniell Clarke are admitted executors to the will of Ephraim Huit. Mrs. Huit p^{r}miseth that if the goods sett apart for the dischardge of debts fall short, that shee will resigne such other goods as are comitted to her, to make yt out.

Robert Bedle is adiudged to restore double for the seuerall thefts acknowledged by him, and to be seuerly whipped and branded in the hand vppō Wensday next.

Ed: Hampson for diuulging slaunderus speeches ag^t Mr. Chester, is fyned fiue pownd to the Country.

In the absence of the officer of the Court, the Constable may searue executions.

Bedle stole frō Mr. Blakman, of gunpowder, ij pownd; Frō wydowe Foote, of Rye, iiij bush; Frō Tho: Welles, 2 sacks; Frō Rich: Mylls, 1 blanket; Frō Tho: Tracy, 1 sacke.

[132] A Generall Court, the xith of Decēber, [1644.]
    Ed: Hopkins Esqr, Go^r.
    Jo: Heynes Esqr. Dep.
    Mr. Webster, Capten Mason, Mr. Welles, Mr. Woolcott.
    Mr. Steele, Mr. Talcoate, Mr. Cullicke, Mr. Westwood,
    Mr. Hill, Mr. Hull, Mr. Trott, James Boosy, Sa: Smith.

Whereas through the blessing of the Lord vppō the paynefull endeauors of these Plantations, incouridgement hath bine giuen for the rayseing some quantity of corne, whereunto many haue addicted thēselues vppon hopes of receaueing some comfortable supply to their necessityes thereby ; But p^rtely through waint of op^rtunity and fitte instruments to transport the same into forraigne p^rts, and partly the aduantages that haue bine taken frō the multitude of sellers and their pinching necessityes, the rate and price of corne is so little and the comodity so vnauaylable for the attaynement of such supplyes as are most sutable to mens needs, that much discouridgement falls vppon the spirits of men in such imployments, wch is like to be more and more increased if some course be not taken for the finding some other way of trade for corne then hath bine hitherto āttended, whereunto not only our owne necessityes call vs, but the complaints of the other Collonyes, both of the Masachusetts and Plymoth, by their Comissioners, who looke vppon thēselues as much p^riudiced by our ouerfilling their marketts, require the same at our hands ; It is therefore, by generall consent, Ordered, and also agreed wth the p^rtyes hereafter mentioned, that noe Englishe grayne shall for the two next yeres ensueing be sould to any out of this Riuer, but Edward Hopkins Esqr and Mr. Williā Whiteing and such other Marchants as they shall take to thē, who do vndertake to endeauor the transportatiō thereof into some p^rts beyond the seas, and to make such improuement of the rest as op^rtunity of these p^rts shall p^rsent, and to pay to the seuerall owners 4*s*. p^r bush. for wheat, 3*s*. p^r bush. for Rye, and 3*s*. p^r bush. for pease ; and it is p^ruided that halfe of that wch is transported this p^rsent yere, if yt be sent into England, the aduenture thereof, in case the ship be taken or otherwise miscary, shall be borne by the owners thereof ; the payment for the said corne to be made by the said March^{ts} at the returne of the shippe, or so soone as returne may any otherway be made, and to be paid in the best and most sutable Englishe comodityes that may be p^rcured for the necessary support of these plantations; they are not to receaue frō, nor be accoumptable to, any owner, vnder a 100 bush. And it is by generall consent Ordered, that whosoever vppon this Riuer shall sell or send out any Englishe corne, vnles such as shall appeare at this p^rsent tyme to be truly and w^thout deceipte ingaged, but to the foresaid company of March^ts, shall forfeit the one halfe of such graine so sould or sent out contrary to the true meaneing of this Order; and halfe of the graine so forfeted shall be to the p^rp^r vse and behalfe of he or they that shall discouer the same deceipte, and the other halfe to the Country: p^ruided that any the Inhabitants of these Plantations may sell or exchaynge the said Englishe graine among thēselves notw^thstanding this Order.

[133] * In the absence of the Officer of the Court, the Constable of the Towne shall searue Executions.

Ed: Harnson for diuulgeing slaunderous speeches ag^t Mr. Chester is fyned 5*l*. to the Country.

William Phillips pl. ag^t Tho. Waples.

---

[134]   Feb: 5th, 1644.

    Ed: Hopkins Esqr, Go^r.
    Jo: Heynes Esqr, Dep.
        Mr. Whiting, Mr. Webster, Mr. Welles, Capten Mason, Mr. Woolcott.
        Mr. Steele, Mr. Talcoat, Mr. Westwood, Mr. Cullicke, Mr. Hill, Mr. Hull, Mr. Gaylard, Mr. Clarke, Mr. Ollister, James Boosy, Sam: Smyth.

Whereas some question hath rysen concerneing vnnessary tryalls by Jury, and found by experience that many such suts might be p^ruented if arbitrations were attended in a more priuat way, according to the nature of the differences, wch is recomēnded by the Court to all the Towns of this Gouerment;

---

* The two entries following are repeated from page [131].

And for the regulateing of Juryes for the future, It is Ordered, that in all cases wch are entered vnder 40s, the sute shall be lefte to be tryed by the Court of Magestrats as they shall judge most agreable to equity & righteousnes; and that in all cases that are tryed by Juryes, the Court of Magestrats shall haue liberty, if they doe not conceaue the Jury to haue p^rceeded according to their euidence, in their verdict giuen in, to cause them to returne againe to a second consideration of the case, and if they continue in their former opinion and doe not in the judgement of the Court attend the euidence giuen in Court, it shall be in the power of the Court to impanell another Jury and comitt the consideration of the case to thē.

It is also lefte in the power of the Court, in any case of tryall to vary and alter the damages giuen in by the Jury, as they shall judge most equall and righteous.

But if any find thēselues agreiued, ether by verdict of Jury, or p^rceedings of Court, they haue liberty to apeale to the Generall Court. It is also left to the magestrats to impanell a Jury of sixe or twelue, as they shall judge the nature of the case to require, but no jury shalbe vnder sixe, and if 4 of thē agree, or 8 in a Jury of 12, the verdict shall stand as if the whole nūber of ether did agree.

It is also Ordered, that the Towns shalbe at liberty to abate two of the 7 men formerly appoynted for the dispose of grownd and Ordering of Fences.

The former Order, concerneing the pryses of corne is repealed, and it is Ordered, that for all bargens hereafter made to be paid in Corne, and for the worke of men and cattle, wheat shall be payable at 4s. p^r bush., rye at 3s., pease att 3s., and Indean att 2s. vid. p^ruided yt be marchantable corne.

For the p^ruenting of differences that may arise in the owneing of Cattle that be lost or stree away, It is Ordered, that the owners of any Catle w^thin these Plantations shall earemarke or brand all their Cattle and swyne that are aboue halfe a yeare old (except horsses) and that they cause their seuerall marks to be registred in the Towne booke; and whatsoeuer cattle shall be found vnmarked after the first of May next shall forfeit 5s. a head, whereof 2s. vid. to him that discouers yt, and the other to the Country.

Whereas yt is expressed in the late bairgen made wth the Marchants, that there shalbe noe Englishe grayne sould out of this Riuer to any other, It is the judgement of the Court and so Ordered, that whatsoeuer wheat shalbe grownd into meale or made into biskett, that all such meale and biskett shall com [135] vnder the said bairgen, as ‖ also malte made of barly, p^ruided the said Marchants giue for such molte an answerable price to other Chapmen.

Whereas it is said in the fundamentall Order,* that the Generall Court shall consist of the Gouernour or some on chosen to moderate and 4 other Magistrats at lest, It is now Ordered and adiudged to be a lawfull Court, if the Gou^r or Deputy wth other Magistrats be p^rsent in Court, wth the mayor part of deputyes lawfully chosen. But no act shall passe or stand for a law, wch is not confirmed both by the mayor part of the said Magistrats, and by the mayor p^rte of the deputyes there p^rsent in Court, both Magistrats and deputyes being alowed, eyther of thē, a negatiue voate. Also the p^rticuler Court may be keepte by the Gouernour or Deputy w^th † other Magistrats.

Whereas vppon an agreement lately contracted‡ by some deputed by this Jurisdiction wth George Fennicke Esqr, for and concerneing the Fort att the Riuers mouth, wth th'apurtenances and disbursements expended there by himselfe and others, this Jurisdictiō is ingadged to pay to the said George Fenwicke Esqr, two pence p^r bush. vppon all graine that shalbe exported out of this Riuer for tenn yeares ensueing, after the first of March next, and six pence p^r C^t vppon all biskett that shall in like manner be exported, as by the said agreeement doth and may more fully appeare; For the p^ruenting of all abuses and indirect courses that may be attempted or taken by any in euadeing the foresaid payment and that the same may be truly and exactly p^rformed, according to the true intent of the said agreements, It is Ordered by this Court, that noe grayne or byskett shalbe laden by any aboard any vessell in this Riuer,

---

* Page [226] 24.
† In the record of the fundamental Orders as amended, in [Vol. ii. p.   ] this blank is filled with the word three.
‡ The articles of agreement bear date Dec 5th, 1644. They were not placed upon Record however, until several years afterward, in [Vol. ii. p. 59.] See Appendix, No. III.

vntill they have made entry of the number of the bush. of
grayne and the kynd thereof, and waight of biskett they intend
to lade aboard any such vessell, and recorded the same in a
booke prouided for that end and purpose, wth such p^{r}sons as by
this Order are appoynted to receaue the same, vnder the penalty of forfeting the on halfe of all such grayne or biskett that
shalbe laden wthout entring of the same as before ; the on halfe
of that wch is so forfeted, to be to the vse of the Country, and
the other halfe to him who shall discouer the same and informe.
And it is Ordered, that euery man who lades any such grayne
or biskett, shall take care and prouide that there be paid to Mr.
Fenwicke or his assignes att Seabrooke, the two pence p^r bush.
and sixe pence p^r C^t, for all graine and biskett so laden by
them, so neere as may be in the same kynd of graine as is laden
by them, or if otherwise, to the content of him or his assignes ;
the laders of the said corne being lefte notwthstanding, in all
bargains for corne made before this time, to compownd or agree
wth those frō whom they receaued the corne so sent away, or in
case of difference, to take any other lawfull course to haue the
said chardge of two pence p^r bush. determined vppon whō, according to the rules of equity and righteousnes, yt ought lastly
[*justly ?*] to fall, for the payment thereof.

And it is further Ordered, that no vessell exporting corne or
byskett, shall depart from any of the seuerall Townes vppon
this Ruier, vntil the M^r thereof, or some frō him, haue taken a
[136] noate vnder the hand of him ‖ that is deputed by this
Court for that searuice in the severall Townes, of what quantities of corne or biskett is laden aboard the said vessell, w^{ch}
noate or noats shalbe deliuered by him to Mr. Fenwicke, att
Seabrooke, or his assignes, and payment made of the two pence
p^r bush. and six pence p^r C^t according to this Order, or satisfaction giuen to Mr. Fenwicke or his assignes for the same ; and
in case any M^r shall refuse or neglecte to take the said noate
according to this Order, yt shalbe lawfull for those who haue
the chardge of the Fort att Seabrooke to make stay of the said
vessell vntill the M^r, or some frō him, haue brought a noate or
certificate as is before exp^{r}ssed. And in case any such vessell
shall, in a surreptitious manner, gett free att the said Fort,
wthout a cleare dischardge frō Mr. Fenwicke or his assignes,

eyther the vessell or the M^r thereof shalbe liable to pay fower pence p^r bush. for all graine and twelue pence p^r C^t for all biskett that is exported w^thout deliuery of such noate as is before exp^rssed, yf eyther the one or the other att any tyme returne agayne into this Riuer. And in regard to the conueniency of the sytuation of their howses, being neere the waterside, wherby the foresaid Records may be made and noates p^rcured by those whō yt may concerne, wth leste troble, Mr. Jo: Plum is appoynted and desiered to attend this searuice at Wethersfield, Edward Stebbing att Hartford and Walter Fyler att Wyndsor.

And whereas further, by virtue of the forementioned agreements, this Jurisdiction is ingaged for the said tearme of tenn yeares after the first of March next, to pay to the said George Fenwicke Esquire twelue pence p^r ann^m for euery hogge that is killed in any of the Townes vppon the Riuer, eyther for mens p^rticuler occasions or to make sale of, as also twelue pence p^r ann^m for euery milch cowe or mare of 3 yeares old and vppwards, that is in any of the Townes or Farmes vppon this Riuer, twenty shillings for euery hogshead of Beuer traded out of this Jurisdiction and paste away downe the Riuer, two pence for euery pownd of Beuer traded w^thin the lymitts of the Riuer, the foresaid payments to be made in Beuer, wampum, wheat, barly or pease, at the most comon and indifferent rates; It is by this Court Ordered, that all the Inhabitants of this Riuer doe take spetiall notice of the said agreements and doe pay in to George Fenwicke Esqr, at Seabrooke, or to his assignes, att or before the first day of March, 1645, and so euery yeare, att or before the first day of the said month of March, vntill the tearme of tenn years be expired, such soms as shalbe due from them vppon any of the foregoing p^rticulers; according to the meaneing of the said agreements, or in case they be respited by the forementioned p^rsons, who are betrusted wth the ordering of these payments, for a longer tyme, that they bring in such payments as shalbe due frō them, to such place or places as shalbe appoynted to them by the said Trustees in ech Towne, vppon 48 howers warneing or notice eyther publickely or priuatly made knowne and giuen. And if any man shall neglecte to make the said payments at the tyme and in the manner before specified, he shall pay two pence in euery shilling alowance p^r month, vntill the whole due be dischardged, and shall, vppon his owne chardge, keepe the grayne or other payment to be made by him, vntill a fitt op^rtunity be offered of conueying the same to Seabrooke, and this signified by the said Trustees. And it is further prouided and ordered, to p^ruent all collusiue dealeing whereby the true meaneing of the said agrements might be frustrated, that if any man shall conceale eyther hoggs, mares, cowes or beuer, and not giue true notice to the partyes forementioned and appoynted by this Order to take record thereof, he shall forfeite the on halfe of what shalbe so concealed by him, or the value thereof, the on halfe of that wch is so forfeted to be to the vse of the Country, and the other halfe to [137] him who shall discouer || and informe of any such indirecte and deceiptfull proceedings.

It is the intent of the Court, and accordingly Ordered, that euery man shall pay for such mares and cowes as are in his hands euery yeare, the first day of February, and those are to be esteemed milch cowes as haue giuen milke the yeare before.

---

[138]   A P^rticuler Court, March the 5th, 1644.

    Ed: Hopkins Esqr, Gou^r.

    Jo: Heynes Esqr, Dep.

        Mr. Webster, Mr. Whiting, Mr. Welles, Cap: Mason, Mr. Woolcott.

    The Jury.   Mr. Androwes, Andrewe Bacon, Will' Westwood, Will' Wodsworth, James Boosy, Sa: Smith, Nath: Dickenson, Tho: Tracy, John More, Sam: Allen, Dauid Wilton, Math: Graunt.

Andrewe Bacon and George Graues testifie in Court, that they being wth Tho: Crumpe when he was sicke, not long before his death, askeing him how he would dispose of his estate, he said, his debts being paid, he desiered his master would doe wth yt as he pleased.

Ed: Hopkins Esqr, Go^r, is admitted to administer the estate of Tho: Crumpe, late of Hartford, deceased.

In the action of Ed: Elmor and Nath: Willett plant^s against

Rich: Trott defen[t], the Jury find for the pl[ts] six pownde, eleauen shillings and sixe pence damages and costs of Court.

In the action of Tho: Steynton pl. against Math: Allen defen[t], the Court haueing hard the witnesses, find that Tho: Steynton bought and paid for the blanketts lefte by Mr. Allens man for Hugh the millwright, and Mr. Allen ought to repay the mony formerly taken by verdict of the Jury, yet in regard of Tho: Steyntons formerly p[r]rūtorines,* not moueing the Court for longer tyme, thereby now occationeing further troble and chardge, the Court adiudgeth Math: Allen to pay to Tho: Steynton twenty shillings and the chardge of this Court, and the other chardge and losse to lye vppon Tho: Steynton.

Rich: Lord being conuented before the Court for altering an execution issued out, his misdemeanor therein is looked vppon as an offence of a high nature, but conceaueing yt a sudden, inconsiderat act, and finding him much humbled and affected therew[th], giueing full acknowledgement of his Offence, he is adiudged to pay to the County fiue marke.†

Daniell Porter for his former thefte is fyned xx$s$.

The said Daniell, Willia Pantry & Rich: Lord acknowledge theselues bownd in the some of ten pownd to the Country; p[r]uided the said Daniell appeare at the Court to be held at Hartford, the first Thursday in June next, then this Recognizance to be voyd.

The Court takeing the cariedge of Jeramy Addoms into consideratio, fynd his misdemeanor great, in adhereing to Tho: Osmor in his misap[r]hensions about the execution, and giueing him incouridgement by p[r]uoking speches to resist the officer, but espetially his passionat distempered speches, lowd languadge & vnmannerly cariedge in the face of the Court, to the great offence of the beholders, Require him to appeare at the next p[r]ticular Court, there to receaue such censure as the Court shall conceaue his misdemeanour to desearue.

The Arbitration vppon the sute of Tho: Dewye pl. ag[t] Tho: Ford deft, is fownd good, and Tho: Ford is to pay the 36s. awarded therein and chardges of the Courte.

Peter Bassaker acknowledgeth himselfe bownd in xx$l$. to the Country, p[r]uided if he appeare at the Court to be held in Hart-

---

*Peremptoriness. †A mark = 13s. 4d.

ford, the first Thursday in June next, then this Recognizance to be voyde.

[139] Susan Coles, for her rebellious cariedge toward her mistris, is to be sent to the howse of correction and be keept to hard labour & course dyet, to be brought forth the next lecture day to be publiquely corrected, and so to be corrected weekely vntill Order be giuen to the contrary.

Tho: Osmore, for some exp^rssions vsed by [*him*] tending to the derogatiō of the justice of the Court vppon an execution issued out of the Court, is fined vi*l*. 13*s*. 4*d*,

Robert Bedle, for his loathsū and beastly demeanor, is adiudged to be brought forth the next lecture day, to be seuerely scourdged, and to be keept in the howse of correctiō a fortnight longer, and then brought forth againe to be publiquely whipped, and then to be bownd to appeare at euery quarter Court to be whipped, vntill the Court see some reformation in him, & shall see cause to release him.

Walter Gray, for his misdemeanor in laboring to inueagle the affections of Mr. Hoockers mayde, is to be publiquely corrected the next lecture day.

The said Walter Gree hath forfeited*

---

[140] THE COURT OF ELECTION THE 10th OF APRILL, 1645.

John Heynes Esqr, Gou^r.

Ed: Hopkins Esqr, Dep.

George Fenwicke Esqr, *Mag*. Roger Ludlow Esqr, *Mag*. Mr. Whiteing, *Tres*", *Mag*. Capten Mason, *Mag*. Mr. Webster, *Mag*. Mr. Welles, *Mag.*, *Secr*. Mr. Woolcott, *Mag*.

[*Deputyes*.] Mr. Steele, Mr. Talcoat, Mr. Trott, Mr. Ollister, Mr. Phelps, Mr. Gaylard, James Boosy, Sa: Smith, Tho: Newnton.

John Byssell is freed frō Trayneing.

Freemen ; Robert Bartlet, Rich: Fellowes, John Halls, Math: Webster, Jo: Welles, Tho: Barbor.

---

* This entry remains thus incomplete.

Whereas yt was Ordered, that the Towns should trayne 6 dayes in the first weeks of seuerall months, It is now Ordered, that the Capten may require the souldears to trayne 3 dayes att any tyme wthin the months of Aprill, May and June, and 3 dayes in Septēber, October & Nouēb^r.

James Boosy is chosen Clarke of the band for Wethersfield.

Henry Gray of Vncowaue, for his many misdemeanors, is adiudged to be imprysoned duereing the pleasure of the Court, and to be fyned ten pownd.

Jehue Burre the elder, and Tho: Barlowes are to be warned to the next p^rticuler Court.

There is a lyberty of two Fayres to be keepte yearely att Hartford, one vppon the second Wensday in Maye, the other the 2^d Wensday in Septēber.

Whereas there hath bine much dispute about the highwaye betweene Wyndsor and Hartford, wch hath bine lately vsed in coming through the meadowe of Hartford wth carts & horses, to the anoyance and p^riudice of the Inhabitants of Hartford that haue lotts in the said meadowe, It is therefore thought meete and so Ordered, that the high waye, as for carts, catle and horsses, be stopped vppe, and that the highwaye betweene the said Wyndsor and Hartford in the vpland be well and passably amended & mayntayned for a continuance, by Hartford as much as belongs to them and by Wyndsor as much as belongs to them; the said highwaye to be amended by ech p^rty by sixe weeks or two months, vppon the penulty of twenty shillings p^r weeke for that p^rty that fayles ether in the whole or in p^rte, as long as it soe lyes not sufficiently repaired and mayntayned; and at the sixe weeks end or two months end, Mr. Webster and Nath: Waird doe seriously surueye that p^rte wch belongs to Wyndsor, and that Henry Woolcott the elder and Jo: Porter doe surueye that p^rte wch belongs to Hartford, and certifie of the sufficiency of the said highwaye, to the next p^rticuler Court, who are delinquents, and the penulty to be leuyed vppon the delinquent p^rty wthout any fauor or affection, both for fayleing att the tyme aforesaid, as also for future the like penulty vppon the p^rsentment of the insufficient mayntayneing thereof.

The Gouernour is content to goe twice this yeare to keepe

Court at the seaside (vppon the motion of Mr. Ludlowe, in the behalfe of the Plantations there,) and hath liberty to take what magistrate he pleaseth to assist him; or in case his occations will not p^rmitt him to goe himselfe, he may appoynt some other in his steed.

The Gou^r & Deputy wth Mr. Whiting, Mr. Webster and Mr. Welles, are desiered to determine and settle any differences that shall arise about the 2d. p^r bush. to be paid for the Corne that shalbe exported.

The Court is adiorned vntill the 2^d Wensday in Maye.

[141] MAY THE 13th, 1645.

It is desiered that the Gou^r, Mr. Deputy, Mr. Fenwicke, Mr. Whiting and Mr. Welles should agitate the busines concerneing the enlardgement of the libertyes of the Patent for this Jurisdiction, and if they see a concurrence of op^rtunityes, both in regard of England   * they haue liberty to p^rceed therein, att such resonable chardge as they shall judge meete, and the Court will take some speedy course for the dischardge and satisfieing the same, as yt shalbe concluded and certified to the Court by the said Comittee or the greater p^rte of them.

The Courts adioyrned to the 2^d Wensday in July, or sooner if the Gou^r see cause to call yt.

JUNE THE 5th, 1645.   THE P^RTICULER COURT.

Jo: Heynes Esqr, Gou^r.
Ed: Hopkins Esqr, Dep.
  Roger Ludlowe Esqr, Mr. Webster, Capten Mason, Mr. Welles, Mr. Woolcott.
The Jury.   Ed: Stebbing, Leonard Chester, *fyned* 5s., John Robins, *fyned* 5s., James Boosy, John Demon, Will:' Gybbins, Nath: Elye, John Willcoxe, Hūphry Pynny, Stephen Terry, Roger Williams, Jo: Banks.

In the action of slaunder of Tho: Sherwood the elder, pl. agaynst Henry Grayc defen^t, the Jury find for the plant^t, costs of Court and damages twenty pownd.

---

*This blank in the original.

In the 2ᵈ action of slaunder of Tho: Sherwood the elder, pl. agᵗ Henry Graye defenᵗ, the Jury find for the planᵗ costs of Court and damages fower pownd.

In the action of slaunder of Tho: Sherwood the elder, plᵗᵉ, agᵗ Jehue Burre the elder, defᵗ, the Jury find for the planᵗ, costs of Court and damages fifteene pownd.

In the action of Jehue Burre the elder, planᵗ, agᵗ Tho: Sherwood the elder, defenᵗ, the Jury find for the defenᵗ, costs of Court.

[142] Nath: Dickenson and Tho: Coleman are to take a prᵗicular of the estate of Mr. Parks man deceased and bring yt to the Court; and for the wages due to him, it may be respited vntill we heare frō Mr. Parks, or his returne.

Baggett Egleston, for bequething his wife to a young man, is fyned 20s.

George Tuckye, for his misdemeanor in words to Eglestons wife, is fyned 40s., and to be bownd to his good behauior and to appeare the next Court.

Tho: Ford acknowledgeth himselfe to be bownd in xl. to this Comonwelth and George Tucky in 20l., that the said George shall appeare at the next Court, and keepe good behauior in the meane season.

The information agᵗ Henry Graye read in Court, is to be inquired into by the Magistrats that goe to Stratford, and he to continue bownd.

Rich: Lord brought Maruins man* into the Court according to his Recognizance.

Tho: Ford pl. agᵗ Josiah Hull and Rich: Oldridge defᵗˢ, in an actiō of the Case, to the damage of 30l.

William Edwards pl. agᵗ Jonathan Rudde, vppon an attachᵗ, 2s. 6d.

Will' Edwards acknowledgeth himselfe bownd in a Recognizance of 5l. to prsecute & make good his actiō.

Tho: Staples pl. agᵗ Clement Chaplin defᵗ.

Rysly agᵗ Watts. Basset agᵗ Tharpe.

Chappell, the Taylar, [agᵗ] Southmead.

---

* Daniel Porter. See p. [138] 123.

JULY THE 9th, 1645.

Ed: Hopkins Esqr, Dep.

Mr. Webster, Mr. Whiting, Mr. Welles, Mr. Woolcott.
[*Deputyes :*]—Mr. Steele, Mr. Talcoate, Mr. Phelps, Mr. Gaylard, Mr. Trott, Mr. Ollister, James Boosy, Sa: Smith.

Whereas Mr. Fenwicke, Capten Mason and James Boosy haue had some treaty wth Math: Gryffen, for fortification att the Forte, who haue reported to the Court how far they haue p^rceeded therein, and the Court doth approue of their p^rpositions, and desire they would take some speedy op^rtunity for the full issueing and p^rfecting the said bairgaine, and there is graunted by the Court a rate of 200*l*. to be leuied on the Plantations, towards the dischardge thereof; and Mr Talcott is desiered to assiste the said Comittee therein, and to take care for the speedy accomplishement thereof, and to p^ruide any necessaryes for the carieing on the same ; the rate is to be paid in, in such grayne and att such prises as the Comittee shall agree to alowe the partyes they contracte wthall aboute the worke.

Will' Smith of Wethersfield is chosen Clarke of the band for that Towne, and to vewe the Arms.

It is Ordered that the Magestrats or the greatest p^rte of the shall haue liberty if they see cause to p^rsse men and munition for a defensiue warre, or to defend the Mohegins vntill the next sitting of this Courte.

There is a Rate of 50*l*. graunted.

[143] Mr. Fenwicke and Mr. Hopkins are chosen Comissioners for the next meeting in September att Newhauen, and for this yeare following.

Its Ordered, that there shall be a letter directed frō the Court to desire Mr. Fenwicke, if his occations will p^rmitt, to goe for Ingland to endeauor the enlardgement of Pattent, and to further other aduantages for the Country.

The P'rticuler Court.   July the xth, 1645.

Ed: Hopkins Esqr.
   Mr. Webster, Mr. Welles, Mr. Woolcot, Mr. Whiting.

Ruth Fishe, for comitting fornicatiō, is adiudged to be twice whipped, once here after the first lecture at this Towne & once at Wethersfield.

Leonard Dyks, whō shee accuseth to be the father of the child, is adiudged to keepe the child, and to be whipped, and vppon his refusall to submit he is to be sent to the howse of correction, there to be held to hard labour and course dyet, and what he can gett aboue the chardge of his dyet is to be keept toward the mayntenaunce of the child.

John Coltman, for his misdemeanour and vnseemely cariedge toward Ruth Fishe, and disobeying the Gouernours comaund, is to be fyned fiue pownd.

Math: Williams, for comitting fornication wth Susan Cole, is adiudged to be twice whipped and to be fyned fiue pownd.

Susan Cole is to be twice whipped, once now and once at the next lecture.

Mr. Allen is to respite his corne in his hand, (demaunded by the powndkeep^r on the north side at Hartford,) and is to bring his action the next Court, ag^t such whose fences were then open when his hoggs were impownded.

The laste will & testament of Edward Vere is brought into the Court.

---

[144]   Sep: 4th, 1645.

   John Heines Esqr, Go^r.
   Ed: Hopkins Esqr.
     Mr. Webster, Capten Mason, Mr. Welles, Mr. Woolcott.
   The Jury.—Mr. Cullicke, Jo: White, Tho: Ford, Rich: Goodmā, Nath: Dickenson, Tho: Coleman, Jo: Stadder, Tho: Hurlbut, Dauid Wilton, Tho: Gunne, Tho: Dewy, Robert Howard.

In the action of John Robins pl. ag^t Leonard Chester defen^t, the Jury find for the defen^t the chardges of the Court.

130

In the action of Sam: Gardner pl. against Leonard Chester deft, the Jury find for the pl. [*costs of*] Corte.

In the action of Berding pl. against Edwards, Edwards is to pay Berding fiue shillings. 5s.

In the action of George Chappell pl. agt Leonard Chester, the Jury find for the deft the chardges of the Court.

Bacon plt.

Will' Colefoxe, for his misdemeanor, is to be fyned xxs.

George Chappell, for abuseing the Constable and excesse in drinkeing, is to be bownd to his good behauior and to be fined fiue pownd. 5l.

Will' Brumfield, for drunkenes and strickeing the watchmen, is to be bownd to his good behauior and fyned fifty shillings.

Mr. Chester, for resisting the Constable and other miscariedges in the Court, is fyned forty shillings. 40s.

James Northā is bownd in 10l., Will' Brumfield in 20l., that Will' Brumfield keepe good behauior and appeare the next Court.

Rich: Belding is bownd in xxl., George Chappell in 10l., that the sd. George keepe good behauior and appeare the next Court.

Sep. xith, 1645.   The Genrll Court.

Jo: Heines Esqr, Gor.

Ed: Hopkins Esqr, Dep.

Roger Ludlowe Esqr, Mr. Webster, Capten Mason, Mr. Welles, Mr. Woolcott.

Deputyes :—Mr. Steele, Mr. Talcoate, Mr. Ollister, Mr. Trott, Ja: Boosy, Sa: Smith, Mr. Phelps, Mr. Hull, Mr. Gaylard, Mr. Roceter, Jehu Burre, Will' Berdsly, Tho: Sherwood.

Mr. Webster is desiered to cause the Constables of Hartford to bring in a iust accoumpte of all the prticuler and seurall chardges of the late warrs,* and for the support of Vncus. Mr.

---

* Against the Narragansetts and Niantics, for the defence and protection of Uncas and the Mohegans. This war was determined upon by the Commissioners of the U. Colonies, at a speciall session in June, 1645, and 300 men were ordered to be raised in the several colonies, of which number Connecticut was to furnish 40. But the timely submission of Pessacus, Ninegret

Roceter to doe the like for Wyndsor, Ja: Boosy for Wethersfield.

Mr. Whiting is desiered to sell the p^ruisions, and make pay to the souldears, and giue accoumpte for the reste.

The p^rticuler Courte is to be held the 2^d Thursday of the next month.

The Gou^r and Mr. Hopkins are desiered to speake or write to Mr. Fenwicke, that in regard there hath not bine a due accoumpte giuen in of all the corne transported this yeare, and in regard of some difficultyes by whō the pay should be made in bargains made before this agreement wth him, that this agreement may not begin vntill the first day of March next; bec. it is found very inconuenient to stay vessells for the deliuery of the [145] corne att the Riuers mouth, that he will assent that a || man may be chosen in ech Towne to rec. and lay vppe such corne as may be due to him vppon the said bargyne, wch shalbe in redines to be sent him att his demaund; and the Court doth agree that whoeu^r doth shippe away corne w^thout giueing due satisfaction, according to agreement, the whole shalbe forfeted, ⅓ to him, ⅓ to him that shall discou^r the fraud, ⅓ to him that keepeth the accoumpte of the corne in the Towne where any such grayne is shipped.

The Court hath Ordered, that 30*l*. in wheat and pease be paid to the Gou^r, and Indean corne.

It is Ordered, that all the swyne, ether hoggs or shouts, in the seuerall Plantations, that are keept att home w^thin the Towne, shall by Aprill next be rynged or yoaked, or kept vppe in their yards, vnder the penulty of fower pence for euery such swyne, to be paid by the owner to the p^rty that shall take the swyne so defectiue and impownd them. Also, all such swyne that are keept by Heards, in the woods, shall not be suffered to abyde aboue on night in the Towne, but yt shalbe lawfull to impownd them in case they com at any tyme home, frō the mydle of March to the mydle of Nouember. Fayerfield & Stratford desire to be included in this Order.

The Court is adiorned to Wednesday com 3 weekes.

---

and their confederates, prevented the further prosecution of hostilities; and on the 27th of August, a treaty of peace was signed at Boston, between the Comm'rs and the principal sachems of the Narragansetts and Niantics. (Records of U. Col., Aug. 1645.)

OCTOBER THE viij^th, 1645.

Jo: Heynes Esqr, Go^r.
Ed: Hopkins Esqr, Dep.
George Fenwicke Esqr, Mr. Webster, Capten Mason, Mr. Whiting, Mr. Welles, Mr. Woolcott.

[*Deputyes :*]—Mr. Phelps, Mr. Steele, Mr. Talcoate, Mr. Roceter, Mr. Trott, Mr. Ollister, Ja: Boosy, Sa: Smith.

Mr. Webster is agayne desiered to call to him the Constables of Hartford and to gather in a true accoumpte of all the expence of the last expedition; James Boosy to doe the like att Wethersfield wth the Constables there, and Mr. Roceter for Wyndsor; and when that is done they are to bring thē to Mr. Hopkins, who, wth Mr. Whiting, Mr. Webster, Mr. Roceter and the said Ja: Boosy, are to examine the said accoumpts, and also to cause notice to be giuen in the seu^rall Townes, that what is due to any frō the Country, in any other respects, be brought in to thē, and to ranke the said debts oweing vnder seuerall heads, both what is payable by this Collony, and w^t belongs to the whole combination, as also, w^t may concerne the seu^rall Townes of theselues to dischardge; and to make returne of the same to the next sitting of this Court, w^n p^ruision shalbe suddenly made to dischardge all the said debts in the best order the Country can.

[146] The accoumpts of the seu^rall Townes are to be brought in to Mr. Hopkins, w^thin 14 dayes at furthest, vnder the penulty of 1*s.* a day as long as yt shalbe omitted, by those who are herein betrusted, and then wth all conuenient speed to be issued by him and the rest ioyned wth him, as before.

THE P^rTICULER COURTE.   OCTOBER THE ix^th, 1645.

Jo: Heynes Esqr, Go^r.
Ed: Hopkins Esqr, Dep.
George Fenwicke Esqr, Mr. Webster, Mr. Woolcot, Capten Mason, Mr. Whiting, Mr. Welles.

Jury :—Henry Clarke, Jo: Byssell, Henry Woolcot, Tho: Thornton, Dauid Wilton, Aron Cooke, Mr. Trott, Mr.

Chester, Ja: Boosy, Sa: Smith, John Ollister, Tho: Coleman.

In the action of Math: Allen pl. ag^t Ed: Hopkins Esqr, def^t, the Jury find for the def^t that he is no trespasser vppon a staunch water, and costs of Court & witnesses.

In the action of Ed: Hopkins pl. ag^t Will' Whiting and Rich: Lord def^{ts}, the Jury find for the pl. 42l. damages, and costs of Court & witnesses.

In the action of John Hewyt pl. ag^t Jo: Demon def^t, the Jury find for the pl. 36s. damages, & costs of Court.

Jo: Demon is to pay Preston 20s. & to be comitted.

Math: Allen, for his mysdemeanor in Court is fined xl.

In the ac. of Tho: Staunton pl. ag^t Math: Allen def^t, the Court adiudgeth Math: Allen to pay the pl. 14s. 2d. & costs of Court.

In the ac. of Hewyt pl. ag^t Demon, the Court adiudgeth Demon to pay 10s. to the pl. & to leaue 10s. wth Tho: Ford vntill y^t appeare whether the other p^{r}tner were formerly paid 10s. and the costs of Court.

---

[147]   DECĒBER THE FIRST, 1645.

Jo: Heynes Esqr, Gou^r.
Ed: Hopkins Esqr, Dep.
   Capten Mason, Mr. Woolcott, Mr. Webster, Mr. Whiting, Mr. Welles.
   [*Deputyes:*]—Mr. Trotte, Mr. Ollister, Ja: Boosy, Jo: Demon, Mr. Hull, Mr. Staughton, Mr. Steele, Mr. Talcott.

Its Ordered, that the Plantation cauled Tunxis shalbe cauled Farmington, and that the bownds thereof shalbe as followeth ; The Esterne bownds shall meet wth the westerne of these Plantations, wch are to be fiue myles on this side the great Riuer, and the Northern bownds shall be fiue myles frō the hill in the great meadow towards Masseco, and the Southerne bownds frō the said hill shalbe fiue myles, and they shall haue liberty to improue ten myles further then the said fiue, and to hinder others frō the like, vntill the Court see fitt otherwise to dispose of yt. And the said Plantā. are to attend the generall Orders formerly made by this Court, setled by the Comittee to whō the same was referred, and other occations, as the rest of the Plantations vppon the Riuer doe. And Mr. Steele is intreated for the p^rsent to be recorder there, vntill the Towne haue one fitt among thēselues. They also are to haue the like libertyes as the other Townes vppon the Riuer, for making Orders among thēselues, p^ruided they alter not any fundamentall agreements settled by the said Comittee, hitherto attended.

The Constables of Hartford are to gather vp the knapsacks, pouches, powder & bulletts, vsed in the last designe, and deliuer them to Mr. Talcott to be kepte, and researue & take a noate in writeing of all the p^rticulers so deliuered, and returne yt to the Secretary.

The like is to be done by John Drake & George Phelps for Wyndsor, and the Constables of Wethersfield for Wethersfield, and deliuer them to Mr. Talcotte, and returne a noate of the p^rticulers to the Secretary.

There is a Rate of 400*l*. graunted to be paid by the Country: Out of this Stratford and Faierfield are to pay 45, as conceaued to be according to their p^rportion; Southampton 10*l*., who are to be warned to com to the Court in Aprill, where their due p^rportions may be determined; Seabrooke is to pay 15, and Tunxis x*l*.; Hartford, 136; Wyndsor, 102; Wethersfield, 102. The Tresurer is to send out his warrants for the leuying these on the seuerall Townes, w^thin one weeke, to be brought in w^thin vi weeks.

Tho: Graues is freed frō Trayneing, watching & warding.

It was also agreed, that in p^rsuance of the bargaine wth Mr. Fenwicke, for this p^rsent yeare, the noats that should be sent by ech vessell to Seabrooke shalbe sent in to Mr. Hopkins as Mr. F. Assigne, and that w^thin six days after the kylling of any hogge or swyne notice shalbe giuen to the p^rsons betrusted in the seuerall Townes thereof, vnder the penultyes exp^rssed in the agreement, who is ether to take p^rsent pay for the same, or if he researue yt in the hands of those that are to dischardge yt, he is to be accoumptable for yt to Mr. Fenwicke or his assignes when yt is sent for; and the like he is also to doe for the rest of the payments that shalbe due. Ed: Stebbing is appoynted for this searuice for Hartford, Walter Fyler for Wyndsor, & Mr. Trotte for Wethersfield.

Nath: Dickenson is appoynted to be Recorder for Wethersfield.

The Court is adiourned to the first Wensday in February, after lecture.

---

[148]   Decē: 4th, 1645.

  Jo: Heynes Esqr, Go^r.
  Ed: Hopkins Esqr, Dep.
    Capten Mason, Mr. Woolcott, Mr. Webster, Mr. Whiting, Mr. Welles.
  The Jury: Andrewe Bacon, Tymothy Standly, James Boosy, John Goutridge, Jo: Hawles, Anthony Howkins, Will' Lewis, Tho: Osmore.

In the action of defamation of John Pratte pl. ag^t Math: Allen defen^t, the Jury find for the plant. thirty pownd damages and costs of Courte.

In the action of the Case of Clement Chaplin pl. ag^t Samuell Smith def^t, the Jury find for the defen^t, costs of the Courte.

John Eauens pl. ag^t M^{ris} Parks; ag^t George Chappell; ag^t Robert Burrowes.

Will' Boreman pl. ag^t Jo: Stadder.

Will' Boreman, for not p^{r}secuting, is to pay the def^t 2s. vi$d$.

Tho: Osmore pl. ag^t Rich: Fellowes.

John Westall is to pay Tho: Osmore fiue bush: of Indean corne, the chardges of the Court & 2s. for witnesses.

John Westall is fyned xs. for entertayneing Brūfield.

Math: Williams is to let his wages that he is to haue of Belding rest in his hands, vntill he take order for the keepeing of the child layd to his chardge by Susan Cole.

The estate of Sam: Wakeman deceased is setled on Nath: Willette, in consideratiō whereof he is to pay 40l. to the eldest sonne w^n he shall attayne 21 years of age, and 20l. a peece to the three daughters w^n they shall attayne the age of 18 yeares: if any dy in the meane, the portiō is to be deuided betwixt the suruiuors: the land to stand ingadged for the p^{r}formance thereof, and if any debts more shall appeare then are now knowne, to be equally borne by him & the children; and if any estate more appeare, that also is to be deuided. *The childrens receipts of their portion is record. in Book D. fo: 19: Decemb^r 23: 1673.*

Samuell Hales, for his mysdemeanor by excesse in drinkeing, is fyned twenty nobles.*

Tho: Hurlebut, for the like is fyned 4l.

Elias Trotte, for accompaning the, and drawing wyne wthout liberty, is fyned 40s.

Will' Crosse, for haueing wyne sould in his howse wthout lycence is fyned 40s.

Samuell Barrett is to searue Arther Smith one yeare after the date hereof, for viij$l$.

---

[149]   March the 5th, 1645.

     Jo: Heynes Esqr, Gou^r.
     Ed: Hopkins Esqr, Dep.
        Mr. Webster, Capten Mason, Mr. Woolcott, Mr. Welles, Mr. Whiting.
     The Jury: Ed: Stebbing, Nath: Waird, Tho: Ford, Jo: Barnard, Jo: Edwards, Jo: Robins, Jo: Notte, Jo: Elson, Jo: Porter, Roger Williãs, Seargeant Fyler, Tho: Dewye.

The Will and Testament of George Willis Esqr, deceased, is brought into the Court by Will' Gybbins.

W^n Mr. Terry hath taken Oath & sent vp a coppy of yt, that the accoumpte giuen in by him is a trewe accoumpte, he shall rec. the goods formerly sequestred for him.

In the ac. of Richard Trotte pl. ag^t Ed: Elmor and Nath: Willet, the Jury find for the pl. 40s. damages & costs of Court.

In the ac. of Clement Chaplin pl^t, ag^t Sa: Smith & Nath: Dickenson defen^{ts}, the Jury find for the plant. damages 2l. 5s. 4d. & costs of Court.

In the ac. of Clement Chaplin pl^t, ag^t Tho: Coleman and Sa: Hales def^{ts}, the Jury find for the plant. damages 8d. & costs of Court.

---

    * Subsequently added,—in the hand writing of John Allyn.
    † £6. 13s. 4d. The noble was equal to 6s. 8d. sterling.

John Byssell, as assigne to John Clarke, pl. agt George Chappell deft, 5*l*. x*s*. damage.

John Byssell & Ja: Eggleston plts, agt William Heyton deft, in an ac. of the Case, to the damage of 10*l*.

In the action of Byssell plant. as assigne to Jo: Clarke, agt George Chappell deft, the Jury find for the defent, costs of Court, and for witnesses, 14*s*. 4*d*.

In the action of Jo: Byssell & Ja: Eggleston plant. agt Will' Heiton deft, the Jury find for the plant. to be paid his prportion of rayleing, three shillings pr rodd, ditching 10*d*. pr rodde, hedgeing 8*d*. pr rodde; costs of Court and witnesses.

The Welchman Lewis, for pilfering Bunces corne, is fined 40*s*.

In the ac. of Berding agt Edwards, the Court adiudgeth Edwards to pay 5*s*. & chardges of Court.

In the ac. of Chappell agt Clarke, the Jury find for the deft. Chappell is to pay costs of Court vii*s*. 4*d*.

In the ac. of slaunder of Edwards pl. against Berding deft, the Jury find for the deft, costs of Court 7*s*. 4*d*.

In the ac. of the Case of Edward pl. agt Berding deft, the Jury find for the deft, costs of Court 7*s*. 4*d*. & witnesses, 4*s*. 8*d*.

Nath: Willett is to haue executiō against Mr. Trott for 3*l*. 6*s*. 8*d*. and to be quit of the 40*s*. damages and costs of the sute agt him by the sd Mr. Trotte.

Mr. Woolcott is desiered to gather vp the debts due to Tho: Marshefield & to husband the estate for the benefit of the creditors, and to be alowed resonable satisfaction.

The Inuentory of Sa. Ierland is brought into the Court by Jo: Edwards, and the wife of Robert Burrowes, who was wife to the deceased, is to administer & to haue the thirds, & the other two prts to be for the children.

---

[150]   Aprill the ixth, 1646.

 Ed: Hopkins Esqr, Gour.
 Jo: Heines Esqr, Dep.
  Roger Ludlowe Esqr, Mr. Webster, Mr. Whiting, Capten Mason, Mr. Woolcott, Mr. Welles.

[*Deputyes :*] Mr. Steele, Mr. Talcoate, Mr. Westwood Andrew Bacon, Mr. Phelps, Mr. Gaylard, Mr. Hull, Dauid Wilton, Mr. Trotte, James Boosy, Sa: Smith, Nath: Dickenson, Jehue Burre, Anthony Wilson, Tho: Fayerchild.

The Court desieres that the Comissio^{rs} should be moued that noe Amunition should be traded wth any that liue out of the Jurisdictions in combinatiō, whereby yt might supply the Indeans, and that some consideration be taken to restrayne Roade Iland frō trading wth thē in such kynd.

Whereas Tho: Thornton of Wyndsor, by haueing his men suddenly taken offe their cauleing, may susteyne great losse, the Court hath freed him frō Trayneing, and desier the Magistrats to take his condition into serious consideration, that he might not be put to extraordinary hassard by imploying his men in publique searuice, and the Capten hath liberty to free his workemen frō one dayes trayneing, p^{r}uided they supply yt in the Artillery. *This not voted.*

Whereas, there is liberty giuen to the Magistrats to mittegat or increase damages giuen in by the verdict of Jury, It is now Ordered, that what alteratiō shall att any tyme be made in that kynd, yt shalbe in open Courte before pl. & def^t, or affedauit made that they haue bine somoned to appeare.

Fayerfiēld eccepte against a Jury of sixe, but subiect to that p^{r}te of the Order that 8 of 12 may giue in a verdicte.

It is Ordered, that if any p^{r}son wthin these libertyes haue bine or shalbe fyned or whippen for any scandalous offence, he shall not be admitted after such tyme to haue any voate in Towne or Comon welth, nor to searue on the Jury, vntill the Court shall manifest their satisfaction.

Whosoeuer shall be comitted for delinquency shall pay two shillings sixe pence to the keep^r of the pryson.

To moue the Comissio^{rs} to make some p^{r}uission ag^t incorigiblenes.

Mr. Ludlowe is desiered to take some paynes in drawing forth a body of Lawes for the gouernment of this Comon welth, & p^{r}sent thē to the next Generall Court, and if he can prouide a man for his occations while he is imployed in the said searuice, he shalbe paid at the Country chardge.

Its desiered by the Court, that the Magistrats would take course that all male pʳsons aboue 16 yeares of age should take the Oath of Fidellity : and that three Magistrats may giue the said Oath & make Freemen, (vppon certificatt of good behauior, as is pʳuided by former Order. This to stand vntill the next Courte.

Whereas Tho: Steynton by his long absence is disabled to attend the Court according to his place, It is now Ordered, his sallery shall cease, and Jonathen Gylbert is chosen to supply the place for this yeare, and the Court will attend him wᵗʰ resonable satisfactiō.

[151] The Gouʳ and Deputy are desiered to be Comissioʳˢ to joyne wᵗʰ the Vnited Collonyes for the meeteing in Septēber next & for this yeare.

It is Ordered, that a Rate be graunted of 50*l*. for the carrieing on the worke of the Forte, in case there should bee need thereof, to be paid by the Townes of the Riuer.

It is Ordered, that there be two pʳticuler Courts held the next pʳceding day before the two standing Generall Courts, that both the assistance of Mr. Ludlowe may be had, and such actions as fall out betwixt any vppon the Riuer and the Townes by the sea side be more comfortably attended.

John Maynard˙ and Williā Westly are freed frō watching.

To the penall Order conserneing the selling of lead, powder etc. to any out of the Jurisdiction is added, That it is lefte to the judgement of the Courte, that where any offence is comitted against the said Order or Orders, ether to aggrauat or lessen the penulty according as the nature of the offence shall require.

Its recomended to the seuerall Townes seasonably to attend the colection for the Colledg, and send it thither in conuenient tyme.

Mr. Hopkins and Mr. Whiting discouering to the Court the wrong recᵈ frō some Indeans in stealeing of theire goods and burneing their howse, it was conceaued that any lawfull course may be taken for the recouery of their losse, according as amongste the Englishe.

The Court being put in mynd of the Indeans that liue in, are recᵈ, and liue among the Englishe in these Townes, it was referred to Mr. Deputy and Capten Mason to take consideratiō of

them, and in case they are willing to submit to the ordering and
gou{r}ment of the Englishe they may accepte of thē vppon such
terms as may be safe and honarable to the Englishe.

The rates at Stratford and Faierfield are to be deuided.

The Freemen finding yt inconuenient to attend the Court of
Election the second Thursday in Aprill, haue ordered yt for
hereafter to be keept the third Thursday in May, and the
Magistrats to hold vntill that day.

Samuell Marten and Williā Androwes acknowledge thēselues
to be bownd to this Comōn welth in a Recognizance of 40*l*. to
appeare at the next Court to be held at Hartford, to answer the
complainte of Edward Stebbing, for lading 97 bush. of Corne
aboarde a vessell at Hartford, w{ch} dep{r}ted the harbor w{th}out
entring the said corne according to Order; then this Recognizance to be voyd, els to stand in force.

---

[152]   June the 5{th}, 1646.

    Jo: Heynes Esq{r}.

    Mr. Webster, Mr. Welles, Capten Mason, Mr. Wool-
cott.

    The Jury :   Tho: Ford, Rich: Goodman, Joseph Magote,
Arther Smith, Frances Styles, Jo: Drake, Roger Willm̄s,
Jo: More, Jo: Edwards, Sa: Marten, Luke Hitchoks,
Tho: Hurlbut.

In the ac. of Rose, pl. ag{t} Robins def{t}, the Jury find for the
pl. ten pownd dam̄ages & cost of Court.

The Jury found these p{r}cells of Corne, forfeited :

    Mr. Woolcott, 28 bush.   Codman, 6.   Lamton, 1. 1p.
Mr. Eauens, 48. 2p.   Jo: Lord, 2.   North, 3.   Coleman, for Smith, 20.   Wm. William̄s, 2.   Jo: Wyet,
11. 2p.

In the ac. of Borman pl. ag{t} Stadder def{t}, the Jury find for the
pl. 5*s*. dam̄ages & cost of Court.

John Drake, for his misdemeanor in p{r}phan execrations, is
fyned 40*s*.

Jo: Carpentor, for breakeing into Will' Gybbins his howse
& drynking wyne, is fyned 10*l*. & stands bownd to his good be-

hauior, & Tho: Osmor stands bownd for him in 10l. & to bring him forth w^n the Court shall call for him.

Williā Ellyt & Will' Yats, for the like misdemeanor, are fyned ten pownd a peece & stand bownd in 20l. a peece for their good behauior, & Will' Gybbins stands bownd for their good behauior in 20l. & for their appearence w^n the Court cauleth for thē.

Stephen Dauis & Symon Smith, for the like misdemeanor, are fyned fiue pownd a peece & stand bownd to their good behauior in 20l. a peece, and Will' Gybbins for thē in 20l. & for their appearance w^n the Court cauleth for thē.

Rich: Belding stands bownd in 20l., Robert Rugge in 40l., that Rugge keepe good behauior & appeare the next Court.

Execution was graunted John Pratte ag^t Mr. Allen, and returne made that yt was executed.

[153]   JUNE THE LAST, 1646.

 Ed: Hopkins Esqr, Gou^r.
  Capten Mason, Mr. Webster, Mr. Welles, Mr. Woolcotte.
 [*The Jury :*] Mr. Phelps, Tho: Ford, Will' Lewis, Jo: Barnard, George Graues, John Hollister, Jo: Demon, Will' Gybbins, *Sa: Smith*,* Jo: Latimore, Mr. Stoughton, Ro: Wynchell, Ro: Hewyt.

In the action of slaunder of John Robins pl. ag^t Leonard Chester def^t, the Jury find for the pl. xij$s$. damages & cost of Court & witnesses.

Rich: Coldecotts ac. ag^t Frances Styles is wthdrawen, and the later Articles to be attended wth reference to the 4 men.

Whereas Tho: Ford, John Byssell, Will' Pantry and Stephen Poste were to sett a Rate or value of the worth of impaileing 2024 rodd of pale according to articles agreed betwixt Mr. Saltingstall & Frances Styles, or to choose a fifthe man if they disagreed, wch hath bine long neglected by the said partyes, It is now Ordered, that if the said partyes doe nott sett downe vnder their hands & determine the rate and value of the foresaid, wthin

---

* A line is drawn about this name.

two months, or chuse a 5th man, according to the said articles, they shall forfeit 100*l*.

Coop^r for his misdemeanor in inuegleing the affect͠ns of Mr. Lee his mayde, wthout her M^r consent, is to pay Mr. Lee 20*s*. damages & 20*s*. fyne to the Country.

John Perkins & Tho: Coop^r vndertake & p^rmise to pay 20*s*. to this Com͠on welth & 20*s*. to Mr. Lee, by the last of March.

In the actiō of Clement Claplin p^{lt} ag^t Dickerson etc. the Jury find for the pl. x*s*. dam͠ages & cost of Court & witnesses.

Robert Bartlett, for his grosse misdemeanor in slaundring M^{ris} Mary Fenwicke, is to stand on the Pillory, Wensday, dureing the lecture, then to be whiped, & fyned fiue pownd & halfe yeares imprysonment.

---

[154] August the 21th, 1646.

   Ed: Hopkins Esqr, Go^r.
   Jo: Heynes Esqr, Dep.
     Mr. Webster, Mr. Welles, Mr. Woolcott.

Richard Fellowes vndertakes to pay ten pownd to the Country wthin 2 months, for Stephen Dauis his fyne.

Tho: Osmore vndertaks to pay fiue pownd for John Carpenter wthin 2 months, and fiue pownd more wthin 3 months after that.

Symon Smith is to stand bownd for his good behauior, vntill the next Court and his M^{ris} vndertaks he shall then appeare.

Jo: Ranolds is to be fyned 5*l*. and p^rsently whiped, for harboring the rouges that brake pryson, in his M^{ris} her howse, and to giue security to appeare at the Court att 3 months end, and then to be agayne corrected, except the Court be certified of his reformation.

Richard Watts vndertaks for the payment of the 5*l*. fyne, and that he the said Jo: Ranolds shall keepe good behauior and appeare the next Court.

Tho: Ford is bownd in a Recognizance of 20*l*. to the Country, to bring in Sa: Drake to the next Court.

Elinor Watts, for the like misdemeanor wth Jo: Ranolds, is fyned 5*l*. and whipped in her M^{ris} howse, and to be brought forth 3 months hence, and then whipped agayne if the Court shall not be informed of her amendment.

Mary Johnson, for theuery, is to be p^{r}sently whipped, and to be brought forth a month hence at Wethersfield, and there whipped.

Elizabeth Fuller, for comitting fornication, is to be seuerely corrected.

Sa: Drake is fyned fiue pownd for concealing Jo: Neuie (?) when he brake pryson.

Ro: Bartlett, for giueing ill counsell to the prysoners, aduiseing they should not peach Drake, is to be whipped.

[155]   OCTOBER THE FIRST, 1646.

Jo: Heynes Esqr, Dep.

Mr. Webster, Mr. Welles, Mr. Woolcot, Mr. Whiting.

The Jury: Hen: Woolcot, Jo: Edwards, Jo: Nott, Sa: Hales, Sa: Boreman, Walter Fyler, Dan: Clarke, Hūp: Pynny, Will: Pantry, Gre: Wilterton, Nath: Waird, Will: Wodsworth.

In the ac. of Whaty pl. ag^t Fellowes, the Jury find for the defen^t; the pl. to pay costs of Court.

In the ac. of Mr. Gylbert pl. ag^t George Chappell def^t, the Jury find for the pl. The def^t is to pay 8l. 8s. damages & costs of Court. Execution graunted ag^t his person.

In the ac. of Will' Whiteing pl. ag^t Tho: Ford def^t, the Jury find for the pl. The def^t is to pay 4l. 12s. 6d. damages & costs of Court.

In the action of Mr. Euens, by his searuant, pl. ag^t Math: Williās def^t, Williams is to pay 19s. damages & costs of Court.

In the action of Mr. Euens pl. ag^t George Chappell, Chappell is to pay 8 bush: of pease & costs of Court.

In the ac. of Mr. Euens pl. ag^t Mathias Trott def^t, the Jury find for the pl. The def^t is to pay 23 bush: 3 pec: of wheat, and cost of Court.

In the action of Mr. Euens pl^{te}, ag^t Carwithy def^t, the Jury find for the pl. 5l. 5s. 6d. damages & cost of Court.

In the action of Henry Smith pl. ag^t Jaruis Mudge def^t, the

Court judgeth Mudge to pay 5 bush: of marchantable dry Indean corne, or the value thereof.

In the action of Rich: Webb pl. ag^t George Chappell def^t, Chappell is to pay 24s. damages & cost of Court.

Tho: Stephenson acknowledgeth himselfe bownd in a recognizance of 10l. to make good his attach^t ag^t Elias Puttmans goods, or satisfie damages.

In the ac. of Webbe pl. ag^t George Chappell def^t, the defe^t is to pay 24s. & cost of Court.

Mr. Chester if freed frō Trayneing.

---

[156]   October the 29th, 1646.

     Ed: Hopkins Esqr, Go^r.
     Jo: Heynes Esqr, Dep.
        Mr. Webster, Mr. Woolcott, Mr. Whiting, Mr. Welles.
     The Jury :—Will' Gybbins, Nath: Richards, Jo: Edwards,
        Tho: Hurlbut, Aron Cooke, John Stadder.

Willm̄ Ellit is to be whipped the next lecture day, and to searue his Master his tyme, & then to returne to pryson.

Will' Fiske is to be whipped the next lecture day, and to restore dubble of what shall be p^{r}ued ag^t him, as yt shall be judged by Mr. Woolcotte.

The ac. of Mr. Whiting pl. ag^t Sa: Smith is respited vntill the next Courte.

     Gybbins pl^t ag^t Read.
     Moody pl^t ag^t Read, for Rent.
     Mr. Moody pl^t ag^t Read, for damages.
     Willit pl^t ag^t Read.
     Judson pl^t ag^t Rescue.

In the action of Mr. Whiting pl. ag^t Tho: Newton def^t, vppon an Attach^t returned by the Constable of Fayrfield, Greene appeared for Newton & the Jury find for the plant. the byll 5l. 16s. and 2s. vid. damages & cost of Court.

In the ac. of Ed: Hopkins pl^t, ag^t Tho: Newton def^t, the Jury find for the pl. The Def^t is to pay 4l. 13s. 4d. in mony according to the bill, 10s. damages & cost of Court,

In the action of John Moody pl. against James Whatly defend^t, the Jury find for the def^t, coste of Court.

Kircū & Carrington are to pay 30s. to the administrators of Vere, for their bargaine of Corne.

Three of the Jury betwixt James Whatly pl. ag^t R. Fellowes d^t, thinke on witnesse cannot cast the cause w^thout some circūstances fall in neare to equalize a witnesse, and they app^r-hend the circūstances on the other side rather the stronger : 1. The p^rty of whō he bought the horse said he knew not of the lamenes : 2. the price giuen might intimat soundness; 3. seuerall that rodde on the horse and that wrought him, did not discouer any lamenes. John White, Tho: Olcoke, Will' Phelps.

The other 3 conceaue the witnesse giuen into the former Court hold out the defen^t might know the lamenes of the horse ; 2. one witnesse testifieing frō his mouth, that he said he was lame.

---

[157]　　　　　　　October the 30th, 1646.

Ed: Hopkins Esq, Go^r.

Jo: Heynes Esqr, Dep.

　　Mr. Webster, Mr. Welles, Mr. Whiting, Capten Mason, Mr. Woolcott.

　　[*Deputyes :*] Mr. Phelps, Mr. Stoughton, Mr. Clarke, Mr. Porter, Mr. Steele, Mr. Talcoat, Mr. Westwood, Mr. Cullicke, Mr. Trotte, James Boosy, Nath: Dickenson, Jo: Demon.

The deputyes are to take into consideration the fenceing uppon the Easte side of the great Riuer, by whō & where they shall see cause.

The Order of the Comissioners concerneing the restreynt of of selling powder, shotte, amunition etc. to any out of the Jurisdiction, w^thout the lycence of two Magistrats, or one Magistrat and 2 deputyes, is confirmed.*

---

* This order of the Commissioners was confirmatory of that made in 1644, (see p. 113, *ante*) which had been approved by the General Courts of all the United Colonies except Plymouth. The present order prohibited, under a heavy penalty, the sale of arms or ammunition to any person out of the confederate jurisdictions, " without lycense under the hands of two.

The Order conserneing the p^rceeding against Indeans is confirmed.†

There is alowed for the searuing of executions 2s. 6d. if vnder 40s. and 5s. if aboue.

Whosoeuer drawes wyne after the publisheing this Order, shall pay to the Country after the p^rportiō of 40s. a Butt for what shalbe drawen.

Mr. Phelps is appoynted to joyne wth the Comittee for the planting Matabezeke.

[158]   J_A: 28th, 1646.

    Ed. Hopkins Esqr, Go^r.
    Mr. Webster, Mr. Whiting, Capten Mason, Mr. Welles, Mr. Woolcott.
    [*Deputyes:*] Mr. Steele, Mr. Talcoate, Mr. Cullicke, Mr. Westwood, Mr. Trott, James Boosy, Nath: Dickenson, Jo: Demon, Mr. Phelps, Mr. Stouton, Mr. Clarke, Mr. Porter.

The Order concerneing paying 5s. a pownd for takeing Tobacco not growing w^thin this Jurisdictiō, is repealed.

Richard Lord for transgressing the Order against selleing lead out of this Jurisdictiō, is fyned seauen pownd.

---

magistrates of the jurisdiction, or at least under the hands of one magistrat and two deputyes, intressed in the publique affaires, & that all & eu'ry such lycense shall from tyme to tyme be kept in a booke or memoriall in writing, that all the parcells or particulers, wth the quantities soe lycensed, the p^rsons to whom, the grounds for weh, upon occasion may be considered by the Gen^rall Courts, or Comissioners for the Colonyes." (Rec. of U. Colonies, Sept. 1646.)

† Providing, that in case of "wilfull & hostile practises against the English, together with the enterteineing, protecting or rescueing of offenders," "the Magistrates of any of the Jurisdictions might, at the charge of the plaintiffs, send some convenient strength of English, & according to the nature & vallewe of the offence & damage, seize & bring away any of that plantacon of Indians that shall entertaine, protect or rescue the offender, though it should be in another Jurisdiction, when, through distance of place, comission or direction cannot be had after notice & due warning given them, as abettors or at least accessory to the iniury & damage done to the English; onely women & children to be sparingly seized vnlesse knowen to be some way guilty. And because it will be chargeable keeping Indians in prison, & if they should escape they would prove more insolent & dangerous after, it was thought fitt that upon such seysure, the delinquent or satisfaction should againe be demanded of the Sagamore or Plantacon of Indians guiltie or accessory as before; and if it be denyed, that then the magistrates of the Jurisdiction deliver up the Indians seized to the party or parties indamaged, either to serve or to be shipped out and exchanged for Negroes, as the cause will iustly beare." [Ibid.] This order will be found incorporated with the code of 1650, in a subsequent part of this volume.

Tho: Staynton, for the like transgressiō, is fyned 5*l*. fiue pownd.

Dauid Wilton, for the brech of the same Order, is to forfeite the lead wch was attached at Wethersfield, being 131 pownd.

Nath: Waird is freed frō trayneing and warding, so long as the infirmity he complaynes of remayneth vppon him.

The Gou^r and Mr. Whiting are desiered to attend the place of Comission^{rs} for the Vnited Collonies, for this next yeare.

There is a Rate of 30*l*. graunted for the Fort.

March the 4th, 1646.

Ed: Hopkins Esqr, Go^r.

Mr. Webster, Mr. Welles.

[*The Jury:*] Tho: Ford, Tho: Osmore, Jo: Nott, Sa: Boremā, Tho: Thornton, Benedict Alford.

In the ac. of Joseph Nubery pl^t, ag^t Ambrowse Fowler def^t, the Jury find for the plan^t, fower pownd x*s*. & costs of Court.

In the actiō of Sa: Smith pl. ag^t John Guteridge, Tho: Rite & Sa: Martin def^{ts}, John Guteridge and Sa: Marten are to pay the pl. xvi bush: Indean.

Mary Williās, for her fowle misdemeanor, is fyned 5*l*.

Joshua Gynings vndertaks to pay this 5*l*.

Tho: Blisse for not trayneing, is fyned 2*s*. vi*d*.

May the 19th, 1647.

Ed: Hopkins Esqr, Go^r.

Mr. Webster, Mr. Whiting, Mr. Woolcoat, Mr. Welles.

The Jury: Mr. Phelps, Mr. Porter, Mr. Roceter, Dauid Wilton, Mr. Parks, James Boosy, Sa: Smith, Will' Wadsworth, Ed: Stebing, Tho: Ford, Andrew Bacon, Nath: Waird.

In the ac. of James Whatly pl. ag^t Tho: Coleman, the Jury find for the def^t, costs of Court, and for witnesses, 2*s*. 6*d*.

In the ac. of Henry Gree pl. ag{t} Sa: Marten def{t}, the Jury find for the pl. debte 15*l*. ii*s*., damages ten pownd, and costs of Court.

MAY THE 21st, 1647.

The Jury : Mr. Talcoate, Gre: Wilterton, Tho: Osmor, Sa: Smith, Will' Wilcoxson, Robert Howard, Dan: Tytterton, Walter Fyler, John Croe, Ed: Haruy, Tho: Judde, John Demon.

In the ac. of John Steele pl. ag{t} Tho: Demon, the said Tho: Demon is to pay six bush: of Indean.

In the ac. of Blysse pl. ag{t} Lyman & Arnold, the defen{ts} are to pay 20*s*. & costs of Court.

Henry Densloe is to attend agayne the next Court, and Wilcoxe to pay him 5*s*. for not p{r}secuting this Court.

In the ac. of Mr. Whiting pl. ag{t} Sa: Smith def{t}, the Jury find for the pl. viij*l*. damages, and cost of Court.

In the ac. of Blachfield pl. ag{t} Spenser, the Jury find for the pl. 50 bush: of Indean, & costs of Court.

In the ac. of Spenser pl. ag{t} Blachfield def{t}, the Jury find for the pl. 31*s*. 3*d*. damages, & costs of Court.

[160] In the ac. of slaunder, of Mr. Whiting pl. ag{t} Tho: Ford def{t}, the Jury find for the pl. 40*s*. & costs of Court.

In the ac. of Will' Fishe pl. ag{t} Aron Cooke, the Jury find for the pl. fiue pownd damages & costs of Court.

In the ac. of Tho: Ford pl. ag{t} Oldige & Hull, the Jury find for the def{ts}, costs of Court.

Henry Gree acknowledgeth himselfe bownd to the Court, in a Recognizance of x*l*. & Tho: Hassard in 20, that Tho: Hassard keepe good behauior vntill the Generall Court in Septēber next, and appeare at the p{r}ticuler Court the day before.

In the ac. of Write pl. against Norton, the pl. is to haue the swyne & pay the chardges for the keeping.

MAY THE 24th, 1647.

Roger Ludlowe Esq{r}, Moderator.
Mr. Woolcoat, Mr. Welles.

Jury : Sa: Smith, Will' Wilcoxsō, Robert Howard, Dan: Tytterton, John Demon, Walter Fyler, Ed: Haruy, Tho: Judde, John Westall, Aron Cooke, Anthony Howkins, Stephen Hart.

In the ac. of M^{ris} Willis pl. ag^t Francis Styles def^t, (Mr. Roceter appeared for Mr. Styles,) the Jury find for the pl. 340*l*. damages & costs of Court.

---

[162]   MAY THE 20th, 1647.

Jo: Heynes Esqr, Go^r.

Edward Hopkins Esqr, Dep. Go^r.

George Fenwicke Esqr, *Magistrate;* Roger Ludlowe Esq. *Mag:* Mr. Webster, *Mag:* Mr. Whiting, *Mag: Tres^r;* Capten Mason, *Mag:* Mr. Woolcoate, *Mag:* Mr. Welles, *Mag: Sec^r;* Mr. Cosmore,* *Mag:* Mr. Howell,* *Mag:*

Deputyes : Mr. Phelps, Mr. Stoughton, Mr. Porter, Mr. Clarke, Mr. Steele, Mr. Talcoat, Mr. Cullike, Mr. Trott, Sa: Smith, Ja: Boosy, Nath: Dickenson, An: Bacon, Mr. Taynter, Ed: Haruy, Dan: Tytterton, Will' Wilcoxsō, Stephen Hart, Tho: Judde.

It is Ordered, that the three Townes on the Riuer & Tunxis shall pay ten shillings to whōsoeuer shall kill any Woolfe wthin any of their libertyes, & so to pay for euery woolfe that shalbe kylled wthin the term of one yeare after the date hereof.

Forasmuch as diuers inconueniences fall out by letting land to the Indeans, whereby they mixe thēselues in their labours wth the Inglishe, and therby the manners of many young men are lyable to be corrupted, It is Ordered, that noe Inhabitant wthin this Jurisdiction shall contracte wth or lette any land to any Indean after the publisheing this Order, nether shall any Indean possesse any land held of the Inglishe after the last of October next, p^{r}uided notwthstanding that such natyves as haue caried thēselues peacebly, and wch will subiecte thēselues to be ordered

---

* John Cosmore and Edward Howell, of Southampton, on Long Island. (See Articles of Combination, in Appendix, No. II; and p. 112, *ante.*)

by the Inglishe, shall haue pruission for planting vppon reasonable terms sette forth for them.

James Pyne hath forfeted his recognizance, for not appeareing at the Court held at Hartford the 20th of May.

James Harwood also hath forfeted his recognizance.

An Attacht is to goe forth for Tho: Sherwood.

A Warrant for Tho: Newton.

Whereas, by an Order of the 14th of January, 1638, it was Ordered, that euery Generall Court, excepte such as through neglecte of the Gor and the greatest prte of Magistrats the Freemen theselues doe call, shall consiste of the Gor or some on chosen to moderate the Courte, and 4 other Magistrats at lest, wth the maior prte of the deputyes of the seuerall Townes, legally chosen, wch hath bine conceaued, that by the example thereof no prticuler Court might be keepte excepte the Gor or Dep: Gor and 4 Magistrats were prsent, wch this day coming into consideration, this Court seeing the many inconueniences thereof to be so restreyned, & considering in case it may so fall out that by reson of the absence of the Gor or Deputy & 4 Magist: noe prticuler Court may be extant to administer justice according to the law of God and humane pollicy, wch is now [163] conceaued to be contrary to the trewe meaneing ‖ of the said former Order, It is therefore now declared and so Ordered, sentenced & decreed, that the Gour or Dep: Gor wth 2 Magistrats shall haue power to keepe a prticuler Court, according to the lawes established, & in case the Gour or Dep: Gor be absent, or some waye or other incapable ether to sit or to be prsent, if three Magistrats meete, and choose on of theselues to be a moderator, they may keepe a prticuler Court, wch to all intents & purposes shalbe deemed as legall, as though the Gor or Deputy did sitte in Courte, and all other Orders that haue bine heretofore in that case made shalbe reduced to this Order.*

It is Ordered, that there shalbe a gard of 20 men, euery Sabboth and Lecture day, compleate in their arms, in ech seuerall Towne vppon the Riuer, and atte Seabrooke and Farmington 8 apeece, ech towne of the sea coast ten, and as the nūber of men increase in the Townes, the gaurd is to encrease.

---

* [*In margin*,] " Added to the 10th fundamentall."

MAY THE 25th, 1647.

The Estreits for the leueing of Fynes shall goe forth once eu^ry yeare, both in the Townes on the Riuer and by the sea-side, and some officer appoynted in ech place to leuy and receaue thē and the accoumpts to be giuen in by the seuerall Plantations of their generall chardges at the Court in Septēber, for the p^rfecting of the accoumpts betwixt them. Mr. Ludlowe is desiered to graunt out warrants for the fynes by the sea-side.

Vppon the makeing vppe of the Rates betwixt the Townes by the sea side, for the last Rate, ther was found to be due frō Stratford, 9*l*. ii*s*. 2*d*.; frō Fairfield, xi*l*. 14*s*. 8*d*.; these Townes being alowed what they had expended vppon the p^rparations of the late warrs, but other expenses shalbe alowed out of the Fynes when the accoumpte of thē shalbe brought vppe.

Its the mynd of the Court that ther should be p^ruision made for entertayneing the Magistrats dureing the sitting of the Court, and the deputyes of Hartford are desiered to find out a fitte man.

Its Ordered that the souldears shall only make choyse of their millitary officers & p^rsent thē to the p^rticuler Court, but such only shalbe deemed Officers as the Court shall confirme.

The chiefe officer in euery Towne shall appoynt the dayes of Trayneing alowed by Order of Court.

[169] Whereas it appeares that diuers, to defeate and defraude their creditors, may secretly and vnderhand make bairgens & contracts of their lands, lotts and accomodations, by meanes whereof, when the creditor thinks he hath a meanes in a due order of lawe to declare against the said lands, lotts and accomodations, and so recou^r satisfaction for his debte, he is wholy deluded and frustrated, wch is contrary to a righteous rule, that euery man should pay his debts wth his estate, be it what yt wilbe, ether real or p^rsonall; This Court takeing it into consideratiō, doe Order, sentence and decree, that for the future that if any Creditor doe suspecte any debtor, that he may p^rue non soluant in his p^rsonall estate, to repair to the Register or Recorder of the Plantation wher the lands, lotts or accomodations lyes, and enter a Caueat against the lands, lotts and accomodations of the said debtor, and shall giue to the said Register or Recorder 4*d*. for the entry thereof; and the said creditor

or creditors shall take out sumons against the said debtor, and in due forme of law the next p^rticuler Court, ether for the whole Collony or for that p^rticuler Plantation wher the said lands, lotts and accomodations lyes, or the next Court ensueing, declare against the said debttors lands, lotts & accomodations; and soe if the creditor recouer, he may enter a judgment vppon the said lotts, lands and accomodations, and take out an extent against the said land, directed to a knowne officer, who may take two honest & sufficient men of the neighbours, to appryse the said lands, lotts & accomodations, ether to be sould out right if the debt so require, or sett a resonable rent vppon the same, vntill the debte be payd, and deliuer the possession thereof ether to the creditor or creditors, his or their assigne or assignes, or any other; and what sale or sales, lesse or lesses, the saide officer makes, being orderly recorded, according to former Order of recording of lands, shalbe as legall and bynding to all intents & purposes as though the debtor himselfe had don the same; p^ruided that if the said debttor can then p^rsently p^rcure a Chapman or Tenant, that can giue to the creditor or creditors satisfactiō to his or their content, he shall haue the first refusall thereof. Also yt is declared, that he wch first enters Caueat as aboue said, and his debte being due att his entring the said Caueat, shalbe first paid, and so euery creditor as he enters his Caueat and his debte becom due, shalbe orderly satisfied, vnlesse at the next Court yt appeares the debters lands, lotts and accomodations p^rue insufficient to pay all his creditors, then eu^ry man to haue a sutable p^rportion to his debte out of the same, and yet notw^thstanding euery man to receaue his p^rte according to the entry of his Caueat; yet this is not to seclude any [165] creditor ‖ to recouer other satisfaction, ether vppon the p^rson or estate of the sayd debtor, according to lawe and custum of the Collony.

And also yt is further decreed, that what sale or bargaine soeuer the debtor shall make concerneing the said lotts, lands and accomodations, after the entering of the said Caueat, shalbe voyde as to defraud the said creditors. It is also further explayned and declared, that if the said debtor be knowne to be an insoluant man before the first Caueat entered against the said lands, lotts & accomodations, and the same appeare at the next pʳticuler Court, then the Court shall haue power to call in all the creditors in a short tyme, and set an equall and indifferent way how the creditors shalbe paid out of the said lands, lotts & accomodations; otherwise, if the said debtor proue insoluant after the first Caueat entered, then this Order to be duly obsearued, according to the pʳmisses and true intent and meaneing thereof. It is also further declared and explayned, that the Recorder or Register of the said Caueat shall, the next pʳticuler Court as aforesaid, returne the said caueats that are wᵗʰ him, at wᶜʰ tyme & Court the enterer of the said Caueats shalbe cauled forth to pʳsecute the next pʳticuler Court following; and if the enterer of the said Caueats fayle to pʳsecute according to this Order, the Register or Recorder of the said Caueat or Caueats shall putt a *vacatt* vppon the said Caueat or Caueats, wᶜʰ shalbe invalled or voyde to chardge the said lotts, lands and accomodations aforesaid.

Forasmuch as it is obsearued that many abuses are comitted by frequent takeing Tobacco, It is Ordered, that noe pʳson vnder the age of 20 years, nor any other that hath not allreddy accustomed himselfe to the vse therof, shall take any Tobacco vntil he haue brought a Certificat, vnder the hand of some who are approued for knowledg & skill in phisicke, that it is vsefull for him, and also that he hath receaued a lycence frō the Court for the same. And for the regulateing those who ether by their former takeing yt haue to their owne appʳhensions made yt necessary to thē, or vppon due aduice are pʳsuaded to the vse thereof, It is Ordered, that no man wᵗʰin this Collony, after the publicatiō hereof, shall take any tobacco publicquely in the street, nor shall any take yt in the fyelds or woods, vnlesse when they be on their trauill or joyrny at lest 10 myles, or at the ordinary tyme of repast comonly called dynner, or if it be not then taken, yet not aboue once in the day at most, & then not [166] in company wᵗʰ any other. Nor shall any ‖ inhabiting in any of the Townes wᵗʰin this Jurisdiction, take any Tobacco in any howse in the same Towne wher he liueth, wᵗʰ and in the company of any more then one who vseth and drinketh the same weed, wᵗʰ him at that tyme; vnder the penalty of six pence for ech offence against this Order, in any of the pʳticulers thereof, to be payd wᵗʰout gainesaying, vppon conuictiō by the testimony of one witnesse that is w^thout iust exception, before any one Magistrate; and the Constables in the seuerall Townes are required to make p^rsentment to ech p^rticuler Court of such as they doe vnderstand and can evict to be transgressors of the Order.

And for the p^ruenting that great abuse wch is creepeing in by excesse in Wyne and strong waters, It is Ordered, that noe inhabitant in any Towne of this Jurisdiction shall continue in any comon victualing howse in the same Towne wher he liueth aboue halfe an hower att a tyme in drinkeing wyne, bear or hotte waters, nether shall any who draweth & selleth wyne suffer any to drynke any more wyne att on tyme then after the p^rportion of three to a pynt of sacke. And it is further Ordered, that noe such wyne drawer deliuer any wyne, or suffer any to be deliuered out of his howse to any who com for yt, vnlesse they bring a noate vnder the hand of some on M^r of some family and alowed inhabitant of that Towne, nether shall any such Ordinary keep, sell or drawe any hotte waters to any but in case of necessity, and in such moderation for quantity as they may haue good grownds to conceaue yt may not be abused; and shalbe reddy to giue an accoumpte of their doeings herein when they are cauled thereto, vnder Censure of the Court, in case of delinquency.

When Mr. Ludlowe hath p^rfected a body of lawes as the Court hath desiered him, it is the mynd of the Court that he should, besids the paying the hyer of a man, be further considered for his paynes.

Yf Mr. Whiting wth any others shall make tryall and p^rsecute a designe for the takeing of Whale, w^thin these libertyes, and if vppon tryall w^thin the terme of two yeares, they shall like to goe on, noe others shalbe suffered to interrupt thē, for the tearme of seauen yeares.

---

[167] June the 3^d, 1647.

 Ed: Hopkins Esqr, Dep.
 Mr. Webster, Mr. Welles.
 The Jury :—Humphry Pynny, Williā Heton, Joseph Magotte, Tym: Standly, John Edwards, John Elsen.

In the action of Aron Cooke pl^t, ag^t John Dawes, the Jury find for the pl^t 4l. & costs of Court.

Henry Densloe is bownd in a Recognizance of 20l. to appear the next Court.

Mr. Math: Allen & Tho: Newton acknowledge themselues bownd in a Recognizance of a 160l. to the Court, to saue the Court & such debttors harmeles & indempnified frō any daynger, losse or inconuenience that may befall thē by any some of mony that shalbe recouered in the Court, of Scippeseyer his debts, in reference to an ac. comenced ag^t Sa: Smith.

In the action of Math: Allen pl. ag^t Peter Jacobe, of 6l. 10s. thers acknowled to be paid,

  by Dauid Prouost, ... 2. 0.
  by Sa: Smith, 1: 2: 7; . . . 1. 2. 7
   more by him in wheat 2l. 8s. . 2. 8.
  behind 19s. 5d. wch the def^t is to pay.

Tho: Sherwood, for his contempte in not appeareing att Court vppō sumons, is fyned 40s.

Tho: Newton, for his misdemeanor in the vessell cauled the Virgin, in giueing Phillipe White wyne w^n he had to much before is fyned 5l.

---

[168]   June the 2, 1647.

 Ed: Hopkins Esqr.
 Capten Mason, Mr. Webster.
 [*Deputyes :*]—Mr. Steele, Mr. Talcoate, Mr. Cullicke, Andrew Bacon, Mr. Trott, James Boosy, Sa: Smith, Mr. Clarke, Mr. Porter.

It was this day Ordered, that all guns and millitary amunition wch this Comon welth by a Comitte haue formerly bought of George Fenwicke Esqr, be deliuered vnto Capten Mason for the vse of the Country, wch being done, the sd. Capten Mason to acquit & dischardge the said George Fenwicke, or his Agent, of the p^{r}ticulers soe deliuered.

It was then further Ordered, that Capten Mason should for the peace, safty and good asurance of this Comon welth, haue the comaund of all souldears and inhabitants of Seabrooke, and in case of alarum or daynger by approch of an enimy, to drawe forth or put the said souldears & inhabitants in such posture for the defence of the place, as to him shall seeme best.

It is this day Ordered, that in case Mr. Whiting, being at p^rsent vppon a voyadge att sea, be by P^ruidence p^ruented of his intended returne, then Capten Mason to be on of the Com̃issio^rs for this Jurisdiction, and to attend the searuice this yeare wth the Comissio^rs of the Vnited Collonyes, in the Bay or elswher, at the tyme or tymes appoynted.

Whereas Capten Mason, at the spetiall instance & request of the inhabitance of Seabrooke, togather wth the good likeing of this Com̃on welth, did leaue his habitatiō in the Riu^r and repaire thither, to exercise a place of trust, It is this day Ordered, that his former sallary of 40*l*. p^r ann. be continued, and after ech of the terms yt hath bine formerly dewe, then at 20 dayes warneing yt be put abord some vessell or vessells as himselfe shall appoynd.

Memorand^m. W^n the Capten doth rec. the guns & millitary am̃unition, he must deliuer a bill of the p^rticulers to the Regester, to be keepte as a record for the Country.

The p^rportions for the composition for the Fort for the full Tearme of 10 yeares is as followth :—

Hartford,	60*l*. 5*s*.	⅓ p^rte wheat, ⅓ p^rte pease, ⅓ Ry.
Tunxis,	15. 5.	in the same kynd.
Wyndsor,	45.	½ wheat, ½ pease.
Wethersflcld,	49. 10.	⅓ p^rte wheat, ⅔ p^rts pease.
Seabrooke,	10.	the same as Hartford.

---

[169]   Sep: 2, 1647.

    Ed: Hopkins, Esqr.
    Mr. Webster, Mr. Welles.
    [*The Jury:*] Nath: Waird, Nath: Ely, Sa: Hales, Jo: Edwards, Jo: More, Aron Cooke.

In the ac. of Wyddowe Kilburne pl. ag^t Peter Blachfield deft, the Jury find for the pl. 40*s*. & cost of Court.

George Abbott is to pay 12*s*. to Rich: Letten.

Vpson is to pay Kerby ix*s*. and the cost of Court, excepte witnesses.

Mrs Whiting is admitted to administer according to the will of her deceased husband.

Trotte ag^t Norton, 2 ac.

Executiō graunted Mrs Willis.

Executiō graunted Aron Cooke.

John Nubery confesseth that he made seuerall attempts of bestiality,* .   .   .   .

John Gynings for resisting the watch seuerall tymes is fyned 40*s*. and to find surtyes for his good behauior.

Peter Bassaker for resisting the watch is fyned 20*s*. and to find surtyes for his good behauior.

Tho: Hubbert for refuseing to watch is fyned x*s*.

Sep. 9, 1647.

Ed: Hopkins Esqr.

Mr. Webster, Mr. Woolcott, Capten Mason, Mr. Welles. [*Deputyes :*] Mr. Steele, Mr. Talcoat, Mr. Westwood, Andr: Bacon, Mr. Phelps, Mr. Clarke, Mr. Stoughton, Mr. Gaylard, Mr. Trott, Liue^t Boosy, Sa: Smith, Nath: Dickenson.

Thers liberty giuen the Comissio^{rs} to forbeare their sett meeting att Septēber, p^ruided they meet once in the yeare.

Also, if no more then syxe of the Comissio^{rs} meet, they may goe on in their occations yf they all agree, and it shalbe as effectuall as if the whole 8 meet, haueing sufficient warneing.

There is a Rate of 100*l*. graunted.

Capten Mason & Jo: Clarke are desiered to carry on the building of the Fort, by hireing men or Cartts or other necessaryes. They are alowed to make vse of the last Rate to be paid by Seabrook.

The Court thinks meet that a Comission be directed to Mr. Wynthrop, to execute justice according to o^r lawes & the rule of righteousnes.

---

* A line omitted.

The deuissiō of the Rate ; Hartford,   35*l*. 10.
         Wyndsor,   24. 10.
         Wethersf^d, 24.
         Seab: 8.
         Farm: 8.
            100. 0.

The Courts adioyrned to the last Wednesday in October.

[170]   October 29th, 1647.

Jecoxe is bownd in a Recognizance of 10*l*., James Pyne in 20*l*., p^ruided Pyne keepe good behauior vntill the Court in May at Fayerfield, and appeare ther.

The Rats to be paid in Englishe graine.

The Courts adioyrned to the first Thursday in March.

      No: the 22th, 1647.

Ed: Hopkins Esqr, Dep: Go^r.

Mr. Webster, Mr. Woolcoate, Mr. Welles.

[*The Jury :*] Tho: Ford, Will: Wodsworth, *fyned* 2*s*. vi*d*., Gregory Wilterton, John Barnard, Mr. Porter, Dauid Wilton, Tho: Dewy, Sa: Marten, John Notte, Sa: Boreman, John Westall, Will: Pantry, Tymothy Standly.

In the action of John Guttridge pl. ag^t Jaruis Mudge def^t, the Jury find for the pl. 20 bush: Indean ; 7*s*. vi*d*. forbearance ; 20*s*. to be deducted for chardge & hazard ; remayneth for the pl. 37*s*. 6*d*. & chardge of Court.

Sa: Gardner is to be alowed frō Mudge vi*s*. for three bush: Indean.

In the action of the Case of Tho: Olcoatte pl. ag^t Mathew Gryssell def^t, the Jury find for the plantife 50*l*. damages & coste of Court, and for witnesses 30*s*. The defen^t to make improuement of the goods that miscaried, for his owne vse.

DECEMBER THE 2ᵈ, 1647.

Ed: Hopkins Esqʳ, Dep: Goʳ.
Mr. Webster, Mr. Woolcoate, Mr. Welles.
The Jury : Mr. Trotte, Mr. Talcoate, Tymothy Standly, John White, Tho: Osmore, Liuetenant Boosy, Sa: Smith, Tho: Coleman, Henry Clarke, Mr. Hill, Mr. Hull, Jo: More.

The Jury find the bill of indictement agᵗ John Nubery, that he is guilty of buggery.

James Whatly, for his contempte in not watching, is fyned 3s. 4d. & the chardge of witnesses.

In the actiō of James Whatly pl. agᵗ Tho: Coleman, the Jury find for the deftᵗ, cost of Court and witnesses.

In the actiō of George Steele pl. agᵗ Will' Corbit deftᵗ, the Jury find for the plᵗ 20s. damages and cost of Court.

In the 2d actiō of George Steele pl. agᵗ Will' Corbit deftᵗ, the Jury find for the pl. 10s. damages, and cost of Court.

Mr. Woolcoate is to giue notice to Tho: Marshfields creditors to pʳfecte the diuissiō of the remaynder of that estate in his hands, by the 24ᵗʰ of June next.

---

[171] FEB: 23ᵗʰ, 1647.

Ed: Hopkins Esqʳ, Dep: Goʳ.
Mr. Webster, Mr. Woolcoat, Mr. Welles.
[*Deputyes :*] Mr. Steele, Mr. Talcoate, Mr. Westwood, Andrew Bacon, Mr. Phelps, Mr. Stoughton, Mr. Clarke, Mr. Trotte, James Boosy, Sa: Smith, Nath: Dickenson.

Forasmuch as yt is obseaured that ther are diuersity of wayghts, yards and measures amoungst vs, whereby damag many tymes ensueth, by comerce wᵗʰ seuerall pʳsons; For the pʳuenting whereof, yt is now Ordered, that no man wᵗʰin these Libertyes shall, after the publisheing this Order, sell any comodity but by a sealed waight or measure, vnder the penulty of xijd. ech defaulte : the Clarke is to haue a penny for sealeing a wayght or yard, ech time, and noe waight or measure is to be accoumpted authenticke that is not sealed or approued by the

Clarke once euery yeare : and the said Clarke is to breake or demolishe such wayghts, yards or measures as are defectiue.

MARCH THE 2d, 1647.

Ed: Hopkins Esqr, Dep: Gor.

Mr. Webster, Mr. Woolcoate, Mr. Welles.

[*The Jury :*] John White, John Byssell, John Drake, Dan: Clarke, Henry Woolcott, John Edwards, Sa: Marten, Sa: Hales, Luke Hitchcoke, Will' Pantry, Rich: Goodman, Rich: Butler.

In the ac. of Will' Gibbins as Assigne to Waterman pl. agt Fra: Norton deft, the Jury find for the deft, costs of Courte.

In the ac. of Peter Jacob pl. agt Sa: Smith deft, the Jury find for the pl. 5l. 7s. 9d. and costs of Court.

In the ac. of Nath: Dickenson pl. agt Peter Jacob deft, the Court adiudgeth the deft to pay 12s. and costs of Court.

In the ac. of John Sadler pl. agt Peter Jacob deft, the deft is to pay ixs. and costs of Court, and 18d. for witnesses.

John Moses acknowledgeth himselfe bownd to this Comon welth in a Recognizance of 20l. and Mathew Allen in xl., pruided that the said John Moses appeare at the next prticuler Court and keepe good behauior in the meane tyme,

Ed: Chancutt, for diuulging misreports agt Hide, is fyned 40s. and Beniamin Nubery for the like is fyned 20s. and Mastens the boy to be corrected.

Anthony Longdon for drunkenes, is fyned 20s.

Nicholas Gynings, for a miscaridge, beateing of a Cow of Ralfe Keelers

Peter Bassaker, 10s.

Ralfe Keeler, Jenings, Ketchrell.

MARCH THE 9th, 1647.

Ed: Hopkins Esqr, Dep: Gor.

Mr. Webster, Mr. Woolcoat, Mr. Welles.

[*Deputyes :*] Mr. Steele, Mr. Talcoat, Mr. Westwood,

Mr. Phelps, Mr. Trott, Mr. Stoughton, Mr. Clarke, Ja: Boosy, Sa: Smith.

Williā Rescue is to be alowed 40s. towards his chardges in keepeing the prysoners.

Ther is a liberty giuen to lett any grownd on the east side the great Riuer and in the Iland, to such Indeans as haue giuen in their names to the Dep: Go^r, and if that p^{r}ue to little it is lefte to the Go^r to dispose of thē as he shall see cause.

The Court thinks fitt that Massacoe be purchased by the Country, and that ther be a Comitte chosen to dispose of yt to such inhabitants of Wyndsor as by thē shalbe judged meet to make improuement therof, in such kynd as may be for the good of this Comon welth, and the purchase to be repaid by those that shall enioy yt, wth resonable alowance. Mr. Hopkins is intreated to be one of the Comittes and Mr. Webster another; and Mr. Steele, Mr. Talcoate & Mr. Westall to vew the foresaid grownd and assist in the dispose therof.

Wheras by former Order there was 2d. p^r pownd laid vppon euery pownd of Beuer traded wthin the libertyes of these Plantations vppon the Riuer, that hath not hitherto been p^{r}formed, It is now Ordered, that whosoeu^r hath traded any wthin these libertyes the last yeare, or shall herafter trade any wthin the tyme specified in the foresaid Order, That they giue notice thereof to Mr. Hopkins before they export yt downe the Riuer, vnder the penulty of forfeting the one halfe, as in the former Order.

[173] It is Ordered, that ther shalbe a Rate of 150l. paid by the Country, whereof noe man shall pay aboue a third part in Indean, and it is intended that the Capten shall haue 60l. therof, for a yeare & halfe, and 40l. to Math: Gressell, and the rest for the Comittee for the Fortte.

The diuission is, for Hartford,   53. 5s.
       Wyndsor,   36. 15.
       Wethersfield, 36. 0.
       Seabrooke, 12.
       Farmington, 12.

Wheras by reson of many waighty occations, expences and chardges are yearely expended by the Go^r, It is therefore Ordered, that ther shalbe yerely alowed to that Place 30*l*. and 30*l*. to the Deputy Go^r for the year past.

Wheras yt was Ordered, that ther should be 20 men to attend the Gaurd at Wethersfield, in regard of the smale number in the Towne yt is now brought to 12 men.

* The Inventoryes of John Elsen & Abrahā Elsen are brought into the Courte.

A Caueat put in ag^t both Wills by Sam: Gardner.

The Wyddow of John Elson is alowed to administer.

Sa: Smith giueth security for the estate.

Tho: Coleman vndertaks the estate of Abraham Elson shalbe p^rsearued vntill the Court settle the administration.

---

[174]   [The date of this Court is not given.]

Ed: Hopkins Esqr.

Mr. Webster, Capten Mason, Mr. Woolcott, Mr. Welles.

The Jury: John White, Williā Lewis, Williā Wodsworth, Tho: Osmor, Tho: Coleman, Mr. Hill, John Byssell, Math: Graunt, Walter Fyler, Sa: Hales, John Demon, Phillip Groues.

In the action of Sarah Lord pl. ag^t Williā Venison* def^t, the Court adiudgeth the def^t to pay the pl. 14*s*. 10*d*. damages & costs of Court.

In the actio of Sarah Lord pl. ag^t Nath: Watson def^t, the Court adiudgeth the said Watson to pay the pl. ten bush: of Wheat & costs of Court.

John Trūble accepteth of Math: Gryssell his Oath and is content to be accoumptable to him for 20 bush: of Wheate.

Will' Colefoxe, for his misdemeanor in laboring to inuegle the affections of Write his daughter, is fyned 5*l*.

In the action of Math: Gryssell pl^t, ag^t Tho: Olcoat def^t, the Jury find for the pl^{te}, That accoumpting the former judgement

---

* The entries which follow, in relation to the estates of John and Abraham Elsen, are in a different hand writing from the rest of the page, and were probably made some weeks subsequently. The Inventory of John Elsen was taken May 16th.

* Vincent ?

graunted Mr. Olcoat to be fully satisfied, the pl. is to receaue backe 30l. of the deft, and costs of Court.

In the action of Ed: Higby pl. agt James Whatly deft, the Jury find for the defent, costs of Court.

In the ac. of Rich: Meaks pl. agt Will' Lewis deft, the Jury find for the pl. ten shillings damages & costs of Court.

The Constables are to make prsentment of the brech of any Orders.

[176]   MAY THE 18th, 1648.

Ed: Hopkins Esqr, Gour.
Roger Ludlowe Esqr, Dep.
George Fenwicke Esqr, *Magestrate;* Mr. Welles, *M: Tr[esr;]* Jo: Heynes Esqr, *M:* Mr. Webster, *M:* Cap: Mason, *M:* Mr. Woolcoate, *M:* Mr. Cullicke, *M: Secr:* Mr. Howell, *M:* Mr. Cosmore, *M:*

[*Deputyes:*] Mr. Talcoate, Mr. Westwood, Andrewe Bacon, Ed: Stebbing, Mr. Phelps, Mr. Allen, Mr. Stoughton, Jo: Byssell, Mr. Trott, Liuetenant Boosy, Sa: Smith, Nath: Dickenson, Stephen Hart, Tho: Judde, Andrew Waird, Mr. Taynter, Phillip Groues.

Whereas ther are certen farms to be sett forth vppon the borders or wthin the limitts of Fayerfield, It is Ordered, ther shalbe no further prceeding in takeing vp any grownd ther aboute vntill it be vewed by some that shalbe appoynted by such as shall keepe the next Court to be held att Fayerfield.

The motion made by Mr. Ludlowe, concerneing Moses Wheeler for the keepeing the Ferry att Stratford, is referred to such as shall keepe the next Court att Fayerfield, both in the behalfe of the Country and the Towne of Stratford.

Wheras Dauid Prouost and other Dutchmen (as the Court is informed,) haue sould powder and shotte to seuerall Indeans, against the expresse Lawes both of the Inglishe & Dutch, It is now Ordered, that if vppon examination of witnesses the said defaulte shall fully appeare, the penulty of the lawes of this Comon welth shalbe laid vppon such as shalbe found guilty of such transgression, the wch if such delinquents shall not subiect vnto they shalbe shipped for Ingland and sent to the Parlament.

It is Ordered, that Capten Mason shall goe to Long Iland and to such Indeans vppon the Mayne as are tributaryes to the Inglishe, and require the Tribuit of thē, long behind & yet vnpaid, and to take some stricte and righteous course for the speedy recouering therof ; and it is judged equall and alowed that he shall haue the on halfe for his paynes.

Mr. Wynthrope the younger is to haue Comission for to execute the place of a Magistrate at Pequoyt.

The Gouernour and Deputy are desiered to execute the place of Comissioners for this Jurisdiction wth the Vnited Collines, for the meeting in September and for on yeare, and in case ether of thē shalbe p^ruented by sicknes or otherwise, Mr. Welles is desiered to supply the place.

Hartford is to make and mayntayne the Bridge leading to Farmington, w^thin the libertyes of Hartford.

---

[177]   JUNE THE FIRST, 1648.*

Ed: Hopkins Esqr, Go^r.

Mr. Webster, Mr. Woolcoate, Mr. Welles.

The Jury : Mr. Parke, Gregory Wilterton, John Barnard, Richard Goodman, Rich: Olmstead, Mr. Pynny, Robert Wynchell, Dauid Wilton, Will' Traull, Nath: Dickenson, Rich: Smith, John Edwards.

In the action of Carpenter pl^t, agt Demon def^t, the Jury find for the pl. 4*l.* damages & costs of Court. *Execution d'd to the pl^t this* 30th *of March,* 1650.

John Byssell is bownd in a Recognizance of 10*l.* and John Bennitte of 20*l.* p^ruided that the said Bennit keepe good behauior and appeare the next Court. He promiseth to acknowledge his fault publiquely at Wyndsor.

John Moses, for miscaridges wth Dauid Wilton his daughter, fyned 20*s.*

---

* With the record of this Court, the official duties of Mr. Welles, as Secretary, terminated. The record of the following session, is in the hand writing of Mr. (afterwards Captain) John Cullick, who had been chosen Secretary in May previous, and who continued in office until 1658.

[178] Att a meeting of the Generall Courte in Hartford, this 12th day of July, 1648.

Whereas seuerall inconveniences doe appeare by reason that the seuerall souldgers of the Trained bands, in each Towne within this Jurisdiction, haue not beene allowed some powder vppon theire training dayes, for their practice & exercise in their seuerall firings: It is Ordered that theire shall bee allowed to euery souldger in the seuerall Trained Bands in each Towne as aforesaid, halfe a pound of powder a peece, for a yeare: and so from yeare to yeare, for the future: to bee prouided by and at the proper costs & chardges of the masters and gouernors of each familie vnto wch the said souldgers doe belong, to bee called forth, improued and disposed of, at the discretion of the Captaine or other principall leaders in each Trained Band.

Att a Perticular Courte houlden in Hartford, the 7th Septembr, 1648.

Magistrates: Mr. Wells, Moderator; Mr. Webster, Mr. Woollcott, Mr. Cullick.

The Jury: Mr. Henry Woollcott, *Jur:* Will: Pantry, Will: Leawis, Will: Gibbens, Rich: Buttler, John Edwards, Sam: Hale, Sam: Smith Junior, Luke Hitchcock, John More, Antho: Hawkins, Aaron Cooke; *Jur.*

George Chappell contra John Goodrich in an action of the Case. *Withdrawne.*

Jeames Wakely plt, contra Nath: Ward defendt, in an action of the Case.

Mrs. Whiting plt, contra Jonathan Brewster defendt, in an action of Debt, 33*l*. 18*s*. Damages 10*l*.

Nicho: Olmsted plt, contra John Halls senior, in an action of the Case; damages, 40*s*.

Tantom Heage, an Indian, plt, contra Jeames Northam & Robert Boltwood defendts; damages, 20*l*.

Jeames Northam plt, contra Jeruis Mudge defendt; damages, 30*l*.

Jeames Northam plt, contra Jeruis Mudge defendt, in an action of the Case; damages 30*s*.

Jeruis Mudge pl^t, contra Jeames Northam defend^t, in an action of the Case ; damages, 3*l*.

In the action of Nicho: Olmsted pl^t, contra Jo: Halls defend^t, the Jury finds for the pl^t, damages 5*s*. and costs of the Courte.

In the action of Tantom Heage, an Indian, pl^t, contra Jeames Northam and Robt: Boltwood defend^{ts}, the Jury finds for the pl^t, damages, 10*l*. and costs of the Courte.

In the action of Jeames Northam pl^t, contra Jeruis Mudge defend^t, damages 30*l*. ; the Jury finds for the pl^t, damages 3*l*. and costs of the Courte.

In the action of Jeames Northam pl^t, contra Jeruis Mudge defend^t, damages, 30*s*. ; the Jury finds for the pl^t, damages, 12*s*. 6*d*. and costs of the Courte.

In the action of Mrs. Whiting pl^t, contra Jonath: Brewster defend^t, the said Jonathan Brewster being called in Courte, or Elias Parkman his p^rtner, neither of them did appeare to answer the action, wherby his Recogniscance is forfeitt.

In the action of Jeames Wakely pl^t, contra Nath Warde defend^t, the action is deferred to the next perticular Courte, by theire joint consent.

---

[179]   ATT A GENERALL COURTE VPPON THE 14th DAY OF SEP-
TEMBER, 1648.

Magistrates: Mr. Wells, Moderato^r, by Vote.
Mr. Woolcott, Mr. Webster, Mr. Cullick.

Deputyes: Mr. Steele, Mr. Taylecoat, Mr. Allyn, Mr. Phelps, Mr. Clark, Mr. Westwood, Jo: Bissell, Andr: Bacon, Mr. Trott, Jeames Boosy.

The Courte is adiourned to the 11th day of October next, except the Gouerno^r see cause to call it sooner.

ATT A SESSION OF THE GENERALL COURTE, THIS 11th DAY OF
OCTOBER, 1648.

Mr. Hopkins Esqr, Gou^rno^r.
Mr. Ludlow Esqr, Deputy.

Mr. Wells, Mr. Webster, Mr. Cullick.

Deputyes: Mr. Phelps, Mr. Allyn, Mr. Steele, Mr. Clarke, Mr. Westwood, Jo: Bissell, Sam: Smith, Andrew Bacon.

Thomas Lord was called vppon for selling Lead to an Indian, and he is to answer the next Courte.

The Courte is adiourned to the 8th day of November next.

---

[180] ATT A PERTICULAR COURTE HOULDEN IN HARTFORD, THIS 17th DAY OF OCTOBER, 1648.

Edward Hopkins Esqr, Gou^{r}no^r.

Magistrates: Jo: Haynes Esqr, Mr. Wells, Mr. Woollcott, Mr. Webster, Mr. Cullick.

Jury: John Tailecoate, Nath: Warde, Will': Wadsworth, Andrew Bacon, Sam: Smith, Nath: Dickerson, Thomas Coleman, John Demyn, Mr. Phelps, Mr. Clarke, Mr. Allyn, John More.

Elias Partman contra Edward Lee, in an action of the Case, damages, 40*s*. Edward Lee is adiudged by the Courte to pay to Elias Partman 20*s*. for a Cannooe Edward Lee acknowledgeth hee bought of Elias.

Judgment is graunted by the Courte to Jeames Northam and Robt Boltwood against Jeruis Mudge.

John Bissell contra John Hawkes in an action of the Case, damages, 40*s*.

In the action of the Case, damages 40*s*., bet: John Bissell pl^t and John Hawkes defend^t, the Courte findeth for the defend^t, costs 3*s*.

John Bissell complaines against John Bennett, for non p^{r}formance of covenant with him.

John Drake complaines against John Bennett for saying he had intised and drawne away the affections of his daughter.

John Griffin complaines against John Bennett for slaundering and defaming of him, by charging him with giuing in to the Courte false euidence and testimonye.

John Bennett being called in Courte, S^{r}geant Fyler appeared in his behalfe, but would not answer to those things that were complained of against Bennett.

George Chappell and Mathew Williams hauing forfeited theire Recogniscance, the judgement is suspended till they shall bee found or knowne to bee at the howse of Thomas Ford or John Sadler: and the judgem^t of the Courte is, that if either George Chappell or Mathew Williams shall hereafter bee in either of the howses aforesaid, and the said Thomas Ford or John Sadler shall not make it knowne to some of the Magistrates within 24 houres after theire or either of theire being in theire howses or either of theire howses, they shall pay the Recogniscance forfeite as aforesaid.

The distribution of the estate of Thomas Dewey, of Wyndsor, deceased, was by this Courte, as follow^th :

To his Relict, 60*l*. 60. 0. 0
To his eldest Sonne by name Thomas Dewy, 30. 0. 0
And to the other fiue children 20*l*. a peece, 100. 0. 0
                                             ———
                                             190. 0. 0.

The daughters portion of 20*l*. to bee paid her at the age of 18 yeares, and the severall sonns portions to bee pd. to them at the age of 21 yeares: the Relict giving in suffitient security to the children, before her marriage againe, for theire severall portions.

---

[181] October 17th, 1648.

Jury: Mr. Phelps, Mr. Clark, Jo: Demyn, Jo: More, Srg^t Fyler, Nath: Dickerson, Tho: Coleman, Sam: Smith, John Hawkes.

In the action of Jeames [*Wakely*] pl^t contra Nath: Warde defend^t, the Jury finds for the defend^t costs of the Courte.

The Courte adiudgeth Peter Bussaker, for his fillthy and prophane expressions (viz. that hee hoped to meete some of the members of the Church in hell ere long, and hee did not question but hee should,) to bee comitt͘d to prison, there to bee kept in safe custody till the sermon, and then to stand in the time thereof in the pillory, and after sermon to bee seuerely whipt.

The Courte gaue order for an attachm^t to issue forth vpon the whole estate of Peter Bussaker, in whose hands soeuer, for the security of his creditors.

William Vincent is adiudged by the Courte to pay 2s. 6d. for neglecting his warde, and Nicho: Clarke is fyned 12d. for concealing it.

The Courte giues Mr. Cullick order to administer vppon the estate of his man Richard Sawyer deceased; there being euidence in Courte that Richard Sawyer said before his death that hee would leaue all that hee had to the dispose of his Ma^r Cullick.

John Lord, Taylor, acknowledgeth himselfe bound in a Recogniscance of 20l. to this Comon wealth, to carry good behauio^r in his course of life; and Thomas Lord his brother is his security in that behalfe.

John Betts acknowledgeth himselfe bound to this Comon wealth in a Recogniscance of 10l. to carry good behauiour in his course of life, and Nicho: Olmsted is his security in that behalfe.

[182] ATT A SESSION OF THE GENERALL COURTE THIS 8th DAY OF NOVEMB^r, 1648.

Magistrates: Jo: Haynes Esqr, *Moderator:* Mr. Woollcott, Mr. Webster, Mr. Cullick.

Deputyes: Mr. Phelps, Mr. Allin, Mr. Clarke, Mr. Steele, Andr: Bacon, Jo: Bissell.

The Courte being mett, was adiourned to the 6th day of December next.

ATT A SESSION OF THE GENERALL COURTE, THIS 6th OF DECEMB^r, 1648.

Edward Hopkins Esqr, Gou^{r}no^r.

Magistrates: Mr. Wells, Mr. Woollcott, Mr. Webster, Mr. Cullick.

Deputyes: Mr. Phelps, Mr. Clarke, Mr. Trott, Mr. Allyn,

Mr. Taylecoate, Mr. Westwood, John Bissell, Sam: Smith, Andrew Bacon, Nath: Dickerson, Jeames Boosy.

The Courte hauing taken into consideration the many occassions that are in veiw at p^rsent, and like to bee for the future, of drawing away Corne from amongst vs, out of the Riuer, or ingaging of it aforehand to those that doe carry it out from amongst vs, before the time of the payment of the Corne to Mr. George Fenwick, for the Fortt Rate, that when diuers people should pay to him, according to order, there corne is gone, wherby Mr. Fenwick hath for the time past susteined some loss, and may doe more for the future :—For the prevention whereof, it is ordered, that the Treasurer shall send out warrants seasonably to the Constables of each Towne vppon the Riuer within this Jurissdiction, for the gathering or otherwise securing of the aforesaid Corne for Mr. Fenwick, by the first of March ; that it may bee in readines, when called for, according to order and couenant, by Mr. Fenwick or his assigne ; and Mr. Wells for Wethersfeild, Mr. Webster for Hartford, and Mr. Woollcott for Wyndsor, are desired to call vppon the Constables in their seuerall Townes, for the returne of their warrants by the aforesaid first of March.

It is ordered, that there shall bee a day of Humilliation kept by all the Churches in this Jurissdiction, to seeke the face of the Lord in the behalfe of his Churches, vppon this day fortnight, wch will bee the 20th day of this instant Decemb^r.

The order concerning the price of Boards, is repealed.

The Courte is adiourned to the last Thursday in Jan^ruary next, being the 25th day thereof.

---

[183] THE PERTICULAR COURTE, THIS 7th DECEMB^r, 1648.
Edward Hopkins Esqr, Gou^rno^r.

Magistrates : Mr. Wells, Mr. Woollcott, Mr. Webster, Mr. Cullick.

Jury : Mr. Phelps, John Tailecoate, Will: Wadsworth, Andr: Bacon, Sam: Smith, Nath: Dickerson, Thomas Coleman, John Demyn, Mr. Clarke, Mr. Allyn, Will: Gibbens, John More.

The Courte adiudgeth Jeruis Mudge to pay to Jeames Northam and Robert Boltwood, for his p^{rt} of the damage they paid to Tantom Heage, if hee had 8 head of cattle trespassers, 37s. 6d. in good, dry, well-conditioned Indian Corne.

Mathius Trott acknowledgeth himselfe bound to this Common wealth in a Recogniscance of 20l. and Thomas Burnham in a Recogniscance of 10l. that hee the said Mathias Trott shall appeare at the next Perticular Courte houlden in Hartford.

It is the judgement of the Courte that John Jennings should serue Jeames Northam first, so long as hee couenanted with him, and when his time is out with Northam, that then hee should serue Stephen Harte in the next place.

The Courte frees John Betts and his security, and John Lord and his security, for theire and either of theire Recogniscances, for the good behauio^r of John Betts and John Lord aforesaid.

The Jury finds the Bill of Inditement against Mary Jonson, that by her owne confession shee is guilty of familliarity with the Deuill.

John Edmonds pl^t contra the wife of Joshuah Jennings defend^t, in an action of slaunder, damages 50l.

In the action of John Edmonds pl^t contra the wife of Joshuah Jennings defend^t, the Jury finds for the pl^t, 5l. and costs of the Courte.

John Bennett appearing to answer the compl^{ts} made against [*him*] last Courte, and expressing his repentance, and promising better carriage for the future, the Courte is willing once more to pass by his corporall punishment; and Will: Edwards acknowledgeth himselfe bound to this Common wealth in a Recogniscance of 20l. that John Bennett shall carry good behauio^r in his course of life for the space of halfe a yeare. *The perticular Courte vppon the first of March,* 1648, *frees John Bennett and William Edwards, his security, from theire Recogniscance for good behauio^r, as appeares by the Records of that Court:*

The Courte frees Henry Palmer from his Recogniscance for his wiues appearing at the last perticular Courte, to answer the compl^t of Mr. Robins: as also, remitt the miscariage of his wife therein, hoping it will bee a warning to her and others for the future.

[184] The Perticular Courte, in Hartford, this 28th day of Decemb^r, 1648.

Edward Hopkins Esqr, Gou^{r}no^r.

Magistrates: Mr. Wells, Mr. Webster, Mr. Woollcott, Mr. Cullick.

Jury: Mr. Trott, Thomas Ford, John White, Nath: Ely, Rich: Smith, Luke Hitchcock, Sam: Hale, Henry Woollcott, Humphry Pinny, Dauid Willton, Walter Fyler, Rich: Goodman.

John Willcock senior, pl^t contra Jeruis Mudge defend^t, in an action of debt, 7*l*.

Rich: Fellowes pl^t contra Will: Vincent defend^t, in an action of debt and damages, 18*s*.

Richard Fellowes pl^t contra Richard Coaker defend^t, in an action of debt and damage, 8*s*.

Jasp^r Gunn pl^t contra Nicho: Olmsted defend^t, in an action of the Case, damages 41*s*.

Beniamin Hilliar pl^t contra Thomas Edwards defend^t, in an action of Slaunder, to the damage of 40*l*.

Jeruis Mudge pl^t contra Will: Colefax defend^t, in an action of debt and damages, 16*l*.

John Cullick pl^t contra George Abbott defend^t in an action of debt & damages, 30*s*.

John Cullick pl^t contra Jeruis Mudge defend^t, in an action of debt and damages 20*s*.

Jonas Wood of Long Iland pl^t contra Thomas Newton of Fairefeild, in an action of the Case, damages 150*l*.

Thomas Newton pl^t contra Jonas Wood defend^t, in an action of the Case for breach of couenants, to the damage of 200*l*.

In the action betwene John Willcock senior pl^t contra Jeruis Mudge defend^t, the Jury findes for the pl^t, 7*l*. costs of the Courte and wittnesses.

In the action betwene Beniamin Hilliar pl^t and Thomas Edwards defend^t, the Jury findes for the defend^t, costs of witnesses.

In the action of Jeruis Mudge pl^t and Will: Colefax defend^t, the Jury finds for the pl^t, his bill, 13*l*. 16*s*., and costs of the Courte.

In the action of Jasp^r Gunn pl^t contra Nich: Olmsted defend^t, the Jury findes for the defend^t.

[185] In the first action of Jonas Wood pl^t contra Thomas Newton defend^t, the Jury findes for the pl^t, that the defend^t shall discharge or cause to bee discharged the bond that the pl^t and his frends lye under at the Monatoes, wch was to answer the defend^{ts} ingage^{mt} there, and to pay unto him 30*l*. besides, and costs of Courte.

In the action of Thomas Newton pl^t contra Jonas Wood defend^t, the Jury findes for the pl^t. The defend^t is to deliuer to the pl^t the two Cowes and the Steare, with theire increase if any, and twenty shillings in wampum, according to the bargaine, and if the said cattle cannott bee gott then the defend^t is to pay him 18*l*. and costs of Courte.

In the action of debt of John Cullick pl^t contra George Abbott defend^t, the Courte findes for the pl^t, 30*s*.

In the action of debt of Capten John Cullick pl^t ag^t Jeruis Mudgē defend^t, the Courte adiudgeth the defend^t to pay twenty shillings damadge to the pl^t, and costs of Courte.

In the action betwene Rich: Fellowes pl^t and Will: Vincent defend^t, the Courte adiudgeth the defend^t to pay to the pl^t 14*s*. 6*d*.

In the action of Rich: Fellowes pl^t contra Rich: Coaker defend^t, the defend^t not appearing to answer the action, the Courte giues order for an attachm^t to issue forth ag^t his body.

Enoch Buck of Wethersfield acknowledgeth himselfe bownd to this Comon wealth in a Recogniscance of 10*l*. to app^r at the next perticular Courte in Hartford. *Enoch Buck appearing at the Courte this first of March is freed from his Recogniscance.*

John Russell seruant to Mr. Robins, acknowledgeth himselfe bownd to this Comon wealth in a Recogniscance of 10*l*. to make his appearance at the next perticular Courte in Hartford.

Beniamin Hilliar acknowledgeth himselfe bownd in a Recogniscance of 30*l*. and Sam: Smith senio^r in a Recogniscance of 20*l*. that the said Beniamin Hilliar shall make his appearance at the next perticular Courte in Hartford & carry in the Interim good behauio^r. *He appearing at ye Covrte ye first of March, they are freed from this Recogniscance.*

Walter Leawis, seruant to M‍rs Hollister, acknowledgeth himselfe bound to this Comon wealth in a Recogniscance of 20l. and Mr. Trott in a Recogniscance of 10l. that the said Leawis shall app‍r at the next perticular Courte in Hartford & carry good behauio‍r.

John Bernard of Hartford is fyned 2s. vid. for not appearing, being called to serue vppon the Jury.

Dauid Willton of Wyndsor is fyned 2s. vid., for not appearing timely at the Courte, to serue on the Jury.

[186] Thomas Newton of Fairefeild acknowledg‍th himselfe bound to this Comon wealth in a Recogniscance of 200l. that hee will answer, truly performe and discharge the verdict of the Jury in the action betwene Jonas Wood pl‍t, and himselfe defend‍t, at or before the last day of Febr: next, and Henry Grey and John Greene, both of Fairefeild are his security in the like sum for his true performance thereof.

And Jonas Wood of Long Iland ingages his interest in the Recogniscance aboue written, that hee will truly performe and discharge the verdict of the Jury in the action betwene Thomas Newton pl‍t, and himselfe defend‍t, at or before the last day of Febr: next.

A SESSION OF THE GENERALL COURTE IN HARTFORD THIS 25th JAN‍r: 1648.

Edward Hopkins Esq‍r, Gou‍rno‍r.
John Haynes Esq‍r.
Magistrates: Mr. Wells, Mr. Woolcott, Mr. Cullick.
Deputyes: Mr. Phelps, Mr. Clark, Mr. Trott, Mr. Allyn, Sam: Smith, Nath: Dickerson, Mr. Steele, Mr. Taylecoat, Mr. Westwood, John Bissell, Jeames Boosy.

John Bissell vnd‍rtakes to keepe and carefully to attend the Ferry ouer the great Riuer at Wyndsor, for the full tearme of seuen yeares from this day, and that hee will provide a suffitient Boate for the carrying over of horse and foott vppon all occasions: And that if his owne occasions should necessitate him at any time to goe out of call from his howse or Ferry, that then hee will provide some able man in his roome to attend that seruice; for wch the said John Bissell is to haue of those that hee Ferryes ouer, eight pence for euery horse or mare, and two pence for euery person that goes ouer therewith, or that hath another passenger to goe ouer the said Ferry at the same time; and three pence for euery person that goes ouer the said Ferry alone, single, or without any more then himselfe at the same time. And the Courte prohibitts all other persons (except the inhabitants of Wyndsor, who haue libberty to carry ouer themselues or neighbo^rs in theire owne Canooes or Boates,) from carrying ouer the said Ferry any passenger or passengers, when the said John Bissell or his Assigne is present, or within call of his howse or Ferry as aforesaid, to attend that seruice. And if any person or persons as aforesaid shall at any time during the aforesaid tearme, goe ouer by Indians or Inglish that haue not Boates or Cannoes of theire owne, that they pass ouer the said Ferry in, they shall as truly pay 8d. for euery horse or mare, and 2d. for euery person, as if they went ouer with him. And the Courte allso giues the said John Bissell liberty to releiue such strangers and passengers as cannot goe to the ordinary, and to take of them convenient and reasonable recompense for the same. This was consented to by John Bissell in Courte.

It is Ordered that Thomas Stanton shall haue paid him yearely by the Country, fiue pownds for his seruice in attending the Courte, or any of the Magistrates, as occassion shall require in any of the 3 Townes, Hartford, Wyndsor and Wethersfeild, to interprett the Indian language: and hee is to bee considered over and aboue, for his extraordinary seruice out of the said Townes. This order to continue till the Courte sees cause to the contrary.

There is a rate of 125l. graunted by ye Courte, to bee deuided as followeth:

Hartford,	35l. 10. 0	Long Iland,	05. 00. 0
Wyndsor,	24. 10. 0	Fairefeild & Stratford,	20. 00. 0
Wethersfeild,	24. 00. 0		
Seabrook,	08. 00. 0		25. 00. 0
Farmington,	08. 00. 0		100. 00. 0
	100. 00. 0	Totall,	125. 00. 0

To bee p^d in 3 month.

The Court adiourned to ye 2d Lecture in Hartford, in ye month of March.

---

[187] THE PERTICULAR COURTE IN HARTFORD THIS FIRST OF MARCH, 1648.

Edward Hopkins Esqr, Gou^{r}no^r.
John Haynes Esqr.
Magistrates: Mr. Wells, Mr. Woollcott, Mr. Webster, Mr. Cullick.
Jury: Mr. Westwood, Mr. Ollcott, Tho: Osmore, Tho: Bull, Tho: Coleman, John Nott, Sam: Smith, Sam: Bourman, Steph: Terry, Arthur Williams, Antho: Hawkins, John Hawkes.

John Webb pl^t contra Ralph Keeler defend^t, in an action of slaunder, damages, 10l.

John Webb pl^t contra Ralph Keeler defend^t in an action of the Case, damages, 10l.

John Bennett pl^t contra William Edwards defend^t, in an action of the Case, damages, 15l.

In the action of slaunder betwene John Webb pl^t and Ralph Keeler defend^t, the Jury finds for the defend^t.

In the action of the case betwene John Webb pl^t and Ralph Keeler defend^t the Jury finds for the pl^t, 4s. damage, and costs of the Courte.

In the action of the case betweene John Bennett pl^t and William Edwards defend^t, the Jury finds for the pl^t, damages 55s. and costs of the Courte.

Nicho: Olmsted pl^t contra Jeames Northam defend^t, in an action of the Case, damages 25s. In the action of Nicholas Olmsted pl^t ag^t Jeames Northam defend^t, the Courte adiudgeth the pl^t to pay to the defend^t, costs 2s. vi$d$. because hee wanted witnesses to proceed in his action ag^t the defend^t.

Ralph Keeler freed John Webb in Courte from his Recogniscance to keepe the peace.

The Courte frees John Bennett and William Edwards his security, from theire Recogniscance for the said Bennetts good behauior.

Beniamin Hilliar is fined 10*l*.

Walter Leawis is fined 40*s*.

Robt Rose is fined for his misdeameano^r, 20*s*.

John Bishop is fined for his boasting of his lying and other misdemeanors, 40*s*.

Thomas Osmore, for not coming seasonably to serue on the Jury, is fined 5*s*.

Enoch Buck is fined 10*s*. for irregular speeches in Courte, ag^t Robt Rose, when hee spake vppon his oath.

Rich: Skinner pl^t contra Peter Bussaker defend^t, in an action of debt 24*s*. 5*d*.; the Courte finds the debt for the pl^t.

[188] Mathias Trott, for making composition about a seruant of Mr. Chesthers and concealing it when it was done, is adiudged by the Courte to pay to Mrs. Chesther, from the time that hee did compound for him, wch they conceiue was about the first of March, to the time that Mr. Chesther sent againe for him, being about the latter end September, in all about 7 months time, 3*s*. p^r weeke.

Wallter Leawis acknowledgeth himselfe bound to this Comon wealth in a Recogniscance of 20*l*. and Mr. Trott in a Recogniscance of 10*l*. that the said Walter Leawis shall carry good behauior and appeare at the perticular Court in June next.

Samuell Comstock acknowledgeth himselfe bound to this Comon wealth in a Recogniscance of 10*l*. and Bray Rosseter in a Recogniscance of 20*l*. that the said Samuell Comstock shall carry good behauior for the space of ten dayes, and then the said Bray Rossiter shall either bring him the said Samuell Comstock to prison and leaue him in chardge with the keeper thereof, or bring him to Mr. Woollcott with such security as hee shall accept for his good behauior for longer time, and for his satisfying what damage Mr. Robins shall susteine for the want of his seruant.

Beniamin Hilliar acknowledgeth himselfe bound to this Comon wealth in a Recogniscance of 20*l*. and Thomas Wright in a Recogniscance of 10*l*. that Beniamin Hilliar shall pay his fyne of 10*l*. when it is required, and carry good behauio^r for the space of one whole yeare.

John Bishop acknowledgeth himselfe bound to this Comon wealth in a Recogniscance of 20*l*. and John Halls Junio^r in a

Recogniscance of 10*l*., that if notice bee giuen to John Halls betwene this and the first Thursday of June next, the said John Bishop shall appeare then to answere the complaint of the Indians against him.

William Comstock acknowledgeth himselfe bound to this Comon wealth in a Recogniscance of 10*l*. and Mr. Trott and Samuell Smith Junior in a Recogniscance of 5*l*. a peece that the said William Comstock shall appeare at the perticular Courte, vppon the first Thursday in June next, and carry good behavio^r in the meane time.

Georg Phillips of Wyndsor, by reason of seuerall weaknesses that for the present attend him, is freed from watching till the Courte sees cause to the contrary.

---

[189] A Session of the Generall Courte in Hartford, this 14th March, 1648.

Edward Hopkins Esqr, Gou^rno^r.
John Haynes Esqr,
Magistrates: Mr. Wells, Mr. Woollcott, Mr. Webster, Mr. Cullick.
Deputyes: Mr. Phelps, Mr. Clark, Mr. Trott, Mr. Allyn, Mr. Steele, Mr. Tailecoat, Mr. Westwood, Jeames Boosy, Sam: Smith, Nath: Dickerson, Andr: Bacon, John Bissell.

The Court desires Mr. Wells and Mr. Cullick to draw vp in writing the whole agreement with Mr. Fenwick, and Mr. Hopkins, about Seabrooke, and that the counterpart thereof vnder Mr. Hopkins his hand, may bee kept and recorded by the Secretary of the Courte.* Also, it is ordered that the Constables in each Towne shall each of them take a receipt vnder Mr Hopkinses hand for so much as is allready paid him, and so euery yeare for such sums as they shall hereafter pay him, in reference to the aforesaid agreement: and shall make returne thereof euery yeare to the Secretary of the Courte, who is to keepe and record the same, for theire security.

---

* See p. 119. [135.]   The agreement was not recorded until 1654.   [Vol. ii. pp. 59–63.]

Mr. John Wenthrop of Pequet was voted to bee in nomination for election to the place of a magistrate.

Whereas by the 6th Article in the Combination of the Vnited Colonyes, in cases proper to the Comissioners, if six agree not, the propositions with the reasons is to bee referred to the foure Generall Courts, and by theire joint agreement to bee determined, It was now recommended by the Commissioners to the seuerall Generall Courts, that if any three of the said Generall Courts agree and conclude any such proposition, it might pass and bee accounted as the conclusion of the vnited Colonyes, as it should haue passed as an Act of the Comisioners if six of them had consented ; wch being duely considered, it was consented to and ratified by the Courte, prouided the Generall Courts of the other Colonyes doe the like.

It was further, vppon the recomendation of the Comissioners, ordered by this Courte, that no peage, white or black, bee paid or receiued, but what is strung, and in some measure strung sutably, and not small and great, vncomely and disorderly mixt, as formerly it hath beene.*

Whereas allso, It was recomended by the Comissioners, that for the more free and speedy passage of justice in each Jurissdiction to all the confederates, if the last will and testament of any person bee duely prooued in, and duely certefied from any one of the Colonyes, it bee without delay accepted and allowed in the rest of the Colonyes, vnless some just exception bee made against such will or the proouing of it, wch exception to bee forthwith duely certefied back to the Colony where the said will was prooued, that some just course may bee taken to gather in and dispose the estate without delay or damage. And allso, that if any knowne planters or setled inhabitants dye intestate, administration bee graunted by that colony vnto wch the de-

---

"Vppon the motion of Mr. Dunster, President of the Colledge at Cambridge, consideracon was had about paym'ts made and received in peage, whether white or black. The Comissioners were informed that the Indyans abuse the English with much badd, false and unfinished peage, and that the English Traders, after it comes to their hands, choose out whatt fitts their m'rketts and occasions, and leaue the refuse to pass to and fro in their Colonies: wch the Indyans, whoe best understand the quality and defects of peague will not willingly take back. Whereupon, (though they see not at present how to propound a full reformacon in all p'rticulars, w'thout much difficulty and inconvenience, yet) they commend it to the severall Generall Courts and to the Plantacons within the Vnited Colonies, that noe peague, white or black, be payd or received, but what is strung," &c. (Records of U. Colonies, Sept. 1648.)

ceased belong, though dying in another colony : and the administration being duely certefied, to bee of force for gathering in of the estate in the rest of the colonyes, as in the case of wills prooued where no just exception is returned. But if any person possessed of an estate, who is neither planter nor setled inhabitant in any of the Colonyes, dye intestate, the administration (if just cause bee found to giue administration) bee graunted by that Colony where the person shall dye and dep^{rt} this life, and that care bee taken by that Gouernm^t to gather in and secure the estate vntill it bee demaunded, and may bee deliuered according to rules of justice :—wch vppon due consideration was confirmed by this Courte, in the behalfe of this Colony, and ordered to bee attended in all such occasions for the future ; prouided the Generall Courts of the other Colonyes yeild the like assent therevnto.

(Court dissolued.)

[190] A Perticular Courte, in Hartford, 24th Aprill, 1649.

Edw: Hopkins Esqr, Gou^{r}no^r.

John Haynes Esqr.

Magistrates : Mr. Wells, Mr. Webster, Mr. Woollcott, Mr. Cullick.

Jury : Thomas Forde, Joseph Mygatt, George Steele, John Marsh, Sam̃: Martyn, John Lattimore. Sam̃: Hale, Tho: Parkes, Robt Winchill, Rich: Birge, John Loomis, Thomas Orton.

William Hurlebutt pl^t contra Jeames Wakely def^t, in an action of the Case, dammages 39s.

Sammuell Steele pl^t contra John Steele defend^t, in an action of debt, 28s., dammages 6s.

Jeames Northam pl^t contra George Chappell defend^t, in an action of the Case.

John Steele pl^t ag^t Nathaniell Kellock defend^t, in an action of debt and dammages, 39s.

John Willcock pl^t contra Jeames Wakely defend^t, in an action of the Case, dammages, 6s.

John Willcock senior pl^t contra Jeames Wakely defend^t, in an action of the Case, dammages 25s.

Mathew Marven pl{^t} contra Mathew Beckwith defend{^t}, in an action of defamation, damages 50*l*.

Richard Fellowes pl{^t} contra William Hill defen{^t}, in an action of debt and damages, 39*s*.

William Bartlitt and Edward Higbye being called in this Courte to appeare vppon theire Recogniscances, and not ansering therevnto, haue both of them forfeited the same.

In the action of the Case betweene William Hurlebutt pl{^t} and Jeames Wakely defend{^t}, the pl{^t} falling shorte of his wittnes, is to loos his sute.

In the action of debt betweene Samuel Steele pl{^t} and John Steele defend{^t}, the Courte findes for the pl{^t}, 34*s*.

In the action of the Case betweene Jeames Northam pl{^t} and George Chappell defend{^t}, the defend{^t} not appearing to answer the pl{^t}, the Courte orders an attachm{^t} to issue forth vppon his two calues in the hands of the plaintiff, for his security vntill the defend{^t} shall answer his sute.

In the action betweene John Steele pl{^t} and Nathaniell Kellock defend{^t}, the Courte adiudgeth those of Farmington that haue not yet paide the pl{^t} theire proportion for the drum hee sould them, to pay double theire proportion, if they doe not satisfie the pl{^t} for the same according to covenant, before the next Courte.

[191] In the action of the Case betweene John Willcock pl{^t} and Jeames Wakely defend{^t}, the Courte adiudgeth the defend{^t} to pay vnto the pl{^t}, 4*s*. 4*d*.

In the action betweene John Willcock, senior, pl{^t} and Jeames Wakely defend{^t}, the defend{^t} hauing satisfied the debt allready, the Courte adiudgeth him to pay the pl{^t}, 16*d*. costs.

In the action of defamation betweene Mathew Marven pl{^t} and Mathew Beckwith defend{^t}, the defend{^t} making his publick penitent confession of his euill in slaundering the said pl{^t}, was remitted by the Courte and pl{^t}.

In the action betweene Richard Fellows pl{^t} and William Hill defend{^t}, the defend{^t} not appearing, the Courte adiudgeth him to pay the pl{^t} the debt and costs 16*d*.

Mr. Newton prooued in Courte that Peter Bussaker owes him the just and full sum of - - - 2*l*. 5*s*. 0.
    Joseph Mygatt, Ditto, - - 0. 9. 0.
    Thomas Forde, Ditto, - - 3. 0. 2.

Rich: Billing,	Ditto, - -	0. 17. 0.
John Cullick,	Ditto, - -	0. 10. 6.
Mr. Wells,	- - -	0. 13. 0.

John Nott, for resisting Nathaniell Dickerson when hee came with a warrant to distreine, was fined - - 50s.

   John Kerby, for the like, is fined - - - 20s.

   Robt Slye, for exchanging a gunn with an Indian, is fined 10l.

   Georg: Hubberd, for ye same, is fined, - - 10l.

   John West, for the same, is fined - - 10l.

   Peter Blatchford, for ye same, is fined - - 10l.

Nicholas Clarke ingages himselfe to deliuer vp his man Vincent vnto the Courte, when his time is out with him, wch he saith will be about Miheltide next.

The Courte and Mr. Robins frees Samuell Comstock and Bray Rosseter from both and either of theire Recogniscances in Courte vppon the first of March, 1648.

Peter Blatchford made oath in Courte, that at the latt^r end of the last yeare, hee deliuered aboard of Chichesters vessell to Mr. Blackleach, by ye order of Jaruis Mudge, for the acco^t of Rich: Belden, six bush: of wheat and three of pease.

Thomas Bunce acknowledgeth himselfe bound to this Common wealth, in a Recogniscance of 5l. provided hee appeare at the perticular Courte vppon the first Thursday of June next, and carry good behauior in the meane time.

---

[195]   A P<small>ERTICULAR</small> C<small>OURTE IN</small> H<small>ARTFORD</small>, <small>THE</small> 16th <small>DAY OF</small>
<small>MAY</small>, 1649.

Edward Hopkins Esqr.

John Haynes Esqr.

Magistrates: Mr. Wells, Mr. Webster, Mr. Woollcott, Mr. Cullick.

Jury: Grego: Willterton, Nath: Ely, John Bissell, Thomas Standly, Thomas Standish, Sam: Smith Junior, John Rose, John Rily, John Drake, Humphry Pinny, Thomas Gunn, Peter Tillton.

John Bissell pl^t contra Jeames Egleston defend^t, in an action of the case, dammages 39s.

Mr. Ollcott pl^t contra Thomas Edwards defend^t, in an action of debt and dammages, 39s. 6d.

Richard Fellows pl^t contra Stephen Beckwith defend^t, in an action of debt and dammages, 30s.

William Frauncklyn pl^t contra Thomas Barber defend^t, in an action of debt and dammages, 6l.

William Frauncklyn pl^t contra Beniamin Nuberry defend^t, in an action of debt and dammages 45l. The pl^t is non-suited and to allow 13s. 4d. costs.

Beniamin Nuberry pl^t contra William Frauncklyn defend^t, in an action of slaunder, to the dammage of 10l.

Nehemiah Olmsted pl^t contra Richard Lyon defend^t, in an action of the case, to the dammage of 12l.

Mr. Ollcott pl^t contra Sammuell Gardiner defend^t, in an action of debt and dammages, 12l.

Bray Rosseter pl^t contra Mr. Henry Woollcott senior, defend^t, in the behalfe of the creditors of Thomas Marshfeild, in an action of trespass, to the dammage of 12l.

William Leawis pl^t contra Thomas Dement defend^t, in an action of slaunder, to the dammage of 50l.

William Leawis pl^t contra Thomas Dement defend^t, in an action of the case, to the dammage of 3l.

Thomas Dement pl^t contra William Leawis defend^t, in an action of slaunder, to the dammag of 51l.

Thomas Dement pl^t contra William Leawis defend^t, in an action of the case, dammages 10s.

Gregory Willterton, Nathaniell Ely, Arthur Smith, are each of them fined 5s. a peece for not appearing seasonably to serue vppon the Jury.

[196] In the action betweene John Bissell pl^t contra Jeames Egleston defend^t, the Courte findes for the defend^t.

In the action betweene Mr. Ollcott pl^t and Thomas Edwards defend^t, the Courte adiudgeth the defend^t to pay to the pl^t 40s.

In the action of Richard Fellows pl^t ag^t Stephen Beckwith defend^t, the defend^t not appearing in Courte to answer his summons, The Courte hath ordered an attachm^t to issue forth vppon his person to answer the pl^t, the next Courte.

In the action of William Frauncklyn pl^t ag^t Thomas Barber defend^t, the Jury findes for the pl^t, 4l. 2s. 6d. to bee pd. in wheat at 4s. p^r bush:, and costs of the Courte, wch the Courte adiudgeth 20s.

In the action betweene Beniamin Nuberry pl^t and William Frauncklyn defend^t, the Jury findes for the pl^t, dammages 2d. and costs of the Courte, wch the Courte adiudgeth to bee 10s.

In the action between Nehemiah Olmsted pl^t and Richard Lyon defend^t, the Jury finds for the pl^t, dammages 11l. and costs of the Courte.

In the action betweene Mr. Ollcott pl^t and Samuell Gardiner defend^t, the Jury findes for the pl^t, his debt of 7l. 11s. 8d. damages 30s. and costs of the Courte.

In the action betweene Bray Rosseter pl^t and Mr. Henry Woollcott defend^t, the Jury findes for the pl^t, damages 3l. 12s. and costs of the Courte.

Thomas Barber testified this day in Courte, vppon oath, that hee being in William Frauncklyns howse last Septemb^r, and the said Frauncklyn speaking to him of Mr. Nuberry's debt, hee tould the deponent that hee had left that debt with Thomas Forde, to doe in it with Nuberry as hee saw cause.

Robert Hayward allso testified this day in Courte vppon oath, that hee being occassionally in William Frauncklyns howse, the said Frauncklyn tould him that hee had left the debt wch Beniamin Nuberry owed him, with Thomas Forde.

Mr. Wells made it appeare in Courte that Peter Bussaker is indebted to him 13s.

[197] William Bartlitt not appearing in Courte, being called, hath forfeited his Recogniscance of 20l. and Edward Higbye, his security, for not bringing him in, hath forfeited his Recogniscance of 10l.

Gouert Locman not appearing in Courte, being called, hath forfeited his Recogniscance of 200l. Sterling ; And Cornelius Vantino and Gisberd Vandict, his security, for not bringing in the said Gouert Lockman, haue forfeited theire Recogniscance of 200l.

William Clarke, being called in this Courte to appeare vppon his Recogniscance of 10l. and not answering therevnto, hath forfeited the same.

[192] At a meeting of the Freemen of the Jurissdiction of Connecticutt, for the choyce of Magistrates, the 17th of May, 1649.

Magistrates:
John Haynes Esqr, is chosen Gou^rno^r.
Edward Hopkins Esqr, Deputy Gou^rno^r.
Rog^r Ludlow Esqr, *Magistrate.* Mr. Webster, *Magist^r.*
Mr. Wells, *Magist^r and Treas-* Mr. Cullick, *Magist^r and Sec^r.*
    urer. Mr. Howell, *Magist^r.*
Mr. Woollcott, *Magist^r.* Mr. Cossmore, *Magist^r.*
Capt. Mason, *Magist^r.*

Deputyes: Mr. Taylecoate, Mr. Steele, Mr. Phelps, Mr. Allyn, Mr. Gayler, Mr. Clarke, Mr. Trott, Edward Stebbing, Andrew Bacon, Jeames Boosy, Nath: Dickerson, Sam: Smith senior, Danyell Tuterton, John Hurd, Mr. George Hull, Mr. Andrew Ward, Steph:Harte, Thomas Judd, John Clarke, Mathew Grisswold.

Cary Lathum being to appeare this day at this Courte vppon his Recogniscance, and the Courte being certefied from Mr. Wenthrope of the said Lathums p^rsent inabillity to trauell, they doe respitt the forfeit of his said Recogniscance, provided hee appeare at the Courte heere vppon the first Wednesday of July next.

Isaac Wylly and Cary Lathum are to bee warned to the Courte the first Thursday in June, for resisting the Constable : and allso Robert Beadle and the aforesaid Cary, for letting an Indian goe that was committed to theire charge.

Vppon the desire of the inhabitants of Pequet, for theire incouragement it is Graunted by this Courte, that they shall bee freed from all publick Country charges, (except such as are occassioned by themselues,) for the space of three yeares next ensuing :

It is allso Graunted, that the bounds of the plantation of Pequett shall be foure myles on each side the Riuer, and six myles from the sea northward into the Country, till the Courte shall see cause and haue incouragement to add therevnto, provided they interteine none amongst them as inhabitants that shall bee obnoxious to this Jurissdiction, and that the aforesaid bounds bee not distributed to less than forty familyes :

And for the setling of some way for the deciding of small differences amongst them, vnder the value of forty shillings, It is ordered by this Courte, that Capt. Mason shall haue power to giue the oath of magistracy to John Wenthrope Esqr, for the [193] yeare ensueing, ‖ and vntill a new bee chosen, whoe shall haue power (taking vnto himselfe Thomas Mynott* and Samuell Lathrop, as Assistants,) to heare and determine the same; prouided if any bee greiued, they shall haue libberty to appeale to the Courte at Connecticutt, if they haue just cause so to doe:

And the Courte will indeauo^r to take order with Vncus, that no trapps shall bee sett by him or any of his men, within the bounds of theire Towne: But to prohibitt and restraine Vncus and his men from hunting and fishing within theire limmitts, they doe not yett see cause to doe; For no Indians are depriued of that libberty in any of o^r Townes, provided they doe it not vppon the Sabath day:

This Courte allso taking into consideration theire proposition for the restraining of others from trading Corne with the Indians within theire Riuer, They doe declare that they cannott restraine any therfrom whoe liue in and are members of any of the Vnited Colonyes; and for others, It is vnder the p^{r}sent consideration of the Commissioners:

The Courte commends the name of Faire Harbour to them, for to bee the name of theire Towne.

Whereas, It is now come to the certeine intelligence of this Courte, that one Hallitt, with one that was Mr. Pheax his wife, are now come into, and liues in the Plantation of Pequett, and (as is conceiued) hath committed in other places, and so liues at this present, in that fowle sin of adultery, wch is odious to God and man, and therfore this Courte cannott but take notice of it; It is therfore ordered, that there bee a warrant directed to the Constable of the same Towne, to ap^{r}hend the said partyes, and to bring them vpp to the next perticular Courte in Hartford, wch will bee vppon the first Thursday of the next month; and the Gouerno^r is desired to write to Mr. Wenthrope and acquaint him with it.

As allso that a like warrant shall bee directed to the Constable

---

* An error of the original record. The name should be *Mynor* or *Miner*.

there for the aprehending and bringing vpp to the next perticular Courte, Mary Barnes of theire Towne.

Thomas Mynott is appointed by this Courte to bee a military Sergeant in the Towne of Pequett, and doe inuest him with power to call forth and traine the souldgers of that Towne, according to order of Courte.

[194] This Courte, taking into consideration the proposition of the Towne of Fairefeild, about a percell of land bought by them of the Indians, that it mighte bee settled vppon them for theire inlargement, doe desire and appointe Danyell Titterton and John Hurd of Stratford to suruey and veiw the said percell of land, and consider therevpon how convenient it is for them and inconvenient for this Comon wealth, to haue the said premisses setled vppon the said Towne of Fairefeild, and make returne thereof to the next Session of this Generall Courte, that they may the better know what is to bee done therein.

The Deputy Gouernor and Mr. Wells are desired to execute the place of Commissioners for this Jurissdiction with the Vnited Colonyes, at theire meeting in July next, and for the yeare ensuing.

William Leawis and Isaack More are presented for Sergeants, by the Deputyes of Farmington, as chosen by the souldgers : and are approued by the Courte : and are to call forth and traine the souldgers at the dayes appoynted.

It is ordered, that there shall bee a dwelling howse erected at Seabrooke, about the middle of the new Forte Hill, at the charge and for the seruice of this Common wealth. And Capt. Mason, Mr. Taylecoate and Jeames Boosy are desired to take care about it, and to see the thinge effected, according to theire best discretion.

The Courte declares that the twenty pound that is now required of the Townes of Fairefeild and Strattford, is in full of all accounts for theire proporcon of country charges to this time.

Concerning Mr. Blackmans meintenance, Mr. Ludlowe is desired (both for what is behinde, as allso for the future,) to take care that it bee leuied, according to the seuerall seasons, as is provided by the order of the Country.

It was reported by the Comittee appointed for the laying out of the lands vppon the Riuer, according to agreement with Mr. Fenwicke, that those of Seabrooke shall runn, in theire deuision of land on the east side the Riuer, from the Riuer eastward, fiue myles; and northward vpp the Riuer, on the east side, six myles: And on the west side the Riuer, northward eight myles.

The Court is adiorned to the first Wednesday in June next.

A Session of the Generall Courte in Hartford, the 6th of June, 1649.

John Haynes Esqr, Gou^rno^r.
Edward Hopkins Esqr, Deputy.
Magistrates: Mr. Wells, Mr. Woollcott, Mr. Webster, Mr. Cullick.
Deputyes: Mr. Phelps, Mr. Gaylerd, Mr. Steele, Mr. Trott, Mr. Clarke, Mr. Taylecoate, Mr. Allyn, Edward Stebbing, Jeames Boosy, Sam: Smith, Andrew Bacon, Nath: Dickerson, Steph: Harte, Thomas Judd.

This Courte being informed (by the Committee appointed to take care about the erecting of a dwelling howse at Seabrooke, aboute the middle of the new Forte Hill, at the charge and for the seruice of this Common wealth,) that there is a want of the hands and abillityes of men of seuerall trades, and labourers, for the carrying on and effecting of the premisses in any reasonable time, doe order that it shall bee lawfull for any Magistrate within and of this Jurisdiction, to send out warrants for the pressing and compelling of such men to worke vppon the premisses, as they shall bee informed to bee fittest and most able to carry on the worke till the same bee effected and compleated, for such wages as the said Magistrate that giues his warrants shall judge meete, any order formerly provided for the regulating of mens wages to the contrary notwithstanding.

For the better preseruing corne and meadow on the east side of the great Riuer; It is ordered by this Courte, that there shall no hoggs or swyne of any sorte bee put ouer thither, or kept there, at any time after the publishing of this order, except they bee kept out of the bounds of the seuerall Townes, or in theire yards, vnder the penalty of two shillings a head for euery hogg or swyne, for euery time they shall bee found there contrary to this Order.

The Courte appoints Thomas Hollibutt of Wethersfeild, Clarke of the Trained Band of that Towne.

[198] Vppon reading the Acts of the Commissioners for the vnited Colonyes at the meeting held at Plymouth the last seuenth month, It was obserued that in the agitacon of the difference betwixt the Massachusetts Colony and this, in reference to the imposition required from Springfeild, vppon some goods passing out at the mouth of this Riuer, towards the charge expended at Seabrooke, tending to the good of all the plantacons vppon the Riuer, It was questioned by the Commissioners of the Massachusetts whether there were any order of this Courte extant, for the payment of any imposition by goods ap^{r}taininge to the inhabitants of Springfeild, brought from thence and so passing downe this Riuer. The Courte doth declare that by express order, of the 5th Feb^r, 1645, all corne laden aboard any vessell vppon this Riuer and passing out to sea at the Riuers mouth, was to pay two pence p^r bush : in the forementioned respects ; and Beauer twenty shillings p^r hogshead ; wherein as Springfeild was intentionally included, so this Courte had due respect therevnto as then considered vnder the Massachusetts Gouernement, that no greater burthen mighte fall vppon those inhabitants then according to cleare grounds of equity and righteousnes, in theire best aprehensions, they ought readily to submitt vnto, and was equall for them to beare ; and no more then they should haue expected to bee imposed vppon themselues in the like case ; which order hath beene since confirmed, and a penalty of confiscation of such goods annexed in case of non-payment : the execution whereof in reference to our brethren of Springfeild, hath only beene deferred vntill the judgement of the Commissioners of the other Collonyes mighte bee vnderstood in the premisses, according to the Articles of Confœderation, wherin provision is made for deciding of any differences that might fall in betwixt any of the Colonyes ; wherevnto they referred themselues in this case, allthough they are yet alltogether vnsatisfied that Springfeild doth properly fall in within the true limmitts of the Massachusetts Pattent, wch they much

desire may with all convenient speed bee clearly issued in a way of loue and peace, and according to truth.

This was voted to bee recorded and sent to the next meeting of the Comissioners, as the Act of this Courte.

---

[199] A PERTICULAR COURTE IN HARTFORD 7th JUNE, 1649.

John Haynes Esqr, Gou^{r}no^r.

Edward Hopkins Esqr, Deputy.

Magistrates : Mr. Welles, Mr. Woollcott, Mr. Webster, Mr. Cullick.

Jury : Sam: Smith, Nath: Dickerson, William Wadsworth, John Crow, John Bernard, Thomas Selden, Antho: Hawkins, William Heydon, Danyell Clarke, George Phelps, Josias Churchell, John Goodrich.

Thomas Newton pl^t contra John Capell, in an action of debt 8*l.* and dammages, 4*l.*

Henry Grey pl^t contra Jonas Wood defend^t, in an action of defamation, to the dammage of 50*l.*

William Edwards pl^t contra Richard Samwis and Stephen Tayler, in an action of the case, damages, 10*l.*

William Edwards pl^t contra John Bennett defend^t, in an action of slander, to the dammage of 5*l.*

William Leawis pl^t contra Thomas [*Dement*] defend^t, in an action of slaunder, to the dammage of 50*l.*

In the action betweene Thomas Newton pl^t and John Capell defend^t, the Jury findes for the pl^t, debt, 8*l.* and 2*d.*, and dammages 40*s.* and costs of Courte. *Execution graunted and deliuered the* 21th *of May*, 1650.

In the action betweene Henry Grey pl^t and Jonas Wood defend^t, the Jury findes for the pl^t dammages, 3*l.*

In the action betweene William Edwards pl^t and Richard Samwais and Stephen Tayler, defend^{ts}, the Jury findes for the pl^t 5*l.* 5*s.* and costs of the Courte. *Execution deliuered to him the* 7th *of Novemb^r*, 1649.

In the action of slaunder betweene William Edwards pl^t and John Bennett defend^t, the Jury findes for the defend^t, and costs of the Courte.

In the action of slaunder betweene William Leawis pl^t and Thomas Dement defend^t, the Jury findes for the defend^t, and costs of the Courte.

William Edwards is fyned, for drawing wine contrary to order of Courte, 30s.

The Courte graunts execution to John Bennett ag^t William Edwards, according to the verdict of the Jury at the Courte houlden the first of March, 1648–9.

The Courte graunts execution to William Francklyn ag^t Thomas Barber, according to the verdict of the Jury at the Courte houlden the 16th day of May, 1649.

The same is graunted to Beniamin Nuberry ag^t Francklyn.

[200] Samuell Pond complaines ag^t Jonas Westouer for misdeameanor.

Jonas Westouer acknowledgeth himselfe bound to this Commonwealth, in a Recogniscance of 20l. and John Bissell and Robert Haward in a Recogniscance of 10l. a peece, provided the said Westouer appeares at the perticular Courte in Septemb^r next and carry good behauio^r in the meane time.

The Courte appoints Mr. Webster to goe to Stratford to assist Mr. Ludlow at the perticular Courte there, next Thursday come fortnight, in the execution of justice.

William Comstock, Mr. Trott and Sam: Smith Junior, are either of them freed from theire and either of theire Recogniscances for the said Comstocks appearing at this Courte.

Walter Leawis and Mr. Trott his security are freed from either of theire Recogniscances, for the said Walter his appearing at this Courte.

This day there was presented to this Courte the last will and testament of John Porter, late of Wyndsor, deceased, and the Inuentory of his estate.

Cary Lathum, of Pequett, acknowledgeth himselfe bound to this Common wealth, in a Recogniscance of 40l. provided hee appeare at any place within this Jurisdiction haueing reasonable warning soe to doe, at any time within this six months, and carry good behauior in the meane while.

William Bartlett acknowledgeth himselfe bound to this Common wealth, in a Recogniscance of 20l. and Cary Lathum, in a Recogniscance of 20l. that the said William Bartlitt shall appeare at the perticular Courte vppon the first Thursday in September next, and carry good behauior in the meane while.

Jonas Woods bond to the Dutch, hee deliuered into this Courte, wᶜʰ was cancelled by order thereof, and the Secr. appointed to certefie the same vnder his hand.

Jonas Wood complaining to this Courte that by reason of Thomas Newtons failing to performe the verdict of the Jury, according to agreement at the Courte in Hartford, vppon the 28ᵗʰ of Decembʳ, 1648, hee was forced, to his great loss and dammage, to satisfie his bond at the Monatoes himselfe; This Courte adiudgeth to bee due to the said Jonas Wood from the said Thomas Newton, according to the aforesaid verdict and dammages,—

For his bond at the Dutch, being 400 Gilders,   38*l*. 00. 0.
For so much the Jury adiudged Newton to
   pay him more then the bond,   .   .   30. 00. 0.
For the charge & dammage about it,   .   .   10. 00. 0.
                                                 ─────────
                                                 78. 00. 0.

out of wᶜʰ the Courte discounts the 18*l*. wᶜʰ Wood was to pay Newton, by the verdict of the Jury, vppon an action of Newtons agᵗ Wood, the same day: so there remaines to Wood sixty pounds. Execution graunted.

---

[201]   A Perticular Courte in Hartford, the 6ᵗʰ of Septembʳ, 1649.

John Haynes Esqʳ, Gouernoʳ.
Edward Hopkins Esqʳ, Deputy.
Magistrates: Mr. Wells, Mr. Woollcott, Mr. Webster, Mr. Cullick.
Jury: Mr. Westwood, John White, Nathaniell Ely, George Graue, John Lattimore, John Rily, Thomas Hollibutt, Luke Hitchcock, Will: Gayler Junior, Will: Phelps Junior, Walter Fyler, Robert Haward.

Thomas Osmore plᵗ contra William Cornewell defendᵗ, in an action of the case, to the damage of 4*l*.

Richard Buttler plᵗ contra William Cross defendᵗ, in an action of the case, to the damage of 6*l*.

Mrs. Chester pl^t contra Wallter Leawis defend^t, in an action of defamation, dammages, 10*l*.

Sam: Gardiner pl^t, for himselfe, Thomas Edwards and the Widdow Louenam, contra Thomas Osmore defend^t, in an action of Trespass, to the dammage of 4*l*.

Mathias Trott pl^t contra John Coleman defend^t, in an action of slaunder, to the dammage of 50*l*.

Mr. Henry Woollcott, senior, pl^t contra Bray Rossiter defend^t, in an action of the case, to the damage of 12*l*.

John Bissell pl^t contra Richard Fellows defend^t, in an action of the case, to the dammage of 40*s*.

Owyn Tuder pl^t contra William Edwards defend^t, in an action of debt, to the value of 20*l*.

Corbitt Piddell pl^t contra Thomas Stanton defend^t, in an action of the case, concerning two cures, to the dammage of 6*l*.

Jeames Wakely pl^t contra Thomas Skidmore and Edward Higby defend^ts, in an action of slaunder, to the dammage of 20*l*.

Thomas Stanton pl^t, contra Joane Sipperance, in an action of slaunder, to the vtter vndoinge of his wiues good name and allmost taking away her life, to the dammage of 200*l*.

Joshuah Jennings, for not watching one night, and other ill carriages to the Constable, is to pay for the watchman in his roome, and is fyned, 2*s*. vi*d*.

Jeames Wakely, for some defects in wattching, is fined 2*s*. vi*d*.

Henry Coale, for sleeping in ye time of his watch, is fyned 10*s*.

Nathaniell Barding, for the same, is fined 10*s*.

Timothy Mercer, of Wyndsor, is fined, for a pound breach, 40*s*.

[202] In the action betwene Thomas Osmore pl^t contra William Cornewell defend^t, the Jury findes for the pl^t, debt 20*s*. damages 13*s*. 4*d*. and costs of the Courte.

In the action betwene Richard Buttler pl^t and William Cross defend^t, the Jury findes for the pl^t, 4*l*. 5*s*. in wampum, and costs of the Courte. *Execution d'd to ye pl^t, ye 15th of May,* 1650.

In the action betwene Mrs. Chesther pl^t and Wallter Leawis is defend^t the Jury finds for the pl^t, 20*s*. and costs of ye Courte.

In the action betwene Sammuell Gardiner pl^t and Thomas

Osmore defend[t], the Jury findes for the pl[t], 20 bush: of Indian corne, two bush: of Indian Beanes, and costs of y[e] Courte. *Execution d'd* 14[*th*] *of May,* 1650.

In the action betweene Mathias Trott pl[t] and John Coltman defend[t], the Jury findes for the pl[t], 30s. and costs of y[e] Courte.

In the action betweene Mr. Woollcott pl[t] and Bray Rossiter defend[t], the Jury findes for the defend[t], costs of the Courte.

In the action betweene John Bissell pl[t] and Richard Fellows defend[t], the Jury finds for the defend[t], costs of the Courte.

In the action betweene Owyn Tuder pl[t] and William Edwards defend[t], the Jury findes for the pl[t], 15 barrills of Tarr and 4*l.* 10*s.* and costs of the Courte. Execution granted, to issue forth within 14 dayes.

In the action betweene Corbitt Piddell pl[t] and Thomas Stanton defend[t], the Jury findes for the pl[t], 20*s.* and costs of the Courte. Execution graunted to bee p[r]sent.

In the action betweene Jeames Wakely pl[t] and Thomas Sckidmore and Edward Higby defend[ts], the Jury findes for the pl[t], damages 2*d.* and costs of the Courte, w[ch] the Courte allowes to bee 9*s.* 8*d.*

In the action betweene Thomas Stanton pl[t] and Joane Sibperance defen[t], the Jury findes for the pl[t], 30*s.* and costs of the Courte.

The Courte appointes the eldest Sergeant of the Trained Band at Wethersfeild, to call forth and exercise the same according to order of Courte, for the present, and that they should make choyce of one amongst them for theire Leiftenant, and p[r]sent him to the Courte.

[203]   Mrs. Chesther complaines against George Chappell and Goody Coleman and Danyell Turner, for misdeameano[rs].

Danyell Turner, for libelling against Mrs. Chesther and for other misdemeano[rs], is committed to prison, and is to bee brought forth and whipt next Lecture day, and then to goe to prison againe for a month from this time, and then publickly corrected againe, and giue good security for his good behauior.

Thomas Willkenson, for disorderly carriage in the meetinghowse, vppon the Saboath day, is to bee committed to prison till the Courte sees cause to free him.

Thomas Rushmore, for the same crime, is committed allso with the former.

This Courte frees Jonas Westouer and his security from theire and either of theire Recogniscances, for Westouers appearance and good behauio^r.

Thomas Burnham acknowledgeth himselfe bound to this Comwealth in a Recogniscance of 10*l.* that Rushmore, his man, shall appeare at the next perticular Courte, and carry good behauio^r in the meane time.

Gregory Gibbs acknowledgeth himselfe bound to this Com̃on wealth in a Recogniscance of 20*l.* and Thomas Parkes in a Recogniscance of 10*l.* that the said Gibbs shall carry good behauio^r for the space of halfe a yeare next ensuing.

The Judgment of the Courte is that Walter Leawis should giue Mrs. Hollister good security to the value of 30*l.* before hee goes from her, that what dammage shee shall susteine for want of his seruice shall bee made good and paid to her, if hee doth not make it appeare in a reasonable time, that hee is not bound to serue her any longer then vntill this time.

William Bartlitt of Pequett is freed from traineing, by reason of his lamenes, prouided hee notwithstanding meinteine his armes as complete and able for seruice as they should bee if hee did traine.

---

[204] A GENERALL COURTE IN HARTFORD, THE 13th OF SEPTEMBER, 1649.

John Haynes Esqr, Gou^rno^r.

Edward Hopkins Esqr, Deputy.

Magistrates: Roger Ludlow Esqr, Mr. Wells, Mr. Woollcott, Mr. Webster, Mr. Cullick.

Deputyes: Mr. Taylecoate, Mr. Steele, Mr. Trott, Mr. Allyn, Mr. Phelps, Mr. Gayler, Mr. Clarke, Mr. Warde, Andrew Bacon, Edward Stebbing, Sam: Smith, Nath: Dickerson, John Demon, Thomas Staples, *absent,* Steph: Harte, Will: Beardsly, *absent,* Thomas Sherratt, *absent.*

This Courte frees John Rockwell senior and John Styles

senior, from watching and training, and Mr. Brancker from watching and wardinge and traininge.

This Courte taking into consideracon the many dangers that the familyes of Thomas Holcombe, Edward Grisswold, John Bartlitt, Francis Grisswold and George Grisswold, all of Wyndsor, are in and exposed vnto, by reason of their remoate liuing from neighbors and nearenes to the Indians, in case they should all leaue theire families together without any guard; doth free one souldger of the foremenconed families from training vppon euery training day; each family aforesaid to share herein according to the number of souldgers that are in them: provided that man wch tarryes at home stands about the aforesaid howses vppon his sentinell posture.

It is ordered by this Courte, that whosoeuer shall take out any warrant from the Secretary thereof, that concernes an action, shall, before hee hath a warrant, enter his action with the Secretary and then take out his warrant for summons to answer the same, for wch they shall pay for euery entry twelue pence, and for euery warrant foure pence, though they agree with their defend^{ts} before the Courte. Allso, if any other magistrate shall graunt a warrant that concernes an action, they shall enter the action in a small booke for that purpose before they graunt the warrant, and shall make a due returne at euery Courte to the Secretary thereof, what such warrants, and to whome, they haue graunted. And all such persons shall bee as lyable to pay twelve pence for euery such action, to the Secretary of the Courte, as if they should haue had theire warrants of him.

It is allso ordered, that whosoeuer shall enter into any Recogniscance in Courte, shall pay to the Secretary of the said Courte for euery entry, six pence; and before hee withdrawes it or bee freed from it, shall pay him for the withdrawing of it, twelue pence.

Whereas by reason that the order about watching hath not beene rightly vnderstood, many differences and inconveniences haue beene occasioned, For preuenting thereof, this Courte doth explaine themselues and order; that whosoeuer within this Jurissdiction that are lyable to watch, shall take a journey out of the Towne wherein hee liueth, after hee hath had timely notice and warning to watch, hee shall provide a watchman for that turne, though himselfe bee absent. And if any man that takes a journey, or goes out of the Towne wherein he liueth, if hee returnes home within a weeke after the watch is past his howse hee shall bee called back to watch that turne past a weeke before.

[205] Jespar Gunn, of Hartford, is freed from watching during the time that hee attends the seruice of the mill.

This Courte, taking into serious consideracõn what may bee done according to God in way of reuenge of the bloude of John Whittmore, late of Stanford, and well weighing all circumstances, together with the carriages of the Indians (bordering therevppon,) in and about the premisses: doe declare themselues that they doe judge it lawfull and according to God to make warr vppon them.

This Courte desires Mr. Deputy, Mr. Ludlow and Mr. Taylecoate to ride to morrow to New Hauen, and conferr with Mr. Eaton and the rest of the Magistrates there aboute sending out against the Indians, and to make returne of their apprehensions with what convenient speed they may.

The Courte is adiourned to next Tuesday at noone.

A SESSION OF THE GENERALL COURTE IN HARTFORD, THE 18th SEPTEMBER, 1649.

Whereas the French, Dutch and other forraigne nations doe ordinarily trade gunns, powder, shott etc. with the Indians, to oʳ great preiudice, and the strengthening and animating of the Indians against vs, as by dayly experience wee finde; and whereas the aforesaid French, Dutch etc. doe prohibitt all trade with the Indians within theire respectiue Jurissdictions, vnder penaltye of confisscation; It is therfore hereby ordered, that after due publication hereof, it shall not bee lawfull for any Frenchman, Dutchman or person of any other forraigne nation, or any English liuing amongste them or under the gouernment of them or any of them, to trade with any Indian or Indians within the limmitts of this Jurissdiction, either directly or indirectly, by themselues or others, vnder penalty of confisscation of all such goods and vessells as shall bee found so trading, or the due value thereof, vppon just proofe of any goods or any vessells so trading or traded : And it shall bee lawfull for any person or persons inhabiting within this Jurissdiction to make seizure of any such goods or vesells trading with the Indians as by this law is prohibited ; the one halfe whereof shall bee to the proper vse and benefitt of the partye seizing, and the other to the publick :

This order, vppon the recomendation of the Comissioners to the Generall Courtes of the seuerall Jurissdictions was confirmed by this Courte.

[206]   The distribution of the souldgers that shall issue forth of each towne, is as followth :

Hartford,	13
Wyndsor,	11
Wethersfeild,	08
Fairefeild & Stratford,	13
	45.

The Comittee chosen by the Courte for the ordering of the setting forth of theise souldgers for ammunition and provision, are as followth :—

Magistrates.   Mr. Haynes, Mr. Hopkins, so farr as his buisines shall p^{r}mitt, Mr. Wells, Mr. Webster.

Deputys.   Mr. Allyn, Mr. Taylecoate, Sam: Smith senio^r.

Mr. Ludlow was desired to take care for preparing the souldgers with provisions and all other necessaryes for the designe in the two   * Townes : and Mr. Hull and William Beardsley are chosen to assist therein.

In the case of Thomas Newton pl^t against John Cabell defend^t the execution of the judgement is to bee suspended vntill the Courte of Election in May, to wch Courte the defend^t doth appeale, and the pl^t is to haue notice to appeare at the said Courte to answer the appeale.

Gouert Lockman appeared at this Courte and desired an issue might bee put to his buisines : hee was tould that notwithstanding the forfeit of his bond, yet if hee could make it appear that hee was hindred by a hand of God, and that there was not a willing neglect of his owne, his case should bee taken

---

* A blank in the original. The words omitted were probably ' sea side'.

into due consideration; wherevnto hee said little, onely professed his innocency in not selling any powder or shott to Indians, but onely the quantity of a pound wch hee once gaue to a Sachem. Hee was allso tould that if hee would enter into a bond to a double valew of what his last was, payable by him in case euident proofe were produced, and that vppon Christian testimonye, (wch hee called for,) that hee is vnder greater guilt then hee yett will acknowledge, by that mischieuous trade, the former ingagement should bee remitted; wch hee refusing, the Courte further propounded to him either to pay the whole forfeiture or to enter into bond to appeare at the Courte in May to answer the charge against him, and to submitt to what shall bee found uppon tryall by suffitient testimonye, and hauing so done, the halfe of the forfeiture should bee remitted him. The said Gouert not attending the propositions made by the Courte, but after the adiournement thereof, applying himselfe to the Gouerno^r for an issue, hee condisscended by way of agreement to pay one hundred pounds, provided hee might not bee ingaged to abide the tryall of the case; wch was accepted by the Gouerno^r, and the said sum̃ receiued.

The Courte is adiourned to the 10th day of the next month.

---

[207] A SESSION OF THE GENERALL COURTE IN HARTFORD, THE 10th OF OCTOBER, 1649.

John Haynes Esqr, Gouerno^r.
Edward Hopkins Esqr, Deputy.
Magistrates: Mr. Wells, Mr. Webster, Mr. Woollcott, Mr. Cullick.
Deputyes: Mr. Phelps, Mr. Trott, Mr. Clarke, Mr. Allyn, Mr. Taylecoate, Mr. Steele, Edward Stebbing, Sam: Smith, Nath: Dickerson, Steph: Harte, John Demon, Andrew Bacon.

It is ordered by this Courte, that the 100*l.* wch is receiued of Gouert Lockman, shall bee sequestred and reserued for the perfecting of the Forte and worke about the same, so farr as it will goe, and that none of it shall [be] expended vppon any other country or common respect.

Mr. Hopkins, Capt: Mason, Mr. Cullick, Mr. Allyn and Mr. Taylecoate are desired to prosecute with effect the worke that is still to bee done aboute the Forte and dwelling howse to bee erected for the vse and seruice of the Country, according to former order of Courte.

It is ordered that Thomas Stanton shall bee allowed and paide fiue pounds for the seruice hee did in interpreting the Indians language the yeare before the last order for his receiuing the like yearely recompence for the future.

The Courte is adiourned to this day month.

A Session of the Generall Courte, this 7th of Novemb^r, 1649.

John Haynes Esqr, Gouerno^r.
Edward Hopkins Esqr, Deputy.
Magistrates: Mr. Wells, Mr. Woolcott, Mr. Webster, Mr. Cullick.
Deputyes: Mr. Phelps, Mr. Trott, Mr. Clarke, Mr. Gayler, Mr. Allyn, Mr. Taylecoate, Edward Stebbing, Sam: Smith, Andrew Bacon, Nath: Dickerson, John Dement.

It is ordered that a warrant shall issue forth to the Constable of Pequet, to repaire forthwith to Chessbrooke of Long Iland, and to let him vnderstand that the Gouernm^t of Connecticutt doth disslike and distaste the way hee is in and trade hee doth drive amonge the Indians : And that they doe require him to desiste therfrom immediately : And that hee should repaire to Capt. Mason of Seabrooke, or some other of the Magistrates vppon the Riuer, to giue an account to him or them of what hee hath done hitherto.

It is further ordered, that East Hampton, of Long Iland, shall bee accepted and interteined vnder this Gouernment according to their importunate desire.

This Courte graunts Sam: Smith and the rest of the owners of the shipp at Wethersfeild, libberty to get and make so many pipestaues as will freight out the said shipp the first voyage, provided they doe it out of the bounds of any of the Townes vppon the Riuer, within this Jurisdiction.

The Courte is adiourned to this day month.

[208]   A Session of the Generall Courte in Hartford, the 5th of December, 1649.

John Haynes Esqr, Gou^rno^r.
Edward Hopkins, Esqr, Deputy.
Magistrates : Mr. Woollcott, Mr. Webster, Mr. Cullick.
Deputyes : Mr. Phelps, Mr. Allyn, Mr. Trott, Mr. Steele, Mr. Clarke, Sam: Smith, Nath: Dickerson, Andrew Bacon, Edward Stebbing, John Dement, Steph: Harte.

There being a petition presented to this Courte, by some of inhabitants of Stratford, complaining against theire way of rating, the Secretary of the Courte is appointed to write to the Constable of Stratford that hee should acquaint the Towne of Stratford with the same, and that the Courte requires the Towne to take order that either theire Deputyes or some others may come prepared to the next Courte of Election in May, to speake to that case.

It is ordered by this Courte, that there shall bee a publick day of Thanksgiving kept by all the Churches within this Jurissdiction that may bee seasonably acquainted therewith, vppon this day fortnight.

The Courte is adiourned to the first Wednesday in February next.

---

[209]   A Perticular Courte in Hartford, the 6th of Decemb^r, 1649.

John Haynes Esqr, Gou^rno^r.
Edward Hopkins Esqr, Deputy.
Magistrates : Mr. Wells, Mr. Woolcott, Mr. Webster, Mr. Cullick.
Jury : William Gibbens, Nath: Dickerson, John Bissell, Sam: Bourman, Sam: Smith, Dauid Willton, Luke Hitchcock, William Wadsworth, Thomas Bull, Thomas Bunce, John More, Antho: Hawkins.

Thomas Burneham pl^t contra John Bennett defend^t, in an action of debt, to the value of 3*l.* 10*s.*

John Sadler pl^t contra John Bennett defend^t, in an action of debt and damages 50*s.*

William Colefax pl^t contra John Sadler defend^t, in an action of the case, to the damage of 4*l.*

William Houghton pl^t contra Jeruis Mudge defend^t, in an action of debt to the value of 6*l*. 10*s*.

John Hudshon pl^t as attorney to Sampson Shorye contra Will: Williams, in an action of debt and dammages 8*l*.

Jeames Wakely pl^t as attorney to Stephen Day contra Thomas Sckidmore defend^t, in an action of debt and dammages, 17*l*. 10*s*.

Thomas Demon pl^t contra Sammuell Martyn defend^t, in an action of the case to the damage of 10*l*.

Jeruis Mudge pl^t contra Edmund Scott defend^t, in an action of the case to the damage of 39*s*.

Richard Samwis pl^t contra Thomas Barly defend, in an action of debt to the value of 5*l*. The defend^t appears not: And the pl^t did not prooue that the warrant was serued.

Sammuell Gardiner and Thomas Edwards pl^ts contra Beniamin Hilliard in an action of the case to the dammage of 3*l*. 10*s*. The defend^t not appearing, the Courte graunts an attachm^t.

John Sable pl^t contra Jeruis Mudge defend^t, in an action of debt to the value of 44*s*. dammages 15*s*. The defend^t is to put in security to answer the pl^t, next Courte.

This Courte doth sequester the howse, homelott and meadow of the relict of Abraham Elsing, now the wife of Jaruis Mudge, wch is mentioned and valued in the Inuentory of Abraham Elsing's estate at 40*l*. 8*s*., for the vse and benefitt of the two daughters of the said Abraham Elsing; and the whole rent of the aforesaid premisses shall bee reserued for the vse of the said children, from this present yeare vntill the Rent of the said land shall make vpp the said 40*l*. 8*s*. to bee two thirds of the sum of the whole estate that the said Inuentory doth ammount vnto.

[210] In the action betweene Thomas Burnham pl^t, and John Bennett defend^t, the Jury findes for the pl^t, debt and damage 1*l*. 18*s*. 2*d*. and costs of the Courte.

In the action betweene John Sadler pl^t and John Bennett defend^t, the Jury findes for the pl^t, debt and dammages, 1*l*. 11*s*. 3*d*. and costs of the Courte. *Execution deliuered to the Marshall, the* 10th *January,* 1649.

In the action betweene William Colefax pl^t and John Sadler defend^t, the Jury finds for the pl^t, dammages 10*s*. and costs of the Courte.

In the action betweene William Houghton pl^t and Jaruis Mudge defend^t, the Courte grauntes the pl^t right to the cowe wch the defend^t had formerly sould him, in satisfaction for the debt.

In the action betweene John Hudshon pl^t and William Williams defend^t, the Jury findes for the pl^t, debt and damages 8*l*. and costs of the Courte. *Execution graunted in* 14 *dayes, and deliuered, the* 8th *Jan^r*, (49.)

In the action betweene Jeames Wakly pl^t and Thomas Sckidmore defend^t, the Jury findes for the pl^t, debt and dammages, 15*l*. 10*s*. and costs of the Courte. *Execution graunted the* 7th *of March* (49.) *and deliuered the* 8th *day of ye same month.*

In the action betweene Jaruis Mudge pl^t and Edmund Scott defend^t, the Court adiudges the defend^t to pay the pl^t 10*s*.

In the action betweene Thomas Demon pl^t and Samuell Martyn defend^t, the Jury findes for the pl^t, debt and damages 41*s*. and costs of the Courte. Execution graunted in a week.

Grego: Gibbs and his security are freed from theire and either of theire Recogniscances for the said Gibbs his appearance at this Courte and good behauior.

John Jennings, for his filthy and prophane speeches and carriages, is adiudged to lye in prison till next Thursday morning after the Catechising, and then to bee publickly whipt, and so returne to prison againe for a month after that, except hee finde bayle to appeare when hee is called for againe to receiue second correction, wch the Courte appoints and thinkes meete to bee next Thursday come month, excepte the Gouerno^r judges the weather vnseasonable.

Joane Sipperance is adiudged to pay double for the lace shee stole, and three fold for the time she absented herselfe from her ma^rs seruice.

S^rgeant Barber, for his disorderly striking Leiftennant Cooke, is adiudged to lay downe his place, and is fined to the Country, 5*l*.

Richard Webb is fined for not appearing at this Courte seasonably to serue on the Jury, 2*s*. vi*d*.

[*Note*. Here terminate the Court Records, contained in Volume I. The remainder of the volume consists of records of Wills and Inventories, and of conveyances of land and lay-outs of grants to individual proprietors. Volume II. contains only the proceedings of the General Court,—and from the period at which it commences, to June, 1663, the Records of the Particular Court, or Court of Magistrates, (including the Probate Records,) have been lost.]

[VOLUME II.]

A SESSION OF THE GENERALL COURTE, 6th OF FEBr, 1649.
John Haynes Esqr, Gournor.
Edw: Hopkins Esqr, Deputy.
Magistrates : Mr. Wells, Mr. Woollcott, Mr. Webster, Mr. Cullick.
Deputyes ; Mr. Phelps, Mr. Clarke, Mr. Allyn, Mr. Steele, Mr. Taylecoat, Sam: Smith, Nath: Dickerson, John Deming, Edw: Stebbing, Andr: Bacon.

It is ordered by this Courte that Nehemiah Olmsted bring in to the Secretary a receipt vnder Mr. Hop[kins] his hand, in full for this yeares payment of that [ ] proportion laid vppon Farmington in reference to the composition for Seabrooke by the first of the next month, and if hee failes so to doe, Mr. Treasurer is desired to send the marshall to distreine the said Olmsted.

The same is to bee done for Jonathan Gillett and Tho: Buckland of Wyndsor, for the yeare 1647.

And for the yeare 1648, Will: Phelps and Will: Hey[ton] of Wyndsor are required to doe the same with the former, or else pay it themselues.

The same allso is to bee done by John Hawkes and Tho: Orton of Wyndsor, for the yeare 1649.

This Courte appointes Sam: Bourman of Wethersfeild, to bee the Towne sealer of all measures and weights in that Towne, according to order of Courte.

It is ordered by this Courte, that Will: Rescew shall bee allowed and paid out of the publique Treasury, ten pounds a yeare during the time hee keepeth the charge of the house of correction.

This Courte, taking into consideraĉon the petition of Tho: Staunton presented to them, haue graunted to him and doe order, that hee shall haue libberty to erect a trading howse at Pawcatuck, with six acres of planting ground, and libberty of feed and mowing, according to his present occasions : and that none within this Jurisdiction shall trade within that Riuer for the space of three yeares next ensuing; provided hee submitt himselfe to such other exceptions and cautions as the Gouerno[r] and Deputy shall judge meett.

The Courte is adiourned to the 20th of next March.

---

[2] A Session of the Generall Courte, this 20th of march, 1649-50.

[John] Haynes Esq[r], Gouerno[r].
[Edw:] Hopkins Esq[r], Deputy.
Magistrates: Mr. Wells, Mr. Woollcott, Mr. Webster, Mr. Cullick.
Deputyes: Mr. Phelps, Mr. Taylecoat, Mr. Trott, Mr. Clarke, Mr. Allyn, Sam: Smith, Nath: Dickerson, Andr: Bacon, John Deming, Edw: Stebbing.

Robert Haward, miller of Wyndsor, is freed from seruing vppon Juryes during his attendance vppon the mill.

The order about the wages of men and cattle is repealed. Allso, the order about the prises of all corne is repealed; whereby all persons are left at libberty to make theire bargaines for corne, provided where no price is agreed betwixt persons, corne shall bee payable according to the former order, that is to say, wheat at 4*s*., pease at 3*s*., rye at 3*s*. and Indian at 2*s*. vi*d*. p[r] bush :

The answer of the Courte to the petitioners in Saybrooke is to bee recorded : and the Comittee appointed to attend further what they shall desire, is as follow[th]:—The Gou[r]no[r], Mr. Wells, Mr. Webster, Mr. Steele, Mr. Allyn and Sam̃: Smith, and such other as they shall see cause to call to them : The answer follow[th] :—

The petition from the Inhabitants of Saybrook, presented by Mathew Grisswold and Tho: Leppingwell, being read and considered, the Secretary was directed to returne the ensuing answer :

Though the Courte yett see not any convincing strength of argument in the reasons alleadged to induce either an allteracõn in theire judgement touching the equity of what is imposed, or a necessity of leauing the determinaçon thereof to others, (the purchase or agreement mentioned not being carried on wholy without the knowledge or consent of the Inhabitants there, vnles the end be severed from the meanes, wch prudence forbids, the interests of that place as really concerned therein as the other plantaçons, and in some respects more, the pretence of this Courts passing sentence in theire owne case, excluding all the inhabitants of the Riuer from a capabillity of acting therein, and vppon the same ground making all Courts vncapeable in many cases of determining by themselues what may concerne theire peace and comforts, without a forraigne assistonce,—the vncomelines, yea, and vnreasonableness whereof is easily obvious,)—yet this Courte, for the further satisfaction of the petitioners are content to giue them full libberty to present in writing any arguments or reasons they haue to lead theire judgements in the present case, wch shall bee taken into due and serious consideraçon, and either owned in theire strength, (if they appeare convincing,) or a returne made therevnto in [3] writing, if the validity bee dissatisfactory; ‖ wherein the Courte shall not deny them any libb[erty they] desire of taking in the aprehensions of others, (not [   ] concerned in the case,) for theire owne reliefe and [satis]faction : being no wayes vnwilling theire actions should bee brought to the light and judged by it, but ever re[sol]ued to give due respect to any beame thereof that [may] bee presented by any, when it shines in its beauty : But in the meane time they advise the petitioners to adress themselues to a ready observaçon of what is imposed, vntill the Courte see cause to make another judgement in the case.

This Courte adds to the Committee chosen to prosecute the worke about a dwelling howse at Seabrooke, at the Courte vppon the 10th of October, 1649, Stephen Post and Thomas Traisy, of Seabrooke :—

And Sammuell Smith senior, of Wethersfeild, to the Comittee about the lands at Mattabeseck, in the roome of Jeames Boosy.

This Courte appoints that next Wednesday come seuen-night shall bee kept a publique day of humilliation throughout all the plantaçons in this Jurissdiction, to seeke the face of the Lord.

Mr. Clarke, of Wyndsor, is propounded by the Deputyes of that Towne to bee in nomination for a Magistrate, at the next Courte of Election.

The Courte is dissolued.

---

[4] A GENERALL COURTE OF ELECTION, THE 16th OF MAY, 1650.

Edward Hopkins Esqr, Gouerno^r.
John Haynes Esqr, Deputy.
Roger Ludlow Esq., *Mag.*   Mr. Cullick, *Mag. & Sec^r.*
Mr. Wells, *Mag. & Treasurer.*   Mr. Clarke, *Mag.*
Capt. John Mason, *Mag.*   Mr. Howell,   } chosen
Mr. Webster, *Mag.*   Mr. Cossmore, } *Magist^r.*
Mr. Woollcott, *Mag.*

Deputyes: Mr. Trott, Mr. Hull, Mr. Gaylerd, Mr. Steele, Mr. Taylecoate, Mr. Allyn, Mr. Hollister, Mr. Warde, Nath: Dickerson, John Bissell, Andr: Bacon, Edw: Stebbing, Dauid Willton, John Deming, Will: Beardsly, Tho: Sherratt, Steph: Harte, Tho: Tomson, Tho: Birchard, *absent*, Nath: Griswold, *absent*.

This day there were made Freemen of this Jurisdiction,
John Wenthrope Esqr, Mr. Jonathan Brewster, Mr. John Russell, John Pantry, Natha: Cooke.

It is ordered by this Courte that no Forreigner, after the 29th of September next, shall retaile any goods, by themselues, in any place within this Jurissdiction: nor shall any Inhabitant retaile any goods wch belong to any Forreigner, for the space of one whole yeare after the said 29th of September next, vppon penalty of confiscation of the value of the one halfe of the goods so retailed, to bee paid by the seller of them.

The Courte is adiourned till Munday next.

The p^{r}sentments of the Grand Jury vnto this Courte are vppon the fyle: wch were fyned by the perticular Courte vppon the 20th of Feb^r, 1650, as appeares by the Records of that Courte.

[5]   A SESSION OF THE GENERALL COURTE, THE 21th OF MAY, 1650.

Edw: Hopkins Esqr, Gouerno^r.
John Haynes Esqr, Deputy,
Magistrates :   Roger Ludlow Esqr, Mr. Wells, Mr. Webster, Mr. Woollcott, Mr. Cullick, Mr. Clarke.
Deputyes :   Mr: Taylecoat, Mr. Steele, Mr. Warde, Edw: Stebbing, Mr. Hollister, Andr: Bacon, Nath: Dickerson, Will: Beardssly, Tho: Sherratt, John Dement, Steph: Harte, Tho: Tomson.

This Courte takinge into serious consideracon, the losse of time that the souldgers pressed vppon the last expedition against the Indians, might sustaine by theire depending therevpon, doe allowe to the common souldgers 6s. 8d. a peece, and the sergeants 10s. a peece.

This Courte graunts execution to Newton against John Cable, according to the judgm^t entred the 7th of June, 1649.

This Courte, considering the Returne of Danyell Titterton and John Hurd, about a percell of land lying neare the Towne of Fairefeild, according to theire order from the Generall Courte of Election, in May, 1649, doe graunt vnto the said Towne of Fairefeild the said percell of land to Sagatuck Riuer : provided the said Sagatuck doe not exceed two myles from the bounds of the said Fairefeild.

Whereas, a thousand acres of ground at Pequett were formerly graunted to Capt: Mason, as a gratuity for his good service at the Pequett warr ; fiue hundred whereof hee gaue to fiue of his well deserving souldgers, wch now the plantation of Pequett hath taken vp at the graunt of the Courte ; this Courte judgeth it meete that those fiue souldgers should bee rationally recompensed and satisfied for the same, either at Niantecutt (if the Courte shall not finde it deepely inconvenient to the Common wealth or the Plantacon of Pequett,) or else in some other place or way.

This Courte vppon request made, adds to the bounds of the plantation of Pequett, two myles from the Sea northward, vppon the same tearmes and cautions that theire former bounds were graunted. And to theire proposition for a further addition of meadow, wch they desire may bee at Niantecutt, this Courte declares that when the said Niantecutt is veiwed, and it doth appeare to the Courte that they may be accommodated there, [6] according to theire desire, ‖ and yet this Common wealth suted allso (as was suggested by some interested in the said Towne of Pequett,) they shall attend theire reasonable satisfaction therein.

Will: Rescews bill of charges for Elizabeth Johnsons imprisonment to the first Thursday of the next month, being 24 weekes, amounting to 6*l*. 10*s*. is allowed and approued: and the Courte desires Mr. Ludlow and Mr. Warde to see the bill discharged to the said Will: Rescew out of her estate.

Whereas Mr. Jonathan Brewster hath set vp a trading howse at Mohigen, this Courte declares that they cannott but judge the thinge very disorderly, neuertheless considering his condition, they are content hee should proceed therein for the present, and till they see cause to the contrary.

This Courte desires the Gouerno^r and deputy to execute the place of Comissioners for this Jurissdiction, with the vnited Colonyes, for the meeting in Septemb^r next and for the yeare ensuing.

This Courte graunts to Capt: John Mason fifty acres of ground neare a brooke, about foure or six myles on this side Mohegin, wch is in consideracōn for the land they graunted him at Pequett vppon the conquest.

Henry Grey is fyned twenty shillings for abusing the Courte.

This day 3 weekes is appointed for a day of Thanksgiuing publicquely, in all the Churches within this Jurissdiction.

The Courte is adiourned till this day 5 weekes.

---

[7] A SESSION OF THE GENERALL COURTE, THE 26th JUNE, 1650.

Edw: Hopkins Esqr, Gouerno^r.
John Haynes Esqr, Deputy.
Magistrates : Mr. Wells, Mr. Webster, Mr. Woollcott, Mr. Cullick, Mr. Clarke.

Deputyes: Mr. Steele, Mr. Taylecoat, Mr. Allyn, John Bissell, Edw: Stebbing, Andr: Bacon, Nath: Dickerson, Dauid Willton, John Deming, Steph: Harte, Tho: Tomson.

John Taylecoat Junior, being presented as chosen En[signe] to the Trained Band in Hartford, this Courte approues and confirmes the said choyce.

Natha: Ely and Richard Olmsted in the behalfe of themselues and other Inhabitants of Hartford, desired the leaue and approbation of the Courte for planting of Norwaake, to whome an answer was returned in substance as followeth :—

That the Courte could not but, in the generall, approue of the indeauo^{rs} of men for the further improuement of the wildernes, by the beginning and carrying on of new plantacõns in an orderly way; and leauing the consideracõn of the just grounds of the proceedings of the petitioners to its propper place, did manifest theire willingness to promoate theire designe by all due incouragem^t, in case theire way for such an vndertaking were found cleare and good : and prouided the numbers and quality of those that ingage therein appeare to bee such as may rationally carry on the worke to the advantage of the publique wellfare and peace; that they make preparations and provisions for theire owne defence and safety, that the country may not be exposed to vnnecessary trouble and danger in these hazardous times ; that the devisions of the lands there to such as shall inhabitt, bee made by just rules and with the aprobacõn of a Comittee appointed for that end by this Courte, or to bee rectified by the Courte in case of aberrations, and that they attend a due payment of theire proportions in all publique charges, with a ready observation of the other wholsome orders of the Country.

The Courte is adiourned till this day month.

---

[8] A GENERALL COURTE IN HARTFORD, THE 12th OF SEPTEMB^r, 1650.

Edw: Hopkins Esqr, Gouerno^r.

Magistrates: Mr. Wells, Mr. Webster, Capt: Mason, Mr. Woollcott, Mr. Cullick, Mr. Clarke.

Deputyes: Mr. Brewster, Mr. Phelps, Mr. Taylecoat, Mr. Allyn, Mr. Steele, Edw: Stebbing, Andr: Bacon, John Bissell, Dauid Willton, Tho: Mynor, Steph: Harte, Nath: Dickerson, Sam: Smith, Mr. Warde, Tho: Judd, Tho: Staples.

Mathew Allyn, appealing to this Courte for justice in reference to the 3 first verdicts of the Jury at the perticular Courte, the 5th day of this instant September, the contents of wch verdicts may and doth fully appeare in the Records of that Courte; They haue taken them perticularly into theire serious consideracon, and therefore haue concluded and determined as followth:—

First, that they see no just cause to varye from or allter the first verdict of the Jury, and therefore doe allowe and confirme the same, namely, that Thomas Allyn should haue his speciallties of Mathew Allyn, with 10s. damage and costs of the Courte:

For the 2d, wch was for vniust molestation and the damage therevpon, wch the Jury found to bee sixty pounds, this Courte declares that they doe judge that Thomas Allyn was vniustly molested by Mathew Allyn, but cannott judge the dammage to bee so great as the Jury did finde, and therefore doe declare and determine that the dammage should bee brought downe to twenty marke and costs of Courte:

For the 3d, wch was for expences about cattle, this Courte approoues of the verdict of the Jury therevpon, wch is that the said Mathew Allyn shall pay vnto the said Thomas, forty fiue pounds and costs of Courte:

And this Courte doth further conclude, adiudge and determine, that Mathew Allyn shall pay vnto his brother Thomas, the full sum of fiue pounds over and aboue what was determined by the severall verdicts of the Jury, wch fiue pounds is for the said Thomas his charges of trauells.

This Courte desires Mr. Gouernor, Mr. Deputy and Mr. Webster to consider of the graunt of land to Thomas Bull and others, and to settle somthing vppon them according to the graunt of the Courte in May last.

Mr. Gayler and John Bissell are chosen by this Courte to

arbitrate in a difference betweene Mr. Richard Collecott and Mr. Mathew Allyn, and to put an issue therevnto.

The Courte is adiourned to next Wednesday come 3 weekes.

---

[9] A Session of the Generall Court, the 9th of October, 1650.

Edward Hopkins Esqr, Gouerno^r.
Magistrates : Mr. Woollcott, Mr. Cullick, Mr. Webster, Mr. Clarke.
Deputyes : Mr. Trott, Mr. Allyn, Mr. Phelps, Mr. Steele, Sam: Smith, Natha: Dickerson, John Bissell, Edw: Stebbing, Andr: Bacon, Dauid Willton, Steph: Harte.

It is ordered by this Courte that the Guards in the [seue]rall Townes within this Jurissdiction, shall bee allowed yearely, halfe a pound of powder a man, to bee prouided by and at the charge of theire seuerall Townes.

The Courte appoints next Wednesday 3 weekes to bee kept a publique day of Thanksgiuing.

The Courte is adiourned till next Wednesday come fortnighte.

A Session of the Generall Courte, the 31st of Octob^r, 1650.

Edw: Hopkins Esqr, Gouerno^r.
John Haynes Esqr, Deputy.
Magistrates : Mr. Wells, Mr. Webster, Mr. Woolcott, Mr. Cullick, Mr. Clarke.
Deputyes : Mr. Phelps, Mr. Allyn, Mr. Steele, Mr. Trott, Natha: Dickerson, Dauid Willton, Sam: Smith, Edw: Stebbing, Andr: Bacon, Tho: Coleman, Tho: Judd.

Thomas Standly, of Hartford, complaining to this Courte of a dissabillity in one of his armes, (wch was broken not long since,) to handle his Armes and to doe his postures in millitary discipline, vppon training days; this Courte frees the said Thomas Standly from his training, till they shall see just cause to allter the same.

The Courte is adiourned till next Munday.

[10]   A Session of the Generall Courte, the 3ᵈ of November, 1650.

Edw: Hopkins Esqʳ, Gouernoʳ.
John Haynes Esqʳ, Deputy.
Magistrates: Mr. Wells, Mr. Woollcott, Mr. Webster, Mr. Cullick, Mr. Clarke.
Deputyes: Mr. Phelps, Mr. Allyn, Mr. Steele, Mr. Taylecoat, Edw: Stebbing, Andr: Bacon, Tho: Coleman, Tho: Judd.

Greenfill Lerreby, for his dissorderly carriage, is fyned fiue pounds,—5*l*.

Stephen Danyell is fyned for the same, forty shillings,—40*s*.

And both of them are required if Joshuah Jennings (whome they rescued or at least conueyed from the power of authority,) come aboard their shipp againe, either vppon the Riuer or at Seabrooke, to deliuer him vp to authority.

It is ordered and concluded, that whereas the Towne of Fairefeild hath not attended this Courte with a just and perfect list of the estate of theire Towne according to order of Courte, as they were inioyned, and required to doe, they shall pay to the Common wealth twenty nobles as a fyne for theire neglect if not contempt therein: and to pay to the Country, by rate for this yeare, according to the estate they formerly gaue in. *The fyne of twenty nobles is remitted, as appeares by the Records of the Courte,* 15ᵗʰ *May,* 1651.

It is ordered, that the Treasurer shall send forth his warrants into the seuerall Townes, for the Country Rate, according to the rule in Courte for this present yeare; and that hee shall keepe a just account how and for what he doth expend the same.

The Courte is adiourned to the first Wednesday in Febʳ next.

---

[11]   A Session of the Generall Courte, this 5ᵗʰ of Febʳ, 1650.

Edw: Hopkins Esqʳ, Gouernoʳ.
John Haynes Esqʳ, Deputy.

Magistrates: Mr. Wells, Mr. Woollcott, Mr. Webster, Mr. Cullick, Mr. Clarke.

Deputyes: Mr. Steele, Mr. Taylecoat, Mr. Trott, Edw: Stebbing, John Bissell, Nath: Dickerson, Dauid Willton, Andr: Bacon, Sam: Smith, Tho: Coleman, Steph: Harte, Tho: Judd.

Whereas there is an order of Courte amongst vs wch prohibitts all perticular persons within this Jurissdiction from buying any land of the Indians, either directly or indirectly, vnder any pretence whatsoeuer; this Courte add^th therevnto and orders, that no perticular person whatsoeuer shall buy of the Indians, either directly or indirectly, any timber, candlewood or trees of any sorte or kinde, within this Jurissdiction, though it bee without the bounds of the seuerall Townes.

Whereas, it doth appeare that much hurte, loss and damage doth acrue to this Common wealth and to perticular persons in the seuerall plantations, by those hoggs that are kept or hearded in the woods, by theire rooting vpp and wronging otherwise the common feed of cattle, and by theire hanging about and breaking through such fences as are suffitient against other cattle, into mens corne, and spoiling the same, It is ordered by this Courte, that if any hoggs or swyne shall bee found within three myles of any dwelling howse, in any of the plantations within this Jurissdiction (except such as are kept in mens yards, wch are to bee ringed or yoaked when found in the streete, according to the order of Courte, in May last,) from the first of March to the middle of October, they shall forfeitt sixpence a peece, for euery time they are soe found.

Whereas, by vertue of an order in May last, each Towne shall chuse among themselues fiue able men, to consider and order the best way of improuing and fencing common lands; It is ordered by this Courte that the seruice committed to them, in all the perticulars thereof, wch appeares more fully in the said order, shall bee attended by the Townsmen, or those men that are chosen to order and attend the affaires of the seuerall Townes wherein they liue, within this Jurissdiction, and whatsoeuer the maior p^rt of the said Townsmen in their seuerall Townes shall agree vppon, conclude, determine and order, according to the former order of fiue men, shall in all respects bynde and bee attended as fully as if it had beene done by the said fiue men.

Thomas Horskins, of Wyndsor, being p^rsented as vnfitt and dissable to attend Trainings, watching and warding, this Courte frees him from the seruices aforesaid, during his dissabillity.

[12] Whereas it doth appeare to this Courte that those Townes that are more remoate are at more and greater charge in bringing the Corne of their Townes, for the ordinary Country Rates, than those Townes or persons that are nearer to the Treasurer, place or places of payment, as occassions shall or may require; It is ordered by this Courte, that for such corne as Wyndsor shall pay to the Rates aforesaid and bring downe to Hartford in corne, they shall bee allowed two pence in the bushell, and for what corne aforesaid they shall carry to Wethersfeild, they shall be allowed three pence p^r bush: And Farmington three pence p^r bush: for what such corne they shall bring to Hartford, and if they carry it further they shall bee allowed reasonable satisfaction for the same, ouer and aboue the aforesaid three pence p^r bushell.

A Committee for the clearing of the agreement with Mr. Fenwick, chosen by this Courte, are as follow^th: Mr. Haynes, Capt. Mason and Mr. John Steele; these are for the clearing of the first agreement, being the Committee that made the said agreement. And for the second agreem^t, Mr. Clarke and Mr. Taylecoate, whoe are to draw out a true coppy of both the said agreements vnder Mr. Hopkins his hand, wch said coppie or coppies shall bee kept vppon record and fyled by the Secretary. And this Courte graunts libberty to each Towne to send any two of theire Inhabitants to the meeting of the aforesaid Committee, to heare the said agitacõns, and to satisfie theire seuerall Townes with the grounds of any conclusions that they may make, that so all scruples may bee remoued and all hearts satisfied and quieted for ye future in the premisses: wch said time of meeting for the Committee aforesaid, is the first Tuseday of the next month, being commonly called March, at the Gouerno^rs howse; and the Deputyes of the seuerall Townes are desired to giue seasonable notice to theire said Townes of the premisses, that so no Towne may plead that they did not know of the same: only speciall notice is to bee giuen to Capt. Mason and the Towne of Seabrooke.

This Courte graunts and orders, that the Secretary shall bee allowed and paid the sum of six pounds, being in p^rt of payment for his great paines in drawing out and transcribing the country orders, concluded and established in May last.

This Courte is adiourned to the 2^d Lecture day in March next, after ye sermon.

---

[13] A Session of the Generall Courte, in Hartford, this 19th March, 1650–51.

Edw: Hopkins Esqr, Gou^rno^r.
John Haynes Esqr, Deputy.
Magistrates: Mr. Wells, Capt: Mason, Mr. Woollcott, Mr. Webster, Mr. Clarke, Mr. Cullick.
Deputyes: Mr. Phelps, Mr. Allyn, Mr. Tailecoat, Mr. Trott, John Bissell, Sam: Smith, Natha: Dickerson, Tho: Coleman, Andr: Bacon, Edward Stebbing, Tho: Judd.

Whereas vppon former information giuen to this Court that William Cheessbrooke (a smith, somtimes an Inhabitant in the Massachusetts, but more lately at Seacunck, alias Rehoboth, in the Jurissdiction of New Plimouth,) had begunn to settle himselfe at Pacatuck, a place within the limitts of this Colonye, order issued out to the said Cheessbrooke,* vppon seuerall weighty consideraçons, either to depart the place, or to make his appearance, and giue an account of his proceedings, whereunto hee submitted, and by a pœnall obligation ingaged himselfe to attend:

The said Cheesbrooke now presented himselfe to this Courte, and in way of Apologie professed his sitting downe there was besides his purpose and intendment, his ayme being to settle at Pequett plantation, but finding that place in seuerall respects vnsutable to his expectations, and hauing disposessed himselfe of his former aboade, hee was in a manner necessitated for the

---

* See page 200, ante.

A Session of the Generall Courts
in Hartford this 19th march: 1650/51

Whereas vppon former Information giuen to this Courts
that william Cheesbrooke (a smith, sometimes an Inhabitant
in the Massachusetts, but more lately at Seacuncke, alias Rehoboth
in the Jurisdiction of new Plimouth had begun to settle him=
selfe at Pawcatuck a place within the limits of this Colony,
Order issued out to the said Cheesbrooke vppon sommons with[y]
Commissioners, either to depart the plantation, or to make his appea=
rance, and giue an account of his proceedings, in reference into
his submittinge, and by a promise obligation Inguage himselfe to
Attend,

John Cullick
(Secretary, 1648–1658.)

preservation of his estate to make winter provision for his cattle there, wherevnto hee was allso incouraged by Mr. John Winthrop, who pretended a Comission from the Generall Courte in the Massachusetts for the planting of those partes. Hee was tould that as the right of that place did clearely appertaine to this Colonye, so his proceeding was vnwarrantable in sitting downe there without the knowledge and approbation of this Gouernem^t, and it carried (in the open face of it,) the greater ground of offence, in that by his calling hee was fitted, and by his solitary liuing advantaged, to carry on a mischeiuous trade with the Indians, p^{r}fessly cross [to] the generall orders of the Country, and extreamely preiudiciall to the publique safety, which was increased by reports of practice in that kinde in the place of his last abode; besides it seemed more than vncomely for a man professing Godliness so to withdraw from all publique ordinances and Xtian society. In his answer, hee acknowledged his former transgression (for wch hee justly suffered,) but affirmed (to take of all suspition in that kinde) that at his remooue hee sould away his tooles, and thereby made himselfe vncapeable of repairing any gun locks, or making so much as a scrue pinn, either for himselfe or others, and that hee was fully resolued not to continue in that sollitary condition, but had to himselfe good grounds of hopes (if libberty might bee graunted,) in a shorte time to procure a competent company of desireable men, for the planting of the place.

The Courte duely considered all that was presented, & though they were willing to make the most favourable construction of his former proceedings, yet they exprest themselues alltogether vnsatisfied in the aforementioned respects, for his continuance there in the way hee is in, and could giue no aprobacõn therevnto, yet they were inclined (hee professing his full agreem^t with the approoued Churches of Christe, in all things) if the necessity of his occassions to his owne apprehensions were such that hee would adventure vppon his owne acco^t and ingage himselfe in a bond of a 100l. not to p^{r}secute any vnlawfull trade with the Indians, they would not comp[el   [to remooue.*

---

* The whole of this last line, (at the bottom of page 13, in the original,) is nearly, and a portion of it quite obliterated.

[14]   And if before the Generall Courte in Septemb[r] next, hee giue in the names of a considerable company of such persons as the Courte shall approoue, who will ingage for the planting of the place and sitting downe there before the next winter, and allso submitt themselues to such wayes and rules as shall best promoate the publique good, all meete incouragement shall be giuen in that way: w[ch] being made knowne to William Cheessbrooke, hee thankfully acknowledged the Courts fauo[r], and acquiessed in theire determinacon.

The Courte is dissolued.

A GENERALL COURTE OF ELECTION, IN HARTFORD, THE 15[th] DAY OF MAY, 1651.

John Haynes Esq[r], elected Gou[r]no[r].

Edward Hopkins Esq[r], Deputy.

Magistrates elected: Roger Ludlow Esq[r], John Winthrop Esq[r], Mr. Wells, Capt: Mason, Mr. Woollcott, Mr. Webster, Mr. Cullick, Mr. Clarke, Mr. Howell, Mr. Tapping.

Deputyes : Mr. Tailecoat, Mr. Phelps, Mr. Steele, Mr. Trott, Mr. Allyn, Mr. Gayler, Mr. Warde, Mr. Hull, Nath: Dickerson, Dauid Willton, Tho: Coleman, John Deming, Edw: Stebbing, Andr: Bacon, John Clarke, Tho: Birchard, Tho: Thorneton, Steph: Harte, Tho: Staunton, John Brunson, Tho: Mynor, [Phil]lip Groues, *absent.*

Samuell Fittch, Jonathan Rudd, John Strong, Moses Ventris, made free.

John Dyer testifieth in Courte, that vppon a time this spring, Mr. Blinman and another of Pequett being at Seabrooke, desired this deponent to carry them ouer the Riuer in a cannooe, towards Pequett, w[ch] hee did; and that when hee had sett them ashore, it being wett weather, hee tarried there awhile, in w[ch] time of his tarrying there came three Indians to him, and that Thomas Leppingwell was with them, w[ch] said Indians desired this deponent to sett them ouer in the cannoe, to Seabrooke, w[ch] hee tould them hee would doe if they would worke, because the cannooe was heauy; so hee brought them ouer, and when hee had turned the point into the North Coue, and came neare the vessells that rode there, the said Indians asked this deponent wch was the Dutch vessell, and hee tould y^m w^ch; then they asked this deponent whether the Dutchman had any coates: hee answered them, *tutta ;* then one of the Indians stood vp in the cannooe and called to the vessell and sayd, Way bee gon coates? Some answered, there was coates: then this deponent tould the Indians, *Nux ;* then they desired and hee sett them aboard, and this deponent tarried in the cannooe: then Mr. Augustine, M^rch^t, called to the skipper to shew the Indians some cloths, so the skipper and the Indians went downe into the hold, as hee supposed, amonge the cloth, & in the meane time Mr. Augustine spake to this deponent to come ouer, wch hee did, and after the said Indians had beene a pretty while in the hold with the skipper, the skipper asked Mr. Augustine how hee sould a coate of two yards: Mr. Augustine answered, twenty shillings: then this deponent asked the said Augustine if hee sould his cloth for ten shillings a yard; hee answered, yes, to the Indians, but for nine shillings to [15] others. or two bushells of wheat: then this deponent replied that two bushells of wheat was worth ten shillings. So hauing tarried some time, hee asked the Indians if [they] would goe ashoare; they answered, by and by: then hee tarried awhile, and asked them againe; then one belonging to the vessell tould this deponent that hee might goe away if hee would, and hee would sett the Indians ashoare, when they desired it. So this deponent went home (and left the Indians aboard) and dyned, and spake nothing to any of any Indians going aboard the Dutch vessell; and allso that hee knew nothing but the Dutch might trade coates, so they did not trade gunns, powder and shott.

Thomas Chapman, William Pratt, Jonathan Rudd, Sacha[ry] Sanford and Christopher Huntington, did all testifie in Courte, vppon theire oaths, that they knew nothing of John Dyers carrying Indians aboard the Dutch vessell, and that that was no ground of theire seizing the vessell and goods.

Whereas Augustine Herriman, by trading with the Indians at Seabrooke, contrary to order of Courte, hath forfeited his vessell and goods, wch was seized by some of the Inhabitants of Seabrooke aforesaid, This Courte hath taken the same into consideracon, and doe adiudge the said Herrman to pay vnto the said seizures the sum of for[ty] pounds sterling, in good pay: And that the said Herriman doe giue it vnder his hand, that vppon the tryall and examination of the buisiness, it did appeare that the English had dealt fairely with him all along in that business; and that there was not any English that drew or caused the Indians to trade with him or in his vessell, to intrapp or insnare both or either of them.

The Gouerno^r, Mr. Cullick and Mr. Clarke are desired to goe downe to Stratford to keepe Courte vppon the tryall of Goody Bassett for her life, and if the Gouerno^r cannott goe, then Mr. Wells is to goe in his roome.

This Courte, considering the great inconveniences that occur by reason of Roade Iland interteining of fugitiues, and such as are guilty of capitall crimes and other misdeameno^rs, from the seuerall vnited Colonyes, cannott but judge the same to bee extreamely preiuditiall to the peace and wellfare of the said colonyes, doe order that the premisses should be recomended to the serious consideracon of the Comissioners, that some effectuall course may bee taken for the redress of the same.

[16] This Courte desires that a letter should be written from the Courte to the Jurissdiction of Plymouth, that they would prepare themselues against the next meeting of the Comissioners, to make appeare vnder wch of the Colonyes the plantations of Warwick and others doe stand.

John Bankes, Edward Adams, Phillip Pinckney, John Hoite and Georg Godding, being fyned twenty shillings apeece, as appeares in the Records of the Courte the 8th July, 1650, this Courte frees the said partyes from theire said fynes, and Thomas Staples fyne of forty shillings is brought downe to twenty.

Whereas in the order of Rating, the Comissioners of Fairefeild and Strattford are not inioyned and required to meete the Comissioners in the seuerall Townes vppon the Riuer; It is now ordered by this Courte that the said Comissioners of Fairefeild and Strattford shall yearely, in the Town of Hartford, two dayes before the Generall Courte in Septemb^r, meete with the Comissioners of the said seuerall Townes vppou the Riuer and bring with [them] the lists of the persons and the estates of theire seuerall Townes, that they may bee jointly examined and perfected, before they are transmitted to the said Generall Courte. And if the said Comissioners should not agree, they are to present the grounds of theire differing and disagreement vnto the said Courte, to bee by them issued and determined; and theire fyne of twenty nobles at the Generall Courte, the 3d of Novembr, 1650, is remitted by this Courte.

There being an occasion of debate in this Courte about Seabrooks non-payment of the proporčon laid vppon that Towne in reference to the purchase and agreement with Georg Fenwick Esqr, John Clarke and Thomas Birchard, Deputyes for that Towne, did ingage themselues in the behalf of the said Towne of Seabrooke, that there shall bee due payment made of the said leuye due by the said Towne of Seabrooke, to bee paid for 5 yeares now past, in October next, provided theire payment of what is due or shall bee due, bee no preiudice to them or the Inhabitants of Seabrooke, in pleading any seeming grounds or reasons they haue for their not paying of all or any parte of the said leuye; the former Comittee are desiered to attend such reasons and allegations as they shall present, as formerly they were desired.

Thomas Thorneton affirmed in Courte, that it was reported there was a hundred beeues killed in Fairefeild last yeare.

This Courte taking into consideračon the proposition of the Inhabitants of Pequett for some inlargemt of meadow at Niantecutt, and whereas there was 500 acres of ground lying in Pequett graunted to fiue of Capt: Masons souldgers at the Pequett warr, wch being taken vp by Pequett, they doe desire may bee recompenced at Niantecutt; the Courte desires and appoints that John Clarke and Thomas Birchard of Seabrooke should goe to Pequett and veiw the said percell of land there [17] giuen to the said souldgers,|| and taken vp by Pequett, as before and then goe to [Niantecutt] and lay out there vnto the said souldgers such and so m[uch] land as may bee fully equiuolent to theire former gr[aunt] of land at Pequett. And for the Inhabitants of Pequett, [the] Courte graunts that theire bounds shall come to Bride Brooke, (the former graunt excepted,) prouided that it doe not come within the bounds of Seabrooke, and provided that what meadow or marshe there is aboue two hundred acres, it shall be reserued for the countrys vse [or] other and further dispose.

Mr. Deputy and Mr. Ludlow are chosen Comissioners for this Jurissdiction to attend the next meeting of the Comissioners of the vnited Colonyes, and so for the yeare ensuing as occassion may require, and if the Deputy should bee gonn out of the Country to England before the said meeting, then Mr. Cullick is to supply his place.

It is ordered, that those that liue in seuerall companyes at farmes remoate from the seuerall Townes, shall haue libberty to keepe one in each quarter at home vppon euery training day, who is of age to bare armes, provided one man, (where more then one is,) shall tarry at home but one training day at a time, and that those whoe doe stay at home bee prouided with armes, according to lawe; and where any one farme is so farre distant from the Towne as Mr. Fenwicks is, at Sixe Myle Iland, then one in like manner may remaine at home, for safety of the place.

This Courte graunts theire consent that Nathaniell Rescew should haue Goodwife Johnsons childe, wch was borne in the prison, as an apprentice to him, till hee is of the age of twenty one yeares, and that the said Rescew shall haue ten pounds with him, out of Newtons estate.

This day there was presented a letter to the Courte, by the Deputy, from John Wenthrop Esqr of Pequett, directed to the said Deputy, the contents whereof fol[lowth:]

Worthy S^r.

It was my intent to haue waited vppon yo^{r}selfe and the Hono^{r}ed Courte, but some occasions of absolute necessity (as Mr. Blinman can informe) require my hasting into the Bay, wch should haue beene sooner if I had beene well to haue gon by land, but I haue expected a passage by water to Providence, wch I am now promissed by a pinnace that I expect to returne from Leiftennant Gardiners this day; therefore I [18] desire to bee excused till some further opportunity.

There hath beene earnest motions to mee, from some well willers to the Comon good, to make some search and tryall for mettalls in this Country, and there is hope that there might bee a stock gathered for that purpose, if there were incouragements from the seuerall Jurissdictions. I have therefore made bould to propound the inclosed graunt to yo^{r}selfe and the Courte; professing this, that I neither know nor haue heard of any

mynes or mettalls within this Jurissdiction, for I haue not yet made any search, but only propound it for incouragement to any that will bee adventurers and joine in the vndertaking of such a designe ; wch is allready done in the Bay, where I know of two places of lead, one at Lynn and the other at Nuberry, but that at Lynn being chalenged by the Towne and so neare the Iron worke, that takes vp all the wood, that it cannott bee wrought there ; and the Towne hath beene at charge for the finding of the veine, but it cannot bee found, and so they are discouraged, for it was onely loose peeces that wee found. I doe not much desire to haue any thinge put in about gold and siluer, yet if it be put in, it may incourage some, but I leaue all to the wisdome of the hono^red Courte, and with my humble seruice to yo^rselfe and the Deputy Gou^rno^r and the Magistrates and Deputies I rest,   Yo^r humble servant,
  May 13th, 1651.   John Wenthrop.

Whereas, in this rocky country, amongst these mountaines and stonye hills, there are probabillities of mynes of mettalls and mineralls, the discouery whereof, may bee for the great benefitt of the country, in raising a staple comodity ;—and whereas, John Wenthrop Esqr doth intend to bee at charge and adventure for the search and discouery of such mynes and mineralls ; for the incouragement whereof, and of any that shall adventure with the said John Wenthrop Esqr in the said buisines, It is therefore ordered by this Courte, that if the said John Wenthrop Esqr shall discouer, sett vppon and meinteine, or cause to be found, discouered, set vppon and meinteined, such mynes of lead, copper or tinn, or any mineralls, as antimony, vitriall, black lead, allom, stone salt, salt springs, or any other the like, within this Jurissdiction, and shall sett vp any worke, for the digging, washing, melting, or any other operation about the said mynes or mineralls, as the nature thereof requireth, that then the said John Wenthrop Esqr, his heires, associates p^tners or assignes, shall injoye foreuer the said mynes, with the lands, wood, timber and waters, within two or three myles of the said myne, for the necessary carrying on of the workes and meinteining of workemen, and prouision of coales for the same ; provided it bee not within the bounds of any Towne allready, or any perticular persons propriety, and provided it bee not in nor bordering vppon any place that shall or may by the Courte bee judged fitt to make a plantation of.

[19]   A GENERALL COURTE IN HARTFORD, 11th OF SEPTEMBr,
1651.
John Haynes Esqr, Gournor.
Magistrates: Mr. Wells, Capt: Mason, Mr. Webster, Mr. Woollcott, Mr. Clarke.
Deputyes: Mr. Allyn, Mr. Phelps, John Bissell, Dauid Willton, Mr. Trott, Sam: Smith, John Demyng, Natha: Dickerson, John Clarke, Mr. Tallcott, Mr. Westwood, Andr: Bacon, Edw: Stebbing, John Bankes, Will: Hill, Thomas Mynott, Wm. Beardsly, Thomas Judd, Steph: Harte.

It is ordered, sentenced and decreed, that Mattabeseck shall bee a Towne, and that they shall make choyce of one of theire inhabitants, according to order in that case, that so hee may take the oath of a Constable, the next convenient season.

It is likewise ordered, that Norwauke shall bee a Towne and that they prouide an inhabitant, according to order, who shall seasonably bee tendred to take the oath of a Constable.

This Courte being informed by the Townsmen of Hartford that John Lord, contrary to naturall affection, hath withdrawne himselfe from his wife, and left her destitute of a bed to lodge on, and very bare in apparell, to the indangering of her health, The said Courte doth herev[ppon] order and giue authority to the said Townsmen to require of the said John Lord the wearing apparrell of his wife, and allso a bed for her to lodge on, and allso to search after the same in any place within this Jurissdiction, and to restore it vnto her, and reasonable satisfaction shall bee giuen if any person shall bee damnified thereby.

It is ordered by this Courte, that the lyne of the Towne of Nameage shall begin on the east side the great Riuer oppositt to the point Mr. John Wenthrop now liues uppon, and so to runn vppon an east lyne to Powcatuck Riuer, together with all the meadow, except it doth exceed foure hundred and ten acres. It is not intended that any prt of the former limmitts of the Towne should bee abridged.

Allso the Iland commonly called Chippachauge,* in Mistick Bay is giuen to Capt: John Mason, as allso one hundred acres

---
*Now called " Mason's Island."

of vpland and ten acres of meadow neare Mistick, where hee shall make choyce.

The Deputyes of Fairefeild haue, according to order of Courte in that behalfe, presented to the Courte a list of theire names and estates, wch in the Totall amounts to the sum of 8895*l*. 3*s*.

Thursday come seuen night is appointed by the Generall Courte for a day of Thanksgiuing in all the Townes in this Jurissdiction.

Vppon petition of Nicholas Olmstead, the Courte frees him from traininge vntill further order. *Repealed : fol.* 21.

The Court is adiourned to Wednesday come 3 weekes, after Lecture.

---

[20] A Session of the Generall Courte in Hartford, the 6th Octob^r, 1651.

Edw: Hopkins Esqr, Deputy.

Magistrates : Roger Ludlow Esqr, Mr. Wells, Mr. Woollcott, Mr. Cullick, Mr. Clarke.

Deputyes : Mr. Phelps, Mr. Trott, Mr. Tailecoat, Mr. Westwood, Edw: Stebbing, Natha: Dickerson, John Bissell, Andr: Bacon, John Deming, Sam: Smith, Steph: Harte, Will: Beardsly, Will: Hill, John Bankes, Tho: Judd.

This Courte considering the motion and request of the Townesmen of Hartford, for some of theire inhabitants to bee freed from training to morrow and next day, they doe graunt and consent that they shall haue libberty to take of so many from theire training aforesaid as are necessary to bee imployed about the raising of the worke prepared for the supporte of the great bridge.

This Courte being informed that there are seuerall Indians amongst vs that are knowne and may bee prooued to bee murtherers of the English before the Pequett warrs, they doe referr the inquiry into the grounds and truth of the premisses vnto the magistrates of this Jurissdiction, and therefore doe desire that ye Gour^nor would write to, or seasonably conferr with Capt: Mason and Thomas Staunton, whether they know any such Indian, that soe they may bee brought to condigne punishment.

This Courte hauing considered the appeale of Thomas Barlowe and Jehu Burr, about the verdict of the Jury at the last Courte in Stratford, whereby they were judged to pay for a colte of Leiftennant Wheelers, they doe determine and conclude that allthough they see not reason to confirme the full verdict of the Jury, yet they judge it meete that the said Barlowe and Burr should pay to Wheeler, for his damage, forty shillings.

Mr. Warde and John Bankes are desired to gather vp and make sale of any estate of that wch was sometimes Peter Johnsons of Fairefeild, and that they shall therewith satisfie the charges of the nursing of the childe of Goody Johnson.

Nicholas Olmsteed, acknowledging to the Courte that by seuerall irregular expressions in his petition, hee hath giuen just cause of offence vnto the Courte, manifesting in his expressions his sorrow for the same, and desiring the Courte to pass it by, They doe remitt and pass by his offence; and doe order that hee shall not bee freed from traininge vppon such a petition, but if hee shall see cause, in time convenient, to present to the Courte the consideracon of his former good service, they shall bee freely willing to attend it, and to allowe him convenient and reasonable incouragem^t ; the petition to bee taken of from the fyle.

Vppon the complaint of the Deputies of Strattford to this Courte, in the behalfe of Richard Buttler, against an Indian named Nimrod, that willfully killed some swyne of the said Buttlers, this Courte consenteth that Mr. Ludlow may p^rsecute the said Indian according to order made by the Comissioners in that respect.

[21] Whereas vppon the motion of Mr. Wells, Treasurer, It was propounded that in regard hee being in the place of Magistrate, doth finde the execution of the Treasurers office to bee [some]what burdensome for both together, and therefore desires [to] bee eased of the Treasurers place, wch this Courte doth desire at the Courte of Election, may bee attended, and that they would thinke of some body else to bee Treasurer in his roome.

Andrew Warde, George Hull and William Beardsly are propounded for Assistants to joine with the magistrates for the execution of justice in the Townes by the sea side.

It was ordered that Thomas Staunton should goe to Narragansett and demaund of Ninigrett 40*l*. for Eltwood Pomryes mare, or Pequoiam to bee d'd vp, according to the determination of the Comissioners in Sept: last.*

William Leawis Junior is confirmed Leiftennant, to order the souldgers at Farmington : John Steele Junior, Ensigne, and Thomas Barnes, Serieant.

A letter being received from Capt: Mason, wherein hee desires, among other thinges, the advice of this Courte touching a motion propounded by some of New Hauen interessed in Dillaware designe, for his assistance of them in that buisiness, with some incouragements for his settling there ; The Courte ordered that answer be returned, in reference to the foregoing particular, to the following purpose :—That it is much in the desires of the whole Courte that hee would not enterteine thoughts of remouing his aboade out of this Colony, wherevnto they cannot giue the least allowance or approbation ; yet if his owne desire bee for the present service of that place, and theire importunities continue for his employment there, the Courte cannott wholy deny him or them, the worke being that wch they are willing to promoate, but are content hee shall attend the service for 3 months, provided hee will ingage himselfe to returne within that time and continue his aboade amongst them as formerly :

---

* See p. 27, *ante*. "Eltweed Pomry, of Windsor, in Connecticutt Jurisdiction, hauing often petitioned the Comissioners about a mare of his, wilfully killed by a Pequott Indyan, called Poquoiam, soone after the fore mentioned warr, when all sorts of horses were at a high price ; concerning which, Mr. Israell Stoughton, Generall for the Massachusetts, made an agreement with Meyantonime, one of the principall Narragansett Sachems, with or under whom the sayd Poquoiam liued, on behalfe of the offendors : * * * * *   Upon consideration of the premisses, the Comissioners thought fitt that the sayd monye be againe demanded of Ninigrett," he being the brother in law of Poquoiam, and heir to Miantonimo, " or that hee deliuer Poquoiam into their hands ; but upon refusall or delay, that some fitt man, duely accompanied, be sent, by order & direction of the Government of Conecticutt, to require it, with allowance of the present charges, and if it be not forthwith paid, to make seizure to the vallew of 40*l*. with the charges, and to bring it away with them ; and hereof the Narraganset Indians now pr'sent were willed to informe Ninigrett ; onely, if after such payment or seizure, Vncas or Wequash Cooke shall by intertaining, pr'tecting or concealing Poquoiam, hinder Ninigrett from recouering the same of him, in such case the said 40*l*. shall be accounted due and be required from them or either of them." [Records of U. Colonies, Sept. 1651.]

The Courte hath allso spoken with Leiftennant Bull, about the land at Nihantecutt, laid out to him and others with him, who hath promised to conferr with Vncas and indeuo^r to giue him reasonable content and satisfaction, in reference to the premisses, wch if they shall not answerably attend, then vppon information the Courte will take further consideraĉon thereof, in seasonable time. And whereas hee certifies in his letter that hee is not satisfied in Saquassens being exalted vnder our power to great Sachemship, this Courte declares that they doe not know of any such thinge, neither doe they or shall they allowe or approoue thereof.*

[22] Mr. Webster and Mr. Cullick are desired to take an acco^t of the Treasurer of the debts of the Country, and how the last Country Rate is dissbursed, and present the same to the next session of the Generall Courte.

It is ordered, that Mattabeseck and Norwauke shall bee rated this p^{r}sent yeare in theire proporĉon, according to the rule of rating in the Country, for theire cattle, and other visible estate, and that Norwaack shall present to Mr. Ludlow, and Mattabeseck to Mr. Wells, in each Towne one inhabitant, to bee sworne by them, Constables in theire seuerall Townes.

It is ordered by this Courte that Wednesday next come fortnight, there bee a day of fasting and humilliation throughout this Jurissdiction, for and in consideraĉon of some diseases or infection that is among o^r neigbors & freinds of the Massachusetts, as allso for and concerninge the affaires of o^r natiue country, and p^{r}sperity of the Gospell of Jesus Christe.

---

* At a meeting of the Commissioners, in September, " Uncas complained that Sequassen some yeares since, as is well knowne, began hostile acts upon him, to the disturbance of the publique peace, whereupon he was occasioned to fight him and in the issue ouercame him and conquered his country, which though he gaue to the English and did not oppose the favour they were pleased to shew him in sparing his life, yet he cannot but looke upon himselfe as wronged in that Sequassen (as he was informed.) is set up and indeavored to be made a great Sachem, notwithstanding he hath refused to pay an acknowledgm^t of wampom to him, according to his ingagements."

"The Commission^{rs} disclaimed any indeavors of theirs to make Sequassen greate, and are ignorant of what he affirmes concerning the other, yet recommend it to the Gouerment of Conecticutt to examine the case, and to p^{r}vide that upon due proofe Vncas may bee owned in what shall bee just and equall, and Mr. Ludlow was intreated to promote the same." [Rec. of U Colonies.]

		£ s.
Hartford estate was presented to this Courte to bee		22404:19.
Wyndsor,		15435:
Wethersfeild,		12748:
Farmington,		04741:
Seabrooke,		04150:
Fairefeild,		08895:3
Strattford,		07118:8:6d.
		75492:10:6

It is ordered, that warrants shall goe out from the Treasurer for a whole rate, and that euery person, according to the order, to bee rated at 2s. vid. p^r head, shall bee brought downe to 18d. p^r head; the whole rate to bee paid $\frac{1}{3}$ in wheat, and $\frac{1}{3}$ in pease, and $\frac{1}{3}$ in good peage or Indian.

The Courte is adiourned to the first Wednesday in Decemb^r next.

[23] A SESSION OF THE GENERALL COURTE, THE 3^d DAY OF DECEMB^r, 1651.

John Haynes Esqr, Gou^{r}no^r.
Magistrates: Mr. Woollcott, Mr. Webster, Mr. Cullick.
Deputyes: Mr. Phelps, Mr. Allyn, Mr. Tailecoat, Mr. Westwood, Edw: Stebbing, Natha: Dickerson, Andr: Bacon, John Bissell, John Demyng, Steph: Harte, Tho: Judd.

The Courte is adiourned to the first Tuesday in March next, by ten a clock in the morninge.

[24] A SESSION OF THE GENERALL COURTE, IN HARTFORD, THE 2^d OF MARCH, 1651-52.

John Haynes Esqr, Gou^{r}no^r.
Magistrates: Mr. Wells, Capt: Mason, Mr. Woollcott, Mr. Webster, Mr. Cullick, Mr. Clarke.
Deputyes: Mr. Tailecoat, Mr. Phelps, Mr. Allyn, Mr. Westwood, Edw: Stebbing, Natha: Dickerson, Dauid

Willton, John Bissell, Sam: Smith, Andrew Bacon, John Deming, Steph: Harte, Tho: Judd.

This Courte orders, that the Treasurer shall pay vnto John Cullick the sum of thirty two pounds nineteene shillings, out of the Country Rate pay, allready graunted and next to bee collected, wch is for so much the Country is indebted to Edward Hopkins Esqr; the pay to bee made in Corne : if any wampum bee paid, it is to bee with so much allowance as shall make the wampum as good as corne.

This Courte considering John Clarks bill of Countryes charges, they doe conclude and order that the Treasurer shall not pay him for the workmens diett aboue six shillings a weeke for one man.

This Courte orders that the Treasurer shall pay to Richard Goodman and John Pratt, for the carrying on of the necessary worke about the prison howse, out of the next Rate, thirty pounds in such pay as the Rate is to bee paid in this Towne.

Thomas Bull and others in the behalfe of the rest, hauing resigned vp to the Courte one hundred acres of the grounds laid out at Niantecutt to them, of that parte thereof wch lyes next to Seabrooke, wch said hundred acres the Courte graunts libberty to the Indians that formerly posessed and planted the same, to posess and plant for the future, so long as they carry peacably and justly towards the English;

This Courte graunts to the said Thomas Bull and the rest of the fiue of Capt: Masons souldgers, that they shall haue two hundred acres of that vpland wch lyes northward, next adioyning to the remainder of land allready laid out to them, wch they accept in full satisfaction for the hundred acres they haue resigned as before.

The Courte is dissolued.

---

[25] A GENERALL COURTE OF ELECTION IN HARTFORD, THE 20th MAY, 1652.

Magistrates elected:
Edward Hopkins Esqr, Gou^{r}no^r.
John Haynes Esqr, Deputy.

Roger Ludlow Esqr, John Wenthrop Esqr, Mr. Wells, Capt: Mason, Mr. Webster, Mr. Woollcott, Mr. Cullick, Sec$^.$., Mr. Clarke, Mr. Howell, Mr. Tapping.

Mr. Tailecoate, *Treasurer*.

Deputyes: Mr. Phelps, Mr. Steele, Mr. Tailecoat, Mr. Warde, Mr. Gayler, Mr. Westwood, Mr. Trott, Mr. Parkes, Edw: Stebbing, Natha: Dickerson, Andr: Bacon, John Deming, John Bissell, Tho: Coleman, Dauid Willton, Will: Hill, Will: Beardsly, Dan: Titterton, John Clarke, Tho: Chapman, Hugh Calkin.

This Courte there was made free,—Robert Lockwood, John Tailecoat, Tho: Whittmore, Tho: Allyn, Tho: Bissell, John Hossford, John Bissell, Will: Beamunt, Will: Waller.

This Courte hauing duely weighed and considered the grounds of John Coopers appeale to the same, in reference to the verdict of the Jury at Southampton in the tryall betweene Mr. Stanborough plaintiffe, and John Cooper senior, defend^t, they finde and hereby doe declare that the said John Cooper had just ground and cause so to appeale; allso, this Courte, considering the bill presented to them of Cooper to Peter Tallman, Dutchman, and assigned by him to Stanborough, according to the euidence giuen in, they find that it was not an authentique bill.

Whereas, by an order in this Comon wealth, there is to bee a perticular Courte in Hartford the day before the two standing Generall Courtes, in May and Septemb^r in each yeare, this Courte finding seuerall inconueniences that followes therevppon, doe hereby order that the aforesaid perticular Courtes shall bee kept in Hartford aforesaid vppon the second day before the said each standing Generall Courte, instead of the former, and that the said perticular Courtes now ordered shall bee ended before each Generall Courte.

This Courte considering the grounds of the seizure of the vessell and goods of Oulsterman, at Fairefeild, Dutchman, by John Cable and some others with him, the parties on both sides haue left themselues with submission to the judgm^t of the said Courte, in reference to the premisses, they doe order that the said Dutchman shall pay to the seizors the sum of fiue pounds, and all theire reasonable costs and charges therevppon, wch being done, then the said seizors are to deliuer vp to the said Dutchman the whole estate, both in vessell and goods seized as aforesaid.

[26] This Courte orders that Nathaniell Rescue shall bee paid fiue pounds more with the Goody Johnsons childe, accordinge to her promise to him, hee hauing ingaged himselfe to meinteine and well educate her sonne without any further demaund of charges either of her or the Country.

Whereas, vppon the motion of the inhabitants of Seabrooke, It was desired that a certeine comon feild by mutuall consent is concluded to bee fenced proporc͠onably, and it so falls out that the said fence cannot goe on comfortably except the Right Worshippfull Geo: Fenwick Esqr doth joine in proporc͠on, by reason of some accomodac͠on that belongs vnto him, wch will necessarily fall in within the fence, and it hath beene obiected by Capt; Cullick, the said Mr. Fenwicks agent, that the same will bee but little beneficiall to the said Mr. Fenwick, and therefore conceiues that the said Mr. Fenwicke is not bound to it ; yet by reason (as the inhabitants plead) the said Mr. Fenwicks land within the said fence will bee benefitted thereby, the Courte therefore, taking into consideration the premisses, doe thinke fitt that there shall bee a Comittee appointed, whoe vppon veiw of the said land shall certefie what benefitt the said Mr. Fenwick or his agent or tennants shall bee advantaged thereby, as the rest of the inhabitants. The Courte makes no doubt but Mr. Fenwick or his agent will bee willing to allowe proportionable fencing for it, wch if it bee refused, the Courte will advise further in it.

Whereas the Courte hath taken into consideration the great abuse that is crept into this Jurissdiction, by the vnlimitted examination of witnesses before the Magistrate in the outward plantations, betweene party and party, sometime before any action in Courte, or process serued before any declaration, It is therefore ordered, that if any that liue in remoate plantations will cause any that mutually liue together in the said remoate plantations to answer them at the Courte in Hartford (seinge there bee ordinary Courtes in the said plantations, to try all actions betweene party and party,) and therefore if any will drawe his adverse party to Hartford, or to the Courte at Connecticutt, hee shall bee a meanes to p^{r}duce his wittnesses to the said

Courte viva voce, and not to examine any before any magistrate before the tryall, except in a speciall case of impotent wittnes or transient wittnes that is goinge out of the Jurissdiction, and in that case the Magistrate may in discretion examine and certefie in silence to the Courte what is examined, and in noe other case.

Forasmuch as the Courte was this day informed there is a necessity that in the plantations of Fairefeild and Strattford that there should bee some joined as Assistants to the Magistrate or [27] Magistrates in the said plantations, ‖ whereby they may bee inabled to keepe a Courte within the said plantations according to the combin[acon,] whoe are to bee sworne before a Magistrate, whoe are to stand for one yeare or the next Courte of Election ; It is therefore ordered, that the said plantations shall or may meete in a convenient time at theire said plantations, and elect such as they see meete to bee Assistants as aforesaid, whoe are to bee sworne before a Magistrate, and are capeable to the intent aforesaid.

Vppon the petition of the inhabitants of the Towne of Pequett, that by reason of the newnes of the saide plantation, there is, and likely to bee some defect of corne for theire necessary provision, notwthstanding there bee Indian corne enough in the place where the plantation is seated to furnishe the inhabitants thereof, if the corne were not traded by some perticular persons that conuey away the corne, and the inhabitants remaine vnfurnished; It is therefore thought meete and so ordered, that the inhabitants shall bee first serued before the Corne bee traded or carried forth out of the Riuer : this order to stand in force vntill Novemb^r come twelue month.

Mr. Ludlow and Mr. Cullick are chosen Comissioners for the yeare ensuing.

The Courte is adiourned to the last Wednesday in June next in the afternoone.

[28] A Session of the Generall Courte, in Hartford, the 30th of June, 1652.

John Haynes Esqr, Deputy.
Magistrates: Mr. Woollcott, Mr. Webster, Mr. Cullick, Mr. Clarke.
Deputyes: Mr. Tailecoat, Mr. Phelps, Mr. Trott, Mr. Westwood, Dauid Willton, Edw: Stebbing, John Bissell, Nath: Dickerson, Andr: Bacon, Tho: Coleman, John Deming.

This Courte, at the request of Mr. Deputy, doe graunte that hee shall haue three hundred acres of ground, meadow and vpland, for a farme lyinge together on the east side of a certeine Coue at Paucatuck where Pequett bounds ends, and abutting in parte or whole vppon the said Coue.

Thomas Lord, hauing ingaged to this Courte to continnue his aboade in Hartford for the next ensuing yeare, and to improue his best skill amongst the inhabitants of the Townes vppon the Riuer within this Jurissdiction, both for setting of bones and otherwise, as at all times occassions and necessityes may or shall require; This Courte doth graunt that hee shall bee paid by the Country the sum̄ of fifteene pounds for the said ensuing yeare, and they doe declare that for euery visitt or journye that hee shall take or make, being sent for to any howse in Hartford, twelue pence is reasonable; to any howse in Wyndsor, fiue shillings; to any howse in Wethersfeild, three shillings; to any howse in Farmington, six shillings; to any howse in Mattabeseck, eight shillings; (hee hauing promised that hee will require no more;) and that hee shall bee freed for the time aforesaid from watching, warding and training; but not from finding armes, according to lawe.

The Courte is dissolued.

---

[29] A Generall Courte in Hartford, the second Thursday of September, being [the] 9th day, 1652.

John Haynes Esqr, Deputy.
Magistrates: Mr. Webster, Mr. Wells, Mr. Woollcott, Mr. Clarke.

Deputyes: Mr. Tailecoat, Mr. Steele, Mr. Westwood, Andr: Bacon, Will: Wadsworth, Steph: Harte, Mr. Trott, Nath: Dickerson, Tho: Coleman, John Deming, Mr. Phelps, Mr. Gaylerd, Dauid Willton, John Bissell, Mr. Horsford, Will Smith, Will: Parker, Robert Chapman.

The Courte being mett, they did adiourne the same to the 6th of the next month.

---

[30]   A Session of the Generall Courte in Hartford, the 6th of October, 1652.

John Haynes Esqr, Deputy.
Magistrates: Mr. Wells, Mr. Woollcott, Mr. Webster Mr. Cullick, Mr. Clarke.
Deputyes: Mr. Phelps, Mr. Gaylerd, Mr. Trott, Mr. Tailecoat, Mr. Westwood, Jo: Bissell, Tho: Coleman, Natha: Dickerson, Will: Hill, John Deming, Andr: Bacon, Will: Wadsworth, Will: Smith.

This Courte orders and appoints, that next Wednesday come seuennights shall bee kept a publique day of thanksgiuing to the Lord for his great mercyes to his people here and elsewhere, by all the plantations within this Jurissdiction.

It is ordered, that notice shall bee giuen to the Sachems of the Indians within this Jurissdiction, that no Indian shall walke or come neare vnto or amongst any English mens howses, in Townes or Farmes, on either side of the Riuer, or elsewhere, vppon the Lords day, except it bee in theire necessary way of recourse to the publique preaching of Gods word, vppon penalty of fyne or imprisonment, as any one Magistrate or more, before [*whom*] such offendors shall bee brought, shall judge meete, and as the nature of theire fact shall appeare to him or them to deserue.

This Courte desires Mr. Hill to acquaint the inhabitants of Norwaack that they require them to giue their reasons why they haue not sent deputyes to the Generall Courte nor made returne of the warrant sent to them for that end, and that neuertheless the Courte expects that they should forthwith make and returne to Mr. Ludlow a true and perfect Liste of the persons and estates in theire Towne, that a due proportion of all Comon charges may be borne by them, with the other Townes in this Jurissdiction.

It is ordered, that warrants shall goe forth from the Treasurer for halfe a Rate for the Country, according to the order of rating, to bee paid $\frac{1}{3}$ in wheat, $\frac{1}{3}$ in pease and $\frac{1}{3}$ in Indian; wheat at foure shillings, pease at three shillings, and Indian at two shillings sixpence, p^r bushell.

The estates and persons of the seuerall Townes, presented to this Courte, were as followeth:—

	£	s.	d.		£	s.	d.
Hartford,	19733.	19.	0.	Seabrooke,	03630.	00.	0.
Wyndsor,	14093.	00.	0.	Strattford,	07040.	19.	0.
Wethersfeild,	11499.	00.	0.	Fairefeild,	08850.	15.	0.
Farmington,	05164.	00.	0.		70011.	13.	0.

The Courte is adiourned to the last Wednesday in Feb^r next, in the afternoone.

---

[31] A Session of the Generall Courte, called by the Deputy Govenor, in Hartford, the 24th Febr. 1652.

John Haynes Esqr, Deputy.

Magistrates: Mr. Wells, Mr. Webster, Mr. Woollcott, Mr. Cullick, Mr. Clarke.

Deputyes: Mr. Talcott, Mr. Phelps, Mr. Steele, Mr. Westwood, Mr. Gayler, John Bissell, Dauid Willton, Nath: Dickerson, Tho: Colman, Andr: Bacon, Stephen Harte, Will: Smith.

Vppon a due consideratyon of the scarsity of prouisions in some of the Plantatyons within this Jurisdictyon, diuers persons already finding they are not suffitiently furnished with corne, flesh, etc. to carry on their family occasyons till the ordinary yearly season for supplyes comes about, It is ordered by this Courte that noe person or persons of what calling or quallity so euer within this Jurisdictyon or any Plantatyon theirof, doe either directly or indirectly ship, put off, transport, carry, send or otherwise conuey out of this Jurisdictyon, upon or under any pretence or coler, plea or reason whatsoever, any quantity greater or smaller, of wheat, rye, pease, Indyan corne, mault, biskett, or any other graine or the p^rcedd of it, or beefe, porke, bacon, butter, cheese, or any the like provisions for meate or drink, before the last of March next, or the next Session of this Courte, which is to be in Aprill next, without the license of the Deputy Goven^r, Mr. Wells & Mr. Webster, or either of y^m with the Deputy, under pen^{lty} of forfiture of the doble value, who are desired in the meane time to consider of some way how those p^rsons that are like to want may be supplyed. Advise also is to be sent to the former plantation excepted, that it may be of vse to them to attend the foresaid order.

---

[32] A SESSION OF THE GENERALL COURTE IN HARTFORD, THE 23 OF FEB: 1652.

John Haines Esqr, Deputy.

Magistrates: Mr. Wells, Mr. Webster, Mr. Woollcott, Mr. Cullick, Mr. Clarke.

Deputyes: Mr. Tailcott, Mr. Steele, Mr. Phelps, Mr. Gaylerd, Mr. Trott, Dauid Wilton, John Bissell, Andr: Bacon, Nath: Dickerson, Steephen Harte, Will: Wadsworth, Tho: Coleman, Mr. Westwood.

Wethersfeild hauing presented Rich: Trott to bee chosen Ensigne to the trained band in that towne, this Courte declares that they approue of the choyse & conferme him in that place.

This Courte considering John Lattimors loss in his horse that dyed in the Bay, being not willing that the whole loss should lye upon him, they are willing to allow him out of the publick treasury the sum of fifteen pounds towards his horse & hire, which hee thankfully accepted in the Courte.

This Courte being willing to attend all the wayes of Gods P^rvidence for the preservatyon & safty of the plantatyon of Sebrooke, with all other within this Jurisdictyon, according to the power & means that is in their hands, doe order that six of the greate guns at Seabrooke shall forthwith, & with all possible speede, be layd up & fitted compleatly vppon able carriages for the servis & defence of the said place & jurisdictyon at all times, as neede shall require, & doe allsoe desire Capt John Mason to see the premisses effected, and for that end they doe impowre him to call forth men & meanes sutable, & upon refusall to press such hands & other meanes that shall be needfull; and Tho: Traisy & Jonath: Rudd are desired to be assistant to Cap: John Mason in what is now desired of him; the charges of all which shall be payd out of the publique Treasury.

This Courte judges the Deputyes actyon in marring Jeames Wakely & the Widdo Boosy to be legall.

The Courte is adiourned to the second Thursday in Aprill next, in the morning.

[33] A Session of the Generall Courte in Hartford, the 14 Aprill, 1653.

Mr. Haynes Esqr.

Magistrates: Mr. Wells, Mr. Webster, Mr. Woolcott, Mr. Cullick, Mr. Clarke.

Deputyes: Mr. Phelps, Mr. Gayler, Mr. Steele, Mr. Tailcoat, Mr. Westwood, Mr. Trott, Jo: Bissell, Nath: Dickerson, Dauid Wilton, Tho: Colman, Andr: Bacon, Will: Wodsworth, Steephen Harte, John Demyng, Will: Smith.

It is ordered that there shall bee speedyly sent downe to Capt: Mason for the use of the Cuntry, as occasion p^{r}sents, for the present one barrill of powder; and that one barrill more of powder from the Bay shall bee left there, when they come up, & w^t else shall be thought meete by Mr. Ludlow & Mr. Cullick; it is allso ordered that 8 able men shall be imp^{r}ssed out of the Townes upon the Riuer, with compleate armes & sent to Sebrooke to bee at the command of Capt. Mason, for the saruis of the Cuntry & defence of the place, by fortefying or otherwise at the Cap: descretion; and this Courte doth farther advise the inhabytants of Seabrooke that are scattered into severall quarters, that they would, till they rec'e farther advice, speedily gather their familyes togeather in to the towne as they tender theire own safty; & if any shall refuse to attend the Courts advice, they are to know that they must runn their own hazzards, the Courte not being able to releiue them in such a scattered way as now they are in.*

Mr. Haines is desired to send downe to Cap:t Mason, for the Corssletts that belong to the Townes, to be speedily sent up to the Treasurer.

It is ordered that this Collonye should haue its proportion of the whole millitary pruision, in all respects, & perticulars sent from the Corporatyon of Eng: to the vnited Colonyes.†

It is ordered by this Courte that all fynes & peanalties of any order, within this Commonwealth, shall be paid, from the time of the publicatyon hereof, in good wheate or pease or Indyon corne, at price currant, or in that which is equiuolent thereunto.

This Courte upon a due consideratyon of the seizure of Symon Yeosens vessell, at Pawcatuck, by seuerall of the inhabitants of Pequett, doe finde & judge that by his owne confession & other testimonys prsented in Courte, according to the order of Courte in that case prvided that forbids all trade by forreigners with any Indyons within this Jurisdictyon, uppon penalty of confisscation, as by the said order more fully appears, the said Symon Yeosens vessell & goods aforesaid to be justly seized & forfited to this Common wealth, out of which the Courte allowes him six pounds in wampom, togeather with his bedding & waring apparrell & chest.

---

* "The commencement of hostilities, the last year, between England and Holland, the perfidious management of the Dutch Governor, with apprehensions of the rising of the Indians, spread a general alarm through the colony." (Trumbull's Hist. of Conn. I. 201.)

† "The Commissioners being informed that the Corporation in England had sent a percell of armes and ammunition, as a supply & for the conveyency of the Vnited Colonyes, did order that the same should be devided as followth:

	£	s.	d.		£	s.	d.
To the Massachusetts,	234.	8.	3;	which at 4d. per shill: is	309.	17.	8.
To Plymouth,	43.	6.	3;	wch at 4d. per shill: is	57.	14.	10.
To Conecticutt,	45.	5.	2;	wch at 4d. per shill: is	60.	6.	10.
To New Hauen,	37.	13	0;	wch at 4d. per shill: is	50.	4.	0.
	358.	12.	8.		478.	3.	4.

For these supplies payment was to be made by such of the Colonies as should receive their proportions, within one or two months thereafter, and the amount received was to be appropriated "for the use of the Indians, as the Commissioners for the Vnited English Colonyes shall from time to time direct." [Records of U. Colonies, May, 1653.]

It is ordered and agreed by this Courte, y^t Capt John Cullick should reserve for the Countrys use, 300 bush: of wheate & 50 bush: of pease ; & the Cuntry is to pay forbearance 8l. p^r centum for one yeare & to repay it at the end of the tearme, in the same grayne ; in like manner is desired ten barrells of porke for the same use & tearms:

This Courte orders that the neighboring Indyons to the seuerall Plantatyons within this Jurisdictyon should be required to giue an evident testimonye of their fidellity to the English, by d'd up their gunns & other armes to the Gouenor or Magistrates, & those that refuse so to doe may iustly bee deemed & looked at by them as their enemies: & that they are not to shoot of any gunn or gunns in the night, or walk in the night, except they come with a message to ye English, & in such cases they are to d'd up themselues to the watch, but if they runn away from the watch, being comãnded to stand, the watch may shoote y^m.

---

[35]   May the 18, 1653.   The Generall Courte.

   John Haynes Esqr, Gou^r.
   Edw: Hopkins Esqr, Deputy, *absent*.
   Magistrates: Roger Ludlow Esqr, *absent ;** John Winthrop Esqr, Cap: Cullick, *absent ;** Cap: John Mason, Mr. Webster, Mr. Woolcott, Mr. Clark, Mr. Howell, Mr. Taping, *absent*.
   Deputyes: Mr. Steele, Mr. Talcott, Mr. Westwood, Andr: Bacon, Mr Phelps, Mr. Gaylard, David Wilton, John Bissell, Mr. Trott, Nath: Dickerson, Sam: Smith, Tho: Coleman, Stephen Hart, Mr. Ward, Mr. Hill, John Clarke, Rob: Chapman, Will: Cheesbruck, Hugh Callkin, John Hall Junior, Rich: Olmsted, Phillip Graues.

The inhabitants of the East side of the greate Riuer are exempted from training with the Towns on the West side, this present time, & are to meete on the East side as Will: Hill shall appoint & traine their together, and so to continnue on theire

---

* Mr. Ludlow and Capt. Cullick were at this time attending a meeting of the Commissioners, in Boston.

training dayes untill the Courte take furder order : & Will: Hill is to returne the names of those that doe not meete according to appointment, as notis shall be giuen them.

Tho: Woodford is freed from watching, during the plesure of the Courte.

Roger Ludlow Esqr and Capt John Cullick are chosen Commissioners for this yeare ensuing, and are invested with full power to agitate such occatyons as concerne the vnited Collonyes in the business of this Jurisdictyon, according to their former Commission.

There are to be prest out of this Collony, 60 men, besides officers, which are to be p^{r}portioned out of the severall Towns p^r Mr. Talcott and Sam: Smith, Mr. Hill & Dauid Wilton; they are also to p^{r}portion for the p^{r}visions sutable for such a servis, for two months time.*

May the 29th, 1653.

Will: Lewis & Will: Phillips doe acknowledg themselues to be a hundred pounds indepted vnto this Jurisdictyon : the condition is, that yf Jo^n: Doyes shall be of good behauior to all peopell within this Jurisdictyon to the end & Terme of tenn days next ensuing, then this obligatyon is voyd, otherwise to stand in force.

Will: Waller is to deliuer vnto John Clarke Junior, of Seabrooke, a pair of carte-wheels that the said Waler hath now in vse, within 8 days after this date, & the wheeles are to be aprised by Francis Bushnell, Steeph: Post & Tho: Tracy, & what the said Waller is indepted upon account vnto the said John Clarke is to be allowed out of the prices of the wheels, & the said Waler is to pay vnto the said John Clarke, for his dammage, 30s, as allso the cost of the Courte.

---

* The Commissioners of the United Colonies, who were at this time in session at Boston, having "considered what number of souldgers might bee requisite if God call the Collonyes to make warr against the Dutch, & concluded that five hundred for the first expedition should bee the number out of the foure Jurisdictyons," apportioned this number to the several colonies as follows; to Massachusetts, 333 ; Plymouth, 60 ; Connecticut, 65 ; New Haven, 42. Captain John Leverett, of Boston, who had been despatched as the agent of the Commissioners, to the Manhattoes, to treat with Gov. Stuyvesant and his Council, was selected as Commander in Chief of the forces to be raised, " with respect to the opportunity hee now hath to veiw & obserue the scituation & fortifycations at the Monhatoes." [Records of U. Colonies.]

Capt: Sebadoe is this day fined tenn pounds for bartring with the Indyons, powder & lead.

Forasmuch as John Dawes hath giuen forth threatning, malitious speeches against Mr. Hopkins his person, for his executing of justice (when hee was Govern^r,) on the said Dawes his wife, this Courte censures the said John Dawes to bannishment; that the said John Dawes shall within tenn dayes ensuing depart from this Jurisdictyon, and not to returne againe to any place within this Jurisdictyon on the perill of his life.

[36] THE GENERALL COURTE, MAY THE 21, 1653.

Searjant Rich: Olmsted is allowed by the Courte to exercise the souldiers att Norworke & to vewe the armes & to make returne to the Courte of the defects.

Whearas ther is a difference betwixt Norwauke & Farfield, each towne is appointed to send two men to vewe the place and debate betwixt themselues, & if they cannot agree they are to make choyce of two inhabitants of Stratford to vew the said difference with them & make returne to the Courte how they finde it, that so there may be an issue of the same, they paying the sayd Stratford men for their time. Will: Berdsly and Phillip Groues are appointed by the Court to that servis.

The Courte hauing received order from the Commissioners that their are to be sixty fiue men to be prepared forthwith*, to be at a day's warning, with prouisions sutable; the Courte rayseth the men out of the severall towns of this Jurisdictyon as followeth, who are to be forthwith impressed to be at a days warning or call, as also that sutable p^ruisions and ammunityon shall be forthwith prepared:—

Winser,	12	Wethersfield,	8
Pequett,	5	Farmington,	3
Mattebezek,	1	Seabroock,	5
Norwack,	1	Farfield,	8
Hartford,	15	Stratford,	6—64

The officers of this Company, that the Courte requires to be over them are as followeth:—

Liuetenant Cooke is to be Commander in Cheiffe;
Liuetenant Bull, to be their Liuetenant;

---
* See note on page 241, ante.

Liuetenant Thomas Wheeler, of Fairfeild, to be their Ensigne; Rich: Olmsteed, of Norwocke, to be a Seriant, & the other Seriant is to be chosen by the officers of this Company; Hugh Wells, to be their drummer.

The Courte orders that there shall be a Committee in each Towne in this Jurisdictyon, with whom the Constables of each Towne shall take their advice in the pressing of men for this present expedition. The names of the Committee are as followeth; For Windsor, Mr. Woolcott, Mr. Chester, Mr. Clarke, Mr. Phelps & Dauid Wilton; for Hartford, Mr. Webster, Mr. Westwood & Good: Bacon; for Wethersfeild, Mr. Wells, Nath: Dickerson, Sam: Smith; for Farmington, Mr. Steele, Good: Harte; for Pequett, Mr. Wintropp (if at home,) Capt: Denison, Good: Calking & the Constables; for Seabroock, Capt: Mason, [37]   Good: Clarke & Good: Chapman; ‖ for Stratford, Good: Groues & Good: Thorenton; for Fairfeild, Mr. Ward & Will: Hill.

The Court orders that the milletary officers of Stratford shall remaine as they ware before Mr. Ludlowe went away, untill Mr. Ludlowe returne againe.

Granted to John Winthrop Esqr, the trees or timber of three or foure swamps where he can finde any Pine, Spruce or Ceder, or any other wood fitt to sawe, & liberty to cutt any other timber in any part of the wast lands for the supply of his saw mill.

The provissions to be prepared by this Jurisdictyon for the present expedityon, are as followeth; 6 bb. of Porke, 4 bb. of Flower, 3500^{lb} of Bread, 4 firkins of Butter, 400^{lbs} of Cheese, a bb. of oat meale, 1 ancor of Licquors, 2 bush: of salt, a tunn of Bear, 2 hh. of pease.

Richard Lettin complayning that his deafnes makes him uncapable of trayning, & hee desiring to be freed, its referred to the Townsmen of Fairfeild to consider of it, & to free him if they see good cause.

The Court is adiorned vnto the last Wensday in June, at one of the clocke, unless the Govornor see cause to call it sooner.

[38] A SESSION OF THE GENERALL COURTE, IN HARTFORD, CALLED BY THE GOVERNOR, THIS 25th OF JUNE, 1653.

It is ordered by this Courte that their shall forth[with] bee presented to the Bay, the present stresses, fears & dangers that the English bordering vppon the Dutch, both upon the mayne & Long Iland, are in:

Secondly, to pʳsent the iudgment of the Courte concerning the power of the Comissioners about making warr:

Thirdly, to present the reasons & grounds of the Courtes judgment, as aforesaid:

Fourthly, humbly to craue that the designe may goe on according to the consult of the Commissioners & therefore that three Magistrates may giue a call to the Commissioners to meete in thes parts for the managing of the present occatyons of the Collonyes, according to the Articles of Confederatyon. & that if thes things bee denyed, then in like manner to desire that we may haue libberty to gather up volunteers amongst them, to inable us to promote oʳ own safty & effect what necessarily conduces thereunto.

JUNE THE 27, 1653.

Whereas there are certaine barrells of powder and ammunityon* that came out of the Bay into this Riuer & Jurissdiction due to this Collony from oʳ friends in England for reasonable pay, it is therefore ordered, that the same be kept intire, not devided, vntill the expedition now in hand bee over, or elce this Courte giue other order to the contrary.

It is ordered that Mr. Haynes & Mr. Ludlow shall treate with Mr. Eaton & oʳ friends of New Hauen, boath about the ship, as also what incouraygment to sende to the English of Long Island & Indyons, as friends.

The Generall Courte is adiorned untell the last Thursday in July, if in the meane time the Governor see not cause to call it sooner.

---

* See note, on page 239, *ante*.

[39]   A Session of the Generall Courte in Hartford, this 28 of July, 1653.

John Haynes Esqr, Governor.
Magistrates: Mr. Woolcott, Mr. Webster, Mr. Cullick.
Deputyes: Mr. Phelps, Mr. Trott, Mr. Tailecott, Mr. Westwood, Edw: Stebbing, John Bissell, Nath: Dickerson, Sam: Smith, Andr: Bacon, Tho: Coleman, Stephen Harte, John Halls.

This Courte desires the Governor to write to Capt. Mason, y^t hee would heare ye difference between James Ellis & Pataquack Indyons, & if hee can, to end it, and to let them know from the Courte that if hee doe not end it they must come up to the Courte.

The Courte is adiorned to this day fortnight, at one of the clock in the afternoone.

A Session of the Generall Courte, 11 Aug: 1653.

Mr. Haynes Esqr, Govenor.
Magistrates: Mr. Wells, Mr. Webster, Mr. Woollcott, Mr. Cullick, Mr. Clarke.
Deputyes: Mr. Gaylerd, Mr. Phelps, Mr. Trott, Mr. Tailcott, Mr. Westwood, Edw: Stebbing, John Bissell, Andr: Bacon, Dauid Wilton, Sam: Smith, Tho: Coleman, Steph: Harte, Will: Smith, John Hall.

Mr. Ludlow & Mr. Cullick are desired to attend the next meeting of the Commissioners at Boston, in Sep^t. next.

This Courte appoints the Govornor, Mr. Webster, Mr. Cullick & Mr. Taillcott, as a Committee to treat with the owners of the Frigott, & agree with them for the use of the same, & to d'd her up to them as soone as they can.

This Courte consents that the Tresorer should receive of Capt. Cullicke, ye some of 10*l.* or 20*l.* for ye Countries vse, which they will repay.

The Courte is dissolued.

[40]   A GENERALL COURTE HELD THE 8 OF SEPTEMBER, 1653.
John Heynes Esqr, Govornor.
   Mr. Webster, Mr. Woolcott, Mr. Clarke, Mr. Welles.
   [*Deputyes :*] Mr. Steele, Steev: Harte, Mr. Talcott, Mr. Westwood, Andr: Bacon, Edward Stebbing, Mr. Gaylard, Dauid Wilton, *absent;* John Byssell, John More, Capt. Dennison, Good: Chesbroock, Andr: Winard, Tho: Morehouse, Rob: Webster, Will: Smith, John Clarke, Robt Chapman, Nath: Dickenson, Sam: Smith, Mr. Trott, Tho: Coleman.

   Liuetenant Cooke is allowed fifty acres of medow in Massacoe. *This Lt Cooke ownes to be in his father Ford's improuem^t, at a Court in May, Anno '61.*

   The Courte doth grant the soulders of these 4 Townes upon the Riuer and Farmington, one day for a Generall Trayning togeather, & they haue liberty to send to Capt. Mason to desire his p^rsence & to giue him a call to command in chief, & to appoint the day; p^ruided that each Towne shall haue power to reserue a guard at home, for the safty of the Townes, as occatyon shall searue.

   It is ordered that Hartford Guard shall be allowed halfe a pound a powder for a man upon the Electyon day, & no person is to desert the Guard that is therein lysted but with liberty from the Govornor.

   The list of the persons & estates in the several Towns :—

Hartford,	19749.	Norwacke,	01968.
Windsor,	15084.	Matabezeck,	01501.
Wethersfield,	12243.	Pequit,	03334.
Farmington,	05157.	Fayerfield,	8822.
Seabrooke,	04268.	Stratford,	7450.19s.

   The Court granteth Mr. Winthrope libberty to improue for his own p^rticuler, ten acres of grownd, where it may sute him for the keeping of goats, betwixt this & Pequet, without the bounds of the libbertyes of the plantatyons ; & likewise he hath libberty to finde out a place for the setting up a saw mill where it may not preiudice the plantatyons or farms allredy giuen out.

   Liuetenant Cooke is to haue 50 acres in Massacoe, on boath sides the Riuer, next aboue the Fauls. John Bissell is allso to haue 60 acres on both sides the aforesaid Riuer, next the Leiftennant.

There is also graunted to Tho: Ford 50 acres at Massacoe, whereof foure & forty hath bine improued by him by plowing & mowing as it was measured by Mathu: Graunt, bounded by the upland south west & compassed round by the Riuer, unless it be about 30 Rodde on the south east against another stripp of meadow.

There is fiue pound to be payd by the aforesaid partyes to the Tresurer, which was formerly disbursed by the Country.

It is desired, that Mr. Woollcott & Mr. Clarke should dispose of the remainder of the ground at Massacoe, to the inhabitants of Wyndsor, as they judg convenient, & to order the laying out of the former grants.

[41] Whereas it is obserued that many seamen, diuers times waygh anker in the harbours of severall Plantatyons within thes libbertyes, & pass out on the Lord's Day, to the griefe & offence of the behoulders; for the preventing whereof, it is ordred, that after the publishing this order, noe vessell shall depart out of any harbour within this Jurisdictyon but the master of the boat or vessell shall first giue notis of the occatyon of his remoue to the head officer of the Towne next the said harbour where they soe ancor & obtaine lysence under the hand of the said officer for his liberty therein; otherwise they shall undergo the censure of the Courte.

The Courte is adiorned to the last Wensday of this month, at 9 a clock.

A GENERALL COURTE IN HARTFORD, CALED BY THE GOVORNOR, UPPON SPECIALL OCCATYONS, 21th OCTOB^r, 1653.

John Hayns Esqr, Govo^r.
Mr. Wells, Mr: Woolcott, Mr. Webster, Mr. Cullick, Mr. Clarke.
Deputyes: Mr. Phelps, Mr. Trott, Mr. Tailcott, Mr. Westwood, Mr. Steele, *absent,* Mr. Gaylerd, *absent,* Edw: Stebbing, Andr: Bacon, John Bissell, Dauid Wilton,

Nath: Dickerson, John Hollister, John Deming, John Coles, Will: Smith, Rob: Webster, *absent*.

This Court desires the Magestrates & Deputyes of the Courte in Windsor to consider of the complainte of some there about the burning of tarr in or neare unto the towne, to their offence & preiudice, & to order the same as they judge meete, for the preventing of inconveniences for the future.

Mr. Gouorno^r, Mr. Ludlow, Mr. Tailcott & Dauid Wilton are chosen for a Committee to goe next seacond day to New-hauen and meete with their Committee to consider aff:*

---

[42] A SPECIALL GENERALL COURTE, CALED BY THE GOVORN-OR, HELD IN HARTFORD, THE 29 OCTOBER, 1653.

John Haynes Esqr, Govorn^r.

Magistrates : Mr. Wells, Mr. Webster, Mr. Woolcott, Mr. Cullick, Mr. Clarke.

Deputyes : Mr. Tailcott, Mr. Westwood, Mr. Phelps, Mr. Trott, Mr. Hollister, Mr. Dan: Clarke, Edw: Stebbing, Andr: Bacon, John Bissell, Nath: Dickerson, Dauid Wilton, John Deming, Steph: Hart, John Coale, Good: Calking, Good: Meads, Will: Beardsly, Tho: Sherwood, Rob: Webster, Will: Smith.

It is ordered by this Courte, that the writings which haue beene read in the Courte, shall be sent to the Bay, and to Colonell Fenwick, Mr. Hopkins & Collonell Haynes,† vnder the

---

* The refusal of Massachusetts to bear any part in the proposed war against the Dutch, which had been resolved upon by the Commissioners of all the other N. England Colonies, at the meeting in September, gave great offence to their confederates, and was announced by the latter as a violation of the articles of confederation and tending to a dissolution of the union. Special sessions of the General Courts of New Haven and Connecticut were convened shortly after the return of their Commissioners from Boston, and the former Colony determined upon seeking redress and aid from England. An address to the Lord Protector was voted, and an agent appointed to solicit from the Parliament, ships and men for the prosecu'ion of the war. A Committee was appointed to confer with Connecticut; to meet with whom, for the purpose of 'considering affairs,' the General Court of Connecticut appointed the Committee named above. The week following, letters were ordered to be addressed to Massachusetts,—and to Col. Fenwick, Mr. Hopkins and other influential friends of the Colony, in England. [New Haven Records· Trumbull's Hist. of Conn. ii. 212.]

† This was probably Hezekiah, second son of Governor Haynes, who (with his elder brother, Robert,) remained in England. In the civil war he sided with the Parliament, and eventually became a major general under Cromwell. [Trumbull's Connecticut,, i. 216 Note.]

Secretary's hand, as from the Generall Courte, for them to doe therein according to their wisdomes & light.

It is ordered & granted that warrants shall issue forth from the Tresurer, to the seuerall Townes in the Jurissdictyon, for the leving of a Rate & halfe, for this yeare, to be payd $\frac{1}{3}$ in wheate, at 4ss. p^r bush: $\frac{1}{3}$ in peass or rye, at 3ss. p^r bush: & $\frac{1}{3}$ in Indyon corne, at 2ss. bd.

Mr. Ludlow, Mr. Wells, Mr. Westwood & Mr. Hull are desiered to keepe a perticuler Courte at Farfield, before winter, to execute justice there as cause shall require.

The Courte is adiorned to the first Wednesday in December next, in the forenoone, except the Govornor see cause to call it sooner.

A SESSION OF THE GENERALL COURTE, IN HARTFORD, THE 23th OF NOVEMB^r, 1653.

John Haynes Esqr, Govor^r.

Magistrates: Mr. Wells, Mr. Webster, Mr. Woollcott, Mr. Cullick, Mr. Clarke.

Deputyes: Mr. Phelps, Mr. Tailcott, Mr. Trott, Mr. Westwood, Edw: Stebbing, Dauid Wilton, Andr: Bacon, John Bissell, Nath: Dickerson, Dan: Clarke, John Hollister, John Deming, Steep: Harte, John Coale, Rob: Webster.

This Courte taking into there serious consideratyon the complainte of the inhabitants of Middletowne, concerning John Willcock, doe order, that John Willcock shall, within 12 moneths from this time, build a tenentable howse upon the home lott giuen him by the Towne or layd out to him by them, & liue therein according to agreement, & so long as other inhabitants in that Towne are injoyned & haue agreed to liue uppon their lotts, if he soe long liue, or elce prouide an inhabitant to liue thereon in his stead for the time aforesayd; which if he shall neglectt to doe, then his home lotts & all his other allotments thereunto ap^rtaining shall returne to the Towne & bee to y^m and at their dispose, as if they had never beene laide out to him.

This Courte approues that the name of the Plantatyon commonly caled Mattabesick shall for time to come bee Middelltowne.

This Courte agrees & concludes that the 20*l*. formerly granted to a fellowship in Harvard Colledg, shall be payd next spring.

This Court is adiorned to Wedensday next, at 9 a clock in the morning.

---

[43] A Session of the Generall Courte in Hartford, the 30th of November, 1653.

Mr. Haynes Esqr, Gouornor.

Mr. Wells, Mr. Webster, Mr. Woollcott, Mr. Cullick, Mr. Clarke.

Deputyes: Mr. Tailcott, Mr. Phelps, Mr. Trott, Mr. Westwood, Dan: Clark, John Bissell, Dauid Wilton, Edw: Stebbing, Nath: Dickerson, Andr: Bacon, John Deming, Mr. Hollister, Stee: Harte, John Coale, Rob: Webster, Will' Smith.

The Courte is adiorned to the first Wednessday in March next, after Lecture.

A Session of the Generall Courte in Hartford, the first of March, 1653–54.

Magistrates: Mr. Wells, Moderator. Mr. Webster, Mr. Woolcott, Mr. Cullick, Mr. Clarke.

Deputyes: Mr. Phelps, Mr. Tailcoat, Mr. Trott, Mr. Westwood, Dauid Wilton, John Bissell, Andr: Bacon, Nath: Dickerson, John Deming, Rob: Webster, Will: Smith, Edw: Stebbing.

Vppon the complaint of Pawcatuck Indyans, this Courte orders, that they shall inioye their planting ground at Paucatuck, prouided they cary friendly & peacably to the English:—

And Goodman Stebbing & Good: White, being to goe to Paucatuck, haue libberty granted them to looke out & finde where Mr. Haynes may haue at Paucatuck the farme of three hundred acres formerly granted, which was then to abutte in p^{rt} or whole uppon Paucatuck Riuer, & they to make report to the Courte of w^t they shall finde & the true bounds of what is desired.

This Courte being informed that the inhabitants of Pequett haue taken possessyon of Vncus his forte & many of his wigwams at Monheag, doe order, that a letter should bee writtē from the Courte to the inhabitants, to acquaint them of Peaquett, to advise them not to mollest the Indyons in their planting ground or other rightfull possessions, & that if they haue done as is complayned, the Courte expects they should giue an account of their soe acting.

The Courte is adiorned till Munday next, at 8 a clock.

[44]   THE 6th OF MARCH, 1653-54.

In respect of a sad breach God hath made amongst us, in regard of the sudden death of o^r late Governor,* & the like mortallity of o^r neibours in the Bay, & some eminent removalls of others, & spreading opinions in the Collonies, the condityon of o^r natiue Countrey, the alienations of the Colonies in regard of the Combinations, It is therefore ordred that ther may be a day of humiliation throughout this Jurisdictyon, on the 15th day of this month.

A SESSION OF THE GENERALL COURTE IN HARTFORD, 6th MARCH, 1653.

Magistrates: Mr. Wells, Moderator. Mr. Ludlow, Mr. Winthrop, Mr. Webster, Mr. Woolcott, Mr. Cullick, Mr. Clark.

Deputyes: Mr. Phelps, Mr. Tailcoat, Mr. Westwood, Mr. Trott, Edw: Stebbing, John Bissell, Dauid Wilton, Nath: Dickerson, Dan: Clarke, Andr: Bacon, John Deming, Robt: Webster.

Mr. Tailcott and Mr. Sam: Willis were voated & passed to be nominated at the next Generall Courte of Electyon, for Magistrates.

---

* Gov. Haynes died March 1st, 1653-4.

It is ordred, there shall be a speciall warrant granted to Jonathan Guilbert to arest Tho: Baxter for his severall misdeameanors committed within this Jurisdictyon, to the disturbance of the peace thereof, & the said Jonathan to haue power to rayse such considerable forces as hee sees meete to execute his warrant.

Mr. Westwood & Rich: Goodman are desired to veiw the prison & cause such reperatyons to be done thereunto as they judge meete.

It is ordered, that Stratford & Fairefild should each Towne chuse a man, to be chosen Assistants to the Magistrates, and present them to the next Courte of Electyon for that end.

The Courte is adiourned to the third Wednesday in Aprill next, by 9 a clock in the morning, except the Moderato^r sees cause to call it sooner.

[45] ATT AN ASSEMBLY OF FREEMEN, IN HARTFORD, THIS 16th FEBU: 1653, TO CHUSE A MODERATOR.*

Mr. Thomas Wells was chosen Moderator for the p^{r}sent Generall Courte vnder adiourm^t: & was invested with full power by them to call the next Generall Courte of Electyon.

A SESSION OF THE GENERALL COURTE IN HARTFORD, THE 6 OF APRILL, 1654.

Magistrates: Mr. Wells, Moderator. Mr. Webster, Mr. Woolcott, Mr. Cullick, Mr. Clarke.

Deputyes: Mr. Tailcott, Mr. Phelps, Mr. Trott, Mr. Westwood, Dauid Wilton, Edw: Stebbing, John Bissell, Natha: Dickerson, John Holister, Dan: Clarke, John Deming, Andr: Bacon, Rob: Webster.

Vppon informatyon of some weaknes that for the present attends the body of Mr. Mathew Allen, this Court frees him from trayning for the present untill they see cause to the contrary.

---

* This was rendered necessary by the death of Gov. Haynes, and the absence of Deputy Governor Hopkins, who was now in England.

This Court hauing duly considered the insufferable, reproach-full speeches of Thom: Baxter against the Cheif of this Jurisdictyon, & his insolent carriages in seuerall p^rticulars (testyfied upon the oath of seaverall credible persons,) to the greate disturbance & breach of the peace of this Common wealth, doe order & sentance, that the sayd Tho: Baxter shall pay as a fine to the Common Treasuory the summ of fifty pounds, besides the 20*l.* allredy seized for the breach of his Recogniscance, & that he shall alsoe putt in 200*l.* bond as security from some able person in this Jurisdictyon, that the Courte shall approue & accept, for his behauior of the space of one whole yeare next ens[uing,] and be farther responsible to Newhaven & Road Iland for what misdemeanors he hath committed in their Jurisdictyons.

Rob: Griffen, of Newport, in Roade Iland, maketh oath in Courte, that hee did supply Tho: Baxter with what meate or provisions hee needed for himselfe & could haue supplyed him and all his men with p^rvisions from October last to this day, whereby it appears that the ground of Baxters running away from Road Iland was not through want of p^rvisions for his men, as he falsly pretended.

[46] This Court uppon the complaint of Mr. Sam: Mayo against Tho: Baxter for his unjust seizure of his vessell, the Desire, of Barnstable, & his goods therein, vnder a pretence of a commityon receved from Roade Iland, hauing duely weighed the premeses & considered all that the said Baxter can or will say in his owne defence, for his soe doing, doe finde, adiudge & declare, that the sayd Baxter hath not acted therein according to his commission or instructyons, & therefore his seizure is vniust, whereby the sayd vessell, with all that belongeth vnto her, is adiudged of right to belong vnto the sayd Mr. Sam: Mayo; & doe allso adiudg the sayd Tho: Baxter to pay vnto Mr. Mayo, for damage in severall respects sustained by him, by reason of the aforesaid vniust seizure, one hundred & fifty pounds; and the cable at Mr. Briants to be d'd to Mr. Mayo; & the said Baxter is to d'd in to Mr. Mayo the 2 bonds, one of 40*l.* & another of 1000*l.* giuen him by Dickenson & Karman, of Hempsted, in reference to the seizure : the perticulars are as followeth :—

Imp[s] For 3 mens wages & himselfe from 18 Aug. last, 68. 0. 0
  For waring cloaths & bedding, . . 10. 0. 0
  For swords & gunns, ... 6. 0. 0
  For 1[bb] of tarr, ... 1. 4. 0
  For expences in trauell in p[r]suance, . . 10. 6. 0
  For sayls & ropes that are lost, . . 12. 0. 0
  For a hh. of meale, ... 2. 10. 0
  For the loss of the use of the vessell, . 40. 0. 0
              ————
              150. 0. 0

Only it is prouided & explained that if the said Baxter shall returne with the vessell to the sayd Mayo the sayls & ropes, with two swords and 4 gunns which are taken from the vessell, they are to be discounted as part of payment out of the 150*l*. damage, at the price of 18*l*.

[47] This Courte, considering the order sent over from the Counsell of State by authority of parliament of England, that as wee expect all due incoridgment, aide and assistance from the said Common wealth of England, as the state and condityons of affaires will admitt, soe it is expected that wee should in all cases so demeane o[r]selues against the Dutch as against those that haue declared themselues enemies to the Comon wealth of England, doe therefore order & declare, that the Dutch howse the Hope, with the lands, buildings & fences thereunto belonging, bee hereby sequestred & resarued, all particular claimes or p[r]tended right thereunto notwithstanding, in the behalfe of the Common wealth of England, till a true tryall may be had of the p[r]mises, & in the meane time this Court prohibitts all persons whatsoeuer from improuing of the premises by virtue of any former title had, made or giuen, to them or any of them, by any of the Dutch natyon, or any other, without the aprobatyon of this Courte, or except it bee by virtue of power & order rec'd from them for their soe doing ; & whatever rent for any part of the premises in any of their hands, it shall not be disposed off but according to what order they shall receive from this Court or the Magistrates thereof.

This Courte considering & beeing deeply sensible of the sad effects & consequences that attend Indyons being supplyed or furnished with liquors or strong water, whereby they haue beene acquainted with and exposed vnto the commission of a grieuous sinn to the greate dishonor of God, abuse of themselues & great hazard of their liues & peace of others, doe therefore order, sentance & declare, that it shall not be lawfull for any person whatsoeuer, male or feamale, one or other, within this Jurisdictyon, either directly or indirectly, to sell, barter, lend, giue or any otherwise, under any plea, coller or pretence whatsoeuer, convay to any Indyan or Indyans, small or greate, any strong water or liquors, sack or any other sort of wine of any kinde, upon penalty of fiue pounds for a pinte, for every pinte of either wine or liquors aforesayd, & forty shillings for the least quantyty; one third part of the penalty to bee & belong to those that shall informe & proue any delinquency, *to the publique Treasury.

[48] It is also ordred, that whatsoeuer Berbados Liquors, commonly caled Rum, Kill Deuill, or the like, shall be landed in any place of this Jurisdictyon, and any part thereof drawn and sould in any vessell, lying in any harber or roade in this Common wealth, after publicatyon of this order, shall be all forfited & confiscated to this Common wealth; & it shall be lawfull for any person in this Jurisdictyon to make seizure thereof, two thirde parts to belong to the publique treasury & the other to the party seazing.

And it is allso farther ordred, that every ancor of Liquors that is landed in any place within this Jurisdictyon, shall pay to the publique treasury 10ss. & every butt of wine 40ss. or hodshede of wine 20ss. or quarter cask 10ss. wheather they are full or noe. *This order repealed, M'rch* 12th, '58–'59.

It is allso ordered, that none shall haue liberty to retaile any quantity of strong waters or wine of any sort without a license from the Courte of Magistrates, uppon peanalty of 20ss. for every default.

The Courte is adiorned till next Wednesday come fortnight, at one of the clock in the afternoone.

---

* " and two thirds," or words equivalent, seem to have been omitted here.

[49] A GENERALL COURTE OF ELECTYON, THE 18th DAY OF MAY, 1654.

Edward Hopkins Esqr, chosen Gouornor. *absent*.
Mr. Wells, chosen [*Deputy*] Govornor.
Magistrates chosen: Mr. Webster, Maior Mason, Mr. Winthop, John Cullick, *Sec^r*; Mr. Woolcot, Mr. Clarke, Mr. Willis, Mr. Tailcot, *Tresu^r*.
Deputyes: Mr. Steele, Mr. Westwood, Mr. Trott, Mr. Phelps, Mr. Fitch, Capt. Denison, Mr. Warde, Hugh Calking, John Bissell, Dauid Wilton, Tho: Foard, Andr: Bacon, Will: Hill, Dan: Titterton, Tho: Coleman, John Hollister, Phill: Graues, John Lattimore, Mathu: Grisswold, John Cole, Rob: Webster, Will: Cornwell, Mathu: Marven, Mathu: Camfield.

The freemen voted that this Generall Courte should haue power to chuse Commissioners for the ensuing yeare.

The freemen voted & ordered to bee added to the Fundamentalls, as followeth :—

That the maior p^{rt} of the Magistrates, in the absence of the Govornor & Deputy, shall haue power to call any Generall Courte; and that any Generall Courte, being legally called & mett, the maior p^{rt} of the Magistrates & Deputyes then mett (in the absence of the Govornor & Deputy,) shall haue power to chuse vnto & from among themselues, a Moderator; which being done, they shall be deemed as legall a Generall Courte to all intents & purposes as if the Govornor or Deputy were present.

The names of those who at this Courte ware mayd free, are as followeth :—

Hartford; Walter Gray, Willam Willams, John Clow, Nathan: Rusco, John Stedman:

Windsor; George Grissell, Samm: Marshall, Joseph Lummis, Thomas Lummis, Nathan: Lummis, Simon Woolcott, Joseph Phelps, Samm: Grant, Walter Lee, Anthony Hoskins, Nicholas Wilton:

Wethersfild; Thomas Wright, James Wright, John Graues, Phillip Smith:

Midletowne; William Harris, George Graues, Samm: Stocking, John Savidge, Samm: Hall, Natha: Browne, George Hubbard :

Norwack ; Mathu: Camphile, Thom: Hanford :

Farmingtone ; John Hartt, Sam: Lomes, Simon Wrothem, Joseph Kelodg, Will: Ventris, Tho: Porter, & Stephen Harte.

[50] It is ordred by this Courte, that Mr. George Hull & Allexander Knowles, of Fairefild, Phillip Graues, of Stratford, & Mathew Camfill, of Norwack, shall be Assistant to such Magestrate or Magistrates as the Courte shall at any time send amoung them, in the executyon of justice, & they hereby impouer them to examine misdeameanors, to graunt out sumons, or binde ouer delinquents to Courte, in this Jurisdictyon, for either of them to marry persons, to press horses by warrant from them as the publick welfaire of this Common wealth & theire perticuler Towns may or shall at any time require ; they giuing an acco^t to this Courte of the same, when required thereunto.

This Courte taking into consideratyon the complaint of Vncus ag^t some in Pequett for laying out & taking up parte of his land which hee conceiues they haue no right unto, doe desire, with the consent of the said Vncus, that Maior Mason would as speedily as hee may, taking Mathew Grisswold, of Seabroocke, with him, goe to Pequett & joyne with Mr. Wintrop to draw the line betwne Pequett & Vncus according to the bounds graunted that towne, beginning their line & soe carrying it on in the most indifferent place & way, that noe aduantage (as neare as can,) may be taken by Points or Coues, either to them or this Jurisdictyon, but that which is most equall on boath sides to be attended ; which being done, they are desired to sett downe where they finde the line to end, & indeavo^r to compose differences bet: Pequett & Vncus, in loue and peace ; and what they shall doe in there premises, in euery respect, they are desired to make repourt of to the Generall Courte.

Mr. Hopkins & Mr. Wells are chosen Commissioners for the yeare ensuing, & if Mr. Hopkins come not in season to attend that saruis, then Mr. Webster is desired to supply his absence.

It is ordred by this Courte, that the Assistants at the sea side shall haue liberty & power to examine those p^{r}sent misdeamenors amongst them, & as they finde cause either to sende up delinquents to come to there tryall at Conettycut, or otherwise to sende up for som Magistrates to goe theither to keepe Courte amongst them. Mr. Deputy, Mr. Webster & Mr. Clarke were desired & appointed to attend that saruis if neede soe require.

[51] Robert Webster is confirmed by the Courte Leiftenant in Middeltowne, for the yeare ensuing accord: to the motyon of the Towne.

Mr. Tailcoate & Andrew Bacon are desired to goe downe to Seabrook & attend the petityon of the inhabitants of this Towne.

It is ordered, that the Secretary of the Courte shall truly in the Country Booke of Records record the agreement of this Jurisdictyon with Colonell George Fenwick Esqr, about the forte.

Whereas, not withstanding an order of this Comon wealth that noe corne or provityons mentyoned theirin shall be transported out of this Jurisdictyon upon penalty of confisscatyon, except they enter the same with the Committy appointed by the Courte, & giue in security to them or either of them that the premises shall be deliuered as in the said order* is expressed, much corne & other provisions contrary to the sayd order is transported, and the end of the order hazarded; for the prevention whereof this Courte doth heereby authorize Capt. Denison, of Pequett, upon all vessells that come into y^t Harber, and for y^t end hee is farther authorized to goe aboard any such vessells & to require an account of theire loading & sight of their Cockett,† & such vessells as hee findes that the Ma^{r}s: of them haue not attended the aforesaid order, hee shall stop and binde ouer the said Ma^{r}s: with suffitient security, to answer the same at the next Courte at Hartford; for which hee shall haue one fourth parte of what the said Courte shall see cause to take from such delinquents, by virtue of the aforesaid order, & the Ma^r of each vessell that lades at that Towne, in p^{r}t or whole, shall enter his cargoe & giue in security to him in the behalfe of this Jurisdictyon, according to that order, to whome hee shall graunte a certificate, for which the Ma^r of each such vessell shall pay unto him 12d.

---

* Page 131, *ante.*   † A custom-house voucher, or permit.

This Courte declareth to Herman Garritt, y^t for the present they judge the proofe about ye land the Country claimes to bee stronger then his, that is in pt. of the Pequett Country, & therefore the grounds of his claime to it not to bee of suffitient strength, & soe consequently at the Countrys liberty to dispose of, & theirfore they aduise Herman Garritt not to molest Mrs. Haynes in the improument of it, hauing suffitient libberty of planting by it for himselfe & his men, & that if he can produce any further or clearer testimony to evince his right, the Court will attend it.

Edwar Stebbing & Tho: Coleman are appointed to draw up some rules for sealing leather etc.

The Courte adiorned to the first Wednesday in Aug: except the Deputy see cause to call it sooner.

[53] A Session of the Generall Courte in Hartford, called by the Deputy Govor^r, this 13th June, 1654.

Mr. Wells, Deputy Gouo^r.*

Maior Mason & John Cullick are chosen Commissioners for the yeare ensuing, and are desired to goe downe to the Bay, and attend the seruice there as occasions p^{r}sent.

The Commission of Maior John Mason, of Seabrooke, and Capt. John Cullick, of Hartford, men of approved fidellity & discretion, now sent from the Generall Courte of Conneticutt, assembled in Hartford aforesaid, this 13 day of June, 1654 :—

Whereas, the Generall Courte of Coñetticutt haue rec'd a letter from his highness Oliuer, Lord Protector of England, Scottland & Ireland, in reference to an expedition which is judged necessary without delay to be attended, wherein all the Colonies are (as is conceiued,) deeply concerned, doe therefore send you as agents from this Collonye to treate with Maior Rob: Sedgewick & Capt: John Leveritt, sent ouer with Comission from his said Highness, now at Boston, or else where, with such other person or persons as are joined in comission or counsell with them, either from his said Highness or any of the Colonies, about all matters and things what soe ever, that may appeare

---
* The names of the other members of the Court are not recorded.

necessary to bee debated, relating to the aforesaid expedityon ; and you are to certifye uppon all occatyons what shall bee the result & issue of y^r negotiations in reference to the premises.*

Instructyons for Maior John Mason & Capt. John Cullick, sent as Agents from the Generall Courte of Connecticutt, now assembled at Hartford, this 13th of June, '54 :—

You are with all convenient speed to trauell to Boston, in the Massachusetts, where you may meete with Maior Rob: Sedgewick & Capt. John Leueritt, togeather with the Agents from the other Collonies, to whome hauing (at request,) shewed y^r Commission, veiwed & p^{r}used theirs, according to the contents thereof you are to treate & negotiate with them about p^{r}suance of an expedition ag^t the Duch &c. If you finde the Massachusetts Colonye shall joyne with their due proportions of men with the other Colonyes, you may ingage o^r meete proportion with them of men as neare as you can, in order to the designe, according to the Articles of Confederatyon, provided the whole number from Eng[land] & all the Colonyes exceed not 1500. If the Massachusetts Collonye shall refuse to joyne in p^{r}portyon in the aforesaid service & uppon debate it appeares the other Colonyes, or those of them that shall joyne, may or are able to carry on the designe with hopefull fruite of success without the Massachusetts, you may ingage this Colonye to joyne therein, p^{r}vided the number of men to goe out from us exceed not 200, wherein you are to avoyde volunteers what you may, but rather then the designe shall fall you may admitt of 4 or 500, p^{r}vided they all ingage to be under the comand & at the dispose of such comanders as you shall approue or appoint ; if neede bee you may ingage, if the rest in counsell see meete, the ordinary wages for souldiers, & their proportyon of the spoile with others in that seruice, if God in his mercy giue us success.

---

* In a letter, of the 10th of June, Mr. Welles writes to Major Sedgewick and Capt. Leveret, " I have received yours of the 5th of this instant, and have given a call for a Generall Courte, but our townes being farr distant wee cannot meete untill the beginning of the weeke. I have sent a messenger to Major John Mason, who lives at Seabrooke, but he is not yet returned. I knowe that our Colony will with all thankfullness imbrace this favour and respect from his Highness, and with all readines attend the counsell and advice of his Commissioners ; wee shall send one commissioner to joine in counsell with yours, and I suppose by this time you understand what concurrence there is from the Bay, that you might informe us what number of men you expect from us and what kinde of provisions you most need," &c. [Hutchinson's Collection, 253.]

OF CONNECTICUT.   261

[52] A Generall Courte caled by the Deputy Govon^r, the 11th of July, 1654.

Mr. Wells, Deputy Govr.
Magistrates: Mr. Webster, Maior Mason, Mr. Woollcott, Mr. Cullick, Mr. Tailcoatt.
Deputyes: Mr. Steele, Mr. Phelps, Mr. Trott, Mr. Westwood, Mr. Hollister, Tho: Coleman, Andr: Bacon, John Latimore, John Coale, John Clarke, Robt Webster, Will: Cornewell.

Mr. Wells, Mr. Webster, Mr. Tailcoat, Mr. Steele, Andr: Bacon & John Cullick & Sam: Fitch are chosen as a Comittee to drawe up and sende one letter to the Coporatyon, one to Generall Monck and one to Mr. Hopkins, & to p^rvide for the Comissioners.

The order for restraint of trade with the Dutch & other forreigne natyons is repealed.

It is ordered, that there shall bee a man p^rvided to bee with Maior Mason uppon the saruice of the Country at Seabroock, adding for the same to his sallery, 20*l*. a yeare.

Dan: Garritt is to attend the prison, as Ma^r thereof.

The Courte is dissolued.

---

[54] A Session of the Generall Courte in Hartford, the 3^d of October, 1654.

Mr. Wells, Deputy Gou^r.
Magistrates: Mr. Webster, Mr. Woolcott, Mr. Cullick, Mr. Clarke, Mr. Willis, Mr. Tailcoat.
Deputyes: Mr. Steele, Mr. Gaylerd, Mr. Trott, Mr. Allen, Mr. Fitch, Mr. Westwood, Edward Stebbing, Nath: Dickerson, John Bissell, Andr: Bacon, John Hollister, Tho: Sherwood, Tho: Fairechild, Tho: Coleman, John Clarke, Rob: Webster, Tho: Chapman, Tho: Whitmore.

The distribution or devision of men to bee pressed out of each Towne to attend the expedition to Narragansett,* according to the conclusion of the Comissioners, is as followeth :—

---

* The Commissioners, at their meeting in September, had resolved upon war with Ninigret,

Windsor,	8 persons.	Wethersfeild,	6.
Pequott,	4.	Farmington,	2.
Mattabeeseck,	1.	Seabroock,	4.
Norwacke,	0.	Fairefeild,	6.
Hartford,	9.	Stratford,	5.–45.

The persons that are to goe first, wch are 24, are to bee out of the Townes following;—Windsor, 4; Pequott, 4; Matabeeseck, 1; Hartford, 6; Wethersfield, 4; Farmington, 1; Seabroock, 4;—24. The remainder of the first numb^r being 21, wch are to attend & be in reddines as a reserue, are to goe out of the towns folowing;—Windsor, 4; Hartford, 3; Wethersfield, 2; Farmington, 1; Fairefild, 6; Stratford, 5;—21.

Mr. Webster, Mr. Stone, Mr. Fitch, Mr. Will: Whiting & Mr. John Whiting, presenting to this Courte a distributyon of Mr. Whitings estate, agreed uppon by them and under all their hands, and baring date the 30th September, 1654, the Courte allowes the said distributyon & orders it to bee recorded.

The Courte allso allowes and approues of the judgment and apprehensions of the Comittee, (viz: Mr. Cullick, Mr. Steele & Mr. Allyn,) about Mr. Whitings will, so farr as they all agree, & order it to be recorded.

This Courte giues Mr. Will: Goodwin libberty to make vse of w^{tt} Timber from the waste land belonginge to the Country, hee shall haue occasion for to keepe his sawe mill in imployment.

This Courte grants Mr. Cullick libberty to draw and sell one hogshead of Clarrett & a quarter casck of red wine to his friends & neighbors, free from the Countryes excise. And this Courte doth allso further graunt unto the said Mr. Cullick, free license and libberty for the futur to draw out or sell to his friends & neighbours w^{tt} wine & liquors hee shall see cause, free from the Countryes excise.

[55] It is ordred by this Courte, that it shall not bee lawfull

---

and had ordered forty horsemen and two hundred and fifty foot soldiers to be forthwith levied from the several Colonies. Of these, Massachusetts was to provide the forty horsemen and 153 foot; Connecticut, 45; Plymouth, 41; and New Haven, 31. A part of this force was to be despatched with all expedition to the Niantic country, and the remainder to hold themselves in readiness to march upon notice from the commander-in-chief,—the selection of whom was conceded by the Commissioners, to Massachusetts. [Rec. of U. Colonies; Hutchinson's History, I, 186, 187, &. Collections, 261; Trumbull's H. of Conn. I. 223, 224.]

for any p^rsons whatsoeuer to draw any Wine, Strong waters of any sorte or kind, stronge Beare or Syder, & sell it out by retaile to any persons whatsoeuer, except such person or persons in each Towne as are licensed so to doe from the Courte.

Whereas, Notwithstanding a former order restraining the selling of all wine & liquors to the Indyans, that greate & crying sinn of Drunkenes reignes amongst them, to the greate dishonor of God & hazard of the liues and peace boath of the English & Indyans, wch as this Courte is informed is by the frequent selling of Syder or strong Beare to them, It is now ordered by this Courte, that it shall not bee lawfull for any person or persons whatsoeuer within these libbertes, directly or indirectly, to sell, lend, barter or giue to any Indyan or Indyans whatsoeuer, small or greate, one or other, any wine, liquors, beare, syder* or metheglin, or any sorte or kinde whatsoeuer except it bee their ordinary howshould beare, for wch they shall haue noe recompence, uppon the former penalty of fiue pounds for euery pinte & 40*ss*. for the least quantity, one third parte to bee to the partyes informing and the other to the publique Treasury.

This Courte orders, that the 5th day of the next weeke bee kept a publique Fast & day of humilliation, throughout all the Plantatyons in this Jurissdiction, to seeke the presence and blessing of the Lord uppon the present expedition to the Narragansetts, according to the conclusion of the Comissioners, wherein o^r future peace & comforts are much concerned.

This Courte desires & appoints the Magistrates to take the most seasonable time to giue order for a publique day of Thanksgiuing throughout this Jurisdictyon.

This Courte frees Thom: Allen, the sonn of Mr. Mathu Allen, from his fine of 20*l*.

The Comittee chosen by this Courte to press men and necessaryes in each Towne, for this expedityon, in each Towne till it bee ended, is as followeth ;—

For Windsor, Mr. Phelps & Mr. Allyn, to joyne with the Magistrates there :

For Hartford, Mr. Webster & Andrew Bacon, to joyne with the Magestrates there :

For Farmingtone, Mr. Steele & the Constable :

---

* [In margin,] " The p^rticuler respecting Sider in this law, is repealed, Mrch 11th, '58–'59."

For Wethersfeild, Mr. Hollister, Thomas Coleman, & Natha: Dickerson, to joyne with the Deputy Govonor :

For Middletowne, Rob: Webster, Tho: Whitmore, with the Constable :

[56] For Seabrooke, John Clarke & Robert Chapman, with the Maior :

For Stratford, Tho: Sherwood & Tho: Fairechild, with the Assistant & Constable :

For Fairefeild, Mr. Ward & Allexander Knowles, with the Constable :

For Pequett, Capt: Denison & Hugh Calkin, with the Constable. One drum & 1 p^r Cullers, frō Pequett :

From Hartford, a Leivetenant, & Surgeon, & 4 hogshd. of Biskett :

From Windsor, a Seriant, & 2 bar: of meale, 1 bar : of peas, & a boate.

The men are to bee uppon there march next Tuesday morning ; and are to meete in Hartford, from Windsor & Farmingtone.

It is ordered, that the size for all Casck for Beefe and Porke, after the 1 of March next, shall bee 31 gall. & $\frac{1}{2}$.

The Courte is adiorned to y^e 1 Wednesday in March next.

---

[57] A SESSION OF THE GENERALL COURTE, AT HARTFORD, SEPTEMB^r 14th, 1654.

Mr. Wells, Deputy Goven^r.

Magistrates : Capt: Cullick, Mr. Woolcott, Mr. Clarke, Mr. Willis, Mr. Talcott.

Deputyes : Mr. Steele, Mr. Trott, Mr. Phelps, Mr. Gaylor, Mr. Allen, Mr. Fitch, Mr. Westwood, Edw: Stebbin, And: Bacon, Mr. Hollister, John Bissell, Natha: Dickerson, Mr. Ward, Will: Hill, *absent ;* Tho: Coleman, Steph: Hart, Tho: Fairechild, Rich: Olmsted, Rob: Webster, Tho: Whitmore, Will: Cheesbroock, Hugh Calkin, John Clarke, Rob: Chapman.

The Lists of the Persons & Estates in the severall Townes within this Jurisdictyon :—

	Persons.	£.		Persons.	£.
	---	---	---	---	---
Hartford,	177.	19609.	Norwoake,	24.	2309.
Windsor,	165.	15833.	Stratford,	74.	7958.
Wethersfeild,	113.	12602.	Fairefeild,	94.	8634.
Midletowne,	31.	2173.	Pequott,		
Farmington,	46.	5519.	Seabrook,	53.	4437.

The lists of the persons & estates of Pequott is to bee perfected & returne thereof bee made to the Magistrates when they keepe the perticuler Courte there, as is after ordered.

This Courte orders that the estate of Capt: Baxter, attached by the Constable of Fairefield for the forfeiture of his recognizance, shall bee remitted.

This Courte orders that when executyon is don uppon the goods of Tho: Staples of Fairefeild, upon a verdict graunted to Capt: Baxter, forthwith attachm^t bee graunted upon those goods for the use of the Country, untill this Courte sees what is to be done in reference to this fine.

Whereas, Notwithstanding former provision made for the conveyance of the knowledge of God to the Natives amongst us, little hath hitherto beene attended through want of an able Interpreter, this Courte being ernestly desirous to promoate & further what lyes in them a worke of that nature, wherein the glory of God & the euerlasting welfare of those poore, lost, naked sonnes of Adam is so deepely concerned, doe order that Thomas Mynor, of Pequott shall bee wrott unto from this Courte & desired that hee would forthwith send his sonne John Mynor to Hartford, where this Courte will provide for his meintenance & schooling, to the end hee may bee for the present assistant to such elder, elders or others, as this Courte shall appoint, to interprett the things of God to y^m as hee shall bee directed, & in the meane time fitt himselfe to bee instrumentall that way as God shall fitt & incline him thereunto for the future.*

---

* " Vppon a motion made to ye Commissioners, by Capt. Cullick, from the Generall Courte of Connecticott, to take into y^r consideration ye instruction of ye Indians in theire Jurisdiction, in ye knowledge of God, and their desire y^t John Minor might bee enterteined as an interpreter to communicate to ye said Indians those instructions wch shall bee deliuered by Mr. Stone, Mr. Newton or any other allowed by the Courte, and allso y^t ye said Minor may bee further instructed and fitted by Mr. Stone to bee a meete instrument to carry on the worke of propagating ye Gospell to ye Indians, ye Commissioners conceiveing ye said propositions to bee much condu-

[58] It is ordered by this Court, that Capt: Cullick, Mr. Steele, Mr. Allen, as a Comitte by this Courte apointed, are to consider of Mr. Whitings will, & a right interpretatyon thereof, togeather with the SuPre[   ]^{rs} of the said will & make report thereof to this Courte.

It is ordered by this Court, that Mr. Talcoat, Mr. Allen, Mr. Hollister, shall joyne with Capt: Cullick in receving the accounts for the forte rate, for the yeare past, of the Constables for the severall plantations uppon the River.

Maior Mason & Capt. Cullick, (if his occasions can permitt him, if not,) Mr. Clarke, are desired to goe to Pequott & with Mr. Winthrop to keepe a perticuler Courte, before winter, to execute justice there as cause shall require.

This Courte graunts power to Maior Mason to call the Traine bands togeather once in 2 years, to exercise in a Generall training on the first or second weeke in September.

It is ordered, that warrants shall goe forth from the Tresurer for a whole rate for the Country, according to the order of rating, to be payd $\frac{3}{4}$ in wheate, $\frac{1}{8}$ in peas, $\frac{1}{4}$ in Indyan : wheatt at 4s. peas at 3s. p^r bush : Indyan at 2s. 6d.

It is ordered by this Courte, that the next Wednesday come three weekes, bee kept a day of Publique Thanksgiuing in the severall Plantations within this Jurisdictyon.

The Courte is adiorned to the first Wednesday in March next except the Deputy Govornor see cause to call it sooner.

---

[59] Articles of Agreement, made and concluded betwixt George Fenwick Esqr of SeaBrooke Fort, on ye one part, and Edward Hopkins, John Haynes, John Mason, John Steele and James Boosy, for and on ye behalfe of ye Jurisdiction of Connecticott River, on ye other part, ye 5th of Decemb^r, 1644.*

The said George Fenwick Esqr doth by these p^{r}sents convey

---

cing to ye propagating of y^t hopefull work, doe desire ye Magistrates of Connecticott to take care y^t ye said Minor bee enterteined at Mr. Stones or some other meet place, and they shall order y^t due allowance bee made for his dyet and education out of the corporation stock." [Rec. of U. Colonies; Sept. 23d, 1654.]

* Recorded here, pursuant to an order of the Court, May 18th. [See pp. 119, 215, 258, ante.]

and make over to yᵉ use and for yᵉ behoofe of yᵉ Jurissdiction of Connecticott River aforesaid, yᵉ Fort att SeaBrooke with yᵉ appertenances hereafter mentioned, to bee inioyed by them for euer :

Two demiculvering cast peeces, with all yᵉ shott thereunto appertaining, except fifty wᶜʰ are reserved for his own use :

Two long Saker cast peeces, with all yᵉ shott thereunto belonging; one Murderer, with two chambʳˢ, and two hammered peeces ; two barrells of Gunpowder :

Forty musketts, with Bandaleers and rests, as allso foure carabines, swords, and such irons as are there for a draw bridge ; one sow of lead, and irons for yᵉ carriages of ordinance ; and all yᵉ housing within yᵉ Palisado :

It is allso provided and agreed betwixt yᵉ said parties, yᵗ all yᵉ land uppon yᵉ River of Connecticott, shall belong to yᵉ said Jurissdiction of Connecticott, and such lands as are yet undisposed shall bee ordered and given out by a Committie of five, whereof George Fenwick Esqʳ aforesaid is allwayes to bee one.

It is further provided and agreed, yᵗ yᵉ Towne of Sea Brooke shalbee carryed on according to such agreements, and in yᵗ way which is allready followed there and attended betwixt Mr. Fenwick and yᵉ Inhabitants there.

It is allso provided and agreed betwixt yᵉ said parties, yᵗ George Fenwick Esqʳ shall have liberty to dwell in and make use of any or all yᵉ howsing belonging to yᵉ said Fort, for yᵉ space of ten yeares ; hee keeping those wᶜʰ hee makes use of, in sufficient repaire, (extraordinary casualties excepted ;) and in case hee remove his dwelling to any other place, yᵗ hee give halfe a yeares warning thereof, yᵗ provision may bee made accordingly ; onely it is agreed yᵗ there shall bee some convenient part of yᵉ howsing reserved for a Gunner, and his family, to live in, if yᵉ Jurissdiction see fitt to settle one there.

It is further provided and agreed bettwixt yᵉ said partyes, that George Fenwick Esqʳ shall inioye to his owne proper use, these pʳticulers following :—

1. The house neare adioyning to yᵉ wharfe, with yᵉ wharfe and an acre of ground thereunto belonging, provided yᵉ sayd acre of ground take not up above eight rodd in breadth by yᵉ water side :

2. The point of land and ye marsh lying under ye barne allready built by ye said George Fenwick:

3. The Island, comonly called Six Mile Island, with ye meadow thereunto adioyning, on ye east syde ye River:

4. The ground adioyning to ye Towne-feild, wch is already taken of and inclosed wth 3 rayles by ye sayd George Fenwick; onely there is lyberty granted to ye said Jurissdiction, if they see fitt, to build a Fort uppon ye westerne point, whereunto there shalbee allowed an acre of ground for a house lott.

[60] It is also provided and agreed, y^t ye said George Fenwick Esqr shall have free warren in his owne land, and lyberty for a fowler for his owne occasions, as allso ye like liberty is reserved for any other of ye Adventurers y^t may come into these parts, with a double howse lott, in such place where they make choise to settle theire aboade.

All ye formentioned graunts (except before excepted) ye said George Fenwick Esqr doth ingage himselfe to make good to ye Jurissdiction aforesaid, against all claymes y^t may bee made by any other to ye premises, by reason of any disbursements made upon ye place:

The said George Fenwicke doth allso promise y^t all ye lands from Narragansett River to ye Fort of Sea Brooke, mentioned in a Pattent graunted by ye Earle of Warwicke to certaine Nobles and Gentlemen, shall fall in under ye Jurissdiction of Connecticutt, if it come into his power.

For and in regard of ye premises and other good considerations, ye sayd Edward Hopkins, Jno Haynes, Jno Mason, Jno Steele and James Boosy, authorized thereunto by ye Generall Courte for ye Jurissdiction of Connecticott, doe, in behalfe of ye said Jurissdiction promise and agree to and with ye said George Fenwicke Esqr, y^t for and during ye space of ten full and compleate yeares, to beginn from ye first of March next ensuing ye date of these presents, there shall bee allowed and payd to ye said George Fenwicke or his assignes, ye perticuler sums hereafter following:—

1. Each bushell of Corne of all sorts, or meale y^t shall passe out att ye Rivers mouth, shall pay two pence p^r bushell:

2. Every hundred of Biskett y^t shall in like manner passe out att ye Rivers month, shall pay six pence:

3. Each milch cow, and mare of three yeares ould or upwards, within any of ye Townes or farmes uppon the River, shall pay twelue pence p^r annū: during ye foresd tearme :

4. Each hogg or sow y^t is killed by any p^rticuler p^rson within ye lymitts of ye River and the Jurissdiction aforesayd, to bee improved eyther for his owne p^rticuler use, or to make marketts of, shall in like manner pay twelve pence p^r annū:

5. Each hoggshead of Beaver traded out of this Jurissdiction, and past by water downe ye River, shall pay twenty shillings :

6. Each pound of Beaver traded within ye lymitts of ye River shall pay two pence, onely it is provided y^t in case the generall trade with ye Indians* now in agitacōn p^rceed, this tax uppon Beaver, mentioned in this and ye foregoing article, shall fall :

7. The sayd Committie doe, by the power aforesayd, consent and agree to and with ye sayd George Fenwicke Esqr, y^t hee ye said George Fenwicke and his heires shall bee free of any imposition or customes y^t may heereafter by the Jurissdiction bee imposed att ye Fort.

It is agreed y^t the aforesaid payments shall bee made in manner followinge :—

What shall bee due from ye graine that is exported shall bee payd in graine according to the proportion of the severall kindes of graine that doe pass away, att the common current price, neyther attending such prises on ye one hand that the Courte may sett, nor yett on the other hand such as Corne may bee sould att through the necessityes of men; and in case of [61] any difference,‖ then the price shall bee sett by two good men the one to be chosen by Mr. Fenwicke and the other by the Courte : what shall bee due otherwise shall bee paid in Beaver, wampom, barly, wheat or pease, the former consideration for the p[rice] to bee herein allso attended ; and it is provided and agreed that a strict order and course shall bee taken in observing what graine is putt aboard any vessell that goeth downe [the] River, from any of the Townes, and due notice being [taken] thereof, every boate or vessell shall bee inioyned to

---

* See page 113, *ante;* Rec. of U. Colonies, in Hazzard's St. Papers, ii. 19.

take note from some deputed by the Courte in each Towne, what quantityes and kindes of graine are aboard the said vessell, and to deliver to Mr. Fenwicke or his assignes att SeaBrooke, so much as will bee due to him according to the forementioned Agreements. And likewise [for the] other payments due care shall bee taken that [they bee] made att the place aforesaid, in as convenient a way as [may] comfortably bee attended, and y^t all indirect courses bee prevented whereby the true meaning of these agreements may bee evaded.

In witness whereof the parties beforementioned have hereunto put theire hands, the day and yeare abouesayd.

      Geor: Fenwick   Edward Hopkins,
                                              Jo: Haynes,
                                              John M[ason,]
                                              John Steel,
                                              James Boosye.

I have examined and compared this writing with the originall and finde it to bee a true Coppy this 4th of March, 1655-56.

                                        John Cullick, Sec^r.

It was afterwards concluded both by the Generall Courte of Connecticutt and Mr. Fenwicke, that in case there should any difference arise touching the Interpretation of any of the within mentioned Agreements, the determination and issuing thereof should bee referred to those who made the sayd Agreements, being best acquainted with theire owne intendments.

It was allso agreed betwixt George Fenwick Esqr and the Committee mentioned, the 11th of Octob^r, 1645, in regard there hath not beene a due and full attendance to the said Agreements this p^{r}sent yeare, by [many,] which in parte arose from the unwillingness in masters of vessels to [stay] allwayes att SeaBrooke for the delivery of the corne due to Mr. [Fenwick,] that the sayd Agreements shall beginn and take place from the [first] of March next, being 1645, to the end and tearme of tenn yeares; [and] for the preventing of the beforementioned difficulty, George Fenwick [Esqr] doth agree & is content to take what corne shall bee due unto [him, att] the Townes of Hartford or Wethersfeild. And the sayd Com[mittee doth, in] behalfe of the Generall Courte, and by vertue of [power committed] to them, [agree] and undertake that att any time [within four]teene days, [after] warning and notice given by [Geo: Fenwick Esqr, or his assignes, there] shall bee delivered to [any vessell he or they shall appoint, such corne] as is due to him by [vertue of this Agreement, att eyther of the Townes aforesaid. Neverthelesse, it is still provided that the Ma^r of every vessell [62] carry a note of the quantityes of grayne,] ‖ with the severall kindes thereof, that are laden by any aboard his vessell from such persons as are deputed by the Generall Courte to that service, and deliver it to George Fenwick or his assignes, before they depart from SeaBrooke, under the penalty mentioned in an order, made by the Generall Courte of Connecticott, for preventing of any indirect or collusive proceedings in violation of the sayd Agreement. And whereas severall penaltyes are by the sayd order to bee inflicted uppon such as shall transgress, or seeke to evade the true meaning of the sayd agreements, It is now agreed and consented to by the aforesayd Comittie, that the one halfe of that wch is so forfeited by any shall bee and appartayne to the sayd George Fenwick Esqr, or his assignes, and the other to such as shall informe.*

E: Hopkins.

I have examined and compared this writing with the originall, and finde it to bee a true Coppy, this 4th of March, 1655-56.

John Cullick, Sec^r.

[63]   Feb^r: 17: 1646.

It was agreed betwixt Edward Hopkins on ye behalfe of George Fenwick Esqr, and John Cullick, John Tallcott, John Porter and Henry Clark, James Boosie and Samuell Smith, on behalfe of ye Jurissdiction of Connecticutt, that the Agreement formerly made with Mr. Fenwick shall bee altered, and what was to bee receaved by him according to that, reduced to the tearmes heareafter expressed : viz : there shall, yearely for ten yeares payd to Mr. Fenwick or his Assignes, one hundred and eighty pounds p^r annum, to bee payd every yeare before ye last of June, as it shall bee required by the Assignes of the sayd G.

---

* Pages 61 and 62, of the record, are much torn and defaced ; the missing portions have been supplied by reference to the original agreement, preserved in Vol. I of 'Towns & Lands,' Doc. No. 3.

Fenwick, either to such vessells as shall bee appointed, or to such house or houses in Wethersfeild or Hartford as hee shall direct and order, to bee payd $\frac{1}{3}$ in good wheat att 4s. p^r B: $\frac{1}{3}$ in pease att 3s. p^r B: $\frac{1}{3}$ in Ry or Barly att 3s. p^r B^{ll}, and if ry or barly bee not payd, then to pay it in wheat and pease in an equall proportion ; only this present yeare, some Indian corne shall bee accepted, but as little as may bee ; Allso there is to bee receaved by the sayd Geo. Fenwick, what shall bee due from Springfeild for the foresayd tearme of 10 yeares, as allso what else may bee due uppon the Beaver trade, according to the former Agreement with him: Allso, whereas the Towne of SeaBrooke is to pay, in this sum of 180l. for this yeare, 10l., when that Towne increaseth so as they pay a greater proportion in other rates, in reference to what these Townes, Windsor, Hartford, Wethersfeild and Farmingtowne doe pay, they shall increase theire pay to Mr. Fenwick accordingly : allso, whereas Mattabesuck may hereafter bee planted, they shall pay to Mr. Fenwick in the same proportion they pay other rates, to these Townes : These foure Townes being accounted at one hundred and seaventy pounds.

   Edward Hopkins,   John Tallcott,
   John Cullick,
      James Boosie.

I haue examined and compared this writing with the originall and finde it to bee a true Coppie, this 4th of March, 1655-56.
            John Cullick Sec^r.

---

[64] A SESSION OF THE GENERALL COURTE IN HARTFORD, THE 7th OF MARCH, 1654-55.

Mr. Wells, Deputy.

Magistrates : Mr. Webster, Mr. Woollcott, Mr. Cullick, Mr. Clarke, Mr. Willis, Mr. Tailecoate,

Deputies : Mr. Steele, Mr. Phelps, Mr. Trott, Mr. Gaylerd, Mr. Allyn, Mr. Westwood, Mr. Hollister, Edw: Stebbing, John Bissill, Andrew Bacon, Nath: Dickerson, Steph: Harte, Tho: Coleman, Tho: Whittmore.

Richard Church is freed from watching, warding & training.

This Courte allowes the souldiers yt went uppon the last expedition to ye Narragansetts, by vertue of the determination of the Comissionrs, as followeth:

 To the comõn souldiers, 16*d*. a day;
 To the Drumẽrs, 20*d*. a day;
 To the Serieants, 2*s*. a day;
 To the Ensigne, 2*s*. 6*d*. a day;
 To the Leiftenant, 3*s*. a day;
 To the Steward, 2*s*. a day.

This Courte desires Mr. Wells & Nath: Dickerson, for Wethersfield; Mr. Webster and Mr. Cullick, for Hartford; Mr. Clarke & Mr. Allyn, for Windsor; Mr. Steele & Steph: Harte, for Farmington; Thomas Allyn and Robert Webster, for Midletowne, to receive, allowe & signe to the Treasurer, such bills of debts from ye Country to any perticular person as shall bee brought in to them in theire severall Townes. And Mr. Webster & Mr. Cullick are desired to audite the Treasurers accot for the yeare past.

This Courte hath considered the acknowledged transgression of lawe, about casting Ballast in an inconvenient place, at Wethersfield, by William King, Marriner; uppon severall grounds they doe mitigate the penalty of the said order, and doe adiudge the said King to pay for his transgression aforesaid, 20*ss*.

This Courte advises that it bee prsented to the Gen: Courte in May next, that it may bee ordered, that notwithstanding the former order wch req: that such goods as are disstreined uppon execution should bee apprized by 3 men, as yt Lawe directs, wch now proves to bee inconvenient & sometimes iniurious to ye creditors, it shall hereafter bee lawfull for ye Marshall to make sale of such goods distreined wthout the apprizemt before specified, as well as hee may, for the good of the debtor, for the same pay that the debtor was to make.

---

[65] A GENERALL COURTE OF ELECTION [IN] HARTFORD, THIS 17th OF MAY, 1655.

 Mr. Thomas Wells, chosen Govrnor.
 Mr. John Webster, Deputy Govrnor.

Mr. Hopkins, *Magistrate*; Maior John Mason, *Magistrate*; Mr. Winthrop, *Magistrate*. Mr. Woollcott, *Magistrate*. Mr. Cullick, *Magistrate & Sec^r*; Mr. Clarke, *Magistrate*; Mr. Willis, *Magistrate*; Mr. Tailecoate, *Magistrate, Treasurer*; Mr. John Cosmore, *Magistrate*; Capt. Thomas Topping, *Magistrate*.

Deputyes: Mr. Steele, Mr. Phelps, Mr. Gayler, Mr. Allyn, John Bissell, Mr. Trott, Nath: Dickerson, Mr. Hollister, John Deming, Mr. Warde, Mr. Hill, Mr. Westwood, Edward Stebbing, Andrew Bacon, Mr. Brewster, *absent*, Will' Cheessbrooke, *absent*, Robert Webster, Will' Smith, *absent*, John Pratt, *absent*, Phillip Groves, Steph: Harte, *absent*, John Clarke, Rich: Webb, Nath: Camfeild, Thomas Fairechild.

The names of those wch were made Freemen of this Jurissdiction, at this Courte, are,—Mr. John Russell Senior, Jacob Gibbs, John Hubberd.

The freemen hath impowered this Generall Courte to chuse Commission^rs for them, for the yeare ensuing.

A letter is to bee sent to East Hampton, in ans: to theires, y^t it can bee no advantage, but rather the contrary, to theire ^devided, shattered condition, not to have dependance uppon or bee under some settled Jurissd: &c. and therefore advise y^m so to doe, &c. and to pay w^tt is theire just dues to this Comonwealth.

Math: Camfeild, for Norwaack, & Phillip Groves, for Stratford, are confirmed Assistants, according to former order, in May (54.)

Maior John Mason & Capt. John Cullick are chosen Commission^rs for this Collony for the yeare ensuing, to agitate with the other Collonyes, according to the Articles of Confederation, and Mr. Tailecoate is chosen as a Reserve.

Mr. Gov^rno^r, Mr. Deputy & Mr. Clarke are desired to goe downe to the sea-side to keepe Courte at Fairefeild or Strattford.

Maior Mason, Mr. Cullick & Mr. Tailecoate, are desired to goe to Pequett, as soone as may conveniently sute them and the Towne, to keepe Courte there, and w^tt other necessary service shall appeare.

This Courte, considering the petition of Capt. John Underhill, in refference to his seizure of ye Dutch Howse, Hope, & lands; they doe, in way of answer, returne as followeth: First, y^t notwithstanding all y^t hath yet appeared to them, they may and doe declare y^t till more appeares, they shall meinteine theire owne seizure of ye p^{r}mises, according to the end and extent thereof. 2dly, y^t they see not cause to warr^t his seizure, neither shall they allowe or approve of his sale thereof, to any person w^{tt}soever, from this Jurissdiction.*

Concerning Mrs. Styles petition, ye Courte declares y^t if the Comittee y^t goes to keepe Courte at Strattford and the Towne of Strattford sees cause, they may settle uppon Mrs Styles w^{tt} shee desires.

[66] This Courte considering the sad complaint of Goody Beckwith, of Fairefeild, in referrence to her husbands deserting of her, doe declare y^t by w^{tt} evidences hath beene p^{r}sented to them of ye manner of her husbands departure and discontinuance, they judge that if the said Goody Beckwith, wife of Thomas, shall uppon her oath testifie to the Magistrates that are shortly to keepe Courte at Strattford, that her husbands departure was as others have testified it to bee; and y^t shee hath not heard from him nor of him any wayes since hee deserted her, the said Magistrates may give her a bill of Divorce & sett her free from her said husband.

This Courte considering the appeale of Jonas Wood, of South Hampton, and well weighing the grounds & causes thereof, doe

---

* In May, 1653, Capt. Underhill was commissioned by the Colony of Providence Plantations, as commander in chief of their land forces, for the prosecution of the war against the Dutch. Under and by virtue of this commission, (and, as he alleges, with the permission of the General Court then in session at Hartford,) on the 27th and 28th of June, 1653, Capt. Underhill seized the Dutch Fort, "The House the Hope," at Hartford, with the lands adjacent. In April, 1654, [page 254, *ante*,] the General Court ordered the Dutch house, with the lands &c. thereunto belonging, to be sequestered and reserved in the behalf of the Commonwealth of England, "*all particular claims or pretended rights thereunto notwithstanding*," "till a true trial may be had of the premises," and in the mean time prohibited all persons from improving the premises by virtue of any title other than should be given them by the Court.

In the petition now presented to the Court, (a certified copy of which is preserved in Vol. I of "Towns & Lands," Doc. No. 81.) Capt Underhill asks permission to sell and convey the property he had seized two years before,—pleading his past services to the Colonies, his straitened circumstances, and the justice of his claim. Notwithstanding the refusal of the Court to grant the prayer of the petition, Capt. U. proceeded to effect a sale, and on the 18th of July following, executed a deed of the premises to Wm. Gibbins & Richard Lord. [Towns & Lands, 1. 82.]

judge and declare, that as things have appeared to them they cannott but justifie the said Woods appeale against John Cooper, and doe judge that Cooper hath vnjustly molested, troubled, greived, and dissparaged the said Wood, in a speciall manner in and about his telling Wood that hee lyed against his knowledge and concience, wch charge of his hath evidently appeared to this Courte to bee alltogether groundless aud scandalous. The p^rmises being considered, they doe adiudge the said John Cooper to pay as followeth :

Im: To Wood, for his charge uppon the first Jury, and all other charges for his owne defence and clearing, at the severall other Courtes at South Hampton, wherein hee was defend^t, and all other charges of evidences, wittnesses and otherwise, in order to his appeale to this Courte, ye sum of thirty pounds,

£30. 0. 0.

2dly To Wood, for slaundering of him, as aforesaid, 05. 0. 0.
3dly To the Country, in p^t of theire charge in attendance uppon ye aforesaid appeals,   05. 0. 0.

40. 0. 0.

It being the true intent & meaning of this Courte, notwithstanding the p^rmises, that John Cooper should pay all the charges of the two last p^rticular Courts at South Hampton and of the Generall Court there, over and above the aforesaid sum of forty pound, that is, so farr as Cooper as plantiff procured ye charge for himselfe or for the maintenance of his cause against Wood ; but so farr as Wood procured any charge for his owne defence & clearing, Wood is to pay out of the aforesaid sum of 30*l*.

If John Cooper shall not satisfie & discharge to Jonas Wood the judgem^t of this Court, viz : the sum of 35*l*. betweene this & the first of July next, then Wood may proceed to execution. The Sec^r. is ordered to deliver execution to Jonas Wood accordingly.

This Courte allowes Cornelius Hull, out of the publique Treasury, for his charge and expence in coming up hither to give in testimonie concerning Baxster, 20*ss*.

John Elderkin, of Pequett, being p^rsented to this Court as chosen by ye Towne of Pequett to keepe an ordinary, according to order of Courte, wch hee hath accepted of to attend after 29 Sep^t: next, the Court confirmes him in that place.

[67] This Courte allowes the keeper of the prison, for his yearly s[alary] 12*l*. & for delinquents 6*s*. 8*d*. ahead.

It is ordered, that the Towne of Norwack shall possess & inioy all ye land wch they purchased of the Indians, not of right belonging to the plantation of Fairefeild.

This Court orders, that in the intervalls of Generall Courts, ye Magistrates shall have power to appointe publique dayes of Thanksgiving & Humilliation, in this Jurissdiction, as they shall judge meete.

It is ordered by this Courte, with the approbation of ye Deputyes from the seaside, viz: Fairefeild, Strattford & Norwacke, that the whole charge of all such Courts as are kept in any of the aforesaid Townes, wherein none are questioned for ye breach of some capitall lawes, shall bee borne by those said Townes, and that all the charge of such Courtes in any of the aforesaid Townes as shall have some charged in them for the breach of any capitall law as aforesaid, shall bee borne one halfe by the said Townes, & the other halfe by the Country.

Whereas, it doth evidently appeare to this Courte that the Secretary thereof, for some yeares past, hath not had sutable recompence for his great paines in the service of his place, by the former provision or allowance they have made in consideration thereof; It is ordered by this Courte, that the Sec^r shall have 18*d*. for every action entred by the taking out of any warrant respecting the same, either from himselfe or any other Magistrate, under the sum of forty shillings, and 6*d*. for every warrant: And for every action, as before, above ye sum of forty shillings, the Sec^r shall have 2*s*.; And that if any Magistrate graunts a warrant respecting any action, they shall bee paid for every warrant, six pence: and they shall take the Secretary's fees of such persons as they graunte theire warrants to, and at every Courte, make due payment thereof to him:

It is allso further ordered, that the Sec^r shall have for every Attachement or Replevin, bond and action belonging thereunto,* 5*s*.; for every Execution under fifty shillings, 2*s*. 6*d*., and every Execution above fifty shillings, 5*s*.; for every Will or In-

---

* [In margin;] " and for coppies of them, halfe so much."

ventory or both, under 50l., 3s. 4d.; & for every under a hundred pound, five shillings; and for every one above a 100l., 6s. 8d. And for the Orders of common concernment in each session of the Generall Court published, 2s. from each Towne where they are published; & what writing perticuler Townes or persons makes y̓e Sec̓r, at any Generall Courte or session thereof, they shall pay and allowe, w̓thout any delay, good recompence & satisfaction to his reasonable content. For every Recognisc: entring in Courte, uppon the entry thereof 2s.

The Courte is adiourned to the 1 Wednesday in July next.

---

[68] A Generall Court in Hartford, the 4th of Octobr, 1655.

Mr. Wells, Gov̓rno̓r.
Mr. Webster, Deputy.
Magistrates: Mr. Cullick, Mr. Clarke, Mr. Willis, Mr. Tailecoate.
Deputyes: Mr. Fitch, Mr. Allen, Mr. Trott, Mr. Hull, Mr. Steele, *absent*, Mr. Woolcott, Mr. Westwood, Mr. Hill, *absent*, David Willton, Edward Stebbing, John Bissell, Andrew Bacon, Nath: Dickerson, Sam: Smith, Tho: Coleman, John Brunson, William Smith, Phillip Grove, Thomas Fairechilde.

Bartho: Barnard, of Hartford, is fyned 5s. for not returning the warrants seasonably for Deputyes, according to order.

The Widdow Gibbs her forfeiture of 4l. as by record of Courte, in Sept. (54) is by this Courte remitted to one halfe, yt is to say, that shee shall pay but 40ss. wch*

Richard Lettin, being called 3 times to appeare at this Courte in answer to his Recognisc: and not answering thereunto, hath forfeited his Recognisc: of 20l.

George Phillips, by reason of severall weakenesses that attend him, is freed by this Courte from Training during his aforesaid weakeness.

The Comissionrs of Strattford & Fairefeild are fyned 40s. a

---

* The original is thus incomplete.

peece, for theire neglect of meeting according to order, for the perfecting the Lists.

Sea-Brooke is fyned forty shillings, for not sending ye Lists of theire estates to the Courte.

Norwacke is fyned in like manner, for ye same defect, 40ss.

The Lists of the persons and estates in ye severall Townes within this Jurissdiction:

	Persons.	Estates: £.		Persons.	Estates: £.
Hartford,	176.	19525.	Sea-Brooke,		
Windsor,	152.	15595.	Norrwake,		
Wethersfeild,	102.	12404.	Strattford,	65.	8165. 10s.
Farmington,	52.	5910.	Fairefeild,	90.	9255. 18
Midletowne,	32.	2315.	Pequett.		

The last Wednesday in this month is appointed by this Courte to bee solemly observed a day of publique Thanksegiving to ye Lord (for renewed mercyes,) by all the Plantations in this Jurissdiction.

This Courte adiudges y^t Wm. Lewis as Attorny to John Cogg[ ] shall pay unto James Wakely thirty shillings for his charges, damages & uniust molestations hee has sustained, by reason of his Attornyshipp to Stephen Day, of Cambridge.*

[69] This Courte graunts a penny in the pound, to bee levied to de[fray the] Country charges & debts, wch is to bee paid three fourths in wheat and pease and one in Indian.

This Courte orders that Danniell Porter shall bee allowed and paid out of the publique Treasury, as a sallery for the next ensuing yeare, the sum of six pounds, and six shillings a journy to each Towne uppon the River, to exercise his arte of Chiurgerie.

The Courte is adiourned to ye last Wednesday in March next.

March 26, 1656.

Deputyes: Mr. Fitch, Mr. Allyn, Mr. Woollcott, Mr. Trott, Mr. Westwood, Edw: Stebbing, Capt: Willton, Nath: Dickerson, Andr: Bacon, Tho: Coleman, John Bissell, Sam: Bissell, Rob: Webster.

---

* [In margin:] " John Cullick dissents from the Court in this Act of theires: John Cullick."

It is ordered by the Courte, that Mr. Wollcott shall assist Mr. Clarke in attending the deffects about trainings in the Towne of Wyndsor, in such cases as 2 Magistrates have power to ishue.

This Courte doth graunt the request of Good: Wadsworth, Good: Lewis, Good: Wilterton, Good: Seager, in freeing them from training & watching.

Capt. Jno: Cullick this day promising to deliver into the Courte the originall agreements betweene Mr. Fenwick & this Collony for what they purchased of him, which being done, this Courte doth order that this Committee now chosen shall give Capt. Cullick a trve coppy of them vnder their hands, which shall be att all times full and good in law to all intents & purposes as the originall writings, which writings shall be sealed with the seale of the Collony.

The names of the Committe now chosen to subscribe ye aforesd coppys are, Mr. Welles, Mr. Webster, Major Mason, Mr. Tallcott, Mr. Steele, Mr. Westwood, Mr. Woolcott, Sam̄: Smith.

Mr. Webster, Mr. Tailcott, Mr. Fitch, Mr. Woolcott, and Sam̄: Smith are chosen to as a Committe for to take in the Accot^s from ye Capt. concerning the monies pd for their purchase of Mr. Fenwick.

The Courte is adjourned to this day fortnight, if the Governo^r sees cause y^n to call it.

---

[70] A GENERALL COURTE OF ELECTION IN HARTFORD, 15 MAY, 1656.

Magistrates elected:

Mr. Webster Esqr, Governo^r.

Mr. Welles Esqr, Dep^t. Governo^r.

Mr. Hopkins Esqr, *Magist.*, Mr. John Winthrope Esqr, Major John Mason, *Magistrate*, Mr. John Cullick, *Magist: & Sec^r.*, Mr. John Clarke, *Magistrate*, Mr. Willis, *Magistrate*, Mr. Tallcott, *Magistrate & Treasurer*, Capt. Topping & Mr. Ogden, *Magist.*

Deputyes: Mr. Steele, Mr. Allyn, Mr. Gaylard, Mr.

Brewster, Mr. Trott, Mr. Ward, Mr. Hull, *absent*, Mr. Westwood, Mr. Newberry, Nath: Dickerson, Sam̃: Smith, Nath: Ward, Edw: Stebbing, Andr: Bacon, Tho: Coleman, Edw: Griswold, Math: Campfeild, Hugh Calkin, John Brunson, John Hurd, John Welles, John Clarke, Robert Webster, *absent*, Tho: Allyn.

Persons made free :—Bartho: Bernard, Wm. Gutteridge, Ben: Harbo^r, Philip Davis, Gabriell Line, Wm. Judd.

This Courte doth graunt that John Bissell shall keepe the ferry at Wyndsor for the next ensuing yeare, being ingaged to performe the former tearms of his keeping the same with this addition, that whosoever in this Jurisdiction shall be listed, with the approbation of the Gen: Courte, from yeare to yeare, for troopers, shall be passage free for horse & man, so long as he keepes himselfe vnder & performes the tearmes of his listing, so often as the said troopers shall with their listed horses travill with them to Springfeild towne or beyond.

Major Mason & Mr. Tailcoate are chosen Commissioners for the yeare ensuing, and Mr. Fitch as a Reserve.

Good: Groves is chosen an Assistant for the towne of Stratford, Ensigne Gold for Fairefeild, Good: Campfeild for Norwalke; Good: Campfeild is ordered to give the oath vnto the other two Assistants.

Mr. Governo^r, Mr. Deputy, Mr. Cullick & Mr. Tailcoat are desired in some convenient time to advise wth the elders of this Jurisdiction about those things y^t are p^rsented to this Courte as grevances to severall persons amongst vs; (and if they judge it nessisary,) to crave their healpe & assistance in drawing up an abstract from the heads of those things, to be p^rsented to the Gen: Courtes of the severall vnited Collonyes, and to desire an answer thereunto as sone as conveniently may be.

This Courte, at the request of Stratford, doe graunt that theire bounds shall be 12 myle northward, by Paugasitt River, if it be att the dispose by right of this Jurisdiction.

Jonas Wood having given to this Courte in writing vnder his hand, severall complaintes ag^t some persons in South Hampton mentioned in the sd writing, & hath given bonds to prosicute his complts. to abide by the judgment of the Gen: Courte in Octob^r next: This Courte desire the Dep. Governo^r to write to Capt. Topping & Mr. Ogden & acqvaint them with the aforesd complaints, and thearfore if the complaints, with the grounds of them, are not timely removed and satisfaction made, it is desired & expected that the respective persons concerned should appeare in theire owne defence at the aforesd Gen: Courte, the first Thursday of Octob^r next.

Geo: Fenwick Esqr, having manifested his respect to this Collony in graunting that the Towne of Seabrooke should have the vse of the Westerne necke, for their young cattle & sheepe or goates, till further order be given by him or his assigne, he reserving to himselfe ye propriety notwithstanding; The Courte declares themselves, that is theire apprihensions y^t ye benefit & advantage of the aforesd graunt should belong only to thos persons that cohabitt in the towne platte, till such time as the aforesd neck be called for again by & for the vse of the aforesd Geo. Fenwick Esqr or his assigne.

This Courte graunts Mr. James Fitch a compitent farme, conteining bet: 2 & 300 Acres, at Menunketeseck, so far as it is within theire power to make the aforesd graunt.

[71] It is ordered by the Courte, y^t the Assistant & Clerke of the Trained Band in each towne of Stratford, Fairefeild & Norwalke, shall hearby have power committed to them to examin & censure all defects of armes, in their severall townes; and allso deffects vpon training dayes, both in not coming late or otherwise; and to graunt out disstresses ag^t the respective delinquents for the same.

The Courte is adjourned to the day before the Quarter Courte in Septemb^r next.

A GENERALL COURTE HELD AT HARTFORD, OCTOB^r 2^d, 1656.

Mr. Webster, Governo^r.
Mr. Welles, Dep. Governor.
Magistrates: Mr. Clarke, Mr. Tallcott, Mr. Willys.
Dep: Mr. Steele, Mr. Allyn, Edw: Stebbing, Wm. Wadsworth, Joseph Mygatt, Rich: Butler, Mr. Gailer, Mr. Clarke, Mr. Newberry, Mr. Hollister, Mr. Robbins, Good: Dement, John Clarke, Mr. Ward, Hen: Grey,

John Herd, John Wells, Lifeten^t Webster, John Brunson, Sam: Haile, Good: Calkin.

Vpon ye complaint of Jonas Wood, this Courte orders, y^t Mr. Ogden shall bee written to frō this Courte to graunt exicution to Jonas Wood, according to the verdict of the Jury, ag^t John Cooper, at a Courte held at South Hampton about a yeare since.

Ordered by the Courte, that Tho. Backsters bill or bond lying in the Courte shall be returned to him by the Secritary, w^n it is or can be found.

It is ordered by the Courte, y^t w^t person so ever, either Indians or English, shall take any Wolfe out of any pit made by any other man to catch wolfes in, whearby they would defraude the right owner of their due from the towne or country, every such offendor shall pay to the owner of the pit 10s. or be whiped on their naked bodyes not exceeding 6 stripes.

Andr: Bacon & John Bernard are exempted from training & watching & warding, by the Courte.

It is ordered by this Courte & ye authority thearof, y^t none in this Common Wealle shall sell any strong liquors after, above 8s. p^r gallon by retail, sil: any y^t are lycenced except ye ordinary keep^rs, who shall not exceed 14s. p^r gallon by retaile: this order to begin at ye 1 Decemb^r next, & this order to continue for one yeare : & none in this Common weale lycenced shall sell wyne at above 18d. p^r qvart, expt to ordinary keep^rs who are not to exceed 2s. p^r quart, & this order to continve for one yeare and to begin 1 of December next.

Good: Mygate is lycenced to sell strong lyquors by retaile.

It is also ordered for one yeare, y^t two Magistrates shall have libertye to lycense such as they see meete, if thos lycenced shall retale* to sell.

It is ordered by this Courte & the authority thearof, that no towne w^thin this Jurisdiction shall entertaine any Quakers, Ranters, Adamites, or such like notorious heritiques, or suffer to continve with them above the space of 14 dayes, vpon the penalty of 5l. per weeke for any towne entertaining any such person; but the townes men shall give notice to the two next

---

*This word should be *refuse*. Several obvious errors and omissions occur in the record of this session, which is not in the hand writing of Mr. Cullick.

Magistrates or Assistants, who shall have power to send them to prison, for the securing of them vntill they can conveniently be sent out of the Jurisdiction.*

It is also ordered, y^t no master of any vessell shall land any such Heritiq^s: but if they doe, they shall be compelled to transport them againe out of this Collony, (by any one Magistrate or Assistant,) at their first setting saile from the port wheare they landed them, duering which time the Assistant or Magistrate shall see them secured, vpon the penalty of 20*l*. for any master of any vessell y^t shall not transport them as aforesd.

[72] It is allso ordered, y^t none in this Collony shall sell any Indian any horse or mare, nor any boate or boate riginge, vpon ye penalty of five for one, for any such default.

It is allso ordered by this Courte, that vpon consideration of w^t was commended to the severall Courtes, to have vpon recorde to posterity the most memorable passages of Gods p^{r}ovidence   †& settlinge & hitherto continuing his people in this Country, for the attaineing hearof, Major Mason, Mr. Stone, Mr. Goodwyn, Mr. Wareham, Mr. Steele & Goodman Stebbing, are desired to meete to collect such remarkable passages; Mr. Pell: & Mr. Ward are desired to send in writing such occurrances by the sea-side.

It is ordered by this Courte, that such Constables‡ within this Jurisdiction shall make returne of their warrants at Octob^r Courte, which they received the spring before, & ishue their accounts with the Treasuror about thos collections which they were adjoyned to attend by thos warrants for Country Levyes, vpon the penalty of 40*s*. to the publike Treasury, for every such default.

The Lists of the persons & estates in the severall Townes within this Jurisdiction :—

---

* This Order, (with the three which next follow,) was made by the General Court in conformity with a recommendation of the Commissioners of the U. Colonies, who, at their session in September, had (upon the suggestion of the Governor and Magistrates of Massachusetts Colony,) " proposed to the severall Generall Courts, that all Quakers, Ranters and other notorious Heretiques be prohibited comming into the Vnited Collonyes, and if any shall hereafter come or arise amongst vs, that they be forthwith secured and removed out of all the Jurisdictions."

" And that no horse or mare, young or old, be sould to any Indian, vnder the penalty of five for one."

" And also that no boates or barkes or any tackling belonging thearvnto be sould to any Indian, vnder the penalty of five for one." [Rec. of U. Colonies.]

† Blank in the original.   ‡ For 'each Constable'?

	Persons.	Estates.		Estates.
Hartford,	188.	19675. 5s. 0.	Stratford,	9033. 0. 0.
Wyndsor,	152.	15531. 0. 0.	Middletowne,	2375. 10. 0.
Wethersfeild,	107.	12504. 10. 0.	Pequott,	6408. 11. 0.
Norwaake,		3154. 10. 0.	Seabrooke,	4931. 0. 0.
Fairefeild,		10053. 4. 0.		

This Courte graunts a Rate in the Country, to bee levyed by virtue of the Treasurors warrants to the Constables in each Towne, for three farthings in the pound, to bee pd halfe in wheat & halfe in pease.

This Courte orders, that when John Elderkin doth lay downe the ordinary att Pequott, yⁿ & not before Geo. Tounge may have a lycence from any one Magistrate to keepe an ordinary according to the orders of this Courte, in the aforesd towne of Pequot.

It is ordered, yᵗ next Wednesday come 3 weekes shall be kept a publique day of Thanksgiving to the Lord, for the gen: concurrances of many mercyes the yeare past, by all the plantations in this Jurisdiction, notice being to be given to yᵉ officers in each towne by the Deputyes of the Courte from the sd townes.

This Courte orders, that in yᵉ action whearin Sam: Smith as Attourny to Tho. Stephenson, did cast Mr. Robbins, 10*l.*, yᵗ execution shall be respited vntill beter proofe appeare, provided he bring it in at yᵉ Quarter Courte in Septem: next.

The Courte is dissolved.

Some other orders made at the Courte in Octob ͬ 4 ͭʰ, 1656.

The names of thos that are appointed by the Courte, to be Leather sealers, for the yeare ensuing: For Hartford, John Stedman, Edw: Grannis; For Wyndsor, Good: Olderige, Jobe Drake; For Seabrook, Jonath: Rudd, John Olmesteed; For Stratford, Good: Groves, & Robert Rice; For Norwaack, Richard Olmesteed.

[73]   Octob ͬ 2 ͩ, (56.)

This Courte taking into serious consideration the severall deceites and abuses which in other places have beene and are commonly practised by the tanners, curiers, butchers and workers of Leather, as also the abuses and inconveniences which acreu to the severall members of this Common wealth by leather not sufficiently tanned and wrought, which is occationed by the necligence & vnskillfullness of thos severall tradesmen, which before, in & after it is in the hand of ye tanner may be much bettered or impayred, for prevention hearof, it is ordered by this Courte and the authority thearof,

That no Butcher, by himselfe or any other person, gash or cutt any hide of ox, bull, steare or cow, in fleaing thearof, whearby the same shall be impayred, vnder the penalty of 12 for every such gash in hyde or skin.

Nor shall any person or persons vseing or which shall vse the mistery of tanning, at any time or times hearafter, offer or put to sale any kinde of leather which shall be insufficiently or not throughly tanned, or which shall not then have beene after the tanning thearof well & throughly dryed, vpon paine of forfiture so much of his or their sd Leather as by any searcher or sealor of leather lawfully apointed shallbe found insufficiently tanned or not throughly dryed as aforesd.

Nor shall any person or persons vseing or occupying the mistery of tanning set any of their fatts in tann hills or other places wheare the woozes,* or Leather put into tann in the same, shall or may take any vnkinde heates, nor shall put any leather into any hott or warme oozes w^tsoever, on paine of 20l. for every such offence; nor shall any person or persons vseing or occupying the mistery or facultye of curreing, burne or scauld any hide or leather in the curreing, but shall worke the same in all respects with good & suffitient liqvor both for quallity & quantity, sutable to the condition of the Leather dreast by him or them, on paine of forfeture, for every such offence or act done contrary to the true meaning of this order, the full value of every such hide marred by his evell workmanship or handleing, which shall be judged by two or more sufficient and skillful persons, curreors or others, and their oath given them for that ende by one Magistrate or Assistant. And every towne wheare neede is or shall be, shall chuse one or two persons of the most able & skillfull within their severall towneshipps, & present them to ye Courte or one Magistrate or As-

---

* Ooze; "the liquor of a tan vat." *Webster.*

sistant, who shall appoint and sweare the sd persons by their
discretion to make search and view within the presincts of their
limmites as often as they shall think good and neede shalbe,
who shall have a mark or seale prepared by each towne for
that purpose: and the said searchers, or one of them, shall
keepe the same & therewith shall seale such Leather as they
shall [*finde*] suffitient in all points, one or other; and if the sd
searchers or any one of them shall finde any Leather sould or
offered to be sould, brought or offered to be searched or sealed,
which shall be tanned, wrought, converted or vsed contrary to
the true intent & meaning of this order, it shall be lawfull for
the sd searchers or any of them to seize all such Leather and to
retaine the same in their custody, vntill such time as it bee tryed by such tryars & in such manner as in this order is appointed, viz: vpon the forfeture of any Leather, ye Officer so seizing ye same shall w^thin 3 dayes call to him 3 or 4 men, honest
& skillfull in such ware, to view the same in the presence of
the perty, who shall haue timely notice thearof, or without him,
who shall certefye vpon their oaths to the next Quarter Courte
or one Magistrate or Assistant, the defect of the same Leather,
except the perty before submit to their judgment. Nor shall
any searchor or sealor of Leather refuse with convenient speede
to seale any Leather suffitiently tanned haveing timely notice;
nor shall any such searchor or sealor seale that which is insuffitiently tanned, vpon the forfeture for every such offence [*of*]
10s; & the fees for searching & sealing of Leather, shall be
2^d p^r hide for every number vnder five, & 12^d for every dicker*
of Leather, which the tanner shall pay vpon the sealing the sd
Leathor, from time to time:

[74] Lastly, its ordered by the authority aforesd y^t ye severall
fynes & forfetvres in this order mentioned, be eqvally devided
into 3 p^rts; one part to the Common Treasuror of the Country,
3† p^rt to the Common Treasury of the towne wheare the offence
comitted, one 3^d p^rt to the seizor or seizers of such Leather
which is insuffitiently tanned, curried or wrought frō time to
time.

---

* *Dicker* or *dicre*; "a quantity of leather consisting of ten hides." *Johnson.*
† Thus, in the Record.

A Generall Court, called by the Gouerno‍r & Magistrates, this 26th of Feb‍r, 1656.

Joh. Webster Esq‍r, Gouerno‍r.
Tho: Wells Esq‍r, Deputy.
Magistrates: Major John Mason, Capt. John Cullick, Mr. Clarke, Mr. Willis, Mr. Tailecoat.
Deputies: Mr. Steele, Tho: Judd, Robert Webst‍r, Geo: Graues, Mr. Trott, Mr. Robbins, John Dement, Mr. Hollister, Cap‍t. Denison, Will: Cheesbrook, Phillip Groues, Willī: Beardsly, Mr. Allyn, Mr. Gailerd, Mr. Phelps, Mr. Clarke, Nath: Ely, Sam: Hale, Cornelius Hull, Henry Grey, John Clarke, Robert Chapman, Mr. Lord, Will': Wadsworth, Joseph Mygat, Richard Butler.

This Court desires that Major Mason doe warne John Olmsteed, Constable in Seabrooke, to appeare at the next session of this Court in Hartford, to answer such irregularities in attending his warrant for choise of Deputies for this Court as shall bee charged & proued, complained of here by William Waller, where the said Waller is also in like mañer to be warned to make good his compl‍t. *Voted.*

This Courte appointe Mr. Steele, Mr. Allin, Mr. Dan: Clarke, Mr. Lord, William Wadsworth, Mr. Hollist‍r, John Deming, Robert Webster, w‍th the Magistrates, to bee Committee, to giue the best safe advice they can to the Indians, if they agree to meete & being mett shall craue the same of them.

This Court doth order that Mr. Warham, Mr. Stone, Mr. Blinman & Mr. Russell bee desired to meet, the first fifth day of June next, at Boston, to conferre & debate the questions formerly sent to the Bay Court, or any other of the like nature that shall bee p‍rpounded to them by that Court or by o‍r owne, w‍th such divines as shall bee sent to the said meeting from the other Collonies; and that they make a returne to the Gen: Court of the issue of their consultations. *Voted.*

It is also ordered, that a coppy of the former order bee sent to the foure Eld‍rs chosen for the Synnod, w‍th a coppy of 12 questions more, w‍ch this Court hath agreed should bee sent by the first opportunity to the Gouerno‍r in the Bay, for the Synnod to consider w‍th the former questions. *Excluded.*

It is also ordered, that the Deputies, wth the Deacons of the Church in each towne, take care that their said Eld^rs bee comely & honorably attended & suited wth necessaries in their journey to the Bay and home againe; and that the same, wth their p^rportion of charge in the Bay, during their abode there vpon this seruice, bee discharged by the Treasurer; and also the Deputies are impowered to presse horses (if need bee,) for the end aforesaid. *Voted.*

It is ordered, that the levy vpon the seu^rall townes for the Country, by the last Court, shall bee made for a penny vpon the pound. *Voted.*

[75] This Court doth grant liberty to Sam^ll Marshall of Windzor, to sell strong liquors by retaile, for the space of one yeare.

This Court confirmes the former grant (prooued to them) of 20 myle Iland, wth the meadow adioyning on the east side the great Riuer, & comonage appertaining, to Robert Chapman of Seabrook.

Robert Webster is confirmed Recorder for the Towne of Middletowne, according to their desire. *Voted.*

Whereas, there is p^ruision made formerly, against all vnlawfull games, but the Court hath not explained themselves so farre as there may bee need, what games they iudge & condemne as altogether vnlawfull, in the very nature of them, It is now ordered, that if any person or persons, of what rank or quallity so euer, in this Jurisdiction, shall after the publishing of this order, play at Cards, Dice, Tables, or any other game wherein that great & sollemne ordinance of a Lott is expressly & directly abused & p^rphaned, the persons playing or that shall play, more or lesse, at any of the aforesaid games, shall pay for euery offence 20*ss*. a peece to the publicke Treasury; & the head of that family where any such game shall bee vsed or played, (if hee or shee know of, bee priuy to & allowe any such playing in their house or houses,) they shall pay in like manner, 20*ss*. for each time any such game is played in part or whole, but if they play w^thout any privity or knowledge of theirs, then that wch otherwise should haue bene paid by them shall bee paid by the said gamesters or play^rs, that is to say that the persons playing shall pay 20*ss*. a time for euery time they play at any of the aforsaid games, more then his former penalty, to the publicke Treasury; onely it is pʳuided that one third part of the penalties shall bee to the party or parties that shall discouer and prooue the same to the Court. *Voted.*

It is ordered, that the sallery formerly allowed Daniell Porter shall bee continued to him for the next ensuing year, after the end of his last sallery. *Voted.*

Mr. Tho: Fitch, of Norwalke, beeing pʳsented to this Court as chosen by that Towne for Clarke of their trained band & Recorder of lands, is confirmed by this Court in the aforesaid respectiue offices & imployments. *Voted.*

This Court hauing read and considered a certificate from Mr. Laurence Cornelius, Dutchman, (& the Townsmen of Pequett,) they doe declare and shew that they allow and confirme the act of the Towne or Townsmen of Pequet in admitting the said Lawrence Cornelius an inhabitant of that Towne, to haue free trade amongst oʳselues; pʳuided in all things hee obserues & kepes all the wholesome lawes and orders of this Jurisdict: that either are or shall be made.

This Court doth order that those that shall hereafter bee made free, shall haue an affirmatiue certificate vnder the hands of all or the major part of the deputies in their seuerall townes, of their peaceable and honest conuersation, and those and only those of them wᶜʰ the Gen: Court shall approue shall bee made free men. *Voted.*

[76] The Deputyes are desired to bring a list of the names of the Freemen in their seuʳall Townes to the Gen: Court in October next.

The Court hereby manifests their desires that the reuerend Eldʳˢ of the Counsell who formerly transacted the differences of Hartford Church,* would giue a meeting to the reuerend Eldʳˢ of the Bay that haue tendred themselues voluntarily to

---

* "It appears, that about the years 1654 and 1655, several councils of the neighboring elders and churches were called, to compose the differences between the parties [in the church at Hartford.] They labored to satisfy them, with respect to the points in controversy. But the brethren at Hartford imagined that all the elders and churches in Connecticut and New Haven were prejudiced in favor of one party or the other, and therefore they would not hear their advice. For this reason it was judged expedient to call a council from the other colonies. Some time in the year 1656, it seems, a number of elders and churches from Massachusetts came to Hartford, and gave their opinion and advice to the church and the aggrieved brethren But it appears, that in the apprehension of the aggrieved, the church did not comply with the result." [Trumbull's Hist. of Conn. I. 297.]

come vp hither to consider and consult wch way may bee most agreeable to the rule, to put an end to the difference.

2. The Court desires that Hartford Church would write to the former Counsell to come together to Hartford to see if they can compose the differences amongst themselues in this Interim: if not the former request to bee attended.

3. That there may be letters gratulatory returned to the reuerend Eld^rs in the Bay, for their respect, & to continue their former resolutions to come vp to helpe in these cases.

4. The Court desires that Mr. Stone & the Church should, together wth their letters of request to the former Counsell, declare also vnto one or more of them, in writing, the p^rticulars wherein they are not sattisfyed wth the determination of the Counsell. Mr. Dan: Clarke is desired to draw the letters to the Eld^rs in the Bay, and to the form^r Counsell.

At the same time, Mr. Gouerno^r, Capt. Cullicke & Mr. Steele, (hauing no hand in the p^rmises,) did seuerall times expresse themselues openly in the Court, to this purpose; that though they did exceeding greatly desire any way that might bee discouered to bee the way of God should bee attended for the healing of those sad differences in the Church of Christ at Hartford, yet being not able, (though oft desired,) to obtaine any thing from the Court that might make it appeare that that wch they haue done was (all things considered) the next way of peace according to God, they w^thheld their votes; but did much & often expressly desire that the former Counsell might bee first showed the grounds & reasons, why the Church at Hartford could not submit to the advice giuen, as the dissenting brethren had done; wherein the Counsell missed any rule of Christ in their aduice for their conviction; and if the Counsell did not returne a sattisfying answer, then they should bee willing further meanes should bee attended; yet none of these things could bee obtained.

[*In the margin;*] The Courte is adjourned to the 2^d Thursday in Aprill.

Whereas, there is great complaint of the damage that doth acrew vnto this Comonwealth by the vnruliness of Swyne, It is ordered by this Court & the authority thereof, that after the publication of this order, no Swyne shall goe w^thout rings, at any time in the yeare, that are out of mens owne yards, or w^{th}in foure miles of any meeting house; And those that shall pound such swyne shall haue sixpence a peice, besides 2*d*. a peice due to the pound keeper & iust damages. The Court doth also referr it to the seuerall Townes, to appoint some that shall attend the execution of this order. This order to take place vpon any swine of aboue a quarter of a yeare old; only it is declared that this order concernes all the Townes in this Jurisdiction, except [77] Windzor, on whom this order takes place if their Swyne shall bee found to goe w^{th}out rings, at any time of the yeare, that are out of mens owne yards or w^{th}in three miles of the great Riuer.

Those that were made free men at this Court, are as followeth :—Mr. John Haynes, Stephen Hopkins, Tho: Butler, John Pratt, Daniell Pratt.

It is ordered by this court, that while the ministry is mainteined at Paucatuck, the charge thereof & of the ministry at Pequett shall be borne as the major part of the inhabitants shall agree and order, that is whether Pawcatuck shall by & of themselues maintaine their minister & Pequett their minister, or whether they shall both maintaine both their Ministers in a joynt way.

Sam: Smith of Pequett is confirmed Leiuten^{t} to the trained band in that Towne.

George Tong is confirmed ordinary keeper in the Towne of Pequett.

This Court orders that a certificate shall be sent to Cuscacinimo,* by the Sec^{r}, to let him vnderstand that this Court allowes him to keep the Mohegins or others of Vncasses men that are

---

* Elsewhere, Cassasinamon, or Robin Cassinomon; a Pequot Indian, and one of the number of tributaries assigned to the government of Uncas, after the conquest. He entered the service of Mr. Winthrop, shortly after the coming of the latter to Pequot. In 1647, Mr. Winthrop presented to the Commissioners of the U. Colonies the complaint of Robin and other Pequots, of the injustice and tyranny of Uncas, with their petition to be taken under the immediate government of the English, and have some place appointed "where they might live peaceably." Their request was not at this time granted; but in 1654, Robin, in consideration of his service promised to the English in the proposed expedition against Ninigret and the Niantics, was freed from his subjection to Uncas or "any Indian Sachem further than the Commissioners should direct, and taken under the protection of the English and freed from tribute." The following year (Sept. 1655,) he was appointed by the Commissioners, Chief or Governor of the Pequot tributaries at Nameag (or Nameoke,) and Nawyunckque (*i. e.* on both sides of Mystic River,) in which post he was continued for many years. [Rec. of U. Col.; Hazzard's Coll. ii. 87, 92, 326, 334.]

wth him, till hee receiues further order from the Gen: Court, or the Comission^rs, to whom they haue writt for advice, except Vncas desires them & they desire themselues to goe to Vncas.

This Court doth order, that by admitted inhabitants, specified in the 7th Fundamentall, are meant only housholders that are one & twenty yeares of age, or haue bore office, or haue 30*l*. estate.

It is also ordered, that not lesse than two Magistrates shall giue the oath of fidellity, at a publicke meeting warned by due & orderly notice giuen for the said publicke meeting.

This Court orders, that no Indians shall make any hostile attempt vpon any Indian or Indians in any Town or house in this Jurisdiction, neither shall they march through any Towne wth theire armes, or in a hostile manner.

This Court orders that next Wednesday come fortnight, being the 25th of this instant, shall bee obserued & kept a day of publicke humilliation, by all the Plantations in this Jurisdiction, to seeke the presence, guidance & direction of the Lord in refference to the Synnod, & the other waighty concernm^ts & difficulties of this Jurisdiction; & the Deputyes in each Towne are desired to acquaint their respectiue Eld^rs wth the same.

---

[78] AN ADJOURNM^t OF THE GEN^ll COURT, APRILL 9th, 1657.

Mr. Webster, Gou^rno^r.
Mr. Wells, Deputy.
Magistrates: Major Mason, Mr. Clarke, Mr. Cullick, Mr. Willis, Mr. Tallcoat.
Deputyes: Mr. Allin, Mr. Phelps, Mr. Gaylerd, Mr. Trott, Mr. Clarke, Mr. Lord, Will: Wadsworth, Mr. Robbins, Leift^nt Hollist^r, Joseph Mygatt, John Deming, Nath: Ely, Henry Grey, John Clarke, Robert Chapman, Sam: Hales, Geo: Graues.

John Packer testifieth vpon oath, that at a Towne meeting at Pequett, the major part of those who were present did vote that the inhabitants of Mistick & Paucatuck should bee a Towne of themselues; and that hee opposed the putting it to vote, and that hee voted against it himselfe.

Nic: Sension is made a freeman.

There being a most horrid murder committed by some Indians at Farmington, and though Mesapano seemes to bee the principall acter, yet the accessories are not yet clearely discou^red, and none brought to a legall triall, It is ordered, that Tekomas, Agedowsick & Wonanntownagun alias Great James, should bee kept as pledges in the prizon till the murtherers & accessaries are brought forth to due triall & judgm^t; only the Court orders that when Tekomas his 2^d sonne shall be deliuered up as a pledge in his Fathers stead, then Tekomas shall be free.

Also the Court orders, that all the estate of Wepaqum in the hands of Mr. Newton, shall bee sequestred for the Countreys security, till the murtherer & accessaries are deliuered vp to the justice of this Court.

Instructions to those who are to goe to Norwootuck & Pacumtuck; that they shall acquaint the Sachem and chiefe there wth the horrible bloody act that is lately done at Farmington, and tell them that wee expect that they and all or any other Indians whatsoeuer shall forthw^th send Mashupanan or any other that are accessary to that bloody act, either wth these o^r messeng^rs or so soone as hee or any other accessary thereto bee p^rcured by them, & tell them that wee shall looke at them or any other that detaine Mashupanan or any that are accessarie in this act, as our enimyes.

The persons the Court appoynts wth all speed to attend this seruice are Jonathan Gilbert & John Gilbert from Hartford, & the Deputies in Windzor are desired to prouide an able man to joyne wth them herein.

It is ordered, that it shall not bee lawfull for aboue two Indians at a time, & they without any armes, to come into any Towne or house in this Jurisdict: till the Court shall take further order.

This Court also desires that the inhabitants of Farmington would vse their best indeauo^rs to search out, app^rhend & bring before the Gouerno^r, either Mesupano, Cherry, or any other that may iustly bee suspected to bee guilty of & accessary to the aforesaid bloody fact.

[79] Nathan Gold is approued by this Court to bee put to

election at the next Gen^ll Court of Election, for to bee a Magistrate in this Jurisdict: for the yeare ensuing.

> The Commission of Major John Mason, of Seabrooke, sent from seu^rall Magistrates & Deputies, as a Committee appointed by the last Gen: Court, to attend any cause or exigent that might accrew wch concernes this Comonwealth, but especially concerning the Indians, before the next Gen^ll Court of Election.

May 15th, 57. Whereas the aforesaid Committee haue receiued credible information of seuerall insolent iniuries & insufferable outrages comitted against the inhabitants of South Hampton, by some Indians vppon Long Iland neare to the said South Hampton, but such as owne the Montacutt Sachem as their Sachem or chiefe, they doe therfore hereby send you (as their Agent, in the behalfe of this Collony,) wth 19 men vnder yor comand, to South Hampton vpon Long Island, where you are to consider of all matters & things whatsoeuer that may appeare necessary to bee considered and attended, according to yor ensuing instructions, & you are to certify vppon all occasions what shall bee the result & issue of yor negotiations, in refference to the p^rmises.

> Instructions for Major John Mason, of Seabrooke, sent wth Commission from the Committee appointed by the Gen: Court of Connecticutt, Aprill, 1657.

You are wth all convenient speed to saile wth yor men to South Hampton, where you may meet wth the Magistrates there belonging to this Collony, taking in Leiften^t Bull, wth such assistants there in counsell as they & you shall agree vpon, who are to consider & attend what shall bee presented in refference to the p^rmises, according to the ensuing instructions :—

You are to get clearly interpreted to the Montacutt Sachem the declaration of the Commission^rs, wch Mr. Ogden will shew you, in the transcript hee hath from hence, & a coppy left wth them :

1. You are to inquire & search out what is the iniury there done & when.

2. You are to inquire & search out by whom such injury is done, & the true vallew of the dammage.

3. If you finde it or any part of it to bee done by the Indians or any of them vnder the Montacutt Sachem, then you are to finde out so farre as you can, by what or how many Indians such injury is done, either as agents or accessaryes.

4. You are to require of the Montacutt Sachem such damage as you shall find done by any Indian or Indians vnder him, or otherwise the iniurious agents & accessaries, according to law & the articles of agreem^t betwene him & vs.

5. If hee declares himselfe vnwilling to attend this, so farre as hee is able, you are speedily to informe thereof.

[80] 6. If hee declares himselfe willing to attend it, but pleades his inability to effect it, and therefore desires the assistance of the English, you are (wth what men shall bee thought meet) to assist him & his men to go to the plantation of Indians vnder him, that haue committed this outrage, of whom it is expected by this Collony that hee should before you require satisfaction for the damage done, which if denyed or delayed, then that hee demands of them the agents and accessaries, (wch you or hee shall find out,) to the aforesaid injury, that they are by them speedily deliuered vp to yo^{r}selfe & the Magistrates in that Towne; if attained, you are to leaue them wth those that are injured, for their satisfaction, according to the act of the Comission^{rs}. If peremptorily denyed, you are speedily to informe the next Gen: Court, Gouerno^r or Magistrates of the same, except the strength wth you & there can compell them. If delayed, then if you see they will come to any termes that will be for the hono^r of the English and the sattisfaction of the injured persons, they may agree wth them as they can, any thing herein to the contrary notwthstanding.

7. You are to take charge of the aforesaid men sent you wth their prouision & amunition, as also all other that you shall see meet to raise there to the furtherance of this worke, who are injoyned to bee vnder yor command at all times & in all things, both for assisting o^r freinds there in their iust defence, by watching, warding, or otherwise, as you & those in counsell wth you shall iudge the case doth require.

8. Wee doe not iudge it convenient that you should in yor owne person make after any Indians in the woods, where you can find or come at them.

Lastly, if you cannot attend this seruice, then Leiften^t Tho: Bull is to attend it, & is invested wth all the power heereby committed to you.

At a Generall Court of Election, 21th of May, 1657.

Magistrates elect:

John Winthrop Esqr, Gouern^r.

Tho: Wells Esqr, Deputy.

John Webster Esqr, *Magist:*   Mr. Tailcott, *Mag:*
Major Jno Mason, *Magist:*   Mr. Nathan Gold, *Mag:*
Mr. Cullick, *Magist & Secrt^r.*   Mr. Gosmore, *Mag:*
Mr. Clarke, *Magist:*   Mr. Ogden, *Magist:*
Mr. Willis, *Mag:*

Deputies: Mr. Steele, Mr. Phelps, Mr. Gailard, Mr. Trott, Mr. Robbins, Mr. Brewster, John Deming, Math: Camfield, James Morgan, John Wells, Rich: Butler.

Were made free before the Court, those whose names are underwritten:

Tho: Hubbard,	Rich: Seager,	Josias Arnold,
Will: Filly,	Nath: Seely,	John Cole,
John Denslow,	Sam: Cheesbrook,	John Butler,
Sam: Bissell,	Will Hought,	Sam: Moody,
Jonath: Gillet, Juni^r,	Tho: Adgate,	Robert Warner,
James Eglstone,	Francis Grizwald,	Willī: Cheeny,
Thomas Huntington,	John Norton,	Willī: Warde,
Ambroze Fowler,	William Goodwin,	John Gilbert,
John Graues,	Robert Lay,	Michael Omphries,
[81] Sam: Rockwell,	Joseph Bird,	James Treat,
Sam: Gibbes,	Rich: Wakely,	John Deming Junīor,
Edw: Andrewes,	Andrew Sanford,	Nath: Graues,
Begatt Eglstone,	Josias Elseworth,	Mathias Treat,
Sam: Church,	Nath: Winchell,	John Palmer,
Tho: Burnham,	Fra: Hall,	Jonath: Smith,
John Baily,	Symon Lobdell,	Sam: Belding,
John Root,	Geo: Woolcot,	Henry Palmer,
Tho: Fitch,	John Harrison,	Tho: Dickerson,
John North,	Enoch Buck,	Mr. Sam: Wells,

Willī: Ventris,   John Belding,   Robert Foot,
Nath: Woodroof, Joseph Smith,   Joseph Dickerson.
James Bird,   Sam: Wright,

This Court doth approue of the place for a farme for Mr. Haines, at Paucatuck, wch Edward Stebbin & John White haue loocked out for him, about a myle & halfe beyond Paucatuck Riuer, as is expressed in an order, March, '53–'54, & for quantity according to Mr. Haines his grant at a Court, June, '52.

This Court doth appoint John Bissell to keepe the Ferry for one yeare,—at his old house.

Thomas Curtis is freed from training, watching & warding.

Jasper Gunn is freed from training, watching & warding, during his practise of phissicke.

This Court orders, that this clause shall bee added to the former order concerning Leather, That no Leather shall bee sold or offered to bee sold before it bee sealed in the Towne where it is tanned, & in case it bee found defectiue, the sealers haue power to fine it or seize it. And in case the owners of such Leather submit not to the iudgment of the sealers, they shall choose 3 or 4 able men as a Jury, who shall iudge of the case, whether it shall bee forfeited or fined & how much,—wch fines or forfeitures shall bee disposed of as in the former order concerning Leather. And that no raw hides shall be transported out of this Collony, vpon the forfeiture of all such hides.

This Court doth approue of the Commission & Instructions wch the Comittee sent wth Major John Mason to Long Island.

[82]   *More acts of this Court, May, '57.*

The testimony of G: Bcon vpon oath, that hee heard it expressed by those that heard it expressed by those that spake in the behalfe of Fairfeild at a Gen^ll Court, that they did not desire the land aboue the path at the Necke.

Mr. Brewster is chosen an Assistant for the Towne of Pequett, for the yeare ensuing.

The Court desires Capt. Cullick to write a letter to Mr. Winthrop, as speedily as may bee, to acquaint him to what place the Country hath chosen him, & to desire his p^rsent assistance as much as may bee.

John Nott, John Cilburne & John Betts & John Dickerson are confirmed to bee Serjeants at Wethersfeild.

Good: Groues }
Good: Fairchild } appointed L. sealers for Fairfeild.

Walter Gailard is appointed Leather sealer at Windzor, instead of old Oldrige.

This Court doth confirme Mr. Gold to bee Leiften^t, Nehe: Olmsteed & Robt Loockuet to bee Serjeants at Fairfeild.

Mr. Deputy & the Magistrates, together wth Mr. Allin, Mr. Steele, Mr. Phelps, G: Migat, Willī: Wadsworth, and Mr. Hollister, are chosen as a Comittee to attend any occasions as the State of Comon wealth in reference to the Indians.

The Court is adjourned vnto the second Thursday in August, except the Magistrates see cause to call it sooner.

Major Mason & Mr. Talcott are chosen Commission^rs for the yeare insuing.

Mr. Steele & Good: Mygatt are appointed by this Court, to demand satisfaction of the Indians at Farmington for such damage wch can bee duely proued to bee done by the late fyering a house, wch was by one of that plantation, as also to acquaint them that the Courts mind is that they should nominate some one to bee a Sachem ouer them, and to make returne hereof at the next Sessions of this Court.

The Courte orders that the chiefe millitary officer of Middletowne, wth Geo: Graues, shall haue power to iudge of the defects in traynings, watchings & armes.

[83] Mr. Clarke & John Allin are desired to p^rsent a list of the names of them that desire to bee troopers, at the next session of this Court, wch said Court is to approue of whom they see meet, there being to bee added to the former preuiledges, that if any troupers horse, being called forth by authority, bee killd in warre, the country shall pay for him; wch troup of horse, as well as the foot companies, are to bee vnder o^r Majors command.

Capt. Denison doth acknowledge in this Court that hee wronged Mr. Blinman & missed his rule, & that hee spake corruptly in saying that Mr. Blinman did preach for Paucatuck & Mistick being a Towne before hee sold his land at Mistick as aforesaid.

This Court doth order, that that the inhabitants of Mistick & Paucatuck shall pay to Mr. Blinman, that wch was due to him for the last yeare, scil: to March last.

Mr. Winthrop, Major Mason, Capt. Cullick, Mr. Tallcott & Mr. Allin are chosen to bee a Committee to meet at Pequett to issue matters betwene the inhabitants of Mistick & Paucatuck, & Pequett, if they can, or else to make a returne how they leaue things, at the next Generall Court.

This Court doth declare that any Assistant, either at Stratford, Fairfeild or Norwake, his power doth extend to any of those three plantations. And order that Good: Camfeild, who is chosen for an Assistant for Norwake, shall giue the oath of freedome & of a Magistrate, to Ensigne Gold.

Math: Camfeild is sworne an Assistant for the yeare ensuing according to the extent of his Comission.

A SESSION OF THE GEN: COURT IN HARTFORD, 12th AUGUST, 1657.

Tho: Wells Esqr, Deputy.

Magistrates: Major Jno. Mason, Capt. Cullick, Mr. Clarke, Mr. Willis, Mr. Tailcoat.

Deputies: Mr. Steele, Mr. Phelps, Mr. Trott, Mr. Gailor, Mr. Allin, Mr. Robbins, Mr. Dan: Clarke, Mr. Brewster, Mr. Lord, Wm. Wadsworth, Joseph Migatt, John Clarke, Robert Chapman, James Morgan, Rich: Buttler.

James Morgan, aged about 50 years, testifyed vpon oath before this Court that hee being last winter at Jacob Waterhouse his dwelling house, in company wth Mrs. Brewster, Goody Waterhouse & Capt. Denison, Thomas Staunton also being p^rsent, hee heard the said Staunton say that the Comission^rs had cast of Vncus, & hee had it in his pockett to shew.

This Court orders & appoints that Leiftent^t Wm. Lewis should to morrow goe to Gilford, & if vpon inquiry there hee vnderstand that Thomas Staunton is gone to Branford & not returned, hee is to goe to Mr. Leet & desire hee would take order that Thomas Staunton, in that Jurisdiction, at Branford or elswhere, shall bee forthw^th sent to Mr. Wells, Deputy Gouerno^r, or else take security for 40*l.* that hee will appeare before the Gen: Court at Hartford, on Tuesday next, & abide the iudgm^t of the Court, in reference to such things as shall bee testify^d against him by Major John Mason.

[84] *Copia.*

You are to bring or cause Thomas Staunton to bee brought before the Gen: Court in Hartford, on Tuesday next, then & there to answere vnto such things as shall bee alleadged against him by Major John Mason & for so doeing this shall bee yor war^t.

By order of the Gen: Court in Hartford,

J: C: Sec^{ry}.

To Leiftin^t Wm. Lewis.

This Court duely & seriously considering what euidence hath bene p^{r}sented to them by Robert Wade, of Seabrooke, in reference to his wiues vnworthy, sinfull, yea, unnaturall cariage towards him the said Robert, her husband, notwthstanding his constant & comendable care & indeauo^{rs} to gaine fellowship wth her in the bond of marriage, and that either where shee is in England, or for her to liue wth him here in New England; all wch being slighted & rejected by her, disowning him & fellowship wth him in that sollemne couenant of God betwene them, & all this for neare fifteene yeares; They doe hereby declare that Robert Wade is from this time free from Joane Wade, his late wife & that former Couenant of marriage betwene them.

This Court orders, that Mr. Winthrop, being chosen Gou^{r}no^r of this Collony, shall bee againe desired to come & liue in Hartford, wth his family, while hee gou^{r}nes, they grant him the yearly vse or profits of the housing & lands in Hartford belonging to Mr. John Haynes, wch shall be yearly discharged out of the publicke Treasury.

Major Mason, Mr. Talcott, John Cullick & Mr. Willis are desired to take the first oportunity to treat wth Mr. Winthrop for that end.

The Court adjourned to Tuesday next, 9 a clocke.

The Narration of Major John Mason, p^{r}sented to the Courte, about the Narragansetts beleaguering of Vncus, at Niantick, is by this Court accepted, thankfullnesse acknowledged, & order the same to bee recorded on the back-side of the said Narration.

This Court ordered the Secr^t to write to the Comission^{rs} in refference to Thomas Staunton, wch letter was read & approued, & the Sec^r ordered to send the same.*

This Court orders that Mr. Brewster shall haue power to put 4 or 5 men into the fort, who shall continue there 2 or 3 dayes for his defence against the Naragansets, & after that bee so in readinesse that if Vncus bee againe assaulted by the Naragansets, they wth 10 or 20 more, prouided by Mr. Brewster, shall beare full wittnesse against the Narragansets carriages, till Vncus his returne home from the Comission^{rs}, & that speedy notice or intelligence shall bee giuen to the Deputy Gou^{r}no^r (if any fresh assault should happen,) or to the Comission^{rs}.

[85] Mr. Tailcoat is desired to write to the Norwuttuck & Pocomtuck Indians to informe them of the time of the meeting of the Comission^{rs} & that if any of them haue ought against Vncus, his purpose & resolution is to bee there to answere them, or any others.

A true coppy of the Counsells answere to seuerall questions sent to the Massachusets from o^r Generall Court, being p^{r}sented to this Court, signed by the Reuerend Mr. Sam: Stone, in the name of the rest of the Counsell, They doe order that coppies should goe forth to the seu^{r}all Churches in this Collony as speedily, & if any exceptions bee against any thing therein, by any Church that shall haue the consideration thereof, the Court desires they would acquaint the next Gen: Court in Hartford, in Octo^r: that so suitable care may bee had for their solution & satisfaction.

This Court considering the ingagem^t of Edward Lay to this Jurisdiction (by 15l. secured in Rich: Fellowes his hand,) of Robert Codnams estate, that the said Lay should appeare, seu^{r}all yeares since, at Hartford, to answere at the Court his abusiue cariage & expressions before seu^{r}all of Seabrooke, wch to this time hee hath not attended, they order that vpon the payment of 5l. to the Treasur^r by the said Codnam hee shall bee free from the aforesaid seizure of Robert Codnams estate in his hands, & the said Edward Lay shall bee free from the forfeiture of bond & contempt therein, wch 5l. being paid by Codnam

---

* See Rec. of U. Col., in Hazzard's St. Papers, ii. 369.

for Edward Layes disappearance, according to ingagem^t, they iudge that Edward Layes estate should satisfy Codnum for the same.

This Court being duly sencible of the danger this Comon wealth is in of being poisoned in their iudgm^t & principles by some loathsome Heretickes, whether Quakers, Ranters, Adamites or some others like them, It is ordered and decreed, that noe Towne or person therein, wthin this Jurisdiction, shall giue any vnnecessary entertainm^t to any of the aforesaid knowne hereticks, vpon penalty of fiue pounds for each Hereticque enterteind, to bee paid by that inhabitant wch giues such intertainment to them or either of them, & fiue pounds a weeke for each Hereticke, to bee paid by each Towne that shall suffer the entertainm^t of any such Hereticks, as also 5l. a person that shall at any time vnnecessarily speake more or lesse wth any of the aforesaid Hereticks, except the Magistrate, Assistants, Eld^{rs} or Constable in this Jurisdiction; all wch fines to bee paid to the publicke Treasury. Also, it is ordered, that any Magistrate, Assistant or Constable, in each plantation, vpon any suspicion of any person to bee such an Hereticke, shall, wth the helpe of their Eld^r or Eld^{rs} in each plantation, examine the said suspected person or persons, & if vpon examination hee or they judge any to bee such Heretickes, the said Magistrate, Assistant or Constable shall forthwth send them to prizon, or out of this Jurisdiction. This order to bee added to the former order in Octob^r, (56.)

[86] This Court orders that if Tho: Staunton comes in the vacancy of this Court, hee shall bee required to put in security for his appearance at the Court in Hartford in October next.

The Court is dissolved.

At a Session of the Generall Court, held at Hartford, August 18th, 1657.

The Indians belonging to Tunksis Sepus, being treated wth about the damage done by fire, occasioned by Mesupeno, they have mutually agreed and obliged themselves to pay vnto the Generall Court in October, or to their order, yearly, for the terme of seauen yeares, the full sume of eighty faddome of wampum, well strungd & mercht^{ble}, the first paym^t to bee made in Octob^r next ensuing, at the Session of the Gen: Court, & so to bee paid yearly at the Sessions in October, vntill the terme bee expired (that is to say) seauen paym^ts. Vnto wch agreem^t the foresaid Indians haue signed, the day & yeare aboue written.

the marke of Nequittacusson : Homs :

the marke of Cowasecutt.

the marke of Taccamus.

the marke of Mamunto.

These haue signed in the name & wth consent of the rest.

A relation of the carriage of the difference that fell out betwixt Vncas & Seoquassen of the one side & Totañimo & the Potunck Indians, At the Generall Court held at Hartford, in May, in the yeare of o^r Lord, 1656.

That vpon the murther of a Sachem of Connecticott dwelling neare Mattapeaset, by a young man called Weaseapano, Seoquassen complained to the Magistrates of Hartford of the wrong that the Potunck Indians did to him in entertaining & maintaining of him against all justice, wch said Seoquassen tooke Vncas in to him for helpe, to bee reuenged for the said Sachems death, who was inraged wth the like accident of entertaining a murtherer that runne from Vnquas to the said Potunck, who complained likewise of wrongs done him, to the Magistrates. Vnquas also had complained to the Magistrates of Connecticot for seuerall wrongs done to him by Tantoñimo, espetially his intising of many of his men & their protecting a Murtherer; & therevpon the Magistrates ordered that the Sachems of both sides should appeare at Hartford at the Generall Court: who all appearing, Seoquassen first declared of the fact done by a meane fellow vppon one that was allyed to him, a great Sachem; and so Vnquas & Foxen iustified, in many words.

[87] The Gouerno^r pressed to know what sattisfaction they required, who answered & pressed hard to haue 10 men put to death of his friends that was the murtherer; the other Sachems pleaded vnjust, because the Sachem that was slayne had murdered the young mans Vncle wilfully. The Court many of them spake their mindes to & fro. The Gouerno^r shewed the Indians what o^r law is in such cases, that onely the murther or any that were accessary to it should bee punished, & so hee & many Deputyes pressed both sides for peace, & not to fight vpon such a quarrell.

The Potunck Sachems p^rffered to giue wampam in way of sattisfaction, wch wholly was rejected, whereupon the Court spent some time to perswade to peace. Then they fell to be sattisfyed wth the death of 6 men. The Court wearied wth their speeches pressed the Potunck Indians to deliuer vp the murtherer, the wch Totannimo p^rmised, but priuately stole out of the Court & went wth the rest of the Sachems to Potunk forte: wherevpon both the English & Indians were offended & agreed to send a messeng^r to deliuer vp the murtherer, as Totañimo had p^rmised in Court. In the meane time the Court appointed 4 Deputyes to bee a Comittee to treat wth the Sachems of both sides, to see what could bee done for peace. This Committee priuately brought Vnquas to accept of the murtherer only, for full sattisfaction. But those Potunck Indians said they could not deliuer vp the said murther^r, his freinds were so many & potent wthin the Forte.

In the afternoone the Comittee & the Sachems made knowne to the Court, who then agreed that by no meanes the English would bee ingaged in either of their quarrells, but would leaue them to themselues, wherevpon the Gou^rnor made a long speech desiring to bee at peace one wth another, & take wampam. If they would not, then hee declared that the Court would not hinder them, but left them to themselues, & whatsoeuer fell out afterwards vpon either of them, they brought vpon themselues. But so were engaged, that they should not fight vpon this side of the riuer of Hartford, nor to hurt any of the English houses or any thing of theirs of the other side of the riuer; wth many expressions more to the same effect, was spoken by the Gouerno^r & also by some Deputies.

Some expressions many times in the agitation thereof was spoken that might carry that sence of advising & counselling of Vnquas not to fight, as some app{r}hended then, but in conclusion the Gou{r}no{r}, as the mouth of the Court, declared his minde fully to the Indians of both sides, as aforesaid.

Wittnesse my hand, this 20${th}$ of August, 1657.
Jonathan Brewster.

Aug: 19${th}$, (57.)

The Court voted that this relation should bee transcribed & asserted vnd{r} the Sec{rs} hand, that to their sattisfaction it was euidenced in Court to bee a true relation.

---

[88] At a Generall Court held at Hartford, October 1, 1657.

Mr. Wells, Dep:

Magistrates: Mr. Webster, Major Mason, Mr. Clarke, Mr. Talcott, Mr. Willys.

Deputyes: Mr. Steele, Mr. Allin, Mr. Phelps, Mr. Lord, Mr. Brewster, *abs.*, Mr. Trott, Mr. Gailor, Mr. Dan: Clarke, Joseph Migatt, Wm. Wadsworth, Rich: Buttler, Mr. Hollister, John Wells, John Hurd, John Clarke, Rob: Chapman, Hugh Caulkin, Michaell Try, John Wheeler, Antho: Howkins, Rob: Webster Geo: Graues, Sam: Hale, Isack Moore, Sam: Wells, Sam: Bourman.

Tho: Staunton, for contempt of the last Gen: Court, in not appearing when sumoned thereunto, for w${ch}$ offence the Court fines the said Thomas, ten pounds.

This Court orders, that the Treasur{r} shall procure convenient supply of corne for the Major this winter, & the charge in procuring it to bee imposed vpon those who are behind of their rate.

The Court doth appoint the Treasure{r} to prouide horses & men to send for Mr. Winthrop, in case hee is minded to come to dwell w${th}$ vs.

This Court appoints Mr. Allin & Jo: Gilbert to goe to Pacomtuck, to declare to the Indians the mind of the Comission{rs} concerning them;* and that there bee a letter sent to Mr. Pinchon to assist them in it; but if hee refuse & Mr. Holliack, then they shall desist from further p^rceeding.

A list of the seuerall persons & estates of the seu^rall Townes w^thin this Jurisdiction :—

    Fairfeild, p^rsons, . estates, 11410. 1. 0
    Stratford, 63. . . 8400. 0. 0
    Seabrooke, 72. . . . 581. 7. 0
    Mr. Fenwicks farme, . . . 200. 0. 0

A note of Mr. Fenwicks cattle vpon the farme, Good: Clarke is to send vp to the Treasur^r, wch are to bee rated according as the law of the Country requires.

The Cattle of Capt. Cullicks farme are to bee rated & a note of them to bee giuen in to the Treasur^r.

The Court appoints Mr. Dan: Clarke to write a letter to the Magistrates of South Hampton, to informe them of the minde of the Comission^rs, & another to the Indians there.

The Major is allowed fiue pounds for his going to Long Iland, besides his expences in that seruice.

This Court doth allow the Treasurer, for incouragem^t of him in his place, 10 pounds p^r annum.

This Court doth grant a rate of a peny vpon the pound, for the defraying of the publicke charges of this Jurisdisdiction. This rate to bee paid three parts in wheat & pease, by equall p^rportion, & one fourth in Indian Corne at 20*ss*. 6*d*. p^r Bush:

This Court doth appoint the fourteenth day of this moneth bee set apart for a sollemne day of thanksgiuing (for the mercyes of God the yeare past,) in the seuerall plantations in this Jurisdiction.

[89] A list of the persons & rateable estate of Connecticutt, taken Septr 23, 1657:

---

 * "It is ordered, that Vnckas bee required to p^rmit the Podunk Indians to returne to theire dwellings & there to abide in peace & safety, w^thout molestation from him or his, & that the said Indians bee incouraged & invited so to do, by the Government of Connecticott."

   * * * * * * * * * *

 "And the Government of Connecticott is desired to signify to the Pocomtick and Norwootick Sachems our charge vpon Vnckas in refference to the Podunk Indians, and our desire of their returne to their dwellings and continuance there in peace; therfore wee desire and expect they will forbeare all hostillity against Vnckas till the next meeting of the Comission^rs. [Records of U. Colonies, Sept. 1657.]

	£. ss.	£. ss. d
Imp^rs the estate of Hartford,	17045. 8	
The persons, 186, that is,	3348. 0	20393. 8. 0
The estate of Windzor is,	12999. 0	
The persons are 161,	2898. 0	15897. 0. 0
The estate of Wethersfeild is,	10758. 0	
The persons come to,	1854. 0	12612. 0. 0
The estate & p^rsons of Farmington come to,	4852. 0. 0	
The estate & p^rsons of Midltowne comes to	2416. 0. 0	

Sume tot'. 56170. 8. 0
p^r nos, Richard Treat,
Henry Woolcott,
William Westwood,
Robt Webster.

This Court orders, that noe person wth in this Jurisdiction shall kepe any Quakers bookes or manuscripts containing their errors, except teaching Eld^rs, vpon the penalty of 10*ss*. a time for euery person that shall kepe any such booke after the publication hereof, & that shall not deliuer such bookes vnto their Eld^rs.

The Court adjourned to the second Thursday of March.

---

[90] A Session of the Gen: Court in Hartford, 11th day of March, 16$\frac{57}{58}$.

John Winthrop Esqr, Gou^rn^r.

Magistrates: Mr. Webster, Major Mason, John Cullick, Mr. Clarke, Mr. Willis, Mr. Talcott.

Deputies: Mr. Steele, Mr. Allin, Mr. Phelps, Mr. Gailor, Mr. Trott, Mr. Lord, Mr. Dan: Clarke, Mr. Brewster, Joseph Mygatt, Wm. Wadswörth, Rich: Butler, Mr. Hollist^r, John Hurd, John Clarke, Robert Chapman, John Wheeler, Antho: Howkins, Sam: Hale, Sam: Wells, Sam: Bourman, Robt Webster, Geo: Graue Junior.

John Hurd is sworne to the office of a Constable for the yeare ensuing, in the Towne of Stratford.

This day 3 weekes, wch is the first day of Aprill, the Court desires the Magistrates to attend the consideration & distribution of such estates of deceased persons as are, or then shall bee exhibited & the Deputies are desired to giue notice thereof in their respectiue Townes.

The listed persons for Troopers presented to, & allowed by this Court, vnder the command of Major John Mason, are as follow :—

In Hartford : Mr. Willis, Mr. Lord, Mr. Tho: Wells, Jacob Migatt, Jonathan Gilbert, Nicho: Olmsteed, John Stedman, James Steele, Dan: Pratt, Andrew Warner, Will: Edwards, Richard Fellowes, Robert Reiue, John Allin.

In Windzor : Mr. Dan: Clarke, Tho: Allin, Sam: Marshall, John Bissell, Geo: Phelpes, Steph: Terry, Willī: Heyden, John Hosford, John Williams, Natha: Loomis, Tho: Loomis, Capt. Aron Cooke, Ensign Dauid Wilton, Symon Woolcott, Tho: Strong, John Moses, John Porter.

In Wethersfeild : John Lattimore, John Belding, Richard Treat, Mr. John Chester, Antho: Wright, John Palmer.

The aforesaid Troopers p^{r}sented to this Court their choise of officers, wch the Court did confirme : Richard Lord, Capt.; Daniell Clarke, Leiften^t ; John Allin, Cornett; Nicho: Olmsteed, Corporall; Richard Treat, Corporall ; Sam: Marshall, Corporall; Mr. Tho: Wells Junior, Quart^r M^r.

Richard Haughton, of Pequett, petitioning this Court for their fauo^r to consent (that hee the said Richard may haue liberty to agree wth Vncus for a certaine neck of land called Massapeag, betwene Pequett & Mohegin,) They hauing considered the low estate of this man, his charge of children, wth other things as further motiues to them, doe hereby declare, that they thus farre consent to his petition or motion, that in [91] case hee fully sattisfie ‖ Vncus for the aforesaid Massapeage & there bee a full & cleare agreem^t betwene them for the same, then this Court shall not mañage the law in this Comonwealth against him for making any such contract wth Indian or Indians, p^{r}uided the said Haughton or his assignes neuer make any further or other vse of it, but only to plant or sowe therevpon in the summer, and kepe cattle therevpon in the winter : and that no swyne shall bee kept vpon the p^{r}misses at any time, neither shall bee any otherwise improued to the trespasse or p^rjudice of Vncus in any such kind, or trouble of this Comon wealth.

This Court grants liberty to the persons already allowed by this Court to cohabite at Bankside, (a place betwene Fairfeild Towne & Norwalke,) to take in as a cohabitant wth them in that place, Robert Beacham, who lately liued at Norwalke.

The Deputies nominated to this Court, to bee p^rpounded at the next Gen: Court of Election for choise to bee Magistrates in this Jurisdiction, Mr. Phelps, of Windsor, and Mr. Mathew Allin; Mr. Treat Senior, of Wethersfeild; Mr. John Wells of Stratford, and Mr Allexand^r Knowles, of Fairfeild.

Phillip Galpin, of Fairfeild, is freed from trayning, but not from watching nor warding, till the Court sees cause to reuoke this their order.

The consideration of the petition from seu^rall inhabitants in Fairfeild, is referred to the next Court of Magistrates there, & they to make returne thereof to the next Gen: Court after the same.

The plantation at Pequet is named by this Court, New London, wth a preāble to bee inserted about the same, (wch is inserted in the closure of ye Acts of this Session.)

The Court frees Thomas Coleman from watching, warding & trayning, if hee makes it appeare that hee is aboue 60 yeares old.

Mr. Russell, of Wethersfeild is also freed.

This Courte doth grant to & agree wth John Bissell Junior, of Windzor, that the Ferry there, ouer the great Riuer, shall bee & belong to him for the space of ten yeares next ensuing, vpon the limitation & termes hereafter expressed, to wch hee doth in Court agree & ingage to attend :—

1. That there shall bee alwayes maintained in readinesse vpon all occasions, an able & sufficient boate & man for the safe passage of horse & men.

2. The said John Bissell shall haue 8*d*. a head for any beast, & 2*d*. a head for any person that commeth wth them, & 3*d*. for any single person.

[92] 3. That each Trooper listed and allowed in the Court, & the horse hee rides, is only freed from the ferridge going to Springfeild Towne, or as farre as Springfeild Towne, or further

4. That no person of Windzor shall haue liberty for to helpe ouer any person or beast of any other Towne, but they shall then pay the Ferryman as much as if they were caryed ouer by him.

5. Vpon consideration wth the inhabitants of Windzor, they are to goe ouer the Ferry for halfe the forementioned price, only that single persons shall pay 3*d*. p^r head for their passage as before.

There was a list of the persons & estates of the west side of Pequett Riuer presented, wch amounted to 3360*l*. 7*s*. 8*d*. & the Court doth expect that a true List of the persons & estates of the inhabitants of the east side of the Riuer shall bee taken & p^rsented to the next Court, that so their list may bee perfected.

Sam: Welles is confirmed Ensigne for the souldi^rs at Wethersfeild.

William Blumfeild is freed from training.

This Court hauing read & duely considered a letter from the Gen: Court in the Massachusets about the land on the east side of Pequet riuer, doe desire the Gou^rno^r & John Cullick to draw vp a letter in an answere therevnto, & send the same signed by the Sec^r in the name of this Court.*

It is agreed by this Court that Wednesday, the last of this moneth is appointed for a day of humiliation.

This Court orders that henceforth no persons in this Jurisdiction shall in any way imbody themselues into Ch: estate, without consent of the Generall Court, & approbation of the neighbo^r Ch^s:

This Court orders that there shall bee no ministry or Ch: administration entertained or attended by the inhabitants of any plantation in this Collony, distinct & seperate from, & in opposition to that wch is openly & publickly obserued & dispenced by the settled & approued Minister of the place, except it bee by approbation of the Gen^rall Court & neighbo^r Ch^s: p^ruided alwayes that this order shall not hinder any priuate meetings of godly persons to attend any duties that Christianity or religion call for, as fasts or conference, nor take place vpon such as are

---

* See Appendix, No. iv.

hindred by any just impedim^ts on the Sabboth day, from the publicke assemblies, by weather or water & the like.

[93] This Court appoints that Will: Waller should bee required forthwith to make due satisfaction to those who are appointed by the Townesmen of Seabrook to leuy the rate for Mr. Fitches maintenance, or otherwise to make his appearance at the Gen: Court in May next to giue an account of his neglect.

It is voted by the Court, that Windzor petition shall bee deferred vntill the next Session of this Court, & then to bee taken into consideration; as also the seu^rall Deputies are desired to acquaint o^r Eld^rs respectiuely that the Court desires them to attend the next Session of the Court to advise & consider what way may bee most requisite to issue the differences that are amongst vs.

This Court orders, in refference to the sad differences y^t are broken out in the seu^rall Ch^s: in this Collony, & in spetiall betwixt the Ch: of Christ at Hartford and the withdrawers, & to p^ruent further troubles & such sad consequences that may issue from the p^rmises to the whole Common wealth, It is desired & required by this Court, that there bee from henceforth an vtter cessation of all further p^rsecution, either on the Ch^s: part at Hartford towards the withdrawers from them, and on the other part, that those that haue withdrawen from the Ch: at Hartford shall make a cessation in p^rsecuting their former p^rpositions to the Ch: at Wethersfeild or any other Ch: in refference to their joyning there in Ch: relation, vntill the matters in controuersy betwixt the Ch: of Hartford & the brethren that haue withdrawen bee brought to an issue in that way that the Court shall determine.

It is ordered, that the Court shall meet together on Wednsday seauennight, being the twenty fourth of this instant, at Hartford, where the neighbo^r Eld^rs are desired to attend the Court, that so their advise & helpe may bee improued to settle vpon some speedy course for the issuing the p^rsent troubles that the Churches, & in spetiall the Ch: of Hartford lyes vnder, in respect of the seperation by them that haue withdrawne from that society.

* Whereas, it hath bene a comendable practice of ye inhabitants of all the Collonies of these parts, that as this Countrey hath its denomination from our deare natiue Countrey of England, and thence is called New England, soe the planters, in their first setling of most new Plantations haue giuen names to those Plantations of some Cities and Townes in England, thereby intending to keep vp and leaue to posterity the memoriall of seuerall places of note there, as Boston, Hartford, Windsor, York, Ipswitch, Brantree, Exeter,—This Court, considering that there hath yet noe place in any of the Collonies bene named in memory of ye Citty of London, there being a new plantation within this Jurisdiction of Conecticut setled vpon ye faire Riuer of Monhegin, in ye Pequot Countrey, it being an excellent harbour and a fit and convenient place for future trade, it being alsoe the only place wch ye English of these parts haue possessed by conquest, and y^t by a very iust war vpon y^t great and warlike people, ye Pequots, that therefore they might therby leaue to posterity the memory of y^t renowned city of London, from whence we had our transportation, haue thought fit, in honour to that famous Citty, to cal y^e said Plantation, New London.

[94] A Session of the Gen: Court, in Hartford, the 24th of March, 16$\frac{5}{3}\frac{7}{8}$.

John Winthrop Esqr, Gou^{r}no^r.
Tho: Wells Esqr, Deputy.
Magistrates: Mr. Webster, Mr. Cullick, Mr. Clarke, Mr. Willis, Mr. Talcott.
Deputies: Mr. Steele, Mr. Allin, Mr. Phelps, Mr. Lord, Mr. Dan: Clarke, Joseph Migatt, W^m. Wadsworth, Richard Butler, Mr. Hollister, Antho: Howkins, Isack Moore, Sam: Wells, Sam: Bourman, Mr. Trott.

This Court desires Mr. Lord & John Cullick to take in the Treasur^{rs} account in the behalfe of this Comon wealth.

This Court appoints & orders that the Constable or Constables in each Towne where there is no Magistrate or Assistant shall, at all times when the Treasurer shall call or require them, deliuer in their account to the Treasurer, vnder his or their owne hand or hands, & the hands of two of the Townes men in their

---

* Here follows the 'preamble,' to the order of the Court changing the name of the plantation of Pequot, referred to, on page 310, *ante*.

respectiue Townes; and where any Magistrate or Assistant dwelleth, vnder their owne hand & the hand of one of the Magistrates or Assistants that liueth in the same Towne wth them.

Sam: Smith, Senior, moouing this Court that hee might bee freed from training as a comon souldier in that Towne, they doe vpon seuerall grounds grant his request, espetially because hee hath bene an antient Serjeant to the trained band in that Towne.

Nath: Ward is freed from trayning, watching & warding

It is desired by this Court, that the Church at Hartford & Mr. Stone should meet together wth those that haue withdrawen, to see if it bee possible by a priuate conference together to issue vpon some mutuall conclusions that may put an end vnto their vnhappy discention. The Gou^rno^r & Deputy Gouerno^r are desired to accompany them in their conference, if it may bee with conueniency attended by the Gou^rno^r & Deputy. And in case the foresaid p^rties at difference cannot agree vpon a way to put an issue to their troubles, that then there bee lett^rs sent to the Bay Eld^rs & to any among vs or in the other Jurisdiction, for advice what the Court should doe in the p^rmises.

The Gou^rno^r, Mr. Willis, Mr. Talcott, & Mr. Stone, & Mr. Lord are hereby desired, that in case there bee no agreem^t amongst the Church & withdrawers, to send lett^rs in the name of the Court, as before.

William Kelsey is freed from watching, warding & trayning.*

---

[95]   At A Gen^ll Court of Election, May 20, 1658.

Magistrates elected:

Thomas Wels Esqr, Gou^rnor.
John Winthrop Esqr, Deputy.

   Mr. Webster,   Mr. Mathew Allyn,
   Maior Mason,   Mr. Phelpes,
   Mr. Clarke,   Mr. John Wels,
   Mr. Willis,   Mr. Treat,
   Mr. Talcot,   Mr. Baker,
   Mr. Ogden,   Mr. Mulford,
   Mr. Cosmore,   Mr. Alex: Knowles.

---

* This is the last entry in the hand writing of Mr. Cullick. In May following, Mr. Daniel Clarke was chosen Secretary, and the records which next follow are in his hand.

Deputies: Mr. Steel, Mr. Brewster, Mr. Lord, Deacon Gaylard, Will' Wadsworth, Joseph Mygat, John Bissel, Dan: Clark, Record", Rich: Butler, Edw: Griswold, L: Hollister, Anthony Howkins,* John Dement, Sam: Wells, Sam: Boreman, Georg Graues, Sam. Stocken, Hugh Caulkin, Jo: Clark, Robt Chapman, John Wheeler, Cornel. Hull, Math: Camfeild, Rich: Olmstead, Will' Beardsley, Joseph Hawley.

Comissioners chosen, for this Colony :—Mr. Winthrop Esqr, Mr. Talcot; Reserue, Maior John Mason.

These p^{r}sons vnderwritten were made free, before the Court :—Sam^{ll} Burr, Obed: Spencer, Thom: Allyn, Eldad Pomrey, John Wiate, John Kelley, Jos: Knowles, Tho: Eggleston, Rob: Reeue, Jos: Arnold, Georg Orvis, Tho: Spencer, Zach: Sanford, Jo: Merrils, Grego: Gibbs, John Pettibone, Sam: Eggleston, Steph: Davis, Joseph Sutton, *Ob:*, John Kerbey, Sam: Richards, Tho: Alcot, John Church, Joseph Nash, Jer: Judson, Will: Warin, John Chester, John Grumwel, James Northam, Cris: Crow, Tho: Clark, John Kelsey, Tim: Traul, Peter Blachfeild, Will' Keney, Rich: Hartly, Matt: Becquet, Tho: Bowen, Tho: Leonards, Pet^r Blachf'ld, John Wadom, Jonath: Deman, Francis Yeates, Ben: Crane, Rich: Smith Junr, James Boswel, Jo: Curtis, Tho: Wickum, Georg Yeates, Sam: Pinney, Rich: Lord Junr, John Sables, Cris: Huntington, John Andrewes, Abrh'. Finch, Jonas Westouer, Beniam: Bur, Renold Maruin, Ren: Maruin Junr, Joseph Judson, John Coleman, Cornel: Gillet, Will'. Edwards, Thomas Brook, Will: Morton, Rob^{rt} Boughtwhord, Peter Browne, Joseph Clark, Raph Parker, Will'. Welman.

[96] This Court orders that Esqr Winthrop, Maior Mason, Mr. Allyn, Mr. Brewster, shal, vpon some seasonable opertunity, attend to keep a Court at Pequit, to settle the affayrs of y place; Mr. Winthrop to appoynt ye time.

Will: Welman, of New London, is discharged from his Recognisanc, about a marriage in Virginia.

The Magestrates graunted Will' Williams, of Hartford, to

---

* The names of Deputies are written, thus far, in the margin of Page [95.] Those which follow, are on page [96,] where the Recorder has *repeated* those already given, down to the name of Anthony Howkins.

dispose of his seruant youth, Math: Young, to another sutable M^r, and the s^d Mathew doth fully consent therevnto and hath p^rmised to giue a ful discharge vnto his Master Williams from ye engagem^t wherein he was bound to teach the sayd Math: the trade of a Cooper.

This Court orders that al seafaring men y^t make it y^{eir} occupation to imploy themselues in Navigatⁿ, they shal for future be freed from trayneings.

This Court voated a confirmation of the Combinatⁿ with Easthampton, and that the Articles of Agreem^t should be signed by the Secretary in the name of the Court and sent ouer vnto them; as also a letter, to signify the mind of the Court.*

This Court orders that ye power of any p^rticuler Magestrate, on the maine and likewise on the Island belonging to this Colony, shall extend itselfe to al and every place and p^rson in this Jurisdiction, as need requires: And that those of Southampton and East Hampton shal ioyne together in the exercise of judicature amongst them, and to summon Juries out of either place: and that they haue liberty to repayr to any Court held at New London for help in any Controuersy

This Court approueing the pious care of the Towne of Fairfeild, in procureing help for Mr. Joanes by his owne consent therevnto, as far as appeares by a pap^r p^rsented by their Deputies to ye Court, doe order, that according to their desires the foresaid paper be kept amongst the Court papers, and desire the Towne not any way therevpon to depriue y^{eir} Reu^rnd ancient Pastor, Mr. Joanes, in sicknes or health, of his comfortable maintenance.

This Court orders y^t out of the sum̃ imposed vpon the Indians of Southampton, to pay for the loss y^t was there susteined by fire, there shalbe the sum̃ of 30*l*. p^r Anñ. for the four first [97] yeares, ‖ and fourty pounds p^r Anñ. for the two last yeares abated. The total abatement amounts to 200*l*. 0*s*. 0*d*.

Its ordered, that Mr. Cosmore, Mr. Ogden, Capt. Tappin and Goodman Clarke, shal make distribution of that paym^t that the Indians make, to them that haue suffr^d loss by fire; only Mr. Fordom is excempted from any part of this pay for the losse of

---

* See a letter to Easthampton, written some months previous to this session of the General Court, in Appendix, No. V.

his owne house and goods therein conteyned: provided, that before distribution be made, the charges that the Countrey hath bin at in y^r exhibited* to ye Island shalbe first defrayed.

John Griffin, now returneing from Pocumtacot, was made free, by consent of the Court.

Robert Allyn and John Gager are released frō their fine for not attending ordinary Town training.

The Court is adiourned til the 3^d Wednesday in August.

Mr. Samuel Stone, Teacher at Hartford, p^rsenting vnto the Gen: Court, M^rch 25, '58, a petition wth certayne p^rpositions, it was vppon his request ordered to be recorded:—

My humble request is that the Quæstions here p^rsented may be sillogistically reasoned before this honor^d Court. I hope that some of o^r withdrawen Brethren, or some other whom they shal p^rvide, wil reason with me, face to face:

Quæs. 1. The former Councel at Hartford June, 56, is vtterly cancild and of no force.

2. There is no violation of the last agreem^t (made when the Reuerend Elders of Massachusets were here,) either by the Ch: of Christ at Hartford or their Teacher.

3. The withdrawen Brethren haue offred great violence to ye formentioned agreement.

4. The withdrawen Brethren are members of the Ch: of Christ at Hartford.

5. Their withdraweing from the Ch: is a sin exceding scandalous & dreadful and of its owne nature destructiue to this and other Churches.

6. The controuersy between the Ch: of Christ at Hartford and the withdrawen p^rsons is not in the hands of the Churches to be determined by them.

Sam: Stone.

---

[98] AT A SESSION OF THE GEN: COURT AT HARTFORD, AUG^s 18, 1658.

Thom: Wels Esqr, Gou:

Esqr Winthrop, Depu:

Magestrates: Mr. John Webster, Maior Mason, Mr. Willys, Mr. Tailcot, Mr. Phelps, Mr. Treat, Mr. Allyn, Dan: Clark, *Secret:*

---

* An error of the Recorder. The word was probably *expedition*.

Deputies: Mr. Steel, Capt. Lord, Deacō Gayl^rd, W. Wadsworth, Jo: Bissel Senr, Jos: Mygatt, Rich: Butler, Edw: Griswold, L: Hollister, Jo: Demāt, Sam: Wells, Sam: Boreman, Antho: Howkins, Jo: Clark, Robt Chapmā, Robt Webst^r, Math: Camfeild.

In reference to a complaynt made by Georg Graues, Georg Stocken, Nath: Willet, Nath: Berdin, contr: Mr. Webster, Capt. Cullick, Mr. Goodwin, Andrew Bacon, in ye name of the rest of ye withdrawers at Hartford, consisting of several p^rticulers, p^rsented the last session to ye consideration of this Court, This Court sees cause to defer the consideration of the compl^t vnto the Court in Octob^r, and haue ordered that then it shalbe attended; in ye meane time, to procure what light and help they can in the case.

This Court appoynted Esqr Winthrop, Major Mason, Mr. Talcot, Mr. Steel, as a Comittee to treat with Capt. Cullick about the purchase of the Riuer, and to p^rpound that in case Capt. Cullick will allow to ye Countrey 500*l.* and demand nothing from Seabrook nor Middletown, and returne such security to ye Countrey as he can or as in his power, that then there shalbe acquittances granted, each to other.

The Comittee is to make report to morrow, w^t the result of ye Treaty is.

19 Day. The Comittee returned answer to ye Court, that Capt. Cullick is willing to quit acc^o wth the Countrey, and if ye arrears yet due to him amount not to 300*l.* he wil make it vp 300*l*. Mr. Talcot sayth 250*l*.

This Court orders, that notice shalbe giuen to ye Indians liueing at Farmington, that in regard of their hostile pursuits, contrary to former ord^r of Court, and considering their entertaynm^t of strang Indians, contrary to their agreem^t wth ye English when they sate downe at Farmington, whence ensues danger to ye English by Bullets shot into the Towne in their skirmishes, That they shal speedily p^rvide another place for their habitation and desert that place wherin they are now [99] garrisoned. ‖ And what Indians refuse to attend this order shalbe returned to ye Courte in October next. Further, it is required by the Court that Farmington Indians shal forthwith send away al such strangers as haue not bin knowne inhabitants in that place, according to forementioned agreem^t.

Mr. Steel, L: Lewis, Ensigne Steel, Thom: Judd, are desired to comunicate the mind of the Court to ye Indians.

Daniel Clark was sworne, according to ye forme of the Secretaries Oath approued by this Court and ordered to be recorded.

A Petition from several of the inhabitants of Wethersfeild* was p^{r}sented to this Court and vpon p^{r}vsall of the same the Court returned this answer :—

In regard of a complayn^t, in the Petition, of a scandalous oath taken by Mr. Russel, whereby the inhabitants seem afrayd to adventure themselues vnd^r his ministery, the Court hath considered the nature of the Oath and ye witnesses, and tho there are diuers app^{r}hensions of it, yet to ye purpose of the allegation to wch Mr. Russel testified, the oath was ambiguous : but that it should be strayned to such a height as in the Petition is declared, this Court iudgeth it not meet, and in that respect the Petitioners blameable, and that he is not hereby rendred so scandalous as not fit to administer in his office. Yet notwithstanding, they iudg that Mr. Russel should speak more playnly for ye future, to ye capacity of the hearers, espetially in way of testimony ; and y^t the Petitioners should carefully avoid all vnnecessary strayneing of words or expressions (y^t are in

---

* This Petition (in "Ecclesiastical" Papers, Vol. i. No. 1,) is signed by John Holister, Thomas Wright Sen., John Demminge Sen., John Edwards Sen., and Richd Smith Sen., and five females, all members of Mr. Russell's church, together with thirty nine others, inhabitants of Windsor. After referring to an order of the Courtp assed in March 1657-8 (see page 311, ante,) that no ministry or church should be entertained or attended by the inhabitants of any plantation, ' distinct and seperate from and in opposition to that which is openly and publicly observed and dispensed by the settled and approved Minister of the place,' the petitioners declare that they cannot regard Mr. Russell as their settled and approved Minister,—first, because, in the preceding spring, he had sent them a writing to provide for themselves,—whereby they consider themselves freed from their former obligations to him : these obligations they profess themselves unwilling to renew, since they "are afrayed to venture [their] soules vnder his ministry." They further represent that he had brought great scandal on the church, by "a greivous oath, acknowledged by himselfe to bee ambiguous, rash and sinfull,—and what more may be made evident." They ask the Gen. Court, that they may not be held in bondage, but may "use their liberty" in procuring another minister "faithfull in the administrations of the Gospell and inoffenciue in his conversation."

For a further account of the dissensions in the Church at Wethersfield, having a similar origin, and intimately connected, with the troubles of the Hartford church, see Trumbull's Hist. of Conn. i. chap. xiii.

y^eir nature dubious) to such a perticuler sense as may occasion trouble.

To ye busines of their liberty, wch the Petitioners think Mr. Russels graunt and their acceptance hath stated them vnder, the Court judgeth, that they had reason to desire help and advice in this case. And it is conceaued that vnles there be some due meanes attended for ye healing of their differenc, that ye fire wilbe more kindled by their address hither, the paper that was sent in to ye Towne by Mr. Russel being of an ambiguous nature, subiect to various interp^rtations, and therefore should be explayned and retracted by Mr. Russel. And the Court adviseth each party, that they walk louingly together, without disturbeing carriage each to other.

In reference to ye differenc twixt the Church at Hartf^rd and the withdrawers, it was ordered, that the ensueing p^rticulers should be p^rsented to each party, as ye mind and desire of ye Court :—

[100] 1. It is conceaued that they should obserue and attend that rule of Christ, Acts, 15, To debate and dispute their differenc amongst themselues, in the first place.

2. That the Quæstions in controuersy should be playnly stated and gathered out of their papers, before they debate as that text holds forth.

3. In case this doth not take nor be embraced, that then each party should chuse three Elders, able and as indifferent as times wil afford, before whom (the Quæst. beinge beforehand playnly stated,) the case in difference shal be publiquely disputed, who shal lend what light and help they can, to ye issueing the controuersy according to God, vnto wch both parties shall peaceably subiect themselues.

4. And in case either the Church or withdrawers refuse to chuse, then the Court to chuse instead of that part y^t discents, leauei ig liberty to ye other part to make choyce for themselues such able and indifferent men as they can agree vpon to be instrumental in issueing these sad differences, by hearing the dispute as before and passing determination thereon. And if either part be dissatisfied wth the determinations of the persons y^t are soe chosen, that then there may be liberty for the dissatisfied

party to obiect, that soe the determination may be vindicated and confirmed by scripture and reason.

These being p^rpounded the withdrawers were willing to chuse, as in 3^d Proposit: The Church at Hartford refused. Soe, in issue, the Court on the one part chose Mr. Cobbit, Mr. Michil, Mr. Danforth, and for a Reserue, Mr. Browne ; and Mr. Street for a reserue to y^m y^t ye withdrawers chose, who were Mr. Dauenport, Mr. Norton, Mr. Fitch.

The seueral Elders forementioned, chosen to assist in the differences at Hartford, are requested to come vp to Hartford by the 17th of September, to assist in that seruice.

Its ordered, that L^rs of request shalbe sent from the Court and both parties, to ye several Elders and y^r Churches, for to effect the same.

Mr. Allyn, Mr. Phelpes, Mr. Henry Clark and the Secretary, are appoynted to write and indite the sayd L^rs, in behalfe of the Court, and to send them.

Mr. John Allyn, Edward Stebbing, Nath: Ward, John Bernard, are appoynted to take in the account of the charge respecting al ye Elders attending the last Council, and the man [101] y^t was maimed, and to distribute it by way || of rate vpon both parties, viz : the church at Hartf: aud ye withdrawers.

In regard that the Court app^rhends y^t the order concerneing the stateing and draweing forth of the Quæstions in controuersy twixt the Church at Hartford and the withdrawers, hath not bene fully attended, it is therfore ordered, that twixt this and the 8^t of September next, each party shal attend the foresayd order, in draweing forth and playnly stateing al such Quæstions as they desire to haue debated before the Council. And in case they attend not to deliuer the sayd Quæstions or Positions each to other, before that day appoynted, whateuer is neglected to be p^rsented as aforesayd shal not be attended by the Council ; and it is also required that each party doe playnly declare what it is that they wil mainteine in their Quæstions, either negatiuely or affirmatiuely, as matter of offence. And in case there be no more Quæstions deliuered in by that time appoynted, then ye quæstions already p^rsented shal stand as that wch the Council is to attend. And both parties are to send in a coppy of their Quæstions or positions to ye Secretary of ye Court.

According to ye desire of Jasper Varleet, manifested to Mr. Gouern^r and Mr. Allyn, in reference to Isbrand Goodheart, It is ordered by this Court, That Isbrand Goodheart, now in durance, shalbe returned vnto Jasper Varleet, to be at his dispose, to improue him for his vse, vntil the remainder of that debt for wch he is now in durance be satisfied,—Provided the sayd Varleet make not sale of the sayd Isbrand to any forreigne Inhabitants or Pagans. And the sayd Jasper is to returne both Isbrand and an account of the debt vnto the next Court.

This Court is adiourned vntil Munday next, 23 Aug^st.

Aug^st 23. This Court, haueing considered the Order about landing Rum and Barbados liquors, doe now impose the forfeiture specified in the sayd order, only vppon draweing out and selling the sayd liquors.

This Court orders that the several Townes where any part of the estates either of Edw: Hopkins Esqr deceasd, or George Fenwick Esqr deceased, be knowne to remayne, shal speedily take an Inventory of the sayd estate and p^rsent it, vnd^r the hands of those y^t order the prudentials of the Towne, to ye Court in Octob^r next.

Its ordered, that the several Constables in the Planta[tions] vpon the Riuer, that haue had to doe in gathering in and deliuering the paym^t for ye purchase of the Riuer, shal bring in their receipts respecting the sayd paym^t, vnto ye Court in October next, if it be not done already.

In reference vnto a General Muster, This Court leaues it vnto the Maior to appoynt the time for calling the companies together this year, as he iudgeth most sutable, || for time and place. And the three p^rticuler training dayes, that are by order and custome to be attended for this latter part of the year, in the Plantations y^t doe assemble at the General meeting, are remitted, and are to issue in the General Muster wch is to be attended for two dayes space. And its also required, that noe souldier that attends the service aforesayd shal deminish any of that p^rportion of powder that ye Order of the Countrey imposeth on him for his store.

This Court Orders, vpon the request of Mr. Allyn, that the case respecting [him] and Mrs. Alcot shalbe attended in the Court in October, and that sumons shalbe granted by the Secretary, for y^t purpose.

On Wednesday, the 8^t of September, is appoynted a solemne humiliation, in al the Plantations in this Collony, to implore the fauour of God towards his people, in regard of the intemperate season, thin harvest, sore visitation by sicknes in several Plantations, and the sad prolonged differences y^t yet remaine vnreconciled in Ch^s: and Plantations; and that God would succeed such meanes as are appoynted to be attended for the healing of the foresayd differences.

Mr. Mathew Allyn is appoynted by the Court, to stand as a Comittee wth Mr. Henry Clark, of Windsor, to act in the disposing of lands at Mussawco, according to former order of Court.

AT A SESSION OF THE GEN^l: COURT AT HARTF: OCTOB^r 7, 1658.

Thomas Wells Esqr, Gou^r.

Magestrates: Mr. Webster, Maior Mason, Mr. Willis, Mr. Tailcot, Mr. Phelps, Mr. Treat, Mr. Allyn.

Secretary; Daniel Clark.

Deputies: Mr. Steel, Capt. Lord, Deacō Gaylard, Will: Wadsworth, Joseph Migat, Rich: Butler, John Bissel Senr, Edw: Griswold, Lieu^t Hollister, Mr. Sam: Wells, Jo: Demant, Sam^{ll} Boreman, Mr. Brewster, Goodm̄: Morgan, Mr. Ward, Mr. Hill, Thom: Fairchild, Joseph Judson, Nath: Richards, Walt^r Hoyt, Goodm̄: Judd, Robt: Webster, Georg Graues, Jo: Clark, Robt Chapman.

It is ordered by this Court, y^t al the receipts respecting the several rates payd for the purchase of ye Riuer, p^{r}sented vnto the Court, shalbe recorded by the Secretary into ye Countrey's booke of Records.

Vpon the motion of Mr. Ward, respecting the estates of p^{r}sons deceased, at Fairfeild, This Court doth appoynt Mr. Ward, Mr. Hill, with the Townesmen of Fairefeild, to assist Mr. John Wells and Assistant Campfeild in proueing Wills and takeing in Inventories, and distributeing estates of p^{r}sons y^t

dyed intestate, and to appoynt administrators; and in case any are vnsatisfied w[th] their determinations herin, they haue liberty to make their address to y[e] next Session of this Court. This ord[r] respects Stratford, Fairfeild and Norwalke.

The list of the Persons and Estates w[th]in this Jurisdiction, p[r]sented to this Court:—

			£
Hartford,	Persons, 187.	Estat,	20547.
[103] Windsor,	Persons, 160.	Estat,	16209.
Wethersfeild,	P[r]sons & Estate,		12397.
Fairfeild,	P[r]sons & Estate,		10509. 13s.
Stratford,	P[r]sons & Estates,		8646.
Norwalk,	P[r]sons & Estate,		3297.
Middle Towne,	P[r]sons & Estate,		2326.
Farmington,	P[r]sons & Estate,		5761.
New London,	P[r]sons & Estates,		5793. 4s.

This Court graunts a Rate of a penny p[r] pound to be levied vppon the estate of this Collony.

This Court haueing considered the former ord[r] about Quakers and such like Heretiques, doe now see cause to leaue it vnto y[e] discretion of the Magestrates or Assistants, within this Jurisdiction, where any such p[r]sons shalbe found fomenting their wicked Tenets and shalbe legally convicted to be disturbeing to y[e] publique peace, to punish the sayd Heretiques by fine or banishment or corporeal punishm[t] as they iudge meete. And the same to be inflicted vppon any p[r]son or p[r]sons that shalbe instrumental to bring any such p[r]sons, viz: Heretiques, by sea or land, into any Plantation in this Collony, P[r]vided the fine for a p[r]ticuler default exceed not the sum of ten pounds.

It is ordered by this Court, that in case there fal out any sudden exigent, in any Plantation in this Collony, by assault of Indians or any other Enemy, to y[e] disturbance and hazzard of the Publique weale, that then it shalbe in the power of the p[r]sent Milletary officers belonging to y[e] place soe disturbed, to require and cal forth the souldiers that are belonging to their comand in y[t] place, to marshal them and order and dispose them as need and p[r]sent occasions shall require to defend the place assaulted and to quit the enemy; and in case need require, to assist a neighbour Plantation in any extremity as aforesayd, that then the miletary officers shal advise wth such Magestrate or Magestrates or Assistants as may conveniently be obteined, what way to act for releif of their neighbouring freinds. And this course to be attended vpon all such occasions vntil the Court shal take further order.

This Court is adiourned vntil the next Wednesday aft^r the p^rticuler Court in March.

The Magestrates appoynted the first Wednesday in Nouemb^r a publique Thanksgiueing, for England's late victories and p^rservation, and for the mercy of God to vs, in o^r continued peace and the abatement of the sore sicknes wherewith many Plantations were visited in this and other Collonies.

[104] THE SEVERAL RECEIPTS RESPECTING THE PAYM^ts FOR Y^e PURCHASE OF SEABROOK FORT ETC.

1647 Windsor. I doe acknowledge hereby to haue receaued of the Constables of Windsor, for ye year 1647, vpon the composition wth Mr. Fenwick, the sum̄ of thirty seauen pounds fiue shilling and seauen penc, I say rec^d. for ye vse aforesayd, 37*l*. 5*s*. 7*d*.
04. 19. 6.

6th Feb: 1647. 42. 5. 1.   Ed: Hopkins.

Rec^d more, of Aaron Cook, 0. 17. 0.
Jno. Bissel, 1. 00. 0.
11½ Bush^ls wheat, 2. 06. 0.
4 Bush: pease, 0. 12. 0.
Jno. Tink^rs Farm, 0. 04. 6.

4. 19. 6.   4. 19. 6.
37. 5. 7.

42. 5. 1.

3^d MARCH, 1655.

1655 Hartford. Receiued of Bartholomew Bernard and Will' Partrigge, Constables for ye Towne of Hartford, in ye yeare (55) the sum̄e of Sixty pounds fiue shillings, for ye vse of George Fenwick Esqr, vpon ye Agreem^t about ye Fort at Seabrook, I say rec^d the day and yeare abouesaid, in part of what is payable to him by the Townes vpon the Riuer for y⁰ yeare past, 60*l*. 05*s*. 00*d*.

John Cullick.

1654 Rec^d of Sam^ll Smith and Jno Demming, Consta-
Wethersfld. bles in Wethersfeild, in ye year 1654, the sum of
Twenty one pound eight shillings six pence, wch was payd in April (54.) And Rec^d of y^m in Corne in April (55) the sum of Twenty eight pounds one shilling and sixpence, both wch payments are made in reference to their p^rportion in Wethersfeild for ye composition for the Fort, and for the aforsaid yeare of their Constableship; both wch paym^ts aforesaid were not made neither for time nor kind according to the Countreyes agreem^t wth Geo: Fenwick Esqr. Witness my hand this seauenth Feb: 1655.

John Cullick.

1654 Rec^d of John Standley, of Farmington, last spring
Farm: twelue month, Thirteen pounds, seauenteen shillings,
and last sumer, one pound eight shillings, wch he payd vpon the acc^o. of the Fort Rate for Farmington, in the year of his Constableship there, wch was 1654. Witness my hand, this 30th Nouemb^r, 1655.

John Cullick.

1656 Rec^d by me, John Cullick of Hartford, of Jona-
Windsor. than Gillet and Abraham Randal, Constables in
Windsor, in ye year 1656, the sum of Twenty six pounds, fifteen shillings and sixpence, part of it being paid to John Bernard for my vse in ye year of their Constableship, and the rest the day of the date of these pr^nts, wch aforesayd sum is in part of payment of their Townes p^rportion, in the afore-
[105] said year of their Constableship, for ye Composition wth George Fenwick Esqr, in reference to ye Fort at Seabrook, I say Rec^d this 25th day of June, 1658, the su of 26*l*. 15*s*. 06*d*.

John Cullick.

Hartford, Rec^d of Richard Goodman and John Bayly, Con-
1656–57. stables in Hartford, the sum of Sixty pounds fiue
shillings, being for that Townes p^rportion in the yeare of their Constableship, of the composition wth George Fenwick Esqr, about the Forte, I say Rec^d as aboue this 16th of March, 1656–57, Witness my hand.

John Cullick.

Hartford, 28th Feb. 1654. Rec^d of Will: Lewis and Gregory Wilterton the sum of Sixty pounds fiue shillings, wch is for Hartfords p^{r}portion (for the yeare of their Constableship,) of the Composition made between this Jurisdiction and George Fenwick Esqr, in reference to Seabrook Fort, I say Rec^d of them, 60d. 5s. 0.

John Cullick.

1652 Farm: Whereas the Constable of Farmington, in the year 1652, did pay vnto me vppon the acc^o: of the Composition for ye Fort at Seabrook betwixt Georg Fenwick Esqr and ye Colony of Conecticut, the sum of Fourteen pounds sixteen shillings and eight pence, and John Brunson, of Farmington, doth now promis to pay the remainder (next March,) wch is eight shillings and fourpence; the said John Brunson alsoe affirming that I gaue him no receipt for the same, I doe hereby declare that I owne the receipt of so much vpon the Acco^t aforesaid, provided no former receipt come in to my p^{r}iudice for the same, and John Brunson aforesayd saue me harmles therefrom. Witness my hand, this 27th day of September, 1658.

John Cullick.

1657. Rec^d of John Root, of Farmington, 14th April, 1657, according to the warrant granted for the gathering of the Rate respecting the purchase of the Fort, The sum of Fifteen pounds fiue shillings.

John Cullick.

Rec^d of John Coal, Constable for this year in Farmington, the sum of Fifteen pounds fiue shillings, wch is for that Townes p^{r}portion in the year of his Constableship, of the composition for the fo$_\wedge$te, I say receaued this 30th of Novemb^r, 15l. 05s. 00d.

John Cullick.

[106]

CONNECTICUT.  For severall good considerations moueing herevnto, It is now ordered and enacted by the General Court of Conecticut, this instant October, the seaventh, sixteen hundred and sixty.

1. That Capt. John Cullick, in behalf of his now wife and her children, shal from henceforth haue ful and free libertie to possess and improue the estate of George Fenwick Esqr, lying in

this Collony, according to ye true intent and meaninge of ye last Will and Testam^t of George Fenwick Esqr, as alsoe this Court graunts vnto the said Capt. John Cullick full power of administring to ye foresaid estate in behalf himself, his wife and h^r children, as legattees to ye foresaid estate.

2. That Capt. John Cullick and his heires, from henceforth, are fully discharged and released from his engagement made in Court, respecting eight hundred pounds estate.

3. The Generall Court doe for themselues and their successors hereby fully remit, release and quit claime all their right and intrest to, and further and future demands respecting a legacy of fiue hundred pounds, specified in ye last will of George Fenwick Esqr.

4. The Generall Court doth hereby, for themselues and their successors, fully and foreuer discharge and secure the said Capt. John Cullick, his now wife, and her children and successors, from all demands and further and future troubles and molestations by any, from, by and vnder vs, both respecting the Legacy forementioned, and respecting moneyes expended by ye Colony or p^rticuler Townes therein, in referenc to ye purchase of ye Riuer, and acquittances giuen for ye said moneyes.

5. And further, this Court doth hereby declare, that Capt. Cullick, his wife and their children and successors, shal from henceforth and for future, be wholly freed from all trouble by sutes of law by any from, by and vnder vs, in reference to ye agreement respecting ye purchase of ye Riuer.

The forementioned graunts are confirmed by the Gen^{ll} Court, vnto Capt. John Cullick, his now wife and her children and successors, vpon consideration of fiue hundred pounds, to be paid by him vnto this Court or their order, and acquittances giuen for moneyes paid and other discharges, more largely specified in specialties giuen by the said Capt. Cullick vnto this Court.

The true intent and meaning of ye fift perticuler grant of ye Court is, that Capt. John Cullick & his wife and heires are freed from all trouble and molestation soe far and noe further then ye estate bequeathed to them had or hath any reference to ye agreement made between Georg Fenwick Esqr and this Gen^{rll} Court.

In confirmation of ẙe p̊rmises & by order of ẙe Gen: Court, I haue caused the seale of ẙe Coll: to be herevnto affixed as aboue appeareth on ẙe margent. Jo: Winthrop, Goůr.

Enacted by the Gen: Court and by their order subscribed, p̊r. Dan: Clark, Secretary to ẙe Collony of Conecticutt.

This writing is a true Coppy of an Orign̊ll d'd p̊r ẙe Gen̊ll Court, to Cap̊t. Jn̊o. Cullick, transcribed p̊r Dan̊ll Clark, Sec̊ry.

---

[107] A discharg from Cap̊t. John Cullick and his wife, to ẙe Gen̊ll Court of Conecticut.*

These p̊nts testifie to all to whom they may be of concernment, that we, John and Elizabeth Cullick, of Boston, in New England, vppon good consideration moueing vs hereunto, doe, for our selues and heires and ẙe legatees to ẙe estate of Georg Fenwick Esq̊r, lying or situate in New England, hereby fully and freely and for euer acquit and discharg the Colony of Conecticut, with ẙe Generall Court and all and every Plantation therein; from all sum̃ or sum̃s of money already paid or any way payable vnto Georg Fenwick Esq̊r, or his assignes by virtue of an Agreem̊t and purchase made of ẙe Riuer; And doe hereby fully discharge and acquit and secure the said Court and all those Plantations that were concerned in ẙe said purchase, from all future demands, troubles or molestations by any from, by or vnd̊r vs or any of vs, in referenc to any moneyes that haue bene alredy paid or ẙt may be deemed to be due by virtue of the said Agreem̊t. In witness to ẙe p̊rmises we, John and Elizabeth Cullick haue hereunto fixed o̊r hands and seales, this instant October the seauenth, 1660.

Signed, sealed and deliv̊rd
  in p̊rsence of vs,
Daniell Clark,
Thomas Bull.

John Cullick.

Elizabeth Cullick.

    Recorded out of ẙe originall, and is a true extract, examined p̊r me   Daniell Clark, Sec̊ry.

---

*See Appendix, No. VI.

[108] At a Session of the Gen: Court, at Hartford, M{r}ch 9, 58-59.

Thom{s} Wells Esq{r}, Gou{r}.
Jo: Winthrop Esq{r}, Deputy.
Magestrates: Mr. Webster, Maior Mason, Mr. Willis, Mr. Talcot, Mr. Phelps, Mr. Allyn, Mr. Treat, Mr. John Wells.
Deputyes: Dan: Clark, *Secret:* Mr. Steel, Mr. Gaylard, Mr. Brewster, Cap{t}: Lord, John Bissel, Will: Wadsworth, Joseph Migat, Mr. Sam{ll} Wells, Goodm̃: Morgan, Goodm̃: Demant, Rich{rd} Butler, Edw{rd} Griswold, Rob{t} Webster.

This Court hath remitted a third part of the fine imposed on Nicholas Palmer, by the Court of Magestrates, for giueing Cider to Indians.

Vppon consid{r}ation about a request of L{t} Hollister, p{r}sented to this Court, respecting the charges of the Ch. of Wethersfeild agaynst him, vpon w{ch} he was excomunicated, the Court finding that former indeauours have not p{r}vayled to obtaine them, doe hereby declare, that this Court iudgeth it agreeable to y{e} General practice of the Ch{s} amongst vs, to deliuer vnto y{e} delinquent the p{r}ticulers of his offence in writeing (if he desire it,) before they proceed to excom: or elce they, by the Elders, seasonably after the sentence, doe giue in the charges for y{e} delinq{nts} benefit and conviction;

The w{ch} this Court doth iudge ought to haue bene attended by the Ch: of Wethersfeild, and the p{r}ticulers wherein L{t} Hollister hath offended (for wh{ch} he was censured,) sent to him from the Church, or elce that the Ch: doe order or enable the Elder to deliuer the said charges to y{e} L{t} Hollister or to some trusty messeng{r} improued by him to fetch them at the Elders house. But in case y{e} motion or advice of the Court p{r}vayle not to procure the charges forementioned, then the Court orders Mr. Sam{ll} Wells and Sam{ll} Boreman seasonably to repaire vnto Mr. Russel, in the behalf of L{t} Hollister, and in the name of the Courte desire, and if need be, require of him and the Ch: of Wethersfeild, the p{r}ticuler charges or offences for w{ch} Mr. Hollister was censured, and hauinge receaved the sayd charges from Mr. Russel and the Ch:, forthwith to deliuer them to Mr. Hollister for his help and conviction.

And whereas Mr. Treat, Mr. Hollister, Jo: Demant, are desirous and willing to attend some regular way for the composing their differences, and to y^t end desire some Ch^s: or p^{r}sons may be thought on, to heare and determine the same ; It is desired by the Court, that Wethersfeild Ch:, wth ye officer, would consid^r the matter and seasonably, wthout delay, conclude if it can be, vpon some way that may effect the issueing their sad differences.

[109] This Court sees cause to repeale that order or orders wherein the selling of Sider was prohibited ; soe far as the ord^r respects Cider, so far it is repealed ; the rests stands in force.

Its ordered by this Court, that there shalbe provided for every Mill in this Collony, a Toll dish, of a just Quart, as alsoe a Pottle dish of 2 Quarts, and a pinte dish, al sealed, and an instrument to strike wth, all fit for the purpose.

Its ordered, that for the future it shalbe left wth the Magestrates in this Jurisdiction, in cases respecting the selling of Liquors to ye Indians, to weigh and consid^r such tests as are p^{r}sented, wth circumstances accompanying the same, and to iudge and determine the cause, as reason and justice in their judgment and app^{r}hension doe require.

Its ordered by this Court, that for the future none shalbe p^{r}sented to be made freemen in this Jurisdiction. or haue the priuilidge of freedome conferd vpon them, vntil they haue fulfild the age of twenty one years and haue 30l. of proper personal estate, or haue borne office in the Comō wealth ; such persons quallified as before, and being men of an honest and peaceable conversation, shalbe p^{r}sented in an ord^{r}ly way at the General Court in October, yearly, to p^{r}vent tumult and trouble at the Court of Election.

It is ordered by this Court, that for al such orders as are of publique concernment, and sent forth into the whole Collony to be published, that the Secretary shalbe payd for his paynes herein out of the publique treasury, and the several Townes to repay the same to the Treasurer. And likewise for al such orders as are by him transcribed into the Countrey booke, there shal be allowed twelue pence for euery order, out of the publique treasury.

Its ordered by this Court, that whateuer wine or liquors are brought in or landed in any part or porte in this Jurisdiction (except such as may be landed for transportation,) shal pay for euery Butt of wine, 20s. to ye publique treasury, and soe p^rportionably for lesser casks. As alsoe, for euery Anchor of Liquors (except before excepted,) there shalbe payd to ye publique treasury, fiue shillings, soe p^rportionably for al greater or lesser casks or quantities. Al wch wines or liquors shalbe entred at such place and by them y^t are appoynted herevnto by the Court. This order to be duely obserued, vpon penalty of forfeiting such wine or liquors as are discouered and proued to be omitted or neglected to be entred. And within one month after the publication of this order, it is to stand in force.

The p^rsons appoynted for entry and recording such Goods as are subiect to Custome, by the forementioned order, are—

For Hartford, Jonathan Gilbert,

[110] Windsor, Walter Filer,
Wethersfeild, Sam^{ll} Boreman,
Fairfeild, Mr. Will: Hill,
Stratford, Richd Butler,
N: London, John Smith,
SeaBrook, John Westall,
MiddleTowne, John Hall,
Norwalk, Mr. Camfield.

These p^rsons appoynted for this service are allowed for ye^r paynes herin, for every Butt of Wine entred, 2s. and for every Anchor of Liquors, twelue pence p^r Anchor; and soe proportionably for other casks.

Its ordered by this Court, that noe p^rson in this Collony shal draw and sel Wine or Liquors to the English, by retayle, wthout licence, vppon penalty of fiue shillings for every Quart. And y^t none y^t are licenced ordinary keepers shal sel liquors for aboue foure shillings by the Quart, and soe p^rportionably, after that rate, for other quantities. And that such as Stil liquors, and are licenced to sel by retayle, shal not sel for aboue two shillings by the Quart, and soe p^rportionably to y^t price, for other quantities.

It is ordered by this Court, that whatsoeuer licences haue bene formerly granted to any priuate p^rsons to retayle liquors, shal stand in force noe longer then til ye General Court in May next, and that whateuer licences of this nature are graunted for the future, they shal pʳceed imediately from yᵉ Genˡ Court; And yᵗ there shalbe 2s. 6d. payd to the Secretary by him yᵗ pʳcures the licence.*

Its ordered by this Court, that if any person be found drunk, and convicted soe to be, in any priuate house, he shal pay twenty shillings for euery transgression of this nature, vnto the publique treasury, and the owner of the house where the person is found and proued to be made drunk, shal pay 10s.

Its ordered and required by the authority of this Court, that the Constables in each Towne shal make diligent search vppon al occasions when there is suspition of miscarriages by disordered meetings of pʳsons in private houses to tiple together; and haueing discouered they are to make pʳsentmᵗ therof to publique authority, and such as are convicted to be guilty of the breach of this order shal pay fiue shillings, one half to yᵉ publique treasury, the other halfe to yᵉ pʳson discouering.

Its ordered by this Court, that there shal not be any corne or malt stild into Liquors, in any Plantation in this Colony.

Middle Towne souldiers are abated one of yᵉ ordinary traineings, that soe they may help him that carries on the Mill there, vp with his heauy worke.

[111] Willᵐ: Wadsworth, Lᵗ: Hollister and George Graues are appoynted by this Court, to discouer what lands are adiacent to yᵉ Riuer, about Thirty Miles Island, on both sides, for the space of six miles vp and downeward the Riuer, as alsoe eastward and westward from the Riuer.

The Treasurer is ordered to send downe Warrᵗ to yᵉ Constable and Townsmen of Seabrook, requireing them to make a valuation of al the land and ratable estate at the Farme at 6 Miles Island, and returne a list thereof to yᵉ treasurer.

This Court, taking into consideration the continued troubles and distance twixt the Ch: at Hartford and the wᵗʰdrawen party, after further indeauours for a concurrenc and vnanimity to cal in some help from abroad, and findeing their labours herin invalid, haue now ordered and appoynted a council to be called by yᵉ Court (leaueing each party to yʳᵉ liberty whether they wil send or noe,) to be helpful in issueing the Questions in controuersy.

---

* [In the margin;] "This order concernes not Ordinary keepers."

Its ordered that those Ch^s: (whose Elders were requested to come hither) should be desired by L^{rs} from ye Secretary, in the name of the Court, to send vs one from each Ch: of their ablest instruments, to be p^{r}sent at Hartford, by the third of June next, to assist in heareing and issueing these differences.

Its alsoe ordered and expected by the Court, that the Quæst^s in controversy shalbe publiquely disputed in the p^{r}sence of the Council, according to former order. And y^t each party, both ye Church at Hartford and ye withdrawers, shal ioyntly concur in bearing the charges of the former Council, and in p^{r}pareing and provideing for this y^t is now to be called.

Edward Stebbing, Jno: Allyn, John Bernard, Nath: Ward, George Graues, or any three of them, are to levy the rate for the charge of the last Council, according to former order, and to make provision for ye entertaynem^t of this Councill.

[112] At the Gen^{ll} Court of Election. Hartford, May 19, 59.

Magistrates chosen:

John Winthrop Esqr, Gou^r.

Thom: Wells Esqr, Deputy.

Mr. Webster, Major Mason, Mr. Hen: Clark, Mr. Willis, Mr. Talcot, & *Treas:* Mr. Phelps, Mr. Allyn, Mr. Tratt, Mr. Jo: Wells, Mr. Gould, Mr. Ogden, Capt. Tappin, Thomas Baker, Robt Bond, Dan^{ll}: Clark, *Secret^{r}y*.

Deputies: Deacon Gaylard, Capt. Lord, Secret^{r}y Clark, Mr. Campfield, Will' Wadsworth, Joseph Migatt, Rich: Butler, Edw: Griswold, Josias Hull, John: Standley, John Hart, Hugh Caulkin, Robt Webster, James Avery, Sam^{ll} Stocken, Cornelius Hull, John Wheeler, Thomas Fairchild, Joseph Judson, John Clark, Robt Chapman, Lt Hollister, John Demant, Sam^{ll} Wells, Sam^{ll} Boreman.

The freemen voted to leaue the choice of ye Com̃issioners with ye Gen^{ll} Court.

Com̃issioners chosen for ye ensueing year; John Winthrop Esqr, Gou^r; Thomas Wells Esqr, Deputy. Reserue, Maior

Mason, who is to act in behalfe of this Collony in y'e busines respecting Mistick & Paucat: at y'e next meeting of y'e Com'rs: The Secret'ry to assist, as occasion shal require.

Mathew Marvin of Norwalk is freed from watching and trayninge.

It is ordered by this Court, that there shalbe Letters sent from y'e Secretary of this Court vnto the Gen'll Court in the Massathuset, to informe them y't it is o'r desire and resolution to bring the case respecting Mistick and Paukatuck, vnto a reveiw, or second consideration, at y'e meetinge of y'e Com'rs, and therefore desire them of y'e Massath: to provide to attend y'e transaction of y'e matter forementioned.

[113] This Court haveing considered the busines respecting the Indians at Paquanack, and the difference twixt Stratford and Fairfield about the sayd Ind's: doe see cause to order, that according vnto y'e desire of the Indians they may quietly possess and enioy from hencforth and for future, that parcel of land called Gold Hill: And that there shalbe forthwith so much land layd out within the liberties of Fairfield as the Comitte appoynted by the Court shal iudge fit, and in as convenient a place as may best answer the desire and benefit of the Indians forementioned, for y'e future. And the sayd Comittee is to see soe much land layd out w'thin y'e bounds of Fairfield, for y'e vse and accomodation of Stratford, as y't Golden hill forementioned is for quantity and quallity, and as may be most convenient for y'e neighbours of Stratford. And in case Stratford men are vnwilling to accept of land, that then y'e Comittee shal appoynt how much and in what kind the inhabitants of Fairfield shal pay vnto Stratford, in way of satisfaction. And it is ordered and concluded, y't this parcel of land called Gold Hill, surrendered by Stratford vnto Paquanack Indians, accordinge to y'e premisses, shalbe ful satisfaction from them vnto the Indians forenamed, and y't neither they nor their successors shal make any further claimes or demaunds of land from Stratford, but shal from henceforth and for future be accounted as Fairfield Indians, or belonging to Fairfield, to be p'rvided for by them for future as is forementioned in the order. And its ordered, y't in case these Indians shal wholly at any time relinquish and desert Gold Hill, that then it shal remaine to Stratford Plantation,

they repaying to Fairfield the one half of y^t wch they receaued in consideration of the sayd land.

The Comittee appoynted by the Court to see this order put in execution, are, of Norwalk, Mr. Campfield, Mr. Fitch, Richard Olmstead, Nath^{ll} Elye, who are to bound out the lands at Gold Hill, about 80 Acres, beginning at ye foot of ye hill where ye Wigwams stood, and soe to run vpwards on the hill and within Fairfield bounds, as is aboue mentioned. And the sayd Comittee is to make returne to ye Court in October, what they doe in reference to this order.

Mr. Campfield p^rsenting from the Towne of Norwalk, Richrd Olmstead for y^r Lieutenant and Walter Hoyt for their Sergeant, they are both confirmed by this Court.

Mr. Talcot, Capt. Lord and Joseph Migat, are appointed to take and p^rsent an Inventory of ye estate of Sam^{ll} Fitch, at ye next June Court, and to be assistant in ye distribution and management of ye sayd estate.

[114] Hartford, May 20, (59) This Court haueing considered the petition p^rsented by the inhabitants of Seabrook, doe declare y^t they approue and consent to what is desired by ye petitioners, respecting Mohegin, p^rvided y^t within ye space of three yeares they doe effect a Plantation in ye place p^rpounded.

The Court ordered the Secretary to send an Attachm^t to be serued on the estate of Arthur Bostock.

Its ordered y^t ye Assistants in this Jurisdiction shal haue power to send forth destreints for levyng rates to grant replevins, to p^rceed according to law in punishing Drunknes, Lying, Theft, wthin their respectiue p^rcincts, as any p^rticuler Magistrate may doe.

Its desired by this Court, That ye Gou^rno^r, Mr. Willis, Mr. Allyn, Mr. Trat, Mr. Brewester, doe assist each other in keeping Court at N: London, on ye first day of June, to transact such occasions as are necessary and shalbe p^rsented vnto them.

Thomas Basset of Fairfield, is freed from watching, warding and traininge.

Vppon consideration of what hath bin propounded by Mr. Baker, respecting East & South Hampton, It is iudged by this Court to be very advantagious to ye safety and comfort of ye Planta^s: aforesayd, that vppon any necessary occasion there should be liberty allowed vnto ye Magistrates, or ye maior part of them, to call a Court in either of those Plantat^s: according as they iudge most meet and to impannel Juries or summon witnesses as need requires, to attend the Court soe called out of either of ye Plantations.

2. It is iudged that noe Magestrate ought to be called to account for any error in transacting matt^rs of Judicat^r, but only by the Gen: Court at Conecticut.

3. That according to ye Articles of Confederation, it is not in ye hands or power of any Magistrate to summon any to Conecticut Court, after triall at Long Island, but by way of appeale, and y^t in all ordinary cases it is very meet and expedient y^t all testimonies should be taken by 2 Magestrates, before Pl^t & Def^t, upon oath, and sent ouer hither, if occasion soe require, and not trouble men to come to giue p^rsonall testimony here.

4. Respecting matter or charge for Magistrates comeing for information in cases to this Court, It is iudged y^t where it redounds to ye p^rticuler benefit of ye Towne concerned in it, the charge should be borne by the Towne to wch he belongs; if any difference arise about ye charges, the Magistrates in ye other Plantation to decide it.

This Court is adiourned to ye 3^d Wednesday in June.

---

[115]   AT A SESSION OF GEN: COURT, HARTFORD, JUNE 15: 59.
  Jo: Winthrop Esqr, Gou^r.
  Tho: Wells Esqr, Dep:
  Magistrates : Mr. Willis, Mr. Talcott, Mr. Allyn, Mr. Phelps, Mr. Goold.
  Deputies : Deacō Gaylard, Capt. Lord, Secret^r: Clarke, Will: Wadsworth, Jos: Migat, Rich: Butler, Jo: Demant Sen:, Mr. Sam: Wells, Edw: Griswold, Josias Hull, Sam^ll Boreman, Cornel: Hull, John Wheeler, John Standley, Joseph Judson, Hugh Caulkin.

The Gouerno^rs Worsh^p manifesting his desires to this Court of a tract of Land at the head of Pocatanack Coue, to ye furtheranc of a Plantat^n at Quinibauge, The Court haueing heard and considered the sayd request, haue answered it to ye number of 1500 Acres vppon the Fresh Riuer together with yᵉ Royalty and propriety of the Riuer, in case it may not be pʳiuditiall to any Plantation, nor take in aboue 150 Acres of Meadow.

This Court doth hereby manifest their acceptance of the inhabitants of Quinibaug vndʳ this Gouernmᵗ, if they desire the same.

Deacon Caulkin, James Morgan, James Avery, are appoynted to lay out yᵉ Gouernours land.

Whereas there hath bin liberty graunted by virtue of a repeale of former orders prohibiting selling Cider to English and Indians, This Court to pʳuent the excess of drinking Cider, and drunknes thereby too frequently obserued in yᵉ Indians, and yᵗ by Cider as is iudged, doe hereby order, that whoeuer sels Cider to Indian or Indians, shal for future sel none by bottles or in Casks, greater or lesser, but only such quantities as they yᵗ sel shal see drunk before their eyes, in yʳ pʳsence, yᵗ drunknes and the evil effects thereof [*may be*] avoided and pʳuented.

Its ordered, that the former order respecting pʳviding Ordinary keepers in each Plantation, shal now stand in force of general concernment to yᵉ whole Collo:

Mr. Willis is requested to goe downe to Sea Brook, to assist yᵉ Maior in examininge the suspitions about witchery, and to act therin as may be requisite.

This Court doth iudge it to be yᵉ duty of the inhabitants of Wethersfield to pʳuide for yᵉ Towne of Wethersfield, in reference to yᵉ ministry.

This Court obseruing the neglect of their former ordʳ in reference to yᵉ Inventories of the estates of oʳ honoʳd freinds deceased, Edward Hopkins and George Fenwick Esqʳˢ, It is therfore now ordered and required by this Court, yᵗ whateuer pʳson or pʳsons in this Collo: haue in yʳ pʳsent possession or improuement any estate yᵗ either is or hath bin reputed or accounted the estate of either of yᵉ aforesaid Gent: sinc their decease, that they secure and pʳserue the said estate in their owne hands, or yᵉ value thereof, (casualties exepted,) to be accomptible to this Court when required thervnto, vntil yᵉ wills and inventories of yᵉ sd Gentl: be exhibited into yᵉ Court, and right owners to yᵉ estate appeare, and administration be graunted according to law.

This Court hath granted a license to yᵉ Marshall to sell wine by retaile, pʳvided he suffer not yᵉ wine that he sels to be drunk in his house.

[116] Its ordered, that yᵉ general heads of the charges against the withdrawers shalbe sent to them, and that they appear at the Court in October, to answer to the sayd charges.

Wednesday, the 29 of this Instant, is appointed to be kept a solemne Humiliation, partly for England and partly for oʳ owne selues, in regard of the vnsetlednes of their and oʳ peace, partly for the season, yᵗ God would pʳuent euills yᵗ may be feared, and respecting yᵉ Council, that God would bless their labours to effect a good issue, if they come vp.

This Court iudgeth it necessary that several of yᵉ Chˢ. of Xᵗ in the Massatuset should be sent vnto, and desired to afford the help of their Reuʳnd Elders and worthy messengers that were of the former Council at Hartford, vnto whom are added, by the nomination of the withdrawers, the teaching Elders of Dorchester and WaterTowne. The Chˢ to be sent to, whose help is requested, are Boston, Camb:, Roxb:, Dorchester, Ipsw:, Dedham, Water T:, CharlesTown, Sudbury; seauen wherof the withdrawers consented to; the Court and Ch: assenting to and desiringe all or as many as the Lord shall incline or enable to attend the worke; vnto whose decisiue power, the withdrawen partie is required, the Ch: at Hartford freely engaging to submit according to the order of yᵉ Gosple.

Its the rather desired that those Reuerend Eldʳˢ and Messengers of yᵉ former Council, with yᵉ other two conioyned, should be requested to be helpful now againe to heare and determine these irreconciled differenc at Hartford twixt the Ch: and wᵗʰdrawen members, bec: of the experimᵗ yᵗ hath bin made of their abillities and labouriousnes, aud the good issue yᵗ was effected therby, working a pacification amongst them yᵗ were at soe vast a distance and being the more apt and ready in yᵉ controuersy to discerne where yᵉ root and occasion of yᵉ breach is.

The Council forementioned is requested to be at Hartford the 19 of Augˢᵗ, the time of their hearing the matters in differenc publiquely debated, according to former ord^r, to be with al convenient speed after their comeing vp.

The former ord^{rs} respecting charges in and about [*the*] former Council, and p^rvideing for this Council, to stand in force.

The Deputy Gouerno^r is desired to inquire into ye busines about ye Monheags comeing and abideing with Seano, and to act by way of advice as his Wors^p shal judge meet.

The petition of James Rogers was read and considered and ye things petitioned graunted, viz: 150 Acres next vnto ye bounds of N. London, p^rvided it doe not damnify the Indians nor ye Planta: of N. London, or any farme now layd out ; Goodm̄: Morgan and Avery to lay it out to him. He hath liberty graunted to possess and improue what land Vncas hath giuen him.

Thomas Burnam is required to appear at ye Court in Octob^r, to answ^r for his former cariage complayned of to ye Court, and Lt Bull is required to p^rsecute his form^r compl^{nt} at ye Court aforesd.

---

[117] AT A SESSION OF THE GEN^{ll} COURT AT HARTFORD, OCTOB^r 6, 59.

John Winthrop Esqr Gou^r.

Thom^s Wells Esqr Dep.

Magestrates : Mr. Willis, Mr. Phelps, Mr. Allyn, Mr. Treate, Mr. Gould.

Deputies : Dan^{ll} Clark, *Sec:* Deacō Gailard, Mr. Rich: Lord, Willm Wadsworth, Mr. Robbins, Joseph Migat, Richrd Butler, Mr. Sam^{ll} Wells, John Deminge, Sam^{ll} Boreman, Edwrd Griswold, Mr. Hill, Josias Hull, Thom^s Fairchild, Joseph Judson, Jehu Burr, John Gregory, Walt^r Hoit, Sam^{ll} Stockin, Nathan^{ll} White, John Clark, Robt Chapman, Thom^s Judd, John Hart.

This Court haueing considered the Petition of Arthur Bostick, and what hath bin p^rsented in behalfe of his wife, according to ye desire and p^rposition of the said Arthur, haue appointed Mr. Blackman, Goodman Beardsley, Mr. Fairchild and Joseph Judson, as a Com̄ittee to consid^r the state and condition of the said Bostock and his wife, and to ord^r what they think sutable therin; and in case Bostick be vnsatisfied wth their act, then he is required to appear at ye next Session of this Court, to render the reason of his dissatisfaction with the act of the fores^d Comittee. And the Comittee to make returne at ye next Session, what their determination is about the p^rmises. But in case Bostock rest satisfied wth what is done by the Comittee, this Court doth free the Attachm^t y^t was formerly laid on ye estate of the said Bostock.

Cromwel Bay being propounded to this Court to be admitted and receaued vnd^r this Gouernment,* The Court considering the same, haue and doe declare their willingnes to accept the said Plantation of Setauk vnd^r this Jurisdiction, soe far as they may not any way intrench vpon the Articles of Confœderation wth the other three Collonies, and therfore desire the inhabitants of Setauk to attend the next sitting of the Com^rs at Newhauen, if they think meet, to act for and in their own behalf in ye p^rmises.

The last wills of Edward Hopkins and George Fenwick† Esq^rs being exhibited into this Court, it is thought meet by the Court y^t ye former restraint layd on ye estates should be taken

---

* The following petition had been presented to the Gen. Court, by the inhabitants of the plantation at Cromwell's Bay:

"Cromwell Bay, alis Setauke, August ye 6. 1659.

It hauing pleased God to dispose the harts of vs the inhabitance of the place aforesaid, to subiect our plantation, persons and estats vnder the p^tection and gouerment of the Colloney of Coneticoke, for the full accomplishment of the p^rmises, wee the said inhabitance doe request the faviour of our trusty and beloved associats Ensigne Alixander Brian and Sammuell Sherman to solicit our vnion wth the sayd Colloney that wee may be accepted a member of the sayd body pollitick; the terms specified in all humblenesse, three years rate free, in respect of our low estate and charge in poynt of purchas, secondly, in regard of our remotenes from the head Court, and the vncertaine passage ou^r the Sound, that like p^rvelege might be granted vs liueing on Long Island equall wth South and East Hampton; the aforesayd terms being granted vnto vs, wee the sayd inhabbitance athorize the sayd Alixander and Sammuell to ratifie and conclud the sayd vnion as if wee the said inhabitance were personally present. Subscribed wth a vnanimos consent, day and date aboue writen." Signed by, John Vnderhill, Richard Wodhull, Roger Cheston, John Jenner, William Fance, Thomas Harlow, James Coke, Johon Diar, Edward Rous, Thomas [   ] Thomas Mabbes, George Wood, Henry Rogers, Roert Acreley. "These in the name of the rest." [Towns & Lands, Vol. i. Doc. No. 9.]

† The Will of Mr. Hopkins, (whose death occurred a day or two before that of Mr. Fenwick,) was executed Mar. 17th, 1656-7. An abstract of it is given in a note to Savage's Winth. Jour. I 228. Mr. Fenwick's Will was *proved*, April 27th, 1657. A copy of it is preserved among the files in the Secretary's Office (of this State,) and an abstract will be found in the Appendix, No. VII.

of, and yt ye debts due to ye said estates be required and gath-
red in, to pruent damadge in ye estates.

This Court takeing into consideration the long and tedious
differences and troubles yt haue bin and are stil continuing
twixt Mr. Russel and severall members of Wethersfield Ch:,
and perticularly twixt Mr. Russel and the Lt,* doe iudge it very
necessary that some course be attended for ye redress of the
same, and haueing long waited to haue ye parties at difference
com to some ioynt agreemt amongst themselues vpon a way
[118] and meanes ‖ of hearing and healeing the said differences, and not concluded of, This Courte doth therfore desire
the 2 Chs of Christ at Hartford and Windsor to send 2 or 3
Messengrs a peice, to examine and search into ye nature of the
differences, and haueing heard what may be said by both parts,
to giue such counsel and advice as God shall direct them vnto
by the light of Scripture and reason, and in case it be not embraced, that then ye determination of ye Messengrs may be
prsented vnto ye Court yt soe it may be duely considered.
And the whole Church belonging to Mr. Russels charge lately
of Wethersfield, is to be acquainted herewith, yt they may prepare ymselues for this hearing. It is further desired that ye
Messengrs may be prsent at Wethersfield ye first Tuesday in
Nobr and that prvision be made for their entertainmt by those
yt are now resideing at Wethersfield.

A list of the Estate of the several Plantations was prsented
and is as followeth :   £

Impr, The Estate and prsons at Hartford,	21128.	: :
of Windsor, .	15345.	: :
of Wethersfield,	12103.	: :
Farmington, . .	05548.	: :
Sea Brook, . . .	05215.	: :
Middle Town, .	02543.	: :
Fairfield, prsons, 80.	10442.	: :
Stratford, prsons, 65.	08434.	: :

Mr. Willis and Mr. Allyn are desired to goe down and to assist in keeping Court at Fairfield, on Thursday, the 20th of this
instant. Mr. Campfield is desired to assist them, espetially in
the busines respecting Mr. Gould and Galpin.

---

* Lieut. Hollister. See page 330, ante.

This Court is adiourned to ye 2^d Wednesday in No^br next.
The estate of Norwalk is 3829 £.

[119] HARTFORD. SESSION OF THE GEN^ll COURT, No^br 9, 50.

This Court doth graunt a Rate of a penny ½ penny p^r £. to to be levied vpon ye estate of ye Collony.

In consideration of Gods goodnes to this Collony, in ye fruitful and seasonable haruest, the general restoration of health to ye Plantations, and the success of ye indeauours of ye Reuerend Eld^rs of ye last Councill, for ye composeing the sad differences at Hartford,—for the foregoinge respects, this Court doth see cause to appoint this day three weeks, being the last of this month, as a publique thanksgiueing throwout this Collony.

Jonathan Gilbert is appoynted to require the paym^t of that wch Farmington Indians are engaged to pay to this Court, in Octo^br yearly, the first payment being due 2 yeares now past.

Mr. Willis, Mr. Talcot, Mr. Stone and Edward Stebbing are desired by the Court to goe downe to Middle Towne, to inquire ye nature of ye troublesom differenc fallen out there, and to indeauour a composition thereof, but if they cannot issue it, the Comitte is desired to make returne to ye next Session, what they shal doe in ye p^remisses.

David the Jew, for his misdemeanour in going into houses when the heads of ye families w^r absent, and tradeing p^rvision from children, and for such like misdemean^rs, is fined 20s.

This Court adiournes to ye last Thursday in Feb^rary next.

[120] AT A SESSION OF THE GEN^ll COURT, FEB^r 23, 59.

Jo: Winthrop Esqr, Go:

Magestrates : * Mr. Willis, Mr. Phelps, Mr. Allyn, Mr. Treat.

Deputies : Mr. Gaylard, Capt. Lord, Dan^ll Clark, *Sec^r*, Willm Wadsworth, Mr. Robbins, Mr. Sam: Wells, Jo-

---

* The name of Deputy Governor Welles, disappears from the list of Magistrates. He died, at Wethersfield, Jan. 14th, 1659-60.

seph Migat, Rich: Butler, John Demant, Edw: Griswold, Sam^ll Boreman, Josias Hull, Thom^s Judd, John Hart.

Michael Griswold is freed by this Court from traineing but he is to maintein watch and ward.

John Allyn and Jacob Migat, in behalfe of the Artillery, pursueing a former graunt of this Court of 300 Acres of land, for incouragem^t to ye Artillery successiuely, doe desire that this Court would be pleased to grant to them 30 miles Island, wth those two parcels of meadow on ye East side of the Riuer, the one next aboue, the other next below the Island, in case the place thereabouts be not found to be sutable for a Plantation, or be not p^rengaged to any perticuler person, by this Court.

This Court considering the low estate of Willm Clarke his family, doe order respecting the fine imposed on him for tradeing Liquors contrary to law, that he shall pay to y^e publique Treasurie 40$s.$ p^r yeare, for foure yeares, the first payment to be made this spring, at y^e demand of the Treasurer.

Daniell Harris is approoued for an Ordnary keeper, in Middle Towne.

To p^ruent future trouble respecting Guards appointed by a former Order, to attend the publique meetings in the several Plantations, This Court now orders, y^t it shalbe in ye power of the milletary officers belonging to each Towne yearely to cal out and appoint soe many of the Traine Band as the order of Court requires for each Plantation, to attend that seruice, provided y^t noe person is to be compelled to attend that service two yeares together. And the Sergeants who are to take care of the said guards, are ordered and required to exercise due care that their respective companies come with their armes wel fixed, and provided with powder and bullets sutable for y^t seruice.

[121] This Court doth order, that all the Podunk Indians shal peaceably enioy al their lands at Podunk with their severall proprieties as formerly, free from any molestation by any in this Collony, according to ye Com^rs orders in 58 & 59, hereby fully ratifyinge and confirmeing their acts therein.

Mr. Willis, Mr. Tailcot, Mr. Allyn, Capt. Lord, William Wadsworth, John Allyn, Ensign Wilton, John Bissel, are appointed a Comittee to lay out and devide Podunk lands formerly possessed by those Indians, and likewise to treat wth ye Indians, that what land there may be that is not or may not be fit for their planting, they may be willing to part with it to those English that have contracted with Tantonimo. And what appeares to ye Comittee to be granted and allowed by the Indians to be Tant^s: perticuler propriety, the Court is willing to allow of and confirme to ye English according to their bargaine, vidz: to Thom^s Burnam and his partners. And what winter graine is sowed on the land, there shalbe liberty and allowance from ye Indians to reap the same by those that haue sowed it. The Comittee aboue haue full power giuen them by this Court to make a ful issue about the p^rmisses accordinge to ye order abouementioned. And if the Indians be willing to part with some planting land, the Comittee may lay it to Tanto: part, for those English abouementioned. And to make returne to ye Court what they doe in and about the p^rmisses.

Whereas there hath bin complaint made and p^rsented by ye inhabitants of Hartf^d, Windsor & Wethersfield in referenc to ye bargain made wth Mr. Fenwick, This Court doth order that a Comittee be chosen to treat with Capt. Cullick, as agent to G. Fenwick Esqr, about the differenc that hath bin and yet is in referenc to ye Agreem^t made with him. Vnto wch Comittee this Court doth grant full power to bring matters in controuersie vnto a full issue by composition or otherwise, as they shal see meet.

[122] The Comittee chosen to treat with and pursue to effect the order of the Court with Capt Cullick, are The Wor^ll Gouerno^r Winthrop, Mr. Willis, Mr. Allyn, the Secretary and W. Wadsworth.

Whereas there hath bin a repealing of ye former restraint laid vpon ye estates of Edw: Hopkins and George Fenwick Esq^rs, that debts due to ye estate might be taken in, Vpon further consideration, this Court orders, that ye estates aforesaid be securd within this Collony vntil the s^d estates be inventoried and ye Inventories p^rsented and administration granted by this Court.

This Court adiournes to ye 2^d Wednesday in Aprill.

[123]   A Session of Gen: Court, Apr^ll 11, 60.

Jo: Winthrop, Esqr, Go:

Magestrats: Mr. Hen: Clark, Mr. Willis, Mr. Allyn, Mr. Phelps, Mr. Treat.

Deputies: Mr. Gailard, C: Rich: Lord, Dan: Clark, Sec^r:, Willm Wadsworth, Mr. Robbins, Mr. S. Wells, Joseph Migat, Richd Butler, John Deminge, Edw: Griswold, Thom: Judd, Jo: Hart, Sam^ll Boreman, Sam^ll Stockin.

A L^r from ye Dutch Gouerno^r to o^r Wor^ll Gouerno^r was read, as also o^r Wor^ll Go: returne thervnto, wch was approued by this Court.

This Court considering the necessity of altering that perticuler in ye 3^d Law, respecting the choice of a Gouerno^r, vidz: That noe person be chosen Gou^r aboue once in two yeares, haue thought meet to propound it to ye consideration of ye freemen of this Collony, and doe order the Secretary to insert the same in the Warr^ts for ye choice of Deputies, and request the return of ye remote Planta^s: (y^t vse to send Proxies, at ye Election, by their Deputies. And it is desired that their proxies may be ordered according to what may be concluded on about ye ord^r forementioned.

This Court appoints Wm. Wadsworth and Jo: Deminge Senr, to assist Mr. Jo: Cotton in administration to ye Estate and as ouerseers of the last will of Thom^s Wells Esqr.

This Court haueing heard the returne of the Comittee for Podunk lands; That since they came to a conclusion respecting Thomas Burnam his contract with Tantonomo, It appeares that part of the lands laid out to the said Burnam and his copartners doth belong to Foxens successors, by a gift from Foxen to his allies: This Court doth therefore order, That those Podunk Indians shal enioy and possess their lands according to former order. And that those English men that contracted with Tantonimo shal enioy and possess according to their bargaine only that wch is ye particuler proprietie of Tantonimo, that the Indians doe yield or that Tanto: can proue to be his propriety.

Mr. John Allyn and Jonath: Gilbert are to bound out ye said Tanton: part to Thos Burnam and his partn^rs and this shal stand vntil further proof appeare about Tantonimo his right.

[124]   This Court haueing heard and considered the Petition from N. London doe at p^rsent soe far accept of the request of the petitioners as to allow of Mr. Tinker for an Assistant in that Plantat^n: and Mr. Bruen, James Rogers, Lt Smith and John Smith, as Com^rs, vntil the Election Court in May next; who with ye assistance of Maior Mason shal haue power to keep Court according to ye contents of ye Petition, in matters of an inferiour nature, and perticulerly about that busines respecting Waterhouse; and the ful answer of ye Petition is deferd vntil ye Court of Election.

Willm Duglas is chosen Packer for N. London, for a ful yeare, and to be allowed for his paines herin according to what is allowed in ye Massachusets collony, and whateuer he packs or repacks shal pass vnd^r his seale.

---

[125]   A Court of Election held at Hartford, May 17, 60.
Magestrates Elect^d.

Jo: Winthrop Esqr, Go:
Maior Jo: Mason, Dep:
    Mr. Henry Clark, Mr. Willis, Mr. Phelps, Mr. Allyn, Mr. Treat, Mr. Gould.
    Long Island. Capt. Tho: Topping, Mr. Ogden, Tho: Baker, Robt Bond.
    Dan^ll Clark, Sec^r.   John Talcot, Treas^r.
Deputies: Wm. Gaylard, Wm. Wadsworth, Jo: Talcot, Joseph Migat, Edw: Griswold, Jo: Deming Sen:, Mr. Sam: Wells, Rich^rd Butler, Josias Hull, Stephen Hart, Antho: Howkins, Sam^ll Boreman, Wm. Gutridge, Mathew Griswold, Robt Chapman, Jno. Tinker, Hugh Caulkin, Math. Campfield, Sam^ll Hall, Wm. Cheny, Robt Warner, Phillip Groues, Tho: Fairchild, Jo: Wheeler, Cornel: Hull.

It was voted by the freemen that ye perticuler in ye 4th Law, respecting the choice of the Gouerno^r, should be alt^rd, and that for future there shalbe liberty of a free choice yearely, either of ye same person or another, as may be thought meet, without p^riudice to ye law or breach thereof.

This Court doth free Michael Try, Richard Vore, Goodman Fossaker and Goodman Stocking, from traineing, watching and wardeing.

This Court doth confirme and establish the conclusion of ye Comittee in reference to ye Paquanack Indians and the Plantations of Stratford and Fairefield.

The choice of ye Com^rs for this Collo: for the yeare ensueing, is left by the freemen to this Court to issue and effect.

The Wor^fl Gouernour and Dep: Gouerno^r are chosen Com^rs for this yeare ensueing, and Mr. Math: Allyn is chosen for a reserue.

Mr. Mathew Allyn is chosen Moderator, to supply the place of ye Gouerno^r and Dep: in case of their occasional absenc from ye Gen: Court.

The Towne of Huntington, on Long Island, p^rsenting their desires to be accepted vnd^r this Gouerm^t, vpon the same tearmes y^t Southampton stands wth vs, and likewise to be freed from publique charges for ye space of three yeares, this Court in order to ye forementioned request, makes this returne; That they accept of ye proposition of ye Towne of Huntington soe far as may be consistent with ye Articles of Confœderation with ye Vnited Collonies, and therfore doe advise the Planta: forementioned to address vnto ye Com^rs at y^eir meeting at N. Hauen, to vnd^rstand the mind of the Com^rs in this matter. And further, this Court expects to be free from publique expense about that Plantat^n for ye space of three yeares after the Confœderation, [126] and that themselues shal beare all the charges ‖ that may be contracted by any occasion wherin this Collo: doth, according to Articles agreed on, afford them assistance.

W^m. Palmer Senr, is freed by this Court from watch: ward: and traineing.

Vppon ye motion of Mr. Josiah Stanborough, This Court doth declare that it is their desire that ye Magestrates of Southampton and Mr. Barret would be pleased to take ye children of ye wife of Mr. Stanborough and the estate belonging to them, and to dispose of both soe as may be conduceable to ye p^rservation of ye estate for ye legatees.

This Court haueing considered the petition of Goodman Jackson, doe accept of his request and are willinge to allowe this libertie, that provided there be 15*l*. fine paid to ye publique treasury by the transgressour, then the form^r sentence adiudging corporall punishm^t vpon ye delinq^t shalbe revoked, but if this fine be not embraced and accepted of, then the corporall punishm^t is speedily to be inflicted, according to ye appointm^t of ye Magestrates.

It is ordered by this Court, that neith^r Indian nor negar serv^ts shalbe required to traine, watch or ward, in this Collo:

In consideration of much inconvenience that appeares to acrew to many in this Collo: by virtue of former orders that in point of execution haue not attayned their end in satisfying creditors in a sutable way, according to ye nature of contracts or bargaines, men conveighing away the kind of pay that many times is preingaged, It is therfore ordered, that it shalbe lawfull for such creditors as haue debts oweing to them in corne or any other spetial pay (vpon ye refusal of pay in kind, when it is due and demaunded,) to take out an attachm^t and lay it (if it can be found out) vpon such estate as is engaged by the debt^r, or other estate y^t may be found such as ye creditor liketh, provided it be not prohibited by law, and secure the said estate attached, to a triall at ye next Court appointed for y^t end. And whateuer estate thus attached vpon a trial and iudgm^t of ye Court comes to be apprized, the said Court y^t issues the case shall appoint those y^t shall prize the estate, the valuation whereof shalbe regulated accordinge to ye worth and nature of ye pay contracted for.

The price of Sheep, in ye list of Rates, shal for future be valued at 15*s*. p^r sheep, vntil the Court further advise on it.

This Court orders that ye Grand Jury hereafter mentioned shal inquire and consid^r of ye misdeameano^rs and breaches of the orders of this Collo: in ye several Townes, and make p^rsentment thereof at ye p^rticuler Court in Octob^r next, and likewise at ye p^rticuler Court in May, (61.) The Grand Jury is as followeth; For Hartford, Willm Wadsworth, Richard Butler; Windsor, Mr. Henry Woolcot, Josias Hull; Wethersfield, John Deming, Sam^ll Boreman; Farm:, Anthony Howkins; Middle T:, John Hall; Sea Brook, Robt Chapman; N. London, John Smith; Stratf^rd, Goodm̄: Groues; Fairfield, Jehu Burr; Norwalk, Richard Olmsted.

It is ordered, that al defects in Armes or neglects in traineing, watch, etc. shalbe determined by any one Magestrate or
Assistant, where such are inhabiting; and by two of them y^t
order the prudentials of ye Towne where is neither Magestrate
nor Assistant; and that those who determine the case shall
haue power to issue forth order to ye Clarke of ye band to levy
the fine imposed. This order to take place notw^thstanding
former orders.

This Court frees the Assistants and ye Deputies chosen to
attend ye severall General Courts, while they stand Deputies,
from traineing, watching and wardeing.

Its ordered, that ye Grand Jury men shal repaire speedily to
some Magestrate or Assistant to be sworne to ye seasonable
and effectual execution and attendanc on their worke.

Its ordered by this Court, that noe Towne in this Collo: shal
suffer any Indians to dwel w^thin a quarter of a mile of it, nor
shal any strange Indians be entertained in any Towne, vpon
penalty of 40s. a month, to be paid to ye publique treasurie by
each Plantat^n which shalbe found transgressours herein. This
order to take place and be of force, in ye begin: of July next.

[128] This Court doth order, that noe man or woman within
this Coll: who hath a wife or husband in forraigne parts, shal
liue here aboue two years, vpon penalty of 40s. p^r month vpon
every such offendor; and any that haue bene aboue 3 years
already, not to remaine within this Coll: aboue one yeare longer,
vpon the same penalty, except they haue liberty from ye Gen:
Court.

This Court obserueing an omission or neglect of a former
order respecting the Inventorying the estates of Edw: Hopkins
and Geo: Fenwick Esq^rs doe now further order, that the select
men of every towne (where any estate that either is, or hath
bin, since the decease of these Gent:, reputed or acco^td part
of that estate y^t is disposed by them or either of them,) shal
make diligent inquiry in their respectiue Plantations to find out
the said estates according to a true value and to inventorie the
said estate and to make p^rsentment thereof at ye p^rticuler Court
in Sept^br next. And all and every person in each Plantat^n, as
before, is hereby required to give in a just acco^t to their select
men, of all the estate that either is, or hath bin in their possession

or improuem^t since ye decease of ye aforesaid Gent:. And whoeuer is knowne to conceale any of the said estates, or not to giue in a true acco^t as before required, or if any select men doe neglect to attend this order, he or they shal pay vnto ye publ: Treasurie, 5*l*. for every such default.

This Court orders, that if any Indians shal bring in Guns into any of the Townes in this Coll: It shalbe lawful for any one of ye English to seize on their guns, and to keep them vntil there be 10*s*. a piece brought to redeem each gun, wch shalbe devided, one half to ye Treasurie, the other half to ye seazer.

Mr. Willis and Goodman Migat and Anthony Howkins are desired and appointed to take in the consideration of ye loss of Lt Lewis and Francis Browne, and according as they iudge requisite to make destribution to both parties of that wch ye Indians haue engaged to pay yearly to make vp their loss by fire, vntil ye whole sum be paid in by ye Indians.

There is liberty graunted that Fairfield, Stratford and Nor-[129] walke shal gather out of their said Townes ‖ a small Troop of Horse, with two meet officers added to exercise them of their owne choseing, and the Troopers to be such as are approued by Mr. Gould and Mr. Fairchild and Mr. Campfield and the officers to be app^rued by the Generall Court. And for proportion they are to take seauen out of Stratford, 7 out of Fairfield and 4 out of Norwalke.

This Court orders y^t none shalbe receaued as Inhabitant into any Towne in the Collony but such as are knowne to be of an honest conversation, and accepted by a maior part of the Towne.

It is alsoe ordered, that noe Inhabitant shall haue power to make sale of his accomodat^n of house and lands vntil he haue first propounded the sale thereof to ye Towne where it is situate, and they refuse to accept of ye sale tendred.

This Court confirmes Robt Chapman for an Assistant at Sea Brooke.

This Court, for many good considerations, doe see cause to allow o^r Wor^fl Gouerno^r 80*l*. for this yeare ensueing.

This Court doth confirme and establish ye Act of the Comittee at Stratford abont Arthur Bostocks estate.

This Court haueing intelligence y^t Jasper Clemens being in

a probable way to enter into the estate of marriage, and confessing that he had a wife in England, and noth: doth appeare to evidenc that she is dead, It is therfore ordered, that the said Jasper and Ellin Browne shalbe forthwith seperated, vntil such evidence be procured that may clearly demonstrate that the couen^t of marriage be dissolued twixt ye said Clemens and his former wife. And the Townsmen of MiddleTowne are required to put this order forthwith in execution.

This Court doth desire and appoint Mr. Gould, Mr. Campfield and Mr. Hill and Mr. Knowles, to issue the busines at Stratford, and alsoe respect: Goodman Rescues horse, y^t he sold.

In reference to the appeale of Mr. Varleet, this Court doth [130] order that Mr. Wells shal returne ‖ to Mr. Varleet the one halfe of what he hath receaued, by virtue of execution, from Mr. Varleet. Its ordered that Mr. Varleet shal pay 40s. to ye Treasurie towards this Courts charges on the Triall. *Execution d˙d the 29 June, '60.*

In answer to ye Petition from N. London, this Court haueing considered the perticulers in it, doe order for ye p^{r}sent, that there should be an Assistant and 3 Com^{rs} in that Towne, who shal haue ful power to issue small causes, and ye punishing smal crimes and offences according to law, provided the cases of debts and fines doe not amount the sum̃ of 2*l*. And the Assistants peculiar power is noe waies hereby infringed.

It is further granted that ye Dep: Gouerno^r & Math: Griswold shal lend vnto N. London two great Guns, from SeaBrooke, wth shot such as y^y judge may be convenient to be let goe from thence. And if they iudge that N. London be capable to secure themselues and the Guns by being thus furnished, they are impowred to lend the Guns vntil the Court see cause to recall them.

Mr. John Tinker is chosen Assistant for N. London, and for Com^{rs}, Mr. Bruen, James Rogers, John Smith, for ye yeare ensueing.

Stebbins, the Constable of N. London, hath liberty of reveiwing his action y^t G: Tong commenct agst him, at ye next Court held at N. London, and ye Wors^{fl} Deputy is desired to assist in keeping a Court for y^t end at N. Lond: and for other occasions as may p^{r}sent themselues.

This Court doth appoint Mr. Gould, Mr. Hill, Mr. Knowles, to hear and determine ye difference twixt Norwalk Inhabit^{ts} and ye Indians there.

This Court doth order, that noe person in Hartford, except Jer: Adams, shal sell wine vnd^r a quart^r cask, nor liquors vnd^r an Ankor.

Robt Lay is desired to take care of any of the estate of Mr. Fenwicks y^t is subiect to loss or damadge, and to improue it, and be ready to render account of the same, when cald thervnto.

This Court haueing heard some orders p^{r}sented by Sea Brook Deputies respect: their Townes, doe approue of them in reference to y^t Towne, and doe grant liberty of a summons to fetch vp several to ye Court y^t haue transgressed those ord^{rs}.

[131] This Court, in consideration of the several affronts of the Indians, and hostile attempts and abuses offred to o^r English subiects, doe order, that the Secretary, in ye name of the Court, shall write to ye Com^{rs} of the severall Coll: to craue their advice, whether it may not concur with their good likeing that we send forth not only to inquire after those Indians, but haueing intelligence who they are, to improue some prudent meanes and effectual, speedily to fetch in such Indians to receaue condign punishm^t, and to intreat a returne to o^r Worshipfull Gouerno^r, to ye p^{r}misses.*

Mr. Bray Rosseter for and in consideration of his paines, in comeing to and attending Mr. Talcot in his sicknes, is allowed fiue pounds, to be paid out of ye pub: Treasury.

SESSION OF Y^e GEN: COURT. OCTO: 4 : 1660. HARTFORD.

Jo: Winthrop Esqr, Go:

Magestrates: Mr. Willis, Mr. Clark, Mr. Allyn, Mr. Phelps, Mr. Treat. *Sec^{r}y*, Dan^{ll}: Clark.

Dep: Capt Rich: Lord, Mr. Gailard, Capt. Tailcot, Mr. Henry Woolcot, W^m. Wadsworth, Joseph Migat, Edw:

---

* See Appendix, No. VIII.

Griswold, John Deming, Sam: Boreman, Wm. Gutridge, Jo: Kilburne, Robt Chapman, Antho: Howkins, Phillip Groues, Sam: Sherman, Cornelius Hull, Jehu Burr, Jo: Tinker, James Avery, Rich: Olmstead, Sam^{ll} Hales, Robert Warner, William Cheny.

This Court vnderstanding the great abuse of y^t liberty y^t hath bin allowed of selling Cider to ye Indians, by virtue of former order, Doe now order the repealing of y^t order any way tollerating that trade, and doe further decree, that what p^{r}son soeuer in this Collony shal hereafter sel, barter or giue any Cider to Indian or Indians, he or she shal forfeit vnto ye Pub: Treasury, twenty shillings p^r pinte, and p^{r}portionably for other quantities, a third part whereof shalbe to him y^t discouers ye offence.

Severall members of this Collony p^{r}senting their desires vnto this Court of setling a Plantation at 30 Miles Island, in consideration thereof, this Court doe order a Comittee to veiw the place, and to dispose of it as may be most sutable for to atteine the end and purpose abouesaid.

The names of ye Committee : For Hartford, Mr. Willis, William Wadsworth; Windsor, Mr. Allyn, Edw: Griswold; Wethersfield, Mr. Treat Senr, Sam^{ll} Boreman; Farmingtō, John Hart.

What right appears that ye Indians haue there, it is left to ye Comittee to ord^r ye purchase thereof.

Eltweed Pomrey hath engaged in Court to rest satisfied with what consideration ye Court shall allow him, in reference to his mare y^t was kild.

[132] This Court, haueing heard and considered the case depending twixt Willm Parker and Wm Waller, about Wallers deteineing a mare and her increase, doe declare this as their sentence, that each party shal beare their own charges about this case; and this to be a finall issue of that matter. And do^e further order the Secretary to send downe summons to Reynold Marvin Senr, to appear at the Perticuler Court in March next, to answer both for loosing the mare into ye woods, and likewise for disposeing of any of those horses wch ye Court had ordered to be marked for ye Countrey, and likewise to prohibit him for medling any more with those horses.

This Court haueing vnd^rstood that there is an estate lying in N. London, the owner or agent whereof is lately drowned, doe order the Secretary to send downe order to Mr. John Tinker and James Rogers to inventory the said goods, and to secure ye estate, and in case any of it be of a p^rishing nature, they are desired to improue it to ye best advantage, vntil the Principals order appear for further dispose of the said goods, and to be accountable for ye same when called therevnto by authority.

In answer to Norwalk Petition, This Court orders, that ye inhabitants there shal attend ye Law provided as a rule of Rateing for ye future.

It is ordered, that the Magestrates, at al times, and ye Deputies, when y^y are vpon pub: imployment, themselues and their horses, shalbe ferry-free, in all places within this Colony.

This Court orders, that it shal not be lawful for any in this Collony to take away by force or otherwise, without ye owners consent, vnd^r p^rtenc of debt, ye corne or other estate from any Indian, vnles it be by virtue of order from lawful authority.

Whereas Quince Smith complaines of Vncas, that he refuseth to pay a fine imposed on him by ye Com^{rs} Court at N. London, This Court orders, that ye said fine be required and recovered of Vncas, according to law in such cases. And Mr. Tinker is desired to haue address to ye Wor^{ll} Deputy Gou^r, that by order from him some course may be taken by him in the busines. Wauwequa being in Court, promised to attend Mr. Tinkers pleasure in ye p^rmisses.

This Court haueing considered the petition of Mr. Tho: Wells, respecting Varleet, in answer thervnto, and in explica[133]tion of a former act, past about y^t case, ‖ doe order, That Mr. Varleet shalbe repaid by Mr. Thom^s Wells only the ouerplus that by execution was taken from Varleet, aboue wompom at six p^r penny, wch amounts to 4*l*. 06*s*. 08*d*; and Mr. Varleet is freed from paying the 40*s*. to ye Treasurer, wch was imposed on him by former act of ye Court.

The Narrogansets are allowed two months longer then ye time agreed on, according to their desires, to bring in ye Wompom that y^y are assess^d by ye Com^{rs} to pay to this Jurisdiction. *This order repeal^d, the* 31 *Octo.* '60.

This Court haueing formerly accepted and manifested their

acceptance of the acco^ts of Jonathan Gilbert, respecting the sequestration and execution served on Goodhearts estate, doe not see cause to alter ye said act. This to be a final issue of that matter.

The Magestrates are desired to heare and determine the case of Thom^s Greenhils Will, and to settle a way for payment of debts.

Mr. Treat, Mr. Tho. Wells and Sam^ll Wels and John Chester are appointed to administer vnto ye estate of Mr. Robins, and to take care to p^rserue it for ye Relicts.

Its ordered by ye Court respecting Mr. Stow of MiddleTown, there appeareing such vnsutablenes in their spirits, that Middle-Town shal haue free liberty to provide for themselues another able, orthodox and pious minister, as soon as they can, who is to be approoued by Mr. Warham, Mr. Stone, Mr. Whiting, takeing in ye help of ye Wor^ll Gou^rn^r and Mr. Willis, wch being done, Mr. Stow is to lay downe his preaching there. The said Towne giueing Mr. Stow Testimoniall L^rs such as the Gent: forenamed iudge fit. In ye meane time the Towne to allow Mr. Stow his vsual stipend, he continueing the exercise of his ministrey, as formerly.

It is ordered that if any in this Collony shall giue, sell or exchang any horse, mare or colt, thereby to conveigh them out of this Jurisdict^n, vnles he first enter the marks both naturall and artificiall, as also the colour and age of ye beast, with ye Recorder of ye Towne where ye beast was taken vp out of ye Comons or kept, he shal forfeit Twenty pounds to ye Pub: Treasury, and ye Recorder is allowed to take sixpence for euery such record or entrey.

The Magestrates haueing considered the case of John Bissel, about tradeing liquors to ye Indians, doe adiudge him to pay (for breaking the Law of this Comō wealth) 40*l*.; the wch he is to pay in two yeares time, in currant countrey pay to ye Pub: Treasury.

Stephen Taylor is allowed 20*s*. for his trouble and expence of time about John Bissels case, to be paid him out of ye Treasury.

It is ordered, y^t Wednesday, the 24th of this instant, be kept a Publique Thanksgiueing to God, for his mercy, in our Peace, Plenty, Health and Liberties y^t we enioy.

[134] It is ordered, that ye Ferrey at Niantecut shal from henceforth belong to ye Farme of o^r Hon^rd Gouerno^r Jno Winthrop Esqr, and, as he shal order, to his Assignes, his Tenants attending the said Ferrey at all times as is necessary, for a reasonable and iust recompenc. Magestrates and ye Deputies of ye Court, ferrey-free, according to order.

It is ordered, y^t the Comittee formerly chosen to treat with Capt Cullick, now haueing ripened their treaty to an issue, are impowered by this Court to p^rfect writings, and what is requisite to be confirmed and signed by ye Court, the Worship^ll Gouerno^r is authorized to act in ye name of the Court, and to fixe ye seale of ye Collony thervnto and to deliver the writings to Capt Cullick, and to receaue in behalf of ye Court those writings y^t Capt John Cullick is to deliver vnto this Court.*

The restraint formerly laid on ye estate of George Fenwick Esqr is now taken of, and free possession and power of administration granted vnto Capt Jno Cullick to ye said estate, in behalf of ye Legatees.

The List of ye Estates p^rsented to this Court are,—

Windsor Estate and p^rsons,	16274.00	SeaBrook,	05724.00
Hartford,	19512.10	Farmington,	06109.00
Wethersfield,	12399.00	Stratford,	08110.00
Middle Town,	02398.00	Norwalk,	03587.00

The Plantat^s of Stratford, Fairfield and Norwalk, haueing failed in transmitting ye List of ye Estates of their Townes according to order, This Court orders the Treasurer to pursue the said order, and to summon ye prsons delinquent to ye Quarter Court in March next, to answer for their transgression herin.

Mr. Willis and Capt Lord are appointed to audit ye Treasurers acco^t for ye year past.

The Treasurer and William Wadsworth are appointed to take in Jeremiah Addams his acco^t.

This Court grants a Rate of a penny p^r £. to be levied vpon ye estate of ye Collony for ye yeare past.

---

* These 'writings' for a final adjustment of accounts between the Colony and Capt. Cullick, are recorded on pages 327–329, *ante*.

This Court allowes libertie to y{e} Treasurer to send forth warrants to y{e} seaside Plantat{s}: to gather their Rates, in such season as may p{r}vent that inconvenience y{t} vsually falls out in failing of their payment.

To p{r}vent future inconvenience and vnnecessary trouble y{t} may ensue by vnwritten grants, bargaines, sales or morgages, It is ordered by this Court, that from hencforth all grants, bargaines, sales or morgages of hous and lands, shalbe in writing and subscribed by the granter with his owne hand or mark, [135] vnto w{ch} mark his name shalbe annexed, and also subscribed by two witnesses at least, w{th} their owne hands or markes, vnto w{ch} marks their names shal be annexed, & that noe grant, sale, bargain or morgage shalbe of value but such as written and subscribed, as abouesaid. It is also ordered, that the said writing shalbe recorded, according to former order. And whereas, by former order there is libertie granted for one Magestrate to commit to prison w{th}out baile, That clause is hereby repealed. And caution giuen in to y{e} Recorder shal secure the intrest of y{e} Grantee, vntil a legall triall hath passed to a finall issue; vpon w{ch} issue according to law, the judgm{t} of the Court being delivered vnto y{e} Recorder, vnde{r} the Secretaries hand, shalbe his Warr{t} to record such grant, bargaine, sale &c. tho y{e} Granter refuse to acknowledge the same.

It is also ordered, that a lawful record of any grant, bargaine, sale or morgage, either in y{e} Countrey Book, or in y{e} Towne Records where y{e} House and Land lieth, shalbe of equal value w{th} a written deed of any grant: Provided the record (if noe other written deed be made as abouesaid,) be testified and subscribed by one witnes at least beside y{e} Recorder.

HARTFORD. SESSION GEN{ll}. MARCH 14. '60.

Jo: Winthrop Esq{r}, Go:
Jo: Mason Esq{r}, Dep:
Magestrates: Mr. Clark, Mr. Willis, Mr. Allyn, Mr. Treat. Sec{r}: Dan{ll} Clarke.
Dep: C. Rich: Lord, C. Jo: Talcot, Mr. Gailard, Mr. Hen: Woolcot, Wm. Wadsworth, Jos: Migat, Edw: Griswold,

Jo: Deming, Sam: Boreman, W^m. Gutridge, Jo: Kilburn, Antho: Howkins, Jo: Tinker, Robert Warner, W^m. Cheny.

M^{rs}. W^m. Thomson, Jo: Cotton and James Rogers were made free at this Court.

This Court orders, that ye Heires of Mr. Wells, of Wethersfield, shal set that part of ye houseing that Mrs. Wells is to enioy for her life time, in p^rsent repaire; and Mrs. Wells is to keep it and to returne it in like repaire.

It is ordered by this Court, that Lt Hollister, Mr. Chester, wth their fellow Townesmen, shal wthin one weeks time after the receipt of this ord^r, p^rfect the gathering the Rate for Tho: Lord, by destreint or otherwise together wth ye Court charges respecting the action of Tho: Lord contra Lt Hollister, and for two executions, wch is thirteen shillings six pence. And in case of neglect of this order, the Secretary is to send out execution vpon ye parties cast in law at ye p^rticuler Court.

The Jurisdiction Power ouer that Land y^t Vncus and Wawequa haue made ouer to Major Mason is by him surrendered to this Colony. Neuertheles for ye laying out of those lands to Farmes or Plantations the Court doth leaue it in ye hands of Major Mason. It is also ordered and provided wth ye consent of Maior Mason, That Vncus & Wawequa and their Indians [136] and successors ‖ shalbe supplied wth sufficient planting ground at all times as ye Court sees cause out of y^t Land. And ye Maior doth reserue for himself a competency of Land sufficient to make a Farme.*

In answer to Mr. Tinkers Petition, it is desired that Maior Mason, Goodman Morgan and Vncus or Wawequa, or some Indian appoined by them, wil veiw the tract of land y^t Mr. Tinker desires, or some other meet for him, not p^ruiditial to others, and to make report thereof to ye Court.

In referenc to Mr. Rosseters desire respecting Land vpon Stratford Riuer, at Paugusset, the Court approues of his purchase, accepts it vnd^r this Gouernm^t, and allowes liberty to purchase one hundred acres more.

It is ordered, y^t Mr. Tinker, James Rogers and Mathew

---

* The informal nature of this surrender to the Colony of the right which Major Mason (as their agent,) had acquired in the Mohegan lands, gave rise to the celebrated "Mason case," which (for nearly seventy years,) occasioned much trouble and expense to the Colony.

Griswold shal examine Stebbins acco^t of N. London, and returne their app^{r}hensions about it to ye next Session.

Jeremiah Adams did resigne all the power of disposeing ye estate (left by Thomas Greenhill to Goodwife Adams) into his wiues hands to be wholly at her dispose.

It is ordered that in case any Trooper die or remoue, whereby his place remaines vacant, it is left to ye Comission officers of ye Troop to accept of such as may be suteable to fill vp the number that ye Court allowes; and such as the officers admit, to stand firme, vnles ye Court, either Gen: or P^{r}ticuler, put a stop to those Troop^{r}s.

John Tinker hath licence to retayle liquors distilled by him, vntil Octob^r, 1662, and to indeauour to suppress others that shal sell by retaile in ye Towne.

In ye appeale of Robert Reeues in ye case twixt him as p^t contr John White, this Court finds for ye Defendant.

In ye case twixt him as p^t contr Wm. Clark, this Court find for ye Defendant, and if there be any land besides the homelot that is expresly bought, such land doth apperteine to John Skinners estate.

[137] It is ordered by this Court it shalbe in the power of the Treasurer, at al times, as cause requires, to issue forth his warrant vnto the Constables in ye respectiue Plantations where any Comissioner or select men shal faile in p^{r}fecting and transmitting the list of Estates according to order, to destreine and leuy the forfeiture required in ye said order provided in this case.

This Court doth impose the fine of 20s. vpon the Town of Norwalk, for y^r neglect in transmitting their list according to order at October Court last.

Receaued by me John Shepherd, of my loving Vnkel Gregory Winterton, Thirty four pounds, wch he receaued of my Bro: Thomas Greenhill for lands I sold him, for wch I made my Vnkel a letter of Attourney, I say receaued by me,

Augs^t 4: 1654.　　　　　　　　　　　　　　John Shepherd.
　　Transcribed out of ye originall.

In answer to Simon Lobdels Petition;
1. This Court admits not a further hearing of ye case.

2. Its ordered that yᵉ spetial verdict drawen vp by the Pʳticuler Court, respecting Simons case agˢᵗ Jared and Hannah Spencer, shal stand firme to issue that busines.

3. In referenc to yᵉ just expences mentioned in yᵉ verdict, Its ordered that Jared Spencer shal pay vnto Simon Lobdell, Fiue pounds, besides the Ten pounds mentioned in yᵉ verdict. All wᶜʰ sum of fifteen pounds shalbe paid in wheat and pease or other estate equivalent: Fiue pounds to be paid by the 10ᵗʰ of Aprill, the other Ten pounds according as is specified in yᵉ spetial verdict. And this is to be a final issue.

Jeremiah Adams acknowledging himself indebted vnto yᵉ estate of Mr. Hopkins the sum of Twenty pounds wherin Mrs. Vrsilla Gibdons stands bound wᵗʰ him for yᵉ payment thereof this Court doth free the said Vrsula from her bond, and doth sequester the said estate in Jer: his hand, til further order proceed for yᵉ paymᵗ thereof.

This Court haueing heard and considered the differenc twixt yᵉ Towne of Middle Town and Mr. Stow, and their allegations [138] and answers, ‖ doe judg and determine, that yᵉ people of Middle Town are free from Mr. Stow as their engaged minister. 2ly. That the people of Middle Town shal giue to Mr. Stow Lʳˢ Testimonial, according as was drawen vp, and pʳsented by the Worshipfull Gouernoʳ in yᵉ Court. And Mr. Stow is not infringed of his liberty to preach in Middle Town to such as will attend him, vntil there be a setled ministrey there.

In reference to former intentions and motions wᶜʰ could not be brought to a ful conclusion for yᵉ manner and meanes to accomplish the same, til this meeting of yᵉ Generall Court, It is concluded and declared by this Court, That (as it was formerly agreed by those Magestrates and Deputies that then could be assembled together,) it is our duty and very necessary to make a speedy address to his Sacred Maiesty, our Soveraigne Lord Charles the Second, King of England, Scotland, France and Ireland, to acknowledge our loyalty & allegiance to his highnes, hereby declareing and professing ourselues, all the Inhabitants of this Colony, to be his Highnes loyall and faythfull subjects. And doe further conclude it necessary that we should humbly petition his Maiesty for grace and fauour, and for yᵉ continuance and confirmation of such privilidges and liberties as are necessary for the comfortable and peaceable settlement of this Colony.

It is ordered, that the Fiue hundred pounds that Capt John Cullick is to pay to ye Countrey, shalbe kept and improued in pursueance of our Address to his Highnes our Soveraigne Lord Charles etc.

Mr. Willis, Mr. Allyn, & Willm Wadsworth are appointed as a Comittee to meet with Capt Cullick when he comes vp, to receaue in such bills as he is to assigne to the Countreys vse.

This Court haueing heard the case respecting Jeremie and John Adams and Edward Stebbing, respecting the sale of ye Homelot of Thomas Greenhill, at Hartford, doe sentence and conclude, that ye said sale of y^t lot by Edward Stebbing to Mr. [139] Goodwin is a legal sale: the sale being ‖ acknowledged by Edward Stebbin in open Court.

In answer to ye close of ye Petition respecting Hoccanum lands, it is ordered, that all ye proprietors of ye wast land shal appoint a time to lay out ye lots according to ye several grants, as they haue agreed in Court to doe.

This Court doth grant and order that there shalbe paid vnto Eltweed Pomry the sum of Ten pounds, out of ye Wompom y^t is come from Narroganset, at six p^r penny, as recompense for his loss in his Mare.

This Court orders, that in case Sarah North hear not of her husband by that ye seauenth year be expired, (he haueing bene absent six, already,) that then she shalbe free from her coniugal bonds.

Its ordered by this Court, that ye people of Middle Town shal pay vnto Mr. Stow, for his labour in ye ministrey the year past, 40l. wch is to be paid vnto him by the 10th of April next.

Its ordered, that ye Wompom y^t the Comission^{rs} ordered to be paid to Mr. Brewster shalbe deliv^{r}d vnto him out of that wch came from Narroganset.

It is ordered that ye Secretary shal send down order to Robt Chapman to giue power and order to ye new Constable at Sea Brook to levy the sum of 9l. 6s. 1d. vpon William Bushnell, and likewise y^t ye Secretary shal send order to require the said Bushnell to levy the said 9l. 6s. 1d. vpon ye estates of such at Norridge as are defectiue in their Rates and to p^{r}fect his Acco^t for ye last yeare.

The Constables in the yᵉ respectiue Plantations are hereby required forthwith to perfect their accoᵗˢ respecting the several levies for yᵉ Countrey Rates yᵗ are yet imperfect ; and in case of defect herein aftʳ the 10ᵗʰ of Aprill next, the Treasurer is ordered to send forth warrants to yᵉ pʳsent Constables to destreine the remaindʳ of yᵉ Levy from the Constable defectiue, also 40*s.* fine for neglect in attending the Countrey order is to to be required of and destreined by the Treasurers Warrant from yᵉ said Constables.

[140] Whereas, it is wel knowne to yᵉ Inhabitants and Churches in these parts that there was a Church orderly gathered at Wethersfield, by yᵉ full approbation and allowance of yᵉ Court and Magestrates then in power, and by the consent and appʳbation of neighbour Churches, and whereas there are diverse of yᵉ members of yᵉ said Church remoued from thence wᵗʰout any notice giuen to, or allowance and appʳbation from this Court or yᵉ Magestrates of this Jurisdiction or the Churches wᵗʰin this Jurisdiction or the neighbouring Churches, soe as the number of yᵉ members of that Church is lessened thereby, and vpon that occasion some, through misappʳhension of the true state of that Church, there still resident and remaineing, haue taken occasion vniustly to question the station and being of yᵉ said Church of Xᵗ: as some of that Church doe complaine, and yet none haue chargᵈ any offence or irregularity vpon the said Ch: or their proceed in their Ch: estate ; & wheras the said Ch: did manifest vnto the former Sessⁿ of this Court, wᶜʰ heard and examined their case openly, the reality and trueth of their continuance in the same membership, Ch: estate & station as formerly ; This Court doth therfore hereby declare that yᵉ said Ch: is yᵉ true and vndoubted Ch: of Wethersfield, and soe to be accountᵈ and esteemed, for any thing doth yet appeare ; yet this Court doth also declare that if any just charg be brought in agaynst them, or any thing be made to appeare that may iustly disaproue or call in question their Ch: estate before the 14ᵗʰ of May next ensueing, and shal orderly declare and regularly prosecute their charge agaynst them, then yᵉ Court will attend the hearing of such charge agaynst them and accordingly iudge of their estate as shal then appeare.

The Magestrates and Assistants in yᵉ respectiue Plantations

in this Colony are desired forthwith to call yᵉ Grand Jury men in their Townes, and to giue them an Oath for yᵉ due discharg of their worke.

[141] The Comʳˢ of N. London is fined 40s. for not transmitting their List of estate, according to order.

It is ordered by this Court, that noe person wᵗsoeuer in this Colony, shal directly or indirectly buy or rent any of yᵉ Lands at Podunk that are laid out and possessed by the Indians there. And respecting Thomas Burnam, it is allowed and granted vnto him, that in case the Indians there shal depart from that place and leaue it, that then the said Thomas, wᵗʰ yᵉ free consent of yᵉ Indians there, shal improue the Indians lands in yᵉ time of their absence, wᶜʰ consent of yᵉ Indians shalbe declared before the Magestrates. Thomas Burnam doth engage to this Court, that whensoeuer yᵉ Indians desire to returne to and improue their lands themselues, he the said Thomas wil freely, readily and without any trouble, surrendʳ yᵉ possession vnto yᵉ Indians agayne. This liberty to continue til his lease be expired.

It is ordered, that Capᵗ Lord and the Treasurer shal leuel accounts, and the Treasurer is to pay what is due to Capᵗ Lord, wᵗʰ dammadges allowed vnto him.

Capt. Cook is required to desist in any further labour on the lower Farme at Mussaco, vntil the matter be issued at Genˡˡ Court, in May next.

Wednesday three weeks is appointed a solemne humiliation to seek the favour of God in yᵉ occasions of yᵉ insueing yeare, and yᵗ God would direct vs in those waies yᵗ may conduce to our settlement in peace and privilidges, and yᵗ peace and truth may be setled in England.

---

[142] COURT OF ELECTION HELD AT HARTFORD, MAY 16, 1661.

Magestrates elected:

Jo: Winthrop Esqʳ, Go:
Jo: Mason Esqʳ, Dep:
    Mr. Henry Clark,   Mr. Gould,
    Mr. Willis,   Mr. Topping,

Mr. Allyn,   Mr. Rainer,
Mr. Phelps,   Mr. Baker,
Mr. Treat,   Mr. Bond.

Treasurer, John Talcot.

Sec'y Dan^ll Clark, *et Dep:*

Dep: C. Rich: Lord, Mr. Henry Woolcot, Mr. Gaylard, Wm. Wadsworth, Joseph Migat, John Moore, Sam^ll Welles, Sam^ll Boreman, John Deming Senr, John Kilburne, John Clark Senr, Math: Campfield, Jehu Burr, John Banks, Rich: Olmstead, Robt Warner, Nath: White, James Rogers, Robt Royce, Antho: Howkins, Thomas Judd, Phillip Groues, Mr. Haul.

The Freemen voted that ye Gen^ll Court should choose Com^rs and invest them wth full power for this year ensueinge:

And likewise that ye Court should choose Assistants, as need requires in ye several Plantations.

Mr. Tinker, Mr. Campfield and Robt Chapman are chosen and sworn Assistants.

The Assistant and Com^rs at New London are desired to take a strickt care to suppress disorders in that place.

The Gou^rnor and Dep: Gou^r are chosen Comissioners for this yeare ensueing, and Mr. Allyn and Mr. Willis for a reserue.

Mr. Allyn is chosen Moderator in absence of ye Gou^r and Dep: Go:, both for Gen^ll and P^rticuler Courts.

This Court remits 4*l.* of ye fine of 8*l.* formerly laid on Wm. Clark.

This Court hath accepted and doe confirme the conclusion of ye Comittee respecting the accounts of Georg Tong & John Stebbin.

This Court remits Ten pound of ye fine imposed on John Bissell for tradeing Liquors.

This Court hath added 20*s.* to that wch the P^rticuler Court allowed to Stephen Taylor out of John Bissells fine.

This Court vnd^rstanding the Com^rs consent thervnto, doe accept of ye Plantation of Setauk vnd^r this Gouerm^t,* vpon ye same Articles of Confederation as are granted to South-

---

* "Libertie is granted to the Jurisdiction of Conecticut, to take Huntington and Setaukett, two English Plantations on Long Iland, vnder their Gouerment." [Rec. of U. Colonies, Sept. 1660.]

ampton; and for two yeares doe free y^t Plantat: from publ: charges, nor must they expect the Countrey to be at charg about them during that time. Mr. Richard Wodhull and Mr. Thom^s Peirce are chosen by the Court to officiate in ye place of Magestrates in that Plantat: for ye yeare ensueing. Mr. Wodhul sworne.

Mr. Pel and Alexand^r Knowles chosen Assistants for Fairfield, and in case either of them refuse, Mr. Wm. Hil is chosen to supply that defect.

[143] This Court doth ord^r, that ye bounds of N. London shalbe measured by the persons that the Court appoints, that soe they may be regulated according to ye grant of the Court.

Mathew Griswold, Thomas Tracy and James Morgan are appointed to try the bounds of N. London, and to make report what is ye extent of ye bounds from the Sea northward into ye Countrey, on ye east side the Riuer, according to ye ordnary way of laying out of bounds in this Colony. N. London people haue liberty to procure the ablest person they can to assist in this matter.

This Court hath chosen Wm. Wadsworth, Mr. Campfield and John Moor as a Comittee to ripen ye case respecting the horses in controuersy twixt Reynold Marvin and Math: Griswold, for ye determination of ye Court.

The former ord^r respecting Mr. Jno Tinker is stil to be attended by him in veiweing a convenient place at or neere Monhegin, to take vp some Land.

Respecting Mr. Bruens letter for advice, the Courts mind is to take the matt^r into furth^r consideration before they giue direction in ye case propounded by him.

In answer to Fairfield Petition, this Court declare their vnwillingnes to admit a further hearing of ye case twixt Fairfield & Stratford.

This Court grants Goodwife Lettin liberty to inhabit in Fairfield, in case that Towne admit her.

Execut^n sent to Fairfield for Twenty pounds, according to ye conclusion of Norwalk Comittee.

This Court remitts 40*s.* of ye fine imposed vpon Nicholas Palmer & his wife.

This Court approues of ye returne of ye Comittee respecting

Math: Griswold and Renold Marvin, and confirm their determination about the Horses.

This Court grants that the one half of ye horses in controuersy shalbe devided twixt Math: Griswold and Reynold Marvin equally, and ye other half the Court ord^r to be to ye Countrey. And its ordered that ye said company of horses shalbe [144] lookd vp by Marvin, and that Robert Chapman, ‖ John Clark Senr, Math: Griswold and Reynold Marvin shal sell the Horses to make paym^t and distribution according to this Order. Goodm̄: Marvin is to see ye Horses brought in, that soe this ord^r may be effected. And ye value of what haue bin sold is to come into this distribution. And this is to issue that controuersy.

John Banks, Richard Olmstead, and Joseph Judson are appointed to run the line from South to ye Northward, twixt Fairfield and Stratford, to ye extent of their bounds, and also ye cross line.

This Court hath remitted fiue pounds of ye fine imposed on Whelpley, for his lasciviousness.

This Court repeales ye ord^r for paying the Indians for such Wolues as they kill or steale.

Respecting Capt Aaron Cooks grant at Mussaco, This Court doth iudg the grant stil in force, and doe order that he shal begin next ye Falls and take meadow, good and bad, wthout exception, except vplands, wch are not intended in ye grant.

In reference to ye Address drawn vp by o^r Gou^{r}nor, This Court doth order that ye said Draft as it is now drawen vp and formed and p^{r}sented to ye Court, shalbe sent and p^{r}sented to his Highnes o^r Soveraigne Lord and King Charles ye 2^d etc., in case the Comittee chose to p^{r}vse and compleat ye said Address see not cause to make any alteration therein, to whom it is fully left to compile or methodize the Instrument as they iudge most convenient, provided ye substance be stil attended and reteined.

The Comittee chosen to compleat ye Address and draw vp the Petition to his Matie or any other L^{rs} to any noble p^{r}sonages in England, and al other matters respecting o^r address, Petition or Patent, are as follow: John Winthrop Esqr, o^r Gou^r;

Also, y*e* Dep: Gou*r*, Mr. Willis, Mr. Allin, Mr. Warham, Mr. Stone, Mr. Hooker, Mr. Whiting and y*e* Secretary.

It is agreed between Cap*t* Topping, Mr. Halsey, Mr. Stanbourough and John Coop*r*, in behalf of all of Southampton [145] vnsatisfied about their bounds, ‖ and Mr. Baker and Mr. Mulford, in behalf of y*e* Towne of East Hampton, That y*e* bounds between the two Plantations shal for euer be and remaine at the stake set down by Capt: How, an hundred pole eastward from a little pond, the said stake being two miles or near thereabouts from y*e* east side of a great pond comonly called Sackaponock ; and soe to run from y*e* South Sea to the stake, and soe ouer the Island by a strait line to y*e* easterne end of Hogneck, according to y*e* true intent and purpose of what is expressed in the grant and deed subscribed and allowed by Mr. James Forret, Agent for y*e* Right Ho*ble* Earle of Sterling. It is further to be vnd*r*stood that what agreem*t* is here made doth noe way intrench vpon any of y*e* rights, privilidges or imunities conferd vpon Southampton by their Patent purchased of the aforesaid James Forret. It is further concluded that y*e* lands on the west side the stake forementioned shalbe and remaine to Southampton for euer, and y*e* land on y*e* east side y*e* stake, being the greater part of y*e* Plaine, to be and belong to y*e* Plantation of East Hampton foreuer. And this to stand as a final conclusion respecting the bounds twixt those two Plantations.

It is ordered, that y*e* Towne of East Hampton shal pay vnto y*e* Cap*t* Topping and his copartners, towards their charges in transacting this case at this Court, the sum of 20 Nobles.

This Court is adiourned til y*e* last Wednesday in Aug*st* next.

Postscrip*t*.

This Court doth desire and authorize o*r* Wor*ll* Gouerno*r* (who speedily intends a voyage to England,) to agitate and transact the affairs of this Colony in reference to o*r* Address & Petition to his Ma*tie*, or respecting o*r* Pattent, according as he shall receaue further instructions from the Comittee appointed to compleat those matt*rs*, takeing in the advice and counsell and consent of such Gentlemen and freinds as may be excited and procured to be actiue w*th* him in and about the premisses.

[146]   HARTFORD. SESSION GEN^ll JUNE 7^t: 61.

Jo: Winthrop Esqr, Go:
Magestrates: Mr. Willis, Mr. Allyn, Mr. Phelps, Mr. Treat.
Sec^r; Dan^ll Clark.
Dep: C. Rich: Lord, C. Jno Talcot, Henry Woolcot, Wm. Gaylard, Wm. Wadsworth, Joseph Migat, Jo: Deming, Sam^ll Wells, Sam^ll Boreman, Tho: Judd, Antho: Howkins, Robt: Warner, Nath^ll White, James Rogers.

This Court haueing considered the Address and Petition compleated by the Comittee, to be sent and p^rsented to his Matie, or Soveraigne Lord Charles the 2d, and also the Instructions drawen vp for o^r Wor^ll Gouerno^r, Agent for this Colony in ye p^rmisses, doe approue of that wch ye Comittee hath done. And doe further add to ye Instructions, that they doe leaue ye matt^rs respecting any L^rs that may be found necessary to be directed to any other Nobles or Gent: who may be stirred vp to be helpful in promoteing the Address, Petition or Pattent, besides them that are nominated in the Instructions, to o^r Wor^ll Gouern^r; and as he shal see cause, to draw vp, and in ye name of the Colony to subscribe, seale and deliuer such L^rs, and to draw vp and p^rsent any further Petition in behalf of this Colony, to his Matie, as may be found necessary.

It is ordered by this Court, that o^r Wor^ll Gouern^r shalbe allowed out of the Treasurie, for this ensuing yeare, the sum̃ of Eighty pounds. And in reference to his intended voiage to England, if his purpose and resolution doe stil continue to goe, in regard this Court hath made choice of his wors^p to be an Agent to further our welfare, in p^rsenting o^r Address & Petition to ye Kings Maiestie, and to improue his abilities to procure vs a Pattent, This Court doth hereby order and enact, that whateuer charges or expenses the attendance on those affaires of this Colony shall require in England, shalbe defraied out of that 500*l.* that is by ord^r of Court appointed and set apart for y^t service.

This Court doth desire and appoint Capt. Lord, Mr. Henry Woolcot, John Allyn, Willm Wadsworth, or a maior part of them, wth ye advice of Mr. Math: Allyn, to order and dispose of ye pay that is to come to ye Col: from Capt. John Cullick, soe as yt it may answer such Bills as may be charged on this Col: by or Worll Gouernor or his order, in pursuance of our Pattent, in England.

[147] The Treasurer is appointed to signe ye Lr of Credit, whereby the Gouernor may be authorized to charge Bills on ye Colony to ye value of 500*l.* according to former act of ye Court. The Treasurer is to giue order to ye Comittee for ye delivery of pay when Bills are charged.

The Secretary is ordered to subscribe in ye name of ye Court, the Address, Petition and Letters to ye Nobles and to ye Corporation, and deliuer to ye Gouernour coppies of ye same; and in case it be iudged expedient the Gouernour is desired to subscribe ye Address and Petition.*

Eltweed Pomrey hath receaued the 10*l.* in Wompom, from ye Gouernor, that the Court formerly granted him.

Session, June 8: 61.

This Court takeing into consideration ye estate yt is in John Coles improuemt, yt formerly belonged to Edward Hopkins Esqr, Doe order, that ye Treasurer shal require and take into his custody and improuement the rent of that house and land at Hartford, from John Cole, and to be accountable for it when ye Court cals him thervnto. And likewise for Willm Hills farme, ye same order is to be attended.

The Treasurer and Willm Wadsworth are desired to acquaint John Cole that ye Court expects that he continue in ye improuement of ye Farme according to his Lease; and its left wth them to informe him that ye Court desires and are ready to incourage him in this busines for ye future.

---

[148]   Hartford.   Session, Augst 17: 61.
Majr Jo: Mason Esqr, D: Go:
Magestrates: Mr. Allyn, Mr. Phelps, Mr. Treat.
Secrety; Danll Clark.

---

* The Instructions to Gov. Winthrop, Letter to the Earl of Manchester, (as is supposed,) and a copy of the Address, will be found in the Appendix, No. X. The Petition, and a Letter to Lord Say & Sele, have been already printed in Trumbull's History of Connecticut, Vol. i., Appendix, Nos. vii. & viii.

Deputies: C. Jo: Talcot, Wm Wadsworth, Joseph Migat, Sam^ll Wells, John Moor, Jo: Deming Sen:, Tho: Judd, Antho: Howkins, Sam: Boreman, John Kilburn, Robt Warner, Nathan^ll White, Mr. Henry Woolcot.

This Court doth order that it shalbe comended to ye consideration of ye Com^rs that an order may be established, That noe Indians w^teuer shal attempt any hostile act, or wage or carry on any warr within ye limits of ye several Colonies or Plantations, but shal first make ye justice of their cause appear to ye Authority of ye Colony wherin the Indians liue, and haue liberty from ye Authority of ye Colonie to proceed on in their warr:

And in case the Indians doe violate ye Com^rs former order, in hostile attempts as before, or in marching throw ye Townes wth armes, what fine or punishment is to be inflicted on offenders, and how we may act in opposeing Indians or pursueing delinquents.

This Court doth appoint Maior Mason, Mr. Allyn, Wm. Wadsworth, C. Jo: Talcot, Joseph Migat, as a Comittee, to whom it is left to settle Podunk Indians in that place, vpon righteous and honerable termes; as also to indeauour to settle Farmington Indians, and to purge out strangers from them. And to enioyne both Podunk and Farmington Indians to cease their warr and not to entertein strang^rs, and also to require ye Captiues.

---

[149]   HARTFORD. SESSION GEN^ll. AUG^st 28: 61.

Mr. Allyn, Moderato^r.

Magestrates: Mr. Phelps, Mr. Treat.

Dep: C. Jo: Talcot, Dan^ll Clark, *et Sec^r*, Mr. Gaylard, Wm. Wadsworth, John Moore, Joseph Migat, Sam^ll Welles, John Deming, Sam^ll Boreman, Anthony Howkins, Thomas Judd.

In reference to ye case depending twixt Caspar Varleet, by way of appeale, contr Edward Palmes, This Court doth determine, That Caspar Varleet shal forthwith make satisfaction to Mr. Palmes for what is vnpaid of ye Bill in Cattle, wth 8*l.* 6*s.* 6*d.* for damadge, with charges. And in case Caspar Varleet doe not satisfie according to this order, This Court grants execution to be delivered vpon ye estate of Varleets that lies vnd^r Attachm^t, and Lt Thomas Bull, Mr. Jos: Wellard and James Steel are appointed to apprize the estate that Mr. Palmes doth receaue from Mr. Varleet; and if any of these three fayle, Thomas is to supply his roome.

This Court hath granted to Jonathan Gilbert a farme, to ye numb^r of 300 Acres of vpland and 50 Acres of meadow, provided it be not preiuditiall where he finds it to any Plantatⁿ y^t now is, or hereafter may be setled.

The Court hath granted vnto Mr. Math: Allyn, 400 Acr^s of vpland and 100 Acr^s of meadow, where he can find it wthin Conect: liberties, vpon ye same termes as to Jonathā Gilbert.

---

[150] HARTFORD: AT A GEN^{ll} SESSION: OCTO^{br} 3: 61.

Maior Mason, D: Go:

Magestrates: Mr. Willis, Mr. Allyn, Mr. Phelps, Mr. Treat.

Sec^r, Dan^{ll} Clark, *et Dep:*

Deput: C. John Talcot, Lt Hollister, L^t Jo: Allyn, Mr. Gaylard, Lt Walter Filer, Joseph Migat, John Moor, John Deming, Sam^{ll} Wells, Sam^{ll} Boreman, Antho: Howkins, Tho: Judd, Robt Chapman, John Clarke, James Morgan, James Avery, Walter Hoit, Joseph Judson, Nath^{ll} White, Robert Warner, Phillip Groues, Mr. Hill, Thomas Staples.

This Court orders, that it may be comēnded to ye consideration of ye Freemen the great cost and burthen y^t lies vpon this Collony by the great number of Deputies that attend ye Gen^{ll} Courts; and if it seeme good to ye Freemen it is desired y^t ye number may be lessened one halfe in each Towne in this Colony. And likewise, in case any occasion necessitate the calling together ye Gen^{ll} Court at such season that may be præiudiciall for the remoter Townes to send their Deputies, that then it may remaine and be in ye power and liberty of these neighbouring Townes on ye Riuer, by their Deputies or a major part of them, wth soe many Magestrates as ye law requires, to keep Court, yt with full power and authority as if the Deputies of ye severall Plantations were prsent altogether.

This Court doth hereby manifest their complianc and consent that ye Comision Court shalbe held but once in three yeares, in ye ordnary course: and ye Secretary is ordered to certifie this order to ye Comrs at yr next meeting.

There is a Levy of a penny pr £ ordered to be raised vpon ye estate of ye whole Colony.

Next Wednesday come fortnight is appointed to be kept a solemne Thanksgiueing throwout the Colony, for Gods merceys in ye remaineing fruits of ye earth, and for or peace, and that God is pleased to free vs from yt mortality yt ye Plantats haue bin afflicted with.

Those that are nominated to be put to election for Magestrates, at the Genll Court in May next, are C. John Talcot, Secr Danll Clark, Lt Jo: Allyn, Mr. Henry Woolcot.

This Court haueing heard and considered the busines respecting Mr. Varleets Still and Worm, wth ye head, yt was destreined for Mr. Palmes his debt, doe see cause to order, that ye said [151] Still etc. be sequestred in ye Marshalls hand or custody, for ye space of three weeks, during wch time it shalbe lawfull and at ye liberty of Mr. Varlet to redeem the Still, by paying the debt to Mr. Palmes or ye Marshall, wth all such charges as haue bene occasioned by executions laid on the Still. And if Caspar Varleet doe not redeem it, or any man elce, in that time, pay more for it then what is due to Mr. Palmes, then ye Still etc. is to be delivered to Mr. Palmes, and he to defray the said charges.

The list of Estate and prsons prsented to this Court:—

Hartford,	£19512. 0. 0.	Wethersfield,	11955. 0. 0.
Windsor,	15902. 0. 0.	Stratford,	8596. 0. 0.
Sea Brook,	05583. 0. 0.	Norwalk,	3527. 10. 0.
Farmington,	06240. 0. 0.	Middle Towne,	2399. 0. 0.
Fairfield,	10423. 4. 0.		

This Court doth ordr and appoint Mr. Gould, Mr. Sherman, Mr. Knowles, Mr. Campfield or any three of them, provided Mr. Gould be one, to examine and issue ye busines respecting Joseph Jeames and Marcy Holbridge and to inflict such punishmt as they iudge meet according to law.

This Court doth confirme and establish yᵉ act of yᵉ Comittee at N. London,* respecting yᵉ east line and lands disposed and to be disposed of; one pʳticuler whereof is yᵗ such land as lies abutteing vpon yᵉ line already disposed to men, shalbe and belong to them, though it lye wᵗʰout yᵉ line.

This Court haueing heard and considered yᵉ contumelioˢ carriage of Mr. Varleet against yᵉ Magestrates, and affront to yᵉ Countries officer in execution of his office, doe fine him 10*l*. to be paid by him to yᵉ Treasurer.

The Worˡˡ D: Gouernʳ, C. Jo: Talcot and Lᵗ John Allyn are appointed and requested to goe to N. London to ioyne wᵗʰ yᵉ [152] Assistant and Comʳˢ there || in keeping Court Pertʳ: and yᵉ Dep: Gouʳ: is to appoint yᵉ time.

It is ordered that the Assistants in this Colony, wᵗʰin their respectiue limits shal haue yᵉ power of one Magestrate vntil yᵉ Genˡˡ Court in May next.

This Court orders yᵉ Secretary to write a Letter to Norridge, to send vp a Comittee in May next, invested wᵗʰ full [*power*] to issue yᵉ affair respecting setling that Plantation vndʳ this Gouerment.

The Will and Testamᵗ of Edward Hopkins Esqʳ, being pʳsented to this Court, legally attested, is accepted as authentick :

This Court doth likewise order and impower Edward Stebbing and Lᵗ Thomas Bull to take yᵉ manadgmᵗ of yᵉ estate of Mr. Hopkins, deceased, into their hands and the gathering in yᵉ debts due to yᵉ estate and to be accountable to yᵉ Court for yᵉ same when called therevnto.

Vpon a proposition pʳsented from Mr. Goodwin, in reference to yᵉ legacy belonging to this Colony, by the last Will of Mr. Hopkins,† and whereas there was, by a writeing, a tendʳ of

---

* [In the margin ;] "17 May, '55."

† Mr. Hopkins, by his will executed Mar. 17th, 1657-8, ("after severall legacies therein bequeathed out of his estate in New England) gave and bequeathed the residue of his estate there, to his father Theophilus Eaton Esq., Master John Davenport, Mr. John Cullick and Mr. William Goodwin, in full assurance of their trust and faithfulnes in disposing of it according to the true intent and purpose of him the said Edward Hopkins, which was, to give some incouragement in those forraigne Plantacons for the breeding up of hopefull youths in a way of learning, both at the Grammar Schoole and Colledge, for the publique service of the Country in future tymes." [Power of Attorney from Henry Dalley, Mr. Hopkins' executor, to the trustees ; in "Colleges & Schools," Vol. i. No. 1.] In addition to this bequest, (estimated at about £1000,)

350*l.* to this Colony, out of that estate; This Court doth declare that they doe not reiect the tender. And further, this Court doth appoint Major Mason, Mr. Mathew Allyn, Mr. Willis and Capt John Talcot, as a Comittee to treat wth ye Trustees of Mr. Hopkins estate about ye foresaid legacy, and what ye maior part of those y^t meet doe conclude, shal stand as an issue of that busines. And ye Secretary is to write a lett^r to ye Trustees to appoint time and place of meeting.

C. John Talcot hath liberty granted to him to retaile liquors provided he attend ye ord^{rs} of ye Countrey therin.

Robt Chapman and Mathew Griswold are appointed to lay out Mr. Allyns Farm according to ye conditions of ye Grant.

Wm. Prat is established Lieutenāt to ye Band at SeaBrook; Wm. Waller, Ensigne; Wm. Bushnel & Reynold Marvin, Sergeants.

[153] Robert Chapman and John Clark Senr are appointed to require Reynold Marvin and Math: Griswold to bring in ye horses soe ordered for the Countrey, and to require ye pay for what are sold, and this to be effected by ye first of Decemb^r next, and to inquire after ye number of them, and to make returne to ye Court in Decemb^r what is done herein.

It is ordered, that ye Indians y^t liue neer ye Townes on ye Riuer haue free liberty to carry their guns, throw ye English Townes, provided they are not aboue 10 men in company. This liberty is granted to Tunxis Indians. Former restreints are repealed.

Willm Wadsworth and Richrd Butler are to iudge of that Beef y^t Varleet doth pay to redeeme ye Still, whether Merchantable or noe, and Joseph Smith to gadge ye cask.

Mr. H. gave from his estate in England, the sum of £500, in further prosecution of "the aforesaid publick ends," "for the upholding and promoting the kingdom of the Lord Jesus Christ in those parts of the earth." This latter sum was considered to belong to Harvard College, and was paid to that institution, under a decree in chancery, in 1710.

The proceeds of the estate in N. England were appropriated by the trustees to the support of Grammar schools in Hartford, New Haven and Hadley.

A letter from Mr. Goodwin, (in the name of the trustees,) to the General Court, in reply to one received from the Secretary requesting the appointment of a time and place of meeting, will be found in the Appendix, No. VIII. [See Savage's Winth. Journal, I. 228, *Note;* Trumbull's H. of Conn. I. 232.]

[154] AT A SESSION OF THE GEN^ll COURT, AT HARTFORD, MARCH 13: 61-62.

This Court hauing read and considered the Petition of Bridget Baxter, in reference to her husbands deserting her and her desire to be divorced from him, doe ord^r Mr. Gould, Mr. Sherman and Mr. Wm. Hill to examine the letter that ye said Baxter sent to his wife in England, and to compare the said writeing wth other of his writeings; and in case they find a true & full concurrence in the said hand writeing, that to their judgm^ts it appeare to be his writeing, then to declare vnto ye said Bridget that this Court hath and hereby doth free her from her coniugall bond to her husband Baxter.

It is ordered, that forty fiue shillings in ye Marshals hands, of Varleets, shalbe a full discharge of ye remainder of his Ten pounds fine to ye Countrey, wch ye Marshal is to discharge to ye Countrey and Mr. Palmes to him.

This Court duely and wth serious deliberation, haueing weighed and considered the nature of the offence of Mr. John Blackleich in his contemptuous expressions against severall p^rsons in authority in this Colony, doe declare, that though the hainousnes of ye transgression deserues a fine of an hundred pounds, yet also considering some weaknes that too evidently appeares that he is incid^t vnto, this Court doth impose the fine of Thirty pounds to be paid by the said Mr. Blackleich to ye publique Treasury.

This Court haue established the line of Farmington to extend to ye mouth of ye Brook at Nod Meadow, at ye northerne end towards Mussaco, and there to be ye devident bounds twixt [155] that plantation and their neighb[ours] at Mussaco, and there to run east and west, to devide twixt both parties.

This Court hath granted vnto Anthony Howkins and Thomas Judd 400 Acres of land betwixt them, whereof 80 Acr^s of Meadow, if it may be found where it may not p^riudice any Plantation y^t now is, or hereafter may be setled.

There is also granted vnto C. John Talcot and L^t Jo: Allyn, 600 Acr^s of vpland and 100 Acr^r of meadow, to be equally devided between them.

There is also granted vnto ye Sec^ry Daniel Clark and John Moor, the number of 400 Acr^s of land, vpon ye forementioned termes, whereof 80 Acres of Meadow, wch is to be devided between them, and if it cannot be found together they haue liberty to seek it out severally.

There is granted vnto Mr. Willys, 200 Acres of land, whereof 50 Acr^s to be Meadow land, vpon ye forementioned termes.

[*In the Margin ;*] C: Lord hath granted from the Court, 350 Acres of vpland & 50 Acres of meadowe, if it : This I find in the Records of this Court, March 13, 61–62, though it be not recorded in their acts in this Booke. As I atest this 11th of Sept^r. '67. John Allyn, Secret^{r}y.

Mr. Phelps, Mr. Gaylard, Jo: Bissell Senr, Sam^{ll} Steell, Lt Hollister, John Wadsworth, doe propound to ye Court for lands.

This Court grants vnto Jeremiah Adams, 300 Acr^s of vpland and 40 Acr^s of meadow, in the place where he kept cattle last winter, going to Monhegin ; and in case there be a plantation there setled, he is to haue a double portion according to his estate out of this land now granted ; the rest he is to surrend^r to ye Towne.

This Court sees cause to repeale the former order respecting allowance for wolues, and y^t each Towne shal pay for ye wolues that are killed in their limits the sum of Fifteen shillings p^r wolfe.

This Court orders, that ye salery for Daniel Porter shalbe paid yearly, out of ye Treasury.

[156] This Court orders, that for future, the leath^r sealers in this Colony shal haue allowed vnto them for each Dicker of Leather they seale, 18*d*. and for half a Dicker, 12*d*. and 4*d*. a hide, for single hides.

This Court declares, that they accept the Towne of Huntington, on Long Island, vnd^r this Gouernm^t. And Mr. Willys, and Capt: Lord are appointed to returne an answer to their Letter.

This Court, vppon further consideration of the frame of ye matter respecting Mr. John Blackleich, and obserueing that there is too much appearance of preiudice in ye testimonies that haue bene p^{r}sented, and how indirect the course was wherby any thing was discouered, i. e. by lying in wait, cannot but see iust cause to acquit Mr. Jo: Blackleich of that fine imposed, there appearing reason to suspect that both Loveridge and Burnam are guilty of yᵉ crime they testifie against Mr. Blackleich.

It is granted and ordered by this Court, vpon the motion and desire of Jeremiah Adams, that yᵉ house that the said Jer: doth now possess and improue for an Ordnary, or house of comon enterteinment, shalbe and remaine for the same end and vse and occupation for the future, both to yᵉ said Jeremie and his successors, provided as hereafter is expressed :

1. That yᵉ said Jeremie, his heires and successors, carry on this worke, by such pʳson or pʳsons inhabiteing in yᵉ said house as shalbe to yᵉ good likeing and approbation of yᵉ Genˡˡ Court from time to time.

2. That yᵉ said house be fitted and made capable to giue sufficient enterteinment as need and occasion shal require, both to neighbours and strangʳˢ.

[157] 3. That there be at all times necessary & comfortable accommodation and provision made for enterteinment of Travellers with horse and otherwise, and that both respecting wine and liquors and other provision for food and comfortable refreshing both for man and beast.

4. It is ordered, that if Jer: Adams shall not attend his agreement in attending the provision made in yᵉ foregoing Articles, he shal not forfeit his licence, but shalbe liable to be censured by the Court as they shal judg most suteable.

AT A COURT OF ELECTION HELD AT HARTFORD, MAY 15, 1662.

Magestrates Elected:

Jo: Winthrop Esqʳ, Gouernʳ.
Jo: Mason Esqʳ, Dep:

    Mr. Math: Allyn, *Moderatʳ*. C. Jo: Talcot, *et Treas:*
    Mr. Willys,   Lᵗ Jo: Allyn,
    Mr. Phelps,   Danˡˡ Clarke, *et Secʳ;*
    Mr. Treat,   Mr. Henry Woolcot.
    Mr. Gould,

Deputies: Wm. Wadsworth, Joseph Migat, Mr. Thomas Wells, Mr. Fitch, C. Benjam: Nubery, Willᵐ Gaylard, John Moore, Edw: Griswold, Samˡˡ Boreman, John Not,

Wm. Goodrich, John Kilburn, Nathan^ll White, Willm Keny, Math: Campfield, Richard Olmstead, Joseph Judson, Isaack Nichols, James Rogers, Sam^ll Smith, Robt Chapman, John Clark, Anthony Howkins, Thomas Judd.

[158] The Freemen haue referred the choice of the Comissioners vnto ye Gen^ll Court. O^r Wor^ll Gouerno^r and Mr. Willys are chosen Com^rs for this yeare ensueing, and Capt John Talcot and Dan^ll Clark are chosen for reserues.

It is ordered by this Court, that whosoeuer for the future shal complaine of and prosecute to effect in a legal way, any poundbreach or rescue, and proue the same, he or they shalbe paid one quarter part of the fine that by the Lawes of this Colony are imposed vpon delinquents that are iudged by the Court y^t heares ye case to be transgressors of any of the said Orders.

This Court doth set at liberty the transportation of Corne.

This Court hath granted the Petition from Huntington, and doe confirme Jonas Wood and Thomas Benedick according to their desire, who are impowred to act in point of Gouerment according to ye liberties granted to that Towne by this Court; And the Secretary is to giue them a Coppy of ye Articles with Southampton, vpon wch termes they are accepted.

The names of the Grand Jury: Willm Wadsworth, Tho: Bull, Deacon Butler, John Moore, Tho: Ford, Ed: Griswold, Anthony Howkins, Tho: Judd, John Kilburn, Sam^ll Boreman, Willm Gutrich, Nath: White.

Bridget Baxter is by the authority of this Court, vpon good consideration and solid reasons and evidenc, freed from her coniugall bond to her husband Thomas Baxter; and whereas the estate that her husband Baxter left with her is sold to pay debts, all excepting a bed and her wearing aparell, This Court doth [159] prohibit all and every of the creditors to ye said estate for seizing, extending or any way troubleing ye remainder, vntil ye Court see cause to ye contrary.

This Court doth release the Com^r of New London from his fine respecting ye list of estates.

This Court vnd^rstanding that several vessels are brought in to ye Ports and Harbours apperteineing to this Colony and vnd^r a p^rtenc of attending the Proclamation sent forth from his Matie oʳ Soveraigne or the Parliamᵗ of England, respecting the transporteing of Tobacco to forreigne nations, and in stead of paying the customes imposed, doe in a clandestine way defeat the law and steale yᵉ custome, and some haue denied to pay any custome, It is therfore ordered by this Court, that whateuer Tobacco is landed in this Colony, there shalbe paid by the Master of the said Vessell, or Merchant importer of yᵉ said Tobacco, vnto the Custome Master of yᵉ place where the vessell is brought in, for evʳy Hogshead, 25*sh*. or 2*d*. pʳ lb. wᶜʰ sum̃ according to yᵉ Law of England shalbe pʳsently discharged, or otherwise, sufficient security shalbe giuen for yᵉ payment thereof wᵗʰin 9 months, otherwise there shalbe noe certificate granted from Authority, respecting the landing of yᵉ said goods.

The Towne of Huntington, on yᵉ Island, is freed from publique charges, for yᵉ space of two yeares from this pʳsent time. Mr. Jonas Wood is appointed Custome Master wᵗʰin and for yᵉ Towne of Huntington.

It is ordered that all the Townes vpon the maine, that are or shalbe vnited to this Gouerment after the publication hereof, shalbe fully compʳhended in yᵉ Order respecting the way and manner of rateinge and raising Countrey Levies.

[160] This Court considering the Petition of Job Drake, respecting the Colt now in the Countreyes possession, formerly handled in yᵉ pʳticuler Court, the said Job pʳtending further evidence to clear his title to yᵉ Colt, Doe therfore appoint and desire Mr. Thomas Wells, Mr. Wadsworth, Mr. Jos: Fitch and Edward Griswold, to heare and consider what Job Drake hath to declare about the colt, and accordingly to determine the mattʳ twixt yᵉ said Job Drake and yᵉ Countrey.

The petition of Mr. Joseph Heines being read and considered, respecting a grant of 1000 Acrˢ of Land to his Honoʳᵈ father in yᵉ Pequot Countrey, This Court orders that yᵉ said grant shalbe fulfilled before any later or further grants be attended or laid out in that part of the Countrey.

This Court graunteth to Mr. Joseph Heines 300 Acrˢ of Land for a Farme, where it may be found not pʳiudiceing a Plantation in being, or that may be, whereof 50 Acrˢ to be mead: land if it can be found.

The Assistants in yᵉ severall Plantations are by this Court established in their respectiue places, for yᵉ yeare ensueing.

This Court orders, that the Bible that was sent to Goodwife Williams be by Sergᵗ John Not delivered to Goodwife Harrison, who engageth to this Court to giue vnto yᵉ children of yᵉ said Williams, a bushel of Wheat a peice, as they shal come out of their time. And John Not doth engage to giue each of yᵉ chilᵈʳn 2 shillings a piece as they come out of their time, to buy them Bibles; and John Not hath hereby power granted him as is ordered, to dispose of yᵉ rest of yᵉ books, to yᵉ children of yᵉ said Williams.

This Court considering the state of the Troop listed by the Countreyes approbation, and yᵉ inconvenience of their meeting in one body, from yᵉ severall Townes, and vnnecessary expence of time to noe profit, Doe therfore order, that yᵉ listed Troopers shall haue ‖ liberty to attend their exercise wᵗʰin yᵉ Plantations where they are resident, wᵗʰ their owne foot company; vpon wᶜʰ consideration their allowance of six shillings eight pence pʳ Trooper is taken of, only the officers for their incouragment are allowed their salery. It is also ordered, that the Troopers in yᵉ respectiue Townes shall attend and obserue the comand of such officers of yᵉ Cavalrey as are cohabiting wᵗʰ them in yᵉ Town where they exercise, except any superior officer of yᵉ Troop shalbe pʳsent at yᵉ exercise. And notwᵗʰ˙ standing this order, they are to be accounted as one intire Troop consisting of severall parts, who are to vnite and attend yᵉ Generall Traineing, as one intire body of Horse.

It is ordered, that for each petition that is pʳsented to yᵉ Generall Court, at any Session thereof, there shalbe paid by the petitioner, or him that pʳsents the same, the sum̄ of 10*sh*. to yᵉ publique Treasury, wᶜʰ shalbe satisfied before the Petition be admitted to be read.

In regard it is found by experience that there is great neglect in veiwinge Generall fences, according to order; It is therfore ordered by this Court, that in every Town in this Colony, there shalbe yearly chosen two men, who shalbe sworne to a due pʳformance of yᵉ work of veiweing fence, and whosoeuer is chosen to yᵉ office of fence veiweing and shal refuse or neglect to attend it, shal pay twenty shilling to yᵉ Town Treasury, vnles it appeareth to some one Magestrate that yᵉ said party be oppressed by the choice, and others vnjustly exempted. And it is likwise ordered, that yᵉ said sworn fence veiwers shal haue power to fine neglects in fenceing, and to require and levy the same, and to deliuer it to yᵉ Townsmen for yᵉ Towns vse where they liue.

[162] This Court grants liberty to yᵉ Marshall, Jonathan Gilbert, to keep an Ordnary at his house, at Cold Spring, for releiueing of Travellers, according to their needs.

This Court desires and appoint the Magestrates of Hartford to agree wᵗʰ a sutable man in Hartford to sel wine by retaile out of doors, at as good a rate as they can.

This Court doe impower Mr. Obadiah Bruen, of N. London, to take Oaths and grant Warrants, in yᵉ Towne of N. London, as occasion requires.

This Court, vnderstanding that there is much preiudice like to ensue to this Colony, by conveighing Tannd Leather out of this Colony, It is therfore ordered, that after yᵉ publication hereof, what pʳson soeuer in this Colony shal transport any Hides that are tan'd either for soles or vpper leather, out of this Jurisdiction, wᵗʰout spetiall order from yᵉ Court of Magestrates, he shal forfeit yᵉ hide or hides or yᵉ value of them, one third part to yᵉ complainʳ, the rest to yᵉ Publique Treasury.

There is liberty granted for yᵉ Town of Huntington to appeale in civil actions, to yᵉ Courts held at Fairfield or Stratford for further triall.

This Court, vpon consideration of Mr. Tinkers incouragmᵗ in his place and imployment, doe order Twelue pounds to be paid to him by the Treasurer out of yᵉ fines imposed on Morton Haughton & Mr. Thomson.

---

[163]   Session Genˡˡ. Hartford, July 22, 62.
               Magestrates:
  Mr. Allyn, *Moderator.*
     Mr. Willys, Mr. Treat, Mr. Talcot, Mr. Allyn, Junʳ, Danˡˡ Clark, *et Secʳ.*

Dep : Mr. Nubery, Willm Wadsworth, Mr. Tho: Wells, Joseph Migat, Joseph Fitch, Edw: Griswold, Tho: Judd, Jo. Kilburn, Jo: Not, Sam^ll Boreman, Willm Keny.

This Court, duely considering the state of this Colony, and espetially the Plantations situate on the Riuer, and iudgeing it very necessary and tending to ye furtherance of o^r p^rsent condition and comfort, Doe order, that after the publication hereof, noe person shal transport and conveigh away out of this River, any Corn or provision from any Plantation w^thin o^r liberties situate on this Riuer, vpon penalty of forfeiting the said Corne or provision or ye value thereof, one 4th part to ye complainer, the rest to ye Publique Treasu[ry.] The Custome masters in each Towne are required and hereby authorized to make diligent search to discouer the transgression of this order. Provided, that this order extends not to any corn or provision y^t shalbe transported by order from ye Treasurer, for any publique concernments respecting this Colony.

This Court doth appoint Sam: Boreman and Serg^t Not to giue notice to those men in Wethersfield that are indebted to ye Countrey in behalf of Capt. Cullick, and likewise C. Beniamin Nubery is to warne Tho: Ford to provide and p^rpare paym^t for the Countrey w^thout delay, that soe ye Countrey may be able to discharge such sums as may be charged on vs by o^r Wor^ll Gouerno^r.

Mr. Jo: Allyn, Mr. H. Woolcot, Wm. Wadsworth, are desired and appointed and authorizd, in case ye p^rsons indebted to ye Countrey doe not provide payment seasonably, as need requires, then ye Comitte or a maior part thereof shal procure corn or provisions as they can agree wth p^rsons: and the forementioned D^rs are to satisfie the said p^rsons accordinge to ye Comitties appointment.

This Court appoints Wm. Wadsworth & James Steel of Hartford, to goe down to Hommanaset and veiw the land there, and if it be not fit for a Plantation, then they are authorizd to lay it [164] out vnto || Mr. Mathew Allyn, Mr. Willys, Capt Talcot, and John Allyn, according to their grants ; and if there be any ouerplus, the Secretary Clark and Mr. Joseph Haines are to haue their proportion there layd out also. Bnt if there be not enough for both of them, it is to be issued by the Generall Court, wch of them two shall haue their proportion there.

At the Generall Assembly or Court of Election held at Hartford, Octob^r 9: 62.

Jo: Winthrop Esqr, Go:
Jo: Mason Esqr, Dep: Go:

Magestrates Elect^d:

Mr. Mathew Allyn,   Capt Talcot, et Treas^r,
Mr. Sam^ll Willys,   Mr. Henry Woolcot,
Mr. Nathan Gold,   Daniell Clark, et Sec^r.
Mr. Treat,   Mr. Jo: Allyn,
Mr. Ogden,   Mr. Baker,
Mr. Tapping,   Mr. Sherman.

Deputies:

Willm Wadsworth,   Sam^ll Smith,   Mathew Campfield,
Joseph Fitch,   James Rogers,   John Gregory,
Edward Griswold,   John Clarke,   Nathan^ll White,
Josias Hull,   Robert Chapman,   Robert Warner,
Sam^ll Boreman,   Phillip Groue,   Thomas Leffingwell,
John Nott,   Joseph Judson,   Thomas Tracy,
Anthony Howkins,   Cornelius Hull,   John Howell.
Thomas Judd,   Sam^ll Drake,

The Pattent or Charter* was this day publiquely read in audienc of ye Freemen, and declared to belong to them and their successors, and ye freemen made choice of Mr. Willys, C: John Talcot and Lt John Allyn to take the Charter into their Custody, in behalf of ye freemen, who are to haue an oath

---

* The Charter bears date April 23d, 1662, and was probably received in Connecticut early in September. The first public exhibition of it seems to have been made to the Commissioners of the U. Colonies, at their Session in Boston, (Sept. 4th--16th,) when "His Maties Letters Pattents granted vnto several Gentlemen of Conecticut, vnder the broad seale of England, was presented and read." In a letter to the Government of Rhode Island, written during the same Session, the Commissioners say, "We have read and p^rvsed a Charter of incorporation vnder ye broade seale of England, *sent over the last ship*, granted to some gentlemen of Conecticut," &c. [Rec. of Comm'rs.] A letter from the General Court of Connecticut to the Commissioners, dated August 30th, 1662, (in "Miscellanies," i. 89) makes no reference to the Charter, but proposes a special meeting of the Comm'rs, in case " any matters needfull to be considered shoul1, at the return of our Wor. Governor and the agents for the Massachusetts, be presented."

The Pattent or Charter was this day on this 8th wherby that
inhabitinc of ye Freemen and Inhabitants to belonging to
them and ye Town purchasors and of ye freesmen made choice
of mr Willis Mr John Talcot and Mr John Allyn to take
the Charter into their Custody in behalfe of ye
freemen who are to have an Oath ministred to them
by the Constable Assembly for ye due[?] Charge of
this trust comitted to them.

Daniel Clark

(Secretary, 1658–1663.)

administered to them by the Generall Assembly, for y^e due discharge of the trust committed to them.

[165] It is enacted and decreed by the Freemen, that y^e Town of Hartford for future shalbe the settled place for the convocation of the Generall Assembly, at all times, vnles it be vpon occasion of epidemicall diseases, sicknes, or ye like.

The Generall Assembly of Assistants and Deputies doe establish all officers in this Collony, both civill and miletary, in their respectiue places and power as formerly, vntill further order be taken.

To ye respectiue Constables :—This Court doth impowre and require you forthwith vpon ye receipt hereof, to gather into yor hands all the corne due from your Towne, to discharge the Countreyes engagem^t for ye Charter. And you are to exercise due care to see that you receaue 2 thirds Wheat and one third Pease, dry & merchantable. And in case any person fayle to pay at ye time that you appoint, that then you destreine any part of ye estate of such person, w^thin doors or without; and ye same to sell at such value as may procure corne to discharge their respectiue rates. And ye Constables are hereby authorized to hire or press any persons, carts, boats or canooes, that may be necessary to carry or transport the Corne from ye severall Townes to ye vessels that are to transport it to N. London. And in case any of the Constables in ye respectiue Townes shall fayle of their duty herein, their estate shalbe destreined to make good what is expected to be discharged by that Constable. And the Deputies in each Towne are desired to excite the Constables to their duty in what is required, and to see that there be receipts taken from ye Pinnace Masters for the whole proportion of Corne for that Towne.

[166] And the Constables are to assigne ye Corne ‖ vnto Mr. James Rogers, Lt Samuel Smith and Ens. Avery, as ye Countreyes Agents to receaue ye Corne, who are desired and appointed to see ye Corne stor'd in ye Warehouse, and also to deliuer it vnto such ship as by order from our Wor^ll Gouernour is to receaue the same, and vpon delivery of ye Corne, to take vp the specialty or Bill from ye Shipmaster, whereby the Countrey or Colony is obliged.

This Court desires Mr. Gould, Mr. Campfield, Mr. Sherman,

or any two of them, to hire vessells to transport the Corne from ye seaside Townes to N: London: and Mr. Wm Wadsworth, Jon: Gilbert, Joseph Fitch, to hire vessels for this Riuer.

And it is ordered, that ye charge of transportation of ye Corne to N: London, shall be discharged out of ye Countreyes Levy the next Spring. And what loss or miscarriage shal happen by shipwrack or other accidts to ye Corne in transport-[ing] shalbe borne by the whole Colony in a Generall way.

This Court doth order and declare, that the Seale* that form-erly was vsed by the Generall Court shall still remaine and be vsed as ye Seale of this Colony vntill ye Court see cause to ye contrary, and the Secretary is to keep ye seale, and to vse it on necessary occasions, for ye Colony.

This Court being informed by C: John Yong and some other Gentlemen of quallity, that ye inhabitants of Southold, ye maior part of them, haue sent up and impowred him to act as their Deputy;† and he as their Agent, tending to submit their [167] persons ‖ and estates vnto this Gouerment, according [to] or Charter; This Court doth owne and accept them, and shalbe ready to affoard them protection as occasion shall re-quire: and doe advise the said Inhabitants to repair to South and East Hampton, to ye Authority there setled by this Court, in case of any necessary occasion, to require the assistanc of Authority. And this Court doth hereby eccept and declare C: John Yong to be a freeman of this Corporatn and doe grant him commission to act in ye Plantation of Southold as need requires, according to his commission. And this Court doth order ye Inhabitants of Southold to meet together, to chuse a Constable for that Towne; and C: Jo: Yong is authorized to administer oath to ye said Constable, for ye due execution of

---

* A fac-simile of this Seal, (from an impression on wax, in the office of the Secretary of State,) is given on the title page of this volume.

† The letter from Southold, presented at this Session of the Court, is as follows: "Southhold, October 4: 1662. Haueing notice from Mr. Willis of Conetticutt Jurisdiction, Long Island comes within yt pattint, and allsoe yt the Court is to be held att Hartford, and thither we ar desired by Mr. Willis to send oure Deputies, from these townes of Long Island: we thearfore, of Southold, whose names are vnderwritten, doe desire, and haue appoynted C. John Youngs, to be owre Deputy; and doe hearby giue him full powre to speake and act in oure behalph, as occasion shall serue." Signed by Thomas More, John Tooker, John Payne, John Budd, and twenty eight others. [Towns & Lands, Vol. i. No. 12.]

his office. And we doe advice and order Capt Yong to see that ye Minister be duely paid his meet and competent maintenance.

Severall inhabitants of Guilford tendring themselues their p^{r}sons and estates vnder the Gouerment and Protection of this Colony, This Court doth declare that they doe accept and owne them as members of this Colony, and shalbe ready to affoard what protection is necessary. And this Court doth advise the said persons to carry peaceably and religiously in their places towards the rest of ye Inhabit^{ts}, that yet haue not submitted in like manner. And also to pay their iust dues vnto ye Minister of their Towne; and also all publique charges due to this day.

This Court doth order and hereby declare all ye Lawes and orders of this Colony to stand in full force and vertue, vnles any be cross to ye Tenour of o^r Charter.

[168] This Court doth order L^t Jo: Allyn to shew Capt Varlet* the Charter granted to this Colony, and to informe him that it is desired by the Court that the Honorable Lord Stevesant would not in any wise incumb^r or molest his Maties subjects comprehended wthin ye extent of our Pattent, by any impositions, that therby more then probable inconveniences may be p^{r}vented.†

This Assembly doth hereby declare and informed the Inhabitants of Westchester, that that Plantation is included in y^e

---

* Capt. Nicholas Varlet (or Varleth,) was an officer in the service of the Dutch W. I. Company, and a brother-in-law to Gov. Stuyvesant. His father, Caspar Varlet, resided at Hartford, (where he died, in 1663.) A sister, Judith Varlet, was afterwards married to Nicholas Bayard, the son of Gov. Stuyvesant's sister. [Rec. of Court of Mag., iii. 2, 4; Rec. of Hoogh Straat church, in N. Y. Hist. Coll., New Series, I. 397.]

† Capt. Varlet had presented to the General Court, a letter from Gov. Stuyvesant (dated Oct. 13th [N. S.] 1662) in which complaint was made that " one John Yonge," professing to act under authority from Connecticut, " had vndertaken (as by his seditious letters may appeare,) to diverte and revoke the English towns in this province, vnder the protection of the high and mighty Lords the Estaats Generall of the Vnited Belgick Provinces & in the jurisdiction of the Right Honnourable Lords of the W. India Compagnie settled, of their oath & due obedience vnto vs, theire lawfull Governour." Gov. S. declares that these procedings of Capt. Young, if authorized or approved by the government of Connecticut, would be regarded as " an absolute breatch and a nullification of the agreement about the limits, Anno 1650," and would give just ground to the States General and the W. India Company " to demand, and by such meanes as they in wisdom shal thincke meete, to recover al that trackt of land between Greenwich and the Fresh River," to which they claimed a right by prior purchase and possession. He requests the General Court to return, by the bearer, their " categorical answer over & aboue the aforementioned John Yongs seditious doings." [Colonial Boundaries, Vol. ii. No. 1.]

bounds of our Charter granted to this Collony of Conecticut. And as it hath pleased his Matie thus to dispose of them, soe we conceaue it most conduceable to their tranquillity soe to demeane in all things as may declare and manifest their readines to subiect to his Royall will and pleasure herein.

The next sett Gen:ll Assembly is to be obserued on ye 2d Thursday in May.

This Court doth hereby declare their acceptanc of ye Plantations of Stanford and Greenwich vnd^r this Gouerment vpon ye same terms and provisions as are directed and declared to ye Inhabitants of Guilford. And that each of those Plantat[ions] haue a Constable chosen and sworne.

Richard Vowles is made free of this Corporation, and sworne to the office of a Constable for and within ye Plantat^n of Greenwich, for ye yeare ensueing, and vntill a new be sworne.

Mr. Mathew Allyn, Mr. Willys, Mr. Stone and Mr. Hooker are chosen a Comittee to goe downe to N. Hauen to treat wth ye Gent: and others of o^r lo: freinds there, according to such instructions as shalbe directed to ye said Comittee by this Court.

[169] Severall of the inhabitants at Southold accepted to be made free of this Colony, vnles any thing appeare to interrupt the same; Mr. Wels, Thomas Terrey, Philemon Dickerson, Goodm̄ Purrier, Goodm̄ Windes, Barnabas Horton, Josph Horton, Lt Glouer, Thomas Moor Senr, Goodm̄ Conclin, Goodm̄ Cory, Goodm̄ Reeues, Goodm̄ Mapes, John Conclin Junr, Jo: Paine, Rich^rd Browne, Joseph Yongs Senr, Joseph Yongs Junr, Jer: Vayle, Jo: Curwin, Richard Terrey, Mr. Elton, Tho: Brush, John Bud, Mr. Tucker.

Mr. Campfield, Mr. Gould, Mr. Sherman, are hereby appointed to keep a Court at Fairfield, when they see cause, for issueing such controuersies as they are capeable of, according to the tenour of our Charter. Stanford, Greenwich and Westchester haue liberty to improue the help of ye Court at Fairfield, to issue controuersies that may arise among them for future.

Mr. Willm Pitkin is desired and appointed as Attourney for ye Gener^ll Court, to p^rsecute Thomas Ford Senr, John Deming Senr, Mrs Lattimore and Thomas Hurlbut, at ye P^rticuler Court to be held at Hartford on Wednesday next.

Persons admitted to be Freemen, by this Court;—Mr. Sam:ll Talcot, Will:m Pitkins, Nathan:ll Goodwin, Mr. Tho: Pell, John Olmstead & John Clarke Jun:r.

Richard Vowles is admitted freeman and sworne to y:e office of a Constable for and within the Plantation of Greenwich, for y:e yeare ensuinge and vntill a new be sworne.

This Court doth hereby declare the free remission of such transgressions of the Lawes of this Colony as haue bene committed by Monsieur Varlet by retaileing liquors in his life time.

This Assembly doth order, that for y:e future, such as desire to be admitted freemen of this Corporation shal p:rsent themselues with a certificate vnder y:e hands of y:e maior part [170] of the Townesmen where they liue, that they are p:rsons of civill, peaceable and honest conversation, and that they attained the age of twenty one yeares and haue 20*l*. estate, besides their person, in the List of estate; and that such persons, soe quallified to y:e Courts approbation, shalbe p:rsented at October Court yearly, or some adiourned Court, and admitted after y:e Election at y:e Assembly in May. And in case any freeman shal walke scandalously or commit any scandalous offence, and be legally convicted thereof, he shalbe disfranchized by any of o:r civill Courts.

This Court doth repeale the late order wherby the Troopers salery was prohibited and taken of.

Robert Vsher is ordered to be sworne to y:e office of a Constable in Stanford, for y:e yeare ensueing, and vntil a new be chosen. Mr. Campfield is to giue him his oath.

It is ordered, that y:e Inhabitants at Mistick and Paukatuck shal from henceforth forbeare to exercise authority by vertue of commissions from any other Colony;* and that in case of any differences that may arise, they repaire to o:r Wor:ll Dep: Gouerno:r for help; and that they chuse a Constable, for the yeare ensueing; and y:e said Constable to repaire to o:r Wor:ll Dep: Go: for his oath. And they [*are*] required to pay vnto Mr. James Rogers, L:t Sam:ll Smith and Ens: Avery, for and in behalf of the charge of o:r Charter, the sum of Twenty pounds, as their Townes proportion, two thirds in wheat, at 4*s*., one third

---

* See Appendix, No. IV.

in pease, at 3s., by yᵉ last of Novembʳ next. The Court orders Lᵗ John Allyn to send a Warrant to Thomas Stanton in yᵉ Courts name, to attend this ordʳ, and if he refuse, Peter Blachford is to gather the rate and destrein according to former order.

[171] C. John Yong is invested wᵗʰ yᵉ power of a Perticuler Magestrate, within yᵉ Plantatⁿ of Southhold, and likewise he is authorizd to sit in Court to assist the Magestrates of South and East Hampton.

It is ordered, that all yᵉ Plantations that shalbe enterteined and embraced vnder this Gouerment, shal according to yᵉ Courts appointment pay their due proportion of yᵉ charge expended in procuring oʳ Charter.

This Court orders yᵉ Secretary to send to yᵉ Plantations of Huntington, Setauk, Oister Bay, that they choose Constables in their respectiue Townes, and to take their oaths, administred to them by Capᵗ Yong for the discharge of their respectiue offices; Thomas Wicks, at Huntington, John Ketchum, at Setauk, Mr. Rigebell, at Oister Bay.

It is ordered, that all yᵉ Plantations, on yᵉ Island as well as on yᵉ maine, shal attend yᵉ established Law of this Colony for yᵉ rule of Rateing, vnles they mutually agree to yᵉ contrary.

C. Yong is desired to giue notice to C: Silvester and Lᵗ Gardner, wᵗʰ yᵉ other Plantations on yᵉ Island, that they attend the Generall Assembly on yᵉ 2d Thursday in May next, to doe their duty to yᵉ Court.

This Court appoints that Wednesday come fortnight be set apart, throwout this Colony, for a solemne day of Thanksgiueing for yᵉ mercies yᵗ God hath extended to this Colony yᵉ yeare past, and pʳticulerly for yᵉ good success God hath giuen to yᵉ indeauours of oʳ Honᵈ Gouernoʳ in obteineing oʳ Charter of his Maiestie oʳ Soveraigne; as also for his gratious answer of oʳ prayʳ in yᵉ late draught, in sending raine; and for abatement of yᵉ sicknes; and for yᵉ hopes we haue of settlement in yᵉ waies of peace and righteousnes.

This Court declares, that Hartford Traine Band shal haue yᵉ prehemenence of all yᵉ Companies in this Colony; And Windsor, the 2d; Wethersfield, the 3d; Then Farmington. This to stand vntill the Court order otherwise.

[172] This Court ordereth, that there shalbe free trade in all places in this Colony. And all former ord^rs imposeing Customes, are hereby repealed.

This Court doth declare these persons hereaft^r named, John Green, Richard Hardey, Joseph Mead, Richard Webb, Joseph Theed, Peter Pheries, to be freemen of this Colony; and Mr. Gould is authorized to giue them ye oath of freedom, at ye next Court in Fairfield.

This Court doth order, that Lt Seely shal haue Fifteen pounds paid to him out of the Publ: Treasurie, & the Countrey house set into repair at Sea Brook, and he to liue in ye house and to take care of ye Amunition.

This Court doth order, y^t a Levy of a penny p^r pound shalbe raised vpon ye estate of ye Colony, and to be paid in wheat, pease, Indian corn or porke, at currant price.

This Court grants Sea Brooke Inhabitants liberty to set vp a Ferrey at Tilleyes Point, and to take 12d. for a man & horse, and 6d. for a single person.

This Court orders each Town in this Colony to chuse an able Inhabitant to ye office of a Pack^r, to pack and repack all such meat as is sent forth of ye Townes, who shalbe deposed on oath to ye faithfull p^rformance of their respectiue offices; wch oath may be administred by any one Magestrate or Comissioner. He shall likewise haue a Brand or Seale, wth these letters, C: R:, wherwith he shall marke each Barrel y^t he packs, and for his paines he is to haue 8d. p^r Barrell.

The Treasurer is required to cause the severall Townes to levell or ballance what is behind of their Levies, or require the fines of ye Constables, and destreine it of them by the Marshall.

Mr. Willys and Mr. Wadsworth are appointed to audit the Treasurers Accounts.

This Court grants to Ens: Olmstead, of Hartford, a farme of 300 acres of vpland and 40 acr^s of meadow, if it be to be had at 20 Miles Riuer, in y^e way to Moheag & N: London.

This Court is adjourned vntil y^e 2d Wednesday in March, vnles o^r Worp^ll Go: return and see cause to call the Assembly sooner.

[173] AT A GEN[ll] ASSEMBLY HELD AT HARTFORD, MARCH
11, 16$\frac{62}{63}$.

Dep: Gou[r]: Major Mason.
Assistants:
Mr. Willys,   Mr. Woolcot,
Mr. Math: Allyn,   Mr. Clark, et *Sec[r]*.
Mr. Treat,   Mr. Jo: Allyn.
Mr. Talcot,

Deputies: Will[m] Wadsworth, Joseph Fitch, Edward Griswold, Josias Hull, John Nott, Sam[ll] Boreman, James Rogers, L[t] Sam[ll] Smith, Thomas Tracy, Hugh Calkin, Antho: Howkins, Thomas Judd, Nathaneel White.

It is ordered by this Court, that after y[e] publication hereof, there shalbe free liberty of transporteinge Corne out of this Riuer, and the former restreint is hereby repealed.

It is ordered, that each Towne in this Col: shal pay for y[e] transportation of their proportion of the Pattent Rate, to N: London. Each Town is to discharge the costs of their owne Corne.

Cap[t] Jn[o] Talcot, Mr. Jo: Allyn and Thomas Tracy are appointed to audit the accounts of James Rogers and L[t] Smith, respecting the Pattent Corne.

This Court haueing duely considered the valuation of y[e] estate of N: London, apprized by Cary Latham and William Douglas, doe judge, that they haue not attended any rule of Righteousnes in their worke, but haue acted very corruptly therein, and therfore doe order the Treasurer that he send forth his Warrant to y[e] Constable of N: London, to levy Four pounds vpon y[e] estate of Cary Latham, and Two pounds vpon Mr. Douglas his estate, as a fine for their corupt and deceatfull actings therein, and fourty shillings more vpon Lathams estate, for neglecting to meet wth y[e] Com[rs] on y[e] Riuer, according to order; w[ch] fines shalbe to y[e] publ: Treasury. And they doe further order the Treasurer to send forth his Warrant to y[e] Constable of N: London, to levy a Rate of a penny p[r] pound vpon Eight thousand, fiue hundred pound estate, w[ch] y[y] judge to be at least y[e] estate of N: London. And doe desire the said Towne of N: London to be more carefull in their choyce of List makers, for the future.

It is ordered, that each Miller in this Collony, or owner of Mill, shalbe allowed for grinding of each Bushell of Indian Corne, a twelf part, and of other graines, a sixteenth part; provided that this order shal noe way preiudice or nullify any agreem^t made in any Towne, respecting grinding.

[174] This Court doth herby declare, that the Treasurer shall not allow of the account p^rsented by ye Constables at Stratford, for searcheing for the Collonels, wch sum amounts to 6*l*. 17*s*. 01*d*. as ye Account specifieth.

This Court hath granted vnto John Gilbert, one acre and half of land lying between the land of Capt Richard Lord and ye land of C. John Cullick; and also one acre of land, more or less, lying at ye landing place on the Rivulet; both parcels being or lying in ye South meadow at Hartford. And the Court doth order John Gilbert to pay vnto the Treasurer, for ye Countreyes vse, Ten pounds, for and in consideration of the two acres and halfe of land granted him by this Court.

This Court, vnderstanding that there is much inconvenience doth yearly ensue vpon the Constables defects in not gathering the Countrey Levies and makeing payments according to the Treasurers order, vnder pretence of a liberty to make vp their accounts by the Court, in Octob^r yearly, Doe therefore order, that the Constables, for the future, in the respectiue Plantations, shal gather their proportion of the Countrey rate and make payment therof, according to order, by the Quarter Court in June in each yeare, vpon the penalty of Fourty shillings fine for every defect herein, and they are also ordered to make vp their accounts wth ye Treasurer according to former order, by October Court yearly, vpon penalty of 40*s*. fine for every defect herein. And the Treasurer is hereby authorized to send forth his Warrant to destreine the estates of the respectiue Constables, for the payment of the fines imposed for the breach of this order.

The conveyance of nine miles square made by Onkos wth other Indians, to Norwich Plantation, is ordered to be recorded, with this proviso, that it shal not preiudice any former grant to o^r Wor^ll Gouerno^r or others.

Thomas Tracy and Lt Sam^ll Smith giue oath in Court, in referenc to laying out the bounds of ye Town of New London, that from ye end of ye eight miles, the measurer run a west line to yᵉ Riuer and there they markt a tree agaynst the north end of Vnkos his fort.

[175] In answer to yᵉ request of John Bissel Junʳ, the Court doth impower the Assistants at Windsor to agree for and with another ferryman to keep the Countrey Ferry, and when they haue pʳvided a sufficient man, and not before, this Court doth release John Bissell of his engagment for keeping the Ferrey.

This Court by their vote gaue liberty to Mr. Pitkin to be a Councelour to plead for Thomas Burnam in his appeale to this Court. They also ordered Mr. Pitkins to giue in al the cheif heads of his plea before he begins to plead vpon the said appeale.

Mr. Pitkins affirmes in Court, if he haue not liberty to make new plea besides what were made in the Perticuler Court, he wil throw vp the case and make noe more plea in it. Mr. Pitkins recals his words, and yᵉ Court passeth them by and fully remits them.

This Court hereby declareth their approbation and confirmation of the purchase of the Town of Farmington, of Fifteen acres of meadow of Thomas Wels Esqʳ, deceased, bounded by the Riuer north, Mr. Newton east, Mr. Howker and John Root Senʳ, southwest.

In reference to Thomas Burnams appeale, the Court doth iudge, that yᵉ Court of Magestrates had sufficient ground to call yᵉ said Burnam to account for his actings in those matters obiected agaynst him; and doe, secondly, approue of the Pʳticuler Courts examination of Thomas Burnam, in referenc to those things charged agaynst him before his accusation was stated agaynst him in Court. 3ly. This Court doth approue of the manner of yᵉ Perticuler Courts proceeding wᵗʰ Thomas Burnam, after his accusation was stated, as wel as before. 4. Respecting the sentence itself, passed vpon Thomas Burnam by the Pʳticuler Court, this Assembly doth approue of the sentence of the said Court and see noe cause to make any alteration thereof.

This Court doth approue of what yᵉ Magestrates haue done formerly, vpon a fame or report of misdemeanour, in calling the persons suspected of delinquency before them, and in examining the case and testimonies, and doe hereby authorize the respectiue Assistants of this Colony, for the future, vpon rumours and fames, to act as aforesaid, and in case the delin-

[176] quency appear ‖ sufficiently proued, they may pass to sentence, according to Law.

It is ordered by this Court, that in case any person in this Colony shalbe convicted and sentenced by the P^rticuler Court for a misdemeano^r, and shal enter an appeale therein to ye Generall Court, and by the judgment of ye said Gen^{ll} Court the said appeale be found to be causeles, the person appealing as aforesaid shal pay Fiue pounds to ye Publ: Treasury. And noe person, in case of delinquency of this nature, shal haue liberty of an Atturney to mannadge his case in any of o^r civil courts.

This Court doth vpon due consideration repeale the order remitting Customes for Wines, Liquors etc., and doe establish the former order requireing the said Customes.

This Court ord^{rs}, that Mr. Steels Bill of 15*l*. baring date 30th of May, 1654, be deliuered vp to ye ouerseers of Thomas Wells Esqr deceased, for ye vse of Mr. Fish, they paying vnto Anthony Howkins the sum of Twelue pounds, he haueing proued in Court a promis of Mr. Wels to ad to the said Howkins his wiues portion, in case her first husband Thomas Thomson had any estate come from England, and he hath made appeare that the said Thompson had to ye value of 30*l*. come from England since this engagement.

This Court doth hereby impower Mr. Obadiah Bruen to administer the oath of a Constable to those y^t are chosen Constables for the Township of N: London for this yeare ensueing.

This Court doth recomend it to ye consideration of the Towne of Hartford, that they would speedily consider of some way to ease the Widdow Lord of her comon fence, it appearing to them y^t she is burthened by mainteineing it hitherto.

Thomas Bull, Thomas Bunc and James Steel are to consid^r of her greivance and report their considerations to ye Court in May next.

This Court doth grant vnto John Adams, 300 acres of land, at ye place where his father Adams took vp land in ye way to N: London, whereof thirty acres of meadow ioyneing to his father or Nicholas Olmsted. He relinquisheth his right at Fairfield.

This Court grants the bounds of Middletown to extend four miles to ye South from ye meeting house, and fiue miles from yᵉ said house, westward; three miles from yᵉ Great Riuer, eastward.

[177] This Court hath voted and desired the Dep: Gouernor, Mr. Math: Allyn, Capᵗ John Talcot and Lᵗ Jo: Allyn, and for a reserue to yᵉ Maior, Mr. Willys, as a Comittee to goe downe to N: Hauen, to treat wᵗʰ oʳ Honoʳᵈ and Lo: freinds about setling their vnion and incorporation wᵗʰ this Colony of Conect: And in case the Comittee cannot effect an vnion, according to instructions giuen them by the Court, that then they indeauour to settle a peace in the Plantations vntil such time as they and we may be in a further capacity of issueing this difference, and to act in referenc herevnto as they iudge most meet.

William Wadsworth and John Deming Senʳ are allowed pʳ the Court, fiue pounds a peice for their care and paines in ouersight of Mr. Wels his estate.

The Magestrates ordʳ Samˡˡ Boreman to deliuer the little Bible and a paper book, vnto Amos Williams, wᶜʰ was giuen to him by his mother, and that he and Willᵐ Goodrich distribute the estate to yᵉ Creditors.

This Court doth grant liberty to Samˡˡ Marshall to sell liquors by retaile, but not to suffer any liquors to be drunk in his house.

It is ordered, that in case the Comittee doe not issue an agreemᵗ wᵗʰ N. Hauen Gent: according to their instructions, before their returne, that then all propositions and instructions from yᵉ Court, respecting vnion wᵗʰ that people, are void and of none effect.

This Court allowes vnto Mr. Rosseter, Twenty pounds, in reference to openinge Kellies child, and his paynes to visit the Dep: Gouernoʳ, and his paynes in visiting and administring to Mr. Talcot. Of this Twenty pounds, he hath already receaued 11*l*. 1*s*. 4*d*. He is to make noe further demands of any pʳticuler pʳsons.

It is ordered by this Court, that the Customasters formerly established by the Generall Court in the respectiue Townes shal attend the worke formerly appoynted to them by order of the Court, and that each Custome master shal giue an account at October Court yearly to yᵉ Treasurer, of what Customes they receaue, and if any Custome master shal neglect to giue an account as aforesaid, he shal pay 40*s*. for every such neglect, wch the Treasurer, shal by Warrant destreine from ye delinquent.

[178] This Court doth order that in ye vacancy of the sitting of the Generall Court, there shalbe a Councill, consisting of the Assistants here on the Riuer, or such as can convene, to ye number of fiue at least, to act in emerg^t occasions that concerne ye welfare of this Colony. And hereby doe authorize the said Councill to act in all necessary concernments, both miletary and civill, according as the p^{r}sent exegents require and call for.

Mr. Willys and Willm Wadsworth are appointed to be a Comittee to order and dispose all matters to issue the busines about the Pattent Rate, and to order the repaying of Wheat borrowed from severall p^{r}sons for the Countreys vse.

This Court doth disallow of Sea Brook Constables Acco^t of charges for witnesses respecting Jennings, and doe not see cause to allow the witnesses pay for their time and travaile, nor to any other vpon such accounts for ye future.

This Court doth order the Marshall to goe downe to Sea Brook, and to destrein the sum of Fifty pounds of the estate of Reynold Marvin, for y^t wch ye Countrey should haue receaued of the said Reynold for horses that he was ordered to seek vp to be sold, and for neglect in attending their ord^r herein. And respecting a mare wth the increase, that Robt Chapman hath, belonging to ye Countrey, the Marshal is ordered to seize on her, wth ye increase, or in want of her, soe much of Chapmans estate, if he giue not an account of the sale of ye mare according to ye Treasurers order. And what estate ye Marshall doth receaue or destrein, he hath power either to bring it vp, or to order prudently that it may be paid to ye Treasurer or his order.

The Town of N: London is to discharge the acco^t of Thomas Tracy, at Georg Tongs, for w^t he expended in laying out N: London bounds.

This Court doth appoint Capt: Nubery, Edward Griswold and John Moore to be as a Comittee, and hereby they are impowred to lay out all those lands that are yet vndevided at Mussaco, to such inhabitants in Windsor as desire and need it.

[179] This Court doth declare, that it is theire mind that the

Marshal haue allowed him for every mile he goeth to serue an execution or attachm^t, four pence forward and fourepence homeward. And this they iudge to be the intent of the former order respecting the Marshals fees.

This Court vnd^rstanding that the hand of God is gone out agaynst the people at New Netherlands, by pestilentiall infections, doe therfore prohibit all persons for comeing from any of those infectious places into this Colony and amongst o^r people, vntil ye Assistants are informed and satisfied that the distemp^r is allayed; and that whoeuer breaks this order shal pay Fiue pound fine to ye publ: Treasury. And if any person shal bring a vessell from thenc and land their men or goods in any harbour in this Colony, the Master of ye vessell shal forfeit Ten pounds to ye Publ: Treasury. And ye Constables in each Town are hereby required and authorized to distrein the fines of such as transgress this order. And whoeuer of o^r people shal goe aboard any such vessell he or she shal pay fiue pounds to ye Treasury for euery such offenc. The Constables in each Town are to informe the Masters of vessels, of this order.

These vnd^rwritten are voted to be put to nomination at ye next Court of Election, in May; Mr. Campfield, Edward Griswold, Mr. Bond.

This Court doth establish and ratifie the former order sent out by the Assistants respecting the Indians, in regard of ye infection of ye Pox.

---

[180] At a Generall Assembly of Election, held at Hartford, May 14, 1663.*

Magistrates elected:

John Winthrop Esqr, Gouern^r.

John Mason Esqr, Dep: Gou^r.

Mr. Mathew Allyn,	Mr. Dan^ll Clarke, *et Sec^ry,*
Mr. Sam^ll Willys,	Mr. John Allyn,
Mr. Nathan: Gould,	Mr. Baker,
Mr. Rich: Treat,	Mr. Shermon,

---

* The record of this and the subsequent sessions, as far as published in this Volume, are in the hand writing of Mr. John Allyn.

Capt Thomas Toppin,   Mr. Howell,
Capt John Talcot, *et Treasurer.*   Mr. Thirstan Rayner.
Mr. Woolcott,

The freemen vote that the Generall Assembly shall choose Comissioners for this Corporation for the year ensuing.

Deputies :

Mr. Wadsworth,	Jehue Burr,	James Rogers,
Mr. Fitch,	Cornelius Hull,	James Morgan,
Capt Nubery,	Richard Olmsteed,	Hugh Caulkin,
L^{nt} Walter Fyler,	John Gregory,	Thomas Tracy,
John Nott,	John Clarke,	Joshua Barnes,
Sam^{ll} Boreman,	Robert Chapman,	Philip Groues,
Anthony Howkins,	Robert Warner,	Joseph Judson,
Thomas Judd,	Nath: White,	

This Court doe make choice of o^r Honoured Gouernour & Capt John Tallcott to be Comissioners for this Colony, for the year ensueing, and L^{nt} John Allyn is chosen as a reserue to Capt John Tallcott, and ye Secret^{r}y Mr. Dan^{ll} Clarke to be a reserue to o^r Honoured Gouernour, to attend that seruice, if the Comissioners by accident faile of goeing.

This Court being sencible of the great charge that this Colony is at, by the Perticuler Courts attending the tryall and issueing of those differences and actions as are presented to their consideration, doe therefore order, that for the future, whateuer actions are comenced to be tryed by a Jury, and are not wthdrawn one day at least before the Court, there shall be payd for euery such action six shillings, (besides what is due by order, to the Secret^{r}y & Jury,) for the use and improuement of the Court that tries the cases, for the discharge whereof the plaintife shall procure a receipt under the hand of that ordinary keeper or inhabitant that prouides for the Court, which receipt shall be deliuered unto ye Secretary or Recorder of the Court, wherby the Court may be sattisfyed that they haue credit giuen for so much wth the sayd ordinary keeper. And there shall be in like manner, two shillings allowed for each action that is to be issued by the Magistrates or Commissioners. And likewise, whateuer fine is imposed by any Court for delinquency in any person, there shalbe so much of the fine abated from the Publique [181] Treasurie as may fully compleat the discharge || of the

Courts expences, wth the ordinary keeper or inhabitant that prouides for them.

There being complaint made to this Court of the unsetled state of the plantation of Sowth-hold, by the ill cariage of seuerall persons there, This Court haue therefore desired and appoynted the Worp^ll Mr. Mathew Allyn and Mr. Willys, to goe to Long Island, to tak in assistance of the Magistrates at Long Island, in setleing affayres at Sowth-hold, and in examining the case respecting Mr. Wells his reuolt since he took oath to this Gouerment; and any other matters, either in setleing the peace of that Plantation or proceding against such as misdemeane themselues, according to their deserts.

Mr. Bond is chosen Comissioner by this Court, and he is hereby inuested wth magistraticall power on the Island.

It is ordered, that three pownds be allowed to the three Plantations of Stratford, Fayrefeild and Norwalke, towards the charge of the transportation of their Corne to New London, which sume shall be allowed out of the next Country Rate, and that the rest of the charge for those Townes be payd by the sayd Townes according to order of Court in March last, which is to be aded to the proportion of the country rate imposed upon those three Townes.

This Court doth order, that the charge of keeping Court since March, 61-62, w^thin the plantations of Fayrfeild, Stratford and Norwalke, which remaines yet to be sattisfyed for, It shall be borne by the Colony in a generall way. The cost of the last Court held at Stratford is comprized in this order. And this Court doth order and hereby graunt, that there shall be liberty to keep Court at Fayrfeild, for the plantations on the seaside, once a year, unles exterordinary occation call for one more in the year. The time of their sett Court is the first Wedensday in Nouember yearly.

This Court doe order & appoynt Mr. Bruen, Mr. Chapman and John Smith, of New London, a Committee to hear and determine the differences betwixt the Indians at Niantick and the English, respecting burning their fence, or any other complaints presented to them respecting those Indians.

This Court doth impower Mr. Toppin, Mr. Gould, Mr. Shermon and Mr. Howell as a Comittee to hear and consider the busines respecting Hamonossitt, and to make reporte of their considerations to yᵉ Court; and likewise the case of the horss in Nicholas Clarkes hand is left according to the premises to the consideration of the sayd Comittee.

This Court doth determine that Jonathan Gilberds Butt of Wine, seazed for the Countrey, to be according to the lawe established forfeited to the Countrey.

This Court doth establish Jeramie Adams to be Custome Master for Hartford, and the liberty graunted unto Jonathan Gilbert by the Perticuler Court, is repealed, respecting customeing his owne wines, liquers, &c.

Whereas this Court, upon the request of Henry Walkely, Attourney to James Wakely, to release the sayd Henry from [182] attending the order ‖ of the Court respecting the sayd estate, these are to declare that this Court doth release the sayd Henry from attending the sayd order, and haue returned to him the letter of attourney granted unto him from James Walkely, and the estate remaines to be ordered according as the Perticuler Court haue prouided.

This Court doth determine that the land at Homonoscitt doth not of right belong unto the Towne of Seabroke.

This Court doth remitt yᵉ Butt of Wine to Jonathan Gilbert that was seized on of his, in behalfe of yᵉ Countrey, & the Marshall doth engage to pay the Custome & to pay 20s. towards yᵉ expence that hath been occasioned therby to yᵉ Countrey.

Wm. Edwards chargeth Mr. Daniell Clerk, for breach of his oath, unfaithfullnesse in yᵉ great trust committed to him by the freemen of this Corporation, to the dishonour of God, infringment of yᵉ royall perogatiue of our Soueraign Lord the King, contempt of yᵉ authority established in this Corporation, & abuse of the members of yᵉ same, to such censure as he shall make appeare according to the lawes established in this Corporation.

Mr. Anthony Hawkins is chosen Commissioner for yᵉ Towne of Farmington, and sworn in Court; Capt Seely is chosen Commissioner for yᵉ Town of Huntington and sworn in Court; and also, Mr. Jonas Wood is chosen a Commissioner for the said Towne, and Capt Seely is to giue him his oath.

Capt John Young is chosen Commissioner for the Town of Southhold, and sworne in Court; and Barnabas Horton is also chosen a Commissioner for Southhold, and Capt Young is to administer the oath unto him.

This Court hath chosen Mr. Bruen and John Smith, Commissioners for ye Town of New London, and the Worship^ll Major Mason is by this Court requested to administer the Commissioners oath unto them.

These may sertify that we Richard Olmstead and Joseph Judson and John Banks, being appoynted by the Generall Court at Hartford to run the line between Stratford and Fairefeild, we accordingly haue begun at the usuall place agreed upon by ye two Townes, and haue run almost two poynts from the North poynt towards the Norwest, and run and measured to the extent of twelue miles, and also haue run the due cross line at the end, which line runs on the South side of a spruse swamp commonly called Monhantik, and so ends at the mouth of ye Brook commonly called by the English the half way Brook, being aboue Pagasitt. Witnesse our hands, this 22 of Nouember, 1662. Richard Olmstead, Joseph Judson,
Joseph Banks.

This was ordered by the Court to be recorded in the Records of the Court.

This Court orders, that Dorathy Lord shall maintaine so much fence (and no more) as doth belong to that proportion of meadow as was graunted to her and her husband by graunt from ye Towne of Hartford.

This Court repeals the order prohibiting commerce wth the people in or about the Manhatoes.

[183] The differences at Southhampton about the land at Quaganantick, is referred to the determination of the Court in May next, and they are to improue the mowing land as formerly, till the case be issued.

This Court orders, that no person in this Colony shall buy, hire or receiue as a gift or mortgage, any parcel of land or lands of any Indian or Indians, for the future, except he doe buy or receiue the same for the use of the Colony or the benefitt of some Towne, with the allowance of the Court.

This Court doth inuest Capt John Young and the rest of the Commissioners on the Island, with Magistraticall power upon the Island.

This Court doth order, that all that are Freemen upong Long Island, and haue not taken the oath of a Freeman, shall haue the oath of a Freeman administred to them by the Magistrates and Commissioners of the Island, or any two of them.

This Court haueing heard and considered the controuersie between Leiu^t Rob: Sealy and the Town of Stratford, doe judge that the Towne of Stratford shall pay unto the said Sealy 25l. in some currant pay, and he to make ouer all his right and title in the lands there, to the said Towne, whether his right there be frō gift of the Towne or Indians or any other wayes; and this to be a finall issue of the controuersie, each man bearing his owne charge.

This Court, haueing presented to their consideration the turbelent carriage of Rich: Latten, doe order, that in case the said Latten do not depart the Towne of Huntington by October next, he shall be summoned to appear to answer the complaint of the said Towne, at October Court ; and the Commissioners are to take the testimonyes that concern the complaint, and send them up wth the said Latten to the Court.

The Court chose Mr. Willys, Mr. Gould, Capt Tallcott and Capt Young as a Comitte to consider and draw up there thoughts and apprehensions conserning the setlement of Westchester & Stanford, and make return to the Court.

This Court doth declare, that notwithstanding the uncomfortable debates that haue been respecting the Major, that the Major stands clear and is in a fitt posture to carry on the affaires of the Court, which this Court doth desire and request him forthwith to attend, according as his place requires.

It is ordered by this Court, that for ye future, each Plantation hath hereby liberty to send their Deputyes to the Generall Assemblies in May and October, according to the tennour of the Charter, and they are not to expect any farther notice to minde them of their liberty herein, and the Deputies are to bring sertificates with them from the Constables, to manifest their choyce.

It is ordered by this Court, that the Constables in each Plantation are hereby impowred to charge the watch and ward in the respectiue plantations, in the name of the authority here establisht, duely to attend there watch and ward, by walkeing in such places where they may best discouer danger by the approach of an enemy or by fire, which if they do discouer, they are to giue notice thereof by fireing their guns and crying Fire, Fire, or Arm, Arm. And in case they meet with any persons walking in the streets unseasonably, they are to examine them, and in case they cannot giue a good accompt of their occasions, they are to returne them to the Constable, who is to require them to appeare before a Magistrate or some Assistant, to giue an accompt of their unseasonable walking.

[184] It is also ordered, that the watchmen shall duely attend to receiue their charge, at the Constables, in the evening by the shutting in of the day light, and they are not to leaue their watch before the break of the day, and whosoeuer shall be found guilty of the breach of this order shall forfeit 1s. for euery defect herein.

This Court ordered that Wm. Waller, as Renol Maruens agent, should be allowed one quarter part of this bill of 50l. as his part of the horses, and Mathew Griswold is not to trouble Wm. Waller or Renold Maruen, for any part of those horses for which the bill is made.

The petition of Mrs. Cullicke was this day read; and the Court voted, that they did not see cause to make any abatement of ye said bill, according as she petitioned.*

This Court appoynted Wm. Wadsworth, Ens: Auery, L^{nt} Smith, as a Committe to veiw the lands at Homonoscitt, and if they judg it be nott fitt for a plantation, and will not be uery prejudiciall to Saybrook, then they are to lay it out to Mr. Math: Allyn, Capt Tallcott, John Allyn, Mr. Willis, and according to the graunt of the Court; but if it be prejudiciall to Saybrook, they are to lay out what they judge right to the Towne of Saybrook and the rest to Mr. Math: Allyn, Capt Tallcott, John Allyn, Mr. Willys, Mr. Joseph Haynes or Mr. Daniell Clerk, according as the Court shall determine, as farr as it will go, according to their graunts, ye 1st graunt to be layd out 1st, and so successiuely; and what any two of this Committe agree to, shall be a finall issue of the case. The time of meeting and attending this seruice is to be appoynted by Saybrook and the Gent: concerned, sometime in June next.

---

* See Appendix, No. XI.

The Court in answer to the request of Thomas Forde, which was to haue some allowance in respect of his land sold to Mr. Fitch, which the said Forde forfeited to the Countrey by mortgage, they graunted him the sume of thirty pownds.

This Court appoynted Mr. Wyllys and   as a Comittee to draw up a letter and send it to the Generall Court of the Massachusetts, about Paukatuck, as an answer to the letter sent to us from their Councill.*

The Court haueing considered the complaint of Wm. Edwards against Mr. Clark, and hauing seriously considered the case, do find him so far falty as to put him out of the Secretary's place untill the next Election Court.

This Court appoynts Thomas Minor, Math: Griswald and Wm. Waller, or any two of them, as a Comitte to hear the case depending twixt Uncass and the Inhabitants of N: London, respecting lands, and to make report to the Court in October next, what they find in the case. This they are to attend between this and the end of June next.

This Court remitts Cary Latham and Mr. Duglas fine, wch was imposed upon them by the Court in March, for there transgression in making their list.

This Court orders, that Rob: Usher and John Meggs shall continue in the place and office of a Constable ouer those that haue submitted to this Gouerment in there respectiue Plantations, untill the Court see cause to alter otherwise, and all those that haue submitted are to attend the former order made in October Court last.

The Court uoted, that they would not send the Patent nor coppy thereof to be read at New Hauen.

[185] This Court orders, that the letter drawne up by the Committe to the Manadoes, be drawn out fair, and sent to the Lord Stephenson,† and signed by the Secretary in the name of the Court, as allso the letter to West Chester.

This Court orders Mr. Willys and John Allyn to draw up a Letter to the Gen^{ll} Court of ye Massachusetts, in refference to Pawkatuck & Mistick, and to desire a return.

---

* The letter from Massachusetts, (of Mar. 8, 1662-3,) and the reply of the Committee are in "Towns & Lands," Vol. I, Nos. 44 & 45.

† Stuyvesant.

This Court appoynts L^nt Rob: Sealy to be the cheife miletary officer in Huntington, to exercise theire trained souldiers.

This Court ordered that Capt John Young should haue 5*l*. allowed him for his seruice on the Island last year.

This Court ordered that Richard Pontons charge at Hartford should be born by the publike Treasury.

This Court orders that Southhold shall haue and enjoy the same priuiledges as Southhampton doth by uertue of their combination.

This Court chose Ln^t John Allyn, Sec^ry for the Colony, untill the next election, and he was sworn in Court.

This Court graunts unto the Major o^r Worp^ll Dep'ty Gouern^r, 500 acres of land for a farme, where he shall chuse it, if it may not be p^rjudiciall to a plantation allready sett up or to sett up, so there be not aboue 50 acres of meadow in it.

The Court orders that those freemen that were presented to the Court in October, from Norwidge, shall be accepted and sworn by o^r Worp^ll Deputy Gou^r.

The Court orders Mr. Math: Allyn and Mr. Willis to write to Setawkit, and settle businesse there, according as they judge best.

The Court also accepts of those freemen p^rsented from N: London, and orders Mr. Bruen to administer the oath unto them, whose names are Sam^ll Roggers, Miles More, Mihell Rice.

The Court is adjourned untill the 3d Wedensday in Aug^st, unless the Gou^r come to us sooner and see cause to call the Court together.

At a Meeting of the Councill, July 10th, 1663.

The Councill doth desire and appoynt Capt John Tallcott to go down to West Chester, and if the eleuen Queries concerning West Chester do appear to be sufficiently proued in the affirmatiue, then the said Capt may and is herby ordered to administer the oath of a Constable unto him whome the Inhabitants shall desire and chuse to that seruice, if he approues of the person; and he hath herby liberty to establish a Serj^nt in the said Town. And it is desired that Capt Tallcott would be pleased to endeauo^r to settle thinges in the Town of West Chester, in as

At a Session of the Gen:ll Assembly holden at Hartford the 14th of Octo:r: 1663

This Court doth desire that those Freemen appoynted to keepe the Charter, do also receive the Duplicate Into their Custody & keep y:t in Behalfe of the Freemen of this Corporation; & the Worshipp:ll ffull Governour is desired to deliver the s:d Duplicate to the said Freinds or either of them,:

This Court doth Nominate & appoynt the Dep: Govern:r, m:r Willys, m:r Dan:ll Clarke & John Allyn or any three or 2 of them to be a Committe to treat w:th o:r honoured ffreinds of N: Hauen, Milford, Brainford & Gilford about setling their union & Incorporation w:th this Colony of Conecticut, & they are Impowred to act according to the Instructions giuen to the Com:tte sent to New: Hauen in March last,

John Allyn Secret:y

(1663-1665.)

peaceable a manner as may be. The forsaid Queries are upon the file.

The Secretary allso is ordered to send a Letter to the Inhabitants of Narraganset in the name of the Councill, and to signify to them, that Mr. Richard Smith Senr, Capt Edwd Hutchinson and Ln^t Jos: Hews are appointed select men at Mr. Smiths tradeing howse; and Mr. Rich: Smith Junr is appoynted Constable for the said Town, and Mr. Rich: Smith Senr is to administer an oath to him for a faithfull discharge of his office.

It is ordered, that the Plantation aforesaid shall for the future be called by the name of Wickforde. The Coppy of the Letter to Wickford, hangs upon the file.

---

[186] At a Session of the Gen^{ll} Assembly holden at Hartford, the 19th of Augst, 1663.

Assist's:

Maior John Mason, Dep^t Gou^r:

Mr. Mathew Allyn,	Mr. Henry Woolcott,
Mr. Sam^{ll} Willys,	Mr. Dan^{ll} Clark,
Capt John Tallcott,	John Allyn & *Sec^ry*.

Deputies:

Wm. Wadsworth,	Tho: Tracy,	Mr. Rob: Chapman,
Capt Benj: Newbery,	Ln^t Walter Fyler,	Sam^{ll} Boreman,
James Rogers,	John Nott,	Mr. Jos: Fitch.
Hugh Calkin,	Nath: White,	

This Court doth desire that those Freinds appoynted to keepe the Charter do allso receiue the Duplicate into their custody, and keep it in behalfe of the Freemen of this Corporation; and the Worshipfull Gouernour is desired to deliuer the s^d Duplicate to the said Freinds, or either of them.

This Court doth nominate and appoynte the Dep: Gouerno^r, Mr. Willys, Mr. Dan^{ll} Clarke and John Allyn, or any three or 2 of them to be a Committe to treat wth or honoured freinds of N: Hauen, Milford, Branford and Gilford, aboute setling their union and incorporation wth this Colony of Connecticut; and they are impowred to act according to the Instructions giuen to the Comitte sent to New-Hauen in March last; and in case they cannot effect a union, they are hereby authorized publikely to declare unto them that this Assembly cannot well recent their proceeding in Ciuill Gouerm^t as a distinct Jurisdiction, being included within the Charter graunted to Conecticut Corporation; and likewise they are publikly to declare that this Assembly doth desire and cannot but expect that the inhabitants of New Hauen, Milford, Branford, Guilford and Stanford do yeild subjection to the Gouerm^t here establisht according to the tennor of o^r Charter, which is publiquely to be read in New Hauen.

This Court being sencible of the great inconueniency that may com to the members of this Colony by Indians walking up and down the Towns, in the night season, to buy liquers, doe order, that whatsoeuer Indian shall be found walking up and down in any Towne in this Corporation, after the day light shutting in, except he giue sufficient reason, shall forfeit twenty shillings, fifteen shillings to the Publiq' Treasury, and five to the person or persons complaining and proueing the same, or else be seuerly whipt six stripes at least; and any one Assist^t or Commissioner hath power to hear and issue any such complaint. And if any Indian shall be found in the night season transgressing this order, the Assist^{ts} or Commissioners, or any one of them, may secure them, by setting a watch upon them or by committing them to prisson for a tryall ye next fitting oppertunity. This is to be published to the Indians in or about each Towne.

Wm. Blumfield appeales from the sentence or judgm^t of the Court held at Hartford, June 15, 63, to the judgment and determination of this Assembly.

The Comitte appoynted to view Hommonoscit, returned a writing under their hands, dated June 3, 1663, wherein they expresst that according to their best judgment it will make a comfortable plantation for the entertainment of thirty families to subsist comfortably. The Comitte were Wm. Wadsworth, Sam^{ll} Smith, James Auery.

John Clow Junr presented a Petition to the Court for the planting of Homonoscitt, and engaged to pay 10s. to the Treasury for it,* according to order.

---

* i. e. for the presentation of the Petition; according to the order of May, 1662. p. 381.

Corporall Marshall is to haue 2*l*. payd him by the Treasurer and deliuer the horse to the Treasurer, and this to be a finall issue of the case.

[187] This Court hauing considered Wm. Blumfeilds appeale, wth the [   ] therof, doe order that Mr. Rogers shall pay unto Blumfeild the summ [   ] pounds in currant pay, and Mr. Rogers to keep the mare and bull and [   ] as his proper estate, and discharge Mr. Louelands debt and pay the cost [*of this*] Court, and the first Court his case was in tryal. Blumfeild is to pay the char[ges of] the special Court.*

This Court orders the Sec^ry to draw out the letter which was read in the [Court,] and subscribe it in the name of the Court, and send it to Capt Hutchinson† and his [   ]

This Court haueing considered the request of Tho: Forde, by their vote d[eclare] that they see no cause to give Goodman Forde the six pownds od, that he d[esires] in refference to his land at Podunck, now in Mr. Jos: Fitches hand.

This Court orders, that the land at Homenoscitt be reserued for a plantation.

This Court orders that the planting of Homonoscit be reffered to October Court.

At a Session of the Generall Assembly at Hartford, [October] the 8th, 1663.

John Winthrope Esqr, Gou^r.
Major John Mason Esqr, Dep:
 Mr. Math: Allyn, Mr. Henry Woolcott,
 Mr. Sam^ll Willys, Mr. Dan^ll Clarke,
 Mr. Rich: Treat, John Allyn,
 Capt John Tallcott, Mr. Sherman.

Deputies :
Mr. Wm. Wadsworth, Capt Ben: Nubery, Mr. Jos: Fitch, Ln^t Walt: Fyler, Samuel Boreman, John Nott,

---

* The corners and outer margins of the two leaves of the original record, paged 187 to 190, are much worn and defaced. On pages 187 and 189, the whole or a part of the words terminating each line is torn off, or has become illegible.

† A letter from Capt. Hutchinson and the other proprietors of the Narragansett lands, with a copy of the reply from the General Court, are in " Colonial Boundaries," Vol. I. Nos. 9 & 10.

Mr. Anthony Hawkins, Thomas Jud, Mr. Jehu Bur, *absent;* John Bankes, Philip Groue, Mr. Math: Campfeild, Nath: White, Rich: Olmsteed, *absent;* Ens: Joseph Judson, *absent;* Wm. Cheny, Tho: Tracy, Tho: Leppingwell, James Rogers, [James] Morgan, Mr. Rob: Chapman, Wm. Waller.

This Court desires and appoyntes Mr. Mathew Allyn, Capt Ta[llcott,] Ln^t Clark, as a Comitty to treat wth the Gent^n come from the M[anhatoes] about the matters in controuersie between this Corporation and the D[utch] at Manhatoes,* and in case Mr. Clark comes not down to the Court, y^e [Secretary to] supply Mr. Clarkes place.

John Griffen haueing made appeare to this Court that he was the first [   ] the art of making pitch and tarre in these parts, doe order that the [said] Griffen shall haue Two hundred acres of lands (where he can find them) between Massacoh and Warranoake, wherof there may be forty acres of [meadow,] if it be ther to be had and be not prejudiciall to a plantation, and not [formerly] graunted.

The list of estates were presented to this Court, as followeth :—

Y^e persons and estates of Hartford,	18917. 06. 00
Y^e persons and estates of Windsor,	16683. 00. 00

---

* With a view to an amicable adjustment of the differences between the New Netherlands and Connecticut, respecting the towns upon L. Island, and the territory between Stamford and Westchester (inclusive of the latter plantation,) to which both Jurisdictions laid claim, Gov. Stuyvesant sent commissioners to Hartford, with full powers " for the composinge and determyninge of all further diffrences in question." In a letter to the General Court (dated Oct. 13, 1663, N. S.) Gov. S. writes, " I therefore thought meete and needfull for the prevention of further troubles, to send the bearers, our lovinge friends and intrusted agents, Cornelys van Ruyven, our faithfull Secretary, Oolvoont Stevenson van Cortland, burge master off the city Amsterdam in New Netherland, and John Lawrence, marchant," &c. [Colonial Boundaries, ii. 6.]

The Committee appointed by the General Court did not assent to the propositions submitted by the Dutch Commissioners, and the latter returned to the Manhadoes, without having attained any satisfactory result of their mission. A correspondence ensued between the General Court and Gov. S., in which the question of jurisdiction was discussed, without however arriving at any positive result, until the claims of the Dutch Government were summarily disposed of, by the occupation of N. York by the English in 1664, and the grant to the Duke of York,—which by the decision of the Royal Commissioners, in Nov. 1664, was made to include the whole of Long Island. The letters of Gov. Stuyvesant, with the propositions of the Dutch agents, and those of the Committee of the Gen. Court, are in ' Col. Boundaries,' Vol. ii. Nos. 3–13. See also, the Journal of the Dutch Comm'ssioners, printed in Hazzard's State Papers, ii. 623–633, from the original in the State Department at Albany.

Yᵉ persons and estates of Weathersfeild, 12258. 10. 00
Yᵉ persons and estates of Farmington,   07044. 00. 00
Yᵉ persons and estates of New London, 07185. 11. 00
Yᵉ persons and estates of Norwalke,   04420. 05. 00
Yᵉ persons and estates of Middletowne, 03017. 00. 00
Yᵉ persons and estates of Norwidge,   02571. 00. 00
Yᵉ persons and estates of Stratford,   09579. 03. 00
Yᵉ persons and estates of Fairfeild,   11030. 09. 08
Yᵉ persons and estates of Saybrook,   08000. 00. 00

Mathew Griswold and Wm. Waller and Tho: Minord are appoynted to [   ] the west bounds of New London, and Ens: Tracy and James Morgan or [   ] whom the two towns of N: London and Norwidge do appoynt are to se[   ] they are to begin at some sutable place as they shall judge m[eet, so that] they may haue as much land without as their is sea [   ]

Timothy Phelpes and Samuel Buell are [propounded to] be made free of this Corporation, according [*to order of Court*]

[188] Serjant Tho: Minor repairing to this Court for aduice, what he should doe or how he should behaue himself to any in the place where he liues that doe pretend authority there ; This Court doth aduise him to carry it peaceably towards them, and at present to be a patient in the case, though they injure him ; this Court engageing to see the said Serjant Minor wrighted for any wrong that he either hath or shall receiue upon this accoᵗ, prouided he attends the directions of this Court, wᶜʰ is that he obey noe authority at Mistick & Pawcatuck but what is or shall be establisht there by this Assembly.

It is ordered by the Court, that the letter drawn up to the Director Genˡˡ at the Manhatoes, be sighned by the Secʳy in the name of the Court, and sent to the said Generall.

This Court doth accept of the town of West Chester as a member of this Corporation, being rece'd and accepted as such by oʳ Councill formerly. This Court doth declare that all the land between the sayd West Chester and Stanford also doth belong to the Colony of Connecticut.

This Court doth desire and appoynt the Major and John Allyn and Mr. Bruen, to keep a Court at New London, for the issuing of such matters as shall be presented to their consideration; they are to appoynte the time.

This Court appoynts Ens: James Auery a Commissioner, to joyne wth Mr. Bruen at New London.

This Court appoynts Mr. Edward Gishop a Commissioner for the Towne of West Chester, and he is inuested with Magistraticall power in that Plantation, untill ye Court in May. Sworn, in Court.

This Court doth appoynte the Sec^ry to draw out the Letter faire, that was read in the Court, and subscribe it in the name of the Court, and send it to Deacon Parks, by him to be presented to ye Gouern^r and Gen^ll Assembly of the Massachusetts.

This Court orders, that the last Wednesday of this Instant October be set apart throughout this Collony for a solemn day of Thanksgiuing for the mercyes God hath extended to us the year past, in the return of o^r Honoured Gouerno^r, the recouery of o^r Deputy Gouern^r out of his late sicknesse, the plentifull haruest, the seasonable abatement of the waters, and continuance of peace and health amongst us.

This Court graunts a rate of a penny on the pound, to discharge the Countrey's debts.

This Court upon the petition of John Tompson, do request Mr. Jones, Mr. Hanford and Mr. Wakeman, to haue a hearing of the difference between the Church of X^t at Stratford and the said Tompson, and to aduise them to the best meanes for an issue therof.

This Court desires and appoynts Mr. Gouernour, Mr. Math: Allyn, Mr. Willys and Capt Tallcott, or any three of them, to consider what is meet to be attended in reffrence to Mr. Hopkins his estate, by him bequeathed for to be improued for ye promoting of learning, and to make reporte of there thoughts the next Court.

Tho: Hunt, John Quinby, Rob: Huested, Nicholas Bayley, Rich: Ponton, Sam^ll Mills, Mr. Rich: Mills, are accepted to be made free, according to order of Courte.

Simon Huntington, Tho: Adgatt, John Post, Tho: Post, Wm. Baccas, Thom: Blisse, John Renols, John Calkin, Jonath: Rice, John Birchard, are accepted to be made free, according to order of Court.

Ens: Steel, John Norton, John Clerk, Joseph Woodford,

Tho: Judd, John Judd, John Woodruff, John Root, John Warner, Tho: Hart, are to stand for their [   ] at the Court in May next, for their freedome.

[189] Lnt John Bud is appoynted Commissioner for the Town of Hastings, and is inuested [with] Magistraticall power within the limits of that Town.

Rich: Vowles is appoynted Constable for the Town of Hastings, and Mr. Bud is to g[iue him his oath.]

This Court doth approue of Deacon Stebbing and Lnt Tho: Bull paying what doth [appear] to be due from Mr. Hopkins estate to Mr. Bournes or Mr. Dallye, with what [   ]ency may bee.

It is ordered by the Court, that Math: Griswald, Wm. Waller and Tho: Minor or [any two] of them, shall settle the bounds between the Town of New London and Uncas, [   ] determine what Uncass shall haue for those of his lands that fall within the [   ] that by the Court haue been confirmed upon the Towne of New London, and issue [   ] case fully, a Munday come four weeks, or as soon as may be.

Frances Brown was sworn Constable for Stanford, in the Court.

Wheras the Court haue formerly graunted Mr. Sam: Stone, of Hartford, a farme, [for his] good seruice to the Countrey both in Pequett warr and since, do now graunt and con[firme] to Mr. Samll Stone his son and Mrs. Eliza Stone, the relict of Mr. Samll Stone, deceased, [in] lieu of the former grant, 500 acres of upland and 50 or sixty acres of meadow, [where] they can find it, prouided it be not prejudicial to any plantation set up al[ready] or place fitt to make a plantation.

This Court appoynts Samll Boreman and James Steele to lay out the bounds [of the] Towne of Middletowne, according to their former graunt, and the [Towne] of Middletowne is to pay the charge therof.

This Court doth leaue the determination of the business respecting [   ] entertainmt of the plantations on Long Island, and the difference between [us] and the Dutch, with the Councill, who are to consider and issue the forementioned [particu]lars, as soon as they haue a return from the Dutch Director Genll or a fort[night] hence, and the people of the Island are to haue a coppy of the proposalls presented [by] the Gen[lls] Messengers.

This Court appoynts John Hurd and Joseph Judson to lay out the bownds [of the] Town of Fairfeild, between them and Norwalk, according to their [former] grant; and the two Townes are to beare the charge.

This Court doth desire and authorize the Councill to draw up and send letters of [   ] to his Majesty or any Noble personages in England, as they see cause.

This Court doth approue of what the Perticular Court did at South H[ampton] September, 1663, and do desire and appoynte the Assis[ts] of South & East Hampton to see that execution be attended according to the determination of the said Court; and in case there be any occasion for the future, the Assis[ts] of South and East Hampton are hereby impowered to go ouer [to South-] hold and keep Court there and deal with all persons (that carry it refractory in the sayd place,) according to lawe; and especially they are desired to consider of Mr. Wells his ill carriage; and in case they cannot sup[press] such ill disposed persons there, they may and are hereby authorized [to send] ouer any such person or persons to the Goal here at Connecticut.

Tho: Tappin is appoynted to joyne with the aforesaid Assis[ts].

This Court doth authorize the Court at Southhold to issue the [   ] respecting Pepper, now in durance there, and to send him to Bar[badoes] or banish him, according as the nature of the offence [requires.]

[190] This Court doth judge that Seabrook hath no right to Hommonoscitt.

This Court doth declare that the former act about Homonoscitts not being a plantation is hereby reuoaked; and the former order, that it should be a plantation is to stand.

The Court doth appoynt S. Willys, Mr. Woollcott, and Wm. Wadsworth as a Commity for the ordering of the plantation at Homonoscitt.

Mr. Willys, Mr. Gould & Ens: Tracy are appoynted by this Court, as a Committy to issue the businesse respecting John Notts appeale.

Ln[t] Lewis doth request this Court for a Farme.

This Court doth order a rate of farthinge & half farthinge upon the pownd, to be paid within 3 weekes, in wheat, for the compleating the charge about procuring the Charter; and the Constables of each Town are to gather the same, and prouide for the transportation of the same to New London, within a month.

This Court doth declare that they can do no less for their own indemnity then to manifest o[r] dissatisfaction wth the proceedings of the plantations of N: Hauen, Milford, Brainford &c., in their distinct standing from us in poynt of Gouerm[t]; it being directly opposite to the tennor of the Charter lately granted to o[r] Colony of Connecticutt, in w[ch] Charter these plantations are included. Wee allso do expect their submission to o[r] Gouerment, according to o[r] Charter and his Majestyes pleasure therin exprest, it being a stated conclution of the Com[rs] that Jurisdiction right allwayes goeth wth Patent. And whereas, the afoars[d] people of New Hauen &c. pretend they haue power of Gouerment distinct from us, and haue made seuerall complaints of wroungs receiued from us, we doe hereby declare that o[r] Councill will be ready to attend them, or a Committee of theirs, and if they can rationally make it appear that they haue such power, and that we have wrounged them, according to their complaints, we shall be ready to atend them wth due sattisfaction. (Y[e] Gou[nr] absent w[n] this vote passed.)

The Court appoynts Mr. Willys and the Sec[ry] to draw up a Lett[r] to N: Hauen Gent[n], and inclose this act of the Court in it.

The return of the Comitty concerning John Notts appeale is, that the land in controuersie between Mr. Russell and the Towne of Weathersfeild doth belong to Mr. Russell, and is confirmed by the Court upon him;

This Court remitts Mr. Russells forfeits for his non recording of his land, all but 5*l*.; and this to be a finall issue of the businesse between Mr. Russell and John Nott and the Town of Weathersfeild.

In answer to the petition of those English Plantations near the Dutch;—This Court being desirous to maintaine his Majesties just interest and the peace of his subjects, and yett to attend all wayes of righteousnesse, that so we may hold good correspondency with o[r] neighbours of the Manhatoes, do herby declare that they will for the present forbear to put forth any authority ouer the English Plantations on the westerly end of Long Island, prouided the Dutch forbear to exercise any coerciue power towards them; and this Court shall cease from farther attendance unto the p^rmises, until there be a seasonable return from the Generall Steuenson to those propositions that his messengers carryed with them, or untill their be an issue of the differences between them and us.

[191] And in case the Dutch do unjustly molest or offer violence unto them, we do hereby declare that we shall not be willing to see o^r Countrey men his Maties naturall borne subjects, and his Maties interest interupted or molested by the Dutch or any other, but we shall adres o^rselues to use such just and lawfull meanes as God shall in his wisdome offer to o^r hands for their indemnity and safety, untill his Matie o^r Soueraigne Lord the King shall please to declare his Royall pleasure for their future settlement, they carrying themselues peaceably and inoffenciuely.

The Court is adjourned to the 2^d Thursday in March, except the Gouerno^r or Councill see cause to call it sooner.

` This Court doth thankfully acknowledge the fauor the Gouern^r hath shewed to this o^r Colony, in his great paynes in procureing o^r Charter of his Matie o^r Soueraigne, and doe hereby discharge him from those seuerall summes of mony that he hath rec^d of the Colony;

And the Worp^{ll} Gouernor doth hereby discharge and acquitt the Colony of Conecticutt from all farther claimes for his paynes and charge about the premises.

At a Session of the Gen^{ll} Assembly at Hartford, March 10th, 1663.

John Winthrop Esqr, Gou^r.

Assis^{ts}.

Mr. Allyn,	Mr. Woolcot,
Mr. Willys,	Mr. Clark,
Mr. Treat,	Mr. Allyn, *et Sec^ry*.

OF CONNECTICUT. 417

Deputies:

Mr. Wadsworth,	Tho: Judd,	John Nott,
Mr. Fitch,	Mr. Jehu Burre,	Wm. Cheny,
Capt. Newbery,	John Bankes,	Tho: Tracy,
Ln^t Fyler,	Nath: White,	Tho: Leppingwell,
Anth: Hawkins,	Sam^{ll} Boreman,	Mr. Rob: Chapman.

This Court doth order that the charge and expence of Mr. John Tinkers sicknesse and funerall shall be payd by the Publiq^e Treasury, which is 8: 6: 4.

This Court doth nominate and appoynte Mr. Willys and Capt Tallcott to take the Marshalls acco^t of what he hath expended on the Contreys acco^t, to the Dutch agents.

This Court upon a consideration of a petition presented from seuerall of the proprietors of the lands on the East side of the Great Riuer, in refference to fencing the said lands, doe therfore see meet to desire and order the said proprietors in the seuerall Townes, to consider of the aduantages and disaduantages that may accrew to the Publique in the premises, and to p^{r}sent their apprehensions and determination of ye m[ajor] part of the said proprietors at the next Gen^{ll} Assembly, in May.

This Court orders Tho: Edwards and the rest of the inhabitants at Hockanum, all aboue sixteen yeares old, to take some speedy oppertunity to make two Bridges, the one ouer the Brook at the place called Sadler Ordnary, the other at Frog Brook, where may be most sutable; in each Bridge to lay three Trees, so hewed that they may be sufficient for horses to passe safe ouer. Thomas Edward is to ouersee the work, and is empowered to call the rest of the p^{r}sons forth to performe the work, according to the Courts expectation herein; and the Court allowes ten shillings towards the work, out of the Publiq' Treasury; it is to be finished before May Court. They are to mark out the way from ye Common way to the Bridge at Frog Brook.

This Court doth remitt John Betts fine of 30*s.*

This Court understanding that trouble is like to ensue upon the apprehension of seuerall inhabitants amongst us respectinge the priuiledge of Freemen, and who are to make choyce of Deputyes and publiq' officers in the Corporation, for preuention wherof, doe declare and order, that only such as haue been or shall be orderly admitted freemen of this Company, by the Gen^ll Assembly, shall haue their votes in chooseing Deputyes and other publique officers for the Corporation, as Gouerno^r, Deputy Gouerno^r, Magistrates.

[192] This Court, upon good advise, doe see cause to take of the sequestration formerly laid upon the estate of Edward Hopkins Esqr, wch for seuerall good reasons was laid under restreint, partly because an authentick coppy of the will of ye s^d Edward Hopkins Esqr did not appeare for ye orderly dispose thereof, and partly because an attested Inuentory of the said estate hath not as yett been exhibited to this Court, yett now being hopelesse, because of the discease of Capt John Cullick, to obteine the said Inuentory, this Court doth order as before mentioned.

This Court grants license to John Westall, to sell wine and liquers by retaile in his house, so he do not suffer men to tipple in his house contrary to lawe, but attends the contrary orders in that respect.

This Court orders, that the letter wth the warrant and instructions to the Marshall respecting Mr. John Scott, that haue been read in the Court, shall be attended.

This Court orders that the bownds of Seabrook shall be six mile and an half from the Neck gate, westward.

This Court doth grant liberty to Mr. Thomas Pell to buy all that land of the Indian proprietors between West Chester and Hudsons Riuer, (that makes Manhatoes an Island,) and lay it to West Chester, prouided that it be not purchased by any before, nor in their possession.

This Court desires Mr. Henry Woolcott, Mr. Willis and Mr. Wadsworth, to go to N: London to assist the Major in keeping a Court at N: London, the 1st Wedensday in Aprill next.

This Court desires the Deputyes of Fairfeild to signify to the Towne of Norwake that the Court will state the bounds between them and Fairfeild, the next Session in May.

To p^ruent future inconueniences that may arise between Saybrook and Homonoscitt plantations, and for a full issue of the case, this Court orders that the bounds between ye said plantations shall be where the common passage ouer Manunketesek Riuer is, and so to run north into the Country and south into the sea. The former vote concerning the bounds of these plantations is retracted. Mr. Rossiter, Mathew Griswold and Joh: West are to lay out the bowndes according to order of Court.

This Court orders, that the Towne of New London shall pay unto Ens: Waller, Mathew Griswald and Thomas Minor what is due unto them for laying out the bounds of N: London; to Ens: Waller, for two voyages, 15s.; to Math: Griswold, 15s.; to Thomas Minor, w^t is his due, at 3s. a day, himself & horse.

This Court grants unto Mr. Mathew Allyn, liberty to take up that meadow at Catch, beyond Goodman Bissell, on the East side of the Riuer, and what upland he pleaseth, so he exceeds not his former grant. What Mr. Allyn takes up at this place is to go onwards of his former grant; and Edward Griswald and Josias Hull are appoynted to lay out this land for Mr. Allyn, he paying of them for their paynes.

This Court grants Mr. Phelps, 200 acres of upland and twenty of meadow, wher he can find it; prouided it prejudice not former grants and plantations sett up and to sett up.

The Deputies of Saybrook presenting to this Court their intendments to set up a plantation on the East side of the great Riuer, and also maintayn a plantation on the West side, and desireing some enlargm^t of their bounds, this Court haueing considered their desires, do enlarge their bownds, fower miles on each side of the Riuer northward, prouided they do make two plantations, as afores^d, within the space of three yeares from the date hereof; and also, o^r Honor^d Gouernor haueing made choyce of the Brook that runs into the great Riuer, near Twelue Mile Island, to sett a saw mill on, and a cedar swamp near adjoyning to the said brook or riuer, by vertue of a former grant, May 21th, 1653, this Court graunts it to him, according to his former grant, and excepts it in the forementioned grant to Seabrooke.

This Court doth nominate and appoynt these to be put to ye election, at May Court next, for Assis^{ts}; Capt Ben: Newbery, Anthony Howkins, Capt Young, Mr. Fayrchild, Mr. Edward Palmes.

[193] This Court orders, that if any person in this Colony shall refuse or neglect to giue in a true acco^t of any sorte of his Cattell to the Listmakers or their agents, when demaunded, in

the respectiue Townes, or shall leaue out any parte of them, he shall forfeit for euery such defect the estate left out, the one half to the Publiq' Treasury, and the other half to the person discouering the same, and prosecuting it to effect.

The Church of Christ at Winsor complaynes of James Enoe and Michaell Humphrey, for seuerall things contayned in a paper presented to the Court. Mr. Clarke, in behalf of the Church complaynes of James Enoe and Michaell Humphrey for a misdameanor, in offering violence to an establisht law of this Colony. Mr. Clark withdrawes this charge.

This Court grants liberty and impowers the Major to take the conuenient time, and what assists he judgeth meet, to purchase what land he can of the Indians for the use and benefitt of the Collony of Connecticutt.

This Court, for the encouragement of any person that will lay out himself for the discouery of any mines or mineralls &c., doe order, that whosoeuer shall make such discoueryes, and purchase it for the Countrey, he shall be honorably rewarded, out of what he doth discouer as aforesayd.

This Court hauing seriously considered the case respecting James Ennoe and Michaell Humphrey, doe declare such practises to be offensiue, and may proue prejudiciall to the wellfare of this Collony, and this Court expects they will readily come to the acknowledgment of their error in the paper by them presented to the Church, wherupon the Court respitts and remitts the sensure due for their offence, prouided answerable reformation doth followe, expecting that their lenity therein will winne upon the spiritts of those concerned in this case. And this Court doth approue of the pious and prudent care of Windsor, in seeking out for a supply and help in the ministry, Mr. Warham growing ancient; and do order all persons in the sayd plantation to allow their proportion towards the competent maintenance of such a supply in the ministry. And the Court desires a friendly correspondency may be maintayned at Windsor, as if this trouble had neuer been; this Court declaring their readyness to mayntayne all the just priuiledges of all the members of this Corporation.

It is ordered by this Court, that ye prticulars complayned agaynst Mr. John Scott, be drawn out and sent downe to the present ciuil officers, the conseruators of the peace of his Maties subjects at New Hauen, Milford, &c., and fully declared unto them, and to demand the said officers, in the Kings name, to apprehend or cause to be apprehended the body of the said Scott, and peaceably to deliuer him unto the custody of o^r Marshall, that he may be brought unto a tryall at Connecticutt, and that he may be proceeded wth according to law, and in case the said officers neglect or refuse to attend o^r demand herein, that then we doe charge them as being guilty of abetting and concealing a malefactor, therby preuenting the execution of justice, and so o^r officer to returne and declare their answer under the hand or hands of such officer or officers to whom the demand is made, unlesse they refuse to declare their answer in writing.

To all his Maties Subjects within these parts of o^r Royall Soueraigne Charles, King of England, Scotland, France & Ireland, his Dominions in New England in America, especially those plantations scituate w^thin the limitts of the Corporation of Connecticutt, These presents doe declare and proclaime, (as followeth :)

That forasmuch as John Scott, inhabitant w^thin the Libertyes of Ashford (alias Setawkit,) on Long Island, stands charged in the Court at Connecticut for sundry hainous crimes and practises seditious, to the great disturbance of the peace of his Maties subjects on the Island aforesayd ; perticularly, as followeth,—

1. Speaking words tending to the defamation of the Kings Majesty ;

2dly. Seditious practises and tumultuous carriages in seuerall Plantations ;

3dly. Abetting and incouraging the natiues in hostile practises against one another ;

4. Vsurpeing the authority of the King in tendring to pardon treason, as Scott called the crime, for bribes ;

5. Threatning his Maties subjects with hanging and banishment ;

6. Grosse and notorious prophanation of God's holy day ;

7. Forgery, and violation of his solemne oath ;

8. Acting treachourously to the Colony of Connecticutt ;

9. Usurpeing authority, upon pretence of a commission ;

10. Calumniating a Commission officer in this Corporation, wth the charge of villanous and felloneous practices ;

We doe therfore in his M^ties name desire and expect all and euery ciuill officer who are conseruators of the peace of his Maties subjects within the Plantations of N: Hauen, Milford, Brainford, Stratford, Fairefeild, &c., whersoeuer the said Scott is resident, forthw^th upon receipt and knowledge of the contents of the premises, to apprehend or cause to be apprehended the body of the said Scott, and peaceably to deliuer him unto the custody of o^r Marshall, Jonathan Gilbert and his aiders, that so he may be conducted securely to Hartford, that so the said Scott may come to a due triall according to law, for the crimes herein specified, according to his Maties Commission to this Corporation of Connecticutt.

God saue the King.

You are hereby authorized, and in his Maties Name required, upon the surrendry made of ye body of John Scott unto yor custody, by any of the ciuill officers within the plantations of N: Hauen, Branford, Milford, Stratford, Fairfeild, &c., to bring the s^d Scott under safe conduct to the goal at Hartford, there to be secured to a triall for seuerall crimes laid to his charge ; and you are further required to make diligent enquiry wher the said Scott is resident, and hauing certaine intelligence, you are forthwith to repair to the ciuill officers or officer in that Towne, and to open the declaration or proclamation, and the same to read unto them, or otherwise cause him to know the contents therof, and so to demand his answer ; and if he or they shall neglect or refuse to obserue and attend what is therin demanded, desire him or them to signify the same unto Authority here establisht, and hauing receiued the answer you are to return unto yor habitation and giue in the accompt of yor p^rceeds to the Worp^ll Magistrates at Hartford. You are further required to desire and demand a speedy answer from the officer or officers to whom you apply yourself for Scotts apprehending ; and in case the answer be unessessarily retarded, you are, in this Courts name to charge the said officer with abetting and concealing a malefactor, therby obstructing the course of justice. But in case Scott be gone beyond Stratford Riuer, you are to attend the execution of yo{r} office by apprehending the said Scott and conducting him safely, as before exprest.

MARCH 19th. It is voated in the Gen{ll} Court that John Gilbert shall be allowed Eleuen pownds out of the Publique Treasury, for and in consideration of his horse that dyed in the Countrey's seruice.

This Court have voated Mr. Willis and Mr. Math: Allyn to go ouer to Long Island to settle the Gouerm{t} on the West end of the Island, according to the aggreem{t} at Hempsted, in Feb{r} last; and those Gentlem{n} are desired to issue the matter twixt J: Scott & Bloomer. And they are farther desired to take in w{th} them the assistance of the Commission{rs} in those Townes, for the regulateing of any disturbances, as occasion is p{r}sented.

[195] The seuerall propositions propounded to the Court for Answer, by Walter Salter.

1 *Qu:* Whether we are taken by Patent right, or not?

1 *A:* The Lines of Connecticutt Patent extending to the adjoyning Islands, and y{e} Townes on the west end of the Island applying themselues to this Gouerm{t} for rule and p{r}tection and settlem{t} in Gouerm{t}, and declaritiuely expressing the same by their Deputies at Hempsted, in Feb: last, upon the grounds foregoing we declare our acceptance of those Townes under the Gouerm{t} of Connecticutt.

2 *Q:* Whether this Court ownes and will mayntayne the Commission of Mr. Allyn,, and what he hath done upon the west end of Long Island?

An: In refference to the p{r}secution of the settlem{t} of Gouerm{t} in those Towns by Mr. Allyn, and the issue that was aggreed on by him, w{th} the Assembly at Hempsted, as specified in a writing w{th} us, wherein the Deputyes of the seuerall plantations there, in behalf of y{e} s{d} Townes, express their joynt submission to this Gouerm{t}, we do own and accept those Townes under o{r} present care and gouerm{t}.

3 *Q:* Whether by what Mr. Allyn brought from Long Island, Connecticut hath power to command us, or not?

An: We judge according to what is returned to this Assembly by Mr. Allen, so farr as we can creditt the coppy attested by Anthony Waters, nominated to be Clark of the Assembly at Hempsted, that this Assembly hath power to require obedience of the persons in those Townes to the authority establisht by o^r Royall Soueraigne Charles the 2^d, in the Corporation of Connecticutt.

These Answers were voted by the Court.

This Court doth order that ye 2^d Wedensday in Aprill next, be solemnly kept a day of publique humiliation, throughout this Collony, to seek to God that he would graciously be pleased to smile upon us, and succeed the labo^{rs} and endeauo^{rs} of his people, in the occasions of the ensuing yeare; that health may be continued amongst us, that peace and truth may be establisht amongst o^{r}selues and throughout his Maties Dominions.

This Court votes that Mr. Allens charges of Mr. Clark, which were presented to the Court, are not proved by Mr. Allen.

    Mr. Allyn,   Capt Tallcott,
    Mr. Willys,   John Allyn.

The Magistrates order the Secretary to giue Mr. Hicks a coppy of the p^{r}clamation against Mr. Scott, and to insert that the plantations of the Island are required by their officers, to act as the plantations of N: Hauen, Milford, Stratford, &c. in the mayne, in refference to the apprehending of Mr. Scott; and Hicks is to haue the exemplification.

The Magistrates doe also desire and aduise the Inhabitants of Hempsted, in case Thomas Rushmore do continue to oppose the Gouerm^t of Connecticutt, to chuse an able and judicious man to the office of a Constable, and Mr. Hicks to administer the oath to him, they haueing first displaced the sayd Rushmore.

And it is also ordered, that all the inhabitants in the English Townes on the west end of Long Island, yeild obedience and submitt to the Gouerment of those officers that were chosen by the respectiue Townes according to the aduise of the Collony of Connecticutt; and all pretended officers are to stand by.

[196] AT A GENERALL ASSEMBLY HELD AT HARTFORD, MAY THE 12th, 1664, FOR ELECTION.

These are to be put to ye election:—John Winthrop Esqr, Major Mason Esqr, Mr. Mathew Allyn, Mr. Samuell Willys, Mr. Richard Treat, Mr. Nathan Gold, Capt Thomas Topping, Capt John Tallcott, Mr. Henry Woolcott, Mr. Danll Clarke, John Allyn, Mr. Samll Shearman, Mr. John Howell, Mr. Thirstin Reynor, Capt Benja: Nubery, Mr. Antho: Howkins, Capt John Younge, Mr. Tho: Fayrechild, Mr. Edw: Palmes, Mr. Bond, Mr. Mulford.

These were elected by the freemen:—

John Winthrop Esqr, Gounr.
Major Mason, Dept: Gouernr.

Assistts.

Mr. Math: Allyn,	Mr. Henry Woolcott,
Mr. Samll Willys,	Mr. Danll Clarke,
Mr. Richard Treate,	John Allyn & Secry,
Mr. Nathan Gold,	Mr. Samll Shearman,
Capt Thom: Topping,	Mr. John Howell,

Capt John Tallcott & *Treasurer*, Capt John Younge.

The freemen voted that the Genll Assembly should chuse the Commissioners for the year ensueing.

The Deputies of the Court are:—

Mr. W. Wadsworth,	Nath: White,	Rich: Olmsted,
Mr. Wm. Gaylerd,	Mr. Joseph Fitch,	Rob: Warner,
Samuel Boarman,	Mr. John Bissell,	Ens: Auery,
Mr. Thom: Pell,	John Nott,	Barnabas Wines,
Thom: Hallsey Senr,	John Bankes,	Mr. Rich: Woodhall,
Hugh Calkine,	John Jessop,	Cary Latham,
Mr. Anth: Howkins,	John Standly,	Capt: Seely,
Mr. Tho: Fayrechild,	Ens: Judson,	John Ketcham.
Mr. Campfield,		

John Norton, John Jud, Samll Buell, Timothy Phelps, Tho: Jud, Mr. Hamlin, Samll Olcott;—these were made free in Court.

Mr. John Hicks, Mr. Rob: Coe, Capt John Coe, Mr. Wm.

Hallett were appoynted by the Townes to which they doe belong to attend the Court.*

This Court orders, that in case the Gouernour or Deputy Goun^r, after ye Gen^{ll} Assembly is once constituted, should by reason of sicknes or other speciall occasions be absent from the Court, that then the Court chuse one to act as Moderator in ye Court, both in ordering speech and silence, and in putting things to vote.

This Court doth nominate and appoynt these to be Comissioners in the respectiue Towns to which they doe belonge ;—Mr. Anthony Howkins, for Farmington ; Mr. Campfield, for Norwalke ; Mr. Rob: Chapman & Mr. John Clark, for Saybrook ; Mr. Bruen & Mr. Palmes, Ens: Auery, for New London ; Mr. Fayrechild, for Stratford; Mr. Burr, for Fayrefeild ; Mr. Jessop, for Westchester.

[197]† They are to repair to the next Magistrate to be sworn, and they are invested with Magistratical power in the several towns.

Zerubabell Phillips appeals from the particular Court at South Hampton, December 1st, 1663, in the action of trespass commenced against him by Joseph Reyner, concerning a pit was digged in the common, whereby he was damnified ; the appeal is to the General Court, but now withdrawn.

This Court doth nominate and appoint Mr. William Pitkin, in the behalf of this Colony, to be their Attorney, to implead any delinquents in the Colony, till October next.

This Court desires the Major, Mr. Wolcott, Mr. Clark, Mr. Sherman and John Allyn, to keep the Court on Monday next, for the trial of such cases or complaints as shall then come under hand, or be presented before them.

Whereas his Majesty hath been graciously pleased to confirm unto this Colony, by Charter, all that part of his dominions

---

* Mr. John Hicks, was from Hempstead ; Mr. Robert Coe, from Jamaica ; Capt. John Coe, from Newtown ; Mr. Wm. Hallett, from Flushing.

†Here occurs the first, and it is believed the only break in the original records, so far as they have been transcribed. A leaf containing pages 197 and 198 has been torn from the volume,—when, or by whose agency, cannot now be ascertaind. The loss is comparatively recent, since the volume was entire so late as 1810, when it was copied by direction of the General Assembly and under the supervision of the Secretary of State. From that copy, which is generally accurate, the missing pages have been supplied.

in New England bounded as in the said Charter is expressed, with the Islands adjoining, This Court doth declare, that they claim Long Island for one of those adjoining Islands expressed in the Charter, except a precedent right doth appear, approued by his Majesty.

This Court doth desire and request the Worshipfull Gouernour, Mr. Mathew Allyn, Mr. Willys and Captain Young to go over to Long Island, and to settle the English plantations on the Island under this Gouerment, according to instructions given them.

The aforesaid Committee are hereby authorized to erect and constitute Quarter Courts, or appoint other fit seasons for the keeping of Court for the administration of justice, that all cases may be tried according to law, (life, limb and banishment excepted,) and to do their endeavours so to settle matters, that the people may be both civilly, peaceably and religiously governed in the English plantations, so as they may win the heathen to the knowledge of our Lord and Saviour Jesus Christ, by their sober and religious conversation, as his Majesty, our Lord the King requires in his gracious Letters Patents granted to his subjects here in this Colony ; and in case of crimes of a capital nature, they are to haue liberty to take the opportunity of the Courts of Fairfield or Hartford ; the like liberty they have in case of review ; they may also give oath to those that are accepted by this Court for freemen on the Island, and to do what else they judge may conduce for the good of the Colony.

This Court orders, that those who were propounded for freemen by the Deputies of Norwich, in October last, shall have the freeman's oath administered unto them, by the Major ;

And that those of West Chester have the oath administered unto them by Mr. Jessop ;

And that those of Farmington have the oath of freedom administered to them by Mr. Hawkins; This Court having accepted of the persons presented by the Deputies of the aforesaid towns, as freemen.

This Court accepts Barnabas Wines Junr, Richard Benjamin, Caleb Horton, Benjamin Horton, Thomas Hutchinson, Thomas Moore, Jeffery Jones, for freemen, and Captain Young is to administer the oath of freemen to them.

This Court accepts John Burr to be made free, and Mr. Gould is hereby authorized to administer the oath of freedom to him.

John Teed, Edward Hornett, Samuel Titus, Thomas Jones, William Williams, Samuel Ketcham, Joseph Whitman, Thomas Brush, Caleb Curwithee, Joseph Bayley, John Rogers, Samuel Wood, Thomas Workes, Henry Whisson, James Chichester, Henry Ludlow, Thomas Scuddor, John Samwayes, Thomas Powell, Jonathan Rogers and Isaac Platt are accepted to be made free, and the Commissioners of Huntington are to administer the oath of freedom to them.

Captain Seely and Mr. Wood are appointed Commissioners for Huntington, and Captain Seely is to administer the Commissioners oath to Mr. Wood.

Ensign Avery is authorized to administer the oath of a Commissioner to Mr. Bruen and Mr. Palmes.

Mr. Woodhall and John Ketcham are appointed Commissioners for Setawkett; and were sworn in Court.

Mr. Thurston Rayner is by this Court chosen a Magistrate, and Mr. John Howell is to administer the oath to him for the faithfull execution of his office.

Mr. Mulford and Mr. Bond are appointed Magistrates for East Hampton, and Mr. John Howell is hereby authorized to administer the oath to them, for the faithful execution of their places.

This Court doth make choice of Barnabas Horton for a Commissioner for South Hold, and Capt. Young is to administer the oath to him.

Mr. Barton, Henry Pering, Robert Ackerly, John Jener, Zach: Hawkens, Ralph Hall, are accepted to be made free.

This Court doth nominate Mr. John Hicks and Mr. Richard Gildersleave Sen[r], Commissioners for the town of Hempstead:

And Mr. Robert Coe and Mr. Thomas Benedict, Commissioners for Jamacoe:

And Capt. John Coe and Mr. Richard Betts, Commissioners for Newtown:

And Mr. William Hallett and Mr. Wm. Noble, Commissioners for Flushen:

And Mr. John Rickbell and Robert Ferman, for Oyster Bay, are Commissioners:

And Mr. James Hubbard and Mr. William Wilkins, for Graves-inn.

This Court invests the several Commissioners on the Island with Magistraticall power on the Island.

This Court appoynts Tho: Minor and Ens: Tho: Tracy to lay out the bounds between Saybrook and New London, according to former grants; and they two are to begin their measure at some indifferent place by the riuer side; prouided if any land be layd out to any of Saybrook, within the bounds of New London, they shall hold their perticuler propriety to those lands, payeing their just dues to the Towne of New London.*

Ensign Avery engageth to pay ten shillings to the Treasurer for New London Petition.

The Court refers it to the next session of this Assembly to grant commission to the several commission officers of the Foot and Horse throughout this Colony, and desire that it may be then attended.

Mr. Daniel Clark was by this Court confirmed Captain of the Troop. And Mr. James Richards is confirmed Leiftenant of the said Troop, by this Court.

This Court confirms the order respecting the penalty laid upon those that neglect or refuse to give in a true account of all sorts of their cattle to the List makers, which order was made March 10th, 1663.

Mr. John Hicks, Mr. Robert Coe, Capt. John Coe, Mr. William Hallett, had the Commissioners oath administered to them, in Court.

For Hempstead, This Court accepts of Richard Gildersleave Sen[r], and Richard Gildersleave Jun[r], Mr. Foredum, John Carpenter, Edward Titus, James Pine, Thomas Carle, Thomas Hicks, John Smithman, Jeremiah Wood, John Smith Jun[r], Henry Persell, William Scuddine, William Yeats, Robert Muruen, to be freemen, if they accept of it.

For Jamaicoe, Mr. Walker, Thomas Benedick, Henry Witny, William Smith, Joseph Smith, Dan Penton, John Bayless, Fulk Davis, Thomas Benedick, are accepted as freemen, if they accept it.

---

* The orthography of this order is made to conform to a copy of it certified by Secretary John Allyn, in 1672. [Towns & Lands, I. 98.]

For Newtown, Mr. Loveridge, Richard Betts, Samuel Toe, Caleb Loveridge, Ralph Hunt, John Burrows, John Ramsden, Nicholas Carter, Gershom Moore, James Christy, are accepted as freemen, if they accept of it.

For Flushin, William Noble, Elias Watty,* Walter Salter, Richard Weller, John Thorne, Nicholas Persell, Thomas [†] Jonathan [†] William Salsbee, John Heeded, are accepted as freemen, if they accept it.

[199]   This Court made choyce of the Worp^{ll} Gouernour and Mr. Math: Allyn for Commissioners for the year ensuing; Mr. Willys is appoynted for a reserue.

This Court doth grant liberty to the Marshall to retaile wine, vntill some other be provided to supply wth wine, that the Court approues of, or the Court call in this lycense; he attending the order in the premises.

The Court made choyce of Jonathan Gilbert for Marshall for the year ensueing.

May 19.   The Court is adjourned till to morrow eight of the clock.

The Major & the Com^{rs} of New London are desired to take a speedy course to secure the fine due from Clay, and to issue any misdemeano^r at New London or Saybrook as speedy as may be, and the Major may desire some other help if he sees it necessary.

This Court doth appoynt Mr. Wadsworth & Mr. Fitch to make an addition to the prison house, so as they judg meete for the conueniency of the Countrey, vpon the Countreys acco^t.

This Court upon due deliberation doth order, that all the estate of Mr. John Scott wthin this Colony be sequestred vntill the Court order otherwise; and ye Com^{rs} in the seuerall Townes are hereby ordered to take an exact Inuoyes of all the sayd Scotts estate as remaynes in their respectiue Townes, and see it be secured and kept from imbezelment dureing the Courts pleasure.

This Court orders that Mr. Hagborns vessell that Ralph Parker and Sam: Chester prized at one hundred pounds, shall be delivered at that prize to Ln^t Bull, (for Mr. Russels vse,) by

---

* Doughty?   Elias Doughty had been a Magistrate in Flushing, the year previous.

† These blanks occur in the copy of 1810.

the Constable of New London, to answer in part the verdict of the Court that Ln^t Bull, as Mr. Russels attourney, recouered ag^nst Samuel Hagborn ; and for the remaynder of the verdict, the Constable of New London is to secure the person of the sayd Hagborn untill he doth produce some currant reall estate to answer ye verdict, which estate when it is produced, it is to be apprized by Ens: Auery, Mr. Palmes, Shepherd Smith, Mr. Duglass, or any three of them, and the estate to be deliuered to Ln^t Bull as afoarsayd. The bills are to be returned agayne to Mr. Hagborn, that are in the Constables hand, and when the debt is answered the sayd Hagborn is to be releassed.

The Court is adjourned till the Gouerno^r, or Dep: Gouernour see cause to call it agayne.

May 24th: 1664 : The Councill order the Treasurer, in those Warrants that now he sends forth to Long Island for the Rate, should be payd in Wheat and Pease, or that which is equiuolent.

[200]   AT A GENERALL ASSEMBLY HELD AT HARTFORD, OCTOB^r 13th, 1664.

John Winthrop Esqr, Goun^r,
Major Mason, Dep^t Gou^r.

Mr. Mathew Allyn,	Capt John Young,
Mr. Sam^ll Willys,	Mr. John Howell,
Mr. Henry Woolcott,	Mr. Sam^ll Shearman.
John Allyn, & Secret^ry.	

Deputies:

Mr. Wm. Wadsworth,	Francis Griswold,
Mr. Jos: Fitch,	Mr. Thomas Fairchild,
Capt. Benj. Nubery,	Mr. Isack Nichols,
Mr. John Moore,	Mr. Rob: Chapman,
John Nott,	Ens: Wm. Waller,
Sam^ll Boreman,	Thomas Hunt,
Mr. Antho: Howkins,	Ln^t John Budd,
Sarg^t John Standley,	Sarg^t Wm. Cornwell,
Mr. Cornel: Hull,	Wm. Cheeny,
Mr. John Bankes,	Ens: James Auery,

Mr. Math: Campfeild,   Mr. James Rogers,
Ln^t Rich: Olmsteed,   Mr. Wm. Chesbrough.

The Major propounding to the Court to take up his former grant of a farme, at a place by the Indians called Pomakuck, neer Norwich, The Court grants liberty to him to take up his former grant in that place, upon the same tearms as it was granted to him by the Court. Ens: Thomas Tracy and Francis Griswold are appoynted to lay it out, according to the former grant.

Whereas, Mr. Wm. Thomson, of New London, is remoueing himselfe from thence to Virginia, and is indebted by Bills the sume of Twenty nine pounds, seven shillings and fower pence, which Bill is in the hands of John Packer, This Court orders the Constable of New London to secure so much of the estate of Mr. Thomson in his hands, as it shall be apprized by indifferent men, and the sayd Constable is to keep it in his hands, till he hath order from this Court or the Court of Magistrates, to dispose of it to the right owner which is according to Mr. Thomsons tender to the Court of Magistrats, Octob^r 11th, 1664.

This Court orders, that if any officer or soldier shall neglect or refuse to attend the command of their chiefe comander in any parte of the time of their exercise, they shall forfeit for euery such defect two shillings, which the clark of the band is hereby authorized to distreine, which fine is to be improued for the use of the company, and in case they haue not where wth all to pay there fine, the officers are hereby impowered to cause such other punishment to be inflicted upon them as the nature of there offence shall deserue.

The list of estates presented :—

For Hartford,   19365 : 18 : 0   For Stratford,   10227 : 11 : 0
For Windsor,   16763 : 00 : 0   For Fayrefeild,   11746 : 11 : 0
For Wethersfeild,   11987 : 02 : 0   For Norwalke,   5230 : 17 : 0
For Farmington,   07021 : 11 : 0   For New London,   8040 : 60 : 0
For Norwidge,   03892 : 00 : 0   For Saybrook,   8397 : 12 : 0
For Middleton,   03583 : 06 : 0

For Fayrefeild, John Bur, Rob: Turny, John Knowles, Joseph Lockwod, Rob: Beecham, Simon Crowch, John Barlow Senr, John Barlow Junr, James Euarts, Peter Cooly, Thomas Sherwood, Wm. Heyden, John Growman, Francis Bradley, John

Hoite, Steuen Sherwood, Nath: Burr, Rich: Lyon, Mr. Wakeman, Thomas Bennit, Thomas Wilson, James Bears, John Odill, Sam[ll] Morehouse, Thomas Morehouse, Mathew Sherwood, Richard Hubbell, were accepted to be made free, and Mr. [201] Gould || and Mr. Sherman are appoynted to administer the oath of freedome to them in [   ] next, if nothing fall in as a just exception in the interem.

For Norwalke, Dan[ll] Kellog, Math: Maruen, Thomas Betts, Mark Senssion, John Bouten, Edward Nash, Thomas Lupton, are accepted to be made free, and Mr. Campfeild is to administer the oath of freedome to them in May next, if nothing fall in as a just exception against either of them in the interrem.

This Court orders, that all dwelling houses and barnes, shall for the future be exempted from the list of estates, and all other houses except warehouses.

For Farmington, Wm. Corbett is propownded for a freeman.

This Court doth grant Mr. John Westall a lycense to keep an ordinary or house of enterteinment, at Saybrook.

This Court appoyntes Ens: Waller to act as an administrator wth John Clarke Sen[r] in the ordering and disposall of the estate of Joseph Clarke, according to his will.

This Court orders Sam[ll] Boreman, Mr. Chester & Sam[ll] Wells to dispose of the estate of Math: Williams his wife, for the payment of what debts are due from the estate, so farr as it will goe.

This Court orders that Colonell Nichols, and the rest of the Com[rs] be presented wth fiue hundred bush: of Corn, as a present from this Colony.

This Court abate John Prentice halfe his fine of fiue pownds, & he is to pay ten shillings for his petition.

Mistick & Pawcatuck haueing by Mr. Cheesbrook petitioned this Court for their fauoure to pass by their offences, the Court haueing considered the same doe hereby declare that what irregularities or abusiue practices haue proceeded from them, whereby they haue seemed to offer contempt to the authority here established, it shall be forgiuen and buryed in perpetuall obliuion and forgetfullness, and this to extend it selfe to all y[e] members of the afoarsayd plantation, Captayn Denison onely except.

ed, whoe hath neglected or refused to submitt himselfe peaceably to the order of the Councill of this Colony.

This Court expects and orders that Mistick & Pawcatuck doe present a true list of their estates to the Treasurer, w^{th}in the space of a moneth, and that they be rated according to their proportions, for this year and the last, wth other Townes; they are to take a list of all the cattell that they had in August last, and those cattell that are left out of their list shall be forfeited, which is according to order of Court; and they are allso to pay twenty pownds, which is their proportion of the Patent rate.

This Court grants Sam^{ll} Gibbs a lycense to sell nine or ten quarter caske of Wine, by the gallon, to his neighbours or those that will buy it; and he freely presents the Court wth an anchor of the best of his wine, which the Court desires him to leaue wth the Gouernour.

The Court appoynted Mr. Campfeild, Deacon More, Mr. Fayrechild, Mr. Hull and Ln^{t} Olmsteed, as a Comittee to ripen the busines respecting the calfe in controuersie between Mr. Lord and Dan^{ll} Cone, whoe returne that they haueing veiwed the sayd beast and the evidences of both sides, doe iudge it to be Mr. Lord's steare. The Court confirmes this y^{r} determination that the stear doth belong to Mr. Lord.

The Maior testifyeth that Vncass did beat out Sunckquasson and his men out of theire country in a just warre (as Mr. Haines and the Major conceiued,) and deliuered vp his right from Tomheganomset upwards to the English, whoe gaue the sayd Sunckquasson and his men leaue to hunt to that Brooke; and there was a parcel of land at Wonggum reserued for the posterity of Sowheage.

The Court orders that Vncass his couenant about the Pequitts &c., and his right to the lands at and about New London, shall be duely considered by the Court, and issued (as allso Quinibage lands,) in some conuenient time the next Court.

Major Mason testifyes that James, alias Allums, did (before Vncass and many other Indians) in his presence affirm that he had giuen all his land to old Mr. Winthrop. It was at the same time when they receiued a letter from Mr. Endicott, wherein he thankt him for land they had giuen him.

[202] This Court doth hereby impower Mr. Wm. Cheesbrooke, Mr. Thomas Stanton and Mr. Thomas Minor, to issue and determine all cases that shall be brought before them, to the value of forty shillings, to grant summons according to lawe to any that desire it, to summon men to appeare before them or at any Court in this Colony, and to marry persons, and punish for criminall matters to the value of forty shillings, or by stocks.

This Court doth nominate and appoynt Major Mason, Mr. Math: Allyn, Mr. Willys, Capt: Tallcott, Capt: Newbery, or any three of them, to be a Committee in the behalfe of this Colony to use their endeauours to issue and setle the bownds of the Colony between the Bay and vs, and Road Island and vs, and o^r Sowth bownds; and this Court doth order and determine that the sayd Committee shall not giue away any parte of the bownds of o^r Charter; and what o^r Committee shall doe in the premises, according to this order, is hereby rattifyed and confirmed. Mr. John Allyn is to attend this seruice in the absence of the Major or his Father.

Mr. James Richards was admitted a freeman of this Corporation, and accordingly the oath of freedome was administred to him.

Mr. Dan^{ll} Clarke refuseing to accept of the place of an Assis^t, Mr. James Richards was chosen an Assis^t for this Colony, till the election in May next, and had the oath administred to him.

Mr. Allyn Senr or Junr, Mr. Gold, Mr. Richards and Capt: Winthrop are desired to accompany the Gouernour to New Yorke, to congratulate his Majesties Honourable Com^{rs}. And if an oppertunety offer itselfe that they can issue the bounds between the Dukes Patten & o^{rs} (so as in theire judgments may be to the satisfaction of the Court) they are impowred to attend the same. Mr. Howell and Capt: Young are desired to atend the same seruice.

The Court orders that Mr. Clarkes paper left in Court shall be giuen to him, or his name rasd out of it by the Secretary.

The Court grants a rate of two pence farthing upon the pound, for all the rateable estate of the Colony.

This Court leaues it wth the Councill to appoint a fitting season for a day of Thanksgiueing.

The Court doe order that the Committee that doe goe to New Yorke shall consider Case his businesse

The Court, upon the complaint of Dan^ll Garrad that Mr. John Scott made an escape from him, being in his debt for dyat and time tending on him, twelue weekes, and for other expences, This Court grants him ten pownds for it, out of John Scotts estate, if he can com at it, and Capt: Young is desired to help him to it.

This Court grants Mr. Pitkin, Twenty Nobles, out of Mr. Scotts fine, for his paines in prosecuteing the sayd Scott.

This Court grants Mr. Sam^ll Sherman a farme of two hundred and fifty acres of land upon New Hauen Riuer, whereof fifty acres may be meadow, so it be out of the bounds of the Towne.

This Court grants Mr. Math: Allyn liberty to take up a lott at Homonoscitt, though he doth not goe to dwell on it, and enjoy it, him and his heirs foreuer.

This Court orders that Ln^t Bud continue in his place of Com^r for Hasting and Rye, vntill the Court order otherwise, or the Goun^r and Gent^n that goe to New Yorke.

This Court orders the Treasurer by his Warrant to require the Constable of Sowthhold to gather a rate upon the inhabitance of the saide Towne, to the same value as he doth on the Towne of East Hampton.

[203] A letter was drawn up and sent to East Hampton, the contents whereof were as followeth:

Gent^n: Respects being presented, these lines are to acquainte you that we are informed by persons of creditt, that there is a mare of Sowth Hampton shott (by some of your inhabitance, as is supposed,) which (if it be true) we cannot but look at it as very vnneighbourly, and doe desire that such unneighbourly and unchristian motions be forborne for the future, and desire that due sattisfaction may be made for such damage as the owner of the mare receiues by her being shott, w^thout any suits of law. We doe allso desire that you would be pleased this winter season to provide and make a sufficient fence about your improueable lands, that soe you may secure your labour from damage by cattell, (water-fences will not be judged sufficient, where it is passable for cattell w^thout swiming, at low water,) and in the mean season, that you doe not exact damage, or trouble men by impounding there cattell, vntill you haue made a sufficient fenc about your feilds, not els. Desiring your complyance wth o[r] desires in the premises, we rest, Your assured freinds, The Gen[ll] Assembly of the Colony of Conecticutt. Signed p[r] their order, p[r] me,

John Allyn, Secret[ry].

This Court desires and appoyntes Mr. Sherman and the Secret[ry] to goe to New Haven, &c. and, by order from this Court, in his Majesties name, to require all the inhabitance of New Hauen, Milford, Branford & Guilford, Standford, to submit to the Gouerment here established by his Majesties gracious grant to this Colony, and to take there answer. And they are hereby authorized to declare all the present freemen of New Hauen, Milford, Brandford, Guilford & Standford, that are qualifyed according to lawe, to be freemen of this corporation, soe many of them as shall accept of the same and take the freemans oath. And they are hereby authorized to make as many freemen as they shall by sufficient testimony finde quallyfyed, according to order of Court, in that respect, and to administer the oath of freedom to them.

They are also to declare, that this Court doth inuest Wm. Leete Esq[r], Wm. Joanes Esq[r], Mr. Gilbert, Mr. Fenn, Mr. Crane, Mr. Treat, Mr. Lawes, wth Magistraticall power, to assist in the Gouerment of those plantations and the people thereof, according to the lawes of this corporation, or so many of theire owne lawes and orders as are not contradictory to the teno[r] of our Charter, vntill May next ; and if any of these aboue named refuse to accept to gouern the people as afoarsayd, then Mr. Shearman and the Secret[ry] are hereby authorized to appoynt some other fitt persons in there roome, and to administer an oath to them for the faythfull execution of the trust committed to them. And to declare that all other military and ciuill officers are established in their respectiue places, vntill the Court in May next.

And they are allso, by order from this Court, to declare that they will not call to acco[t] what hath formerly passed to an issue in their courts of judicature.

This Court desires Mr. Allyn and Mr. Richards to attend the searuice that Mr. Shearman and the Secret[ry] were to attend at Standford.

This Court vnderstanding by a writing presented to them

from seuerall persons of this Colony, that they are agrieued that they are not interteined in church fellowship; This Court haueing duely considered the same, desireing that the rules of Christ may be attended, doe commend it to the ministers and churches in this Colony to consider whither it be not their duty to enterteine all such persons, whoe are of an honest and godly conuersation, haueing a competency of knowledg in the principles of religion, and shall desire to joyne wth them in church fellowship, by an explicitt couenant, and that they haue their children baptized, and that all the children of the church be accepted and acco^{td} reall members of the church, and that the church exercise a due christian care and watch ouer them; and that when they are growne up, being examined by the officer [204] in the presence of the church, || it appeares, in the judgment of charity, they are duely qualifyed to perticipate in that great ordinance of the Lords Supper, by theire being able to examine themselues and discerne the Lords body, such persons be admitted to full comunion.

The Court desires y^t the seuerall officers of ye respectiue churches, would be pleased to consider whither it be not the duty of the Court to order the churches to practice according to the premises, if they doe not practice wthout such an order.

If any dissent from the contents of this writing they are desired to help the Court wth such light as is wth them, the next Session of this Assembly.

The Court orders the Secret^{r}y to send a copy of this writing to the seuerall ministers and churches in this Colony.

The Court is adjourned till the Gouernour or Dep: Gouernour see cause to call it againe.

AT A GENERALL ASSEMBLY HELD AT HARTFORD, APRILL
20th, 1665.

John Winthrop Esqr, Goun^r.

Mr. Math: Allyn,   Mr. Henry Woolcott,
Mr. Sam^{ll} Willys,   Ln^t James Richards,
Mr. Rich: Treat,   Ln^t John Allyn, Sec^{r}y.
Captn John Tallcott,

Deputies:

Mr. William Wadsworth,	Mr. Isack Nichols,
Mr. Joseph Fitch,	Mr. John Clarke,
Capt Benj: Nubery,	Mr. George Clarke,
Deacon John More,	Sarj^t W^m. Cornwell,
Samuel Boreman,	W^m. Cheeny,
John Nott,	Tho: Cooke,
Mr. James Rogers,	Mr. Robert Chapman,
Mr. Anthony Howkins,	Mr. James Bishop,
Ens: James Auery,	John Cooper,
Sarj: John Standley,	Ln^t Sam^{ll} Swaine,
Mr. John Bankes,	John Wilford,
Mr. Cornel: Hull,	John Fowler.
Mr. Thomas Fayrechild,	

Sr Robert Carr, Colonel Georg Cartwright, Samuel Mauerick Esq^{rs}, his Majesties Honourable Com^{rs} propositions were presented to this Court and read, and are as followeth:

1. That all householders inhabiting this Colony take the oath of allegiance, and that the administration of justice be in his Majesties name.

To this we returne, that according to his Majesties pleasure exprest in o^r Charter, o^r Gouernour formerly hath nominated and appoynted meet persons to administer the oath of allegiance, whoe haue, according to their order, administred the s^d oath to seuerall persons allready; and the administration of justice amongst us hath been, is and shall be in his Majesties name.

2d. Propos: That all men of competent estates and of ciuill conuersation, though of different judgments, may be admitted to be freemen, and haue liberty to chuse or to be chosen officers, both military and ciuill.

To the 2d, our order for admission of freemen is consonant wth that proposition.

3. Propos: That all persons of ciuill liues may freely injoy the liberty of their consciences, and the worship of God in that way which they thinke best, prouided that this liberty tend not to the disturbance of the publique, nor to the hindrance of the mayntenance of ministers regularly chosen in each respectiue parish or township.

To the 3d. propos: we say, we know not of any one that hath bin troubled by us for attending his conscience, prouided he hath not distu^{r}bed the publique.

4. Propos: That all lawes and expressions in lawes, derogatory to his Majestie, if any such haue bin made in these late troublesome times, may be repealed, altered and taken off the file.

To the 4th prpos: we return, we know not of any lawe or expressions in any law that is derogatory to his Majesty amongst us; but if any such be found, we count it or duty to repeal, alter it, and take it off the file, and this we attended upon the receipt of our Charter.

[205] This Court, upon the humble petition of Jasper Gunn, haue granted fiue pownds to be paid unto Mr. Crow next yeare, in leiw of parte of his fine.

This Court frees Isack More from training, he haueing formerly bin cheif officer of the Traine Band of Farmington.

This Court doth repeal the former order, which constituted and impowred a Councill, made March the 11th, 166$\frac{2}{3}$.

This Court orders that Mr. Wm. Leete, Mr. Wm. Joanes, Mr. Benjamin Fenn, Mr. Math: Gilbert Mr. Jasper Crane, Mr. Alexander Bryant, Mr. Lawes, shall be read at the Election for nomination for Assistants. Mr. Rot: Treat allso is nominated for election; Mr. Welles, Mr. Newbery & Mr. Howkins were allso nominated, and Mr. Clarke.

This Court doth hereby declare that all former actings that haue past by the former power at New Hauen, so farr as they haue concerned this Colony (whilst they stood as a distinct Colony,) though they in their own nature haue seemed uncomfortable to us, yet they are hereby buryed in perpetuall obliuion, neuer to be called to account.

This Court doth approue of the inhabitants of Midleton's endeauours to enter into church fellowship, and doe desire that they would proceed therein according to the order of the gospell, and take the aduice of the neighbour elders and churches.

This Court doth appoynt Ensigne Auery, Ensigne Thomas Tracy, and John Gallop, Thomas Minor, or any three of them, to lay out a conuenient percell of land, for Robin and his company to plant vpon, at or near the head of Mistick Riuer, prouided it be not in the bownds of any of the plantations, & to make returne hereof to ye Court in May next.

In refference to ye motion of Coll: Richard Nichols to or

John Winthrop (Governor.)
John Mason (Depr Governor.)
(Assistants.)
Mathew Allyn
Sam:ll Willys
Nathan Gold
Henry Wolcut
John: Allyn
John Talcott
Samuell Sheawrman
James Richards
Will'm Leete
Wm Jones.
Beniamin ffen   Jasper Crane
Danll Clark:

Gentlemen, for assistance, in case of forraigne inuassions, it being a matter of waighty importance, it is left to the serious consideration of the Gen^ll Assembly in May next.

In refference to what was moued about Captn Scotts fine, the Deputies declare that they feare his fine will not sattisfye the charge and damage which he put this Colony to, but when that is issued the case may be farther considered.

Respecting what was moued about a speedy conuayance of of Lett^rs, the Court will consider & aduice wth neighbour Colonyes, what will be best in that case.

The Court desires Mr. Willys and Mr. Richards to draw vp a writing in answer to what was moued about Duke Hambleton's Petition, and to present it to the next Courte.

[*Note.* The General Court of New Haven Colony, at their session in December, 1664, had assented, conditionally, to the necessity of union, and voted that, " in loyalty to the King's Majesty, when an authentic copy of the determination of his Majesty's Commissioners is published, to be recorded with us, if thereby it shall appear to our Committee that we are, by his Majesty's authority, now put under Connecticut Patent, we shall submit, by a necessity brought upon us, by the means of Connecticut aforesaid; but with a *salvo jure* of our former rights and claims, as a people, who have not yet been heard in point of plea." A Committee was accordingly appointed to confer with Connecticut and to complete the union. In a letter to Connecticut, Jan. 5th, 1664–5, Mr. Bishop, (a member of the New Haven committee, and by their order) writes that " having seen the copy of his Majesty's Commissioners' determination (deciding the bounds betwixt his highness the Duke of York and Connecticut charter,) we do declare submission thereunto, according to the true intent of our vote, unto which we refer you." &c.

The union of the two colonies was now virtually complete. The Magistrates of New Haven, having been formally " invested with Magistratical power to assist in the government of those plantations & the people thereof," by the General Court of Connecticut, and " all other military and civil officers established in their respective places," continued to exercise their former authority in New Haven Colony, until the General Election in May : at which time the union was finally consummated, and the following Magistrates chosen to office for the ensuing year:

John Winthrop Esq., Governor. John Mason Esq., Deputy Governor. Assistants; Mathew Allyn Esq., Sam^ll Willys Esq., Mr. Nathan Cold, Capt. John Talcot (& Treasurer;) Mr. Henry Wolcott, Lt. John Allyn, Mr. Samuel Sherman, Lt. James Richards, Mr. William Leete, Mr. William Jones, Mr. Benjamin Fenn, Mr. Jasper Crane. Capt. Daniel Clarke, Secretary.

Of the Assistants, the four last named had been Magistrates in New Haven colony, the year preceding.

A list of such documents relating to the union, as have been preserved in the office of the Secretary of this State, with a partial abstract of their contents, is given in the Appendix, No. XII.]

WILLS AND INVENTORIES.

[From Colonial Records, Vol. I.*]

[52] The last Will and Testament of RICHARD LYMAN, being in p^{r}fect memory, I giue vnto my wife all my howseing & lands dureing her life, and one third p^{r}te of my lands to dispose at her death amongst my children as shee pleaseth, and I giue to her all my moueable goods, as Cattell and howshold stuffe, and all other impliments or mouables. And the other two p^{r}ts of my land I giue to my elder sonne Richard, and to his heires forever, and if he dy wthout an heir, then I giue yt to my sonne Robert and to his heires for ever. For my sonne Richard my mynd is that the Cattell I haue formerly giuen him, that he shall enioy. To my daughter Sarah, besids the Cattell I formerly haue giuen her, my will is that my wife shall pay her twenty pownds, to yeres after my death. To my sonne John Lyman I giue him thirty pownds, to be paid him by my wife, att two & twenty yeres of age, and the hoggs that I formerly haue giuen him, I giue vnto my wife, and if he contends wth her and will not be content my wife should enioy the hoggs, then yt is my will that shee should not pay him the thirty pownds. To my sonne Robert I giue twenty fower pownds, to be paid him at twenty two yeres of age; and to my daughter Fillis, the wife of Williā Hills, I giue tenne shillings; and I make my wife sole Executrixe to this my will.

Dated the 22th of Aprill, 1640.

---

* Such wills and inventories as were recorded prior to the close of the year 1644, were entered in various parts of the first Volume, wherever a convenient blank page offered itself to the Secretary, and without any regard to chronological sequence. These are here brought together, and transposed so as to follow somewhat more nearly the order in which they were originally recorded. Such as are recorded by themselves, on pages [228] to [271] of the first Volume, are printed without transposition. The record, as far as page [250,] inclusive, is in the hand writing of Secretary Welles; the remainder, in that of John Cullick.

The two p^rts of my land and howse I give to Richard Lyman my sonne: the reson of writeing this is because the word howse was not formerly exp^rssed.

Read, sealed and del^d   Richard Lyman.
in the p^rsents of vs
     Tho: Bull, John Moodie,
     Andrewe Bacon.

July 24th.

The wydowe Lymans mynd is that her sonne Richard Lyman should p^rforme her husbands will, and that her sonne Robert should liue wth him till he be twenty two yeres of age, and then she giues Robert Lyman the third p^rte of the howsen & grownds, & for p^rformance of her husbands will, shee giues Richard all her moueable goods both w^thout the howse and w^thin, only her weareing Cloathes and some of her lining shee will dispose of.

                         John Moody,
                         Andrew Bacon.

[53] *A Inuentory of the goods of Richard Lyman deceased, made the vi^th of Sept͞eber, 1641.*

	£		
Imp^rs· A Cow & a Cow calfe,	8.	10.	00
It: a heifer of a yere & halfe old,	4.	00.	00
It: a bull, 4*l*. 10*s*.; It: a goate & 2 kids, 1*l*. 13*s*.,	[6.	03.	00
It: 8 hoggs and halfe a sowe, & the pewtre,	10	00.	00
It: one acre of mislin,*	3.	10.	00
It: an acre of sumer wheat, 2*l*. 10*s*.; an acre of oats, 2*l*.	[4.	10.	00
It: 3 roods of pease and barly,	1.	10.	00
It: 5 acres of Indean Corne,	8.	15.	00
It: for squared tymber, planke & board,	1.	05.	00
It: a Cart & plow & tacklin belonging to them,	1.	08.	6
It: a Tabell, forms & chaires, 8*s*.; It: a Cubberd, 15*s*.,	[1.	03.	00
It: 4 chests, a trunke; a old one,	0.	18.	6
It: 2 beare vessells, 5*s*.; It. 4 old firkins, 3*s*.;	[0.	8.	00
It: 1 payle & a wooden platter, 2*s*.; an old byble, 2*s*. 6*d*.,	[0.	4.	6
It: 3 kettells, 2 skillits, an old brasse pot,	2.	4.	00
It: 2 brass pans & a bakeing pan,	0.	12.	00
It: a pestell, a mortar and old kettell,	0.	6.	6
It: 4 platters, 2 cansticks, & drinkeing pott, wth some other smale peeces of pewter,	1.	2.	00
It: a warmeing pann, a chaffin dishe and pewter bottell,	0.	9.	00
It: 2 frying pans, 6*s*.; It: 3 Iron potts, 1*l*. 4*s*.,	[1.	10.	00

---

* *Mislin* or *Meslin*; a mixture of wheat and rye. *Webster.*

It: a Cob iron, a gridiron, a trammell, a fire pan &
doggs & some other old iron, . . 0. 11. 00
It: 2 fier locke peeces, a sowrd & belt, . 2. 3. 00
[54] It: a sacke & wool, . . . 0. 8. 00
It: 2 bedds and bowlsters & pillowes, . 6. 00. 00
It: 3 Couerlids, 4 blankets, 3 straw bedds, . 4. 8. 00
It: 8 Curtens, 1*l*. ; 3 bedsteads, 6*s*. ; Tewed* skins, 8*s*., [1. 14. 00
It: 2 Wheeles, 5*s*. ; It: 9 p^{re} of sheets & one odde one,
3*l*. 8*s*. 8*d*., ... [3. 13. 8
It: 4 table cloathes and a dossen and halfe of napkins, 1. 9. 00
It: 7 pillobers and 2 other smale peeces of linnen, 0. 13. 6
It: a Coate, a Jergen, 2 dubletts, and a p^{re} of breeches, 1. 10. 00
It: 2 sythes wth their tacklin, 6*s*. ; It: 2 ladders, 6*s*., 0. 12. 00
It: a Churne & meat in yt, 10*s*. ; It: 4 howes, 6*s*., 0. 16. 00
It: 2 wedges, 2 betel rings, 2 sawes, . . 0. 16. 00
It: a broad axe, 2 narrow axes, wimbell & chessells, 0. 11. 00
It: a powdring trofe, . . . 0. 01. 6

Some is 83*l*. 16. 2*d*.

John Moodie,
Andrew Bacon,
John Barnard.

---

[70] OCTOBER THE 27, 1639.

A Inuentory of the goods and Cattle of JOHN BRUNDISH of Wethersfield.†

	£	s	d
Imp^{rs.} his weareing apparrell,	3.	0.	0
It. his two bedds compleat,	6.	0.	0
It. two p^{re} of sheets wth two pillowberes,	1.	0.	0
It. in brasse and pewter,	5.	0.	0
It. one chest, a boxe, a small cubbert & a table,	3.	0.	0
It: cushens, stooles & chaires,	0	10.	0
It. Tramels, tongs, fier pan, bellowes, cobirons, rostiron, spitt and frying pan,	1.	5.	0
It in working tooles,	4.	5.	0
Itē twelue bushells of Rye,	4.	16.	0
It. about fourscore and ten bush^s of Indean corne,	18.	0.	0
It. one horse and a mare,	48.	0.	0
It. one cow, 2 heifers, 2 calues,	55.	0.	0
It. in hay,	7.	10.	0
It. in debts due vnto him,	15.	0.	0
It. books,	2.	0.	0
	174.	6.	

Debts due to be payd out 62*l*. 10.
her howse and land valued at 130*l*.

---

* *Tewed* or *tawed*; i. e. dressed white.   † See pp. 40 and 45, *ante*.

She hath 5 children, the 2 eldest girls, the next a boy, the other 2 girles.

Andrew Ward,
Richard Gyldersly.

A noate brought in Court since the Inuentory, as followeth:
Rachell Brundishe hath 14 acres of meadow, her howse lott 3 acres, and w^t vpland belongs thereunto in euery diuysion, saueing w^t her husband and shee hath sould, vizt. her shaire beyond the Riuer and 6 acres in Penny wise.

Debts appereing since the Inuentory was made,		4*l.*
Debts paid,	. .	41*l.* 16. 4*d.*

Remayneing of the stocke of Cattle, 2 Cowes, on mare.

---

[68] A true Inuentory of all the goods, corne and cattell that were in the hands of ABRAHAM FYNCH, when he deceased, taken the 3 of Sep. 1640.

	£	s.	d.
Imp^{rs} his apparrell,	2.	6.	0
It. one Cow,	20.	0.	0
It. one Heifer,	10.	0.	0
It. four swyne shoots,	2.	0.	0
It. one cutting saw, one axe,	0.	10.	0
It. 3 p^rre of sheets, 2 p^rre of pilloberes,	1.	10.	0
It. 5 napkins,	0.	3.	0
It. 2 kettles and 1 potte,	1.	8.	0
It. his howse lott, wth all deuisions thereunto belonging,	100.	0.	0
The prisers, Sam: Smith, Nathaniell Foote. The some,	137.	17.	0

A noate of the debts that Abraham Fynch owed at his decease.

	£	s.	
To Mr. Michell,	3.	1.	0
To Goodman Boosie,	1.	12.	0
To Goodmā Sticklin,	1.	9.	0
For Towne Rates,	4.	15.	6
To Goo: Lawes,	1.	10.	0
Wydow Kilborne,	0.	5.	0
Goo: Smith,	0.	3.	0
Leasly Bradfield,	0.	9.	0
To Mr. S	0.	11.	0
To goodmā Daggett,	1.	3.	0
	14.	18.	6

It [*is*] Ordered, that the Relike of Abraham Finch deceased shall administer & possesse the Estate lefte in Goods, and also hold the land & howseing vntill the Child com to the age of one and twenty yeres, and then the Child of the said Abraham to haue two p^rts, & the said Relick duering her naturall life the third ; the said Relick is to mayntayne the Child, or to comitte him to his Grandfather Abrahā Fynch, who tenders to educate yt as his owne Coste.

Decēber the 3^d, 1640.

---

[64]   The last will and Testament of J<small>AMES</small> O<small>LMSTEAD</small>, late of Hartford, decesed.

This is my wyll, to giue my Estate betweene my two sonns, that is to say, the on halfe to my sonn Nicholas, and the other halfe to my sonne Nehemiah, equally deuyded betweene thē both, wth this reseruation, that if my brother Lum̄us doe make his word good to make my sonne Nicholis wifes portion as good as any child he hath, for so I vnderstand his p^rmise is, but if he shall refuse so to doe, I shall then refuse to giue my sonn any p^rte of my moueable goods, cattell or debts, but my will is to leaue the thing wth Richard Webb and William Wodsworth to see my Brother Lum̄us doe p^rforme his p^rmise, and as the said Richard Webb and Will' Wodsworth shall doe I shall be content. And if my Brother Lum̄is doe p^rforme his p^rmise, then my will is their portions shall be a like, only Nicholis shall abate so much as I gaue him before. And my will is that my sonne Nehemiah shall giue out of his portion ten pownd to my Cossen Rebeca Olmstead that now dwelleth wth me, and he shall pay yt her w^thin three yeares after my dicease, and I leaue her to be disposed by Richard Webb and Will' Wadsworth, and as shee shall carry herselfe, yt shall be in their power ether to giue her the tenn pownd or to deteyne yt frō her. I doe giue my searuant Will' Corby fiue pownd, to be paid when his tyme coms forth, and I doe will my sonne Nehemya to pay him out of his owne portion: And I doe will that Will' Corby doe searue his tyme wth my sonne Nehemiah. And I leaue my sonne Nehemiah wth Richard Webb and Will' Wodsworth, intreating thē to haue the ouer sight of him, and the disposeing of him as their owne child. But if my sonne Nehemiah shall goe contrary in bestowing himselfe any way contrary to the judgement of my two frinds, Rich: Webb and Will' Wodsworth, then yt shall be in their power to comaund and take a hundred pownd of his Estate, and dispose of yt as they thinke fitt. I giue to my two frynds Richard Webb and Will' Wodsworth, wch I put in trust, six pownds and a marke to be paid equally betwixt thē, and my two sonns shall pay thē, the one pay the one halfe and the other pay the other halfe.

    Witnesse, the 28th of September, 1640,   Ja: Olmstead.
    Richard Webb,
    Will' Wodsworth.

[65] Wee whose names are hereunder written, the frynds intrusted by the decesed wthin named, haueing litell acquayntance wth things of this nature, and being by him suddenly caled hereunto, in a sore stresse and pang of his sicknes, wherein he expected a p^{r}sent dep^{r}ting, he being senceble of his owne weakenes, hasted to an issue of this busines, did seuerall tymes desire vs to aduise him what he should doe, and many tymes did wishe us to doe what we thought meet o^{r}selues.

Now we haueing since his disease, togather wth his two sonns, Nicholas & Nehemiah, to whō he hath bequethed his estate, taken into more serious consideration what is done, and obsearueing some things to be ouerpast, of wch we are p^{r}swaded that if ether they had com to his owne mynd, or otherwise had then bine suggested by vs, he would redily and cherefully haue attended thereunto: Wee therefore, togather wth the reddy & free consent of his sonns abouesaid, (well knowing, out of long and good experience, the disposition and constant practice of their father,) hath mutually agreed, as desierus to fulfil that wch we conceaue to be his mynd, to ad to those bequethed wch are spesified wthin, these legases following:

That is to say, to his Kynsmen Richard Olmstead fiue pownd, and to his Kynsman John Olmstead fiue pownd, to be paid vnto them wthin three yeres after his disease. And vnto the Church of Christ in Hartford, Twenty pownds, to be paid at the same tyme of three yeres after the decease of there said father. In witnesse whereof we haue sett to our hands.

    Will' Wadsworth.   Nicholas Olmstead,
                                       Nehemiah Olmsted.

[66] Sep: 28th. *An Inventory of the goods and Cattell of James Olmestead of Hartford, deceased in the yere of o^r Lord, 1640.*

	£	s	d
Imp^r^s one horse,	20.	0.	0
It. one mare,	15.	0.	0
It. one mare colt,	10.	0.	0
It. one yoke of steeres,	30.	0.	0
It. one single steere,	13.	0.	0
It. four cowes,	47.	13.	4
It. three calues,	10.	10.	0
It. thirteene hoggs,	18.	0.	0
It. eightscore bush^l of Indean corne,	24.	0.	0
It. 30 bush^l of sumer wheat,	7.	0.	0
It. 12 bush^l of pease,	2.	10.	0
It. 15 load of hay,	10.	0.	0
It. 8 bush^l of molt,	2.	0.	0
It. one young heifer and on young steere,	13.	0.	0
It. one young steer at Paq'nuck,	8.	0.	0
It. one cow hide,	0.	10.	0
It. 3 ewe goats & a wether,	7.	0.	0
It. one wayne,	3.	0.	0
It. 2 yoaks & the Iron worke,	0.	6.	0
It. one plow, two plow irons, & a chayne,	1.	12.	0
It. one gang of harrow tynes,	0.	16.	0
It. one smale chest wth old iron & some tooles,	3.	0.	0
It. old sithes & on new on,	0.	10.	0
It. one pyke & Costlitte,*	1.	10.	0
It. two hand sawes, one frameing saw, one hack saw,	1.	0.	0
It. one nayle boxe,	1.	10.	0
It. four howes,	0.	7.	0
It. two mattocks, on,	1.	0.	0
It. one chese p^rsse, old hogsheads & a pype,	1.	3.	0
It. 2 beare hogsheads, two beare barrells, 2 powdring tubbs, 4 brueing vessells, 1 cowle, 2 firkins,	2.	0.	0
It. wymbles, chysells, hammers, pynsers,	0.	13.	0
It. collers & harnes, saddell and pannell,† halters & brydle,	1.	7.	0
It. fiue pyke forks, one rope, on fanne,	0.	8.	0
It. 3 axes, 2 wedges, 2 ryngs for a beetell,	0.	13.	0
It. 4 brasse, 3 skilletts, one skimer, on ladle, on candlestick, on morter, all of brasse, 1 brasse pott,	5.	0.	0
It. 7 small peuter dishes, 1 peuter bason, 2 chāber potts, 6 poringers, 2 peuter candlesticks, 1 frudishe, 2 little sasers, 1 smale plate,	1.	12.	6
It. 7 bigger peuter dishes, one salt, 2 peuter cupps, one peuter dram, 1 peuter bottle, 1 warmeing pan, 13 peuter spoones,	2.	3.	0
It. 2 Iron potts & a pott posnette, 1 dripping pan, 1 frying pan, 1 gridiron, one squar, 2 spitts,	2.	2.	0
It. 2 Irons, 2 tramells, 1 perre of tongs, 2 perre of pothooks, 2 perre of cobirons, 1 fier pan, 1 cole dishe and a perre of bellowes, one peale,	1.	13.	0
It. one stupan, 3 bowles & a tunnell, 7 dishes, 10 spoones, one woodden cuppe, 1 woodden platter, wth 3 old latten‡ pans, & 2 doz. and halfe of trenchers and two wyer candlesticks,	0.	11.	1

---

* Corslet. † A kind of rustic saddle. *Webster.* ‡ Sheet iron covered with tin. *Webster.*

It. 2 Jacks, 2 bottells, two drinkeing horns, 1 little pott,	0.	10.	0
It. 3 bibles & 3 other bookes,	2.	5.	0
It. one payle, one pecke, one halfe bushell,	0.	3.	8
It. one smoothing iron, two brushes,	0.	2.	8
[67] It. 3 musketts, one fowleing peece, 3 perre of bandaleres, one sword, one rapier, 1 dagger, 2 rests, 2 pistolls, wth powder, shott & match,	6.	0.	0
It. one Table, one Chire, sixe cushions and one little forme,	1.	7.	0
It. fiue sacks,	0.	10.	0
It. two fether bedds, two flockebedds,	6.	10.	0
It. 3 ruggs, one Couerled, 6 blanketts, one p^re of curtens & curten rods, & a course bedcase,	7.	15.	0
It. 2 fether pillowes, 1 flocke pillow, 1 bedsteed,	0.	19.	0
It. 3 p^re of fyne sheets & 5 p^re of course sheets,	3.	10.	0
It. 3 course pillowbeers, & 2 fine ons, 1 doz. of napkins,	1.	3.	0
It. two shorte Table Cloathes & two course ons, 2 towells,	0.	11.	0
It. diuers smale things in a trunke,	3.	0.	0
It. 20 little smale peeces of childing lyning,	0.	10.	0
It. 15 quire of paper,	0.	6.	3
It. 27 yards of course Canuas,	1.	0.	10
It. 19 yards of Lockrū,*	1.	4.	0
It. 5 yards of woollen cloath,	1.	5.	0
It. 2 trunks, one chest and 2 smale boxes,	1.	6.	0
It. 12 Caps, 8 bands,	1.	2.	0
It. 3 shirts,	0.	15.	0
It. one little peece of course Lockrū,	0.	4.	6
It. 3 suits of apparrell, wth hatts, stocking & shues,	13.	5.	0
It. 2 acres of Englishe corne of the grownd,	4.	0.	0
It. 13 acres of grownd broke vp,	12.	0.	0
It. in mony and debts,	55.	0.	0
It. one case of bottells,	00.	15.	0
The whole some,	£397.	19.	2

John Steel,
Edw: Stebbing.

[60] March the iiijth, 1640.

A Coppy of the will & Testament of Williā Spenser, late of Hartford deceased, p^rsented in Court vppon Oath, by John Taylcott & John Pratt of the said Towne.

A noate of the mynd and Will of Williā Spenser for p^rsent the 4th of May, 1640.

Imp^{rs} his Will is that the Estate that he hath in New Ingland, and also that wch may com to his wife hereafter, that is any

---

Lockram,—"a sort of coarse linen." *Webster.*

p^rte of his wifes portion yf any doe com, that all the Estate be dyuyded as foloweth :

I giue to my wife one third p^rte of all my Estate :

I giue to my sonne Samuell one third p^rte :

I giue to my two daughters Sarah and Elizabeth one third partte :

The children to be brought vppe wth the improuement of the whole estate that I leaue both to my wife and children ; The portion wch I leaue to my sonne to be paid him when he is of the age of twenty yeres; Also the portion of my daughter Sarah and my daughter Elizabeth to be paid to them at the age of   * yeres of age. Also yt is my mynd that if ether of my children doe dy before the tyme their portions be due to them, that the portion of the p^rty desesed be equally devyded to the p^rtyes or p^rty that shall suruife the other.

Also my mynd is, my Cosen Mathew Allen, my brother John Pratt and John Taylcoate, that these three partyes, or any two of them, shall haue the Ouersight of my Estate, and in case that they shall see in theire judgements the Estate to be wasted, that they shall haue power to take the children and their portions   † for their bringing vppe, and to pay the Children their portn͠s that remayne at the seuerall tymes aboue written.

Also my mynd is, that my wife shall haue no power to alienatt or make sale of my howse or any p^rte of my land I leaue, w^thout the consent of two of the p^rtyes that are to ouersee my Estate.

The Inuentory of the Estate of the said Will' Spenser.

	£	s.	d.
Imp^rs in weareing Cloathes,	5.	8.	0
in the Hall, the planks & two chayres,	0.	11.	0
in the Closett, on trundell bedd and blankett,	0.	15.	0
one sadell and brydle, and waight & skalls,	0.	15.	2
in sythes, axes, wimbles, horsse harnis & other working tooles,	3.	0.	0
in the Parlor chamber, one chest, two plancks,	0.	9.	0
one fetherbedd, boulster, two pillowes,	3.	0.	0
In sheets and tabell lynen,	2.	0.	0
in the Sisler, in seuerall peeses of peuter,	1.	10.	0

* Blank.   † Blank.

in brasse kettells and iron potts & other implements, and on hogshead and barrell,	4.	15.	0
In the lodgeing roome, one bedsteed & curteens,	1.	5.	0
two chests,	0.	15.	0
One muskette, bandalers, two sowrds,	1.	5.	0
One fowleing peece,	1.	4.	0
One Cowe and on Cow calfe,	28.	0.	0
In swyne of seuerall sorts,	13.	0.	0

[67. 12. 2]

Seuerall debts lefte vncroste in his booke, oweing in the Bay, the wch the most of thē are denyed, and those that are confessed are very doubtful whether much of yt will be paid, being in the hands of some of his kindred that are pore, in all to the value of . 44l.

Also, the howse and howse lott conteyneing aboute 2 acres, wth some outhowses; also seuerall p^{r}sells of vpland lotts, to the value of 74 acres, as may apeare by the records to that purpose, whereof, besids the right wch he had in any other lands to be deuyded.

Also, eleuen acres of meadow and swamp, lying in the north meadow.

Also, one p^{r}cell lying on the East side of the great Riuer, conteyneing tenne acres.

Also, there is land yet remayneing at Concord in the Bay, wch while he liued he esteemed at . . . . 120l.

Out of this estate there is lefte to be paid, . . 50l.

Also, a debt wch is of an old recknoing, the wch we haue no clere accoumpts of, but yet himselfe doubted that it would be 10.

The goods and estate estimated by these p^{r}tyes here expreste.

John Tallcott,
John Pratt.

The destribution of the estate appeares in the Records of the perticular Courte, the 24th June, 1650, fol: 10: and the Coppyes of the bills giuen to the Courte for the payment of 30l. to the chilldren, are in the Booke of Records of Lands for the seuerall townes, at ye other end of it; the original Bills are vppon the fyle of wills and Inventoryes.*

---

[62] March the 4th, 1640. The last will of Joyce Ward.

I, Joyce Ward, of Wethersfield, being sicke in body but whole in mynd, doe make my last will and Testament, this 15th day of Nouember in this p^{r}sent yeare of o^r Lord Christ, 1640, in manner of forme as foloweth :—

Imp^{rs}. I giue to four of my sonns, that is to say, to Anthony Ward, Williā Ward, Robert Ward & John Ward, ech of thē

---

* These last four lines were added subsequently, in the hand writing of Secretary John Allyn.

a pare of sheets, and to my eldest sonne Edward I giue vnto him twelue pence of mony; furthermore I make my sonne in law, John Flecher, my whole and sole Executor, to pay and dischardge all those debts and legaces wch I am bownd to p^rforme, and for to see my body to be brought to the grownd in a decent manner; In witnesse whereof I haue sett my hand the day and yeare aboue written.

Memorand^m. That I Joyce Ward haue lefte my sonne Roberts portion, wch his father gaue him, wch is twenty pownd, in England, in the hands of my sonne Edward Ward; I haue made Mr. Wollersloue, of Clipsum, in England, in the County of Rutland, my Atturny for to receaue yt for my vse; if he haue gott yt then my sonne Robert shall haue the whole twenty pownd, but if yt be not gotten, then the sixe pownd wch I paid for the puting out of the said Robert Ward to an Aprentice shall be p^rte of that twenty pownd.

Joyce Ward, her marke.

This was done in the p^rsence of vs,
    Nathaniell Dickenson,
    Roger Prichat.

An Inventory of all and singuler the goods, chatells, Cattle, belonging to Joice Ward, wydow, late of Wethersfield, made, taken and found, the 24th of February, 1640, by George Hubberd and Leonard Chester.

	£	s.	d.
Imp^rs. 7 yards of Hemppen cloath at 2s. p^r yard,	0.	14.	0
It. one p^re of flaxen sheets,	1.	0.	0
It. four p^re of hemppen sheets,	2.	0.	0
It. her apparrell vizt. 2 gownes, one hatt, one p^re of bodyes wth other,	5.	0.	0
It. one bedd, two boulsters, two pillowes, two Couerings, two Curtens,	10.	0.	0
It. one boxe wth a litle hand Trunke,	0.	3.	6
One brasse pott,	0.	16.	0
One brasse panne,	1.	0.	0
One Iron pott,	0.	2.	0
One Chamber pott,	0.	2.	0
One brasse Coal dishe,	0.	2.	0
[63] One sowe, wth three piggs,	1.	0.	0
Two table cloathes, wth 4 napkins,	0.	16.	0
One bond or specialty,	30.	0.	0
Som: tot^s:	52.	15.	6

    p^r Leonard Chester,
      George Hubberd.

[75] The Inuentory of THO: JOHNSON,* as the p^rticulers were sold by Andrew Bacon & John Barnard, appoynted by the Court to make sale of them.

	£.	s.	d.		£.	s.	d.
To Gudm^n Hill, a Coat,	1.	10.	0	a peece of leather, a perre of stockings and other things,	0.	8.	7
2 p^re of stockings, a shirt & band and hose yarne,	0.	12.	0	2 bush^l of maslin,	0.	12.	0
a p^re of high shues,	0.	5.	0	some smale peeces of leather,	0.	6.	0
a peece of leather,	0.	2.	6	3 hatchets,	0.	4.	1
5 bands, a shirt, a redde wascoat, a perre of start ups,†	0.	12.	0	one shurt,	0.	5.	2
				1 paire of shues and boots,	0.	5.	0
a shute of apparrell, a pestell,	0.	18.	0	2 peeces of leather,	0.	3.	0
				3 perre of boots,	0.	9.	0
a hatte,	0.	6.	0	Mr. Welles distreyned a muskett, a sword, bandaleres & a rest,	1.	5.	0
3 peeces of leather, halfe a pownd of pepp^r, a seefe bottom,	0.	12.	1				
					10.	13.	5
a syth,	0.	2.	0				
a shuet & two bands,	1.	13.	0				
2 perre of breeches,	0.	3.	0				

Abated the Partyes for a mistake in their accoumpte, To be alowed the^m for their paynes in keepeing & selleing the p^rticulers, ... 9s. 5
The debte he owed vppon the distresse & for Recording the Inuentory, ...
Goodm^n Hill owed him 10*l*.

---

[71] The 6th of Nouember, 1643.

The last Will and Testament of THO: SCOTT, of Hartford, deceased, as yt was spoken by him to Edward Stebbing and Tymothy Standly who were sent for by him for that end, to who^m he expressed his will as followeth :—

I doe giue to my wife and sonne Thomas, the one halfe of my howse and halfe of my barne and halfe of my howse lott : I doe also giue vnto them my two lotts in the North meadow, and my lott in the litle meadow, as also the swamps at both ends : I doe in like manner giue vnto them all my corne in my howse and barns, both here at Hartford and at Tunxis Cepus, as also two Cowes and my two elder steers and fiue hoggs, wth halfe my howshold stuffe : I doe also giue them my Carts and ploughs and

---

* See pages 49, 53, ante.   † A kind of high shoe.

the tacklin belonging to thē. And my mynd is that if my sonne Tho: depart this life before my wife, at his death that the one halfe of the meadow, catle and howshold stuffe before giuen to him and my wife, shalbe equally diuided betwixt my other children then liuing; and my mynd is that my wife shall haue power at her death to dispose of and giue away the other halfe of that wch is giuen to her and my sonne as shee seeth fitt, except my howseing and land, wch my mind is shall then com to the rest of my children, at the death of the longest liuer of my wife or my sonne Thomas. I doe also make my wife executrixe to receive and pay my debts; and my mynd is that my youngest daughter doe remayne wth my wife so long as shee seeth meete, wth the advice of those that ouersee my will. My mind also is, that all my daughters be disposed of, both in searuice and mariedge, by my wife and ouerseers, and that my daughters shall receaue their portions, ether at the day of their mariedge or at twenty yeares of age, wch shall first happen, my mynd being that all the remaynder of my estate wch is not by this my will giuen to my wife and sonne Thomas, (after my debts are discharged,) shall be equally diuided among them.

The sume and substance of this was exp^rssed by Tho: Scott aforesaid in the p^rsence of vs.

But before he had named the ouerseers of his will, the Lo: pleased to put an end to his life and p^ruented him in that and what els he would haue said, and therefore the Relict of the said Thomas wth the app^rbacōn of the Court hath desiered John Talcott, Wm: Westwood, Ed: Stebbing and Andrew Warner to assist in seeing the Will of the dead p^rformed. And these Ouerseers, vnderstanding frō these that are the witnesses of his will, that he often expressed that his mynd was his wife and sonne Thomas should be comfortably p^ruided for, and finding that no p^ruission is made for fuell or fireing, doe thinke fitt and very agreable to the mynd of the deceased, though p^ruented by death frō exp^rsseing himselfe in that p^rticuler, wch yet they leaue to the consideration and confirmation of the Court, That the Widdow & Thomas should haue liberty to cutt & fetch fire-wood for their owne vse out of that field comōnly cauled the Aduenturers field, vntill the other children, or some for them, do diuert yt to such impruement as will receaue priudice if this liberty should be continued; and that they should haue liberty to cutt & fetch any such fuell for their owne vse out of that peece of ground cauled the Ox pasture, dureing ech of their naturall liues. They also thinke fitt and agreable to the mynd of the deceased, that the boy searuant shall continue wth the Relict of the said Thomas, dureing his tyme. All wch they leaue to the consideration and confirmation of the Court, if they approue thereof.

[72] *A Inuentory of the goods of Tho: Scott deceased, taken January the 6th, 1643, deliuered to the Wydow Scott for her vse.*

One fetherbed & fether boulster,	3. 5. 0
one greene Rug & Couerled,	3. 0. 0
one blanket and strawe bed,	0. 10. 0
one pre of sheets & pillowe, 15s.; one bedsteed & curtens, 2l. 10s.,	[3. 5. 0]
4 pre of sheets, 2l. 5s.; 2 table cloaths, 12s. 6d.,	[2. 17. 6]
3 dyeper napkins, 6s.; 5 flaxen napkins, 5s.,	[0. 11. 0]
2 fyne pillowbeers, 12s.; in wearing cloaths that were her husbands, 5l.; 2 chests, 12s.,	[6. 4. 0]
40 pownd of cotten wooll, 1l. 6s. 8d.; 3 sawes, 1l.,	[2. 6. 8]
severall peeces of old Iron,	0. 10. 0
1 flockbed, 2 boulsters, 2 blanketts,	2. 10. 0
1 couerled & blanket, 1 pillowe,	1. 6. 0
in seu'all peeces of pewter, and one brasse candlesticke,	1. 17. 5
in brasse kettells & iron potts: 1 iron dripping pan,	2. 7. 6
1 pre of pothooks & a glasse bottell,	0. 2. 6
1 brasse skimmer, 1 laten lampe, 2 latten panns,	0. 5. 4
1 spit, 1 trammel, 1 pre of bellowes,	0. 8. 0
1 pre of tongs, fyer pan, cob iron, andiron, & a iron to make wafer caks, 10s.; 1 smothing iron, 1 fowleing peece, 1l. 5s.,	[1. 15. 0]
1 match locke muskett, 13s. 4d.; 1 sword, 1 pre of bandalers, 9s. 2d.,	[1. 2. 6]
1 lether bottell, 1 warmeing pan,	0. 13. 0
1 chafin dishe, 1 frying pan, 1 shreding knife,	0. 5. 10
4 hows, 4 axes, 1 bill, 2 cleuers, 1 mattoke,	1. 2. 0
1 spade, 1 hobing iron, 5 siues,	0. 12. 0
in brueing vessells, barrells; 2 churns, 1 tabell,	2. 6. 0
wimbells & chissells, 3 wheels, 1 glasse botle,	0. 16. 0
4 chayrs, 2 tabells, 1 forme,	0. 13. 0
In the seller, vessells & seu'all goods,	0. 14. 0
In the lenetoe, potts, pans, vessells & other implements,	2. 3. 0
In the seller without dores, dyet vessells,	1. 0. 0
	48. 18. 3

1 grinston & winch, 6s.; 1 great bible & other smale
 books, 1l.,   [1. 6. 0]

Goods of Tho: Scotts sett aparte for his 3 daughters.

3 pʳe of flaxen sheets, 2 pʳe tow sheets,	3. 5. 0	
3 diapʳ napkins, 4 flaxen napkins,	0. 10. 0	
1 flaxen tabell cloath, 2 fine pillobers, 1l. 4s.; 2 boxes, 8s.	[1. 12. 0]	
In the little chamber, 1 fether bed,	4. 10. 0	
1 bedkase, 1 bedsted, 19s.; 2 fether bolsters, 1 pillow, 1 blanket, 2l. 8s. 4d.; 1 couerlitt, 1l. 10s.,	[4. 17. 4]	
In the garret, 1 fether bed, 1 fether bolster, 1 fether pillow,	3. 12. 0	
1 yellow & red couerlitt, 1 pillow,	1. 14. 0	
1 quart pot, 2 porringers, 3s. 2d.; 2 dishes, 1s. 8d.,	[0. 4. 10	
2 sasers, 1 smale salt seller,	0. 1. 4	
4 smale platters, 3 great platters, 18s. 6d.; 1 pewter bowle, 1s.,	0. 19. 6	
1 laten candlesticke, & tunell, 1s.; 1 pewter candlestick, 2s.	[0. 3. 0]	
1 great pewter bason & chāberpott,	0. 6. 6	
1 great brasse kettle, 15s.; 1 brasse posnit, 1 iron pott, 18s. 4d.,	[1. 13. 4]	
1 litle brasse kettle, 1 brasse potte,	0. 11. 8	
1 pʳe of pot huks, 2 latten pans,	0. 2. 2	
1 spit & tremell, 1 smothing iron,	0. 6. 0	
1 snaphanc* smale peece, 15s.; 1 cok mach musket, 13s. 4d.	[1. 8. 4]	
1 rapier, 2 pʳe of bandelers,	0. 10. 8	
1 frying pan, 1 shreding knife, 2s. 8d.; 1 brasse morter & iron pestill, 7s.,	[0. 9. 8	
1 glasse bottell, 1 couerd drinking pott,	0. 2. 6	
	27. 3. 1	
Corne for the Widdowe Scott, at Sepose & Hartford,	30. 0. 0	
2 Cowes for Wydow Scott, at Sepose,	10. 0. 0	
2 steers, 16l.; 2 hoggs, 9l.,	[25. 0. 0]	

For the three daughters.

2 steers, 12l.; 1 Cow, 5l.; 1 mare, 8l.; 2 calfs, 3l. 6s.,	[28. 6. 0]	
4 hoggs, 3 piggs,	5. 5. 0	
The Wydowes Some,	65.	
The daughters,	33. 11	
Totall,	174. 12. 4.	

besids Carts & 3 Ploughs.

---

* *Snaphance*; (German, *Schnap-kahn*;) a musket with a flint-and-steel lock. *Bailey.*

[54]   The Will of BLAYNCH HUNT deceased.

I, Blaynch Hunt do make my last will. Imp^{rs}, I giue my best suite of weareing Cloathes to my Cossen Mary Robins, & a p^{re} of my best blanketts; Itē, I giue my Cossens in the howse, twenty shillings a peece, in gold or sylver if yt can be made vpp att my decease; Itē, for the rest of my estate in howshold stuffe & debts, I comitt to the dispose of my Vnckle Welles, only I remit 40s. I lent my Cossen Mary Robins; I make my Vnckle Welles my Executor; I giue my Cossen Mary Baylding vi yards of kersey.   Blaynch Hunt.

[55]   *A Inuentory, taken the 20th day of September, 1644, of the goods of Blaynch Hunt deceased, by Andrewe Waird & Will^l Gybbins.*

	£. s. d.		£. s. d.
Imp . in mony,	5. 14. 3	6 yards of kersy,	2. 0. 0
A debt oweing frō Mr. Hill,	4. 0. 0	a debt frō John Fishe,	0. 16. 0
A debt frō John Robins, now on her Vnckles accoumpt,	3. 10. 0	3 yards of cloath,	1. 0. 0
		a Cloke,	0. 10. 0
		mittens & stockings,	0. 5. 0
		paper,	0. 1. 0
Lent her Cossen Mary Robins,	2. 0. 0	table cloaths & lynine cloath,	0. 15. 0
Her cloath shute of weareing cloathes,	1. 10. 0	three white aporns, 7 napkins & a Towell,	1. 0. 0
Her stuffe shute,	1. 0. 0	2 ap^{r}ns, 2 pilloberes & small lynine,	1. 5. 0
A greene Couering,	1. 0. 0		
A p^{re} of blanketts,	1. 10. 0	a trunke & a boxe,	0. 10. 0
one blankett,	0. 6. 8	a p^{re} of course sheets,	0. 10. 0
A fetherbed, a bolster and 2 pillowes,	3. 0. 0	shues,	0. 4. 0
		gloues, pyns, laces, kniues & a spoone,	0. 9. 0
2 Cloath petticoats,	1. 15. 0		
5 old petticoats & 4 p^{re} of bodyes,	2. 2. 0	a glasse & a byble,	0. 6. 0
		sheets,	2. 0. 0
4 wastcoats & 4 aporns,	1. 7. 4		
4 hatts,	1. 10. 0		43. 16. 3
3 shifts,	0. 12. 0	A ketle, a torne & a hatchet, left out and omitted.	
brasse and pewter,	1. 3. 0		
yarne,	0. 5. 0		

[69]   A Inuentory of the goods of JOHN CATTELL, deceased, taken and prysed by John Coleman, and Samuell Hales, the 17 of July, 1644.

	£. s. d.
Imp^{rs}. a Bedde, boulster, and furniture to yt,	4. 0. 0
Itē: Woollen and Lynnen Cloathes,	5. 8. 0

Itē: Brasse & Pewter & 2 potts & other tooles,	2. 0. 0	
Itē: a gun, sword and bandaleres,	1. 10. 0	
Itē: a Calfe, 2. 0. 0 ; It: a Cowe, 5. 0. 0 ;	[7. 0. 0]	
Itē: oweing frō George Chappell a debt of	5. 0. 0	
It: Swyne, 6. 10. 0 ; It: a debt of Good: *1. 0. 0.	[7. 10. 0]	
It: a debte of goodman Boosye, 1*l*.; It: a debte of Corne, 5*l*.,	[6. 0. 0]	
It: the home lott and barne,	12. 0. 0	
It: 6 ac: in myle meadowe,	6. 0. 0	
It: 3 ac: in the great mea: 12*l*.; It: the garden, 12*s*.	12. 12. 0	
	69. 0. 0	
Debts he owed,	10. 0. 0	
	59. 0. 0	

Witnes hereunto,
  Tho: Tomson.   Tho: Coleman,
                       Sam: Hale.

P'sented to the Court by Will': Gybbins, and the Relicke of the deceased admitted to administer.†

---

[97] The last Will and Testament of MR. EPHRAIM HUIT, of Wyndsor, in Conectecotte.

Impr^s. I giue vnto my loueing wife my dwelling howse and homelott, downe vnto the swampe, wth all the howseing thereon; also I giue vnto her my meadowe lott conteyneing by estimation fowerteene acres more or lesse, likewise I giue vnto her my lott of fifteene acres wth the vast swampe adioyneing thereto. Ite: I giue vnto her Tho: Staires his howse and the square plot of gardens lying beyond the swampe to the highway. Ite: I give vnto my daughter Susanna, and to my daughter Mercy, my great lott lying behind the hog pen, adioyneing to Daniell Clarke on the one side and Humphrey Hids on the other, to be diuided betweene thē equally. It: I giue vnto my two younger daughters, Lydea and Mary, my great lott at the Falls, conteyneing fowerscore and two rodde in breadth, to make them two lotts, togather wth the meadowe grownd that lyes therein, to be diuyded also equally betweene them. Pruided alwayes, and it is my full intent, that these my fower daughters shall not enter vppon these said portions of land vntill they ech of them shall com to the age of one and twenty, and in the meane tyme yt shall be to my beloved wife whateuer p^{r}fit shall accrewe thereby; and as ech of thē shall com to the age of one and twenty, so ech shall enter accordingly vppon her portion.

---

* Blank.   † Page 110, *ante*.

P^ruided also, that if either or any of them, shall dy before they com to the said age of one and twenty, then the portion intended to her or the͞ so dying, shall desend vppon my wife and be at her dispose.

Also, I giue vnto my daughters Susanna and Mercy, all my interest, right and benifit that shall arise fro͞ the graunt of the Towne, made me, of fifteene acres of meadowe, when yt shall com first into their hands, about Pequanucke, if they shall liue to the age of on and twenty yeares; if ether dy in the interim, then her portion to descend vppo͞ my wife.

Ite͞: my great Iland at the Falls, I giue to the Court at Hartford, for the vse of the Country.

Ite͞: I appoynt that my debts be paid out of my p^rsonall estate, and all the rest, both w^thin dores and w^thout, whatsoeuer, I wholy giue to my beloued wife, whether land or goods.

Lastly, I appoynt Dauid Wilton and Daniell Clarke to be the Executors of this my last will and Testament, only they shall not medle wth any thing w^thin dores. And the Ouerseers of this my Will, I intreat the Deacons of our Church to be.

Ep: Huit.

An Inuentory of the Goods of Ephraim Huit, late of Wyndsor, taken the 9th October 1644, by vs whose names are vnderwritten.

	£	s.	d.
In the *Parlour*, 1 Bedstead, w^h bed and furniture thereunto belonging, all valued at	10.	0.	0
1 table & forme, 1 chest, 2 trunkes, 1 case of bottles, vall:	02.	10.	0
Carpitts, Cushions,	02.	12.	0
6 veluet couers for stooles & Chaires,	01.	10.	0
8 yards Kitermaster, 16s.; 3 yards Cotton att 10s. 6d.	[01.	06.	6]
1 childs blanket & wascoat cloath,	01.	06.	8
the weareing apparrell,	04.	10.	0
[98] in bucrum, 10s.; 9 doz. of napkins, fine course, 5l. 19s. 4d.	[06.	09.	4]
4 towels at 1l. 4s.; 14 pillobears at 3l. 10s.	[04.	14.	0]
5 table cloaths, 1 towell,	3.	17.	
14 pair sheets, fine and course,	16.	14.	
3 table cloaths, 2 short towels, 8 napkins, 1 sheet, vall:	1.	5.	
In plate, 2 Bec Bowls, 2 wyne bouls, 1 salt, 1 trencher, salt seller, 4 siluer spoons, att	14.	0.	
13 spoons giuen to children, hauing their names on them, & 1 silver dishe;			
2 desks, 2 boxes, 1 small trunke, & other smale things,	0.	6.	8
In chamber ouer parlour; 2 bedsteeds, wth beds & furniture,	9.	0.	

another bed wth boulsters, pillowes, ruggs & blanketts,	4.	0.
3 chests, 1 box, 9 doz. trenchers,	0.	16.
In the corne chamber, in rye and pease,	0.	13. 4
In the hall, 3 spinning wheels,	0.	10. 4
one table board & forme, & 2 peir of bellowes,	0.	6. 0
2 fowleing peeces, 2 muskets, 4 chayres,	4.	5.
in lynnen yarne, 2l. 6s. 8d.; in pewter, 4l. 10s.	[6.	16. 8]
1 cullender, 2 pudding pans, 2 swords, 1 p^{re} of bandalers,	0.	15. 0
In kitchin, in brasse & Iron potts & brasse panes, ladles, skim^{rs}, dripping pans & posnet and other pans, vall:	6.	16. 0
a pair of Andirons, 1 Brandii:* 2 pair Crooks, 5 pair of tongs & iron spitts, pothangers,	1.	0. 0
a Fornace,	2.	0. 0
In tubbs, pales, churns, butter barrells & other impliments,	2.	0. 0
2 thwart saws, axes, pitchforks,	1.	0. 0
3 stocks of bees, 3l.; 1 cow, 1 heifer, 9l.; 4 goats, 2l.	[14.	0. 0]
2 sowes, 5 piggs, vall: at 6l.; 2 pownd of powder, 6s.	[6.	6. 0]
2 thousand planks at Elias Packmans, & 5 C. at the Falls,	8.	10. 0
In the Barne, in wheat, pease, oats, hay, flaxe,	7.	5. 0
The Howse and barne, wth other howseing & homelott, vall:	100.	0. 0
Som:	247.	2. 8
16 acres & ½ of meadowe in the great meadd:	66.	0. 0
The land at the Falls, ouer the great Riuer,	30.	0. 0
80 acres of land neere Mr. Phelps,	15.	0. 0
In books, valued by Mr. Smith and Mr. Warham,	13.	0. 0
A grinding stone wth iron spindle & turne,	00.	12. 0
A share & culter, 13s.; a ferry boat, 2l. 10s.	[03.	03. 0
	374.	18. 0
More a Lease for the Tole at the Mill, the wch valued at 259.	1.	1

[633. 19. 1.]   Will' Gaylard, Will' Hill,
Henry Clarke.

I owe Mr. Willis 100, wch I make accoumpt wilbe paid thus: thirty pownd is coming to me frō Piscataq' Company, and there is Guns sold to do yt. A Rafte of Planke is goeing downe, I think will be 40. What is wanting may be made vp out of the Loder.

I owe 100 to John Fishe wch he will haue keept in New Ingland.
I owe Mr. Lummas 20; he will take nothing but mony.
I owe Mr. Woolcott about 12.
I owe John Eares, 25.
I owe for Tho: Sters his howse and land, about 17.

Oweing me.

The butcher, for goats, 6l. 13s.; Gudwife Whithead for all Rats since her husband went, & for my Canow. Mr. Williams, 2l. Mr.

---

* Qu. Brand-iron? "a trivet to set a pot on."—*Webster.*

Rossiter, 2l. Tho: Dewe, 1l. 10s. Mr. Whiteing owes something as the accoumpt will show. Mr. Hill, 3. He hath power to receaue yt of Mr. Maio.

[100] Jo: Fishe his 100, if Henry Clarke will take yt, it shall be paid in wheat now.

John Banks owes me about 5 or 6 pownd.
Daniells accoumpt is lefte to himselfe.
Mr. Phelps owes 1l. 18s. debt confest.
*Yf Henry Clarke will not, then yt must be keept, as the rest of the Towne mony is.
The towne owes me 25l.
Richard Sexton oweth me 16l. and for the 2 yeares to come.
The Townes Rate and his debte must be husbanded by the Executors.
Old Eagleston owes 2l. to be paid in wheat & pease.
Mr. Hull witnesse to yt.
My wife and children must liue vppon the Lott set out for that purpose.

Nouember the 20th, 1644.

An Inventory of the goods and Lands of NATHANIELL FOOTE of Wethersfield deceased, being truly taken and Indifferently prised by Richard Tratte, Samuel Smith and Nath: Dickinson.

		£. s. d,
Imp^r	His purse and apparrell,	7. 16. 00
It	In neat Cattell and in hay,	93. 00. 00
It	in horsse fleshe,	34. 00. 00
It	in hoggs,	66. 60. 00
It	in debts,	29. 03. 04
It	in Englishe corne,	70. 00. 00
It	in goats,	3. 15. 00
It	in carts, ploughs and the furniture belonging theretoo,	6. 00. 00
It	in nayles,	1. 10. 00
Ite	Indean Corne,	8. 00. 00
It	in old wheat and pease,	6. 06. 00
It	for certain things in the chamber,	2. 00. 00
It	for amunition,	5. 00. 00
Ite	for fower beds wth the furniture,	13. 06. 08
It	in fyne Lynnen,	5. 10. 00
Ite	2 table boards, 2 chests, 1 Trunke wth other Imple^{ts},	5. 00. 00
It	pewter & brasse and other vseful vessells,	12. 00. 00
It	in husbandry tooles,	3. 00. 00
It	in beife, buttor and cheese and other necessary p^rvision for the howse,	8. 10. 00

---

* This clearly ought to follow "John Fishe his 100," &c., four lines above. The entries were probably separated by an error of the recorder.

Ite In poultry,		1. 00. 00
Som:		380. 17. 00

The debts of Nath: Foote of Wethersfield wch he did owe at his disease.

Imp^{rs}. for goats, 2*l*. It; another debt, 3*l*. 10*s*. It; 12*s*. It; 1*l*. 3*s*. 4*d*. It; 12*s*. 6*d*. It; 1*l*. 10*s*. . 9 7 10

The Land.

Ten acres of home lotts wth one dwelling howse and 2 barnes wth other buildings therevppon,

4 acres of home lotts,
6 acres of meadow wth an acre of swampe,
20 acres of plaine fenced in being 14 ac. broke vp,
7 acres of the plaine meadow plowed vp,
20 acres in the great meadow of hay grownd,
4 acres in bever meadow,
27 acres of swampe grownd,
81 acres of vpland in the weste field,
32 rod broad beyond the Riuer being three myles in length.

      Richard Trott, Samuell Smith,
       Nathaniell Dickenson.

3 sowes, 6 young shoats prysed 17*l*. One young mare prysed at 5*l*. A company of nayles wth other smale things, 1*l*. 10*s*.

Land devided to the Wydowe Foote.

4. ac. home lott where her howse is,	20. 00. 00
The howseing,	50. 00. 00
2 ac. vnsubdued,	4. 00. 00
7 ac. plaine broke,	28. 00. 00
3½ plaine med:	20. 00. 00
14 ac. meadow,	70. 00. 00
3 ac. plaine not broake up,	5. 00. 00
30 ac. vpland in westfield,	15. 00. 00
Som:	212. 00. 00

Land devided to the eldest sonne.

3 ac. homelott next her,	15. 00. 00
2 ac. vnsubdewed,	4. 00. 00
7 ac. plaine broke vp,	28. 00. 00
3½ of meadow,	20. 00. 00
3 ac. in great med:	24. 00. 00
4 ac. in beaver med:	4. 00. 00
27 ac. swampe,	1. 10. 00
2 ac. not broke vp,	5. 00. 00
30 ac. vpland west field,	15. 00. 00
Halfe the east side,	10. 00. 00
	126. 10. 00

Land for the youngest sonne.

3 ac. homelott,	15. 00. 00
6 ac. mea: in the swamp,	30. 00. 00
21 ac. west field,	10. 00. 00
halfe on the east sd,	10. 00. 00
	65. 00. 00

A Debt formerly forgotten wch the said Deceased Nath: Foote did owe, ... 1. 10. 00

The age of the 5 children Dwelling with their mother.

Nath: Foote,	24 yeares,
Rob Foote,	about 17.
Frances,	about 15.
Sarah,	about 12.
Rebecka,	about 10.

The wyddowe of the said Nath: Foote is admitted to administer the Estate, and the eldest sonne is to have the lands before mentioned as they are valued at 126*l*. 10*s*. wch is to be made vppe 148*l*. & the youngest sonne the pticuler landes above mentioned for him at 65*l*. wch is to be made vppe 74*l*. and the daughters disposed in marriedge are to have the 30*l*. a peece wch they have receaued made vppe 74*l*. and the other Children are to have 74*l*. a peece p^ruided it is lefte at the dispose of their mother to detracte from any of them if shee see just cause 5*l*. of the portion here sett downe, and to adde yt to such of the other as best deseaue yt.

---

[228]   The last Will and Testament of E<small>D</small>: V<small>EIR</small> of Wethersfield, wch he being in p^rfect memory hath established, the 19th of July, 1645.*

Imp^{mis} I giue to Mr. Shareman of Totocott, 4 pownds. Ite: to Mr. Smith of Wethersfield, 4 pownds, of wch two legaces my will is that my cow wch is at Totocott shall be parte, so far as yts worth, to be deuided betweene the two. It: I giue to Lysly Bradfield 3 pownds. It: to John Robins and his wife, I giue three pownds. It: I giue to Mary & Hannah the daughters of John Robins, my two acres of meadow, wch I had of John Robins in exchaynge for my howse and homelott. It: my mynd is that John Carington and Tho: Kirkeman shalbe no loosers by the bargaine of pease and wheat they bought of me. Itē: I

---

* See page 129, *ante*.

make Mr. Shareman & Mr. Smith my executors to whō I giue the rest of my estate. Memorand: yt is my mynd that John Carington and Th: Kirkeman shall vse their indeauor that they loose not any thing in their Corne through their owne default. It: my mynd is that John Carrington & Tho: Kirkman shall haue 20s. for makeing my Coffen. It: my mynd is that there shalbe 20s. bestowed vppon p^ruissions of wyne, bear, caks and such like of what may be had for my buriall. It: I giue to Mr. Swayne all my workeing tooles. The marke of
In the p^rsence of Ed: Veir.
Nath: Dickinson.

His land prysed by Richard Trotte & Nath: Dickenson, Dec: 2: 1645.

Two acres of meadowe,	6: 14: 0	
A peece of land in Pennywise,	1: 10: 0	9£.
One Sowe, . . .	0: 16: 0	

Goods at Totocutt prysed by Will' Swayne & Robert Rose.			
A heifer, . .	4:	10:	0
a barrell, . .	0:	4:	0
an old brasse potte,	0:	7:	0
in bedding, . .	0:	8:	0
a locke and key,	0:	1:	8
a peece of a bears skinne,	0:	3:	6
an old cheste, .	0:	1:	0
a frying panne,	0:	3:	6
	5:	18:	8

Goods prysed by Gyles Smith & Samuell Nettleton.			
Two smale sawes,	0.	5:	0
one long playne,	0:	2:	0
one plough playne,	0:	2:	0
2 old smale playnes,	0:	1:	0
1 priker & chessell,	0:	1:	0
an old axe, . .	0:	2:	0
1 adds, . , .	0:	1:	8
2 smale augers, .	0:	1:	6
	16:	2	

[229] Oweing the foresaid Veare at Totocutte.

Tho: Whitway,	0:	6:	8
Tho: Blachly,	0:	0:	10
Will' Palmer for 6 bush: Indean, . -	0:	15:	0
Tho: Fenner, .	0:	4:	0
Lysly Bradfield, .	0:	4:	0

Oweing him at Wethersfield.

From Mr. Robins 10 bush: Indean, 10 bush: pease, & of wheate,	3:	7:	6
and 8s. 8d. in corne for worke, . .	0:	8:	8
By Rich: Hill, as appeareth by bill, in corne at March, & a sowe 2 yeares, to halues,	2:	16:	6
John Carrington & Tho: Kircū a debt of 12 bush: of wheat and 8 of pease,	3:	12:	0
Henry Palmer, 3£. in Corne, . .	3:	0:	0
frō Ab: Elsing in Corne,	3:	0:	0

[230] WILLIAM FROSTE his laste will and testament, wherein the said Williā doth giue and bequeth all his lands and goods now inioying, the vi[th] of January, 1644.

I giue and bequeth to my eldest sonne Daniell Frost, two p[rt]s of my meadowe and vpland outte and to lay oute, (the home lotte excepted,) and also to the said Daniell Froste all my parte of the swampe and Redye ponds, and also fifteene acres of meadowe that I bought of John Graye, lying att Muchuncohsor Sasqug, comonly so cauled, and also my cloake and warmeing pan, I giue to the said Daniell Frost his heires for euer; I giue and bequeth to Rebecka & Sarah Frost that blacke heiffer that Daniell Frost hath to wynter; I giue and bequeth to my sonne Abraham Frost all that lotte and howse, wth all the land laid out and to be laid out, that I bought of John Stickling, wth those moueālls I bought of him, and also those cloathes on my bedde and my little chest, and also my two great Oxen and my two greate yearleing Calues, wth all that is in my little chest, and on third part of my howshold goods. I giue and bequeth to my daughter Elizabeth and John Graye the sowe that he hath to winter and all her increase and [the third part of my howshold goods; & to Luke Watson] the two yeare old blacke heifer that goodman Close hath to the halfes for fower yeares, the p[r]fite to be for the said Luke. And to Susanna and Johana Watson, daughters to Elizabeth Graye, one blacke heifer that John Graye hath to the halues for fower yeares, and the profit to them both equally. And the redde heifer that Daniell Froste wintereth, I giue to John Grayes owne two children, and the profit equally to them both. I giue and bequeth to Henry Graye and Lydea Graye for their liues and after them to Jacob their sonne, all my howse and home lott, w[th] that part that I chaynged w[th] John Foster, and the third p[rt]e of my meadowe and vpland, laid out and to lay out; and to Mary Graye, daughter to Henry Graye, I giue and bequeth my redde heifer that Goodman Close hath to wynter. And to Mary Rylie and her children, I giue and bequeth all my goods and lands that I haue in Old Ingland. And to the Towne of Vncowah, I giue and bequeth tenn pownds, in good

---

[In margin] 'These words enterlyned, the third parte of my howshold goods, and to Luke Watson.'

pay, towards the building a Meeteing howse, to be paid when yt is halfe built. Furthermore I ordeyne and make Henry Graye of Vncowauh, my lawfull executor, to pay and dischardge my legaces & debts, and also power to receaue what is due to me, and I giue the foresaid Henry Graye full power to sue and dischardge for any debts or goods, that these p^rsents should stand in force, after my decease and not before, and I entreat Ephraim Weeler and Daniell Frost to be my Ouerseers to see my will p^rformed according to the intent thereof, and they are to haue ten shillings for their paynes. Whereto I haue sett my hand and seale, the day and date hereof.

 Witnes, Ephrā Weeler,   William Froste.
  Frances Purdy,
  Mary Purdy.

[529] *On the backe side of Frosts Will.*

These are to explayne my meaneing of howshold goods; all my moueable goods or tables, excepte corne and cattell and swyne. Further, I would haue Abraham my sonne to receaue to his vse the rent of all the howseing and land that I bought of John Sticklin; further, I will that Abrahā my sonne pay no rent to Henry Gray my sonne, nor Henry to him, but all former ingadgements to be voyd betwixt thē, in or about the lease. I will that the two third p^rts of my land be deuided as soone after my death as may be, yet so that my sonne Henry his leace be not disturbed. Witnes my

 Witnes, Ephraim Wheeler,   Willm̄ Frost.
  Frances Purdy,
  Mary Purdy.

---

[231] The last Will & Testament of J<small>OHN</small> P<small>URKAS</small>.

I the said John Purkas doe appoynt my wife to be my sole executor, to administer vppon my whole estate, to bring vp my children, and it is my mynd & will that my wife shall possesse my howse and land for her p^rper vse for the whole tyme of her life, p^ruided that shee shall haue noe power to alienat yt or make sale of my howse or any of my land w^thout the consent of John Talcotte and Richard Goodman, or one of them if ether of them shall dy. Also yt is my mynd that if the child my wife goeth wth shalbe a sonne and shall suruiue & continue vntill the death of my wife, that he shall possesse my howse and all my land in Hartford for himselfe and heires; but if the Lord giue me noe sonne my mynd is that my howse and land be equally deuided among my daughters that shall suruiue and continue after the death of my wife. Also, my mynd is, that my daughter Mary & Elizabeth shall haue ech of them a whole and seruiceable pear of sheets and ech of the a pewter platter at the age of eighteene yeares. And if God giue me a sonne wch my wife goeth with all, my mynd is that if my sonne shall liue to the age of eighteene yeares, that he shall haue my gunne, wch is a fierlocke, and my sowrd and bandaleres and rest, and my long crosscutt sowe, and my betell rings and three wedges. Also my mynd is, that my howshold shall be deuided to my daughters that shall suruiue & continue vntill the death of my wife, only the bedde and blanketts and one pair of sheets and one trunke, I leaue wholy to my wife to dispose on at her death. Witnesse hereof I haue sett to my hand the 15th of October, 1645.

Witnes hereunto, Jo: Talcott,   Jo: Purkas.
    Rich: Goodman.

Nouember 26: 1663. Know all men by these presents that I, Jaret Spicke doe acknowledg my self receiued of Nicholas Palmer, the full and just sume of ten pownds, which is the acquiting all acco^ts between us two concerning my wiues portion, which was due to her by her father John Purkis his will.
                 Jerret Speck.
 Witnes, Thomas Butler, Robert Sanford.

Whereas there haue bin an appoyntment that Nicholas Palmer was to pay his daughter in lawe Elizabeth Purchass tenn pownds &c. These presents doe testify, that I Richard Case of Windsor doe acknowledg that I haue receiued of Nicholas Palmer of Windsor afoarsayd Tenn pownds in pay to my content and sattisfaction, & doe hereby acquitt & dischardge the sd Nicho: of all debts and demands, as witness my hand this 17 December: 1663:

Signed, & deliuered in the   The marke of Richard M Case
presence & witnes of us,
   John Moore,
The marke, Antho: C Hoskins.

These are true coppyes of the origanell receipts, being compared therew'th Octob^r 20th: 64: p^r me, John Allyn, Secret^ry.

[232] *An Inventory of the goods of John Purkas, deceased in October, 1645.*

	£	s.	
One bedde & bolster, 2 blanketts, one on rag, one pair of sheets, 2 fetherbed, pilloberes & 2 pilloberes, one coverlett,	4.	15.	0
Two pair of new sheets & one pair of old sheets and one halfe sheet & two old pilloberes,	2.	5.	0
His weareing cloathes,	4.	0.	0
6 pewter dishes and some smale things,	1.	0.	0
one great brasse kettell, one iron pott, one brasse pott, one posnett, brass ladle, driping pan & other implements,	4.	10.	0
in barrells, tables and pailes,	1.	0.	0
one trunke and chest, chaiers, frying pan & gridiron,	1.	5.	0
one fier locke musket, bandalers, rest & sowrd,	2.	0.	0
one crossecutt sawe, 3 wedges, two betell ryngs, & other implements,	1.	10.	0
one Cow & 6 pyggs, and corne for the yeare.	8.	10.	0
	30.	15.	0

FEB: 27th: 1645.

A trewe Inuentory as neere as we can find out of all the goods, corne and cattle and lands of SAMUELL IERLAND, deceased the 20th of May, 1639.

His Howse and lotte wth 8 acres of meadowe & all other diuidents vnsold prysed at,	40£. 0. 0
His Apparell and p^rsonall estate,	10. 0. 0
His Hoggs,	20. 0. 0
Tho: Vffoote Som:	70£. 0. 0
Jo: Edwards.	

[233] Whereas I, GEORGE WILLIS, of Hartford vppon Conectecutt am by a gratious & mercifull visitation of the Lord sumoned to expect my chainge, to the end therefore that I might p^rforme my duty and continue loue and peace among those I shall leaue behind, being at the p^rsent through the gentle and tender dealeing of the Lord in full and p^rfecte

memory, I doe dispose of that estate the Lo: hath giuen me, and make my last will and testament as followeth:—

I giue all my buildings, lands, tenements and heredetaments in Hartford bownds and at Tunxis Cepus, vnto my beloued wife Mary Willis and vnto my sonne Samuell and vnto the heires of his body, and in the want of such heires, then vnto my heires as yt is exp^rssed vppon record:

I doe giue vnto my sonne George and the heires of his body, all my land and buildings vppon the west side of the great Riuer in the bownds of Wethersfield, now in the hands and occupation of diuers men, p^ruided he doe com ouer into New England and settle himselfe and his family heare, according as I haue wrote him by letter, dated the 28th of October laste, (a coppy whereof is among my papers and subscribed wth my owne hand,) and p^ruided that he make payment and send ouer hither in goods, according to the tenour of the said letter, to the vallue of three hundred pownds; it being my will, that if he attend the terms p^rpownded by me in the letter aforsd he shall inioy and there shalbe made good to him what I haue offered and tendred to him in my said letter, wch is the buildings and land aforesaid, as also on hundred pownds to be paid him in corne and cattle w^thin three months after his arriuall here, researueing only twenty pownds a yeare out of the said lands, wch my will is he shall pay to my beloued wife Mary Willis dureing the tearme of her life. But in case my sonne doe not attend my aduise in transplanting himselfe and family into these p^rts, or p^rforme not the conditions p^rpownded by me as afore, then my will is that the buildings and land aforesaid shalbe and remayne at the whole dispose of my beloued wife Mary Willis.

My will is further, that my sonne George shall injoy and possesse my lands and buildings att Feny Compton, in Old England, according to a deed made to him by my feoffees, and the heires of his body after him, and in case of the want of such heires, then to fall to my sonne Samuell and the heires of his body, and for want of such heires then to the right heires of me, George Willis.

[234] And whereas vppon the makeing ouer of the moity of my lands att Feny Compton aforesaid and the reuersion of the other moity after on & twenty yeares to my sonne George, I

researued to my selfe on third p^rte of his mariedge portion, my will is that in case my sonne George shall giue to me or my executrixe a generall and full relesse of all claimes and disbursments expended by him for me and mentioned in his last accoumpte sent me, that then he shall enioy to himselfe and his owne p^rper vse, that third part of his mariedge portion so researued. But in case my sonne shall not accepte of this third p^rte of his mariedge portion, in full satisfaction of all claimes and demaunds of monyes due to him frō me, then my will is that the third parte of his mariedge portion due to me as aforesaid shalbe and remayne to the vse of my executrixe, and that shee pay and dischardge vnto my sonne the fower hundred pownds claimed by him frō me, in his accoumpts, out of the estate bequethed to her, in this my will.

I doe giue vnto my daughter Hester, fower hundred pownds, whereof two hundred pownd shalbe paid at the day of her mariedge, in mony, and the other two hundred pownds in such goods and comodityes as the Country doth afford, eighteene months after the day of her mariedge, prouided shee or any issue of her body be liueing at that tyme ; but if it please the Lord otherwise to dispose, then my will is that the said two hundred pownds shalbe paid to my daughter Amy and the heires of her body.

I doe giue vnto my daughter Amy, three hundred and fifty pownds, whereof on hundred and fifty pownd shall be paid in mony at the day of her mariedge, and one hundred pownds twelue months after that, and the other hundred pownds twenty fower months after the day of her mariedge, p^ruided shee or any issue of her body be aliue at the seuerall tymes of payment as aforesaid ; the two last hundred pownds to be paid in such comodityes as this Country doth aford.

My will is that my loueing wife Mary Willis shall haue and inioy to her owne p^rper vse and to her assigns, the lease of the moity of Feny Compton, for one and twenty yeares ; and my will is that shee pay tenn pownd a yeare to my daughter Hester, and tenn pownd a yeare to my daughter Amy, for the said tearme of the lease, p^ruided they continue so long in this life, but when ether of thē shall departe this life, then the said anuity to cease.

I doe giue vnto my sonne Samuell, all my land on the east side of the great Riuer, w^{th}in the bownds of Wethersfield, he paying to my daughters, Hester and Amy, forty pownds a peece, sixe yeares after my decease.

I doe giue vnto my loueing fryends Mr. Fenwicke, Mr. Heynes, Mr. Hopkins, Mr. Welles, Mr. Webster, Mr. Whiting, Capten Mason, Mr. Hooker, Mr. Stone & Mr. Wareham, twenty shillings a peece, as a token of my loue.

[235] I doe giue vnto M^{ris} Huet, fiue pownd, out of the debte due to me frō her deceased husband, and to Mr. Smith fiue pownd, out of the debte he oweth me, and to William Gybbins tenn pownd, out of Mr. Smiths debt, to be paid to him twelue months after my decease. George Willis.

I doe further giue to my sonne Samuell, ten pownd in mony, and all my books, and my watch.

I doe giue vnto ech of my two daughters, a bedde and furniture, wch I leaue at the ordering of my wife.

It is my will that my two daughters take the aduise & counsell of my loueing wife, att their dispose in mariedge.

I doe giue and bequeth vnto my beloued wife all my debts, cattell, chatells, vtensells, mony, plate, wth all other moueables not otherwise disposed of by this my will. And for the payment of my debts and p^{r}formance of this my will, I doe make my beloued wife sole executrixe.

This was published by Mr. George Willis, as his last will and testament, the 14th of December, 1644, in the p^{r}sence of,   Ed: Hopkins, & Will' Gybbins.

George Willis.

Whereas, I haue expressed before my will to be that my sonne Samuell should pay to ech of my two daughters, Hester & Amy, forty pownds w^{th}in sixe years after my decease, now my will is that the said forty pownds be paid w^{th}in on yeare after my sonne Samuell shall com to the age of one & twenty yeares, to ech of my said daughters, and not before.

This last clause was added the 22th of Febr. 1644, in the p^{r}sence of,
    Ed: Hopkins.

George Willis.

March the 4th, 1644.

My will now is that the two hundred pownds giuen to my daughter Hester by this my Will, in comodities of this Country, and made payable eighteene months after the day of her mariedge, if shee or any issue of her body be liueing at that tyme, that the said two hundred pownd be paid in manner following, vizt. one hundred pownds eighteene months after the day of her mariedge, and the other hundred pownds eighteene months after that, pruided shee or any issue of her body be liueing at the seuerall dayes of payment, as before; but if otherwise it please the Lord to dispose, my will is that it be paid to my sonne Samuell and daughter Amy, and equally diuided betwixt them. And my will is that so long as both or ether of my daughters remayne vnmaried and my wife continue in this life, besids their, or ether of their dyet, there be paid to thē fifteene pownds a peece, pr ann: in this Country comodityes, for and towards their mayntenaunce. And my will is that they or ether of them remayneing vnmaried att my wyues death, that sixe months after her discease the portion that is giuen by this my will to them, or ether of them, payable at the day of mariedge, shalbe paid to thē or ether of them that soe remayne, to be at their owne dispose; ‖ and if they afterwaird marry, then the resdue of the portion giuen to them or ether of them by this my will, to be paid according to the tenor and true meaneing thereof.

I doe further giue & bequeth twenty Nobles to the poore in the Towne of Hartford, fiue marke to the poore in Wethersfield, forty shillings to the poore att Wyndsor, and forty shillings to the pore at Tunxis Cepus, to be paid in Country comodits and disposed according to the discretion of my Executrixe.

These explications and additions of the 4th of March were made in the prsence of, Ed: Hopkins,
    Will' Whiteing.

George Willis.*

---

* " George Wyllys Esq. late of Fenny Compton, in old England, dyed March 9th, 1644." (*Hartford Records.*) From the record of the Particular Court, (page 122, ante,) it appears that Mr. Willys' Will was brought into Court, March 5th, 1645–6.

[240]   March 20th, 1645.

A pʳticuler of all the debts oweing to WILLIAM LOTHAM, as also by him oweing:

	£	s.
Impʳˢ. Debts to him oweing, first from Mr. Robins, for deliuʳing Robert Bedle at Fishers Iland, according to Mr. Robins desire,	1.	14.
Itē: to him due frō Goodman Comstocke, for Tobaco,	0.	6.
Itē: also frō Walter Baker, for Tobaco,	0.	6.
Ite: frō Seargeant Bryan, vppon Mr. Tapens accoūpt,	1.	9.
Ite: more frō Seargent Bryan, for transporting 2 butts of sacke frōm Mr. Leches,	0.	16.
Itē: frō Seargeant Bryan more in sope,	3.	0.
Itē: from Henry Townsend 1*l*. Itē: frō John Ogden,	1.	15.
Ite. frō Mr. Mitchell for carrieing goods,	3.	19.
Itē: frō Goodmā Carman, 0. 6*s*. Itē: frō Mr. Olderton,	1.	0.
Itē: frō Frances Homes, 36 pownd of Iron.		

Debts by him oweing to the pʳsons followeing :—

Impʳˢ. To one Elias, his seruant formerly, about	3.	0.
Itē: to on Michaell Chatterton,	0.	10.
To Frances Homes,	0.	6.
Itē: To Lathā as long as he is myne after sixe and twenty shillings a month.		

A pʳticuler of his goods, as followeth :

Impʳˢ: 3500 of Planke, 6000 Trunnells, 500 of Iron, part att Frances Homes, part att Mr. Tappings, the rest in a grapnell lying att the Waterside.

Itē: a barrell and three quarters of tarre and pitch, lying att the waterside.

Itē: a sow in Edmund Sticlins hands.

Itē: a boate of tenn tun, wᵗʰ two roads, an anker, a grapnell, mainesale and foresale, a iron pott, a new sute of cloathes, shues, hatt, stockins, three shirts, 6 handcharses, 2 bands, a gunn, one hundred nynty three pickes, on auger, one draweing knife.

---

2 chessells, 2 caukeing irons, some heads for clinke worke, a scraper, a brest wimble, one iron wedge, a frying pan, a skellette, a sacke wᵗʰ some bisket in yt, another old sacke vsed for a bedd, an axe, a perre of pinsers, 2 hamers, a gymlett, 2 Indean baggs, a file, a butter tub, a powder horne, a pʳre of old stockings, an old buckett, an old kettell to make fyer in, a mallett, a woodden dishe, a platter, a litle box, on gouge, on narowe chessell, a chest, an iron candlesticke, 2 owers, 2 setting poles, an halespeare, a pockett compasse, a skife & two Owyres.

These seuerall pʳticulers appeareing under the lyne were added vppon a vewe taken in the boate the same morneing the Testator dyed by others & Will' Wells.

WILLS AND INVENTORIES.

[241]   Wheras on the other side herof ther is p'ticulers of the debts & creditts and goods of Williā Lothā, wch apeares best vnder ech p'ticuler matter, and therunto as his memory may be [   ] being now visited by the hand of the almighty Jehouah, wth sicknes, haueing in p'sence of vs whose names are hereunder subscribed, declared his mynd and will to be, that in case a period be put to his dayes before alteratiō hereof, then his just debts being defrayed out of his p'sonall estate, the remaynder hereof is by him giuen & bequethed to John Clarke and John Ogden, who he maks joynt executors of this his last will and Testament, equally to be deuided betwixt thē. Witnes my hand the day and yeare wthin written.
  In the p'sence of vs,
    Will' Wells, Ed: More,
    Isacke Nicholls, George Allsoope.

Septēber the 27th, 1645.
An Inuentory of the goods of Will': Lothā late deceased.

	£ s. d.
Imp^{rs}: a Boat, 8 tun, more or lesse, valued at 30s. p^r tun,	12. 0. 0
On grapnell, on anker, about a C. and ¼,	3. 10. 0
Maynsale & foresale,	5. 10. 0
about halfe a C. wayght of rigging, wth the oares,	1. 0. 0
a Skife, 1. 10. for old tooles & nayles, 0. 10.	2. 0. 0
Som:	24*l*.

also, a chest prised att	0. 3. 0	Ed: More,
a Coat, drawers & cap,	0. 17. 0	Will' Carrose,
a doublet, breches, stockings, shues & hatt, & some other old cloathes,	2. 7. 0	Tho: Trecy.
an Iron pott,	0. 10. 0	
	3. 15. 0	

prised and witnessed by
  Tho: Burchwood, Stephen Poste.

---

[242]   A Inuentory of the goods of E$_D$: Harrison, latly deceased.

	£ s. d.		£ s. d.
one chest,	0. 6. 8	one p^{r}e of stockings,	0. 2. 0
in mony,	3. 19. 5	one stuffe sute,	0. 6. 8
in Wampum,	0. 13. 4	one wascoate,	0. 5. 0
two shirts,	0. 8. 0	one p^{r}e of shues,	0. 3. 4
two hats,	0. 6. 0	one p^{r}e of boots,	0. 7. 0
one old Coate,	0. 2. 4	one p^{r}e of drawers,	0. 0. 6
			7. 0. 3

prysed by Nath: Waird & Andrewe Warner,
  Townsmen, John White, Gregory Wilterton.
    Mr. Whiting speaks of some Beauer, viij*l*. & boards, 8 C.

There was testimony giuen in Courte vppon the 28th March, 1650, in reference to this estate, as appeares by the Records of the said Courte, in the Booke of Perticuler Courtes. fol: 5:

[244]   Anno: 1648: Aprill 20th.

Imprimis, This is the last Will and Testament made by mee, JOHN PORTER, of Wyndsor, allthough now weake and sick in body yet in p^rfect memory, doe bequeath my Soule to God that gaue it, and my Body to bee buried, and my Goods as followeth :—

Item, I giue to my eldest sonne, John Porter, one hundred pounds; and to my second sonne Jeames Porter, I giue threescore pounds; and to my other six children, to witt, Sammuell Porter, Nathaniell Porter, Rebecka Porter, Rose Porter, Mary Porter, Anna Porter, I giue to each of them thirty pound a peece; wch is to bee raised out of my whole estate, as howseings, lands, cattells and houshold goods, and is to bee paid as they come to bee twenty yeares of age or sooner if my ouerseers sees just cause, without whose consent I would not haue them to marrye; wch if they doe, it shall bee in the power of my ou^rseers to abate of theire porc̃ons, and giue it to the other that are more deseruinge. And in case any of my children dye, before they bee married or bee twenty yeares of age, theire portion shall bee equally devided amongst the rest, vnless the ou^rseers see cause to abate it vppon the eldest. In case my estate shall bee founde vppon perticular veiw to arise to bee more in valew then these portions aboue giuen, or less then the summ, my will is that it shall bee proportionably added or abated to my childrens seuerall portions, except my ou^rseers see cause to abate my eldest, that hath the bigger portion, or likewise my second. The particular goods wherein each childe shall haue his porc̃on paid out of my whole estate, I leaue to the discretion of my ou^rseers.

My sonn Joseph Judgson is to take twenty shillings of Thomas Thornton, the next winter.

Allso, I giue fifty shillings to the pore of Wyndsor Church.

My desire is that these my beloued freinds would bee the ou^rseers of this my last will and Testament; Mr. Warham, of Wyndsor, Mr. Goodwyn, of Hartford, Goodman White, of Hartford, Mathew Graunt, of Wyndsor.

Wittnesses: John Porter.*
Henry Clarke, Abigaill Branker.

---

* See page 191, ante.

Vppon consideracon of the buisnes referred to o{r} consideracon, touching the chilldren of John Porter of Wyndsor, deceased, wee findinge some expressions of his, that hee would make the portions of his two eldest daughters as good as his younger, allso wee conceiue the eldest were helpefull to the estate, and that the Lord hath taken away one of the younger daughters, and that the rest of the chilldren are disposed of without damage to theire portions; o{r} apprehensions are (if the Courte see meete) that the two eldest daughters portions bee made vp thirty pounds a peece.

March 7th, 1650.   John Taillcott,
This is a true coppye of an originall   Will': Westwood.
writing, ordered by the Courte to bee recorded with the Will and Inventory.

J. C. Sec{ry}.

[245]   APRIL 27th: 1648.

An Inuentory taken of the whole estate of John Porter, of Wyndsor, late deceased, as howsing, lands, and all moueables, according as they were valued by the men imployed to prise them, whose names are underwritten:

	£	s.	d.
Item: All the howsing was valued at sixty pounds,	60.	0.	0
Item: The homelott pertaining to the Howse, w{ch} is seuen acres, valued at twenty eight pounds,	28.	0.	0
Item: The meadow before the howse containing sixteene acres, valued at sixty eight pounds,	68.	0.	0
Item: All his land on the east side the great Riuer, fifty eight rodd in bredth, from the Riuer eight score back in length, with an addition fifty rodd in bredth, and in length two myles and a halfe, valued at sixty fiue pounds fiue shillings,	65.	5.	0
Item: Three acres of meadow, valued at	6.	15.	0
Item: of woodland, forty six acres, valued at thirteene pounds, twelue shillings,	13.	12.	0
Item: eight acres in a swamp, valued at two pounds,	2.	0.	0
Item: sixty acres, remoate in the woods, valued at one pound ten shillings,	1.	10.	0
Item: for plowing and seed in the ground, nineteene pounds,	19.	0.	0
Item: Cattle valued; foure cowes, foure oxen, four young beasts, one mare, nine swyne, at seuenty seuen pounds, two shillings,	77.	2.	0

Item: All the furniture for carte and plow, valued at six pound fiue shillings,	6. 5. 0	
Item: Corne in the howse, twenty pound seuenteen shill:	20. 17. 0	
Item: Hopps, ten shillings,	0. 10. 0	

Goods within howse valued: In the parlour:

Item: One standing bedstead, with a featherbed and all thinges belonging to it, with a trundle bed vnderneath it; foure paire of sheets, with pillow beers; table linnen; wearing cloaths of his owne, and wearing cloaths of his wiues; and other furniture about the room; valued at thirty two pound two shill: . . . 32. 2. 0

Item: In the Chamber ouer the parlour:

One standing bedstead, with a featherbed and all things belonging to it; one halfe headed bedstead and bedding to it; with some cushions and cotton wooll; valued at 11. 14. 0

In the Chamber ouer the Kittchin:

Item: Some bedding for children, valued at . 3. 9. 0

In the Kittchin:

Item: Fiue siluer spoones; and in pewter and brass, and iron, and armes, and ammunition, hempe and flax and other implements about the roome and in the sellar, valued at thirty fiue pound, 14 shill^s: 35. 14. 0

Item: In the new Roome, seuerall sortes of tooles for husbandry and seuerall other vses, valued at 7. 0. 0

Item: In debts owing to the estate, . . 12. 2. 0

                   470. 17. 0

Debts to bee paid out of the estate, 20*l*. 17*s*.

       Henry Clarke, William Phelps,
       Dauid Willton, Thomas Forde.

---

[246] An Inuentory taken of the goods of THO: FENNER, deceased May the 15, 164[7].

Att G^n Luffuns:

Imp^{rs}. a peece of Trucking cloath of about 4 yards, 32*s*.—A Jackette, & p^{r}re of breches, 30*s*.—1 Fowleing peece, 30*s*.—1 Racoone skine coate, 12*s*.—11 Beauer skins atte 8*s*. p^r p^d.—21 kniues att 4*s*. a dozen, 7*s*.—2 lookeing glasses, 0. 8*d*.—An old hat, stockings & shues, 3*s*.—a little iron potte, 6*s*.

Prysed by G^n Luffun & G^n Northam, May the 17.

A p^{r}cell of wooden ware about 6*l*. Itē: His boate and lyne wch he brought vp. Itē: a p^{r}cell of wampū about 20*l*. & 16 peeces of Dutch mony in Mr. Whitings hand. The boate & loading.

Goods att Totokett of the sd Tho: Fenners, prysed by Robert Rose & Jo: Plum.

Imp^{rs}. one peece of trucking cloth con. 24 yards at 7s. 6d.
p^r yard, ... 9. 1. 10
one peece more of vyolet cullered trucking cloath,
of 21 yards, at 7s. 6d. p^r yard, . . 7. 17. 6
Itē: on other peece of damask coulered trucking cloath,
con. 13 yards, at 6s. 6d. the yard, . 4. 4. 6
Itē: one smale & course fetherbed tecke & boulster, wth
some fethers put into them, . . 2. 0. 0
It: one course Cou^{r}lette, . . . 0. 12. 0
It: 2 blanketts, on cotten, the other cotton & lynnen, 0. 14. 0
It: on weareing coate, 1: 5: 0. It: one coate made of
Catte skins, ... 0. 10. 0
It: one coate made of Racoone skins, . . 0. 10. 0
It: two deer skins, one foxe skin and a pair of Indean
stockins, ... 0. 11. 0
It: one old sowrd, 0: 0: 5. It: one pair of shues, 0. 5. 6
It: 11 traplines 0: 1: 0. It: a litle oyle, in a halfe firkin, 0. 1. 6
It: a smale kettle, he vsed to boyle tar in, . 0. 2. 0
It: one short coate made of darnixe, . . 0. 6. 0
It: one Portingale cap begun made & vnlyned, wth a smale
piece of cloth of the same, . . 0. 4. 0
Itē: in Wampum, ... 1. 0. 0
It: 2 yards of blewe lynen, 0: 6: 0. It: 4 bands, 0. 4. 0
It: 4 handkercheifs, cut out, vnmade, . . 0. 6. 0
It: on ketell, wch will hold about a pint, . 0. 2. 0
It: 2 dozen & a halfe of Jues trumps, 0: 4: 0. It: his Chest, 0. 4. 0
It: 3 yards one halfe of red broad cloath, at 18s. p^r yd. 3. 3. 0
24 bush: of Indean trucked wth Indeans, at 2s. 6d. p^r
bush: 3. 0. 0

Concerneing his debts, we cannot yet certenly find what they are. The writings in his chest you wrote for, are sent wth this Inuentory & are found to be somewhat imp^{r}fect, wch is like, had we had tyme & the booke he had wth him, they myght haue bine p^{r}fected. Mr. Swayne ought him 4l., towards the wch payment he appoynted him to receaue 20 bush: of pease of Sa: Gardner.

Concerneing what is owed, we fynd he owes to a Country Rate, 18s. 8d.; besids there is another Rate come out, yet vngathered of any; and also some fenceing wch he hath lett out, & 22 weeks dyet to Mr. Swayne; also some other.

Robert Rose,
The 17th of the 3^d month 1647. Jo: Plum.

[247] The Inuentory of the goods and lands of ABRAHAM ELSEN, lately deceased in Wethersfield, prysed the 8th of May,* 1648, by Sa: Smith, Nath: Dickenson, Tho: Hurlebutt.

	£	s.	d.		£	s.	d.
Impr^{is}: his apparell att	9.	0.	0	It: his brasse, in potts &			
Itē: in wheat & pease,	3.	5.	0	kettells, .	2.	10.	0
It: in Indean, att	1.	10.	0	It: his arms & munition,	1.	15.	0
It: in meale & molte,	1.	0.	0	It: his house, homelotte			
It: one bed & bedding,	5.	0.	0	& mea: att	40.	8.	0
It: his husbandry tooles,	3.	10.	0	It: his cattell, att	18.	10.	0
It: chests & a bed ticke				It: his hoggs, att	5.	10.	0
& wooden vessell,	2.	10.	0	It: that wch is due to him frō other, .	5.	3.	0

                                             Som: 99. 11. 0
                  The debts wch he oweth   17. 11. 0

                                  Remayn: 82. 0. 0

    The wyddow is admitted to administer. She hath two daughters, on 3 year old, the other a yeare and halfe.

This 6th of June, 1655. An account of ye House and Land of ye Heires of Abraham Elsen desceased in Wethersfeild, rented out by us, Nath: Dickinson and Sam: Smith, foure yeares, for ye raising of ye childrens portions, according to ye appointment of this Court, unto Thomas Hurlbutt, at foure pounds ten shillings ye yeare, voth ye use of 4*l*. 10*s*. for three yeares : y^t is to say, ye Rent is eighteene pounds, ye use is two pounds one shilling and seauen pence,   18. 00. 00
                                                02. 01. 07

                                                20. 01. 07
Layd out for groundselling ye house, one pound three and fourepence, . .   1. 03. 4
And for other necessary charges, layd out of purse, . . .   0. 06. 8
                                                01. 10. 00

        The charges substracted there remaines,   18. 11. 07

    For wch eighteene pounds, eleaven shillings and seauen pence, wee ye said Nath: Dickinson and Sam: Smith, doth by o^r hands, ye day and yeare abouesaid, secure ye said portions unto ye Courte, for ye best improvement of ye said portions for ye children, either till they come at age, or till ye Courte bee pleased to call us to acco^t.

                                             p. nos { Nath: Dickinson,
                                                          { Samuell Smith.

---

* See pages 162, 202, ante.

[248]   The Inuentory of the goods and land of JOHN ELSEN,[*] of Wethersfield, on Conectecott River, wch he was cesed on when he dyed, prysed the sixteenth of May, by Sa: Smith and Nath: Dickenson.

Imp^is his Apparrell,	6. 18. 0	
Itē: his cattell, hoggs & a mare,	67. 10. 0	
Itē: his cart and plows, wth husbandry tooles,	8. 10. 0	
Itē: his brasse and pewter and iron vessell,	5. 0. 0	
Itē: his tables and forms, chests & tubbs and other woodden vessell and some other things,	5. 10. 0	
Itē: his corne and meat and molte,	6. 0. 0	
Itē: his bedds and bedding, woollen & lynin wth some leather,	14. 10. 0	
Itē: his arms and ammunition,	2. 0. 0	
Itē: his corne vppon the grownd,	8. 13. 4	
Itē: his howse & barne & homelott & other land,	87. 0. 0	
Itē: debts wch were owing him,	8. 10. 0	
Itē: his books,	1. 0. 0	
	221. 1. 4	

A coppy of the dispose of his estate, before Mr. Smith.

To my B. Gardners children, land att the meadowe gate ; To my Br: Gardner my coate ; To Mr. Smith, 5*l*.; My loueing wife all the rest. Only the howse and land to her two sons, after her life ; 11 acres of meadowe, howse & lotte ; 3 roods of meadowe to B. Gardners boy. The howse & home lett to Ben: The meadowe to be deuided betweene him & Job.

Robert Parke
Henry Smith

John T Elsin
his marke.

The Wyddow is admitted to administer.

---

[249]   May the 19th, 1648.
An Inuentory of THO: DEWYS Estate.

	£. s. d.
Imp^rs: One howse and barne, wth the home lott, in quantity about one acre & quarter, to the foote of the hill,	40. 0. 0
Itē: one p^rcell of meadowe adioyneing thereunto, about 7 acres,	20. 0. 0
Itē: another p^rcell in the great meadow, 4 acres & one quarter,	13. 0. 0
Itē: another p^rcell in the great meadowe, 3 acres and on quarter,	10. 0. 0
Itē: another p^rcell in the great meadowe, about 5 acres, 8 rodde & halfe,	15. 0. 0
Itē: two p^rcells of vpland, about 29 ac: & halfe,	20. 0. 0
Itē: one yoake of oxen,	15. 0. 0
Itē: two mares & a colte,	18. 10. 0

[*] See page 162, *ante.*

WILLS AND INVENTORIES. 481

Itē: two cowes and on young beast,		12. 0. 0
Itē: one sowe & two piggs, 1: 0: 0. Itē: 2 stocks of bees, 2: 10: 0.		[3. 10. 0]
Itē: 5 acres of corne vppon the grownd,		5. 0. 0
Itē: 7 other acres of corne vppon the grownd,		5. 0. 0
Itē: in bedding, bedsteed and lyning,		9. 10. 0
Itē: his weareing cloathes, 5: 10: 0. Itē: Pewter, 1: 8: 0.		[6. 18. 0]
Itē: a chest, a boxe, a cubberd,		0. 11. 0
Itē: one fowleing peece, sword, powder & bullits,		1. 15. 0
Itē: wedges & betle rings, 0: 4: 0. Itē, axes, spads & other tooles, 1: 10: 0.		[1. 14. 0]
Itē: potts, kettells of brasse & Iron,		7. 0. 0
Itē: hempe & flaxe, 1l. Itē: a saddell & pillion, 1l. 4s.,		[2. 4. 0]
Itē: meal trow, tables, payles & other smale things,		2. 1. 0
Itē: a table board, 0: 6: 0. Itē: a syth, 0: 5: 0,		[0. 11. 0]
Itē: part in a sawe & shott mold,		0. 6. 0
Itē: a cart, plowe, harowe, howes, and other things,		3. 10. 0
	Som,	213£

The distribution of this estate was by the Courte the 17th October 1648, as appeares by the Records of that Courte:[*] and prouision made for the childrens portious at yᵉ Courte the 6th of June, 1650. fol: 9.
Dauid Wilton,
Robert Wymbell.[†]

Syxe children, 4 boyes, 2 gerlls; one gerle, Mary Clark, 12 yeare old; one sonne, Thomas Dewye, 8 yeare. Josiah Dewey, 7 yeare old; Annah Dewye, 5 yeare old; Isreall Dewey, 3 yeare old; Jydidiah Dewey, 3 quarters of a yeare old.

---

[250]   A trew and pʳfecte Inuentory of the goods and Chattells of SETH GRANT, of Hartford, deceased.

Impʳⁱˢ: In the parlowre, one great table, 10s.: 3 joyned stooles, 6s: two chaire, 4s. 6d: on chest, 6s.	£. s. d. 1. 6. 6
It: in the lodgeing roome, 1 fetherbed & bolster, 3 pillowes,	3. 10. 0
It: one rugge, 20s: one flock bolster 10s: 3 blanketts & one couerlett, 1l. 10s.,	[3. 0. 0]
It: 5 curtens, 12s. 6d: one bedsted and strawe bedd, 1l.	1. 12. 6
It: one trundle bed, 7s: fower sheets & one board cloath, 3l. 10s.	3. 17. 0
It: 3 sheets, 3l. 10s: fower sheets, 1l: 5 perre of pillobers, 1l. 10s.,	6. 0. 0
It: a parcell of linen cloath, 2l. 0: one table cloath & 3 napkins, 12s.,	2. 12. 0
It: 1 graue cloath, 3s: three towells, 4s. 6d.	0. 7. 6
It. one smale boxe, wᵗʰ some child bed linnen,	0. 5. 0
It: 2 chests, 4 boxes, 13s. 4d: one cubberd, 5s: one warmeing panne, 6s. 8d.,	1. 5. 0

---

* Page 168, ante.   † Wynchell?

It: in the Hall, one Table, 2 forms, 1 chaire, . 0. 6. 8
It: one muskett, bandalers, & sowrd, . . 1. 5. 0
It: 1 pair of cobirons, 1 slyce,* 1 pair of tongs, 1 p're of bellowes, 2 perre of trammells, . . 0. 14. 0
It: 7 smale books, 8s: one spit & gridiron, 4s., . 0. 12. 0
It: 2 brasse kettells, 1l. 5s: three brasse posnetts, 10s., 1. 15. 0
It: on paile wth an iron baile, 1s. 6d: 2 iron potts & potthooks, 1l., . . . 1. 1. 6
It: one bell mettell morter & iron pestell, . . 0. 5. 0
It: 2 smale bear vessels, 4s: a cowl, 2s. 8d: an hower glasse, 2s., ... 0. 8. 8
It: 2 wedges, 2 axes, 2 betel rings, 8s: It: 10 pewter dishes, 2l. 4s., . - . . . 2. 12. 0
It: 1 pewter quarte, 1 halfe pinte, 1 beker, 1 candlesticke, 2 salts, 3 porringers, 2 saucers & 1 bason, 0. 15. 10
It: 4 smale dishes, 4s., ... 0. 4. 0
It: 2 peir of new shoos, 10s: one peir of boots, 7s. 0. 17. 0
It: 4 cushens, & his weareing apparrell, . . 2. 6. 8
It: in the chambers, 7 bush: Indean corne, . 0. 17. 0
It: 29 bush: of wheate, 5l. 16s: 10 bush. of pease, 1l. 10s., 7. 6. 0
It: two bush: of Indean molt, 5s: 7 bush: of oats, 12s. 0. 17. 0
It: 13^lb of towe, 6s. 4d: 25 pownd of hempe teare, 1l. 5s., 1. 11. 4
It: in the yards, 1 Cowe, 6l: two hoggs, 1l. 10s. 7. 10. 0
It: on dwelling howse, wth the barne & homelott, cont: 1 acre, 1 rood, ... 40. 0. 0
It: in the north meadow, 1 p'cell of meadow, cont: 3 roods, 4. 10. 0
It: on p'sell of meadowe & swampe, cont: 3 ac. 3 roods & 27 p'ches, ... 20. 0. 0
It: 2 roods 4 p'ches of meadow, on the east side the great Riuer, . - - . . . 2. 0. 0
It: 1 acre of swampe, 2l: and 32 acres of vpland, 30l., 32. 0. 0

                 The totall sume as ther cast vppe, 141. 10. 8
March the 4th, 1646.

---

[251] The last Will and Testament of WILLIAM BUTTLER, late of Hartford, deceased.

I William Buttler of Hartford, in Connecticutt, doe make and ordaine this my last will and Testament, wherein I giue my earthly goods as followeth:

And first, I make my brother Richard Buttler dwelling in Hartford, my whole executor, and all that is left of my lands and goods, when hee hath paid all these legacies vnderwritten, I giue to him.

---

* A peel, or fire shovel.

It: I give my sister Wests children that are now liuing in old England, fiue pounds a peece. Item, I give my sister Winters children, that are now living in old England, fiue pounds a peece. Item, I giue my louing frends of Hartford, Mr. Stone and Mr. Goodwyn and Mrs. Hooker and Mr. John Steele, ten pounds a peece. Item, I giue to the Church of Hartford, threescore pounds. And further, I doe earnestly desire my two frends, Mr. John Cullick and William Gibbens, both of Hartford, to see that this my last will and testament bee fullfilled; and for theire loue and paines, I doe bequeath to each of them three pounds a peece. In wittnes whereof, I the said William Buttler haue set to my hand, this eleuenth of May, 1648.

William Buttler.

A true and perfect Inventory of the goods and estate of William Buttler, late of Hartford, deceased: appr'sed by John Cullick and William Gibbens.

Imp^s: wearing cloaths and mony in his purse,	.	12. 0. 0
It: one bed and furniture, . . .		10. 0. 0
It: one gunn, one sword, powder and shott, .	.	2. 0. 0
It: 4 yards of searge 1*l*. 10*s*. It: land at Wethersfeild, 60*l*.		[61. 10. 0]
It: Land at Hartford, 90*l*. It: In debts, 193*l*. 13*s*.		[283. 13. 0]
	Summa Totalis,	429. 03. 0*

[252] The last Will and Testament of JOHN HORSKINS, of Wyndsor, deceased.

I, John Horskins, of Wynsor, doe make this my last will and testament, as followth: Item, I give vnto the Church, three pounds, to bee distributed by the Deacons vnto the poore, to bee paid in wheat or pease, as wee are able. Concerning my man seruant, Sammuell Rockwell, my desire is that hee should serue in my howse one quarter of a yeare after his covenant is out, which hee hath formerly made; and in case hee is willing so to doe, my will is that at the end of his seruice, hee shall haue six pounds of mee, as wee are able to pay it; but in case hee is not willing, then my will is that hee shall haue foure pounds, when hee hath compleated his tearme of searuice allready cou-

---

* An error of the original record. The amount of the Inventory, as recorded, is £369. 3. 0

enanted. Some persons owe mee some small sums of corne, wᶜʰ I shall leaue to the disposing of my wife and my sonne. Fiue bushells of Indian Corne and seauen pecks of pease is due to mee from Robert Winchell, and Thomas Hollcombe owes mee seuen bushells of pease; and Sammuell Gaylerd owes mee two bushells of pease, and eight shillings or thereabouts of an old reckoning; and Abraham Randall owes mee foure shillings. And all the rest of my goods, moueable or immoueable, cattell, howses and lands, and any thing growing thereon, I leaue to my wife and my sonn Thomas, assininge them to receaue my debts, and allso to make payment of theise things forenamed, or any other ingagement of mine. In wittnes whereof, I have herevnto put my hand, this first of May, 1648.
In the pʳsence of,   John Horskins.
    Thomas Horskins,
Sammuell Rockwell, Abraham Randall.

An Inventory of the goods of John Horskins deceased, June this 29 : 1648.

Impʳ: the howse and two barnes, with the homelott of 12 akers of land,	52. 0. 0
Item, 12 akers of meadow, 42*l*: Item, a great lott, 27 akers, 6*l*. 15*s*.,	48. 15. 0
Item, at Pyne meadow, 14 akers, 30*l*: Item, a parcell of swamp, 3 akers, 3*l*.,	33. 0. 0
Item, 6 akers of wheat sowen, 10*l*: Item, 14 akers of diuerse sortes of graine, 18*l*.,	28. 0. 0
Item, 2 paire of wheeles, one carte, one tumbrill, wᵗʰ a plough & tackling therevnto belonging,	6. 0. 0
Item, halfe a Boate,	0. 10. 0
Item, two axes, howes, sawes, wedges, and hookes, with other things,	2. 0. 0
Item, two swyne,	1. 6. 8
Item, in the Hall, one bed & a bedcase, and the furniture,	7. 0. 0
Item, two beds more with the furniture,	6. 0. 0
Item, in Leather, 1*l*: Item, in sheets, 3*l*: Item, two table cloaths, 6*s*.,	4. 6. 0
Item, in napkins, 6*s*: Item, in holland, 1*l*. 2*s*.,	1. 8. 0
Item, his wearing cloaths, 16*l*: Item, in cotton cloath and kniues, 5*l*. 8*s*.,	21. 8. 0
Item, in baggs and bottells, 1*l*. 6*s*: Item, in chests and boxes, 1*l*.	2. 6. 0
Item, a table, formes, stooles and wheeles, 1*l*. 2*s*: Item: in bookes, 10*s*.,	1. 12. 0
Item, one furnace pann, 2 brass panns, 1 warming pann & other things,	3. 15. 9
Item, in pewter, 1*l*. 2*s*: Item, 3 brass potts, 3*l*.	4. 2. 0

Item, 1 frying pann, crooks, pot hookes and other things,	1.	0.	0
Item, 3 peeces, 2 swords, powder, bandleers and bullitts,	2.	10.	0
Item, a barrill of pitch,	1.	0.	0
Item, in barrills, tubbs, pailes, hogsheads & other things,	1.	10.	0
Item, a cart rope, hemp, flax, yarne, and cushions,	2.	10.	0
Item, in corne, meale, mault and bacon,	9.	0.	0
Item, in salt, siues, meale troughs, one hyde, sadle & other lumber,	2.	10.	0
Item, 2 kine, 11*l*. 10*s*: Item, one Cowe, 4*l*. and two steeres, 6*l*.,	21.	10.	0
Item, two steares, 9*l*. and one Cowe, 4*l*. 10*s*: Item, one Bale, 4*l*.	17.	10.	0
Item, one yoake of oxen, 16*l*. 10*s*: Item, one mare and colt, 14*l*.	30.	10.	0
Item, 2 yearlings and two calues, 4*l*. 10*s*: Item, in debts, 20*l*. 18*s*.,	25.	8.	0

Will: Gaylerd, Thomas Stoughton, Dauid Willton. Totall sum is 338.[6. 8]

---

[253]   An Inventory of the goods and estate of RICHARD SAWYER, deceased July 24, 1648.

	£.	s.	d.
Imp^r: 1 musck colored cloth doublitt & breeches,	1.	00.	0
It: 1 bucksleather doublett, at 12*s*: It: 1 calues leather doublitt, at 6*s*.,	0.	18.	0
It: 1 liuer coloured doublett & jacket & breeches,	0.	07.	0
It: 1 haire coloured jackett & breeches,	0.	05.	0
It: 1 p^r of canuas drawers, 1*s*. 6*d*. It: 1 old coate & 1 p^r of old grey breeches, 5*s*.	0.	06.	6
It: 1 stuff jackett, 2*s*. 6*d*. It: 1 paire greene knitt mens hose, 2*s*.,	0.	04.	6
It: 1 old coloured hatt, 3*s*. It: 1 p^r old knitt cotton hose, 1*s*. 6*d*.,	0.	04.	6
It: 1 new coloured hatt, at 7*s*. It: 10 bands, at 15*s*.	1.	02.	0
It: 3 shirts, at 12*s*. It: 1 paire of old bootts, at 5*s*.	0.	17.	0
It: 1 paire of old shoes, at 2*s*.,	0.	02.	0
It: 1 chest, 1 paire of cloth buskins and other th:	0.	04.	6
It: in siluer, 2*s*. 3*d*. in wampum 23½*d*. It: in debts, 2*l*. 2*s*. 8*d*.,	2.	06.	10½

John Bernard, Arthur Smith.   Totall sum is   07. 17. 10½

Octob^r 17th 1648, The Courte gaue Mr. Cullick pow^r to administer vppon the estate abouesd. as appears by the Records of that Courte.*

---

* Page 169, *ante*.

[254] A true and perfect Inventory of the goods and chattells of RICHARD RISSLY, late of Hockanum, deceased.

	£.	s.	d.
In the yarde, Imp[rs]. two milch cows and a heifer,	14.	0.	0
Item, 3 heifers, 9*l*. and one steare, 3*l*.,	12.	0.	0
Item, one Bull and two young Bullocks 6*l*; one calfe, 20*s*.	7.	0.	0
Item, one steare, 5*l*., one spotted hogg 50*s*.,	7.	10.	0
Item, 2 sowes, 4*l*., younge hoggs, 9*l*.; 6 stores, 4*l*., and 6 shotes, 3*l*.,	20.	0.	0
In the Hall, Item, 1 muskitt, 15*s*., and one sword, 7*s*.,	1.	2.	0
Item, 2 frying pans, 6*s*., and one kettle, 16*s*.,	1.	2.	0
Item, 1 kettle, 13*s*. 4*d*., and one small kettle, 3*s*.,	0.	16.	4
Item, 1 posnett, 2*s*. 6*d*.; one iron pott, 7*s*.,	0.	9.	6
Item, one small iron pot, 3*s*.; pott hooks and trammells, 4*s*.,	0.	7.	0
Item, 3 platters and a plate, 8*s*., one pewter pott, 3*s*.,	0.	11.	0
Item, 1 pewter cupp, 12*d*.; six spoones, 12*d*.; earthen ware, 7*s*.,	0.	9.	0
Item, 2 payles, 2*s*. 6*d*.; 2 old payles, 12*d*.,	3.	6.	0
Item, 2 Indian trayes, 4*s*.; 2 platters, 2 bowles and dishes, 3*s*.,	0.	7.	0
Item, 1 great wooden platter, 2*s*.; 1 lattin dripping pann, 18*d*.,	0.	3.	6
Item, 1 paire of bellowes, 2*s*.; one joined table and formes, 10*s*.,	0.	12.	0
Item, 2 chaires, 3*s*.; 1 childes chaire, 18*d*.; a forme, 6*d*.,	0.	5.	0
Item, 6 trenchers, a scummer, a cleansing dish, & chaffing dish,	0.	1.	6
Item, 1 smoothing iron, 12*d*.; 1 great Bible, 13*s*. 4*d*.; 1 small Bible, 2*s*.,	0.	16.	4
Item, 1 narrow axe, 3*s*.; a broad axe, 2*s*.; a hattchett, 12*d*.	0.	6.	0
Item, 1 handsaw, 12*d*.; 1 hammer, 8*d*.; 2 augers and a beetle ring, 2*s*.,	0.	3.	8
Item, 1 charne, 3*s*.; 1 coule, 3*s*.; 1 keeler, 2*s*.; 1 powdering tubb, [3*s*.]	0.	12.	0
Item, 2 beare barrills, 5*s*.; 1 powdering trough, 4*s*.; 2 payles, 12*d*.,	0.	10.	0
In the Parlour: Item, 1 bedsted, 10*s*.; a featherbed, strawbed & 2 boulsters, 5*l*.,	5.	10.	0
Item, 1 pillow, 5*s*.; 1 paire blanketts, 30*s*,	1.	15.	0
Item, curtaines, 20*s*.; 3 paire new sheetes, 3*l*.,	4.	0.	0
Item, 6 yards of lynsy woollsy, 12*s*.; a flock bed and boulster, 30*s*.,	2.	2.	0
Item, 1 paire of blanketts, 15*s*.; 1 cradle, 2*s*.; 3 pillows, 8*s*.,	1.	5.	0
Item, 3 pillow beeres, and a warming pann,	0.	15.	0
Item, wearing clothes, and mony in his purse,	3.	0.	0
Item, 3 chests and a box, 12*s*.; a hogshead & meale tubb, 6*s*.,	0.	18.	0
Item, 1 peece of sole leather,	0.	3.	0

In the chamber ; Item, one fann, 6*s.*; one great Indian
    bagg, 4*s.*, ... 0. 10. 0
Item, 6^lb of hopps, 4*s.* 6*d.*; rough hemp, 10*s.*, . 0. 14. 6
Item, 3 baggs, 3*s.*, & 1 spade, 2*s.*; a corne baskitt, 12*d.*, 0. 6. 0
Item, 1 saw, 1 old sithe, 7*s.*; 1 iron bayle & old how, 12*d.*, 0. 8. 0
Item, halfe a bushell, ... 0. 2. 0
In the Barne ; Item, 55 bush: wheate, . . 11. 0. 0
Item, 40 bush: of pease and rye, . . 6. 0. 0
Item, 15 bush: of Indian corne, . . . 1. 10. 0
Item, a Howse at Hartford, with the homelott, 4 akers of
    swamp, and 2 of woodland, . . . 26. 0. 0

       John Cullick,   Totall sum is 135. 5. 10
       Will: Gibbens.

There are 3 children, viz. one daughter, by name Sarah Rissly, betweene 7 and 8 yeares old ; one sonne, by name Sammuell Rissly, about 2 yeares old ; and one sonn, by name Rich: Rissly, about 3 months old.

The distribution of the estate by the Courte, the 7th of Decemb^r, 1848, is : To the 3 children, 16*l.* a peece, to bee pd to the daughter at the age of 18 yeares, and to the sonns at the age of 21 years, William Hill bringing of y^m vpp to write and read, and giuing security to the Courte for the payment of the seuerall childrens portions.

[255]   *Debts owing p'r the estate of Richard Rissly deceased.*

	£.	s.	d.		£.	s.	d.
				To Joseph Mygatt,	2.	6.	5
To Mr. Olcott,	9.	1.	9	Thomas Selden,	1.	13.	11
Rich: Lord,	0.	13.	0	Capt: Cullick,	0.	17.	0
Sam: Smith, *Weth:*	1.	4.	0	Phillip Dauis,	0.	13.	10
Will: Gibbens,	0.	4.	0	Rich: Fellowes,	0.	15.	0
Mr. Moody,	0.	3.	0	Will: Wessly,	3.	8.	0
Will: Houghton,	0.	12.	6	Andr: Warner,	1.	3.	0
John Lyman,	0.	6.	0	Robt. Ely,	1.	12.	0
Mr. Stone & Mrs.				Mr. Edw. Hopkins,	16.	15.	8
Hooker,	0.	11.	0	To John Hopkins,	0.	4.	0
Knott,	0.	10.	6	Thomas Woodford,	0.	3.	0
Patience Smith,	0.	9.	0				
John Sabell,	10.	0.	0		53.	07.	05

---

[255]   May 20th, 1648.

The will of ROBERT DAY hee being sick and weake, yet in perfect memory, doth order and dispose of his estate to his wife and children, in the manner following :

Imp^rmis I give vnto my beloued wife Edatha Day my now dwelling howse and howsing thereto adioyning, howse Lott,

Allso all my land whereof I stand possessed, or that of right doth belong vnto mee, lying in Hartford, during the tearme of her naturall life: And at the end of her life, my will is that the said howse and land shall bee for the vse of my children that then shall bee liuing, to bee deuided in an equall proportion: my will allso is that all my howsehold stuff, and Cattle and other moueable goods shall bee my wiues to bring vp my children: And in case my wife should bee married to another man, then my surviers of my will shall haue power if they thinke good to take security for the bringing vp of the children, and for so much estate as shall bee thought meete by them, and to this my last Will and Testament I make my wife my Executrix, and I doe desire my Deare Brethren, Mr. Tailecoate, Willterton, and Stebbing, to take care of and Assist my wife in the ordering her selfe and my children, and I give them power to doe what in their Judgements may bee for the best, to bring vp my Children and dispose of them, and that I leaue, for theire good. And to this my will I sett to my hand the day aboue written.

Edward Stebbing,   Robert Day.
Wallter Gaylerd.

[256]   14th OCTOBER, 1648.

An Inventory of the Goods of Robert Day Deceased.

	£. s. d.
In the Chamber. Impr. one Bedstead; one feather bed, and feather Boulster and flock boulster: 2 pillowes, & bedcase & Curtaines,	07. 00. 00
Item: 2 blankitts, one red & yellow Couerlitt,	
Item: 1 chest 10s. 1 Box 3s. 1 desck box 3s.	00. 16. 00
Item: 1 table 5s. 1 Cubberd 5s. and chaiers,	00. 16. 90
Item: 3 paier of sheetes,	02. 00. 00
Item: 6 table napkins 12s. 1 table cloth 5s.,	00. 17. 00
Item: 6 pillow beeres,	01. 10. 00
Item: the wearing clothes with 3 skinns,	05. 00. 00
Item: in Linnen yearne and Cotton wool yearne,	01. 10. 00
Item: 2 Cushins 6s. 1 paire of Bellowes 3s.,	00. 09. 00
Item: 1 Little Baskitt 12d. 1 warming pann 6s.,	00. 07. 00
In the Hull. Item: 1 Brass Kettle,	02. 10. 00
Item: 1 Little kettle 12s. 1 little brass kettle,	00. 15. 00
Item: 1 brass possnett 4s. 1 brass pott 16s. 1 Iron pott 14s.,	01. 14. 00
Item: 1 brass Chaffin dish 3s. one skumer,	00. 05. 66

Item: 7 pewter dishes, and some broken pewter; 1 saser: 2 pewter potts: 1 Candlestick: 1 salte: 1 small bottle: 6 ockumy* spoons, 2 porringers and 4 old spoones, ...	01. 10. 00
Item: 1 Lattin dripping pann: 1 spitt, 1 pistoll: 1 smoothing Iron, ...	00. 10. 00
Item: in earthen ware, and wooden ware, . .	00. 10. 00
Item: 1 muskitt Bandleers and sword, . .	01. 00. 00
Item: 1 table and 2 chaires, . . . ,	00. 05. 00
In the sellar. Item. in tubbs and Tables and formes,	01. 00, 00
In y[e] little chamber. It: one flockbed, 2 blankitts: 1 Couerlitt, 1 feather boulster, 2 feather pillowes, 2 bedsteads, ...	04. 12. 00
Item: 3 hogsheads, 2 Linnen wheeles, 1 woolen wheele, one Barrill, ...	00. 19. 00
Item: 1 table, 1 wheele, 1 hatchett, . . .	00. 05. 00
Item: in working tooles, ...	01. 08. 00
Item: 1 Leather Bottle 2s. vi d. 1 paire of tongs: fier pann, grid Iron: frying pann, one trammell,	00. 15. 00
Item: in Bookes, and Sackes, and Ladders, .	01. 00. 00
Item: one Cow: 1 3 yeare ould heifer: one 2 yeare old heifer, with some hay to winter them, . .	14. 10. 00
Item: 2 hoggs 3l., ...	03. 00. 00
Item: in seuerall sortes of Corne with some hemp and flax, ...	15. 00. 00
Item: the dwelling howse and out howsing, howse lott and Garden, ...	45. 00. 00
Item: about 6 Akers of meadow, in severall parcells with vpland, ...	26. 00. 00
Summa Totalis	142. 13. 06

John Tailecoate,
Gregory Willterton,
Edward Stebbing.

---

[257]   October 16th, 1648.

An Inventory of the Goods of Timothy Standly, of Hartford, deceased.

	£. s. d.
Imp[r]: *In the kitichin chamber;* One standing bedstead, one feather bed and feather boulster, one red and blue couerlitt, one paire blankitts, 2 pillowes, . .	7. 18. 08

---

* *Ochimy,* (alchemy) a mixed base metal.

Item, one trundle bed, 1 flock bed & 2 boulsters, 1 white blankitt, 1 straw bed case, one yello and white couer litt, 1 feather pillow, 1 flock pillow, 2 little feather pillows,	5. 18.	08
Item, 4 yards ½ of blankitt cloth at 3s. p^r yard, and one trundle bed,	0. 18.	06
Item, one paire of flaxen sheetes,	1. 04.	00
Item, 1 paire of course sheets, 12s. 1 paire sheets more, 12s.,	1. 04.	00
Item, 2 paire of hempen sheets,	2. 10.	00
Item, 1 paire more of towing sheets, 16s. 1 single sheete, 12s.,	1. 08.	00
Item, more 4 paire of course sheets, 8s. pr,	1. 12.	00
Item, 1 long table cloth, 10s. 2 shorte table cloths, 10s.,	1. 00.	00
Item, 3 holland pillow beeres, 12s. 3 flaxen pillow beers, 10s. 2 flaxen hand towels, 9s. 1 course towell, 2s.,	1. 13.	00
Item, 1 course board cloth, 2s. foure course towing towells, 6s.,	0. 08.	00
Item, 6 flaxen napkins, 12s. 1 chest & box, 4s. 3 chaires, 4s.,	1. 00.	00
Item, 6 cushins, 12s. 1 paire bellows, 2s.,	0. 14.	00
In the *Hall chamber*; one chest, 12s. 1 paire curtans, 20s. 1 little chest, 3s. 1 shipp chest, 2s. 6d.,	1. 17.	06
Item, one trunck, 5s. one old trunck, 3s. one little chest, 2s.,	0. 10.	00
Item, one Fann, 10s. foure hogsheads, 8s. 10 yards of course lyning at 18d. pr.	1. 13.	00
Item, 5 great platters, 20s. 4 small platters, 10s.,	1. 10.	00
Item, 3 sasers, and 2 bigger dishes,	0. 05.	04
Item, pewter bowle, 2 small potts, 4s. foure porringers, 21s. one salte, 3s. one dozen of spoones, 2s. vid.,	0. 11.	06
Item, one chamber vessell, 2s. vid. 12 skinns for cloaths at 5s. p^r. 3l.,	3. 02.	06
Item, the wearing cloaths, valued at	6. 00.	00
In the *Garritt chamber*; 1 flock bed & 4 blankitts,	2. 10.	00
Item, 8 sacks,	1. 00.	00
In the *Kittchin*; 1 kettle, 30s. one, 16s. one, 12s,	2. 18.	00
Item, 3 skilletts, 10s; 3 iron potts, 1 iron kettle,	1. 14.	00
Item, one spitt, one lattin dripping pann,	0. 04.	00
Item, one brass sckumer; in earthen ware and wooden dishes,	0. 06.	08
Item, one iron morter and pessell,	0. 05.	00
Item, 1 kneading trough, 1 forme, 1 table,	0. 08.	00
Item, 2 tramells, fier pann, tongs & cobiornes,	0. 11.	00
Item, 1 tosting iron, 2s. two linnen wheeles, 6s.,	0. 08.	00
Item, 3 siuefes,* 3s. one treuett, 18d. 1 chaffin dish,	0. 05.	06
Item, 1 cross cutt saw, 6s. 2 muskitts, 24s. 2 paire bandleers, 4s. 1 fowling peece, 15s.,	2. 09.	00

* sieves?

Item, more one woollen wheele,	0. 03. 00
Item, in seuerall bookes, 20s. and one sword, 4s.	1. 04. 00
In the Hall; one table, 10s. one press, 10s.,	1. 00. 00
Item, one warming pann, 5s. 1 halfe bushell, 2s.,	0. 07. 00
Item, one great seife, 2s. in mony and wampum, 2l.,	2. 02. 00
In the chamber ouer the shopp; 1 flock bed, 2 boulsters, 2 blankitts, 1 yello: and white couerlitt,	4. 00. 00
[258] Item, *In the working shopp;* in lasts, axes, handsaw, beetle rings, iron wedges & other toolls,	1. 15. 00
Item, in 3 backs and halfe of leather, and one peece;	10. 00. 00
Item, one parcell of leather, sould for 13l.,	13. 0J. 00
Item, one paire of Bootts,	00. 10. 00
Item, in Cartes and wheeles, & chaines & plow irons,	2. 10. 00
Item, 6 oxen valued at,	38. 00. 00
Item, 2 cowes, 11l. one heifer, 2l. 10s. two calues, 2l.,	15. 10. 00
Item, 1 yeare old horse colt, 4l. 4 sheepe, 5l. one blankitt more, 10s.,	9. 10. 00
In wheat at Farmington, valued at 100 bush: out of which the family is to bee provided and some small debts paid.	
Item, 6 hoggs at 25s. p^r, and 3 piggs,	9. 00. 00
Item, 2 hiuefes of bees,	1. 10. 00
Item, the dwelling howse, home lott, and little meadow lott, and outhowsing, with uplands,	75. 00. 00
Item, 8 akers of meadow and swamp, in the northmeadow,	40. 00. 00
Item, 3 akers of meadow and some vpland on the east side of the great Riuer,	12. 00. 00
Item, land and howsing at Farmington,	40. 00. 00
Totall sum is	332. 18. 10

John Tailecoate,   Will: Westwood,
Edward Stebbing,   Thomas Standly.

The distribution of the estate by the Court, the 7th Decemb^r, 1648, is as followeth: To the two eldest daughters, 50l. out of the moueables. To the eldest sonn, Calib, the howses and lands in Hartford, at the age of 21 yeares; hee paying to the youngest daughter, if shee liues, 30l. To the youngest sonn, Isaack, after the decease of his mother, the land and howsing at Farmington.

These presents witnesse, that we Thomas Portter & Lois Porter haue fully receiued of o^r brother Caleb Standly of Hartford, that portion that was alotted or distributed to Lois by the Honoured Court as her portion due to her of her father Timothy Standly his estate, and we doe by these presents fully acquitt, exoneratt and discharge our sayd brother Caleb Standly, his heires, executors and administrators of all debts, dues and demands whatsoeuer dew from him the sayd Caleb Standley, by vertue of any guift or distribution made of the estate of o^r Honoured Father Timothy Standly deceased; as witness oʳ hands this first day of December, in the the year of oʳ Lord, one thowsand, six hundred and seuenty.

Witness, Samuel Cowles, Thomas Porter,
    Abigail Cowles. Lois Porter.

This is a true coppy of the originall, being examined & compared therewith, this 5ᵗʰ of January, 1670, pʳ me,

                          John Allyn, Secret'y.

---

[259]   October 17ᵗʰ, 1648.

The Testament of Edward Chalkwell.

Impʳ: I doe bequeath vnto Nicholas Sension my gunn and sword and bandaleers and best hatt and forty shillings : Item, to John Moses, my best sute and coate and stockings and shoes : Item, to Mr. Warham, forty or fifty shillings, according as my goods doe hould out, after my debts bee paid : Item, to Georg Phelps, three pounds, and if any thing bee left, I giue it to the poore of the Church, and I doe make George Phelps executor to this my will and testament.

    Wittnes, Henry Woollcott,
           Nicholas Sension.

An Inventory of the goods of Edward Chalkwell, December 5ᵗʰ, Anno Dmni: 1648.

Impʳ A cotton sute, breeches and jackett,	00. 12. 00
Item, a cloth sute, breeches and jackett,	00. 12. 06
Item, a coate, jackett and breeches,	3. 00. 00
Item, a leather doublitt, 8s. a cloth doublett, 5s,	0. 13. 00
Item, a red jackett, 16s. Item, worsted stockings, 6s. 6d.,	1. 02. 06
Item, a chest lock, 1s. 6d. and 1 paire of gloues,	00. 04. 06
Item, a peece of trading cloth, 6s. 6d. 1 pʳ shoes, 3s. 8d. 1 pʳ stockings 3s.,	00. 13. 02
Item, 2 old paire stockings, 1s. Item, 2 shirts, val'd 6s.,	00. 07. 00
Item, a band and strings, 2s. Item, 7 yards of Lockrum, 12s.,	00. 14. 00
Item, a gunn 12s. a cuttlas, 24s. a belt, 2s.,	1. 18. 00
Item, his best hatt, 14s. an old hatt, 1s.,	0. 15. 00
Item, an axe howe, 6s, and chest, 2s. vid.,	0. 08. 06
Item, bandleers and powder horne,	0. 03. 00
Item, wheat, 2 bush: pease, 2 bush:	0. 14. 00
Item, pʳt of a pott, frying pann, old payles, bedstick & barrill,	0. 09. 00
Item, seed wheat, 3 bush: ½, and 1 day ¼ worke,	0. 16. 00
Item, a bible,	0. 05. 06
Item, in flax,	13. 07. 08

[260]   March 20th, 1643.

Whereas by the Providence of God, I William Whiting doe intend a voyage presently vnto sea, mans life being allwayes incident to change, but so much the more in regard of my voyage, therfore, I did thinke good, if God should not returne mee with safety, to leaue some lynes in generall, as my last Will and Testament. And whereas that estate I haue doth lye in such a manner as it is vncerteine what it will bee, therfore my will is it should bee thus devided: I giue vnto my loving wife, halfe my houshould stuffe of all kinds, and one fourth parte of my whole personall estate; and her widdowes estate in my now dwelling howse and lands at Hartford, vntill my sonne William bee the age of twenty and one yeares, and after, if shee continue a widdow, I giue her the one halfe of my said howse and land for her life. I bequeath vnto my sonne William, one hundred pound more then I giue vnto either my sonne John or my sonne Samuell. I bequeath vnto my sonne John one hundred pounds more, and my sonne Samuell, one hundred pounds more a peece, then I giue vnto my daughter Sarah or vnto my daughter Mary. The fourth parte of my estate being taken out for my wife, one hundred pound for my eldest sonne not being accounted with the rest, hee hauing an equall proportion with my two other sonns in the estate, my other two sonns and hee taking one hundred a peece, I bequeath the rest of my estate thus; first, to haue 20*l*. paid vnto Mr Hooker, towards the furtherance of setting forth for the benefitt of the church his worke vppon the 17th of John,* with any else hee doth intend. I desire Mr. Stone may haue added vnto the 5*l*. I did promise him, 5*l*. more. Allso, I bequeath 5*l*. towards the mending of the high wayes betwixt my howse and the meeting howse. Allso, I giue 5*l*. to some godly poore in the Towne. These sums being taken out, I doe bequeath the rest of my estate vnto my fiue children to bee equally deuided amongst them, that is, euery one a like proportion; and this my said estate to bee improued vnto the best advantage for the breeding vpp of my children in learning, to

---

* This work of Mr. Hookers, so far as it was completed before his death, was first published in London, in 1657, under the title of "Christ's Prayer for Believers, a Series of Discourses founded on John xvii. 20-26."

schoole, and in the feare of God; and theire portions to bee paid before the age of twenty and one yeares, as the providence of God shall giue occasion. And my will is that if any of them dye before the said tearme of yeares, the portion should bee deuided among the rest of my children. And that this my will may bee performed, I doe earnestly intreat my much hono^red frends and beloued in the Lord, Mr. John Haynes, Mr. Edward Hopkins, Mr. John Webster, with o^r deare and louing Pastor, Mr. Thomas Hooker and Mr. Samuell Stone, to bee ou^rseers of this my last will and Testament, not doubting they will indeauo^r the performance of the same. In testimony of my loue to them, I doe bequeath, out of my whole personall estate, 10*l*. a peece. Allso, I doe bequeath vnto my Father and Mother, 20*l*., and if they bee dead my minde is it should bee giuen vnto my brother and his children. My meaning is, my land and howse shall bee accounted a parte of my sonne William, his portion. And my will is, if those my ou^rseers doe thinke my second sonne fitt to make a schollar, for his naturall parts, and allso in the gifts of his mind hopefull to keepe the fire vppon the Alltar, my will is hee should bee sett aparte for that seruice.

This is my last will, as wittnes my hand, the day and yeare aboue. William Whiting.

Aprill 2^d, 1646. Whereas by the providence of God, I am intending a voyage, my will is that my sonne Joseph shall haue an equall portion with my sonne John and my sonne Samuell, out of my whole personall estate. Allso, I giue my sonne William, 50*l*. more. I giue vnto my daughter Mary, 10*l*. more. Allso, I giue vnto my sister Wiggen, 5*l*. and vnto her children, 3*l*. a peece. I giue vnto Margery Parker, 10*l*. My former will, my mind is, it should bee in force; and these last legacies should bee paid at the age of 21. The rest to bee paid in one yeare after my decease. p^r mee,

This was done in the presence William Whiting. of Mr. Edward Hopkins.

[261] In a letter to Mr. Hopkins hee did further express himself, as follo^th:

S^r, I left my last with you. God hath increased my number. My mind is that the last should haue an equall proportion with the rest. And whereas I did referr some trust with Mr. Haynes, I doe now referr all vnto you, and the rest expressed therin.

William Whiting.

And vppon his death bed hee did declare, as followth:

It is my minde, if the Lord take mee away at this present, before I can draw vp any further will, that the children wch God hath giuen mee since the will was made wch I haue in Mr. Hopkins his hands, shall haue an equall proportion in all my estate, together with the rest of my children, as I haue there deuised. Allso, I confirme ten pounds giuen to Mr. Hopkins, ten pounds giuen to Mr. Webster, ten pounds to Mr. Hookers children, ten pounds to Mr. Stones children, ten pounds to the pore, fiue to Hartford and fiue to theise other two townes Wyndsor and Wethersfeild, and fiue pounds to Mr. Smiths children, of Wethersfeild.

July 24th 1647. William Whiting.*

In the presence of Henry Smith,
                        Jeames Cole.

APRIL 24th, 1649.

The Courte taking into serious consideration Mr. Whitings Will, and judging it necessary for the preuenting of future difference to express theire judgements therevpon, doe conceiue that it was according to his true meaning and intent that the last sonne borne after his death should haue an equall portion with the rest of his sonnes, except the eldest; And they doe conceiue that twenty pound should be paid to Mr. Hooker vppon a speciall consideration, viz: for the putting forth of his worke vpon the 17th of John; and the ten pound giuen in his last writing to Mr. Hookers children, to bee in leiw of the ten pound giuen in his first writing to Mr. Hooker as ouerseer. Allso, they doe conceiue that the fiue pounds giuen to Mr. Stone, in his first writing, should bee paid, and the ten pounds giuen in his last writing to Mr. Stones children, to bee in leiw of the ten pounds giuen Mr. Stone, in his first writing, as ouer-

---

* Administration granted to the widow of Mr. Whiting, Sept. 2, 1647. The estate distributed, Oct. 3d, 1654. See pages 157, 262.

seer. To his Father etc. twenty pounds, fiue pounds to his sister Wiggen, and three pounds a peece to her children. Ten pounds to Margery Parker; fiue pounds to Mr. Smiths children; fiue pounds to the mending of the highwayes, and fiue pounds to the pore of Hartford; fifty shillings to the pore of Wyndsor, and fifty shillings to the pore of Wethersfeild.

That legacy giuen to Mr. Haynes is left to further consideration.

Theise are the aprehensions of the Courte for the present, till other and better lighte appeares.

It was further declared by the Courte, this 24th of March, 16$\frac{50}{51}$, that it is theire aprehensions, according to their present lighte, that whereas Mr. Whiting giues his wife her widdowes estate in her howse & land in Hartford, vntill his sonne William comes to the age of 21 yeares, that it was his intent and meaneing that his said wife should injoye his said howse and land vntill William bee of the age aforesaid of 21 yeares, though shee bee marryed before.

And whereas, hee giues her one fourth p^{r}t of his whole personall estate, It is in like manner theire aprehensions, the 24th March, 16$\frac{50}{51}$, that it was his intent & meaning that his said wife should not haue a fourth p^{r}t of his howsing & lands.

[262]   April 20th, 1649.

An Inventory of the Estate of Mr. William Whiting, deceased.

	£. s. d.
In the parlour; It: A featherbed, 2 flock bedds, 2 p^r of sheets, blankitts, stooles, a clock, a safe, a bedstead, cradle, cobirons &c. valued at,	17. 06. 00
In the Hall; It: a table, a courte cubberd, 6 joint stooles, 3 chaires, 6 cushions, and andirons &c. valued at,	04. 17. 00
In the parlour Chamber; It: 2 flock beds and boulsters,	03. 00. 00
It: 2 featherbeds, boulsters and pillowes,	14. 00. 00
It: 6 blankitts, 1 p^r sheets, 2 coverlitts & a trundle bed,	07. 01. 00
It: a coverlitt, vallance, curtaine, cubbert cloth, 2 small carpets,	09. 00. 00
It: a bedstead, 2 chaires, and 4 stooles,	02. 06. 00
It: a cubberd, a window cushion, cobirons and 3 p of bellowes,	02. 02. 08
It: 8 paire of fine sheets, 6 large table cloaths, 12 pillow beers, 4 doz. fine napkins, and 6 shorte table cloaths,	19. 06. 00
It: a chest contayning seuerall remnants of wollen and linnen, intended for the vse of the family, valued at,	10. 00. 00

It: a trunck and 4 window curteines,		00. 18. 00
In the Hall Chamber ; It: 6 cushions, 2 greene carpetts, a coverlitt, a sett of curtaines and valence of greene say, 5 old curtaines and valence,		07. 12. 00
It: a chest & 4 truncks 1*l*. 10*s*.; 2 remnants of Kithermast^r stuff, 2*l*.,		03. 10. 00
In the closett ; It: seuerall pewter dishes cont: 91*lbs*.; a flagon, 2 candlesticks & a chamber pott, valewed at,		06. 10. 00
In the garritt ; It: a flockbed, 2 boulsters, a blankitt, 2 ruggs, 2 pillows and a bedstead,		05. 00. 00
It: 5 p^r of sheets and 5 doz: napkins,		05. 00. 00
In the kitching chamber ; It: a bed, 2 couerings, a p^r of sheets, and two bedsteads,		03. 10. 00
In the Kittching ; It: 2 brass potts, 5 iron potts and an iron kettle, 4 brass panns and 6 brass kettles and 9 skilletts,		14. 10. 04
It: a pott posnett, a brass morter & chafing dish,		01. 00. 00
It: 12 old pewter dishes, 6 porringers, 2 quart potts, 1 pinte, 2 chamber potts & a roster,		02. 03. 04
It: a frying pan, gridiron, 3 spitts, a jack, racks and cobirons,		01. 17. 00
It: a furnace, 2 dripping panns, and a grater,		03. 04. 00
It: in tubbs and keelers &c.,		02. 10. 00
It: a new iron kettle & a warming pann,		00. 13. 04
It: in plate and mony,		14. 10. 00
		161. 06. 08
In the closett, more ; It: in wampum,		39. 09. 00
It: in howes and hatchetts, shoes, nayles, pinns, paper, shott, fish hooks, and all blades,		16. 19. 00
It: in Beauer, 10*l*. 4*s*.; It: in Amunition & gunpowder, 7*l*. 10*s*.,		17. 14. 00
It: in shagg cotton, stockings, hollands, deare skinns & 9 yards stuff,		19. 03. 00
It: in hatts, capps, gilded looking glasses, 7 peeces tape, tinn cupps and dram cupps,		04. 13. 06
It: 25 yards greene tammy, 2*l*. 18*s*. 4*d*.; 13 peeces of duffles, 130*l*.,		132. 18. 04
It: in looking glasses, pewter bottles, brass ladles, brushes, bells, thimbles, boxes, kniues, sissers, combs, Jewes harps,		19. 06. 02
It: 4 small brass kettles,		01. 06. 08
It: 2 Racoone coats, 1 Wolf skin coate, 4 Bear skinns, 3 Mooss,		06. 10. 00
It: one small haser, 2*l*.; It: 2 p^r of stilliars, 1*l*. 10*s*.,		03. 10. 00
It: Tobacko pipes, 1*l*. 10*s*.; It: in bookes and apparell, 25*l*.		26. 10. 00
It: in beauer, mooss and wampum, more,		250. 00. 00
It: in 2 great gunns, anker, a cable, & hides, vppon Cariso:* adventure,		61. 11. 06

* Curacoa ?

It: in skinns, and debts, vppon a voyage to Verginia, in
    anno 1647, yet due, ... 67. 10. 00
It: in Tobacko, at Verginia, . . . 65. 00. 00
It: in the proceed of corne and porke, sould in anno 1648, 48. 00. 00
Il: in oyle, soape, vinegar and other goods from Dela-
    war, ye last yeare, ... 30. 00. 00
It: in trade at Long Iland, . . . 30. 00. 00
It: in stock for trade at Waranoco, . . 100. 00. 00
It: in goods sent from England, . . . 65. 19. 03
It: in p^rt of a pinnace, ... 40. 00. 00
It: in debts in the book, whereof ⅛ is doubtful, . 372. 00. 00
It: in debts at Dillaware, wch are harserdous, . 90. 00. 00
It: in debts heere, vppon Mr. Whitings last voyage to
    Dillawar, ... 15. 00. 00
It: a debt of Steph: Luxford, very doubtfull, 15. 12. 00
It: a hhd. of Beauer, very haserdous, at least in great
    p^rt, sent for England, in Trerice, valued at, . 50. 00. 00
It: goods and debts at Piscataway, very haserdous, 150. 00. 00
It: 7 cowes, a bull stagg and a young bull, 5 calues, and
    9 other cattle, at Warranoco, & 1 at the sea side, at 102. 00. 00
It: 2 mares, 3 horses and 3 colts, . . . 77. 00. 00
It: 20 hoggs, small and great, that were killed, . 45. 00. 00
It: 23 store hoggs, 20*l*.; It: beefe in the tubb, 10*l*., . 30. 00. 00
It: howsing and land at Wyndsor, at . . 300. 00. 00
It: howsing and land in Hartford bounds, . . 400. 00. 00

                                                    2854. 00. 00
    Debts owing by this estate, about 97*l*.

This aprizement was made the day and yeare before expressed, according to the best light that then appeared, by vs,

                                Nathaniell Warde,
                                John White.

---

[263] The last Will and Testament of Mr. THOMAS HOOKER, late of Hartford, deceased.

I Thomas Hooker, of Hartford, vppon Connecticutt in New England, being weake in my body, through the tender visitation of the Lord, but of sound and perfect memory, doe dispose of that outward estate I haue beene betrusted withall by him, in manner following :—

I doe giue vnto my sonne John Hooker, my howsing and lands in Hartford, aforesaid, both that which is on the west, and allso that wch is on the east side of the Riuer, to bee inioyed by him and his heires for euer, after the death of my wife, Susanna

Hooker, provided hee bee then at the age of one and twenty
yeares, it being my will that my said deare wife shall inioye and
possess my said howsing and lands during her naturall life:
And if shee dye before my sonne John come to the age of one
and twenty yeares, that the same bee improued by the ou^rseers
of this my will for the maintenance and education of my children not disposed of, according to theire best discretion.

I doe allso giue vnto my sonne John, my library of printed
bookes and manuscripts, vnder the limitations and provisoes
hereafter expressed. It is my will that my sonne John deliuer
to my sonne Samuell, so many of my bookes as shall bee valued
by the ou^rseers of this my will to bee worth fifty pounds sterling, or that hee pay him the some of fifty pounds sterling to
buy such bookes as may bee vseful to him in the way of his
studdyes, at such time as the ouerseers of this my will shall
judge meete; but if my sonne John doe not goe on to the perfecting of his studdyes, or shall not giue vpp himselfe to the seruice of the Lord in the worke of the ministry, my will is that
my sonne Samuel inioye and possesse the whole library and
manuscripts, to his proper vse for euer; onely, it is my will that
whateuer manuscripts shall bee judged meete to bee printed,
the disposall thereof and advantage that may come thereby I
leaue wholly to my executrix; and in case shee departe this life
before the same bee judged of and setled, then to my ouerseers
to bee improued by them in theire best discretion, for the good
of myne, according to the trust reposed in them. And howeuer
I do not forbid my sonne John from seeking and taking a wife
in England, yet I doe forbid him from marrying and tarrying
there.

I doe giue vnto my sonne Samuell, in case the whole library
come not to him, as is before expressed, the sum of seuenty
pounds, to bee paid vnto him by my executrix at such time, and
in such manner, as shall be judged meetest by the ouerseers of
my will.

I doe also giue vnto my daughter Sarah Hooker, the sum of
one hundred pounds sterling, to bee paid vnto her by my executrix when she shall marry or come to the age of one and twenty
yeares, wch shall first happen; the disposall and further educa-

tion of her and the rest, I leaue my wife, advising them to attend her councell in the feare of the Lord.

I doe giue vnto the two children of my daughter Joannah Shephard deceased, and the childe of my daughter Mary Newton, to each of them the sum of ten pounds, to bee paid vnto them by my sonne John, within one yeare after hee shall come to the posession and inioyment of my howsings and lands in Hartford, or my sonne Samuell, if by the decease of John, hee come to inioye the same.

I doe make my beloued wife Susanna Hooker, executrix of this my last Will and Testament, and (my just debts being paid,) doe giue and bequeath vnto her all my estate and goods, moueable and imoueable, not formerly bequeathed by this my will. And I desire my beloued frends, Mr. Edward Hopkins and Mr. William Goodwyn, to affoard theire best assistance to my wife, and doe constitute and appoint them the ouerseers of this my will. And it hauing pleased the Lord now to visitt my wife with a sicknes, and not knowing how it may please his Matie to dispose of her, my minde and will is, that in case shee departe this life before shee dispose the estate bequeathed her, my aforesaid beloued frends, Mr. Edward Hopkins and Mr. William Goodwyn, shall take care both of the education and dispose of my children (to whose loue and faithfullnes I commend them,) and of the estate left and bequeathed to my wife, and do committ it to theire best judgment and discretion to manage the said estate for the best good of mine, and to bestow [264] it vppon any or all of them in such a proportion || as shall bee most sutable to theire owne ap^{r}hensions; being willing onely to intimate my desire that they wch deserue best may haue most; but not to limmitt them, but leaue them to the full scope and bredth of theire owne judgments; in the dispose whereof, they may haue respect to the forementioned children of my two daughters, if they see meet. It being my full will that what trust I haue comitted to my wife, either in matter of estate, or such manuscripts as shall bee judged fitt to bee printed, in case shee liue not to order the same herselfe, bee wholly transmitted and passed ouer from her to them, for the ends before specified. And for mortallity sake, I doe put power into the hands of the forementioned beloued freinds, to constitute and appoint such other faithfull men as they shall judge meete, (in case they bee depriued of life or libberty to attend the same, in theire owne persons,) to manage, dispose and performe the estate and trust comitted to them, in as full manner as I haue comitted it to them for the same end.

This was declared to bee the last Will and Testament of Mr. Thomas Hooker, the seuenth day of July, 1647,

Thomas Hooker.

In the presence of
    Henry Smith,
    Samuell Stone,
    John White.

[265] *An Inventory of the estate of Mr. Thomas Hooker, deceased, taken the 21st Aprill,* 1649.

In the new Parlour ; It: 3 chaires, 2 stooles, 6 cushions, a clock, a safe, a table, window curtaines &c.,   05. 00. 00

In the Hall ; It: a chest of drawers, and in it, 2 dozen of dishes, a pewter flagon, basons, candlesticks, sawcers, &c., ... 06. 00. 00

It: in ammunition, 4*l*. It: in a table, & forme, and 4 wheeles, 1*l*., ... [05. 00. 00]

In the ould Parlour ; It: 2 tables, a forme, 4 chaires, 4 stooles, 4 table carpetts, window curtaines, andirons and doggs &c. in the chimny, . . 09. 00. 00

In the Chamber ouer that ; It: a featherbed and boulster, 2 pillowes, a strawbed, 2 blankitts, a rugg, and couerlitt, darnix hangings in 7 peeces, window curtaines, curtaines and valence to the bed, a bedstead, 2 chaires, and 3 stooles, andirons &c. in the chimny, & a courte cubberd, . . . 14. 05. 00

It: curtaines and valence to the same bed, of greene say, and a rugg of the same, with window curtaines,   05. 00. 00

In the Hall Chamber ; It: a trunck of linnen, cont: 20 p^r sheets, 8 table cloaths, 5 doz. napkins, 6 p^r of pillow beers, and towells, ... 27. 00. 00

It: a bedstead, two truncks, 2 boxes, a chest & a chaire, 03. 05. 00

In the Kittchin Chamber ; It: a featherbed, a quilt bed, 2 blankitts, 2 couerlitts, 1 boulster, a flockbed and boulster, a rugg and blankitt, a chest & ould trunck, and a bedstead, ... 12. 00. 00

In the chamber ouer the new Parlour ; It: 2 featherbeds, 2 boulsters, a p^r of pillows, 5 blankitts and 2 ruggs, stript valence and curtaines for bed & windowes, a chest of drawers, an Alarum, 2 boxes, a small trunck, 2 cases of bottles, 1 p^r of dogs, in the chimney, ... 21. 00 00

In the garritts ; It: in corne and hoggsheads and other
  houshould lumber, . . . 14. 15. 00
It: in apparrell and plate, ... 40. 00. 00
In the Kittchin ; It: 2 brass kettles, 3 brass potts, 2 cha-
  fing dishes, 2 brass skilletts, a brass morter, a brass
  skimmer, and 2 ladles, 2 iron potts, 2 iron skilletts,
  a dripping pann, 2 kettles, 2 spitts & a jack, a p^r of
  cobirons, a p^r of andirons, a p^r of doggs, fire shouell
  and tongs, 2 frying panns, a warming pann, a gridiron, 7 pewter dishes, 2 p⌄rringers, 1 p^r of bellowes,
  a tinn dripping pan, a roster, & 2 tyn couers, potthooks and trammells ; all valued at . 12. 10. 00
In the Brew howse ; It: a copper mash tubbs, payles,
  treyes, &c. 04. 10. 00
In the sellars ; It: 2 stills and dairy vessells, . 06. 00. 00
It: in yearne ready for the weauer, . . . 03. 00. 00
It: 2 oxen, 2 mares, 1 horse, 2 colts, 8 cowes, and 2
  heifers, 3 two yeares ould and 6 yearlings, val-
  ued at, ... 143. 00. 00
It: husbandry implements, ... 05. 00. 00
It: Howsing and Lands within the bounds of Hartford,
  on both sides the Riuer, . . . 450. 00. 00
It: Bookes in his studdy &c., valued at . . 300. 00. 00
It: an adventure in the Entrance, . . . 50. 00. 00

                                                                  1136. 15. 00

The foregoing perticulars were prised the day and yeare aboue written, according to such light as at p^{r}sent appeared,
                                   by Nathaniell Ward,
                                         Edward Stebbing.

---

[266] The last Will and Testament of Mr. HENRY SMITH, late of Wethersfeild, deceased.

I Henry Smith, of Weathersfeild, being at present in health of body and soundnes of minde, considering my mortallity, and knowing it to bee my duty to prouide for my family and settle my estate, that I may leaue no occasion of trouble to my children when I am gonn, and that I may free myselfe from distractions of this kinde, if it shall please God to visitt mee with sicknes before I dye ; I doe therfore leaue this testimony vppon Record, as my last Will and Testament.

First, I doe professe my faith and hope to bee in the free grace aloane of God in Jesus Christe, whose I wholly am, and to whome I haue for euer giuen vpp my selfe, both soule and body, being fully perswaded of his vnchangeable loue and goodwill, both in life and death to mee and mine, according to his covenant, viz : I am thy God, and the God of thy seed after thee.

Then for my owtward estate, wch because it is but little, and I haue well prooued the difficultyes of this Country, how hard a thinge it will bee for a woman to mannage the affaires of so great a familye as the Father of Mercyes hath blessed me withall ; and haue had allso experience of the prudence and faithfullnes of my deare wife, who shall, in parting with me, parte allso with a great parte of her liuelihood ; I do therfore bequeath and giue vnto her, the full power and dispose of all that estate wch God hath giuen mee, in howses, lands, cattells and goods whatsoeuer, within dores and without ; onely providing, that in case shee marry againe, or otherwise shee bee able comfortably to spare it from her owne necessary maintenance, that shee giue vnto my sonne Samuell that parte of my howselott that was intended for my sonne Perrigrine, lyinge next to the burying place, and the land I haue beyond the great Riuer eastward ; and allso, to him and my second sonne Noah, fiue acres apeece of meadow, with vplands proportionable therevnto, and to the rest of my children vnmarried twenty pounds apeece, at the age of one and twenty yeares, or at the time of her death, wch shall come the sooner. And for my two daughters that bee married, my desire is, that they may haue twenty shillings a peece, and euery one of theire children, fiue shillings a peece, either in bookes or such other thinges as my wife shall best please to parte withall. And I desire the Church, whose seruant I now am, to take the care and ouersight of my family, that they may bee brought vp in the true feare of God ; and to see that this my will bee faithfully p^rformed. In witnesse hereof, I haue subscribed my name, the 8th May, 1648.

Henry Smith.

[267] *The Inventory of Mr. Henry Smith of Weathersfeild, lately deceased.*

Imp^r: wearing clothes,	20. 00. 00
It: Bookes,	
It. 3 feather beds, with all thinges belonging to them, two sutes of linen,	40. 00. 00

It: 2 flock beds, with two sutes of Linnen, and all things
    belonging to them, ...   08. 00. 00
It: Table linnen, 4*l*. It: one carpett, 1*l*. It: chests and
    truncks, 1*l*. 10*s*., ...   06. 10. 00
It: 4 cushion stooles, 15*s*. It: 9 cushions, 1*l*. 10*s*., 02. 05. 00
It: Tables, chaires, stooles, and other things belonging
    to them, ...   01. 10. 00
It: Cob irons, trammells and other fire irons, .   02. 08. 00
It: Brass, iron potts, & pewter and such like, .   15. 00. 00
It: Beare vessells, tubbs, and other wooden vessells, 02. 00. 00
It: Armes and Ammunition, . . .   04. 00. 00
It: Axes, howes and other husbandry tooles, .   03. 10. 00
It: in Corne, 14*l*. 10*s*. It: in Maulte, 2*l*, 8*s*., .   16. 18. 00
It: Meate and Bacon, 6*l*. It: Bees, 8*l*., . .   14. 00. 00
It: Howses and lands, 180*l*. It: a Horse and Mare, 23*l*., 203. 00. 00
It: 3 Cowes, 15*l*. It: one last yeare heifer, 1*l*. 10*s*., 16. 10. 00
It: one sow and 2 piggs, . . .   01. 10. 00
It: due to the estate in debts, . . .   40. 00. 00
                                          ───────────
                                          397. 01. 00
              Owing from the estate,   026. 02. 06
                                          ───────────
              The sum remaining is   370. 18. 06
Jeames Boosy,
Sammuell Smith.

---

[268]   The last Will and Testament of GYLES GIBBS, of
              Wyndsor, deceased.

Know all men by these presents that I, Gyles Gibbs, of Wyndsor, on Connecticutt, yeoman, being weake in body but of perfect vnderstanding and memory, doe ordaine this my last will and Testament, as followth:

Imp^r: my will is, that my sonne Gregory bee put forth an Apprentice to some godly man, for the space of fiue yeares, at the discretion of my execut: and the ouerseers of this my last will; and if hee submitt therevnto and stay out his time to the likinge of my ouerseers, I doe then bequeath vnto him my lott ouer the great Riuer, to him and his heires foreuer, in case my said ouerseers haue any incouragement to judge him worthy; otherwise at theire discretion, I bequeath him 5*l*. to bee paid him at the age of 21 yeares. Allso, I giue to my two sonnes, Sammuell and Beniamin, 20*l*. a peece, and to my daughter Sarah, 20*l*., to bee paid them at the age of 21 yeares. And to

Jacob, my sonne, I giue my howse and lotts, meadow, home-
lotte and great lott and lottes whatsoeuer on this side the great
Riuer, after his mothers life. And to my wife, I giue all my
lottes, howses, all my househould goods, cattells and chattells,
my debts being discharged; provided that in case my said
ouerseers haue no good incouragement concerneing the disposition of my sonne Gregory, but doe judge him vnworthy a
fathers blessing, vnder theire hands, my will is that my execut:
shall haue the said lotte towards the education of my children,
vntill my sonne Jacob shall attaine the age of 21 yeares; and
then my will is that my sonne Jacob shall haue it to him and
his heires for euer. And Executrixe of this my last Will, I
appointe Katherine, my wife. And ouerseers of this my Will
and Testament, I appointe the Deacons of the Church of Wyndsor, at all times in being. Blessed bee God.

May 18th, 1641. Witness,   Gyles Gibbs.
      John Warham,
      Ephraim Huitt.

    Postscript: I giue to Elizaphatt Gregory, 10 bushells of
Corne, in case hee discharge the debt I gaue my worde for him
to Mr. Huitt. And to Richard Wellar, I giue 40s., by 20s. a
yeare, begininge from September next.
   Witness,
      John Warham,
      Ephraim Huitt.

---

[269]   Wyndsor, 8th Septembr, 1648.

An Inventory of the estate of SAMUELL ALLYN, late of Wyndsor,
                       deceased.

	£
Impr: the howsing and homelottes, 11l.; It: 4 acres of meadow, 7l.	18. 00. 00
It: 15 acres ouer the great Riuer,	15. 00. 00
It: 18 acres of vpland,	04. 10. 00
It: in goodes; one bed with his furniture,	05. 00. 00
It: two beds more, &c.	02. 14. 00
It: one pillowbeere, one table cloath and napkins,	00. 10. 08
It: his wearing apparrell,	05. 05. 00
It: 3 iron potts, 2l. 5s.; in brass, 1l. 10s.; in pewter, 1l.,	04. 15. 00

It: in hogsheads, payles, tubbs and earthen ware,	00. 19. 00	
It: 2 spinning wheeles,	00. 07. 00	
It: in crookes, Grid iron, fire pan and tongs,	00. 13. 00	
It: his working tooles, 2*l.* 2*s.* ; It: a muskitt and sworde, 13*s.*,	02. 15. 00	
It: a table, and forme, and other lumber,	00. 10. 00	
It: in cattle; one cowe, one heifer, 1 yearling,	12. 00. 00	
It: two swynes,	04. 00. 00	
Henry Clarke,	76. 18. 08	
Dauid Willton,		

[270] The last Will and Testament of THOMAS NOWELL.

I Thomas Nowell, of Wyndsor on Conecticutt, being righte in vnderstanding and of perfect memory, in regard of my age and weaknes desiringe to sett my howse in order, as my last Will and Testament and a token of my loue and respect, doe bequeath vnto Robert Willson my kinsman, one steere and one cowe; and vnto Isable Phelps my kinswoman, one cowe. And in case my wife shall after my decease marry againe, then it is my will and Testament that at the time of marriage forespecefied, the said Elizabeth, ouer and aboue my foresaid gifts, shall pay to the said Robert and Isable each of them, ten pownds a peece   Item, as a token of my loue, I bequeath vnto my wife Elizabeth all the rest of my estate in goods, debts or dues of what kinde soeuer, to her full and finall dispose as shee shall see best; as allso I bequeath vnto her my dwelling howse, with all my lands thereto p^{r}taininge in Wyndsor aforesaid, for and during the tearme of her life. And after her decease, as a token of my love, I bequeath my said howse and land vnto Christopher Nowell, son of Edward Nowell, of Wakefield, in Yorkshire in England, deceased, to him and his heires for euer. And to this my last Will and Testament, wittnes my hand, subscribed this present November 3^d, Anno Domini, 1648.

Wittnes, Isable Phelps,   Thomas Nowell.
   Bray Rosseter.

An Inventory of the Estate of Thomas Nowell, late of Wyndsor deceased, prized by vs whose names are heere vnderwritten, Febr. 22th, 1648.

	£	s.	d.
Imp^r: The dwelling howse, barne, outhowses, with the homelott, orchyard, with an addition of meadow adioining,	75.	00.	00
Item, 13 akers of meadow, 3*l*. 10*s*. p^r acre,	45.	10.	00
Item, 66 akers of vpland, with some additions,	03.	00.	00
In the Parlour ; Item, one standing bed, with its furniture,	17.	00.	00
Item, one trundle bed, with its furniture,	10.	00.	00
Item, one couerlitt, 4 p^r of sheets, 3 p^r pillow beers,	06.	12.	00
Item, 3 table cloaths, 15 table napkins,	02.	18.	00
Item, 14 yards ½ of new linnen, with some cotton cloath,	02.	03.	06
Item, more new cloath, 5 yards ½,	00.	13.	09
Item, a cubberd, a table, a chaire, a small box, 3 stooles,	02.	10.	00
Item, 2 truncks, one chest, 1*l*. 6*s*. ; Item, 15 cushions, 2*l*. 6*s*.,	03.	12.	00
Item, 2 Bibles, and some other bookes,	00.	14.	00
Item, a p^r of gold waights,	00.	03.	00
Item, his wearing apparrell, 11*l*. 11*s*. ; Item, 2 carpetts, 2*l*.,	13.	11.	00
Item, in mony and plate,	34.	00.	00
[271] Item, a pewter flagon, 2 platters, 3 saltes, 2 pintes,	01.	00.	00
Item, a pr. of andirons, tongs and other things,	00.	13.	00
Item, 33 yards of kersy, 11*l*. 4*s*. ; Item, 5 yards ½ of searge, 1*l*. 15*s*.	12.	19.	00
In the Kittchin ; Item, in Pewter,	04.	00.	00
Item, in Brass,	04.	03.	04
Item, one iron pott, one fryinge pann,	00.	12.	00
Item, 2 peeces, a p^r of bandleers,	01.	06.	00
Item, one broiling iron, one cleaver, 1 spittle iron, 2 spitts, one smoothing iron, one gridiron,	00.	18.	06
Item, 2 p^r of andirons, fire shouell and tongs,	00.	18.	00
Item, 2 chaffing dishes, potthookes and hanging,	00.	05.	06
Item, one chaire, one p^r of bellowes, 7*s*. ; Item, 2 linnen wheeles, 6*s*.,	00.	13.	00
In the sellar ; Item, 2 beare barrills, one butter churne, 2 Runletts,	00.	13.	00
Item, one case of bottles, one salting trough,	00.	08.	00
Item, in Porke, 2*l*. 10*s*. ; Item, in tubbs and other lumber, 1*l*.,	03.	10.	00
In the Parlour Loft ; Item, one bed with its furniture,	05.	00.	00
Item, 7 bush: rye, 3 bush: maulte, 20 bush: pease,	04.	13.	00
Item, 22 bush: wheat,	04.	08.	00
Item, 2 sacks, 2 baggs, 1 hogshd., some old tooles,	00.	18.	06
Item, yearne, linnen and cotton,	01.	14.	00
Item, 12 yards of okam cloath,	00.	18.	00

In the Kitchin Lofts and Garritts ; Item, 10 bush: Indian corne, ... 01. 05. 00
Item, in Bacon, ... 01. 00. 00
Item, 1 saddle, 1 cloakbag, 1 pillion, 1 sidesaddle and pillion cloath, ... 02. 06. 00
Item, 2 horse collars, and other geares, . 00. 12. 00
Item, 3 pillowes, one blankitt, . . 01. 00. 00
Item, 3 hogshds, 2 sythes, flax, and other lumber, 02. 00. 00
In the yardes and outhowses ; Item, 2 horses, one colte, 27. 00. 00
Item, 2 oxen, 2 steares, . . . 23. 00. 00
Item, 3 cowes, one heifer, one young bull, 18. 05. 00
Item, 3 swyne, ... 02. 00. 00
Item, waine, wheeles, expinns, cops and pin, . 01. 10. 00
Item, 2 yoakes with theire irons, 2 chaines, 2 p^r yoake crooks, ... 01. 00. 00
Item, one plow, one harrow, one grynding stone, 01. 05. 00
Item, 4 stocks of Bees, ... 03. 00. 00
Item, (more abroad) 2 cowes, one steare, . 15. 00. 00
Item, one iron crow, a saw, beetle and wedges, with some other things, ... 01. 10. 00

  Henry Clarke,   Totall sum is,   368. 11. 01
  Dauid Willton,
  John Moore.

CODE OF LAWS,

ESTABLISHED BY THE GENERAL COURT, MAY, 1650.*

[Recorded in Vol. II.]

[6*] FORASMUCH as the free fruition of such Libberties, Immunities, Privileges, as Humanity, Civillity and Christianity, call for, as due to euery man in his place and proportion, without Impeachm' and infringement, hath euer beene and euer will bee the Tranquillity and Stabillity of Churches and Common wealths, and the denyall or deprivall thereof, the disturbance if not ruine of both :—

It is therefore ordered by this Courte and Authority thereof, that no mans life shall bee taken away, no mans honor or good name shall bee stained, no mans person shall be arrested, restrained, banished, dismembered nor any way punnished; no man shall bee deprived of his wife or children, no mans goods or estate shall bee taken away from him, nor any wayes indamaged, vnder colour of Law or countenance of Authority, vnless it bee by the vertue or equity of some express Law of the Country warranting the same, established by a Generall Courte, and sufficiently published, or in case of the defect of a Law in any perticular case, by the word of God.

---

* In April, 1646, the General Court desired Mr. Ludlow "to take some paynes in drawing forth a body of lawes for the gouernment of this Commonwelth. & present them to the next Generall Courte." (p. 138, ante.) The request does not appear to have been immediately complied with,—at least, the work was not completed in time to be presented for the action of the Court, before May, 1647; it was then ordered, that when the body of laws should be perfected, as the Court had desired, Mr. Ludlow "should, besides the paying the hyer of a man, be further considered for his paynes." (p. 154.) No further mention of the progress of the work, or of its completion, occurs upon the records, until Feb. 1651, when an order of the Court, granting extra-compensation to the Secretary for "drawing out and transcribing the country orders, *concluded and established in May last*," enables us to fix the date of its adoption.

This Code, (usually cited as 'Mr. Ludlow's code,' or 'the code of 1650,') is recorded at the end of Vol. II. of the Colony Records, and separately paged. The orders subsequently passed, were, from time to time, added at the end, or occasionally inserted under the appropriate title, by the Secretary. Prefixed to the Laws is a copy of the Fundamental Orders, or Constitution of 1639, already printed, on pages 20—25 of this volume.

[7*]   ABILLITY.

It is ordered by this Courte, that all persons of [the age] of twenty one yeares and of right vnderstanding, whether excomunicated, condemned or other, [shall] haue full power and libberty to make theire W[ills and] Testaments, and other lawfull alienations of theire [lands] and estates, and may bee Plaintiffes in a civill case.

ACTIONS.

It is further ordered and decreed, that in all Actions brought to any Courte, the Plaintiff shall haue libberty to withdraw his Action, or to bee non suted, before the Jury haue giuen in theire verdict, in wch case hee shall allwayes pay full costs and charges to the Defend^t, and may afterward renew his suite at another Courte, the former non suite being first recorded.

AGE.

It is ordered by this Court and the Authority thereof, that the Age for passing away of Lands or such kinde of Hereditaments, or for giuing of voates, verdicts or sentences in any civill Courtes or causes, shall bee twenty and one yeares, but in case of chusing of Guardians, fourteene yeares.

ARRESTS.

It is ordered and decreed by this Courte and Authority thereof, that no person shall bee arrested or imprisoned for any debt or fyne, if Law can finde any competent meanes of satisfaction otherwise from his estate; and if not, his person may bee arrested and imprisoned, where hee shall bee kept at his owne charge, not the Plaintiffs, till satisfaction bee made, vnless the Courte that had cognisance of the cause or some Superior Courte shall otherwise determine; provided neuertheless, that no mans person shall bee kept in prison for debt but when there appeares some estate wch hee will not produce, to wch end any Courte or Commissioners authorized by the Generall Courte, may administer an oath to the party or any others suspected to bee priuye in concealing his estate; [   ] shall satisfie by service, if the Creditor require [it,] but shall not bee sould to any but of the English Nation.

[8*]   ATTACHEMENTS.

It is ordered, sentenced and decreed, that the ordinary summons or process for the present within this Jurissdiction and vntill other provision made to the contrary, bee a warrant fairely written, vnder some magistrate or magistrates hand or hands, mentioning the time and place of appearance, and if the said party or partyes doe not appeare according to the said warrant or summons vppon Affidauit first made of the serving of the said person or persons, the Courte shall graunt an Attachement against the person or persons delinquent to arrest or apprehend the said person or persons for his or theire willfull contempt; and in case no sufficient securitye or bayle bee tendred, to imprison the said party or partyes, returneable the next Courte that is capeable to take cogniscance of the said buisnes in question; and vppon returne of the said Attachement, the said Courte to doe therein as according to the Lawes and orders of this Jurissdiction; and in that case allso the party delinquent to beare his owne charge.

It is also ordered, that Attachements to seize vppon any mans Lands or estate bee onely graunted for, or against, such goods as are Forreigners and doe not dwell or inhabitt within this Jurissdiction; or in any case vppon credible Information it appeare that any Inhabitant that is indebted, or ingaged, goe about to conuey away his estate to defraud his Creditors, or to conuey away his person out of this Jurissdiction, so as the process of this Jurissdiction may not bee serued vppon his person; in that or any other just causes there may bee Attachement or Attachements graunted vppon the Limmitations expressed; provided that in all cases of Attachements, all or any of the Creditors haue libberty to declare vppon the said Attachement, if hee come in at the returne of the said Attachement; provided allso that if any Attachement laid vppon any mans estate, vppon a pretence of a great sum, and if it bee not prooued to bee due in some neare proportion to the sum challenged, and mentioned in the Attachement, then the security giuen shall bee lyable to such damages as are susteined therby.

It is further ordered and decreed by this Courte, that whosoeuer takes out an Attachement against any mans persons, goods, chattles, Lands or Hereditaments, sufficient security and caution shall bee [9*] giuen by him to prosecute his Action in C[ourte] and to answer the defendant such Costs as shall [be awarded] him by the Courte; and in all Attachments of g[oods or] lands, legall notice shall bee giuen vnto the P[arty] or left in writing at his howse or place of vsuall [abode] if hee liue within this Jurissdiction, otherwise [his] sute shall not proceed. And it is further ordered and declared, that euery man shall haue libberty to Repleuye his Cattle or goods impounded, distreined, seized or extended, (vnless it bee vppon execution after Judgment and in payment of Fynes,) prouided in like manner hee put in good security to prosecute his Replevy and to satisfie such damage, demaunds or dues as his Adversary shall recouer against him in Lawe.

BALLAST.

It is ordered by this Courte and Authority thereof, that no Ballast shall bee taken from any shoare in any Towne within this Jurissdiction, by any person whatsoeuer, without Allowance vnder the hands of those men that are to order the affaires in each Towne, vppon the Penalty of six pence for euery shovell full so taken, unless such stones as they had laid there before. It is allso ordered by the Authority aforesaid, that no shipp nor other vessell shall cast out any Ballast in the Channell or other place inconvenient, in any harbor within this Jurissdiction; vppon the Penalty of ten pounds.

BARRATRY.

It is ordered, decreed and by this Courte declared, that if any man bee prooued and adiudged a Common Barrater, vexing others with vniust, frequent and needless sutes, it shall bee in the power of Courtes both to reiect his Cause, and to punish him for his Barratry.

BILLS.

It is ordered by the Authority of this Courte, that any Debt or Debts due vppon Bill or other speciallty, Assigned to another, shall bee as good a debt and estate to the Assignee as it was to the Assigner, at the time of its Assignation, and that it shall bee lawfull for the said Assignee to sue for and recouer the said Debt due vppon Bill and so assigned, as fully as the originall Creditor might haue done; provided the said Assignement bee made vppon the backside of the Bill or Speciallty, not excluding any just or cleare interest any man may haue in any Bills or Specialtyes made ouer to them by Letters of Attornye or otherwise.

[10*] BOUNDS OF TOWNES AND PERTICULAR LANDS.

Forasmuch as the Bounds of Townes and of the Lands of perticuler persons are carefully to bee meinteined, and not without great danger to bee remoued by any; wch notwithstanding by deficiency and decay of markes may at vnawares bee done, whereby great jealousies of persons, trouble in Townes and incumbrances in Courtes doe often arise, wch by due care and meanes might bee prevented;

It is therfore ordered by this Courte and Authority thereof, that euery Towne shall sett out theire Bounds within twelue months after the publishing hereof, and after theire Bounds are graunted ; and that when theire Bounds are once sett out, once in the yeare three or more persons in the Towne, appointed by the Select men, shall appoint with the adiacent Townes to goe the bounds betwixt theire said Townes and renew theire markes, wch markes shall bee a great heape of stones or a trench of six foott long and two foott broad, the most Auncient Towne, (wch for the Riuer is determined by the Courte to bee Wethersfeild,)* to giue notice of the time and place of meeting for this perambulation, wch time shall bee in the first or second month, vppon paine of fiue pounds for euery Towne that shall neglect the same ; provided, that the three men appointed for perambulation shall goe in theire severall quarters, by order of the select men and at the charge of the severall Townes. And it is further ordered, that if any perticular proprietor of Lands lying in Common with others shall refuse to goe by himselfe or his Assigne, the bounds betwixt his land and other mens, once a yeare, in the first or second month, being requested thereunto vppon one weekes warning, hee shall forfeit for euery day so neglecting, ten shillings, halfe to the party mooving thereto, the other halfe to the Towne. And the owners of all impropriated grounds shall bound euery perticular parcell thereof with sufficient Meare stones, and shall preserue and keepe them so vppon the former penalty.

BURGLARY AND THEFT.

Forasmuch as many persons of late yeares haue beene and are apt to bee iniurious to the goods and liues of others, notwithstanding all care and meanes to prevent and punnish the same ;

It is therfore ordered by this Courte and Authority thereof, that if any person shall committ Burglary, by breaking vp any dwelling howse, or shall robb any person in the feild or high wayes, such a person so offending shall for the first offence bee branded on the forehead with the Letter (B) : If hee shall offend in the same kind the second time, hee shall bee branded as before, and allso bee

---

* This early decision, by the General Court, of the question of priority of settlement of the River towns, seems to have been hitherto overlooked by writers on our colonial history. The clause within the parenthesis is, in the original record, interlined. As however the hand writing is that of Capt. Cullick, who ceased to be Secretary in 1658, the interlineation must have been made within a few years after the adoption of the code of 1650. The clause is retained in the first printed revision, of 1672-3, and in that of 1702 ; but is omitted in subsequent revisions.

[11*] severely whipped; and if hee shall fall [into the same offence] the third time, hee shall bee put to death [as being incorridg]able. And if any person shall committ [such Burglary or] rob in the feilds or howse on the Lords day, beside the former punnishments, hee shall for the first offence haue one of his eares cutt of, and for the second offence in the same kinde, hee shall looss his other eare in the same manner; and if hee fall into the same offence the third time, hee shall bee put to death.

2. Secondly, for the preuention of Pillfring and Theft, It is ordered by this Courte and Authority thereof, that if any person, whether Children, Servants or others, shall bee taken or knowne to Robb any orchyards or garden, that shall hurte or steale away any grafts or fruite trees, fruites, linnen, woollen, or any other gooods left out in orchyards, gardens, backsides, or other place in Howse or Feilds, or shall steale any wood or other goods from the Waterside, from mens dores or yards, hee shall forfeitt treble damage to the owners thereof, and such seveere punishment as the Courte shall thinke meete.

And forasmuch as many times it so falls out that small thefts and other offences of a criminall nature are comitted, both by English and Indians, in Townes remoate from any prison or other fitt place to wch such malefactors may bee committed till the next Courte; It is therfore hereby ordered, that any Magistrate, vppon complaint made to him, may heare and vppon due proofe determine any such small offences of the aforesaid nature, according to the Lawes heere established, and giue warrant to the Constable of that Towne where the offender liues to leuye the same, provided the damage or fyne exceed not forty shillings; provided allso it shall bee lawfull for either party to appeale to the next Courte to bee houlden in that Jurissdiction, giuing sufficient caution to prosecute the same to effect at the said Courte. And euery Magistrate shall make returne yearely to the Courte of the Jurissdiction wherin hee liueth, of what Cases he hath so ended. And allso the Constable, of all such fynes as they haue receiued; And where the offender hath nothing to satisfie, such Magistrate may punnish by Stocks or whipping, as the Cause shall deserue. It is allso ordered that all servants or workemen imbeazling the goods of theire Masters, or such as sett them on worke, shall make restitution, and bee lyable to all Lawes and Penaltyes as other men.

CODE OF LAWS.   515

CAPITALL LAWES.

[Of the Capital Laws, fourteen in number, the first twelve agree, word for word, with those adopted in Dec. 1642, and recorded on page [92] of Vol. I, (p. 77, ante.) It has not been thought necessary to repeat them here. The others follow :—]

[13*] 13. If any Childe or Children aboue sixteene yeares old and of sufficient vnderstanding, shall Curse or smite theire naturall father or mother, hee or they shall bee put to death, vnless it can bee sufficiently testified that the Parents haue beene very vnchristianly negligent in the education of such Children, or so prouoake them by extreame and cruell correction that they haue beene forced therevnto to preserue themselues from death [or] maiming. Exo: xxi: 17; Levit: xx. [9]; Exo: xxi. 15.

14. If a man haue a stubborne and rebellious sonne of sufficient yeares and vnderstanding, viz: sixteene yeares of age, wch will not obey the voice of his father or the voice of his mother, and that when they haue chastened him, will not hearken vnto them, then may his Father and Mother, being his naturall parents, lay hold on him and bring him to the Magistrates assembled in Courte, and testifie vnto them that theire Sonne is stubborne and rebellious and will not obey theire voice and chastisement, but liues in sundry notorious crimes, such a Sonne shall bee put to death. Deut: xxi. 20, 21.

It is allso ordered by this Courte and Authority thereof, that whatsoeuer Childe or Servant, within these Libberties, shall bee convicted of any Stubborne or Rebellious Carriage against their Parents [14*] or Governours, ‖ wch is a forerunner of the aforementioned euills, the Gouernor or any two Magistrates haue libberty and power from this Courte to committ such person or persons to the howse of Correction, and there to remaine vnder hard labour and severe punnishm^t so long as the Courte or the maior parte of the Magistrates shall judge meete.

And whereas frequent experience giues in sad euidence, &c.

[This provision is precisely as enacted in Dec. 1642, and follows immediately after the twelve capital laws recorded on page 78.]

CASCK AND COOPER.

It is ordered by this Courte and Authority thereof, that all Casck vsed for Tarr or other Comodityes to bee put to sale, shall bee Assized as followth, viz: euery Casck commonly called Barrills or halfe hogsheads shall containe twenty eight gallons wine measure, and other vessells proportionable; and that fitt persons shall bee appointed from time to time, in all places needfull, to gage all such vessells or

Cascks and such as shall bee found of due Assize shall bee marked with the gagers marke and no other, who shall haue for his paines four pence for euery Tunn, and so proportionably.

And It is allso ordered, that euery Cooper shall haue a distinct Brandmarke on his owne Casck, vppon paine of forfeiture of twenty shillings in either case, and so proportionably for lesser vessells.

[15*]   CATTLE, CORNEFEILDS, FENCES.

Forasmuch as complaints haue beene made [of] very euill practice of some disordered persons in the Country, who vse to take other mens Horses, sometimes vppon the Commons, sometimes out of theire owne grounds, common feilds and Inclosures, and ride them at theire pleasure, without a leaue or priuity of theire owners:—

It is therfore ordered and enacted by the Authority of this Courte, that whosoeuer shall take any other mans Horse, Mare or drawing Beast, out of his Inclosure, vppon any Common, out of any common feild or elsewhere, except such bee taken damage faisant, and disposed of according to law, without leaue of the owners, and shall ride or vse the same, hee shall pay to the partyes wronged treble damages, or if the Complainant shall desire it, then to pay onely ten shillings, and such as haue not to make satisfaction shall bee punnished by whipping, imprisonment or otherwise, as by law shall bee adiudged, and any one Magistrate may heare and determine the same.

It is allso further ordered, that where Lands lye Common, vnfenced, if one shall improue his Lands by fencing in seuerall, and another shall not, hee whoe shall so improue shall secure his land against other mens Cattle, and shall not compell such as joine vppon him to make any fence with him, except hee shall allso improue in severall, as the other doth; and where one man shall improue before his neighbour, and so make the whole fence, if after his said neighbor shall improue allso, hee shall then satisfie for halfe the others fence against him, according to the present value, and shall meinteine the same. And if either of them shall after lay open his said feilds, (wch none shall doe without three months warning,) hee shall haue libberty to buy the devidend fence, payinge according to the present valuation to bee sett by two men, chosen by either party one. The like order shall bee [attended] where any man shall improue Land against any Towne Common, provided this order shall not extend to howse lotts not exceeding ten acres: But if in such, one shall improue, his neighbour shall [bee] compellable to make and meinteine one halfe of the fence betweene them, whether hee improue [or not.]

[16*] Provided allso, that no man shall bee lyable to satisfie for dammage done in any ground not sufficiently fenced, except it shall bee for dammage done by Swyne vnder a yeare old, or vnruly Cattle wch will not bee restreined by ordinary fences, or where any man shall put his Cattle, or otherwise voluntarily tresspass vppon his neighbors ground. And if the partye damnified finde the Cattle dammage faisant, hee may impound or otherwise dispose of them. 6*th* *Octo:* (52.) *The Courte declares & explaines this order doth not reach the Lands on y*e *east side of the Great Riuer.*

CATTLE TO BEE MARKED.

For the preventing of differences that may arise in the owning of Cattle that bee lost or stray away,

It is ordered by this Courte, that the owners of any Cattle within this Jurissdiction shall eare marke or brand all theire Cattle and Swyne that are above halfe a yeare old (except Horses,) and that they cause theire severall markes to bee registred in the Towne Booke, and whatsoeuer Cattle shall bee found vnmarked after the first of July next, shall forfeitt fiue shillings a head, whereof two shillings sixpence to him that discouers it, and the other to the Country.*

COMMON FIELDS.

Whereas the condition of these seuerall plantations in these beginnings wherein wee are, is such that necessity constraines to improue much of the ground belonging to the seuerall Townes in a Common way, and it is obserued that the publique and generall good, (wch ought to bee attended in all such improuements as are most propper to them, and may best advance the same,) receiues much prejudice through want of a prudent ordering and disposing of those seuerall Common Lands so as may best effect the same ;—

It is ordered by this Courte and Authority thereof, that each Towne shall chuse from among themselues fiue able and discreet men, who by this order haue power giuen them, and are required, to take the Common Lands belonging to each of the severall Townes respectiuely into serious and sadd consideration, and after a through disgesting of theire owne thoughts, sett downe vnder theire hands in what way the said Lands may, in theire judgements, bee best improved for the common good. And whatsoeuer is so decreed and determined by the said fiue men in each Towne, or any three of

---

* Enacted Feb. 5, 1644-5. p. 118.

them, concerning the way of improuem¹ of any such Lands, shall bee attended by all such persons that have any propriety or interest in any such Lands so judged [by the said Committee.]

[17*] And whereas allso, much dammage hath risen not onely from the vnrulines of some kinde of Cattle [but allso] from the weaknes and insufficiency of many fences, whence much variance and difference hath followed, wch if not prevented for the future may bee very preiuditiall to the publique peace ;—

It is likewise therfore ordered, that the said fiue men so chosen or at least three of them shall set downe what fences shall bee made in any Common grounds, and after they are made to cause the same to bee veiwed, and to sett such fynes as they judge meete vppon any as shall neglect or not duely attend theire order therein ; and where fences are made and judged suffitient by them, whatsoeuer dammage is done by hoggs or any other Cattle, shall bee paid by the owners of the said Cattle. And the severall Townes shall haue libberty once euery yeare to allter any three of the former fiue, and to make choyce of others in theire roome. It being provided that any perticular man or men, shall haue libberty to inclose any of theire perticular grounds, and improue them according to theire owne discretion by mutuall agreement, notwithstanding this order.* This service is committed to the Townsmen, as appeares by an order of Courte, 5th of Feb^r, 1650, on the other side of this booke.†

CAVEATS ENTRED.

Whereas it appeares that diuers to defeate and defraude theire Creditors may secreetly and vnderhand make Bargaines and Contracts of theire Lands, Lotts and Accomodations, by meanes whereof, when the Creditor thinkes hee hath a meanes in due order of Law to declare against the said Lands, Lotts and Accomodations, and so recouer satisfaction for his debt, hee is wholy deluded and frustrated, wch is contrary to a righteous rule that euery man should pay his debt with his estate, bee it in what it will bee, either reall or personall, this Courte taking it into consideracon doe order, sentence and decree, That if any Creditor for the future doe suspect any debtor, that hee may prooue non soluant in his personall estate, hee may repaire to the Register or Recorder of the plantation where the Lands, Lotts or Accomodacons lyes, and enter a Caveatt against

---

* Enacted Feb. 14th, 1643-4. (p. 101.) with an amendment authorizing the appointment of *five* men, in place of *seven*, Feb. 5th, 1644-5. (p. 118.)   † Page 214.

CODE OF LAWS. 519

the Lands, Lotts and Accomodacons of the said debtor, and shall giue to the said Register or Recorder foure pence for the entry thereof: And the said Creditor or Creditors shall take out summons against the said debtor, and in due forme of Law, the next perticular Courte, either for the whole Colony or for the perticular plantation where the said Lands, Lotts or Accomodations lyes, or the next Courte ensueing, declare against the said debtors Lands, Lotts and Accomo-
[18*] dations.|| And so if the Creditor recouer, hee may enter a judgement vppon the said Lotts, Lands and Accomodations, and take out an extent against the said Land, directed to a knowne officer, whoe may take two honest and sufficient men of the neighbours, to aprize the said Lands, Lotts and Accomodations, either to bee sould outright if the debt so require, or sett a reasonable rent vppon the same vntill the debt bee paid, and deliuer the possession thereof either to the Creditor or Creditors, his or theire Assigne or Assignes, or any other; and what sale or sales, lease or leases, the said officer makes, being orderly recorded, according to former order of recording of Lands, shall bee as legall and binding to all intents and purposes as though the debtor himselfe had done the same; provided that if the said debtor can then presently procure a Chapman or Tennant that can giue to the Creditor or Creditors satisfaction to his or theire content, hee shall haue the first refusing thereof. Allso it is declared, that hee wch first enters Caveatts as abouesaid, and his debt being due at his entring the said Caveatt, shall bee first paid; and so euery Creditor as hee enters his Caveatt and his debt becomes due, shall bee orderly satisfied, vnless it appeare at the next Courte, the debtors Lands, Lotts and Accomodacons proue insufficient to pay all his Creditors, then euery man to haue a sutable proportion to his debt out of the same, and yet notwithstanding euery man to receiue his parte according to the entry of his Caveatt. Yet this is not to seclude any Creditor to recouer other satisfaction, either vppon the person or estate of the debtor according to Lawe and Custome of the Colony. As allso it is further decreed, that what sale or bargaine so euer the debtor shall make concerning the said Lotts, Lands and Accomodations, after the entring of the said Caveatt, shall bee voide, as to defraude the said Creditors.

It is allso further explained and declared, that if the said debtor bee knowne to bee a non solvant man before the first Caveatt entred against the said Lotts, Lands and Accomodations, and the same appeare at the next particular Courte, then the Courte shall haue power to call in all the Creditors in a shorte time, and sett an equall and indifferent way, how the creditors shall bee paid out of the said Lotts, Lands and Accomodations; otherwise, if the said Debtor prooue insolvant after y'e' first Caveatt entred, then this order to bee dulye obserued, according to the premisses and true intent and meaning thereof.

It is allso further declared and explained, that the said Recorder or Register of the said Caveatt, shall, the next perticular Courte as aforesaid, returne the said Caveatts that are with him; at wch time and Courte the enterers of the said Caveatts shall bee called forth to prosecute the same the next perticular Courte following, and if the enterers of the said Caveatts faile to prosecute according to this order, the Register or Recorder of the said Caveatt or Caveatts shall putt a Vacatte vppon [the said Caveatt or Caveatts] wch shall bee invalid or voide to [charge] the saide Lotts, Lands and Accomodations aforesaid.*

[19*]   DISSORDER IN COURTE.

It is ordered by this Courte that whosoeuer doth disorderly speake priuately during the sitting of the Courte, with his neighbo'r', or two or three together, shall presently pay twelue pence, if the Courte so thinke meete.†

SECREETS IN COURTE.

It is ordered and decreed, that whatsoeuer member of the Generall Courte shall reueale any secreett wch the Courte inioynes to bee kept secreet, or shall make knowne to any person what any one member of the Courte speakes concerneing any person or businesses that may come into agitation in the Courte, shall forfeitt for euery such fault ten pounds, and bee otherwise dealt withall at the discretion of the Courte. And the Secretary is to read this order at the beginning of euery Generall Courte.‡

CHILDREN.

Forasmuch as the good Education of Children is of singular behoofe and benefitt to any Common wealth, and whereas many parents and masters are too indulgent and negligent of theire duty in that kinde;—

It is therfore ordered by this Courte and Authority thereof, that the Select men of euery Towne, in the seuerall precincts and quar-

---

*Enacted, May 25th, 1647. p. 151:   †Mar. 9th, 1637-8. p. 13.   ‡Oct. 1639. p. 39.

CODE OF LAWS. 521

ters where they dwell, shall haue a vigilant eye ouer theire brethren and neighbours, to see first, that none of them shall suffer so much Barbarisme in any of theire familyes as not to indeauor to teach by themselues or others theire Children and Apprentices so much Learning as may inable them perfectly to read the Inglish tounge, and knowledge of the Capitall Lawes, vppon penalty of twenty shillings for each neglect therein; Allso, that all Masters of familyes doe once a weeke at least, catechise theire children and servants in the grounds and principles of religion; and if any bee vnable to doe so much, that then at the least they procure such Children or Apprentices to learne some shorte orthodox Catechisme, without booke, that they may bee able to answer to the questions that shall bee propounded to them out of such Catechismes by theire parents or Masters or any of the Select men, when they shall call them to a tryall of what they haue learned in this kinde. And further, that all Parents and Masters doe breed and bring vp theire Children and Apprentices in some honest lawfull [calling,] [20*] labour or imployment, either in husbandry, or some other trade proffitable for themselues and the Common wealth, if they will not nor cannott traine them vp in Learning to fitt them for higher imployments. And if any of the Select men, after Admonition by them giuen to such Masters of familyes, shall finde them still negligent of theire duty in the perticulars aforementioned, wherby Children and Seruants become rude, stubborne and vnruly, the said Select men with the helpe of two Magistrates shall take such Children or Apprentices from them, and place them with some masters for yeares, boyes till they come to twenty one and girles to eighteene yeares of age compleat, wch will more strictly looke vnto, and force them to submitt vnto gouernem^{t}, according to the rules of this order, if by faire meanes and former instructions they will not bee drawne vnto it.

CONSTABLES.

It is further ordered by the Authority aforesaid, that any person tendred to any Constable of this Jurissdiction by any Constable or other officer belonging to any Forreigne Jurissdiction in this Country, or by warrant from any such Authority, such shall presently bee receiued and conueyed forthwith from Constable to Constable, till they shall bee brought vnto the place to wch they are sent, or before some magistrate of this Jurissdiction, whoe shall dispose of them as the Justice of the Cause shall require; and that all Hue and Cryes shall bee duely receiued and dilligently persued to full effect.

It is ordered by the Authority of this Courte, that euery Constable within our Jurissdiction shall henceforth haue full power to make, signe and put forth persuits or Hue and Cryes, after Murthers, Malefactors, Peacebreakers, Theeues, Robbers, Burglarers and other Capitall offendors, where no magistrate is neare hand. Allso, to apprehend without warrant such as are ouertaken with drinke, swearing, Saboath breaking, slighting of the ordinances, lying, vagrant persons, night wallkers, or any other that shall offend in any of these, provided they bee taken in the manner, either by sighte of the Constable or by present information from others : As allso to make search for all such persons either on the Saboath day or other, when theire shall bee occasion, in all howses lycenced to sell either Beare or Wyne, or in any other suspected or disordered places, and those to apprehend and keepe in safe custody till oppertunity serues [21*] to bring them before one of the next Magistrates || for further examination ; Provided, that when a[ny Consta]ble is imployed by any of the Magistrates for [appre]hending of any person, hee shall not doe it [without] warrant in writing ; And if any person shall refuse to assist any Constable in the execution of his office in any of the things aforementioned, being by him required thereto, they shall pay for neglect thereof ten shillings to the use of the Country, to bee leuyed by warrant from any Magistrate before whome any such offendor shall bee brought ; and if it appeare by good testimony that any shall willfully, obstinately or contemptuously refuse or neglecte to assiste any Constable, as is before expressed, hee shall pay to the vse of the Country forty shillings ; and if any Magistrate or Constable, or any other vppon vrgent occasions shall refuse to doe theire best indeauor in raising and prosecuting Hue and Cryes, by foott, and if need bee, by horse, after such as haue committed Capitall crimes, they shall forfeit to the vse aforesaid for euery such offence, forty shillings.

And it is allso ordered, that the Constables in each Towne shall bee chosen from yeare to yeare before the first of March, and sworne to that office the next Courte following, or by some Magistrate or Magistrates.

CONVEYANCES FRAUDULENT.

It is ordered by this Courte and Authority thereof, that all Covenons or fraudulent Alienations or Conveyances of Lands, tenements or any hereditaments, shall bee of no validity to defeat any man from due debts or legacyes, or from any just Title, clayme or possession of that wch is so fraudulently conveyed, and that no conveyance, deed or promise whatsoeuer shall bee of validity, if it bee gotten by illegall violence, imprisonment, threatening or any kinde of forcible compulsion caled Dures.

CRUELTY.

It is ordered by this Courte and Authority thereof, that no man shall exercise any tiranny or cruelty towards any brute creatures wch are vsually kept for the vse of man.

[22*] DAMMAGES PRETENDED.

It is ordered by this Courte, that no man in any Sute or Action against another shall falsely pretend great dammages or debts, to vexe his Adversary ; and if it shall appeare any doth so, the Courte shall haue power to sett a reasonable fyne on his head.

DEATH VNTIMELY.

It is ordered by this Courte and Authority thereof, that whensoeuer any person shall come to any very sudden, vntimely or vnnaturall death, some Magistrate or the Constable of that Towne shall forthwith summon a Jury of Jury of sixe or twelue discreet men to inquire of the cause and manner of theire death, whoe shall present a true verdict thereof vnto some neare Magistrate vppon theire oath.

DELINQUENTS.

It is ordered, that all persons hereafter comitted vppon Delinquency, shall beare the charges the Country shall bee at in the prosecution of them ; And shall pay to the Ma^r of the prison or Howse of Correction, two shillings six pence before hee bee freed therefrom. Vide *Execution vppon Delinquents.*

ECLESEASTICALL.

Forasmuch as the open contempt of Gods word, and messengers thereof, is the desolating sinne of Ciuill States and Churches, and that the preaching of the Word by those whome God doth send is the chiefe ordinary meanes ordained by God for the converting, edefying and sauing the soules of the elect, through the presence and power of the Holy Ghost therevnto promised ; and that the ministry of the Word is sett vp by God in his Churches for those holy ends, and according to the respect or contempt of the same and of those whome God hath set aparte for his owne worke and imployment, the weale or woe of all Christian States it much furthered and promoated ;—

[23*] It is therfore ordered and decreed, that if any Christian (so called,) within this Jurissdiction shall contemptuously [behave] him-himselfe towards the word preached or the messengers th[ereof,] called to dispence the same in any Congregation, when hee faithfully execute his seruice and office therein according to the will and word of God, either by interrupting him in his preaching, or by charging him falsely with an error wch hee hath not taught in the open face of the Church, or like a sonne of Korah, cast vppon his true doctrine or himselfe any reproach, to the dishonor of the Lord Jesus whoe hath sent him, and to the disparagement of that his holy ordinance, and making God's wayes contemptible or ridiculous, that euery such person or persons, (whatsoeuer censure the Church may passe,) shall for the first scandall, bee convented and reproved openly by the Magistrate, at some Lecture, and bound to theire good behauiour: And if a second time they breake forth into the like contemptuous carriages, they shall either pay fiue pounds to the publique Treasure, or stand two houres openly vppon a block or stoole foure foott high, vppon a Lecture day, with a paper fixed on his breast written with Capital Letters, AN OPEN AND OBSTINATE CONTEMNER OF GODS HOLY ORDINANCES, that others may feare and bee ashamed of breaking out into the like wickedness.

It is ordered and decreed by this Court and Authority thereof, that wheresoeuer the ministery of the word is established according to the order of the Gospell throughout this Jurissdiction, euery person shall duely resorte and attend therevnto respectiuely vppon the Lords day, and vppon such publique fast dayes and dayes of Thanksgiuing as are to bee generally kept by the appointment of Authority. And if any person within this Jurissdiction shall without just and necessary cause withdraw himselfe from hearing the publique ministry of the word, after due meanes of conviction vsed, he shall forfeit for his absence from euery such publique meeting, fiue shillings: All such offences to bee heard and determined by any one Magistrate or more, from time to time.

Forasmuch as the peace and prosperity of Churches and members thereof, as well as Ciuill rights and Libberties are carefully to bee maintained,—It is ordered by this Courte and decreed, that the Civill Authority heere established hath power and libberty to see the peace, ordinances and rules of Christe bee obserued in euery Church according to his word ; as allso to deale with any Church member in a [24*] way of Ciuill [justice] ‖ notwithstanding any Church relation, office or interest, so it bee done in a Ciuill and not in an Eclesiasticall way : nor shall any Church censure degrade or depose any man from any Ciuill dignitye, office or authority hee shall haue in the Commonwealth.

ESCHEATS.

It is ordered by this Courte and Authority thereof, that where no heire or owner of howses, lands, tennements, goods or chattells can bee found, they shall bee seized to the publique Treasury till such heires or owners shall make due clayme therevnto, vnto whome they shall bee restored vppon just and reasonable termes.

EXECUTIONS.

Whereas by reason of the great scarcity of mony, Execution being taken of seuerall persons goods that haue beene sould at very cheape rates, to the extreame dammage of the Debtor ;

It is therfore ordered, that whatsoeuer Execution shall bee graunted vppon any debts made after the publishing of this order, the Creditor shall make choyce of one partye, the Debtor of a second, and the Courte of a thirde, whoe shall prise the goods so taken vppon Execution aforesaid, and deliuer them to the Creditor,

EXECUTION UPPON DELINQUENTS.

It is ordered, that the Gouerno^r or any other Magistrate in this Jurissdiction shall haue libberty and power to call forth any person that hath beene publiquely corrected for any misbehauio^r, to doe execution vppon any person or persons by whipping or otherwise, and that at any time hereafter as occasion doth require ; and in case of defect or want of such, any other person as hee or they shall thinke meete.

FENCES.

For the preventing of differences that may arise in making or setting downe of Fences as well in meadowes as vpland,—

It is ordered, that in the setting of posts and rayles or hedges in the meadow and homelotts, there shall bee a libberty for either partye of twelue inches from the dividend lyne, for breaking of the ground to sett the posts on, [or] for the laying on the hedge ; but the stakes and postes are to bee sett in the devident lyne ; and in vpland there is allowed a libberty of foure foott for a ditch from the devidend

[25*] lyne for either of the bordering partyes where the proportion of Fences belongs vnto them.*

FYNES.

It is ordered by this Courte, that the Estreits [for] the levying of Fynes shall goe forth once euery yeare, both in the Townes on the Riuer and by [the] seaside, and that some officer in each place shall bee appointed to levye and receiue the same, [and] the Acco^{ts} to bee giuen in by the severall plantations of theire generall charge, at the Courte in September, for the perfecting of the Acco^{ts} betwixt them: Mr. Ludlow is desiered to graunt out Warrants for the Fynes by the seaside.†

FYRE.

It is ordered by this Courte and the Authority thereof, that whosoeuer shall kindle any fire, in woods [or] grounds lying in common or inclosed, so as the same shall runn into such Corne grounds or Inclosures, before the tenth of the first month, or after the last of the second month, or on the last day of the weeke, or on the Lords day, shall pay all damages, and halfe so much for a fyne; or if not able to pay, then to bee corporally punnished, by a warrant from one Magistrate or more, as the offence shall deserue, not exceeding twenty stripes for one offence; provided, that any man may kindle fyre vppon his owne ground at any time, so as no dammage come thereby, either to the Country or to any perticular person. And whosoeuer shall wittingly and willingly burne or destroy any frame, timber hewne, sawne, or riuen, heapes of wood, charcoale, corne, hay, strawe, hempe, flaxe, pitch or tarr, hee shall pay double dammages.

FORGERIE.

It is ordered by this Courte and Authority thereof, that if any person shall forge any Debt‡ or Conveyance, Testament, Bond, Bill, release, acquittance, Letter of Attorneye, or any writing to prevent equitye and justice, hee shall stand in the Pillorye three severall Lecture dayes, and render double damages to the partye wronged, and allso bee disabled to giue any evidence or verdict to any Courte or Magistrate.

---

* June 3d, 1644. (p. 105.) The accidental substitution of *on*, for *or*, was made in transcribing this order for the code of 1650, and is followed in the printed revision of 1673.

† May 25th, 1647. p. 151. ‡ Deed?

[26*]   FORNICATION.

It is ordered by this Courte and Authority thereof, that if any man shall committ fornication with any single woman, they shall bee punished either by inioyning to marriage, or fyne, or corporall punnishment, or all or any of these, as the Courte or Magistrates shall appoint, most agreeable to the word of God.

GAMING.

Vppon complaint of great disorder by the vse of the Game called Shuffle Board, in howses of Common Interteinement, whereby much precious time is spent vnfruitfully and much waste of Wyne and Beare occasioned,—

It is therefore ordered and enacted by the Authority of this Courte, that no person shall henceforth vse the said Game of Shuffle Board, in any such howse, nor in any other howse vsed as Common for such purpose, vppon payne for euery keeper of such howse to forfeitt for euery such offence twenty shillings; and for euery person playing at the said Game in any such howse to forfeitt for euery such offence fiue shillings. The like penalty shall bee for playing in any place at any vnlawfull game.

GUARDS AT MEETING.

It is ordered by this Courte, that there shall bee a Guard of twenty men, euery Saboath and Lecture day, compleat in theire Armes, in each severall Towne vppon the Riuer; and at Seabrooke and Farmington, eight a peece; each Towne vppon the seaside in this Jurissdiction, ten; and as the number of men increase in the Townes, theire Guards are to increase.*

And it is further ordered, that each man in the Guards aforesaid shall bee allowed halfe a pound of powder yearly, by their seuerall Townes.†

HIGHE WAYES.

Whereas the mainteineing of high wayes in a fitt posture for passage according to the severall occasions that occurre, is not onely necessary for the comfort and safety of man and beast, but tends to the proffitt and advantage of any people, in the issue,—

It is thought fitt and ordered, that each Towne within this Jurissdiction shall euery yeare chuse one or two of theire inhabitants as

---

* May 20th, 1647. p. 150.
† Oct. 9th, 1650. (p. 212.) This order was made subsequently to the adoption of the code, and inserted under its proper title by the Secretary.

Surveyors, to take care of, and ouersee the mending and repairing of the High wayes within theire severall Townes respectiuely, whoe haue hereby power allowed them to call out the severall cartes or [27*] persons fitt for labour in each Towne, || two dayes at least in each yeare, and so many [more] as in his or theire judgements shall bee found necessary for the attaining of the aforementioned end, to bee directed in theire worke by the said surveyor or surveyors, and it is left to his or theire libberties either to require the labour of the severall persons in any familye, or of a teame and one person, where such are, as hee finds most advantageous to the publique occasions, hee or they giuing at least three dayes notice or warning before hand of such imployment; and if any refuse or neglect to attend the service in any manner aforesaid, hee shall forfeit for euery dayes neglect of a mans worke, two shillings sixpence, and of a Teame, sixe shillings, which said fynes shall bee imployed by the Surveyors to hire others to worke in the said wayes; And the Surveyors shall within foure dayes after the severall dayes appointed for worke, deliuer in to some Magistrate a true presentment of all such as haue beene defectiue, with their severall neglects, who are immediately to graunt a distresse to the Marshall or Constable, for the levying of the incurred forfeiture, by them to bee deliuered to the Surveyors for the vse aforesaid. And if the Surveyor neglect to performe the service hereby comitted to him, either in not calling out all the inhabitants in theire severall proportions as before, or shall not returne the names of those that are deficient, hee shall incurr the same penaltye as those whome hee so passes by are lyable to by vertue of this order, wch shall bee imployed to the vse aforesaid, and to bee levyed allso by distress vppon information and proofe before any one Magistrate.*

IDLENES.

It is ordered by this Courte and Authority thereof, that no person, howseholder or other, shall spend his time idlely or vnproffitably, vnder paine of such punnishment as the Courte shall thinke meet to inflict: and for this end, It is ordered, that the Constable of euery place shall vse speciall care and dilligence to take knowledge of offendors in this kinde, especially of common Coasters, vnproffitable fowlers, and Tobacko takers, and present the same vnto any Magistrate, who shall haue power to heare and determine the case or transferr it to the [next] Courte.

---

* An order for the appointment of Surveyors of highways in the several towns, and impowering them to call out persons and teams, was passed July 5th, 1643. (p. 91.)

[28*]   INDIANS.

It is ordered and decreed, that where any company of Indians doe sitt downe neare any English plantations, that they shall declare whoe is theire Sachem or Chiefe, and that the said Cheife or Sachem shall pay to the saide English such tresspasses as shall be comitted by any Indian in the said plantation adioyning, either by spoyling or killing any Cattle or Swyne, either with trapps, doggs or arrowes : And they are not to pleade that it was done by strangers, vnless they can produce the partye and deliuer him or his goods into the custody of the English : And they shall pay the double dammage if it were done voluntarily.* The like ingagement this Courte allso makes to them in case of wrong or iniurye done to them by the English, wch shall bee paid by the partye by whome it was done, if hee can bee made to appeare, or otherwise by the Towne in whose limmitts such facts are committed.

Forasmuch as o^r lenity and gentlenes towards Indians hath made them growe bold and insolent, to enter into Englishmens howses, and vnadvisedly handle swords and peeces and other instruments, many times to the hazzard of limbs or liues of English or Indians, and allso oft steale diuerse goods out of such howses where they resorte ; for the preventing whereof, It is ordered, that whatsoeuer Indian shall hereafter meddle with or handle any English mans weapons, of any sorte, either in theire howses or in the feilds, they shall forfeitt for euery such defaulte halfe a fathom of wampum ; and if any hurte or injurye shall therevppon follow to any persons life or limbe, (though accidentall,) they shall pay life for life, limbe for limbe, wound for wound, and shall pay for the healing such wounds and other dammages. And for anythinge they steale, they shall pay double, and suffer such further punnishment as the Magistrates shall adiudge them. The Constable of any Towne may attache and arrest any Indian that shall transgress in any such kinde beforementioned ; and bring them before some Magistrate, whoe may execute the penalty of this order vppon offendors in any kinde except life or limbe ; and any person that doth see such defaults may [29*] prosecute, and || shall haue halfe the forfeiture.†

It is ordered by this Courte and Authority thereof, that no man within this Jurissdiction shall, directly or indirectly, amend, repaire, or cause to bee amended or repaired, any gunn, small or great, belonging to any Indian, nor shall indeauo^r the same ; nor

---

* Thus far, ordered, Apr. 5th, 1638. p. 19.   † June 11th, 1640. p. 52.

shall sell nor giue to any Indian, directly or indirectly, any such gunn, nor any gunpowder, or shott, or lead, or shott mould, or any millitary weapon or weapons, armor, or arrowe heads; nor sell nor barter nor giue any dogg or doggs, small or great; vppon paine of ten pounds fyne for euery offence, at least, in any one of the aforementioned perticulars; and the Courte shall haue power to increase the fyne, or to impose corporall punnishment where a fyne cannott bee had, at theire discretion.*

And it is allso ordered, that no person nor persons shall trade with them at or about theire wigwams, but in theire vessells or pinnaces, or at theire owne howses, vnder penalty of twenty shillings for each default.†

Whereas, It doth appeare that notwithstanding the former Lawes made against selling gunns and powder to Indians, they are yet supplyed by indirect meanes, It is therfore ordered and declared, that if any person after publishing of this order shall sell, barter or transporte any gunns, powder, bullitts or lead to any person inhabiting out of this Jurissdiction, without license of this Courte, or from some two Magistrates, hee shall forfeit for euery gunn ten pounds, for euery pound of gunpowder fiue pounds, for euery pound of bullitts or lead forty shillings, and so proportionably for any greater or lesser quantity‡; provided notwithstanding, that [it] is left to the judgment of the Courte, that where any offence is committed against the said order, either to agravate or lessen the penalty, according as the nature of the offence shall require.

Whereas diuerse persons departe from amongst vs, and take vp theire aboade with the Indians, in a prophane course of life; for the preventing whereof,

It is ordered that whatsoeuer person or persons that now inhabiteth, or shall inhabitt within this Jurissdiction, and shall departe from vs and settle or joine with the Indians, that they shall suffer three yeares imprisonment at least, in the Howse of Correction, and vndergoe such further censure, by fyne or corporall punishment, as the perticular Courte shall judge meete to inflict in such cases.§

[30*] Whereas the French, Dutch and other Forraigne Nations

---

* Dec. 18th, 1642,—except the clause "nor sell &c. any dogg or doggs, small or great," which was added subsequently. pp. 79, 80.
† Oct. 12th, 1643. p.95.
‡ Dec. 18th, 1642. p. 80. The proviso was added subsequently.
§ Dec. 1642. p. 78.

doe ordinarily trade gunns, powder, shott etc. with the Indians, to oᶠ great preiudice, and the strengthening and animating of the Indians against vs, as by dayly experience wee finde ; and whereas the aforesaid French, Dutch etc. doe prohibitt all trade with the Indians within theire respectiue Jurissdictions vnder penalty of confiscation ;

It is therfore hereby ordered by this Courte and Authority thereof, that after due publication hereof, it shall not bee lawfull for any Frenchmen, Dutchmen, or person of any other forraigne nation, or any English liuing amongst them or vnder the gouernmenᵗ of them, or any of them, to trade with any Indian or Indians within the limmitts of this Jurissdiction, either directly or indirectly, by themselues or others, vnder penalty of confisscation of all such goods and vessells as shall bee found so trading, or the due value therof, vppon just proofe made of any goods or any vessells so trading or traded : And it shall bee lawfull for any person or persons inhabiting within this Jurissdiction, to make seizure of any such goods or vessells trading with the Indians as by this law is prohibited, the one halfe whereof shall bee to the propper vse and benefitt of the partye seizing, and the other to the publique.*

This Courte, judging it necessary that some meanes should bee vsed to conuey the lighte and knowledge of God and of his Worde to the Indians and Natiues amongst vs, doe order that one of the teaching Elders of the Churches in this Jurissdiction, with the helpe of Thomas Stanton, shall bee desired, twise at least in every yeare, to goe amongst the neighbouring Indians and indeauoʳ to make knowne to them the Councells of the Lord, and thereby to draw and stirr them vp to direct and order all theire wayes and conversations according to the rule of his Worde : And Mr. Gouernoʳ and Mr. Deputy, and the other Magistrates are desired to take care to see the thinge attended, and with theire owne presence so farr as may bee convenient, incourage the same.

This Courte hauing duly weighed the joint determination and argument of the Commissioners of the United English Colonyes at New Hauen, in Anno 1646, in reference to the Indians, and judging it to bee both according to rules of prudence and righteousness, doe fully assent therevnto, and order, that it bee recorded amongst the [31*] Acts of this Courte, ‖ and attended in future practice as occassions may present and require : The said conclusion is as followeth ;—

---

* Passed, Sept. 18th, 1649, upon the recommendation of the Comm'rs of the U. Colonies. p. 197.

The Comissioners seriously considering the many willfull wrongs and hostile practices of the Indians against the English, together with theire interteineing, protecting and rescuing of offendors, as late our experience sheweth, (wch if suffered, the peace of the Colonyes cannot bee secured,) It is therfore concluded, that in such cases the Magistrates of any of the Jurissdictions may, at the charge of the Plaintiff, send some convenient strength of English, and according to the nature and value of the offence and damage, seize and bring away any of that plantation of Indians that shall interteine, protect or rescue the offendor, though it should bee in another Jurissdiction, when through distance of place, commission or direction cannott bee had, after notice and due warning giuen them, as actors, or at least accessary to the iniurye and damage done to the English : onely women and children to bee sparingly seized, vnless knowne to bee some way guilty. And because it will bee chargeable keeping Indians in prison, and if they should escape they are like to prove more insolent and dangerous after, It was thought fitt that vppon such seizure, the delinquent or satisfaction bee againe demaunded of the Sagamore or plantation of Indians guilty or accessary as before ; and if it bee denyed, that then the Magistrates of the Jurissdiction deliuer vp the Indian seized to the party or partyes endammaged, either to serue or to bee shipped out and exchanged for neagers, as the case will justly beare. And though the Comissioners foresee that such severe though just proceeding may provoake the Indians to an vniust seizing of some of ours, yet they could not at present finde no better meanes to preserue the peace of the Colonyes, all the aforementioned outrages and insolences tending to an open warr : Onely they thought fitt that before any such seizure bee made in any plantation of Indians, the ensuing Declaration bee published, and a Coppye giuen to the perticular Saggamores :

The Commissioners for the Vnited Colonyes, considering how peace with righteousnes may bee preserued betwixt all the English and the severall plantations of the Indians, thought fitt to declare and publish, as they will doe no iniurye to them, so if any Indian [32*] or Indians of what plantation so euer, doe any willfull dammage to any of the English Colonyes, vppon proofe, they will in a peaceable way require just satisfaction, according to the nature of the offence and dammage. But if any Saggamore or plantation of Indians, after notice and due warninge, interteine, hyde, protect, keepe, conuey away or further the escape of any such offendor or offendors, the English will require satisfaction of such Indian and

Saggamore or Indian plantation ; and if they deny it, they will right themselues as they may, vppon such as so meinteine them that doe the wrong, keeping peace and all tearmes of Amity and Agreement with all other Indians.

INKEEPERS.

Forasmuch as there is a necessary vse of howses of Common Interteinement in euery Common wealth, and of such as retaile wine, beare and victualls, yet because there are so many abuses of that lawfull libberty, both by persons interteining and persons interteined, there is allso need of strict lawes and rules to regulate such an imployment ;

It is therefore ordered by this Courte and Authority thereof, that no person or persons licensed for Common Interteinement shall suffer any to bee drunken or drinke excessiuely, viz: aboue halfe a pinte of wyne for one person at one time, or to continue tipling aboue the space of halfe an houre, or at vnseasonable times, or after nine of the clock at night, in or about any of theire howses, on penalty of fiue shillings for euery such offence. And euery person found drunken, viz: so that hee bee thereby bereaued or dissabled in the vse of his vnderstanding, appearing in his speech or gesture, in any of the saide howses or elsewhere, shall forfeitt ten shillings; and for excessiue drinking, three shillings, foure pence ; and for continnuing aboue halfe an houre tipling, two shillings six pence ; and for tipling at vnseasonable times, or after nine a clock at night, fiue shillings, for euery offence in these perticulars, being lawfully conuicted thereof ; and for want of payment, such shall bee imprisoned vntill they pay, or bee set in the stocks, one houre or more, in some open place, as the weather will permitt, not exceeding three houres at one time : Provided notwithstanding, such licensed persons may interteine seafaring men or land trauellers in the night season when they come first on shoare, or from theire journye, for theire necessary [33*] refreshment, or when they prepare for ‖ theire voyage or journeye the next day early, [if there] bee no disorder amongst them ; and allso strangers and other persons in an orderly way may continnue [in] such howses of Common Interteinement during m[eal] times or vppon lawfull buisines, what time their occassions shall require.*

And it is also ordered that if any person offend in drunkenes, ex-

---

* Some of the provisions of this section are included, in substance, in the order of May 25th, 1647.

cessiue or long drinking, the second time they shall pay double fynes: And if they fall into the same offence the third time, they shall pay treble fynes: And if the parties bee not able to pay theire fynes, then hee that is found drunke shall bee punnished by whipping to the number of ten stripes, and hee that offends by excessiue or long drinking, shall bee put into the stocks for three houres, when the weather may not hazzard his life or limbs; and if they offend the fourth time they shall bee imprisoned vntill they put in two sufficient sureties for theire good behauiour.

And It is further ordered, that the severall Townes vppon the Riuer within this Jurissdiction, shall provide amongst themselues in each Towne, one suffitient Inhabitant to keepe an Ordinary, for provision and lodging in some comfortable manner, that passengers or strangers may know where to resorte. And such inhabitants as by the seuerall Townes shall bee chosen for the said service shall bee presented to two Magistrates, that they may bee judged meete for that imployment. And this to bee effected by the severall Townes within one month, vnder the penalty of forty shillings a month for each month that either Towne shall neglect the same.*

And It is allso further ordered, that euery Inkeeper or Victuailer shall prouide for interteinement of strangers horses, viz: one or more inclosures for summer, and hay or provender for winter, with convenient stable roome and attendance, vnder penalty of two shillings sixpence for euery dayes default and double dammage to the partye thereby wronged, except it bee by inevitable accident.

Lastly, It is ordered by the Authority aforesaid, that all Constables may and shall, from time to time, duely make search throughout the limmitts of their Townes, || vppon Lord's dayes and Lecture dayes, in times of exercise, and allso at all other times so oft as they shall see cause, for all offences and offendors against this Law in any the perticulars thereof: And if vppon due information or complaint of any of theire Inhabitants or other credible persons, whether Tauerner, Victualler, Tabler, or other, they shall refuse to make search as aforesaid, or shall not to theire power performe all other things belonging to theire place or office of Constableship, then vppon complaint and due proofe before any one Magistrate, within three months after such refusall or neglect, they shall bee fyned for euery such offence ten shillings, to bee levied by the Marshall as in other cases, by Warrant from such Magistrate before whome they

---

* June 3d, 1644. p. 103.

are convicted, or Warrant from the Treasurer vppon notice from such Magistrate.

It is ordered by this Courte and Authority thereof, that no Inkeeper, Victualer, Wine drawer, or other, shall deliuer any Wyne, nor suffer any to bee deliuered out of his howse, to any wch come for it, vnles they bring a noate vnder the hand of some one master of some familye and allowed Inhabitant of that Towne; neither shall any of them sell or draw any hott water to any but in case of necessitye, and in such moderation for quantity as they may haue good grounds to conceaue it may not bee abused; and shall bee ready to giue an account of theire doings herein, when they are called thereto, vnder censure of the Courte in case of delinquency.

INDITEMENTS.

If any person shall bee indicted of any Capitall crime (whoe is not then in durance,) and shall refuse to render his person to some Magistrate within one month after three proclamations publiquely made in the Towne where hee vsually abides, there being a month betwixt proclamation and proclamation, his lands and goods shall bee seized to the vse of the Common Treasury, till hee make his lawfull appearance, and such withdrawing of himselfe shall stand in stead of one wittnes to prooue his crime, vnless hee can make it appeare to the Courte that hee was necessarily hindred.

[35*]   JURYES AND JURORS.

*It is ordered by the Authority of this Courte, that in all cases wch are entred vnder forty shillings, the sute shall bee left to bee tryed by the Courte of Magistrates as they shall judge most agreeable to equity and righteousnes. And in all cases that are tryed by Juries, It is left to the Magistrates to impannell a Jury of sixe or twelue, as they shall judge the nature of the case shall require; and if four of sixe, or eight of twelue, agree, the verdict shall bee deemed to all intents and purposes sufficient and full; vppon wch judgement may bee entred and execution graunted, as if they had all concurred; but if it fall out that there bee not such a concurrence as is before mentioned, the Jurors shall returne the case to the Courte with theire reasons, and a speciall verdict is to bee drawne therevpon, and the voate of the greater number of Magistrates shall carrye the same; and the judgement to bee entred and other proceedings as in case of a verdict by a Jury.

---

* [In margin,] "In old Book, Feb: 5, '44." See p. 118, *ante.*

And it is further ordered, that the Courte of Magistrates shall haue libbertye (if they doe not find in their judgements, the Jury to haue attended the euidence giuen in, and true issue of the case, in theire verdict,) to cause them to returne to a second consideration thereof; and if they still persist in theire former opinion, to the dissatisfaction of the Courte, it shall bee in the power of the Courte to impannell another Jurye, and committ the consideration of the case to them. And it is allso left in the power of the Courte to varye and allter the dammages giuen in by any Jurye, as they shall judge most equall and righteous, prouided, that what allteration shall at any time bee made in that kind, bee done in open Courte, before Plaintiff and Defendant, or Affidauitt made that they haue beene required to bee present, and that allteration wch is made bee done either the same Courte, or provision made to secure the verdict of the Jury vntil the case bee fully issued. And whereas many persons, after theire seuerall causes in Courte haue beene tryed and issued, haue slipt away or otherwise neglected, if not refused, to pay the charges of the Courte, according to order; for preventing thereof for the future, It is ordered, that whosoeuer shall haue any action or sute in Courte, after the publishing hereof, shall, as soone as his cause is issued pay [36*] the whole charges of the Courte, that concernes either Jury or Secretary, before hee departes the same. And the like allso shall bee done by all those whose Actions are not taken vp, and withdrawne before the sitting of the Courte wherein they were to bee tryed; or otherwise, for neglect or non performance of either, bee committed to prison, there to remaine till hee or they haue satisfied the same.

GRAND JURY.

It is ordered and decreed, that there shall bee a Grand Jury of twelue or fourteene able men warned to appeare euery Courte yearely in Septemb^r, or as many and oft as the Gouerno^r or Courte shall thinke meete, to make presentment of the breaches of any Lawes or orders or any other misdemeanors they shall know of in this Jurissdiction.*

LANDS; FREE LANDS.

It is ordered, and by this Courte declared, that oure Lands and Heritages shall bee free from all fynes and lycenses vppon Alienations, and from all Harriotts, Wardships, Liveries, Primer seizins,

---

* July 5th, 1643. p. 91.

yeare, day and waste, escheats and forfeitures vppon the death of parents or ancestors, bee they naturall, vnnaturall, casuall or juditiall, and that for euer.*

LEVYES.

Forasmuch as the Marshalls and other officers haue complained to this Courte that they are oftentimes in great doubt how to demeane themselues in the execution of theire offices;

It is ordered by the Authority of this Courte, that in case of fynes and assessments to be levyed, and vppon execution in Civill Actions, the officer shall demaund the same of the party or at his howse and place of vsuall aboade; and vppon refusall or non payment, hee shall haue power (calling the Constable, if hee see cause for his assistance,) to breake open the dore of any howse, chest or place where hee shall haue notice that any goods lyable to such Levye or Execution shall bee; and if hee bee to take the person, hee may doe the like, if vppon demaund hee shall refuse to render himselfe; and whatsoeuer charges the officer shall necessarily bee put vnto, vppon [37*] any such occassion, ‖ hee shall haue power to levye the same as hee doth the debt, fyne or execution; and [if] the officer shall leuye any such goods vppon execution as cannott bee conuayed to the place where the party dwells for whome such execution shall bee leuyed, without considerable charge, hee shall leuye the said charge allso with the execution. The like order shall bee obserued in leuying of fynes; provided, it shall not bee lawfull for such officer to leuye any mans necessarye bedding, apparrell, tooles or armes, neither implements of houshold, wch are for the necessary vpholding of his life; but in such cases hee shall leuye his Land or person, according to Law; and in no case shall the officer bee put to seeke out any mans estate further then his place of aboade: But if the party will not discouer his goods or Land, the officer may take his person. And it is allso ordered and declared, that if any officer shall doe iniurye to any, by colour of his office, in these or any other cases, hee shall bee lyable vppon complaint of the party wronged, by action or information, to make full restitution. *See* MARSHALL.

LYING.

Whereas truth in words as well as in actions is required of all men, especially of Christians whoe are the professed seruants of the

---

* From the Massachusetts " Body of Liberties," of 1641.

God of Truth ; and whereas all Lying is contrary to Truth, and some sortes of Lyes are not onely sinfull, as all Lyes are, but allso pernicious to the publique weale and iniurious to perticular persons ;

It is therfore ordered by this Courte and Authority thereof, that euery person of the age of discretion, wch is accounted fourteene yeares, who shall wittingly and willingly make or publish any Lye wch may bee pernicious to the publique weale, or tending to the damage or iniurye of any perticular person, to deceiue and abuse the people with false newes or reportes, and the same duely prooued in any Courte or before any one Magistrate, who hath hereby power graunted to heare and determine all offences against this Lawe, such persons shall bee fyned for the first offence ten shillings, or if the party bee vnable to pay the same, then to bee sett in the Stocks, so long as the said Courte or Magistrate shall appointe, in some open place, not exceeding three houres ; for the second offence in that kind, whereof any shall bee legally convicted, the sum of twenty [38*] shillings, ‖ or bee whipped vppon the naked body not exceeding twenty stripes : and for the third offence that way, forty shillings, or if the party bee vnable to pay, then to bee whipped with more stripes, not exceeding thirtye. And if yett any shall offend in like kinde and bee legally convicted thereof, such person, male or female shall bee fyned ten shillings at a time more then formerly, or if the party so offending bee vnable to pay, then to bee whipped with fiue or sixe stripes more then formerly, not exceeding forty at any time. And for all such as being vnder age of discretion, that shall offend in Lying, contrary to this Order, theire Parents or Masters shall giue them due correction, and that in the presence of some officer, if any Magistrate shall so appointe. Provided allso, that no person shall bee barred of his just action of slaunder or otherwise, by any proceeding vppon this Order.

MASTERS; SERVANTS; SOJOURNERS.

It is ordered by this Courte and Authority thereof, that no Master of a Familye shall giue interteinment or habitation to any younge man to soiourne in his familye, but by the allowance of the inhabitants of the Towne where hee dwells, vnder the penalty of twenty shillings p^r weeke. And it is allso ordered, that no young man that is neither married nor hath any servant, nor is a publique officer, shall keepe howse of himselfe without the consent of the

Towne for and vnder paine or penalty of twenty shillings a weeke.*

It is allso ordered by the Authority aforesaid, that no servant, either man or maid, shall either giue, sell or truck, any commodity whatsoeuer, without license from theire master, during the time of theire service, vnder paine of fyne or corporall punnishment at the discretion of the Courte, as the offence shall deserue. And that all workemen shall worke the whole day, allowing convenient time for food and rest.

It is allso ordered, that when any Servants shall runn from theire Masters, or any other inhabitants shall priuately goe away with suspition of ill intentions, It shall bee lawfull for the next Magistrate, or the Constable and two of the chiefest inhabitants, where no Magistrate is, to press men and boates or pinnaces, at the publique charge, to persue such persons by sea or land, and bring them [39*] back by force of armes.

And whereas many stubborne, refrectary and discontented Seruants and Apprentices, withdraw themselues from theire Masters services to improue theire time to theire owne advantage ; for the preventing whereof, It is ordered, that whatsoeuer Servant [or] Apprentice shall hereafter offend in that kinde, before theire Covenants or tearme of service are expired, shall serue theire said Masters, as they shall bee apprehended or retained, the treble terme or threefold time of theire absence in such kinde.†

MANSLAUGHTER.

It is ordered by this Courte and Authority thereof, that if any person in the just and necessary defence of his life, or the life of any other, shall kill any person attempting to rob or murther in the feild or highe way, or to breake into any dwelling howse, if hee conceiue hee cannott with safety of his own person otherwise take the Felon or Assailant, or bring him to tryall, hee shall bee houlden blameless.

MAGISTRATES.

This Courte being sensible of the great dissorder growing in this Common wealth, through the contempts cast vppon the Civill Authority, wch willing to prevent, doe order and decree :

That whosoeuer shall henceforth openly or willingly defame any

---

* Feb. 21st, 1637. p. 8. The words 'for and,' in the line before the last, were probably substituted for 'first had,' by an error of the compiler, or recorder, of the code of 1650.
† June, 1644. p. 105.

Courte of Justice, or the sentences and proceedings of the same, or any of the Magistrates or judges of any such Courte, in respect of any Act or sentence therein passed, and being thereof lawfully convicted in any Generall Courte or Courte [of] Magistrates, shall bee punnished for the same by fyne, imprisonment, dissfranchisement or bannishment, as the quality and measure of the offence shall deserue.

MARRIAGE.

Forasmuch as many persons intangle themselues [by] rashe and inconsiderate contracts for theire future joininge in Marriage Covenant, to the great trouble and greife of themselues and theire freinds ; for the preventing thereof,

[40*] It is ordered by || the Authority of this Courte, that whosoeuer intends to joine themselues in Marriage Covenant shall cause theire purpose of contract to bee published in some publique place, and at some publique meeting in the severall Townes where such persons dwell, at the least eight dayes before they enter into such contract whereby they ingage themselues each to other, and that they shall forbeare to joine in Marriage Covenant at least eight dayes after the said contract.*

And it is allso ordered and declared, that no person whatsoeuer, male or female, not being at his or her owne dispose, or that remaineth vnder the gouernement of parents, masters or guardians, or such like, shall either make, or giue interteinment to, any motion or sute in way of marriage without the knowledge and consent of those they stand in such relation to, vnder the seuere censure of the Courte in case of delinquency, not attending this order ; nor shall any third person or persons intermeddle in making any motion to any such, without the knowledge and consent of those vnder whose gouernment they are, vnder the same penalty.†

MARRIAGES AND BIRTHS ; *See* RECORDS..

MARSHALL.

It is ordered by this Courte, that the Marshall shall be allowed for euery Execution hee serues, wch is under the sum of fiue pounds, two shillings six pence, and foure pence for euery myle hee goes to serue the said Execution out of the Towne where hee liueth : And for euery Execution hee serues of or aboue fiue pounds and under the sum of ten pounds, hee shall be allowed three shillings foure

---

* Apr. 10th, 1640. p. 47, 48.   † July 5th, 1643. p. 92.

pence, and foure pence for euery myle, as before: And for euery Execution hee serues of or aboue the sum of ten pounds, hee shall bee allowed fiue shillings, and foure pence for euery myle as before. Allso hee is to bee allowed his other just and necessarye charges; onely it is provided that if hee bee excessiue therein, vppon due complaint and proofe made, it shall bee redressed. And it is allso further ordered that the Marshall shall bee allowed for euery Attachement hee serues halfe so much as is before allowed him for Executions, onely hee is to haue foure pence for euery myle hee goes to serue the Attachement as before.

It is further ordered by the Courte and Authority thereof, that euery Officer* that shall at any tyme bee fyned for the breach of any pœnall lawe or other just cause, such person or persons so of-[41*]fending ‖ shall forthwith pay his or theire fyne or penalty [or giue] in security speedily to doe it, or else shall bee imprisoned or kept to worke till it bee paid, that no loss may [come] to the Commonwealth; and what other fynes or debts allready due or shall bee due to the Country, the Marshall for the time being, vppon warrant from the Treasurer, and according to his oath, shall bee faithfull in doing the duty of his place in levyinge and returning the same, vppon paine of forfeiting two shillings of his owne estate for euery pound, or else such fine as any Courte of Justice shall impose on him for neglect.

MEASURES AND WEIGHTS.

Forasmuch as it is obserued that there are diuers of Weights, Yardes and Measures amongst vs, wherby dammages many times ensueth by commerce with seuerall persons; for the preventing whereof,

It is now ordered, that no man within these libberties, shall, after the publishing of this order, sell any comodityes but by sealed weight or measure, under the penalty of twelue pence each default. The Clarke is to haue a penny for sealing a weight or measure each time; And no weight or measure is to bee accounted authentick that is not sealed or approoued by the Clarke, once euery yeare. The said Clarke is to breake or demolish such Weights, Yards or Measures as are defectiue.†

---

* In the (printed) revision of 1672–3, the word 'person' is substituted for 'officer.'
† The substance of this order is contained in an order of Feb. 14th, 1643–4. p. 100.

MILLITARY AFFAIRES.

It is ordered and by this Courte declared, that all persons that are aboue the age of sixteene yeares, except Magistrates and Church offi_cers, shall beare Armes, vnless they haue, vppon just occassion, exemption graunted by the Courte ; and euery male person within this Jurissdiction aboue the said Age, shall haue in continuall readines, a good muskitt or other gunn, fitt for service, and allowed by the Clark of the Band, with a sword, rest and bandaleers, or other seruiceable provision in the roome thereof, where such cannott bee had ; as allso such other millitary provision of powder, match and bullitts as the lawe requires, and if any person whoe is to prouide Armes or Ammunition cannott purchase them by such meanes as hee hath, hee shall bring to the Clarke so much Corne or other merchantable goods as by aprizement of the said Clarke and two others of the Company (whereof one to be chosen by the partye) [as shall bee judged [42*] of a greater value by a fifth part] then such Armes or Ammunition is of, hee shall bee excused of the penalty for want of Armes (but not for want of appearance) vntill hee bee provided. And the Clarke shall indeauor to furnish him so soone as may bee by sale of such goods so deposited rendring the ouerplus to the partye. But if any person shall not bee able to provide himselfe Armes or Ammunition through meere poverty, if hee bee single hee shall bee put to service by some Magistrate, and the Constable shall appointe him Armes and Ammunition, and shall appointe him when and with whome to earne it out.

And it is ordered that all the Soulgers within this Jurissdiction shall bee trained at least six times yearely, in the months of March, Aprill, May, Septemb^r, Octob^r or November, by the appointment of the Captaine or Chiefe officer in the seuerall townes : And the times of theire meeting together shall be at eight of the clock in the morninge. And the Clarke of each Band shall, twise euery yeare at least, veiw the Armes and Ammunition of the Band, to see if they all bee according to Lawe ; And shall vppon euery Traininge day giue his attendance in the feild, euery day, (except hee hath speciall leaue from his Captaine or Cheife Officer) to call ouer the Roll of the Souldgers and take notice of any defect by theire absence or otherwise : And hee shall duely present to the Gouernor or some of the Magistrates, all defects in Armes or Ammunition, at least once in each yeare, and oftner if it bee required. And it is left to the judgement of the Magistrates to punnish all defects in that kind according to the nature of the offence, wherein due regard is to bee had of willfull neglects in any, that such may not pass without a severe censure, And whosoeuer shall bee absent any of the dayes appointed for traininge, after the houre appointed, or shall not continnue the whole time, shall forfeitt the sum of two shillings six pence for euery default, except such as are licensed vnder the hand of two Magistrates. The Clarkes of the severall Bands are to distreine the delinquents, within fourteene dayes after the forfeiture; whereof six pence shall bee to himselfe and the remainder for the maintenance of Drums, Cullers &c. And if any of the said Clarkes shall omitte to distreine any delinquents, aboue the said terme of fourteene dayes, hee shall forfeitt and pay to the vse of the Publique, double the fyne so neglected by him.

[43*] It is ordered, that the Souldgers shall onely make choyce of theire Millitary Officers, and present them to the Perticular Courte; but such onely shall bee deemed officers as the Courte shall confirme.

The state and condition of the place where [we] liue, by reason of the Indians and otherwise, requiring all due meanes to bee vsed for the preservation [of the] safety and peace of the same, this Courte judgeth necessary that there should bee a Magazine of Powder and Shott provided and mainteined in the Country, in each Towne within this Jurissdiction; And doe therefore order and decree, that there shall bee two barrills of Powder and six hundred weight of Lead provided by this Commonwealth, before the Generall Courte in Septemb^r next, wch shall bee meinteined and continued and accounted as the Country stock. And it is allso further ordered, that the severall Townes within this Jurissdiction shall provide and mainteine as followth, viz:—

Wyndsor, one barrill and halfe of Powder, four hundred and fifty pound of Lead, one hundred fathom of m[atch,] nine Cotton Coates or Corseletts and suffitient serviceable Pikes to either of them.

Hartford, two barrills of Powder, six hundred weight of Lead and six score fathom of Match, and twelue Cotton Coates or Corseletts with serviceable Pikes to either of them.

Wethersfeild, one barrill of Powder, three hundred weight of Lead, eighty fathom of Match, and eight Cotton Coates or Corseletts with serviceable Pikes to either of them.

Seabrooke, halfe a barrill of Powder, one hundred and fifty pound of Lead, forty fathom of Match, and three Cotton Coates or Corseletts with serviceable Pikes to either of them.

Farmington, the same in each perticular with Seabrooke.

Fairefeild and Strattford, in each Towne, one barrill of Powder three hundred weight of Lead, one hundred fathom of Match, and six Coates or Corseletts with serviceable Pikes to either of them.

South hampton and Pequett, in each Towne, halfe a barrill of Powder, one hundred and fifty pounds of Lead, forty fathom of Match, with three [Coates or Corseletts with serviceable Pikes to either of them.]

[44*] Each Towne allso shall provide so many good firelocke muskitts and good backswords or Cuttlasses, as the Corseletts are they are charged with by this order. All wch shall bee provided by the seuerall Townes by the Courte in September next, and meinteined constantly for the future, vppon the penalty of ten shillings p^r month for each Townes defect or neglect herein.

Allso it is further ordered, That euery male person within this Jurissdiction, that is aboue the age of sixteene yeares, whether Magistrates, Ministers or any other, (though exempted from training, watching and warding,) shall bee allwayes provided with, and haue in readiness by them, halfe a pound of Powder, two pound of serviceable Bullitts or shott, and two fathom of Match to euery Matchlock, vppon the penalty of fiue shillings a month for each persons default herein : provided notwithstanding, that if the proportions of powder laid vppon each Towne and person either doth not at present or shall not, (by reason of the increase of theire numbers,) for the future, amount in all to three pound of powder for euery Souldger, then each Towne shall, vppon the former penaltye, provide so much more as shall bee three pound of powder for a Souldger, and other provision of Lead &c. increase in each Towne according to the same proportion.

Whereas many inconveniences doe appeare, by reason that the severall Souldgers of the Trained Bands in each Towne within this Jurissdiction haue not beene allowed some powder vppon theire Training dayes, for theire practice and exercise in theire severall firings :—

It is ordered by the Authority of this Courte, that there shall bee allowed to euery Souldger in the seuerall Trained Bands in each Towne as aforesaid, halfe a pound of powder a peece for a yeare, and so from yeare to yeare for the future, to bee provided by and at the propper costs and charges of the Masters and Gouernors of each familye vnto wch the said Souldgers doe belong, to bee called forth,

CODE OF LAWS.   545

improued and disposed of, at the discretion of the Captaine or other principall leaders in each Trained Band.

It is allso ordered, that the Captaines, Leiftennants and Ensignes shall bee freed from watching and warding, and the Serieants from warding and halfe theire watch.

[45*]   MINISTERS MEINTENANCE.

Whereas the most considerable persons in [these Colonyes] came into these partes of America that they [might] inioye Christe in his ordinances, without dis[turbance ;] And whereas amongst many other pretious [mercies] the ordinances haue beene and are dispensed amongst vs with much purity and power ; this[Courte] tooke it into theire serious consideracon how due meintenance, according to God, might bee provided and setled, both for the present and [future,] for the incouragement of the Ministers who [labour] therein ; And doe order, that those who are [taught] in the word, in the severall plantations bee [called] together, that euery mann voluntarily sett downe what hee is willing to allowe to that end and [vse :] And if any man refuse to pay a meet proportion, that then hee bee rated by Authority in some [just] and equall way ; and if after this any man withhold or delay due payment, the Civill power to bee exercised, as in other just debts.*

OATHS.

[The oaths for the Governor, Magistrates, Constables, Freemen, and Jurymen, are the same as originally recorded, pages 25, 26, 62, 57. Those which follow, were inserted after the adoption of the code, and are in the hand writing of Secretary Clark.]

[47*]   *Commissioners Oath.*†

You doe sweare by the great and dredfull name of the euerlasting God, that for this yeare ensuing [and] vntill new bee chosen, you shall faithfully execute the place and office you are chosen unto, according to the extent of your Comission : So helpe you God, in the name of the Lord Jesus Christ.

Secretaries Oath.

A. B. You being chosen Secretary for this Jurisdiction, dureing this year, doe sweare by ye great name of God, that you shall keep

---

* Ordered, Oct. 25th, 1644, upon the recommendation of the Commissioners of the U. Colonies. p. 112.

† This and the two following Oaths, were subsequently recorded, (as appears by the hand writing) by Secretary Clark.

the secrets of the Court and shall carefully execute the place of a Secretary, and shal truly and faythfully record all Orders of the Court; and (fixe the Seale vnto ye orders sent forth to ye respectiue Townes &*) shall deliuer true copies and certificates when they shalbe necessarily required. So help you God, in our Lord Jesus Christ.

Grand Juryes Oath.

You doe sweare, by the great and dreadful name of God, that you will wth all due care and faithfulnes make presentment according to order, at ye Quarter Court in September next, such misdemeanours and transgressions of ye Lawes and Orders of this Commonwealth as shal come to your cognisance; as also to doe your indeauour to find out such things as are contrary to religion and peace: So help you God, in o^r Ld. Jesus Christ.

[48*] PEAGE.

It is ordered by this Courte and decreed, that no Peage, white or black, bee paide or receiued, but what is strunge and in some measure strung sutably, and not small and great, vncomely and disorderly mixt, as formerly it hath beene.†

POORE.

It is ordered by this Courte and Authority thereof, that the Courte of Magistrates shall haue power to determine all differences about lawfull setling and providing for poore persons, and shall haue power to dispose of all vnsetled persons, into such Townes as they shall judge to bee most fitt for the maintenance and imployment of such persons and families for the ease of the Countrye.

POUND; POUND BREACH.

For prevention and due recompense of dammage in Corne feilds and other inclosures done by Swyne and Cattle, It is ordered by this Courte and Authority thereof, that there shall bee one suffitient Pound or more made and meinteined in euery Towne and Village within this Jurissdiction, for the impounding of all such Swyne and Cattle as shall bee found in any Cornefeild or other Inclosure: And whosoeuer impounds any Swyne or Cattle shall giue present notice to the owners, if hee bee knowne, or otherwise they shall bee cryed

---

* The words in the parenthesis are interlined.

† Recommended by the Commissioners of the U. Colonies; and approved by the Gen. Court, Mar. 1649; p. 179.

at the two next Lectures or Markitts. And if Swyne or Cattle escape out of the pound, the owner, if knowne, shall pay all dammages, according to lawe.

And whereas impounding of Cattle in case of Trespasses hath beene allwayes found both needfull and proffitable, and all the breaches about the same very offensiue and iniurious:—It is therefore ordered by this Courte and Authority thereof, that if any person shall resiste or rescue any Cattle going to the Pound, or shall by any way or meanes conuey them out of Pound or custody of the law, whereby the party wronged may looss his dammage and the Lawe bee deluded, that in case of meere Rescues, the party offending shall forfeitt to the Treasure, forty shillings ; and in case of Pound breach, fiue pounds ; and shall allso pay all damages to the party wronged : And if in the Rescue any bodily harmes bee done to the person of any man or other, they shall haue remedye against the rescuers : And if either bee done by any not of abillitye to answer the dammage and forfeitt aforesaid, they shall bee [   ] whipt, by warrant from any Magistrate ‖ before whome the offender is convicted, in the Towne or Plantacon where the offence was committed, not exceeding twenty stripes, for the meere Rescue or Pound breach, and for all dammages to the party they shall satisfie by service, as in case of theft : And if it appeare there were any procurement of the owners of the Cattle therevnto, (and that they were Abettors) they shall all pay forfeitures and damages as if themselues had done it.

PROFANE SWEARING.

It is ordered and by this Courte decreed, that if any person within this Jurissdiction shall sweare rashly and vainely, either by the holy name of God, or any other oath ; and shall sinfully and wickedly curse any ; hee shall forfeitt to the Common Treasure, for euery such severall offence, ten shillings : And it shall bee in the power of any Magistrate, by warrant to the Constable, to call such persons before him, and vppon just proofe to pass a sentence, and leuye the said penalty, according to the vsuall order of Justice : And if such persons bee not able, or shall vtterly refuse to pay the aforesaid fyne, hee shall bee committed to the Stocks, there to continue not exceeding three houres and not less than one houre.

RATES.

It is ordered by this Courte and Authority thereof, that euery Inhabitant shall henceforth contribute to all charges both in Church and Common wealth whereof hee doth or may receiue benefitt, and euery such Inhabitant who doth not voluntarily contribute proportionably to his abillity with the rest of the same Towne to all common charges, both Ciuill and Ecleseasticall, shall bee compelled therevnto by assessments and distress, to be leuyed by the Constable or other officer of the Towne as in other cases; And that the Lands and Estates of all men, whereuer they dwell, shall bee rated for all Towne Charges, both Ciuill and Ecleseasticall as aforesaid, where the Lands and Estates shall lye, and theire persons, where they dwell.

For a more equall and ready way of raising means [for] defraying of publique charges in time to come, and for preuenting such inconueniences as haue fallen out vppon former assessments;—It is [50*] ordered and acted by the Authority of this Courte, ‖ That the Treasurer for the time being shall, from yeare to yeare, in the first month, without expecting any other order, send forth his Warrants to the Constables of euery Towne within this Jurissdiction, requiring the Constable to call together the Inhabitants of the Towne, whoe being so assembled shall chuse three or foure of theire able Inhabitants, whereof one to bee a Comissioner for the Towne, whoe shall some time or times in the sixth month then next ensuing, make a list of all the male persons in the same Towne from sixteene yeares old and vpwards, and a true estimation of all personall and reall estates being (or reputed to bee,) the estate of all and euery the persons in the same Towne, or otherwise vnder theire custody or managing, according to just valuation, and to what persons the same belong, whether in theire owne Towne or other where, so neare as they can by all lawfull wayes and meanes wch they may vse, viz: of howses, lands of all sortes, as well vnbroken vp as other (except such as doth or shall lye common, for free feed of Cattle, to the vse of the Inhabitants in generall, whether belonging to the Townes or perticular persons, but not to bee kept or hearded vppon it to the damage of the proprietors,) mills, shipps and all small vessells, merchantable goods, cranes, wharfes, and all sortes of Cattle, and all other knowne estate whatsoeuer, as allso all visible estate either at sea or on shore; all wch persons and estates are by the said Commissioners and select men to be assessed and rated as heere followth, viz: Euery person aforesaid, (except Magistrates and Elders of Churches) two shillings six pence by the head, and all estates both reall and personall, at one penny for euery twenty shillings, according to the rates of Cattle hereafter mentioned. And for a more certeine rule in rating of

Cattle, euery Cowe of foure yeare old and vpward shall be valued at fiue pounds; euery heifer and steare, betweene three and four yeare old, foure pounds, and betweene two and three yeare old, fifty shillings, and betweene one and two yeare old, thirty shillings; euery Oxe and Bull of foure yeare old and vpwards, six pounds; euery Horse and Mare of foure yeare old and vpwards, twelue pound; of three yeare old, eight pounds; betweene two and three yeares old, fiue pounds; of one yeare old, three pounds; euery Sheepe of one yeare old, thirty shillings; euery Goate aboue one yeare old, eight shillings; euery Swyne aboue one yeare old, twenty shillings; and all Cattle of all sortes vnder a yeare old, are hereby exempted, as allso all Hay and Corne in the husbandmans hand, because all meadow, earable ground and Cattle are rateable as aforesaid. And [51*] for all such persons as by the advantage of theire Artes and Trades are more able to helpe beare the publique charge then Common Labourers and workemen, as Butchers, Bakers, Bruers, Victuailers, Smiths, Carpenters, Taylors, Shoemakers, Joiners, Barbers, Millers and Masons, with all other manuall persons and Artists, such are to bee rated for their returnes and gaines proportionably vnto other men for the produce of theire estates. Provided that in the Rate by the Poll, such persons as are dissabled by sickness, lameness or other infirmities shall bee exempted; and for such servants and children as take not wages, theire parents and masters shall pay for them, but such as take wages shall pay for themselues.

And it is further ordered, that the Comissioners for the severall Townes vppon this Riuer shall yearely meet vppon the third Thursday in the sixth month at Hartford, and the Comissioners for the Townes of Fairefeild and Strattford shall meett the same day in one of those Townes, (and two dayes before the Generall Courte in Sept: they shall meete ye Comissioners vppon ye Riuer in Hartford,*) and bring with them, fairely written, the just number of males listed as aforesaid, [and] the Assessment of estates made in theire seuerall Townes according to the rules and directions in this present order expressed; And the said Comissioners being so assembled shall duely and carefully examine all the said Lists and Assessments of severall Townes, and shall correct and perfect the same, according to the true intent of this order, and the same so perfected they shall transmitt vnder theire hands to the Generall Courte, the second Thursday in September, and then, directions shall bee giuen to the Treasurer for gathering of the said Rate, and euery one shall pay

---

* The clause in parenthesis, is interlined.

theire Rate to the Constable of the Towne where it shall bee assessed ; nor shall any land or estate bee rated in any other Towne but where the same shall lye, is or was improued to the owner's, reputed owner's, or other proprietor's vse or behoofe, if it bee within this Jurissdiction. And for all peculiars, viz: such places as are not yet laid within the bounds of any Towne, the same Lands, with the persons and estates therevpon, shall bee assessed by the Rates of the Towne next vnto it ; the measure or estimacon shall bee by the distance of the meeting howses.

And if any of the said Comissioners or of the select men shall willingly faile or neglect to performe the trust committed to them by this order, in not making, correcting, perfecting or transmitting any [52*] of the said Lists or Assessments, || according to the intent of this order, euery such offendor shall bee fyned forty shillings for euery such offence, or so much as the Country shall bee damnified thereby, so as it exceeds not forty shillings for one offence ; provided that such offence or offences bee complained of and prosecuted, in due course of law, within six months.

And it is further ordered, that vppon all distresses to bee taken for any of the Rates and Assessments aforesaid, the officer shall distreine goods or Cattle, if they may bee had ; and if no goods, then lands or howses ; if neither goods nor lands can bee had within the Towne where such distresses are to bee taken, then vppon such returnes to the Treasurer hee shall giue warrants to attache the Body of such persons to bee carried to prison, there to bee kept till the next Courte, except they put in security for theire appearance there, or that payment bee made in the meane time.

And it is further ordered, that the prises of all sorts of Corne to bee receiued vppon any Rate by vertue of this order, shall bee such as the Courte shall sett from yeare to yeare, and in default thereof they shall bee accepted at the price current, to bee judged by the said Comissioners.

And it is further ordered, that all Estates of land in England shall not bee rated in a publique assessment.

It is allso provided and ordered, that all Towne Rates shall bee made after the same manner and by the same rule as the Country Rate.

Whereas much wrong hath beene done to the Country by the negligence of Constables, in not gathering such Leuyes as they haue receiued Warrants from the Treasurer, during theire office :—It is therfore ordered, that if any Constable shall not haue gathered the

Leuyes committed to his charge by the Treasurer then being, during the time of his office, that hee shall, notwithstanding [*the*] expiration of his office, haue power to leuye by distress all such Rates and Leuyes; and if hee bring them not in to the old Treasurer, according to his warrants, the Treasurer shall distreine such Constables goods for the same; and if the Treasurer shall not so distreine the Constable, hee shall bee answerable to the Country for the same. And if the Constable bee not able to make payment, it shall be lawfull for the Treasurer, old or new respectiuely, to distreine any man or men of that Towne where the Constables are vnable, for all Arrearages of Leuyes; and that man or men, vppon petition to the Generall Courte, shall haue order to collect the same againe, equal- [53*] ly, of ye Towne, || with his just dammages for the same.

It is further ordered by this Courte, that all Collectors and gatherers of Rates shall appoint a day and place and giue reasonable warning to the Inhabitants to bring in theire proportions, vppon wch every man so warned shall duely attend to bring in his Rate, or vppon neglect thereof shall forfeitt two pence in the shilling for what hee falls shorte; and the said Collector shall haue authority hereby to distreine the delinquents, or bee accountable themselues for the Rates and penaltyes so neglected by them.

RECORDS.

It is ordered by this Courte and Authority thereof, that the Towne Clarke or Register, in the several Townes of this Jurissdiction, shall record all Births and Deaths of persons in theire Towne: And that all parents, masters of servants, executors and administrators, respectiuely, shall bring in to the Register of theire severall Townes, the names of such persons belonging to them or any of them, as shall either be borne or dye; and allso that euery new married man shall likewise bring in a certificate of his Marriage, vnder the hand of the Magistrate wch married him, to the said Register; And for each neglect the person to whome it doth belong shall forfeitt as followth, viz: If any person shall neglect to bring in a noate or certificate as aforesaid, together with three pence a name, to the said Registers, for all Births and Deaths, and six pence for each Marriage, to bee recorded, more then one month after such Birth, Death or Marriage, shall forfeitt for euery default fiue shillings, and the penalty further increased vppon longer neglect, according to the judgement of the Courte. And the Register of each Towne shall yearely conuey to the Secretary of the Courte a true transcript of the Births, Deaths and Marriages, giuen vnder theire hands, with a third parte of the aforementioned fees, vnder the penalty of forty shillings for euery such neglect, all wch forfeitts shall bee returned in to the Treasury; Allso the Grand Jurors may present all neglects of this order.

It is ordered by the Authority aforesaid, that the seuerall Towns within this Jurissdiction shall each of them provide a Ledger Booke, with an Index or Alphabett, vnto the same: Allso shall chuse one [54*] whoe shall bee a Towne Clarke or Register, ‖ whoe shall, before the Generall Courte in September next, record euery mans howse and lands allready graunted and measured out to him, with the bounds and quantity of the same. And whosoeuer shall neglect three months after notice giuen, to bring in to the said Towne Clarke or Register a noate of his howse and land, with the bounds and quantity of the same by the nearest estimacon, shall forfeitt ten shillings; and so ten shillings a month, for euery month hee shall so neglect; the like to bee done for all lands hereafter graunted and measured to any. And if any such Graunter, being required by the Grauntee, his Heires or Assignes, to make an Acknowledgm^t of any Graunt, Sale, Bargaine or Morgage by him made, shall refuse so to doe, it shall bee in the power of any Magistrate to send for the partye so refusing and committ him to prison without Bayle or Maineprise, vntill hee shall acknowledge the same: And the Grauntee is to Enter his Caution with the Recorder, and this shall saue his interest in the meane time. And all Bargaines or Morgages of lands whatsoeuer shall bee accounted of no value vntill they bee recorded, for wch Entry the Register shall receiue six pence for euery percell, deliuering euery owner a Coppy of the same vnder his hand, wherof foure pence shall bee for himselfe and two pence for the Secretary of the Courte. And the said Register shall, euery Generall Courte in May and September, deliuer into the same a Transcript fairely written of all such Graunts, Bargaines. or Ingagements recorded by him in the Towne Booke; And the Secretary of the Courte shall record it in a Booke fairely written, prouided for that purpose, and shall preserue the Coppy brought in vnder the hand of the Towne Clarke. Allso the said Towne Clarke shall haue for euery search of a percell, one penny, and for euery Coppy of a percell, two pence; and a Coppy of the same vnder the hand of the said Register or Towne Clarke and two of the men chosen to gouerne the Towne, shall bee a suffitient euidence to all that haue the same.*

---

* Oct. 10th, 1639. p. 37.

CODE OF LAWS. 553

For the better keeping in minde those passages of Gods Providence wch haue beene remarkeable since o^r first vndertaking of these Plantacons, Mr. Deputy, Capt. Mason, Mr. Stone, with Mr. Goodwyn, are desired to take the paines seuerally in theire seuerall Townes, and then jointly together, to gather vp the same and deliuer them in to the Generall Courte in September next, and if it bee judged then fitt, they may bee recorded, and for future times, whatsoeuer remarkeable passages shall bee, and if they bee publique, the said parties are desired to deliuer in the same to the Generall [55*] Courte : || But if any perticular person doe bring in any thinge, hee shall bring it vnder the hands of two of the aforementioned parties, that it is true, then present it to the Generall Courte, that if it bee there judged requisitt it may bee recorded : provided that any Generall Courte for the future may allter any of the parties before mentioned or add to them, as they shall judge meett.*

It is allso ordered by this Courte and decreed, that after the death and decease of any person possessed of any estate, bee it more or less, and whoe maketh a will in writing or by word of mouth, those men wch are appointed to order the affaires of the Towne where any such person deceaseth, shall within one month after the same at furthest, cause a true Inventory to bee taken of the said estate in writing ; as allso take a Coppy of the said Will or Testament and enter it into a Booke or keepe the Coppy in safe custody ; as allso enter the names vppon record of the Children and Legatees of the Testator or deceased person. And the said orderers of the affaires of the Towne are to see euery such Will and Inventory to bee exhibited into the publique Courte, within one quarter of a yeare, where the same is to bee registred. And the said orderers of the affaires of the Towne shall doe theire indeauours in seeing that the estate of the Testator bee not wasted nor spoiled, but improued for the best advantage of the Children or Legatees of the Testator, according to the minde of the Testator, for theire and euery of theire vse, and by theire and every of theire allowance and approbation. But when any person dyeth Intestate, the said orderers of the affaires of the Towne shall cause an Inventory to bee taken, and then the publique Courte may graunt the Administracon of the goods and chattles to the next of kinn, jointly or seuerally, and devide the estate to wife (if any bee,) children or kindred, as in equity they shall see meett. And if no kindred bee found, the Courte to administer for the publique good of the Common: provided ther

---
* Oct. 10th, 1639. p. 39, 40.

bee an Inventory registred, that if any of the kindred in future time appeare, they may haue justice and equity done vnto them. And all charges that the publique Courte or the orderers of the affaires of the Towne are at, about the trust committed to them, either for writing or otherwise, is to bee paid out of the estate.*

Whereas allso, It was recomended by the Commissioners, that for [56*] the more free and speedy passage of Justice || in each Jurissdiction, to all the Confederates, If the last Will and Testament of any person bee duely prooued in, and duely certified from any one of the Colonyes, it bee without delay accepted and allowed in the rest of the Colonyes, vnless some just exception bee made against such will or the proouing of it, wch exception to bee forthwith duely certefied back to the Colony where the said Will was prooued, that some just course may bee taken to gather in and dispose the estate without delay or dammage. And allso that if any knowne planters or settled inhabitants dye Intestate, Administracon bee graunted by that Colony vnto wch the deceased belong, though dying in another Colony. And the Administracon being duely certefied, to bee of force for the gathering in of the estate in the rest of the Colonyes, as in the case of Wills prooued, where no just exception is returned. But if any person possessed of an estate, who is neither planter nor setled inhabitant in any of the Colonyes, dye Intestate, the Administracon (if just cause bee found to giue Administracon,) bee graunted by that Colony where the person shall dye and departe this life, and that care bee taken by that Gouernement to gather in and secure the estate, vntill it bee demaunded and may bee deliuered according to rules of justice:—Which vppon due consideracon was confirmed by this Courte, in the behalfe of this Colonye, and ordered to bee attended in all such occasions for the future: provided the Generall Courtes of the the other Colonyes yeild the like assent therevnto.†

SCHOOLES.

It being one chiefe project of that old deluder Sathan, to keepe men from the knowledge of the Scriptures, as in former times keeping them in an vnknowne tongue, so in these latter times by perswading them from the vse of Tongues, so that at least the true sence and meaning of the originall might bee clouded with false glosses of saint seeming deceiuers; and that Learning may not bee

---

* Oct. 10th, 1639. p. 39.

† Recommended by Comm'rs of the U. Colonies, Sept. 1648, and confirmed by the General Court, Mar. 14th, 1648-9. p. 179.

CODE OF LAWS. 555

buried in the Graue of o' Forefathers, in Church and Common wealth, the Lord assisting our indeauors,—It is therfore ordered by this Courte and Authority thereof, that euery Towneshipp within this Jurissdiction, after the Lord hath increased them to the number of fifty houshoulders, shall then forthwith appoint one within theire [57*] Towne to teach || all such children as shall resorte to him, to write and read, whose wages shall bee paid either by the parents or masters of such children, or by the Inhabitants in generall by way of supplye, as the maior parte of those who order the prudentialls of the Towne shall appointe; provided that those who send theire children bee not oppressed by more then they can haue them taught for in other Townes. And it is further ordered, that where any Towne shall increase to the number of one hundred families or housholders, they shall sett vp a Grammer Schoole, the masters thereof being able to instruct youths so farr as they may bee fitted for the Vniversity. And if any Towne neglect the performance hereof aboue one yeare, then euery such Towne shall pay fiue pounds p^r Annũ, to the next such Schoole, till they shall performe this order.

The propositions concerning the maintenance of Schollars at Cambridge, made by the Comissioners, is confirmed. And it is ordered, that two men shall bee appointed in euery Towne, within this Jurissdiction, whoe shall demaund what euery familye will giue, and the same to bee gathered and brought into some roome, in March, and this to continue yearly as it shall bee considered by the Comissioners.*

SECRETARY.

It is ordered and decreed, that within twenty dayes after the session of euery Generall Courte, the Secretary thereof shall send forth Coppies of such Lawes and orders as are or shall bee made at either of them, wch are of generall concernement for the gouernement of this Commonwealth, to the Constables of each Towne within this Jurissdiction, for them to publish within fourteene dayes more, at at some publique meeting in theire seuerall Townes, and cause to bee written into a Booke and kept for the vse of the Towne. And once euery yeare the Constables in each Towne shall read or cause to bee read in some publique meeting all the Capitall Lawes, and giue notice to all the Inhabitants where they may at any time see the rest of the Lawes and orders and acquaint themselues there-

---

* Confirmed by the General Court, Oct. 25th, 1644. p. 112 ; *Note.*

with: And the Secretary of the Courte shall haue twelue pence for the Coppy of the orders of each Session aforesaid, from each of the Townes.*

[58*] And it is further ordered that the Secretary of the Courte shall record such Wills and Inventoryes as are exhibited into the said Courte, and shall fyle the originall of them, and giue a Coppy thereof to such as desire it, for wch hee shall haue for euery Record of any Will or Inventory, or both, wch is aboue the sum of forty pounds, three shillings foure pence ; and for euery coppy of them or either of them, one shilling eight pence : And for euery search or supervising of them six pence : allso for recording of euery Will or Inventory, or both, wch is aboue the sum of thirty pounds and vnder the sum of forty pounds, two shillings six pence ; and for euery coppy of them, or either of them, fifteene pence ; and for euery search or supervising of them foure pence : Allso for euery Attachem^t, twelue pence, and for euery Bond or Recogniscance in or about the same, six pence : Allso for euery Execution above fiue pounds, the Secretary shall haue twelue pence, and for euery Execution vnder fiue pounds, six pence : Allso for the entry of euery or any Recogniscance in Courte, six pence, and for the withdrawing of it twelue pence, wch shall bee paide before the bounden bee freed from his said Recogniscance.

It is allso ordered, that whosoeuer shall take out any Warrant from the Secretary of the Courte, that concernes an Action, shall, before hee hath a Warrant, enter his Action with the Secretary, and then take out his Warrant for summons to answer the same ; for wch they shall pay for euery entry twelue pence, and for euery Warrant, foure pence, though they agree with theire defend^{ts} before the Courte. Allso if any other Magistrate shall graunt a Warrant wch concernes an Action, they shall enter the Action in a small Booke for that purpose, before they graunt the Warrant, and shall make a due returne at euery Courte to the Secretary thereof, what such Warrants and to whome they haue graunted ; and all such persons shall bee as lyable to pay twelue pence for euery such Action to the Secretary of the Courte as if they should haue had theire Warrants of him.

STRAYES.

It is ordered by this Courte and Authority thereof, that whosoeuer shall take vp any straye beast or find any goods lost, whereof the owner is not knowne hee shall giue notice thereof to the Constable

---

* Oct. 10th, 1639 ; (p. 39 ;) amended.

of the same Towne, within six dayes, whoe shall enter the same in a [59*] booke, and take order that it bee cryed || at theire next Lecture day or generall meeting, vppon three seuerall dayes, and if it bee aboue twenty shillings value, at the next Markitt, or two next Townes publique meetings, where no Markitt is within ten miles, vppon paine that the partye so finding and the said Constable hauing such notice and failing to doe as is here appointed, to forfeitt, either of them, for such default one thirde parte of the value of such straye or lost goods.

And if the finder shall not give notice as aforesaid, within one month, or if hee keepe it more then three months, and shall not aprize it by sufficient men, and allso record it with the Register of the Towne where it is found, hee shall then forfeitt the full value thereof. And if the owner appeare within one yeare after such publication hee shall haue restitution of the same or the value thereof, hee paying all necessary charges, and to the Constable for his care and paines, as one of the next Magistrates or one of the Townesmen shall adiudge; and if no owner appeare within the time prefixed, the said straye or lost goods shall bee thus devided, one fourth parte thereof with his reasonable charge shall bee to the finder, one fifth parte thereof or ten shillings to the Constable, at the choyce of the Courte, and the rest to the Common wealth; provided there bee three streakes clipt in the haire of the neare buttock six inches long, that they may bee knowne.

SWYNE.

It is ordered by this Courte, that all the swyne, either hoggs or shoates, in the severall plantations that are kept at home within the Towne, shall by September next bee ringed or yoaked, or kept vp in theire yards vnder the penalty of foure pence for euery such swyne, to bee paid by the owner to the party that shall take the swyne so defectiue and impound them; allso all such as are kept by heards in the woods, shall not bee suffered to abide aboue one nighte in the Towne, but that it shall bee lawfull to impouund them, in case they come at any time home from the middle of March to the middle of November. Fairefeild and Strattford desires to bee included in this order.

For the better preserving Corne and meadow on the east side of the great Riuer, It is ordered by this Courte, that there shall no hoggs nor swyne of any sorte bee put ouer thither or kept there at [60*] any time, after the || publishing of this order, except they bee kept out of the bounds of the severall Townes or in theire yardes vnder the penalty of two shillings a head for euery hogg or swyne, for euery time they shall bee found there contrary to this order.

TIMBER.

It is ordered by this Courte, that no Timber shall bee felled within three myles of the mouth of Mattabeseck Riuer, nor at vnseasonable times, viz: from the beginning of Aprill to the end of September, and that it bee improued into pipestaues or some other merchantable comodity, within one month after the felling thereof, or carted together : and that the Timber so improued shall not bee transported from the Riuer but for discharge of debts or fetching in some necessary provision.

TOBACKO.

Forasmuch as it is obserued that many abuses are crept in and comitted by frequent taking of Tobacko, It is ordered by the Authority of this Courte, that no person vnder the age of twenty yeares, nor any other that hath not allready accustomed himselfe to the vse thereof, shall take any Tobacko, vntill hee hath brought a certificate vnder the hands of some who are approued for knowledge and skill in phisick, that it is vsefull for him, and allso that hee hath receiued a lycense from the Court for the same. And for the regulating of those whoe either by theire former taking it haue to theire owne aprehensions made it necessary to them, or vppon due advice are perswaded to the vse thereof, It is ordered, that no man within this Colonye, after the publication hereof, shall take any Tobacko publiquely in the street, high wayes, or any barne yards, or vppon training dayes in any open places, vnder the penalty of six pence for each offence against this order in any the perticulars thereof, to bee paid without gainsaying vppon conviction, by the testimony of one wittness that is without just exception, before any one Magistrate. And the Constables in the severall Townes are required to make presentment to each perticular Courte of such as they doe vnderstand and euict to bee transgressors of this order.

[61*] TRESPASSES.

It is ordered by this Courte and Authority thereof, that if any horse, or other beast, trespass in Corne or other Inclosure, being fenced in such sorte as secures against Cowes, oxen, small calues, and such like orderly cattle, the party or parties trespassed shall procure two able men of good reporte and creditt to veiw and adiudge the harmes, wch the owner of the beast shall satisfie (when knowne,) vppon reasonable demaund, whether the beast were impounded or not ; but if the owner bee knowne and neare residing, as in the same Towne, or the like, notice shall bee left at the vsuall place of his aboad, of the Trespass, before an estimacon bee made thereof, to the end hee, or any others appointed by him, may bee present when the judgement is made ; the like notice allso shall bee left for for him of the damage charged vppon him, that if hee approue not thereof hee may repaire to the select Townsmen, or some of them, whoe shall in such case nominate and appointe two able and indifferent men, to reveiw and adiudge the said harmes, wch being discharged, together with the charge of the notice, former and latter veiw, and determination of dammages, the first judgement to bee void, or else to stand in lawe.

TREASURER.

It is ordered, that the Treasurer shall deliver no mony out of his hands to any person, without the hands of two Magistrates, if the sum bee aboue twenty shillings ; if it bee vnder, then the Treasurer is to accept of the hand of one ; but if it bee for the payment of some bills to bee allowed, wch are referred to some Comittees to consider of, whether allowed or not, that such bills as they allowe and sett theire hands unto, the Treasurer shall accept and giue satisfaction.*

VOATES.

It is ordered by this Courte and decreed, that if any person within these Libberties haue beene or shall bee fyned or whipped for any scandalous offence, hee shall not bee admitted after such time to haue any voate in Towne or Common wealth, nor to serue on the Jury vntill the Courte shall manifest theire satisfaction.

VERDICTS.

That loue and peace, with truth and righteousnes may continue and [62*] flourish in these confœderated Colonyes, || It was, vppon the recomendation of the Commissioners, ordered, that any Verdict or sentence of any Courte within the Colonyes, presented vnder authentique testimony, shall haue a due respect in the severall Courtes of this Jurissdiction, where there may bee occasion to make vse hereof, and

---

* Jan. 14th, 1638–9. p. 26.

shall bee accounted good euidence for the partye, vntill better euidence or other just cause appeare to allter or make the same voide : And that in such case, the issueing of the cause in question bee respited for some convenient time, that the Courte may bee advised with where the verdict or sentence first passed. Provided notwithstanding, that this order shall bee accounted valid and improued onely for the advantage of such as liue within some of the confœderated Colonyes; and where the verdicts in the Courts of this Colony may receiue reciprocall respect by a like order established by the Generall Courte of that Colonye.*

WYNE AND STRONG WATER.

Whereas many complaints are brought into the Courte, by reason of diuerse abuses that fall out by severall persons that sell wyne and strong water, as well in vessells on the Riuer as allso in severall howses ; for the preventing hereof, It is now ordered by the Authority of this Courte, that no person or persons, after the publishing of this Order, shall neither sell Wyne nor strong water by retaile, in any place within these Libberties, without lycense from the perticular Courte or any two Magistrates,† or where there is but one Magistrate, by a Magistrate and one of those appointed to order the affaires of the Towne.

WATCHES.

It is ordered by this Courte and decreed, that there shall bee a suffitient Watch meinteined in euery Towne, and that the Constable of each Towne shall duely warne the same and see that the inhabitants or residents doe severally in theire turnes obserue the same, according as the inhabitants doe agree.‡ And this Courte doth explaine themselues and order that whosoeuer within this Jurissdiction, that is lyable to watch, shall take a journeye out of the Towne wherein hee liueth after hee hath had timely notice and warninge to watch, hee shall provide a watchman for that turne, though himselfe bee absent ; and if any man that takes a journye, or goes out of the Towne wherein hee liueth, if hee returne home within a weeke after the Watch is past his howse, hee shall bee called back to watch that turne past a weeke before.§

[63*] And for the better keeping Watches and Wards by the Con-

---

* Approved by the General Court, Oct. 25th, 1644. p. 113.
† Feb. 14th, 1643-4. p. 100. The clause which follows was added subsequently.
‡ June, 1636. p. 2.   § Sept. 1649. p. 196.

stables in time of peace, It is ordered by this Courte and Authority thereof, that euery Constable shall present to one of the next Magistrates the name of euery person whoe shall vppon lawfull warninge refuse or neglect to watch or warde, either in person or some other fitt for that service: And if, being convented, hee cannott giue a just excuse, such Magistrate shall graunt warrant to levye fiue shilliugs on euery such offender, for euery such default: the same to be imployed for the vse of the Watch of the same Towne. And it is the intent of the lawe that euery person of able body (not exempted by lawe,) or of estate to hire another, shall bee lyable to watch and warde, or to supply it by some other, when they shall bee therevnto required. And if there bee in the same howse diuerse such persons, whether sonnes, seruants or soiourners, they shall all bee compellable to watch as aforesaid. Provided that all such as keepe families at theire farmes, being remoate from any Towne, shall not bee compellable to send theire seruants or sonns from theire farmes to watch and warde in the Townes.

WOLUES.

Whereas great loss and dammage doth befall the Common wealth by reason of Wolues, wch destroy great numbers of our Cattle, notwithstanding provision formerly made by this Courte for suppressing of them; therfore, for the better incouragement of any to sett about a worke of so great concernement, It is ordered by this Courte and Authority thereof, that any person, either English or Indian, that shall kill any Wolfe or Wolues, within ten myles of any plantacon within this Jurissdiction, shall haue for euery Wolfe by him or them so killed, ten shillings paid out of the Treasurye of the Country: provided, that due proofe bee made thereof vnto the plantacon next adioyning where such wolfe or wolues were killed, and allso bring a certificate under some Magistrates hand, or the Constable of that place, vnto the Treasurer.

WRECKS OF THE SEA.

It is ordered and decreed and by this Courte declared, that if any shipps, or other vessells, bee it freind or enemye, shall suffer shipwreck vppon o^r Coasts, there shall bee no violence or wrong offered to theire persons or goods, but theire persons shall bee harboured and releiued, and theire goods preserved in safety, till Authority may [64*] bee certefied and shall take further order therein.

VESSELLS.

It is ordered by this Courte and Authority thereof, that no Vessell nor Boate shall haue libberty to goe from any Porte in any Towne within this Jurissdiction, before they haue entred with the Register or Recorder in each Towne what quantity of powder and shott they carry forth with them in theire said vessells, and shall take a Certificate, vnder the said Registers or Recorders hand, of the same, paying to him for every Certificate, foure pence: And if any vessell shall attempt to goe from the said Towne or Porte, or Townes and Portes, before hee hath entred as aforesaid, or shall bee found with any more or greater quantity of powder and shott aboard the vessell or vessells then they had a Certificate to shew they had entred, shall forfeitt and pay for each default the true value of all such powder and shott as they should haue entred as aforesaid. And all such persons or Ma^{rs} of such Vessells shall giue a true account, vppon theire returne, to the said Recorder where they have entred the premises, how they haue disposed thereof, vppon the former penalty: And if the said Towne Register or Recorder shall haue just cause to conceiue that hee or they carry forth more of the premises then in an ordinary way is requisitt for theire necessary defence and safety in theire intended voyage, then the said persons or Ma^{rs} of Vessells shall giue in security vnto the said Recorder, (if by him required therevnto,) that hee shall giue a due account to this Commonwealth of the same, vppon his returne.

FORREIGNERS.

It is ordered by this Courte, that no Foreigners, after the twenty ninth day of September next shall retaile any goods by themselues in any place within this Jurissdiction, nor shall any Inhabitant retayle any goods wch belongs to any Forreigner, for the space of one whole yeare after the said twenty ninth of September next, vppon penalty of confisscation of the value of one halfe of the goods so retailed, to bee paid by the seller of them.

[65*]   HOME LOTTS.

Whereas there is creeping in, in severall Townes and plantations within this Jurissdiction, a great abuse of buying and purchasing Home Lotts and laying them together, by meanes whereof great depopulations are like to follow, It is ordered that all dwelling or mansion howses that are or shall bee allowed in any plantation or Towne within this Jurissdiction, shall bee vpheld, repaired and meinteined sufficiently in a comely way : As allso, whosoeuer shall possess and inioye any homelotts within any such plantation or Towne, that is not yet built vppon, shall, within twelue months after the making of this order, erect and build a howse there, fitt for an inhabitant to dwell in, vnless the Courte, vppon knowledge of the case, finde cause to abate, or giue longer time for building.

It is ordered, that the prises of Corne for the yeare ensuing, for all Country Rates, (except where ingagements to the contrary are expressed,) shall bee as followeth :

Wheat, foure shillings six pence p^r bush:
Pease, three shillings six pence p^r bush:
Rye, three shillings six pence p^r bush:
Indian, three shillings p^r bush:
And that there shall bee libberty for all men to pay one thirde parte of such Rates, in good Wampum.

State of Connecticut, ss.

Office of Secretary of State.

I hereby certify, that I have caused the printed matter contained in the foregoing pages of this volume, to be diligently compared with the original Records of the Colony of Connecticut, prior to its union with New Haven; and that I find the same to be (except where otherwise indicated and expressed,) a true, full, and literal copy of the said Records.

In testimony whereof, I have hereunto set my hand
L. S.   and affixed the Seal of the said State, at Hartford, this 29th day of January, A. D. 1850.

ROGER H. MILLS,
Secretary of State.

APPENDIX.

No. I. (p. 68.)

LETTER FROM SIR WILLIAM BOSWELL, RELATING TO THE ENCROACH-
MENTS OF THE DUTCH.

[In 'Colonial Boundaries,' Vol. II. Doc. No. 1.]

HAGHE, 22 Jan: $164\frac{1}{2}$, st. vet.

Worthy Doct^r Wright,

You cannot but imagine of how small effect any instructions [*to me*] or motions of myne heer are like to be, vntil our aff^{res} shalbe better settled at home; yet is it vnfit wee should forbeare to keep any right wee haue on foot, or to set forth in due manner to the States th' encrochem^t of their West-Ind^a Comp^{ny}, (vnder whose wing the traders vpon Conecticut & Planters in New Netherl^d, if any be, doe sheltre themselues,) vpon his Mat^{ties} sub'ts th'abouts. Wherfor my aduise (the best I can offre for present,) is,—

1. That the Parties interested, (by whom the Mem^{all} enclosed hath been drawne) procure some Declaracon or Act, from the Parlem^t, at least from the Howse of Commons, or their Comittee for these buisinesses; wherby it may appeare, that they take notice & care of our people & plantacons in those p^rts.

2. That they procure lettres likewise, from the Lords of the Con^{cll} vnto mee, wth this Mem^{all} or the like enclosed, requiring mee to represent the same, in wholle or p^rt, as I shall see requisit, to the States G'rall, & West-India Comp^{ny}, or others, whom I shall think propre. As also, to doe what else I shall iudge necessary, for atteyning the end, & quiett correspond^{ce} between the English & Dutch desired: And to make report.

3. They acquaint the States Amb^r in London with the summe of these l'res, Mem^{all}, & Act. And to make him sensible of the inconueniences & harmes wch may & certainly will befall the West India Comp^{ny}, &c., if any quarrells should arise & spread from those quarters. This to be done by p^rsons of qu[ality.]

4. That in the mean tyme, th' English there doe not forbeare to put forward their plantacons, and crowd on, crowding the Dutch out of those places where they haue [occupied,] but without hostility or any act of violence. I will not doubt but they are so wise as to stand vp, on their guard, with sufficient caution, and force to resist any suddaine attempt by frends or foes vpon them.

I shall heartily contribute the best of my powre vnto their & your content; praying you to pardon mee for not answering yo{r} l're sooner, hauing indeed hoped to haue learned something more to purpose, by the time I haue taken, I rest

Yo{r} assured ould frend & seru{t},
Willm Boswell.

Dr. Laur{ce} Wright &c.   At Chartrehowse.
For yourself.

[Sir William Boswell, was at this time English ambassador to the States General. How this letter found its way to the Colonial files, does not appear. It is probable, however, that the 'Memorial' to which it refers, was one drawn by Gov. Hopkins, (at that time in England,) and transmitted through the agency of his friend, Dr. Wright, to the English ambassador; and that the letter itself (indicating a course of policy which seems to have been closely adhered to by the Colony, in their subsequent dealings with the Dutch,) was brought to Connecticut, by Gov. Hopkins, on his return, some months afterward. The Dr. Wright to whom it is addressed, is probably the same to whom Mr. Hopkins, in his will, bequeathed a piece of plate of the value of £20, desiring " his honored friend Dr. Wright, to whom he owed much more than that, being much engaged, to accept it only as a testimony of his respect."]

No. II.   (p. 112.)

A COPPIE OF Y{e} COMBYNATION OF SOUTHAMPTON W{th} HARFORD.

[From 'Towns & Lands,' Vol. I. Doc. No. 7.]

Whereas formerly sume Ouerturs haue by letters paste betwixt sum deputed by the Jurissdiction of Conectecote and others of y{e} plantation of Southampton vpon Long Iland, concerning vnion into one boddy and gouernment, wherby y{e} said Towne might be interested in y{e} general combination of y{e} vnited Collonies, for prossecution and issuing wherof, Edward Hopkins & John Haines being authorised w{th} power from y{e} Generall Corte for y{e} Jurisdiction of Conecticute, & Edward Howell, John Gosmore and John More deputed by y{e} Towne of Southampton, It was by the said parties concluded & agreed, And y{e} said Towne of Southampton doe by their said deputies, for themselues and their successors, assotiate and joyne themselues to y{e} Jurisdiction of Conecticote, to be subiect to al the lawes there established, according to y{e} word of God and right reson, w{th} such exceptions & limmitations as are hereafter expressed.

The Towne of Southampton, by reson of ther passage by sea being vnder more difficulties and vncertainties of repayreing to y{e} seueral Corts held for y{e} Jurisdiction of Conectecote vpon y{e} mayne land, wherby they may be constrained to be absent both at y{e} times of election of Magistrats and other ocations, w{ch} may proue p{r}judicial to them; for p{r}venting wherof, it is agreed, y{t} for y{e} p{r}sent vntil more plantations be settled neere to y{e} Towne of Southampton w{ch} may be helpful each to other in publike occations, (and y{t} by mutual agreement betwixt y{e} said Towne and y{e} Generall Corte for y{e} Jurisdiction of Conectecote it be otherwise ordered,) there shalbe yearly chosen two Magistrats inhabbiting w^{th}in ye said Towne or liberties of Southampton, who shal haue ye same power wth ye P^rticuler Courts vpon ye Riuer of Conectecote, though no other Magistrats of ye Jurisdiction be p^rsent, for ye Administration of Justice and other ocations wch may concerne the welfare of ye said Towne, offences only wch concerne life excepted, or limbe, wch always shalbe tryed by a Courte of Magistrats to be held at ye Riuers mouth, wch said Magistrats for ye Towne aforesaid, shalbe chosen in manner following:

The Towne of Southampton, by ye freemen therof shall yerely p^rsent to sume Generall Courte for ye Jurisdiction of Conectecote or to ye Gouerner thereof, before ye Court of Election, wch is ye second Thursday in Aprill, the names of three of their members of their said Towne, and such as are freemen therof, whome they nominate for Magistrats the yeare ensuing, out of wch ye Generall Courte for ye Jurisdiction shall chouse two, who vpon oath taken before one or both of ye Magistrats for ye p^rcedent yeare at Southampton, for ye due execution of their place, shal haue as ful power to proceede therin as if they had beene sworne before ye Gouernor at Conectecote. It is also provided y^t ye freemen of ye said Towne of Southampton, shal haue libertie to voat in ye Courts of Election for ye Jurisdiction of Conectecote, in regard of ye distance of ye place, by proxie. But in case the Towne of Southampton shal, by any extreordinarie hand of Providence, be hindred from sending ye names of ye three p^rsons to be in Election for Magistrats, vnto ye Generall Court in Aprill, or hauing sent, ye same doe miscarrie, it is in such case then prouided & agreed, y^t ye two Magistrats for ye precedent yeare shal supply ye place vntill ye next Generall Court for election.

It [is] agreed and concluded, y^t if vpon vewe of such orders as are alreddy established by ye General Court for ye Jurisdiction of Connectecoate, there be found any difference therin from such as are also for ye present settled in ye Towne of Southampton, the said Towne shal haue libertie to regulate themselues acording as may be most sutable to their owne comforts and conueniences in their own judgment, provided those orders made by them concerne themselues only and intrence not vpon ye interestes of others or ye Generall Combination of ye vnited Collonies, and are not cross to ye rule of riteousness. The like powre is also reserued vnto themselues for the future, for making of such orders as may concerne their Towne ocations.

It is agreed & concluded, y^t if any party find himselfe agreved by any sentence or judgment passed by ye Magistrats, residing at Southampton, he may appeale to sum p^rticuler or General Court vpon [the] Riuer, p^rvided he put in securitie to ye satisfaction of one or both of ye Magistrates at Southampton spedily to prosecute his said appeale, and to answer such costs and dammages as shalbe thought meete by ye Court to which he appeals, in case there be found no just cause for his appeale.

It is agreed & concluded, y^t ye said Towne of Southampton shal only beare their owne charges in such Fortifications as are necessarie for their owne defence, maintaining their owne officers and al other things that concerne themselues, not being lyable to be taxed for fortifications or other expences y^t only apertaine to the plantations vpon the Riuer, or elswheare. But in such expences as are of mutuall & common concernment, both ye one and the other shal beare an equall share in such proportion as is agreed by the vnited Collonies, vizt. according to the number of males in each plantation, from 16 to 60 years of age.

The oath to be taken at Southampton.

I, A. B. being an Inhabitant of Southampton, by ye P^{r}vidence of God, combined wth ye Jurisdiction of Conectecote, doe acknowledg myself to be subiect to ye Gouernment therof & do sweare by the greate and dreadfull name of the euerliuing God to be true & faithfull to the same, and to submit both my person & estate therunto, acording to al the wholesum lawes and orders y^t are or hereafter shalbe made and established by lawful Authority, wth such limmitations & exceptions as are expressed in ye Combynation of this Towne wth ye aforesaid Jurisdiction, & that I wil nether plot nor practice any euil against ye same, nor consent to any that shal so doe, but wil timely discouer it to lawful authority there established; and y^t I wil as I am in duty bound maintaine the honner of the same and of ye lawfull Magistrats therof, promoteing ye publike good of it, whilst I shal continue an Inhabbitant there; & whensoeuer I shal giue my voate or suffrage touching any matter wch concerns this Common Wealth, bein cald therunto, I wil giue it as in my consience I shal judg may conduce to ye best good of ye same, wthout respect [*of*] p^{r}sons, or fauor of any man; soe help me God in ye Lord Jesus Christ.

The forementioned agreements wear concluded ye day & yeare aboue written, betwene ye parties aboue mentioned in behalf of ye Jurisdiction of Conectecott and ye Towne of Southampton, wth refference to ye aprobation of ye Commissioners for ye vnited Collonies, wch being obtayned the said agrements are to be atended and obserued, according to ye true intent and purpose thereof, or otherwise to be voyde and of noe effect; and in testimonie thereof haue interchangably [   ] put to their hands.

[*Endorsed, in the hand writing of Secretary Clark.*] A coppy of ye Combination with Southampton.

No. III. (p. 119, 266.)

THE AGREEMENT WITH MR. FENWICK.

Writers upon our colonial history, almost without exception, have referred to the contract with Mr. Fenwick, as a purchase by Connecticut of the *jurisdiction right* to the territory included in the Earl of Warwick's grant to Lord Say & Sele and his associates,—or in other words, as an assignment to the Colony, of the 'Old Patent' of 1632, held by Mr. Fenwick and his co-proprietors. Dr. Trumbull has given authority to this version, by stating that "the Colony, on the whole, paid Mr. Fenwick £1600, *merely for the jurisdiction right*, or *for the old Patent of Connecticut;*" (H. of Conn. 1. 150.) elsewhere, that the settlers of Connecticut and N. Haven were the *patentees* of Viscount Say and Seal, &c., to whom the patent was originally given;" (p. 28.) and again, (p. 118,) that "as the colonists, both in Connecticut and New Haven, were the *patentees* of Lord Say & Seal, Lord Brook and the other gentlemen interested in the old Connecticut patent, and as that patent covered a large tract of country, both colonies were desirous of securing the native title to the *lands*." Mr. Dwight, (who seems rarely, if ever, to have questioned the authority of Dr. Trumbull, in matters connected with the early history of the colony,) repeats the statement, that the colony paid Mr. F. £1600, "merely for the jurisdiction right, or for the *old patent*." (H. of Conn. p. 109.)

It will be seen, however, on referring to the agreement itself, that it is merely a contract of sale, of the fort at Saybrook and its appurtenances, and the land upon the River,—with a pledge on the part of Mr. F., to convey to the Colony '*if it come into his power,*' all the land between Saybrook and Narragansett River, included in the old patent. Such conveyance does not appear ever to have been made; on the contrary, repeated admissions of the General Court, show that it was *not* made, and that so far from receiving any legal assignment or transfer of the old patent, the Colony was (so late as 1661,) without even a *copy* of it, and not fully informed as to the rights and privileges which it was supposed to confer. In the Instructions to Gov. Winthrop,* the agent of the Colony for procuring the charter of 1662, the General Court desire him "to use all due means to procure a *copy of the Patent referring to these parts*, granted unto those Nobles and Gentlemen whom Mr. Fenwick did represent in his sale to this Colony;" and in case the copy could be obtained, Gov. F. was "to consider both what privileges, rights and immunities are therein granted, and to compare it with the Bay Patent," &c. In the letter to the Earl of Manchester,† the General Court represent the Colony as "having *neither Patent or copy of it*, nor aught else that may ensure us of future continuance of our present privileges." And if further evidence is necessary that the conditional engagement of Mr. Fenwick, to procure an assignment of the patent, was never performed, it is furnished in the conditions of the settlement between the Colony and Capt. Cullick, (Mr. F.'s brother-in-law and executor,) and in the admissions of Mrs. Cullick, in her petition to the General Court in 1683, (after a copy of the old patent had been found by Gov. Winthrop, among the papers of Mr. Hopkins.)‡

The settlers of the River towns had not,—*before* or *after* the agreement with Mr. Fenwick,—any right of jurisdiction except such as grew out of occupation, purchase from the native proprietors, or (in

---

* See Appendix, No. X, (1.) † App. No. X, (3.)
‡ Pages 327–329, *ante*; and App. Nos. VI. and XI.

the case of the Pequot territory,) of conquest. Their policy seems to have been to dispose as *quietly* and as *cheaply* as possible of the claims of such as challenged their title,—into the exact nature of which they were not disposed to provoke too close an investigation ; assenting to the conditions of settlement imposed by Mr. Fenwick, (as the agent of the Patentees,) until they were enabled by the purchase of Saybrook, to relieve themselves from present or possible exactions made in the name of his employers, and to conciliate the only rival claimant to jurisdiction whom they had then reason to fear ; waiting patiently for some favorable turn in the affairs of the mother country, which should enable them to obtain from the Sovereign, a recognition and confirmation of the right to self-government, which they had from the first asserted and maintained.

No. IV.   (pp. 311, 389.)

CLAIMS OF MASSACHUSETTS TO THE PEQUOT COUNTRY.

The right of jurisdiction to that portion of the Pequot territory lying between Pequot (Mystic) River, on the West, and Wecapaug, (a brook about four miles east of Pawcatuck River,) was, for many years, warmly contested by Massachusetts and Connecticut. In 1646, the question being referred to the decision of the Commissioners, as to which Colony the jurisdiction of Mr. Winthrop's new plantation at Pequot rightfully appertained, "The Commissioners for the Massathusets p'pounded an intrest by conquest ; the Commissioners for Conecticot by Patent, purchase and conquest. It was remembred that in a treaty betwixt them at Cambridge, 1638, not p'fected, a p'position was made that Pequot River in reference to the conquest should be the bounds betwixt them." As the new plantation was upon " the west syde of Pequott, & soe within the bounds at first p'pounded for Conecticott," the Commissioners decided that "unlesse the Massathusets hereafter shewe better title, the Jurisdiction should belong to Conecticott."

The next year, the question again came up for review, when the decision of the former year was confirmed and established in relation to the new plantation ; Mr. Winthrop " expressing himselfe as more indifferent," having probably effected some satisfactory arrangement with the General Court of Connecticut, (by whom he was shortly after commissioned as a Magistrate, at Pequot.)

Some ten years later, a considerable number of settlers who had located themselves farther to the eastward, (within the limits of the present town of Stonington,) under grants from Massachusetts, were invested by the General Court of that Colony, Oct. 1658, with town privileges, by the name of *Southertown*. To this settlement, or rather, to the whole of the territory which it in part occupied, the General

Court of Connecticut had given the name of 'Mystic and Pawcatuck,' and claimed over it exclusive jurisdiction right, as embraced within the limits of their purchase from Mr. Fenwick, as well as by right of conquest. Massachusetts did not, however, abandon her claims, until after the charter of 1662 had confirmed to Connecticut the eastern boundary claimed under their "old patent," the Earl of Warwick's grant,—' Narragansett River, commonly called Narragansett Bay.'

The following documents relating to this controversy are preserved among the files, in the State Department:—

1. A certified copy of an order of the Gen. Court of Massachusetts, May 6th, 1646, empowering Mr. Winthrop, to appoint some place "on the other side, that is on the east side of the great River of the Pequot Country," " for the convenient planting and subsistence" of such Indians as should be willing to remove thither, from within the limits of the new plantation; and to set out lots, and to govern the people of the plantation; associating with him, Mr. Thomas Peters, " for the better carrying on of the worke." [Towns & Lands, 1. 39.]

2. Letter from Massachusetts, (by Edward Rawson, Secretary,) to the General Court of Connecticut, dated October 21st, 1657; complaining of the exercise of jurisdiction by Connecticut, over the territory east of Pequot River, which had been established by the Commissioners in 1646 and 1647, as the boundary between the two Colonies; and desiring Connecticut to " friendly yield up those aforesaid lands on the east side of Pequot river," and to forbear further exercise of authority there, without the consent of the inhabitants, until the matter should be determined by the Commissioners. A petition which had been recently presented by the inhabitants of the disputed territory, is referred to, as giving occasion for the letter. [Ibid. No. 40.]

3. Copy of a letter from the General Court of Connecticut, in reply to the foregoing, (dated, May 10th, 1658,) denying that Massachusetts had ever " challenged an interest" in the Pequot country, "either by protest or letters, or so much as the least intimation by word, or any act whatsoever, since that case was fully & clearly determined by the Commissioners in the year 1647, at which time they declared that Jurisdiction goeth constantly with the Patent;" claiming to have hitherto enjoyed uninterrupted possession of the territory in question, and to have exercised authority there, with the consent of the inhabitants, most of whom had " by oath of fidelity submitted thereto;" expressing surprise that Massachusetts should pretend a claim to those parts, and impower persons to lay out lands there. An assent is given " in a friendly manner," to the proposition of Massachusetts to refer the question to the Commissioners, with the understanding that that colony should meanwhile forbear to exercise jurisdiction or authority, until their better right by conquest should be made to appear. [Ibid. No. 41.]

4. A letter from the Commissioners of the United Colonies, to Connecticut, (dated Sept. 18th, 1658,) in reply to one received from

the General Court, dated Aug. 2d, (a copy of which has not been preserved,) " intimating a difference between the Government of the Massachusetts and them, concerning the division of the Pequot country ;" accompanying which was sent a copy of the decision of the Commissioners, in the premises. By this decision Mystic River is made the boundary between the colonies " soe far as the Pond by Lanthorne hill, and thence from the middle of the said pond, to run away upon a north line." [The letter is filed in 'Indians,' Vol. 1. No. 3. The decision may be found in the Records of the U. Colonies. Both are printed (with some errors,) in Hazzard's S. Papers, 2. 395–397.]

5. Proceedings of the Commissioners, in September, 1659, upon the application of Connecticut for a 'review of the case respecting Mystic and Pawcatuck.' [Rec. of U. Colonies. A part of the original minutes of the Commissioners, (with their signatures,) are in 'Miscellanies,' Vol. 1. No. 88. See Hazzard, 2. 415.]

The General Court in May, had ordered letters to be sent to Massachusetts, 'to inform them that it is our desire and resolution to bring the case respecting Mystic and Pawcatuck, unto a review, or second consideration, at the meeting of the Commissioners,' and appointed Major John Mason, 'to act in behalf of the Colony, in the business.' (page 335, *ante*.) Accordingly, in September following, Major Mason presented to the Comissioners the plea of Connecticut, claiming right to exclusive jurisdiction 'by patent, conquest, possession and allowance.' The Commissioners having 'duly weighed and considered' the application, with the reply of the Commissioners of Massachusetts, and the ensuing replication and rejoinder, decided that they ' saw no cause to vary from the determination given, in the last year.'

No. V. (p. 316.)

LETTER TO EASTHAMPTON.

[In 'Towns & Lands,' Vol. I. Doc. No. 8.]

Gen: & Lovinge Friends,

We havinge received your Letter and findinge recorded a Court order of 1649, wherein ye Court declared their acceptance of your Towne vnder this Government; a coppy whereof we have herewith sent you ; and havinge received a full resignation of your Towne vnder this goverment, by your Agents, Life^t Gardner etc: we shall present ye same to our next Gen: Court for a further and full confirmation thereof: And in ye meane tyme did take y^t case wh^{ch} was presented from you into serious consideration ; and there hath passed a legall tryall therevpon ; wherevpon, tho there did not appeare sufficient evidence to proue her guilty yet we cannot but well approue and commend the Christian care & prudence of those in Authority with you, in searchinge into y^t case, accordinge to such just suspicion as appeared.

Also we thinke good to certify y^t it is desired & expected by this Court, y^t you should cary neighbourly & peaceably, without just offence, to Jos: Garlick & his wife, & y^t y^y should doe ye like to you. And ye charge wee conceive & advise may be justly borne as followeth : 1. Y^t Jos: Garlick should beare ye charge of his wives dyete & ward at home, with ye charge of her tranceportation hither & returne home ; 2ly, y^t your Towne should beare all theire owne charges at home & the charge of theire messengers & witnesses in bringinge the case to tryall here & theire returne home ; the Court beinge content to put ye charge of the tryall here, vpon ye Country's account.

[The copy of this letter preserved on file, is believed to be in the hand writing of Gov. Winthrop. It is not dated, but must have been written sometime in the spring of 1658. The reference to the case of Jos. Garlick and his wife is important, as furnishing evidence of the action of the General Court upon the first case of *witchcraft* (an *imported* case, by the way,) brought before them for trial. At a town meeting in Easthampton. Mar. 19th, 1657–8. it was " ordered, and by a major vote of the inhabitanrs of this Towne agreed upon, that Thomas Baker and John Hand [should] go into Keniticut for to bring us under their government according to the terms as Southampton is; and also to carry Goodwife Garlick, that she may be delivered up unto the authorities there for the triall of the cause of Witchcraft which she is suspected."*
" This poor woman," says Mr. Gardiner, " had had a trial in Easthampton, for witchcraft, but nothing was done. It was referred to the General Court at Hartford." The grounds of the accusation and further particulars of the case, may be seen in Woods, Thompson's, and Prime's Histories of Long Island.]

No. VI. (p. 238.)

THE SETTLEMENT WITH MR. CULLICK.

Dr. Trumbull, referring to the final adjustments of accounts with Capt. Cullick, remarks, that " it appeared that Mr. Cullick and the heirs of Mr. Fenwick were indebted five hundred pounds sterling to the colony, which had been paid them, more than what was due according to the original agreements with Mr. Fenwick." (Hist. of Conn. 1. 238.) This statement is not strictly correct,—as reference to the terms of settlement, and to the previous action of the General Court, will show. Mr. Cullick, (as the agent of his brother in law, Mr. Fenwick, after the return of the latter to England,) had received from the several towns their annual payment to the ' Fort rate,' stipulated for in the agreement between Mr. F. and the colony, in 1644. By one of the articles of this agreement, Mr. Fenwick had engaged to secure to the Colony, ' if it came into his power,' the right of jurisdiction to the territory embraced in the Earl of Warwick's grant to Lord Say & Sele and his associates. This engagement remaining

---

* See Gardiner's Notes on Easthampton &c. in Doc. Hist. of N. York, Vol. 1, page 683.

unfulfilled at the death of Mr. Fenwick, the General Court sought to recover from his agent, a portion of the monies which had been paid, as was alleged, without valid consideration. They therefore refused to surrender Mr. Fenwick's estate, which by his will had been devised to his sister, (Mrs. Cullick,) or to grant administration thereon, until an equitable settlement of accounts should be effected. By the conditions of this settlement, Capt. Cullick compromised with the colony, by the repayment of £500, and an acquittance of all claims against the colony growing out of the agreement for the purchase of the River: and the Court released the estate of Mr. Fenwick from the restraint formerly imposed, and discharged Mr. and Mrs. Cullick from all existing liabilities, ' so far and no further, as the estate bequeathed to them had any reference to the agreement.' [See pages 318, 329, 338, 341, 345, 357; Petition of Mrs. Cullick, App. No. XI; Agreement with Mr. Fenwick, App. No. III. The " repaying of £500" of " the monies expended in our agreement with Mr. Fenwick," is alluded to in the Instructions to Gov. Winthrop, App. No. X.]

No. VII. (p. 341.)

GEORGE FENWICK'S WILL.

A certified copy of Mr. Fenwick's Will, (probably the same that was exhibited to the General Court, October, 1659,) is preserved in Vol. 1. of ' Private Controversies,' Doc. No. 9. The introduction is as follows :

"The councell which the Prophett gave to King Hezekiah, upon ye Lord's message to him that hee should dye and not live, is seasonable for all, it being as true of all others as of him that they must dye and not live, the truth of which is not more certain then ye time uncertain ; whereof by mercy being sensible, though att present in good health, I make this my last Will and Testament, as followeth :"

First he gives to his " dearely beloved wife Katherine,"* the remainder of his term of years in Worminghurst, in lieu of that part of her jointure in Morton, (Co. of Durham,) which was yet in lease for five or six years ; several articles of furniture and household stuff, two suits of hangings ' one of Cæsar, the other of Diana,' ' a green embroidered bed,' & all the plate and pewter marked with their arms ; all the pictures, and such books as she might choose to take ; with the coach and horses, &c.

To his " most naturall and deare mother, Mrs. Dorothy Claveing," an annuity of £10. during her life.

---

* Mr. Fenwick's first wife died before his return to England, and was buried at Saybrook. The second was probably the daughter of Sir Arthur Haslerigge, (who is subsequently referred to as the ' father in law' of the testator.)

To his brother Claudius, and his heirs male, lands in Brenckborne and Nether Frawlington, in Northumberland.

To his nephew Thomas Ledgard, and his heirs male, lands in Thirston and Tillington, Northumberland.

To his sister Ledgard and his sister Cullick, each £50, and to their husbands, £10 each : and to his sister Cullick's children, £100 a piece.

To his "niece Clifton," and to his "niece Bootflower's boy," each £50.

To his daughter Elizabeth, "the suit of Landscape hangings," and to his daughter Dorothy, "that of Susanna;" the remainder of the household stuff to be divided between them. Elizabeth, he made sole executrix of his will, and gave to her the remainder of his personal estate and chattels. A hundred pounds per annum to be paid Dorothy, "out of [his] lease of the lands in Sussex."

To Ralph Fenwick; "now scholar of Christ Church in Oxford," £10 per annum, for six years.

To every servant 20 shillings, for each year they had been in his service.

Lands in Sussex, which descended to his daughters from their uncle Edward Apsley Esq. deceased, some houses in Hartshorne, land in Middlesex, and some salt marsh in Kent, near Upchurch, after the lease expired, his daughters were advised to divide equally between them, Elizabeth, the elder, being allowed the first choice.

This will was executed Mar. 8th, 1656-7, in presence of Robert Leeues, Moses Fryer.

A codicil added, the next day, revokes £50 per annum given his daughter Dorothy, from the lands in Sussex;—and "all gifts of sum or sums of money, by will, to Sister Cullick and her children," bequeathing, in lieu thereof, "all lands, chattels, real & personal, that are in New England, and my debts that are oweing there unto mee, to bee divided amongst them and in such manner as y^t her eldest sonne may have a double portion; *and likewise, that out of itt may bee had fiue hundred pound, which I doe hereby give to ye publique use of that country of New England,* if my loueing friend Mr. Edward Hopkins think it fitt : And to bee imployed and used to that end as my said loueing friend Mr. Edw. Hopkins shall order and direct."

To his "deare and loueing wife Katherine," £500.

To his "loveing friend Mr. Robert Leeues," £20, to buy books ; and desires him to assist his executrix, in managing her estates in Sussex, Middlesex and Kent.

To "Dame Eleanor Selby, of Barwick," £10 ; with the request that his 'much honored good friend' would undertake the care and education of his daughter Dorothy.

To his "deare friend and father in law Sir Arthur Haslerigge," and to each of his children ; to his "very good friend" his "cousin Lawrence & his wife," and to his "cousin Strickland & his lady," "as the remembrance of an affectionate friend;" to his "dear & good friend, Mr. Edward Hopkins, late warden of the Fleete ;" and

to his "father in law, Mr. Claveringe & to Thomas Burrell, Brinke-
barne" (Northumberland,) 40 shillings each, to buy rings :

To his "ancient acquaintance & dearely beloved friend, Sir
Thomas Widdrington," £5, for the same purpose.

To his good friend, "Aron Gourdon, Doctor of Phisick, £10.

To his "good friend Mr. Tempest Milner, Alderman of London,
and to his kinsman, Mr. Robert Key," £5, each.

£6 per annum, to Tristram Fenwicke, for life ; 40 shillings per
annum, to "Mrs. Ogle, of Leith, Scotland," and 20 shillings per
annum, to " Widdow Clarke, of Weldon," for life.

The codicil witnessed by John Stratford, Ro: Leeues and George
Hargripe.

The will was proved at London, and administration committed to
the executrix, his daughter Elizabeth, April 27th, 1657.

The copy is attested (for Thomas Walker,) by Rob Howard, Not.
Publique, Massachusets Col., Mar. 1st, 1658[9], from a former copy
certified by Leonard Browne, Not. Publique.

No. VIII. (p. 353.)

LETTER TO THE COMMISSIONERS OF THE U. COLONIES, COMPLAINING OF
AFFRONTS RECEIVED FROM THE NARRAGANSETTS.

[Indians, Vol. I. Doc. No. 4.]

Honord Genl:

The former insolent and proud cariage aud manifold abuses that
o^{r} people in this Colony haue (as yor Wors^{rs} wel vnd^{r}stand,) haue
sustained from the Vncircumcised Heathens round ab'ut vs, haue
bin noe small exercise to o^{r} spirits quietly, though not contentedly,
to beare. Yet hoping after soe much paines taken by the Wor-
shipf^{l} Com^{rs} at ye last sess^{n} at Hartford, both by Messuages sent to
severall of them, and impositions and iniunctions vpon them, for
wrougs done, and ye intimations of yor minds in reference to such
carriages manifested and declared vnto them, that it might haue
p·vayled to haue curbed their proud humors and in issue haue accomplished a peaceable correspondence in point [of] neighbourly carriage towards the English for ye future. But all candidnes and clemency towards these beastly minded and mannered Creatures seemes
rather to embolden them in (not only vnciuil and inhumane) but in
tendency to bloody practices ; for not many weeks now past, wee
are by sufficient information certified, that one night at ye New
Plantat^{n} at Monheage, some Indians, (as wil appeare, of the Narragansets,) shott 11 Bullets into a house of o^{r} English there, in hopes,
as they boasted, to haue slaine him whome we haue cause to hono^{r},
whose safety we cannot but take o^{r}selues bound to promote, o^{r} Deputy Go:, Maior Mason ; as also, slew another at Robt Layes, to y^{e}

great affrightment and terror of Goodwife Lay. W^ch outrages, tho' we cannot but iudge cals vnto vs to be awakened and to take some speedy course for distribution of justice to those y^t haue thus carried towards vs, in o^rs, yet bearing due respect to o^r neere vnion to and confœderation with ye other Collonies, to whom o^r liues and comforts are (we hope,) p^rcious, we thought meet to acquaint your Worsh^ps wth the p^rmisses, desiring if it may be, some speedy redress of the wroungs done vnto vs in this Collony, and provision for o^r indemnity and security, wch if yor Worships, after yor serious consideration on what hath now as an addition to former matters bene p^rsented to yor Worsh^ps, see not cause to stir or act on o^r behalfe, we cannot but take ye best advice y^t God shall direct vs vnto what God requires and cals for at o^r hands, to provide for o^r peoples safety, not onely in indeauouring to discouer the guilty but alsoe to vse just and lawful meanes to p^rvent such abuses and affronts for y future. O^r earnest desire is that yor Worsh^ps would be pleased to expedite a returne to o^r Gouernor Winthrop or Deputy Gouernor, Maior Mason, what your Wors^ps doe iudge in ye p^rmisses. We intreat you to consider how incongruous and cross it would haue bin 20 yeares agoe to an English spirit, to beare svch things as now we are forct to beare, or whether ye Indians would not haue exspected a visitation upon less occasions then these that haue of late bene met with by several of ours. We cannot but conceaue it is high time to renew vpon the memory of these Pagans the obliterate memorials of ye English. We desire not vnnecessarily to enlarge, but rather refer yor thoughts to a reduplicate animadversion on ye p^rcedent lines ; hoping for a speedy intimation of yor advice therin ; wherein we commend you to ye Infinite Wisdom of ye wond^rfull Counseller, to guide and direct you ; and subscribe, Gent:

Yo^rs in a ready discharge of relatiue obligations.

The p^rmisses ordered to be sent to ye Com^rs of ye other Collonies, June 9th, '60.

[The copy of this letter, preserved on file, is in the handwriting of the Secretary, Mr. Clark.
The Commissioners, at their next meeting, (Sept. 6–17th, 1660,) upon consideration of the premises, and of similar complaints preferred by the English residents of the new plantation at Mohegan, resolved "to require and force the Narrogansetts to a just satisfaction ;" and for that end, commissioned Capt Geo. Denison, Thomas Stanton, Thomas Mynor and others, to repair to Ninigret and the Narraganset sachems and require of them the punishment of the offenders and full reparation of injuries done to the English ; that "at least foure of the chiefe of them that shot into the English house at Monhegin should be proceeded with and punished, according to justice ; and in case they cannot be drawn thereunto." that five hundred fathoms of wampum should be exacted, in expiation of the offence; and that speedy payment should be made of a quantity of wampum, which the Commissioners, the year before, had required of the Narragansets, "for insolencies comitted at Mr. Brewster's, in killing an Indian servant at Mrs. Brewster's feet, to her great affrightment, and stealing corne, and other affronts." [Rec. of Comm'rs ; in Hazzard, ii. 433.]

The General Court, in October following, (p. 355, ante,) allowed the Narragansets "two months longer than the time agreed on, according to their desire, to bring in the wampum that they are assessed by the Commissioners to pay to this Jurisdiction." The payment appears to have been made not long afterwards,—as, at the next session of the Court, in March, 1661, it was ordered that "the wampum that the Commissioners ordered to be paid to Mr. Brewster, shall be d clivered unto him out of that which came from Narragansett." (p. 362.)]

No. IX. (p. 374.)

LETTERS FROM MR. GOODWIN, RESPECTING GOV. HOPKINS' LEGACY.

[Colleges & Schools, Vol. I. Doc. Nos. 2 & 3.]

To ye Honored Courte that is to be held at Hartford, in March next following ye date heerofe.

Much Honored,

We receaued wrytings from you, sygned by ye Secretary, wherein you desire ye trustees to appointe a tyme & place to meete with a Comittee which you haue chosen to treate with them, and to put a fynall issue to ye busines respecting y^t Legacy. I am desired in ye name of all ye trustees, to informe ye Courte, y^t we cannot entertaine y^t motion, both for y^t we are not able to vndertake such travell, nor do we see any vse at all of it (if we were able;) for we haue ordered Three hundred & fifty pownds, sett out of Mr. Hopkins estate committed to our trust, to be alowed to Hartford, vpon these conditions & termes following:

(1.) That it be by them improued, according to ye minde of ye donor, exprest in his will. (2.) That ye Court do also engage to remooue all obstructions out of our way, that we may not be disturbed, nor any way hindred, from, by, or vnder them, in ye managem^t of ye rest of y^t estate, according to o^r trust: that so loue & peace may be settled & established between vs. (3.) That you will deliuer us back ye attested coppy of ye Will sent vs from England, or els a true Coppy of it, vnder ye Seale of ye Collony.

Now if it please the Honored Courte (or there Committy) to accept of this Tendry of 350L., as is abouesaid, and shall deliuer vnto vs, or to our atturnies, an instrum^t drawne vp in wryting, & sealed with ye Seale of ye Collony, whearin all ye conditions of ye Tendry abouesaid shalbe fully & plainly exprest and confirmed by the Courte as abouesaide, before ye last of March next ensueing ye date heerofe, that then this grante of 350L. to Hartford, as abouesaid, shalbe settled vpon them, to be improued by them, according as is exprest in ye will of the doner. But if ye Courte do not fully & plainely declare ther acceptance, according as is aboue exprest, then we heerby declare our grante to them heer inserted to be a nullyty & voyde; and thus I humbly take leave of you,

Subscribing myselfe, yor Worshipps' in all due observance,

Hadley, February 24th, 1661.

Will: Goodwin, in ye name of ye rest of ye Trustees.

[The General Court did not, at this time, decide to accept the conditions imposed by the Trustees; and the order of Feb. 23d, 1659-60, (p. 345,) "that the estate of Mr. Hopkins should be secured within this Colony until the said estates be inventoried, and the inventories presented, and administration granted by this Court," remained in force. Oct. 8th, 1663, Gov. Winthrop, Mr. Allyn, Mr. Willys & Capt. Talcott, were appointed by the General Court, " to consider what is meet to be attended in reffrance to Mr. Hopkins estate by him bequeathed for to be improved [for the promoting of learning, and to make report of their thoughts the next Court." (p. 412.) The following letter appears to have been written in reply to some communication addressed by this Committee to the Trustees. At the next session of the General Court after its receipt, (Mar. 10th, 1663-4,) the restraint laid upon Mr. Hopkins' estate was removed, and administration seems to have been surrendered to the Trustees.]

To the Honoured Court at Hartford.

Much Honoured,

Yours of Novemb: 16, 1663, I received, and not to trouble you with my answer unto your severall motives to induce us to be of youre minde, my finall returne to all is this, That as I haue noe cause, soe I doe in noe sort consent to that which you were pleased to move me unto, but doe desire that your selves would returne the estate unto us, who only haue right to dispose therof, with due satisfaction for all damage that shall appeare to be done unto it, since it hath been taken out of our hands; which being timely performed, I doubt not but the three hundred and fifty pound tendred unto you in Feb: 1661, may yet be setled upon Hartford, on such like conditions as be therein expressd, tending to the securing of the estate from any farther obstructions by your means, and ordering of the improvment of it according to the Doners end, expressed in his will, as our duty bindeth us to doe. Now herunto I doe humbly desire the Honoured Court speedily and plainly to declare themselves to me (or to our Attourneys) whither they doe now accept of this tendery or noe, without any farther agitations about the disposall of it, which hath already been a great wrong to the estate and Doner therof, as also to us, the Trustees, and whole Country besids; the which if you shall decline to doe betwixt this and the end of March next ensueing the date hereof, this tendery also is to be judged a nullity, and we shall forthwith endeavour the freeing of the estate elsewhere, as the great betrustment committed to us, in all respects considered, in duty bindeth us to doe thus. Hoping and heartily wishing that you would accept of my motion, though I cannot accept of yours, I rest,

Hadley, Feb: 1st, 63. Yours to love & serve you as I may,

Will: Goodwin.

No. X. (p. 370.)

THE CHARTER OF 1662.

[For. Correspondence, Vol. II. Nos. 1-3.]

Instructions for o^r Wor^{ll} Gou^r, Agent for and in behalf of the Generall Court at Conect^t, both for p^{r}senting o^r Address and Petition to ye Kings Matie, and also for procureing a Pattent for this Colony.

Imp^r: For advice and counsell, it is desired that you would be pleased to address vnto these noble and gentlemen, The Right Honerable Lord Sea,* Earle of Manchester, Lord Brooke, and alsoe Mr. Nathan[ll] Fines, Mr. Sam[ll] Peck, Doct of Phisick, and Mr. Floid, of y[e] Corporation; vnto whose advice and counsell the Comittee doth refer you, according to y[e] ord[r] of y[e] Generall Court, to act or to desist.

2d. It is desired that you would be pleased to vse all due meanes to procure a Coppy of the Pattent referring to these parts, granted vnto those Nobles and Gent: whom Mr. Fenwick did represent in his act of sale to this Collony. And in case the Coppy of this Pattent can by noe meanes vsed be obteined, then you are desired to advise wth y[e] Counsell forementioned, what to doe in reference to y[e] heires of Mr. Fenwick for y[e] regaining such sums as haue bine disbursed for y[e] purchase of Jurisdiction Right.

And in case the forementioned Pattent can be procured, our desire is, that you would be pleased to consid[r] both what privilidges, rights and imunities are therein granted, and to compare it w[th] y[e] Coppy of y[e] Bay Pattent; and what is conduceable in both to y[e] welbeing and future comfort of this Colony, our desire is may be inserted and comp[r]hended in the Pattent granted and confirmed to this Colony. [But in case vpon rep[r]sentation of our Purchase and moneyes expended vpon it, the heires of Mr. Fenwick, or any other y[e] Pattentees, doe tender the confirmation of the Pattent, (y[t] we conceiue we bought,) we shal rest satisfied w[th] that Pattent, provided it may be compleated and y[e] confirmation finished w[th]out further expense to this Colony.

But in case a Pattent be yet to be procured for the Collony, our desire is, that it may comp[r]hend al y[e] rights, privilidges, authority and imunities that are granted in y[e] Massachuset Colonyes Pattent. And that, respecting the Pattent, it may be granted and confirmed to severall Pattentees, together with theire Associates and such [as] may be adioyned to them, their heires and successors, for euer. The Extent of y[e] bounds to bee; from y[e] limits or bounds of y[e] Massachuset and Plimouth, vnto y[e] Delliway Riuer south, or as far as may be granted that way. And that, respecting the quallificat: of such as may be added as Freemen to this Company of Pattentees and associates, who only shall haue power to choose any officers that are requisite and necessary to carry on the Affaires of the Colony—

Those who are desired to be Patentees are the p[r]sent Gouernour, Dep: Gouernour, Mr. Henry Clark, Mr Sam[ll] Willis, Mr. Mathew

---

* Lord Say & Sele, who had done much to promote the restoration of Charles II, was, shortly after the king's return, made Lord Privy Seal. In a letter to Gov. Winthrop, (printed in Appendix to Trumbull's Hist. of Conn. No. IX,) he professes himself desirous of doing his good friends in New England, the best service he could, and regrets that the state of his health was such as to prevent his going to London, in person, to aid in procuring the charter; but informs Gov. W. that he had written to the Earl of Manchester (at that time Lord Chamberlain of the household,) " to give the best assistance he may." Lord Say & Sele died April 14th, 1662. His son, Nathaniel Fiennes (Fines,) had been one of the Commissioners of the great seal, under the Parliament, and subsequently, a member of Cromwell's privy council and lord privy seal. After the restoration, he retired to his estates in Wiltshire, where he died Dec. 16th, 1669. (Wood's Ath. Oxon. II. 454.) The Lord Brooke, here mentioned, was Robert, son of Robert (second Lord Brooke,) one of the original proprietors of Connecticut, under 'the old Patent', or the Earl of Warwick's grant.

Allyn, Mr. Richard Treat, Mr. William Phelps, Nathan Gold, together wth their Associates hereafter named, M[rs] John Warham, Sam[ll] Stone, John Whiting, Sam[ll] Hooker, James Fitch, Rich: Lord, Henry Woolcot, John Steele, Edw: Stebbin, John Talcot, Beniamin Nubery, Dan[ll] Clarke, Mathew Campfield, Will[m] Wadsworth, John Hawley, John Allyn.]*

The p[r] sons whom we desire to be nominated in y[e] Pattent, to whom it should be granted and confirmed are, John Winthrop Esq[r], and Maior John Mason Esq[r], Sam[ll] Willis, Henry Clark, Math: Allyn, William Phelps, Richard Treat, Nathan Gould, John Talcot, Daniell Clark, John Deming Sen[r], Anthony Howkins, Robert Warner, John Clark Sen[r], Robert Royce, Phillip Groues, Jehu Burr, Mathew Campfield ; to them and their Associates and successors.

The Bounds y[t] we doe p[r]sent to be inserted in o[r] Pattent, if it may be obtained, are, eastward to Plimouth line, northward to y[e] limits of y[e] Massathusets Collony, and westward to y[e] Bay of Delloway, if it may bee.†

And respecting liberties and privilidges inserted in the Pattent, not to be inferiour or short to what is granted to y[e] Massachuset.

And respecting Customes, that if it may be obtained, we, in regard of our meane and low condition, may be freed for w[t] may be exported from hence to England, and from thence to vs, for y[e] space of 21 yeares or as long as can be procured.

And also y[t] y[e] Islands adjacent, y[t] are not already granted to any other, may be included in o[r] Patent.

And likewise respecting the moneyes expended by o[r] agreement wth Mr. Fenwick, to take y[e] best advice you can meet w[th] from the Noblemen mentioned or others whom you think meet to address vnto, what is requisite to bee done for to regaine y[t] money if it may bee ; declareing, as cause requires, the repaying of 500£.‡

Our desire is, that if it can be procured there may be a resolution of y[t] p[r]ticuler in y[e] Bay Pattent, where they are to begin to run their line twixt themselves and vs.

We desire as oppertunity tenders itself, that there may be a declaration of the carriage of Capt. Fernes, both respecting Hartford shipp taken by Rupert and Fernes, as also his stealing away the Indians.

Respecting the Dutch, we desire that his Ma[tie] may be informed of their setling upon the Maine, and stil incroaching vpon the English.

---

* The whole of the portion here included in brackets, (from "But in case," &c., on the preceding page,) is, in the original draught, marked across, with lines,—and what follows appears to have been substituted on a subsequent revision.

† Next follow three lines, which were afterwards partially erased, by lines drawn across them ; " But if it cannot be granted that the bounds may extend at least to Hudsons Riuer, we doe not judge it requisite to expend money vpon a Pattent."

‡ By Capt. Cullick, as Mr. Fenwick's executor. See pages, 329, 573, *ante*.

[*The Address to the King.*]

Most Dread Soveraigne,

It was far from our purpose to be of the latest of yor Maties subiects, in these o^r humble aproaches vnto yor Royal p'sence. We are not only seperated by soe vast an Ocean from our deare English Brethren that [*have a*] place vnder ye immediate influence and splendor of soe great a Monarch, in y^t princely Pallace of his renowned imperial City, the glory of ye whole earth, but also, by a lone tract of a dismall wild'ness, are very remote from o^r other English Americans of ye parts of ye ordnary recourse of shipping; wherby we were depriued by the too soone approaching Winter, together with some other impediments, of the timely effecting of y^t which was long since concluded o^r duty and desire, namely to prostrate o'selues by an humble Address at our soueraigne Princes feet.

Our Fathers & some few yet aliue of their associates in so great an vnd^{r}taking, of transporting themselues, their wiues and children, into this westerne world, had certainly very pious and publique ends, the propagation of the blessed Gosple of the Lord Jesus amongst the Heathen, who til then had neuer heard the sound thereof, as also the the honour and further extent of the British monarchy; And thervpon came ouer, vpon the full and free consent, allowance and spetial fauour of his Highnes, our euer lamented late Soveraigne Lord, your Royal father of glorious memory, expressly declared in his gratious L^{rs} Pattents granted to ye vndertakers of ye Plantation of ye Massachusets Bay, in New England. In y^t part of the Countrey, neer the port of their first arrival they setled for a time, till vpon experience they found that place would be too streight for soe great a number if they should continue all there long together. They therfore vndertooke a troublesome, hazardous and chargeable discouery of the more inland parts of ye Countrey; where comeing to ye great faire Riuer of Conecticut, haueing opertunity by the free tender of ye sale of some larg tracts of lands fit for ye setling of diuers Plantations or Townes, profered unto them by ye Sachems or Heathen Princes and with y^t concurrence of ye other natiues vnd^r them, the then proprietors of those places, they thought it very convenient to purchase those lands of them who appeared to be the owners and possessors of ye same; which could not but tend to y^t enlargment of his Maties Dominions, and be a good step towards ye yet further extent thereof, and ye benefit of ye English people. And therevpon transplanted themselues and vs to this place, where we were but now in a manner vpon our very beginnings of takeing possession and inhabiting ye places wch we had brought at noe smal expences, when those sad and vnhappy times of troubles and wars begun in England, which we could only bewaile wth sighes and

---

* Dr. Trumbull seems to have overlooked this document, and to have confounded the *Address* and *Petition*. He speaks of the latter as having been presented by the Governor to the Court, in May. (H. of Conn. I. 240.) It will be seen, on reference to the Records, that the Address was 'drawen vp and formed and presented' by Governor Winthrop to the Court, and referred by them to a Committee, *subsequently* appointed, ' to peruse and compleat the Address and draw vp the *Petition*.' (page 367, *ante*.)

mournfull teares: And haue euer since hid our selues behind the Mountains, in this desolate desert, as a people forsaken, choosing rather to sit solitary and wait only vpon the Divine Providence for protection than to apply ourselves to any of those many changes of powers, o^r hearts as wel as o^r stations stil remaining free from illegal ingagements and intire to yor Maties intrests, euen now at ye returne of o^r Lord ye King to his Crowne and dignities. The beames of whose soueraignty (like y^t admired star y^t appeared at noonday at his happy nativity,) haue filled the worlds hemisphere and appeared also ouer ye great deeps in this our Horizon; wherby we are newly animated and incouraged to take vpon vs this boldnes to implore your Maties fauour and gratious protection, y^t you would be pleased to accept this Collony, your owne Colony, a little branch of yor mighty Empire; y^t as we haue hitherto (by ye great goodnes of ye Almighty,) since ye ouerpassed difficulties and hardships of our beginnings, enioyed peace and prosperous proceedings, we might yet be made more happy in ye fruition and continuance of ye same, through yor Maties goodnes and bounty in granting o^r humble Petition, when we shall haue liberty to p^{r}sent ye same by a person herewith sent from amongst vs, to attend yor highnes pleasure, that therby you may haue a more ful account of whateuer concernes yor poor Pilgrims here.

That we p^{r}sumed publiquely and solemnely to proclaime and declare for yor Matie here, before we had a forme and express order for ye same, we humbly craue yor gratious pardon. The expectation of y^r Royall Comand therein, caused vs a while to defer, but not receaueing it by ye ships before winter, it made vs thus presume vpon yor fauourable acceptance of o^r publisheing to ye world o^r true allegiance to o^r Lord the King.

Most illustrious S^r, be please to excuse o^r poverty, that haue nothing to p^{r}sent yor Matie from this Wild^{r}nes but o^r hearts and loyall affections, wch stir vs vp to supplicate ye Eternall Matie, the King of Heauen and Earth, for all happiness and blessings both temporall and spirituall to be plentifully and abundantly powred downe from Heauen vpon yor Royal Throne, that soe we therby, together wth all those numberles members of yor Maties subjects, may liue vnder yor protection a quiet and peaceable life in all Godlines and honesty.

With all humble acknowledgm^t of o^r Loyalty, real and due subiection and allegiance to yor Matie, we craue leaue in all submission to subscribe o^{r}selues,

Yo^r Maties most faythful and loyall
subiects & servants.

[Letter to the Earl of Manchester.]

[The draught of this letter preserved on file, is without address. There can, however, be no doubt that it was designed for the Earl of Manchester, to whom Gov. Winthrop had been referred for 'advice and counsel'; whose 'gracious inclination, and spirit towards the sons of Zion' were well known to the petitioners; and whose position and influence were such as to make it highly important to the Colony to secure his good offices in their behalf. The Earl of Manchester had heartily concurred in the restoration of Charles II, and on the King's return was received into especial favor, made a lord of the bed chamber, and of the privy council, knight of the garter, lord lieutenant of Huntingdonshire, and subsequently, lord chamberlain of the household; "in which great charge he behaved himself with that honour, candour and great civility, as he justly obtained the affection and respect of all men." (Walker's H. of Kts. of the Garter.) He died May 5th, 1671, æt. 69.]

Right Ho^{ble}:

O^r p^{r}sent station and condition being by the wise step-ordering Providence of ye Almighty setled in this remote wild^{r}ness, strang^{r}s in a strange land, far distant from such opertunities that might be advantagious to vs and o^r posterity in a familiar access by o^{r}selues or rep^{r}sentatiues vnto his Highnes o^r gratious Soveraigne, for ye obtayneing such fauours as may tend to o^r safety and settlement, we are necessitated to embrace opertunities to implore the aid and countenance of such as ye Lord may stir vp to be fauourers of the work of God amongst vs. And the abundance and plenary test, y^t we haue soe frequently bene furnished wth, not only respecting ye gratious inclination and disposition of yor Honours spirit towards the sons of Sion, but also doth not a little incourage vs in o^r owne behalf and as rep^{r}senting the whole Colony, humbly to p^{r}sent o^r desires and earnest requests vnto yor Lordship, to afford vs yor fauour in countenancing and vshering into ye Kings Maties audience o^r Address and Petition, if yor Honour judge it seasonable ; and o^r further request is that we may obtaine yor counsell and advice to o^r Agent, in such p^{r}ticulers as may be by him p^{r}sented to yor Honours consideration, either respecting monies disbursed by this Colony to Mr. Fenwick for Jurisdiction Power etc., and also respecting the obtaining of a Pattent for this Colony. For although ye Honerable Committee of Lords and Commons did owne this a distinct Colony, and soe we haue euer stood since our begin: in administracon and confæderation wth o^r Brethren of ye Massachuset, yet we want a Pattent to secure o^r standing and to confirme o^r privilidges, and to strengthen vs against such as may oppose o^r p^{r}sent intrests in civil polecy. Honerable Sir, wee can thus far excuse o^r boldnes in p^{r}senting o^r humble requests at this time to yo^{r}self, together wth some others of noble quallity, whose intercession if we can obtaine we hope wilbe of great availe on o^r behalfe. The great disappointment y^t we meet wth about an Agreem^t y^t was made by this Colony wth ye forementioned Mr. Fenwick, doth necessitate vs thervnto. We disbursed a considerable sum of estate, to ye value of 1600l., vnto Mr. Fenwick. He p^{r}tending power and authority, as a Pattentee, ouer ye Riuer and the lands adjacent, when he intended to returne to England, propounded to this Court at Conecticut, the sale of Sea Brook Fort, wth ye lands vpon ye Riuer and other lands more remote ; w^{ch}, if refused by ye Colo: or Court, he would (as it was reported, frequently,) otherwise dispose of, either by imposeing taxes, customes etc., or else (as was feared,) sell it to ye Dutch, wch as was conceaued would haue bene very destructiue to o^r comforts, occasioning broyles and contests twixt them and vs. We therfore, conceaueing it would tend to o^r peace and settlement, were willing to attend his propositions ; and out of desires to lay a good foundation of enioying the advantage both of Civil and Ecclesiastick rights, privilidges and imunities, for o'selues and posterities, vnder ye shadow of Patent Right, (by vertue whereof, he p^{r}tended, and could haue noe other way, power or authority to make sale vnto vs of w^t he agreed to confirme vnto this Jurisdiction,) we willingly disbursed (tho' much disabled, by reason of o^r meanes and pouerty,) the sum forementioned; wch tho' it hath much oppressed vs, yet could we but haue enioyed what we expected, it would haue satisfied; but now we see o'selues as naked as before, haueing neither Pattent or Coppy of it, nor ought elce y^t may ensure vs of future continuance of o^r p^{r}sent piivilidges. And therfore are necessitated from several other respects, to lay out o'selues, and to improue all the interest y^t we can raise in o^r natiue soyle, for obtaineing reliefe in this o^r state and condition, w^h humane frailty hath in a great measure cast vs into. Had we not bene too credulous and confident of ye goodnes and faithfulnes of that Gent: we might possibly haue bin at a better pass. But we shal craue leaue to refer further enlargm^t to o^r Agent, only reduplicating o^r earnest request that yor Hon^r would be pleased to afford vs the great fauour of yor aduice and counsell, as need requires, and occasion offers itself.

If this poor people may find such acceptance, and o^r request such entertainment, wth yo'self, as that throw yor Hon^{rs} help and mediation we may find grace and audience wth o^r Gratious Soueraigne, we shall therby be refreshed, as wth the sweet smiles of o^r father, and be excited to returne the tribute of daily prayer for yor Lordships prosperity; and humbly subscribe, &c.

No. XI. (p. 404.)

MRS. CULLICK'S PETITION, TO THE GENERAL COURT, IN MAY, 1663.

[Towns & Lands, Vol. I. No. 68.]

To the Hon'rd Generall Court of Connecticott Jvrisdiction, now assembled, the humble petition of Elizabeth Cullicke, relict to Captayne John Cullick, deceased,

Humbly sheweth:

That whereas there weare entred into (by yor Petitioner's husband,) certayne obligations for the makeing of paym^t the sum of fiue hundred pownds vnto this hono'rd Co^{r}t, according to the tymes specifyed in the twoe obligations given for the same, together wch the paym^t of interest in case of falure in poynt of tyme, one of wch obligations hath beene satisfyed & taken vp, & the other in p^{r}t satisfyed, viz: one hundred pounds, foure shillings, tenpence, being payde, so that there remaynes one hundred fourty & nine pounds, fiftene shillings, twoe pence, by the sayd obligation, for yor petitioner to pay, as executrix vnto her late husband. And forasmuch that the grownd of those obligations given by yor petitioner's husband, was vpon the apprehention that there had beene a totall falu^r in the brother of yor petitioner, George Fenwicke Esqr, respecting his procuring of a Pattent for the Collony, since which it hath appeared that there was a mistake therin, for that there was found wth the Executor of Mr. Edward Hopkins some such writing, wch was delivered to the Hon^{r}d John Winthrop Esqr, Governor and Agent for the Collony, whereby he was advantaged in the soliciting the Kyngs most excellent Majesty for, and in the procuring of, those Letters Pattent now obtayned,—

Wherefore yor Petitioner doth pray this Hono^{r}d Gen'rall Co^{r}t, that they will please to accept of what hath beene already payde ; and that you would remit the one hundred fourty nine pounds, fiftene shillings twoe pence, by obligation remaineing ; which wilbe an acceptable clemency before the Lord towards yor petitioner, and noe stratening to the Treasury of this Hono'd Court. And yor petitioner shal pray.

Elizabeth Cullick.

[The petitioner was Mr. Fenwick's sister, and married Capt. John Cullick, May 20th, 1648. This document is of historical interest, as exhibiting the nature of the settlement with Capt. Cullick, and as an admission of the fact (elsewhere sufficiently established, but which our historians have very generally lost sight of,) that no transfer of *jurisdiction right* or assignment of the Earl of Warwick's grant, was ever made by Mr. Fenwick to the Colony,—the latter not being in possession even of a *copy* of the " old Patent" until after Gov. Winthrop's return from England, where he had procured from Mr. Dalley, the executor of Mr. Hopkins, a copy found among that gentleman's papers after his death. This copy, the writer has been so fortunate as to discover among the old files in the State Department, and satisfactorily to identify. It is informal, having no certificate of authentication ; but at the top of the first page is written, in the hand writing (as believed,) of Gov. Winthrop. " *The copye of the Patent for Connecticutt, being the copy of that copy wch was shewed to the people here by Mr. George Fenwick. Found amongst Mr. Hopkins' papers.*" A copy of this document made by Capt. John Talcot, not long after Gov. Winthrop's return, and attested as " Vera Copia of that copy which was in Mr. Hopkins his custody ;"—with a subsequent copy made from this latter, by Secretary Allyn,—have been often referred to and cited. The omission of two or three words, and some other slight errors, made by Capt. Talcot, have been closely followed by every subsequent transcriber, whence it appears that the copy "which was in Mr. Hopkins' custody" has hitherto escaped observation.]

No. XII. (p. 441.)

THE UNION.

The correspondence between the General Courts of the two colonies, the committees appointed by each, orders of the Council, and such other documents relating to the union, as have been preserved on file in the State Department of Connecticut, are to be found in the first volume of "Miscellaneous" papers, Nos. 67 to 87. The proposed limits of this volume not admitting of their insertion here, (several of them, especially, "New Haven's Case stated," and the reply of Connecticut, being of great length,) a list is subjoined, for the purpose of facilitating reference.

[Doc. No. 67.] A letter from the Committee of the General Court, appointed at the October session, 1662, " To our much Honored and Reverend Friends of New Haven, Milford, &c. to be communicated to all whom it may concern."

APPENDIX. 587

Announcing the receipt of the Charter, (a copy of which accompanied the letter,) and expressing the desire of the General Court for "a happy and comfortable union" between the two colonies; "that inconveniences and dangers may be prevented, and peace and truth strengthened and established, through our suitable subjection to the terms of the Patent, and the good blessings of God upon us." Without date,—but written between Oct. 9th and 17th, 1662.

[No. 68.] Letter from the New Haven, in reply to the foregoing, dated Oct. 17th, 1662.

The Committee do not find the Colony of New Haven to be expressly included in the Patent, (a copy of which had been read to them,) but ' to shew [their] desire that matters may be issued in the conserving of peace and amity, with righteousness,' they promise to communicate the copy of the Patent and the letter of the Committee to the freemen of the colony, & with all convenient speed, return their answer. They wish the issuing of the matter deferred until they have opportunity of receiving fuller information from Gov. Winthrop (who had not yet returned,) "or satisfaction otherwise,"—the Colony of N. Haven to remain meanwhile " distinct, entire and uninterrupted." Signed by Gov. Leete, Mathew Gilbert, Benjamin Fenn, Jasper Crane, Robert Treat, Wm. Jones, and Rev. Messrs. Davenport, Steele, Pierson and Newton. [Copies of these two letters are in Trumbull's H. of Conn., 1. 252.]

[No. 69.] " Some proposals to the Gentlemen of N. Haven &c., in reference to their firm settlement and incorporation with us of Connecticutt."

By the Committee appointed by the General Court, Mar. 11th, 1663, (see page 396, *ante*,) to treat with New Haven. These proposals are in the hand writing of Mr. Allyn, who was one of the Committee. Dated, New Haven, Mar. 20th, 1662–3.

[No 70.] Reply of the New Haven Committee (by Gov. Leete,) to the propositions of Connecticut. March 20th, 1662–3.

"Our answer in general is, that we are not in a capacity" to " conclude the matter, at this present meeting." 1st. Because having appealed to the king, they were unwilling to proceed further, " until his Royal determination be known, in the question depending between us." 2d. Because the consent of the other confederate colonies must be first obtained. 3d. Because they were prohibited by the freemen from " concluding any thing for altering their distinct colony state and government, without their consent." They promise, however, to consider further of the propositions and communicate them to the Freemen. They complain that *Stamford* is not named in the propositions of Conecticut, " as if it were no member of vs," and profess themselves ' unsatisfied with that omission.'

[No. 71.] Queries proposed by the N. Haven Committee, "to the Honored Committee from the General Assembly of Connecticut, Mr. Willis, Mr. Clark & Mr. Allyn." Aug. 26th, 1663.

For the appointment of, and instructions to, the Connecticut Committee, see page 407, *ante*. The propositions made in March, were now repeated, (as appears by an endorsement of Mr. Allyn's thereon, dated Aug. 26th;) and this gave occasion for the committee of N. Haven to propound certain inquiries, " in order to a friendly treaty, and amicable composure of matters in difference ;" with the express stipulation, however, that no treaty shall be binding without the assent of their General Court of Freemen, and of the confederate Colonies.

[No. 72.] Reply of the Connecticut Committee to the foregoing ; Aug. 27th, 1663.

They " declare the propensity and readiness of their spirits fully and finally to obliterate the memorial of all former occasions administered to us as matters of grievance or offence respecting any of you," referring especially to alleged grounds of offence given to New Haven, by proceedings at Stamford and Guilford. The queries proposed by N. Haven, are replied to, in order, and at considerable length.

[No. 73.] " At a meeting of the Council of ye Colony of Conecticut the 28th of December, 1663.

The Council did nominate & appoynt Mr. Willys, John Allyn & Mr. Wayt Winthrope to goe to Guilford, and treat wth Mr. Leet (and any others whom Mr. Leet shall desire to joyne wth himselfe) about indemnitie of the persons and estates of those whoe haue actually joyned to o^r Gouernment according to these following instructions.

       Extracted out of the records of ye Council, p^r me
Mr. James Richards is   John Allyn, Secret'y.
desired to attend ye seruice also."

Following this, is a certified copy of the " instructions for ye aforesayd Committee :"

1. If Mr. Leete will give security (by his word,) for the indemnity of the aforesaid persons, the Committee were to propose terms of union. But if not,

2. They were to appoint a meeting at Middletown, for concluding a treaty with New Haven and the rest.

3. If neither proposition were acceded to, then to forbid all proceedings against those persons who had united themselves to the government of Connecticut ; and to administer an oath to a Constable.

[No. 75.] A note from the Committee to Mr. Leete, requesting a meeting at Guilford. Dated Dec. 30th, 1663.

[No. 74.] A brief reply from Gov. Leete, (of the same date,) referring the Committee to some former communication, which was ' in earnest,' and ' from which he cannot recede.'

[No. 76.] Extract from Records of Council, of the appointment of another Committee to treat with N. Haven, (Feb. 6th, 1663–4,) who are instructed to tender to New Haven the enjoyment of all privileges not repugnant to the tenor of the Charter. If these terms are not acceded to, the Committee are " ordered to read the Charter at a public meeting, if they can attayne it, and to declare that we expect their submission to his Majesties order therein conteined," &c.

[No. 78.] A letter from the New Haven committee, (Feb. 24th, 1663–4,) requiring, as a preliminary to further treaty, that Connecticut should "redintegrate the Colony, by restoring our members at Stamford and Guilford."

[No. 77.] Reply of Connecticut committee,—agreeing, in order " to preuent divisions," that " divers persons of Guilford and Stamford" " be ordered to submit to the same authority with their neighbours in these places :" and making further propositions for union. Same date, with preceding.

[No. 79.] Feb. 25th. The New Haven committee inquire if the concession (as to Stamford & Guilford,) is " an authentic act," unless confirmed by the General Court of Connecticut. On which, Mr. Allyn, for the Connecticut Committee, endorses an assurance that, " we are ready to make authentick what we have proposed to you."

[No. 80.] " New Haven's Case stated." Mar. 9th, 1663–4. " From the Committee, By order of the General Court of New Haven Colony. James Bishop, Secretary." The New Haven Court, Jan. 7th, 1663–4, desired " Mr. Davenport and Mr. Street to draw up in writing all our grievances, and then, with the approbation of as many of the committee as could come together, to send it to Connecticut, unto their General Assembly,—which accordingly was done in March next." (N. Haven Rec.) A brief abstract of this document, is given by Dr. Trumbull, (Hist. of Conn., i. 264,) and a part of it, (three of the seven pages of the original,) has been published by Dr. Bacon, in the Appendix to his Historical Discourses, pp. 359–365. Dr. B. had been informed that "the original is not found, among the archives of the State, at Hartford," and supposed the partial transcript, upon the New Haven Records, to be all that had been preserved.

[No. 81.] Reply of Connecticut; (seven pages, in hand writing of Mr. Allyn ;) Mar. 1663–4.

[Nos. 82–84.] Petitions of Bray Rosseter, (Mar. 19th, & May 20th, 1664,) and of sundry inhabitants of Guilford, (Mar. 29th,) asking protection and support from the General Court of Connecticut.

[No. 85.] Letter from the General Court of Massachusetts, to Connecticut, (May 28th,) proposing to settle the differences between the latter colony and New Haven, by arbitration, &c.

[No. 86.] Letter from Connecticut to the Commissioners of the U. Colonies, (Sept. 2d,) protesting against their recognition of Commissioners from New Haven colony.

[No. 87.] Warning to the inhabitants of Milford (Nov. 17th, 1664,) to meet, "to attend such occasions with Mr. Sherman" and Mr. Allyn, as had been given them in charge by the General Court of Connecticut. Following which, is recorded the submission of the town of Milford to Connecticut government, "by a general vote," "no one person voting against it."

INDEX OF NAMES.

※※ Names of *localities*, of *Indian tribes* and their *sachems*, and of a few individuals who are most frequently referred to in the pages of this volume, and whose history is inseparable from that of the colony, have been included in the *General Index*. Special references to the names of *magistrates* and *deputies* prefixed to each session of the Court, would have swelled the Index to an inconvenient bulk, and, as there seemed no absolute necessity of their insertion, have been omitted. Reference to names occurring in the list of *jurors*, has been made only in cases where no previous mention of the individual had appeared on the pages of the record.

Abbott, George, 49, 156, 172.
  Robert, 55, 66.
Ackerly, Robert, 341, 428.
Adams, Jer. 17, 19, 123, 357, 360, 361, 377, 378, 401.
  Edward, 220.
Adgate, Thomas, 297, 412.
Alcock, 83, 115. See Olcott.
Allen, Math. 28, 43, 66, 123, 106, 110, 111, 133, 155, 211, 252, 323, 348, 372, 404.
  Thomas, 4, 14, 33, 43, 45, 211, 231, 263, 309, 315.
  Robert, 317; Sam. 122, 505.
  John, 299, 309, 321, 344, 346, 373, 376, 383, 384, 404, 406.
Alvord, Benedict, 83, 89, 102, 103, 108.
Anadowne, Roger, 94.
Andrews, William, 122, 140.
  John, 315; Edward, 297.
Arnold, Jos. 148, 297, 315.
Astwood, 68.
Avery, James, 338, 385, 412, 426, 429.

Baccas, (Backus) Wm. 412.
Bacon, And. 49, 55, 66, 74, 94, 258, 261, 263, 283, 318.
Bailis, Thomas, 82.
Baily, John, 297, 326.
Band, Robert, 112.
Banks, John, 85, 220, 226, 367.
Barber, Thomas, 8, 124, 183, 184, 191, 203.
Barclet, 84.
Barnard, John, 49, 55.
Barding, (Berding,) 130, 137.
  Nath. 193, 318.
Barlowes, Thomas, 125.
Barlow, John, Sen. 432.
  John, Jr. 432.
Barly, Thomas, 202.

Barnard, Jo. 81. 174, 283, 321.
  Barth. 278, 281, 325.
Barnes, Mary, 187.
  Thomas, 227.
Barrett, Samuel, 136.
Bartlemewe, Henry, 89.
Bartlet, Rob. 124, 142, 143.
  John, 196.
  William, 181, 184, 191, 195.
Barton, 428.
Bassaker, Peter, 102, 111, 114, 123, 157, 160, 168, 177, 181.
Bassett, Thomas, 46, 102. 336.
  (Goody) 220.
Bassum, William, 4, 5.
Baxter, Thomas, 252, 253, 265, 283, 379.
  Bridget, 376, 379.
Bayley, Nich. 412.
Beacham, Rob. 310, 432.
Beadle, Rob. 115, 124, 185.
Beardsley, Will. 130, 198, 226, 340.
Bears, James, 433.
Beaument, William, 231.
Beckwith, Math. 29, 81, 110, 181.
  (Becquet) 315. Steph. 183.
Belden, Rich. 88, 130, 141, 182.
  Samuel, 297.
  John. 298, 309.
Benedick, Thomas, 379, 428.
Benjamin, Richard, 427.
Bennitt, John, 29, 164, 167, 171, 190, 201. Thos. 433.
Betts, Thomas, 433.
  Richard, 428.
  John, 169, 171, 299, 417.
Billing, Richard, 182.
Birchard, 29; John, 221, 412.
Bird, Jos. 297. James, 298.
Birge, Richard, 180.
Bishop, John, 177.

Bissell, John, 55, 75, 137, 174, 211, 231, 246, 298, 281, 309, 310.
  Tnomas, 231. Samuel, 297.
Blackleach, John, 376, 377.
Blackman, (Rev. Adam) 187, 340.
Blachfield, (Blachford) Peter, 33, 108, 182, 156, 315.
Blinman, (Rev. Richard) 218, 288, 299, 300.
Bliss, Lidea, 82.
Blisse, Thomas, 147, 412.
Bloomer, 423.
Blumfield, Will. 311, 408, 409.
Boltwood, Robert, 165, 167.
Bond, Robert, 398, 400, 428.
Boosy, James, 30, 42, 47, 60, 69, 125, 238.
Boreman, William, 135.
  Samuel, 143, 204, 332, 349, 379, 396, 413.
Boscom, Thomas, 106.
Boswell, James, 315.
  William, 565.
Bostock, (Bostwick) Arthur, 336, 340, 351.
Boughtwhord, Robert, 315.
Bouten, John, 433.
Bowen. Thomas, 315.
Bradley, Francis, 432.
Branker, 87, 98, 196.
Bratfield, Lisley, 83, 84, 463.
Brewster, Jona. 165, 166, 207, 209, 298, 301, 306, 362.
Brocke, John, 89.
Brook, Thomas, 315.
Browne, Nath. 257. Peter, 315.
  Francis, 351, 413.
  Ellen, 352. Richard, 388.
Browning, Henry, 43.
Bruen, Obad. 347, 352, 366, 382, 400, 426.

INDEX OF NAMES.

Brumfield, William, 130, 135.
Brundish, John, 40, 45, 444.
  Rachel, 45, 46, 445.
Brunson, Mary, 45, 50.
  John, 327.
Brush, Thomas, 388, 428.
Bryant. Alex. 440.
Buck, Enoch, 173, 177, 297.
Buckland, Thomas, 109, 204.
Budd, John, 386, 388, 413, 436.
Buell, Samuel, 411, 425.
Bull, Thomas, 29, 211, 228, 230, 242, 379, 413.
Bunce, 137. Thomas, 182.
Burnham, Thomas, 195, 201, 202, 297, 340, 346, 364.
Burr, Jehu, 12, 112, 125, 127, 130, 226, 349, 426.
  Benjamin, 315; Samuel, 315.
  John, 428, 432.
  Nathaniel, 433.
Burrowes, Robert, 135, 137.
Bushnell, Francis, 241.
  William, 362, 375.
Butler, William, 75, 482.
  Richard, 88, 192, 226, 332, 349, 482.
  Thomas, 292. John, 297.

Cable, (Cabell, Capell,)
  John, 54, 190, 198, 208, 231.
Calkin, Hugh, 243, 264, 338.
  John, 412.
Campfield, Math. 257, 274, 281, 300, 323, 332, 336, 398, 426.
Capell, (see Cable.)
Carpenter, 164. Jo."140.
Carr, Sir Robert, 439.
Carrington, John, 107, 115, 145, 463.
Carter, Joshua, 70, 92.
Cartwright, George, 439.
Carwithy, 143, (see Curwithee.)
Cattell, John, 102, 110, 457.
Chalkwell, Edward, 492.
Chancutt, Edw. 160.
Chapman, John, 43.
  Thomas, 219.
  Robert, 264, 349, 351, 362, 375, 397.
Chaplin, Clem. 6, 12, 39, 51, 97, 135, 136, 142.
Chappell, Geo. 8, 127, 130, 135, 137, 143, 165, 168, 180, 194.
Chatterton, Michael, 473.
Cheeny, William, 297.
Chesebrough, (Chessbrooke.)
  William, 200, 216, 235, 240.
  Samuel, 297.
Chester, Leo. 56, 75, 93, 117, 130, 141, 452.
  Mrs. 177, 193.
  John, 309, 315, 356, 359.
Chichester, 182 ; James, 428.
Church, 56 ; Richard, 272.
  John, 315 ; Sam. 297.
Churchill, Josias, 88, 190.
Cilburne, (Kilburne) John, 299.
Clarke, William, 41, 92, 344, 360, 365.

Henry, 46, 70, 112, 207, 321, 323.
Nicholas, 92, 169, 182, 401.
Thomas, 315.
Joseph, 315, 433.
John, 66, 221, 367, 241, 264, 426, 137, 389.
Daniel, 115, 143, 288, 291, 307, 309, 319, 373, 376, 383, 401, 404, 429, 435.
Clemens, Jasper, 351.
Clow, John, 256, 408.
Codman, Rob. 302.
Coe. (Coo) Rob. 2, 425, 428.
  John, 425, 426.
Coggen, John, 66, 67, 72.
Coker, Rich. 54, 172.
Coldecott, Rich. 141, 212.
Cole. John, 297, 327, 370.
  Henry, 193.
Colefoxe, Will. 130, 162, 172, 201.
Coleman, Thomas, 41, 44, 83, 111, 127, 140, 147, 259, 310.
  John, 193, 315, 457.
Coles, Susan, 124, 129, 135.
Collecott, Rich. 141, 212.
Coltman, John, 129.
Comstock, (Combstocke-)
  Will. 109, 114, 191.
  Samuel, 177, 182.
Concklin, 388 ; John, 388.
Cone, Daniel, 434.
Coaker, (see Coker.)
Cooke, John, 108.
  Aaron, 87, 148, 155, 242, 246, 309, 364, 367.
  Nathaniel, 207.
Cooly, Peter, 432.
Cooper, Thomas, 8, 142.
  John, 231, 276, 368.
Corbitt, Will. 159, 433, 446.
Cornelius, Law. 290.
Cornwell, Thomas, 29.
  William, 192.
Cory, 388.
Cosmore, John, 316, 566.
Cotton, John. 346, 359.
Craddock, Math. 43.
Crane, Benj. 315.
  Jasper, 437.
Cross, Will. 136, 192.
Crow, John, 41, 148.
  Christo. 315, (see Clow.)
Crowch, Simon, 432.
Crump, Thomas, 102, 122.
Cullick, John, 76, 172, 318, 327, 345, 357, 573.
  Elizabeth, 404, 585.
Curtis, Thomas. 298.
  John, 315.
Curwin, Jo. 388.
Curwithee, Caleb, 428.

Daniell, Stephen, 213.
Davis, Philip, 281.
  Steph. 141, 142, 315.
Dawes, John, 155.
Day, Stephen, 202, 279.
  Robert, 487.

Deming, (Dymon, Demon, Dement,) 81, 102, 109, 133, 164.
Thomas, 148, 183, 190, 202.
  John, 288, 297, 315, 349, 388,
Denison, Geo. 243, 258, 264. 299.
Denslow, John, 297.
  Henry, 115, 148, 155.
Dewey, Thomas, 81, 123, 168, 480.
Deynton, 63.
Dickenson, Nath. 76, 95, 115, 135, 182, 243, 264, 273.
Dickerson, Thomas, 297.
  Joseph, 298 ; Philemon, 388.
Disborough, Nicholas, 45.
Douglass, Will. 34, 392, 405.
Doyes, John, 241 ; (Dawes,)242.
Drake, John, 88, 134, 140, 167.
  Samuel, 142, 143.
  Job, 285, 380.
Dyblie, Thomas, 46.
Dyer, John, 218, 341.
Dyks, Leonard, 129.

Edmonds, John, 28, 171.
Edwards, John, 55, 56, 115, 137, 319.
  Will. 107, 115, 190, 193, 309, 315, 401, 405.
Thomas, 172, 190, 202, 417.
Eggleston, James, 137, 182, 297.
  Baggett (Begat) 127, 297.
  Thomas, 315 ; Samuel, 315.
Elderkin, John, 276, 285.
Eldridge. 75, 76, 89.
  Nathaniel, 95.
Ellis, James, 245.
Ellison, Laurence, 88.
Ellyt, (Ellit) 141, 144.
Elmore, Edw. 82, 122, 136.
Elsen (Elsing) John, 83, 110, 162.
  Abraham, 162, 202, 479.
Elseworth, Jos. 297.
Elton, 388.
Ely, Nath'l, 43, 83, 126, 183, 210, 336.
Ennoe, James, 420.
Evarts, James, 432.
Evans (Euens) 143.
  John, 55, 135.
Ewe, John, 103.

Fairchild, Thomas, 264, 299, 340, 419, 426.
Fellowes, Rich. 92, 112, 124, 135, 142, 145, 302, 309.
Fenn, Benj. 437, 440.
Fenner, Thomas, 477.
Fenwick, George ; See GENERAL INDEX.
Ferman, Rob. 428.
Ferris, Jeffery, 29, 43, 44.
  (Pheries) Peter, 391.
Filly, William, 297.
Finch, Daniel, 1, 4, 5, 6.
  Abraham, 315, 445.
Fishe, Ruth, 129.

INDEX OF NAMES. 593

Fishe, William, 144, 148.
Fitch, Samuel, 218, 261.
  (Rev.) James, 282, 312, 321.
  Thomas, 290, 297.
  Joseph, 380, 409.
Flecher, John, 452.
Foote, Nath'l, 10, 56, 87, 93, 109, 115, 461.
  (Widow) 115.
Foot, Robert, 298.
Ford, Thomas, 17, 60, 83, 148, 168, 247, 379, 383, 388, 405, 409.
Forret, James, 368.
Fossaker, 348.
Foster, John, 465.
Fowler, 68.
  (Ambrose) 147, 297.
Franklin, (Frauncklyn.)
  Will. 183, 191.
Froste, Will. 465.
  Daniel, and Abraham, 465.
Fuller, Elizabeth, 143.
Fyler, Walter, 55, 76, 109, 121, 135.

Gager, John, 317.
Gaines, Thomas ? 29.
Gaylord, Will. 44, 87, 89, 104, 112, 211 ; Walter, 299.
Galpin, Philip, 310, 342.
Gardner, Sam. 66, 130, 158, 193, 202.
Garritt, Daniel, 46, 261.
  (Garrad.) 436.
Gibbons, (Gibbins) Will. 42, 83, 110, 136, 140, 160.
Gibbs, John, 17 ; Jacob, 274.
  Gregory, 195, 203, 315, 504.
  George, 82 ; Giles, 504.
  Samuel, 297, 434, 504.
Gilbert, William, 46.
  Jona. 139, 252, 295, 309, 332, 343, 346, 372, 382, 401, 430.
  John. 295, 297, 306, 393, 423.
  Mathew, 437, 440.
Gildersleeve, Rich. 3, 5, 40, 51, 65, 428.
Gillett, Cornelius, 315.
  Jona. 204, 297, 326.
Gishop, Edward, 412.
Glover, 388.
Godding, George, 220.
Gold, (Gould) Nathan, 281, 294, 299, 342, 353.
Goodheart, Isbrand, 322.
Goodman, Rich. 88, 230, 252, 326.
Goodridge, (Goodrich) John, 97, 135, 147, 165.
  William, 281, 379.
Goodwin, William, 20, 39, 262, 297, 318, 362, 374.
  Nath'l, 389.
Grannis, Edward, 285.
Grant, Samuel, 256 ; Seth, 481.
  Math. 122, 162, 247.
Graves, Geo. 104, 122, 299, 318.
  John, 256, 297.
  Thomas, 134 ; Nathaniel, 297.

Grey, Henry, 125, 126, 127, 148, 174, 190, 209, 465.
  John, 465.
  Walter, 124, 256.
Green, John, 174, 391.
Greenhill, Thos. 356, 360, 362.
Gridley, Thomas, 33.
Griffin, John, 167, 317, 410.
  Robert, 253.
  Mathew, 128.
Griswold, (Gryssell) Math. 158, 161, 162, 205, 352, 404, 419.
  Edward, 196, 379, 380, 397, 398, 419.
  Francis, 196, 297.
  George, 196, 256.
  Michael, 344.
Groves, Philip 162, 242, 243, 257, 274, 281, 285, 349.
Growman, (Gruman) John, 432.
Grumwell, John, 315.
Gunn, Jasper, 172, 197, 298.
  Thomas, 102, 111, 129, 182.
Gybbert, Thomas, 82.
Gynings, John, 157.
  Nicholas, 160 ; Joshua, 147.
  (See Jennings.)

Hagborn, (Mr.) 430.
Hales, Sam. 92, 95, 136, 143.
Hall, John, 66, 332, 349.
  Sam. 257, Francis, 297.
  Ralph, 428.
Halls, John, 124, 165, 177.
Hallet, 186 ; James, 84, 110.
  William, 426, 428.
Halsey, 368.
Hamlin, 425.
Hanford, Thos. 257, 412.
Hampson, (Harnson) Ed. 115, 117.
Harbor, Benj. 281.
Hardey, Rich. 391.
Harris (–on) Rich. 110.
Harris, Daniel, 344.
Harrison, John, 297 ; Edw. 474.
  (Goodwife) 381.
Hart, Steph. 149, 243, 257.
  John, 257, 354.
  Thomas, 413.
Hartly, Rich. 315.
Harvey, Edward, 148, 149.
Hassard, Thomas, 148.
Haughton, Rich. 309.
  Morton, 382.
Hawkens, Zach. 428.
Hawkes, John, 167, 176, 204.
Haynes, John ; See GENERAL INDEX.
  (Col.) Hez. 248.
  Jos. 380, 383, 404.
  John, 292.
Hayward, Rob. 184, 191, 205.
Herriman, Augustine, 219.
Hews, Jon. 407.
Hewyt, (Hewitt) 133, 141.
Heyton, Wm. 92, 137, 154, 204, 309, 432.
Hicks, John, 424, 425, 428.
Higby, Ed. 163, 181, 184, 193.

Hill, Will. 181, 241, 243, 332, 353, 366, 442.
Hilliar, Benj. 172, 173, 177.
Hitchcock, Luke, 140, 160.
Hoite, (see Hoyt.)
Holbridge, James, 373.
  Mercy, 373.
Holcombe, Thomas, 196.
Holibut, Thos. 93, 114, 189.
  (See Hurlbut.)
Hollister, (Ollister) 81, 115, 141, 264, 288, 330, 342, 359.
  (Mrs.) 174, 195.
Holt, Mary, 28, 29.
Hooker, Thomas, 498.
Hopkins, Edw. See GENERAL INDEX.
  William, 53, 71.
  John, 49, 92 ; Steph. 292.
Hornett, Edw. 428.
Horskins, Thos. 215, 484.
  John, 483.
Hoskins, Anthony, 256.
Hosford, William, 44.
  John, 231, 309.
Horton, Barnabas, 388, 402, 428.
  Jos. 388, Caleb, 427.
  Benj. 427.
Hosmer, (Osmore) Thomas, 70, 76, 107, 123, 124, 142, 177, 193.
Hought, William, 297.
Houghton, William, 202.
Howard, Robert, 88, 107, 129.
Howell, Edward, 149, 566.
  John, 428.
Howkins, Anth. 349, 351, 376, 379, 401, 419, 426, 440.
Hoyette, Simon, 49.
Hoyt, John, 220, 433.
  Walter, 336,
Hubbard, Geo. 2, 5, 7, 17, 20, 39, 42, 57, 182, 257.
  William, 89.
  Thomas, 157, 297.
  John, 274 ; James, 429.
Hubbell, Rich. 433.
Hudshon, John, 202.
Huested, Rob. 412.
Huit, Eph. 46, 70, 76, 91, 109, 115, 458.
Humphreys, Mich. 297, 420.
Hull, Geo. 20, 44, 198, 226, 249, 257.
  Jos. 127, 349, 419.
  Corn. 276.
Hullett, Jas. 82.
Hungerford, Thos. 110.
Hunt, Thos. 412 ; Blaynch, 457.
Huntington, Chris. 219, 315.
  Thos. 297 ; Simon, 412.
Hurd, Jo. 112.
  John, 187, 208, 308.
Hurlbut, Thos. 81, 82, 102, 136, 129, 388 ; Will. 180.
Hutchinson, (Widow) 76, 81, 83, 88.
  Edw. 409, 407 ; Thos. 427.

Ireland, Samuel, 33, 137.

INDEX OF NAMES.

Jackson, 348.
Jacob, Peter, 155, 160.
Jecoxe, 158.
Jener, John, 341, 428.
Jennings, Nich. 160.
  Josh. 171, 193, 213.
  John, 157, 171, 203.
Jessop, John, 12, 425, 426.
Johnson, Thos. 49, 55, 453.
  Mary, 143 ; Peter, 226.
  Elizabeth, 209.
  (Goodwife) 222, 232.
Jonson, Mary, 171.
Jones, (Rev.) 316.
  Jeffery, 427 ; Tho's. 428.
  William, 437, 440.
Judd, William, 281.
  Tho's. 319, 376, 379, 413, 425.
  John, 413, 425.
Judson, 144 ; Will. 112.
  Jer. 315.
  Joseph, 315, 340, 367, 475.

Keeler, 160 ; Ralph, 176.
Kelley, John, 315.
Kellock, Nath. 180.
  Jos. 257 ; Daniel, 433.
Kellodg, Jos. 257.
Kelsey, Will. 314.
  John, 315.
Keney, Will. 297, 315.
  (See Cheeny.)
Kerby, 157 ; John, 182, 315.
Ketchrell, 160.
Ketchum, John, 390, 428.
  Samuel, 428.
Ketling, Tho. 109.
Kilburne, (Widow) 156, 445.
  John, 299, 354, 379.
King, Will. 273.
Kircum, (Kirkman) 145,163.
Kitwell, Sam. 29.
Knowles, Alex. 257, 264, 310.
  Jos. 315 ; John, 432.

Latham, Cary, 185, 191, 392, 405.
Lathrop, Samuel, 186.
Latimore, John, 29, 110, 141, 180, 237, 309, 388.
Lay, Rob. 297, 353.
  Edw. 302.
Lawes, Rich. 20, 43, 437, 440.
Lee, 142 ; Edw. 167.
  Walter, 256.
Leete, Will. 437, 440.
Leffingwell, Tho. 205, 384.
Leonard, Tho. 315.
Lerreby, Greenfill, 213.
Letten, (Lattin.) 156, 243, 278.
  (Goodwife) 366, 403.
Leverett, John, 259.
Lewis, 137 ; Will. 43, 66, 96, 187, 227, 300, 327.
  Walter, 174, 177, 191, 193.
Line, Gabriel, 281.
Lobdell, Symon, 297, 360.
Lockman, Gouv. 184, 198, 199.
Lockwood, Rob. 231, 299.
  Jos. 432.

Loockuet, Rob. 299.
Lomes, Sam. 257.
Longdon, Andrew, 92.
Longdon, Anth. 160.
Loomis, (see Lummis.)
  John, 180.
Lord, Rich. 17, 33, 43, 55, 72, 94, 123, 146, 309, 315, 377, 434.
  John, 140, 161, 171, 224.
  Tho. 167, 234, 359.
  (Mrs. Dorothy,) 402.
  Sarah, 162.
Lotham, William, 473.
Lovenam, (Widow.) 193.
Lummis, Jos. 81, 110, 256.
  Thomas, 256, 309.
  Nathaniel, 256, 309.
Ludlow, Henry, 428.
  Roger ; See GENERAL INDEX.
Lupton, Tho. 433.
Lyman, Rich. 33, 81, 114, 442.
  John, 81 ; Rob 81, 443.
Lyon, Rich, 183, 433.

Maggott; (see Mygatt.)
Mapes, (Goodman,) 388.
Marsh, John, 180.
Marshall, Sam. 256, 289, 309, 396, 409 ; Ann, 28.
Marshfield, Tho. 76, 82, 87, 107, 115, 137.
Martyn, Sam. 140, 147, 180, 202.
Marvin, Math. 43, 111, 181, 334, 433.
  Renold, 315, 354, 367, 375, 397, 404.
Mason, Capt. John ; See GENERAL INDEX.
  Edward, 43, 57.
Mastens, 160.
Maynard, John, 139.
Mayo, Samuel, 253, 254.
Mead, Jos. 391.
Meaks, Rich. 163.
Meggs, John, 405.
Mercer, Timothy, 193.
Merricke, Thomas, 17.
Merrills, Jo. 315.
Mills, Rich. 109, 110, 114, 115, 412 ; Sam. 412.
Minor, Thomas, 186, 187, 265, 405, 411, 419, 435.
  John, 265.
Minott, (Minor) Tho's. 186.
Mitchell, Math. 6, 40, 48, 51, 55.
Moody, John, 29, 33, 81.
  Samuel, 297.
Moore, Thomas, 28, 388, 427.
  John, 366, 376, 379, 397.
More, Thomas, 46, 386.
  John, 46, 76, 112.
  Isaac, 137, 440.
  Miles, 406.
Morehouse, Samuel, 433.
  Thomas, 433.
Morgan, Jas. 300, 338, 366.
Morton, Will. 315.
Moses, John, 160, 164, 309, 492.

Mudge, Jarvis, 102, 115, 143, 165, 202.
Mulford, (John,) 428.
Munson, Thomas, 66.
Mygat, (Magott,) Jos. 87, 104, 283.
  Jacob, 309, 344, 351.

Nash, Edw. 433 ; Jos. 315.
Neuie, (Nenie ?) 143.
Newbery, Thomas, 44.
  Benj. 160, 183, 191, 397, 419, 440 ; Jos. 147.
Newton, Tho. 144, 150, 155, 172, 190, 192.
Nicholls, (Sergt.) 36.
Nicholls, (Col Rich.) 440.
Noble, William, 428.
North, 140.
  John, 297 ; Sarah, 362.
Northam, James, 45, 165, 167, 176, 315.
Northum, (Norton ?) Jas. 110, 130.
Norton, James, 49, 109.
  Francis, 41, 44, 97, 86, 160.
  John, 297, 412, 425.
Nott, John, 55, 182, 299, 381, 414, 415.
Nowell, Thomas, 506.
  Christopher, 506.

Odill, John, 433.
Ogden, 280, 282, 295, 316.
Olcott, (Thomas,) 83, 92, 96, 158, 162, 183, 315.
  Samuel, 425.
Oldham, (John,) 3–6, 12, 43, 91.
Oldridge, Rich. 127.
Oldige, 148.
Olderige, 285.
  James, 446.
Olmsted, Nich. 50, 226, 309, 446.
  Nehe. 183, 204, 299, 447.
  Rich. 210, 242, 285, 336, 349, 367, 391, 447.
  John, 45, 285, 389, 447.
Omphries, Mich. 297.
Orton, Thomas, 95, 110, 204.
Orvis, George, 315.
Osmore, (see Hosmer.)
Oulsterman, 231.

Packer, John, 293, 432.
Packs ? Henry, 56.
Paine, Jo. 386, 388.
Palmer, Will. 81, 89, 348, 464.
  John, 297, 309.
  Henry, 297, 464.
  Nich. 330, 366, 467.
Palmes, Edw. 371, 373, 419, 426.
Pantry, Will. 93, 107, 123.
  John, 207.
Parker, Will. 354.
  Ralph, 315, 430.
Parke, (Parks) 46, 55, 84, 127, 135, 180, 412.

INDEX OF NAMES. 595

Parkman, (Putman) Elias, 14, 16, 46, 81, 144, 166, 167.
Parsons, Rich. 46.
Partridge, Will. 325.
Patten, Nathaniel, 87.
Peerce, John, 45.
Pell, Tho. 366, 389, 418.
Pering, Henry, 428.
Perkins, John, 142.
Perwidge, Will. 102, 107, 110.
Pettibone, John, 315.
Pheax, 186.
Phelps, Geo. 28, 134, 309, (see Phillips.)
  Will. 1, 32, 54, 145, 419.
  Timo. 411, 425 ; Jos. 256.
Pheries, (Ferris) Peter, 391.
Phillips, Will. 117, 241.
  Geo. 178, 278, 309.
  Zerub. 426.
Piddell, Corbitt, 193.
Pierce, Tho. 366.
  John, 45.
Pincheon, Wm. 10, 13, 16, 18, 19, 20, 43.
Pinney, Humph. 126, 143.
  Samuel, 315.
Pinckney, Philip, 220.
Pitkin, Wm. 388, 389, 426, 436.
Platt, Isaac, 428.
Plum, Jo. 3, 13, 18, 41, 44, 56, 69, 97, 121.
Pomrey, Eltweed, (Eldad) 27, 104, 227, 315, 354, 362, 370.
Pond, Samuel, 191.
Ponton, Rich. 406, 412.
Porter, John, 28, 43, 75, 191, 309, 475.
  Daniel, 123, 127, 377.
  Thomas, 257, 491.
Post, Stephen, 206, 241.
  John, and Thomas, 412.
Powell, Tho. 428.
Pratt, John, 93, 108, 135, 219, 230, 292, 450 ; Wm. 375.
  Daniel, 292, 309.
Prentice, John, 433.
Preston (Presson) 102, 109, 133.
Provost, David. 155, 163.
Prudden, Mr. 36.
Purdy, 466.
Purkas, John, 466.
Purrier, 388.
Putnam, (see Parkman.)
Pyne, James, 150, 158.

Quicke, William, 6.
Quinby, John, 412.

Randal, Abraham, 326.
Rayner, (Reyner) Thurston, 3, 13, 17, 428 ; Jos. 426, 388.
Read, 144.
Reeves, Jo. 6.
Reive, Rob. 309, 315, 360.
Rescue, (Rusco) Nath. 222, 232, 256, 352.
  Will. 70, 110, 161, 204, 209.
Reynolds, (Renols) Robert, 2.
  John, 142, 412.

Rice, Robert, 285.
  Jonathan, 412.
Mihell, 406.
Richards, James, 429, 435.
  Samuel, 315 ; Nath. 92, 144.
Rigebell, Mr. 390.
  (Rickbell,) 428.
Rily, John, 182.
Rissly, Richard, 127, 486.
  Samuel, 487.
Robins, John, 88, 93, 95, 109, 129, 141, 356.
  Mary, 457, 463.
Robinson, Thos. 54.
Rocester, 48, 49, 55, 81, 83 ; (see Rossiter.)
Rockwell, John, 195.
  Samuel, 297, 483.
Rogers, Jas. 340, 352, 359, 385, 392, 409 ; Sam. 406.
  John, and Jona. 428.
Root, John, 297, 413.
Rose, Rob. 42, 43, 60, 97, 109.
Rossiter, Bray, 76, 81, 83, 88, 102, 177, 353, 359, 396.
Rowlins, Jasper, 56, 82.
Rudd, Jona. 45, 127, 218, 219, 238, 285.
Rugge, Robert, 141.
Rushmore, Tho. 195, 424.
Rusco ; (see Rescue.)
Russell, Henry, 288, 319, 330, 342, 415.
  John, 173, 207, 274.
Rysly, 127.

Sable, John, 202, 315.
Sadler, John, 93, 108, 160, 168, 201.
Salter, Walter, 423.
Saltington, } Robert, 62, 66, 67,
Saltingstall, } 70, 72.
Samwis, Rich. 190, 202.
  John, 428.
Sanford, Andrew, 297.
  Zachary, 219, 315.
Savidge, John, 257.
Sawyer, Richard, 169, 485.
Scippeseyer, 155.
Scott, Thomas, 18, 42, 70, 103, 453.
  Edmund, 202.
  John, 418, 420, 424, 430, 436, 441.¶
Scudder, Thomas, 428.
Seager, Rich. 297.
Sebadoe, (Capt.) 242.
Sedgewick, (Maj.) Rob. 259.
Seely, Robert, 4, 5, 9, 10, 43, 49, 391, 401, 403, 406.
  Nath. 297.
Seldon, Thomas, 46, 190.
Senthion, (Sension) Nich. 55, 294, 492.
  Mathew, 95, 114 ; Mark, 433.
Shepherd, John, 360.
Sherman, Jo. 2, 49, 463.
  Sam. 425, 426, 436.
Sherwood, Tho. 126, 150, 155, 264, 432.

Sherwood, Stev. and Mark, 433.
Shorye, Sampson, 202.
Sipperance, Joan, 193, 203.
Skidmore, Thomas, 193, 202.
Skinner, Rich. 177.
Slye, Robert, 182.
Smith, Arthur, 62, 92, 136, 183.
  Edward, 89, 93, 96.
  Henry, 86, 90, 97, 98, 106, 143, 502.
  Simon, 141, 142.
  Samuel, 54, 106, 155, 191, 200, 206, 285, 292, 314, 503.
  William, 114, 128.
  Philip, 256 ; Jonathan, 297.
  Joseph, 298, 375.
  Quince, 355.
  John, 332, 347, 349, 352, 400, Rich. 164, 315, 319, 407.
Southmead, 127.
Spencer, Obed, 315.
  William, 449 ; Samuel, 450.
  Thomas, 81, 315.
  Jared, 361.
Speck, Jared, 467.
Stadder, 135, 140 ; see Stodder.
Stanborough, Jos. 348, 368.
Stanley, Timothy, 69, 489.
  Tho. 87, 212.
  John, 326 ; Caleb, 491.
Stanton, Tho. 108, 193, 300, 435. See GENERAL INDEX.
Staples, Tho. 127, 220, 265.
Stares, (Serg't) 17 ; Tho. 458.
Starke, Aaron, 28, 55, 84.
Stebbing, Edw. 18, 43, 47, 112, 121, 135, 250, 259, 321, 362, 413.
Stebbins, 352, 360, 365.
Stedman, John, 256, 285, 309.
Steele, John, 48, 134, 148, 180, 227.
  George, 75, 87, 107, 159.
  James, 309, 372.
  Samuel, 180.
Stephenson, Thomas, 144, 285.
Stickland, Jo. 2, 6.
Stocking, 348.
  Samuel, 256 ; George, 318.
Stoder, Jo. 81, 83.
Stone, Samuel, 20, 39, 317, 356, 413.
Stoughton, Thomas, 7, 48.
Stow, Mr. 356, 361, 362.
Strong, John, 218.
  Thomas, 309.
Styles, Henry, 1, 2.
  John, 108, 195.
  Francis, 3, 6, 8, 33, 62, 70, 76, 83, 86, 91, 107, 141, 149.
Sutton, Jos. 315.

Talcott, John, 9, 75, 210, 231, 251, 353, 373, 375, 383, 384, 404, 406.
  Samuel, 389.
Tallman, Peter, 231.
Tarpe, Mr. 68.
Tapping, Thomas, 29, 30, 218, 316, 368, 414.

INDEX OF NAMES.

Taylor, John, 106, 108.
  Steph. 190, 356, 365.
Terry, Steph. 18, 93, 136, 309.
  Thomas, and Rich. 388.
Theed, Jos. 391.
Teed, John, 428.
Tharpe, 127.
Thomson, Wm. 359, 432.
Thornton, 56.
  Thos. 83, 138, 221, 243, 475.
Tillton, Peter, 182.
Tinker, John, 82, 114, 347, 352, 359, 366, 382, 417.
Titterton, Daniel, 148, 187, 208.
Titus, Samuel, 428.
Tompson, John, 412.
Torrey, William, 88.
Toung, (Tong) George, 285, 292, 352, 365, 397.
Tracy, Thomas, 106, 115, 206, 238, 241, 366, 393, 397.
Traull, Will. 164; Tim. 315.
Treat, Jas. and Math. 297.
  Robert, 440; Rich. 309, 310.
  (Trott) Rich. 75, 76, 80, 88, 93, 112, 123, 135, 237.
  Elias, 136; John, 76.
  Math. 143, 171, 177.
Trumble, John, 162.
Try, (Tray) Mich. 46, 348.
Tucker, (Tooker) 386, 388.
Tuckye, George, 127.
Tuder, Owyn, 193.
Turner, Daniel, 194.
Turny, Robert, 432.

Uffoote, (Ufford) Tho. 95, 110.
Underhill, John, 275, 341.
Upson, 29, 157.
Usher, Rob. 389, 405.

Vandict, Gisberd, 184.
Vantino, Cornelius, 184.
Varleet, (Varleth) 322, 352, 355, 371-6, 387.
Vayle, Jer. 388.
Venison, (Vincent?) Wm. 162.
Ventris, Moses, 218.
  Will. 257, 298.
Vere, Edw. 129, 145, 463.
  (Veare,) 50, 81.
Vincent, Wm. 162, 169, 172, 182.
Vore, Richard, 348.
Vowles, Rich. 388, 389, 413.

Wade, Robert, 46, 301.
Wadom, John, 315.
Wadsworth, Wm. 12, 55, 288, 349, 379.
Wakely, (Whately) James, 180, 238, 279, 401; (see Whately.)
  Richard 297.
Walkely, Henry, 401.
Wakeman, Sam. 1, 2, 3, 7, 135.

Waller, Wm. 231, 241, 312, 354, 375, 404, 411, 419.
Walston, Thomas, 115.
Waples, Thomas, 117.
Ward, Andr. 2, 12, 226. 243, 264, 284, 323.
  Joyce, 451.
  Nath'l, 18, 60. 93, 112, 125, 147, 165, 314, 321.
  William, 297, 451.
  Anthony, Robert, John, and Edward, 451.
Warham, (Rev.) John, 288, 420.
Warin, William, 315.
Warner, Andr. 14, 43, 60, 309.
  Robert, 297.
  John, 413.
Waterhouse, Jacob, 40, 95, 300.
Waters, Anthony, 424.
Watson, Nathaniel, 162.
  John, 114.
Watts, 127; Thomas, 108.
  Ellinor, 142; Rich. 142.
Waynewright, Thomas, 88.
Webb, Henry, 82, 87.
  John, 176.
  Rich. 93, 110, 144, 203, 391.
Webster, Math. 124.
  Robert, 258, 264, 288, 289.
  John, 9, 27, 36, 49, 263, 273, 280, 318.
Weed, Jonas, 2.
Welman, William, 315.
Welles, Jo. 124; Edw. 107.
  Hugh, 243; Thomas, 309, 346, 359; John, 310, 323.
  Samuel, 297, 311, 356.
West, John, 182, 419.
Westall, John, 87, 135, 332, 418, 433.
Westcoat, Rich. 40, 41, 44, 111.
  William, 41.
Westly, William, 139.
Westover, Jonas, 191. 195, 315.
Westwood, Will. 18, 252.
Whately, (see Wakely.)
  James, 109, 110, 111, 115, 145.
Wheeler, Isaac ; (see Wylly.)
  Ephraim, 112, 466.
  Moses, 163 ; Thos. 243.
Whisson, Henry, 428.
White, John, 83, 93, 108, 145, 250, 298, 360.
  Philip, 155 ; Nath. 379.
Whitehead, Robert, 55.
Whiting, Will. 10, 18, 55, 62, 116, 131, 133, 493.
  (Mrs.) 165 ; Giles, 99.
  John, 262, 493.
Whitman, Jos. 428.
Whitmore, John, 44, 197.
  Thomas, 231, 264.
Wiate, John, 315.
Wichfield, 56, 89.

Wicks, Thomas, 390.
Wickum, Thomas, 315.
Wilcoxson, William, 148, 149.
Wilkenson, Thomas, 194.
Wilkins, William, 429.
Wellard, (Willard) Jos. 372.
Willcock, John, 126, 148, 172, 180, 249.
Williams, John, 28, 309.
  Roger, 43, 76, 87, 106.
  Arthur, 46, 95, 176.
  Math. 129, 135, 143, 168, 433.
  Will. 140, 202, 256, 315, 428.
  Amos, 396 ; (Mrs.) 381.
Willis, George, 27, 52, 64, 68, 71, 136, 469.
  Sam. 251, 377, 383, 404, 415, 469.
Willet, Nath. 88, 89, 122, 135, 137, 318.
Wilson, Anthony, 84.
  Thomas, 433 ; Rob. 506.
Wilterton, Grego. 55, 183, 327, 360.
Wilton, David, 102, 107, 115, 147, 164, 174, 309.
  Nicholas, 256.
Winchell, (see Wynchell.)
Windes, 388.
Wines, Barnabas, 427.
Winthrop, John ; See GENERAL INDEX.
Wolcott, Henry, 1, 12, 18, 55, 56, 76, 81, 88, 89, 102, 125, 184, 193, 349.
  George, 55, 297.
  Simon, 256, 309.
Wood, Jonas, 172, 174, 190, 192, 275, 281, 283, 379, 380, 401, 428.
  Samuel, 428.
Woodcocke, John, 33, 34, 66.
Woodford, Tho. 112, 241.
  Joseph, 412.
Woodhull, Rich. 341, 366, 428.
Woodroofe, Nath. 88, 298.
  John, 413
Woods, John, 29.
Workes, Thomas, 428.
Wright, Samuel, 298.
  Anth. 309.
  Thomas, 92, 147, 177, 256, 319.
  James, 256.
Wrothem, Simon, 257.
Wylly, (Wheeler) Isaac, 185.
Wynchell, Rob. 109, 141.
  Nath. 297.

Yeates, Fra's and Geo. 315.
Yeosen, Simon, 239.
Young, Mathew, 316.
  John, 386, 390, 402, 406, 419.
Youngs, Joseph, 388.

GENERAL INDEX.

Adamites; see Quakers.
Address to the King; see Charter.
Adultery; how punished, 77.
Administration; see Estates.
Agawam, 12, 13, 14, 19; see Springfield.
Alarms; impressment of men, arms, &c. authorized, in case of, 94.
Allegiance, oath of, to be taken, 439.
Ammunition; see Military Stores.
Apparel, excess in, prohibited, 64.
Appeals, from inferior courts, regulated. 37, 118, 186, 395.
Appraisal of property attached, 349, 525.
Apprentices, orders concerning, 8, 105, 349, 222, 316, 538.
Armour; provision and survey of, 15, 17, 30.
Aramamett, complains of Lt. Holmes, 16.
Artillery; see Military.
Ashford; see Setauket.
Assistants; appointment of, at Pequot, 186; to join with magistrates, on the seaside, 227, 233; appointed for several towns, 281, 351, 352, 365, 381, 435; powers of, 324, 336, 350, 374, 394, 397; Gen. Court to appoint, 365.
Attorney for the Gen. Court, 388, 426.
Auditors of treasurer's accounts appointed, 30.

Ballast, orders respecting, 273, 512.
Banishment, sentence of, 242, 324.
Bankside, inhabitants admitted at, 310.
Baptism of children; advice to the churches respecting, 438.
Bay; see Massachusetts.
Beaver; duty on, 20; trade with Indians for, prohibited, 20; order respecting, 161.
Beef cattle, number of killed in Fairfield, 221.
Bestiality, how punished, 77.
Bible, sent to goodwife Williams, 381; given to Amos Williams, 396.
Births, to be recorded, 106, 551.
Blasphemy, how punished, 77.
Boundary of the Colony; committee appointed to ascertain and settle, 435.
Brands; see Cattle.
Breach of Promise; law against, proposed, 80.
Bride brook; a bound of Pequot, 221.
Bridges, to be built, at Hoccanum, 417; at Farmington, 164.

Cannon to be provided, 70; loaned by Mr. Saltingstall, 72; carriages to be made for, 74; to be purchased, for public use, 104.
Capital Laws, 77, 515.

Casks; size of, regulated, 264, 515.
Cassasinamon; see Robin.
Cattle, to be restrained, 60, 517; to be marked, 118, 517.
Caveat may be entered, when, 151, 153, 518.
Charter, measures for procuring, 360, 367, 368–370; instructions to Gov. Winthrop, &c. 579; received and publicly read, 384; committee entrusted with custody of, 384, 407; payment of rate for, 385, 390, 392, 397, 400, 415; not to be sent to New Haven, 405; thanks to Gov. W. for procuring, 416.
Children, stubborn, how punished, 78, 515.
Chippachauge Island, granted to Capt. Mason, 224.
Church; see Ecclesiastical Affairs.
Cider; orders respecting sale of, 331, 354.
Clerks of train bands; appointment and duties of, 73, 75, 97, 282.
Code of 1650; Mr. Ludlow desired to prepare, 138, 154; when adopted, 216, 509; recorded, 509.
Collectors of rates; duties of, 12, 113, 550.
Combination; see United Colonies.
    with Southampton, 566; with Easthampton, 316, 572; with New Haven; see Union.
Commissioners, of U. Colonies; first appointment of, 90; to meet yearly, 157; see United Colonies.
    for the plantations, 53; powers of, 408; on L. Island, powers of, 402.
Common lands; orders concerning, 100, 108. 118, 214, 517.
Communion; respecting the subjects of, 438.
Composition, for Saybrook; see Saybrook.
Conscience; liberty of, to be secured, 439.
Constitution of 1639, 20; amendments of, 96, 119, 140, 150, 346, 347.
Contempt of Court, punished, 44, 155.
    of ordinances, 80. 524.
Contracts; see Debts.
    of marriage, 47, 48, 540.
Conveyances, of land, to be in writing, &c. 358. See Deeds, and Records.
Corn, price of, established. 11, 18, 61, 79, 100, 116, 118, 205, 563; trade with Indians for, prohibited, 11, 13, 68, 81; plantations, how to be supplied with, 13, 16, 18, 19; to be received in payment of debts, 69, 72; orders respecting exportation of, 116, 258, 379, 383, 392; not to be distilled, 333; measure of, regulated, 104.
Corselets, to be provided by the towns, 14, 546,

GENERAL INDEX.

Costs, when allowed, and by whom payable, 37, 55, 113.
Cotton; trade therein proposed and encouraged, 59, 75.
Council, constituted, and its powers, 397; repeal of order erecting 440;
Ecclesiastical; see Ecclesiastical Affairs.
Court, General, times of holding, 16, 21; how constituted, 150; how called, 256.
of Election, in April, 21; in May, 140; to be held at Hartford, 385.
Particular; times of holding, 71, 81, 231; how constituted, 119, 150.
Cromwell's Bay; see Setauket.
Cupheag; tribute from Indians there, 52; orders respecting bounds of, 53, 62; commissioner appointed. 53; see Stratford.
Customs; see Duties.

Damages, may be varied by the Court, 118; double, when to be paid, 19.
Deaths, sudden; inquests on, 42, 523.
Debts; committee appointed to examine the public debts, 228; in the several towns, 273; notice to be given of, 383.
remedy of creditor against debtor, 151, 349, 511, 518; debts payable in corn, 61.
Deeds, how to be executed and recorded, 37, 552.
Delinquents, to pay cost of prosecution, 113; fee to prison keeper, 138; appealing, after conviction, to be fined, 395; execution upon, how performed, 103, 525.
Deputies, to General Court; to be sent by the towns, 22, 23, 403; number of, 23, 372; exempt from training &c. 62, 350, 355; their powers, 24; vacancies, how filled, 51.
Dice; see Gaming.
Disability, consequent on conviction of scandalous offences, 138, 389.
Distillation of corn &c. prohibited, 333.
Divorces granted; to —— Beckwith, 275; Robert Wade, 301; Sarah North, 362; Bridget Baxter, 379.
Dollars, (rix) value of, 86.
Dorchester, bounds of, 2; named *Windsor*, 7; see Windsor.
Drunkenness, how punished, 333, 533.
Dutch; letters to be sent to Dutch Governor, 52, 75, 346; settlement of differences with, to be agitated, 68; cattle of, impounded, 51; liable for trespasses of their swine, 83; arms, &c. not to be sold to, 114; prohibited from trading with Indians, 197; prosecuted for such trade, 163, 198; House the Hope sequestered, 254, 275; repeal of orders restricting trade with, 261; proposed expedition against, 241, 244, 259; vessel seized at Saybrook, 219; at Fairfield, 231; the charter to be shown to Capt. Varlet, 387; committee to treat with, 410; other orders relating to, 346, 402, 405, 411, 413, 415; controversy respecting L. Island, 410, 413, 416; letter from Sir W. Boswell, relating to, 565.
Duties; on beaver, 20, 31; on drawing of wine, 146; custom masters appointed, 332; their duties, 332, 383, 396; wines &c. to pay duties, 255, 332, 395; tobacco, 380; repeal of acts imposing, 391.

East Hampton; articles of combination with,

approved, 96; accepted under jurisdiction, 200; letter to be sent to, 274, 572; power of magistrates there, 336; of commissioners, 402; bounds with Southampton stated, 368; letter to, 436.
Ecclesiastical Affairs:
formation of church at *Watertown*, approved, 2; Mr. Allyn's complaint against ch. at Hartford, 106, 111; orders respecting maintenance of ministers, 111, 112, 545; difficulties in church at *Hartford*, 288, 290, 312, 314, 317, 318, 320–333, 339, 343; at *Wethersfield*, 87, 90, 97, 330, 338, 342, 363; petition of Mr. Russell, 319; committee to present complaints to the other colonies, 281; council at Boston, 288; answers from Massachusetts, to be submitted to the churches, 302; churches not to be formed without consent of Gen. Court, 311; petition from *Windsor*, 312; church at *Middletown* and Mr. Stow, 356, 361, 362, 440; ministry at *Southold*, 387; at *Guilford*, 387; ch. at *Stratford* and John Tompson, 412; complaint from ch. at *Windsor*, 420; recommendations of Gen. Court, respecting half-covenant privileges &c., 438.
Education; contributions to support of scholars at Cambridge, 112, 139; to fellowship at the college, 250; schools to be established in each plantation, 554; children to be instructed, 520.
Election, Court of; see Court.
of deputies, who to vote in, 21, 96, 417; how determined, 24.
of governor &c. when and how made, 21, 22.
alteration of law respecting, 346, 347.
warrants for, issue and return of, 23, 24.
Estates, orders respecting settlement of, 3, 5, 38, 42, 179.
administration, where to be granted, 179; distribution of, to be attended, 309;
testate; see Wills and Inventories.
intestate; of Sam. Allen, 505; John Brundish, 40, 45, 444; John Cattell, 110, 457; Jos. Clark, 433; Tho. Crumpe, 122; Tho. Dewey, 168, 480; Abr. Elsen, 163, 202, 479; John Elsen, 162, 480; Tho. Fenner, 477; Abr. Finch, 445; Sam. Fitch, 336; Nath. Foote, 115, 461; Seth Grant, 481; Tho. Greenhill, 356, 360; Edw. Harrison, 474; Blaynch Hunt, 457; Samuel Ireland, 136, 468; Thomas Johnson, 49, 55, 453; William Lotham, 473; Edward Mason, 57; Thomas Newbery, 44; John Oldham, 3, 5, 91; Rich. Rissly, 486; Mr. Robins, 356; Rich. Sawyer, 169, 485; Timo. Standly, 489; Mr. Stoughton, 83; Sam. Wakeman, 135; Tho. Welles, 346, 359, 395, 396; Goodwife Williams, 396, 433.
Evidence, orders respecting the introduction of, 232, 337.
Executions; how served, 115, 117, 540; fees for levying, 146, 398; appraisal of goods taken, 273, 525; sales by officer, 273.

Fairfield; excepts against order relating to juries, 138; orders respecting lands there, 163, 187; bounds with Norwalk to be laid out &c. 414, 418; grant of land on Sagatuck River to, 208; Dutch vessel seized there, 231; difference with Norwalk. 242; constables, fined for neglect, 278; deposition respecting land a.

GENERAL INDEX. 599

the neck, 298; petition of inhabitants, referred, 310; provision for maintenance of Mr. Jones, approved, 316; boundary with Stratford, 367, 402; enlistment of troop, 351; bounds with Norwalk, 414, 418.
See Pequannoc; and Golden Hill.
Fairs, twice a year, at Hartford. 125.
False witness, how punished, 77.
Farmington, named and bounded, 133; Mr. Steel appointed recorder, 134; bounds, 376;
Indians; hostilities of, 294, 299, 303, 318; payment required of, 343.
see Tunxis.
Fast days, appointed, 98, 99, 170, 206, 228, 251, 263, 293, 323, 339, 364, 424.
may be appointed by magistrates, in recess, 277.
Fees, of jurors, 9; of Secretary and Registers, for recording, 37, 106. 151, 196, 277; on entry of actions, 39, 277; for copies of laws, 39, 331; on licenses, 333; on attachments &c. 100, 277; for warrants, 105, 277; of prison keepers, 138, 277; of leather sealers, 287, 377; of pound keepers, 292; of packers, 347, 391; of custom masters, 332; of marshall, 398; of courts, in civil actions, 399; on entry of petitions, 381.
Fences; orders respecting, 101, 105, 381, 516, 518; on east side of the river, 417.
Fence viewers, to be chosen, 381.
Fenwick, George; committee to confer with, 30; his reply, respecting union, bounds &c., 31; nom. for magistrate, 36; invited to join the plantations, 82; comm'r to U. Colonies, 90; payment to, for repairs of fort, 95; agreement with for purchase of Saybrook, 113, 119, 170, 178, 215, 258, 266, 280, 345, 568; letters to be sent to, 248; grant to Saybrook, from, 282; will of, 341, 574; final settlement with heirs of. 318, 325, 327, 362, 573.
Ferry; at Niantecut, granted to Gov. Winthrop, 357. See *Windsor* and *Saybrook*.
Fidelity, oath of, by whom to be taken, 139.
Fisheries; on Long Island, agreement with Mr. Fenwick concerning, 68; whale, exclusive right for, granted Mr. Whiting, 154.
Fisher's Island; grant, to Gov. Winthrop, 64.
Flax; raising of, enjoined, 61, 64.
Flushing; deputy sent from, 426; comm'r appointed, 428; freemed admitted, 430.
Foreigners, not to retail goods in the colony, 207; sale of arms &c. to, prohibited, 139, 145.
Fort, at Saybrook; see Saybrook.
Fort rate; receipts for, 325–7; orders respecting, 170, 178, 204, 221, 280, 345.
Freemen; oath of, 62; qualifications of, 21, 23, 96, 290, 331, 389, 439; to be nominated at October court, 331, 389; how disfranchised, 138, 389; to be admitted by the Gen. Assembly, 418.
French; sale of guns, &c. to, prohibited, 130; trade with Indians by, prohibited, 197.
Fundamental Orders; see Constitution.

Gaming, prohibited, 289, 527.
General Court; see Court, General.
Golden Hill, set off to Paquannack Indians, 336.
Goodwin, William, trustee of Mr. Hopkins' legacy; letters from, 374, 578.

Governor; how elected, 21; oath of, 25; qualifications for office, 22; powers of, 23, 25; alteration of law respecting election, 346, 347; allowance of salary to, 69, 131, 161.
Grain; see Corn.
Grand Jury; appointment and duties of, 91, 536, 349; to be sworn, 350, 364; names of, 349, 379.
Grants of land; to Jer. Adams, 377; John Adams, 395; John Allyn, 376; Math. Allyn, 372, 375, 419, 436; John Bisssll, 246; Rob. Chapman, 289; Dan. Clark, 376; Aaron Cook, 246, 367; Fairfield, 208; Jas. Fitch, 282; Tho. Ford, 72, 246; Jona. Gilbert, 372; John Gilbert, 393; John Griffin, 410; Gov. Haynes, 82, 234, 250, 298 : Jos. Haynes, 380; Eph. Huit, 70 : Anth. Howkins, 376; Tho. Judd, 376; Rich. Lord, 377; Capt. Mason and his soldiers, 70, 208, 221, 230; John Mason, 209, 224, 406, 432; John Moor, 376; Ens. Olmstead, 391; Pequot (town of,) 208; Mr. Phelps, 419; Jas. Rogers, 340; R. Saltingstall, 72; Sam. Sherman, 436; Saybrook, 419; Mrs. Stone, 413; John Talcott, 376; John Tinker, 359; Sam. Willys, 377; John Winthrop, 64, 223, 243, 246, 337.
of Niantecut Ferry to John Winthrop, 357.
Greenwich, admitted to jurisdiction, 388.
Guards, on Sabbath days, 73, 95, 96, 150, 162,344; to be supplied with powder, 212;
of the Governor, to be allowed powder, 246.
Guilford, admitted to jurisdiction, 387; constable confirmed, 405.

Hastings; officers appointed there, 413, 436.
Hartford, named, 7; bounds of, 8; constable sworn, 43; bounds with Wethersfield, 69; building of the great bridge, 225; allowance to the Governor's guard, 246; ordinary, licensed, 378; train band to have the pre-eminence, 390; difficulties in the church, (see Ecclesiastical Affairs.)
Harvard College; see Education.
Haynes, John, sent to the River's mouth, to treat with the Bay, 10; sent to the Bay, 82; to keep court at the sea side, 126; requested to endeavor to procure an enlargement of Patent, 126; grant of land to, at Pawtucket, 234, 250, 298; death of, 251.
Hemp, cultivation of, enjoined, 61, 64, 79.
Hempstead; 423; constable to be displaced, 424; deputy from, 426; comm'r for, appointed, 428; freemen from, accepted, 429.
Heresy, how punished, 283, 303, 308, 324.
Herman Garrett; claims at Pawcatuck, 259.
Hides; see Leather.
Highways, between towns, how repaired. 91, 527; between Windsor and Hartford, 17, 51, 56, 125; surveyors of, to be appointed, 91, 527.
Hockanum; petition respecting lands there, 362; bridges to be built at, 417.
Homonoscitt, (Hammonasset,) committee to inquire concerning, 400; Saybrook no right to land there, 401; land to be laid out there, 404; petition of John Clow, for lands, 408; orders respecting planting of, 409, 414; bounds with Saybrook, 418.
Hopkins, Edward, allowed to trade at Warranoke, 57; his mill attached, 67; proposes a trade in cotton, 59, 75; desired to adjust dif-

GENERAL INDEX.

ferences with the Dutch, 68, 566; sent to further a union of the colonies, 90; to press soldiers for defence of Uncas, 94; engagement for exportation of corn, 116; comm'r of U. Colonies, 128; agent for Mr. Fenwick, 132, 134; proposed departure for England, 222; absent, 257; letter to be sent to, 261; his death, 341; legacy to the colony, 374, 578; orders respecting his estate, 322, 338, 341, 345, 350, 370, 374, 418.

Horses, penalty for selling to Indians, 284; not to be exported without entering marks, 356.

House of correction to be built, 47; allowance to keeper of, 204.

Householders; unmarried men not to be, 8; not to entertain young men in families, 8.

Huntington; inhabitants of admitted under this government, 348, 377, 379; exempted from taxes, 380; order respecting, 382; officers appointed, 401, 406, 428; freemen admitted, 428.

Idleness, to be punished, 528.

Impressment of men, arms &c. when authorized, 94; for war with the Dutch, 241.

Indians; orders regulating trade with, in arms, &c., 1, 74, 79, 138, 163; in corn, 11, 13, 19; for beaver, 20; in venison, 74; on L. Island, 72; in timber, 214; in liquors, 47, 263, 338, 354; a general trade with, proposed, 113; trade with Dutch and French prohibited, 197, 218; sale of horses, boats &c. to, prohibited, 284; rights of, protected, 14, 355; sachems answerable for their tribes, 19; Indians not to enter houses, handle arms &c., 52, 73, 106, 235, 294; in plantations, at night, may be shot, if they resist, 46, 240; not to bring arms into the towns, 294, 351; smiths not to work for them, 74, 79; measures for redress of wrongs done by, 139, 146; admitted under the government of the English, when, 139; lease of lands to, prohibited, 142, 161; ordered to deliver up their arms, 240; instructors provided for them, 265, 531; committee to counsel and advise them, 288, 299; purchase of land from, prohibited, 402; towns not to permit stragglers to be harbored, 350; other orders relating to, 293, 371, 375, 529.

of Stamford; war declared against, 197.

Nimrod, prosecuted for killing swine, 226.

letter to commissioners, respecting hostilities of the Narragansetts, 353, 576.

murders committed by, at Farmington, 294; plot of 1642, 73.

See Pequots, Mohegans, Narragansetts, Uncas, Sowheag, Sequassen, &c.

Inhabitants; admission of, 21, 96; qualifications of, 293, 351; not to sell lands, without consent of town, 351.

Inquest in case of sudden death, 42, 523.

Insolvent estate; caveat how entered, 151, 518. of Tho. Marshfield, 76, 89, 115, 137, 159.

Inspection, of pipe staves, 67; of yarn, 104; of leather, 75, 287; of weights, and measures, 16, 85, 100, 104, 159, 541.

Interpreter; Tho. Stanton appointed, 10, 175; an allowance made to, 200; Jon. Gilbert appointed, 139.

Invasion, or insurrection; penalty of, 78; provisions in case of hostile, 324.

Inventories of estates of deceased persons, when and how taken, 31, 553; fees for recording, 31, 105. See Estates; and Wills and Inventories.

Jamaica; deputy sent from, 426; comm'r appointed for, 428; freemen admitted, 429.

Jurors, oath of, 57; fees of, 9; how paid in civil actions, 55.

Juries; a majority may give verdict, 84; may be sent out a second and third time, 118, 536; may consist of six or twelve, 118, 138, 535.

Killingworth; see Hammonasset.

Kettle Brook; a bound of Windsor, 7.

Labor; price of, regulated, 52, 65, 205; repeal of order regulating, 61.

Lands, to be recorded, 37; bounds of, to be marked, by owners, 53; not to be sold without consent of the town, 351; not to be purchased of Indians, 402; nor leased to them, 142; tenure of, 536; may be extended, for payment of debts, 151.

Laws, to be revised and recorded, 36; how enacted, 119; Mr. Ludlow desired to prepare a code, 138, 154; adoption of code, and compensation for recording, 216; how to be published, 39; to remain in force under the charter, 387, 440. Code of 1650, 509.

Leather; manufacture and inspection of, 60, 75, 162, 259, 285, 287, 298; sealers of, their appointment and duties, 285, 286, 299, 377.

Letters, respecting the conveyance of, 441.

Licenses, to retailers, &c. 283, 289, 360, 375, 396, 418, 430; may be granted by magistrates, 283; by Gen. Court, 332. See Taverns; and Spiritous Liquors.

Lists, orders respecting, 360, 419, 429, 433. See Rates.

Long Island; orders respecting plantations on, 388–390, 423; taxes, how to be paid, 431; power of magistrates there, 316, 336; payment for losses by fire, 351; powers of comm'rs there, 402; freemen's oath to be administered, 403; controversy with the Dutch respecting, 410, 413; Connecticut officers to forbear exercising authority there, 416; propositions respecting jurisdiction, 423; towns ordered to submit to Conn., 424; declared within charter limits, 427; freemen admitted, 427, 428; proceedings against John Scott, 418, 420, 421, 424, 430, 436. See Southampton, Easthampton, Setauket, Southold, &c.

Ludlow, Roger; sent to treat with the Bay, about the Pequot country, 10; deputy governor, 27; commences a plantation at Uncoa, 35; desired to prepare certain laws, 42; moderator of Part. Court, 86; requested to prepare a body of laws, 138, 154; comm'r to the U. Colonies, 222, 241.

Lying, to be punished, 68, 537.

Magazines, of ammunition to be provided, 15.

Magistrates, how elected, 22; to be nominated previously, 22; oath of, 26; exempted from training &c. 350, and from ferriage, 355; certain powers and duties of, 14, 21, 52, 58, 96, 277, 324, 350, 408.

Malt; distillation of, prohibited, 333.

Manhatoes; see Dutch.

GENERAL INDEX. 601

Manstealing, punishable with death, 77.
Market; weekly, at Hartford, 91.
Marriages; contract to precede covenant, 47, 48; to be recorded, 48, 106; without consent of parents &c. prohibited, 92, 540.
Maratime Affairs; employment of ship carpenter, proposed, 74; supply of cordage, provided for, 79; building of a ship, proposed, 80; encouragement to owners of Wethersfield ship, 200; masters of vessels not to weigh anchor on Sunday, 247; seamen exempted from training, &c. 316.
Marshall; fees of stated, 398, 540.
Mason, John; commander against the Pequots, 9; sent to Agawam, 14; appointed military officer, 15; sent to Warranoke, 17, 19; to demand tribute from L. Island Indians, 70, 164; to press soldiers for defence of Uncas, 94; moves to Saybrook, 155, 156; Chippachaug granted to him, 224; proposes to move to Delaware, 227; sent to L. Island, to deal with the Montauks, 295, 307; sent to examine suspicions of witchcraft at Saybrook, 338; surrenders land bought of Uncas, 359; acquitted of charges brought against him, 403; grant of farm to, 406; liberty to take up farm at Pomakuck, 432.
Massachusetts; combination with, proposed, 30, 82, 91; letter to be sent to, 412; boundaries with Conn., 435; claims the Pequot country, 311, 389, 570.
Massacoe, 31; lands there to be disposed of, 71; to be purchased, 161; committee to dispose of lands there, 323; grant to Lt. Cooke, 246, 364, 367; bounds with Farmington, 376; lands there to be laid out to inhabitants of Windsor, 397.
Massapeage; contract of Richard Haughton for purchase of, 309.
Mattabeseck, 31; settlement proposed, 146; committee, about lands there, 206; made a town, 224; to be rated, 228; named *Middletown*, 250.
Mattanag; residence of Sequassen, 56.
Measures; see Weights and Measures.
Menunketeseck, land at, granted Mr. Fitch, 282.
Middletown, named, 250; mill there, 333; committee to settle differences, 343; ordinary keeper, 344; bounds of, 395, 413; church of, (see Ecclesiastical affairs.)
Military Force; repeal of former orders respecting, 16; provision for training, 4; orders respecting, 15, 30, 97, 125, 151, 222, 241; subjects of, 15, 75, 542; who exempt, 15, 62, 316, 349, 350; general trainings, 266, 322; enrolment of troopers, 299, 309; their privileges, 299, 381, 389; rank of companies determined, 390; penalty for disobedience to officers, 432.
officers; Capt. Mason appointed, and salary stated, 15; officers, how chosen, 151; free from watching, &c. 48; commissions to, how issued, 429; of troops of horse, may fill vacancies, 360; officer appointed at *Pequot*, 187; at *Farmington*, 187; at *Wethersfield*, 194.
stores, to be provided, and how, 3, 4, 15, 30, 91, 93, 134, 165, 543; inspection of, 282, 350; cannon to be procured, 70, 74; pikes, 74; arrow-proof coats to be provided, 75;

arms or military stores not to be sold to foreigners, 138, 139, 145, 163;
ammunition &c. rec'd from England, 239, 244.
Mills and Millers; toll dishes to be provided, 331; toll regulated, 393; saw mills, 246, 262.
Mines and minerals; letter of John Winthrop respecting, 222; encouragement to discoverers of, 223, 440.
Ministers; see Ecclesiastical Affairs.
Moderator, of Gen. Court, when to be appointed, 256, 426.
Mohegan; men to be impressed, for the protection of Indians there, 128; see Uncas.
Mr. Brewster's trading house, 209; petition respecting a settlement there, 336; land for John Tinker, at or near, 366. See Norwich.
Money; value of rix dollars stated, 86.
Montacut (Montauk) Indians; 295, 296.
Murder, punishment of, 77.
Mystick and Pawcatuck; order respecting Wm. Chesebrough, 200, 216; he appears before the Court, 216; vessel seized at Pawcatuck, 239; ministry there, 292; Indians, to retain planting ground, 250; proposed separation from Pequot, 293, 299; to pay Mr. Blinman, 300; order respecting, 389; controversy with Massachusetts, about jurisdiction, 389, 405, 570–572; instructions to Serg. Minor, 411; their offences pardoned, 433; ordered to return lists of estate, 434; commissioners appointed there, 435. See Pequot; and Pawcatuck.

Nameage, bounds of, 224.
Narragansetts; expedition against, 261, 263, 273; hostilities with Uncas, at Niantic, 301; letter to Comm'rs of U. Col. relating to, 576; payment of wampum by, 355, 362. See Ninigret.
New Haven; committee to confer with about measures against the Indians, 197; about the ship &c. 244; to confer about union, 396; charter or copy not to be sent there, 405; committee to treat with, 407; declaration of Gen. Court respecting, 415; letter to be sent to, 415; to be required to submit, 437; magistrates continued in office, 440; documents relating to the union with, 586–590.
New London; named, 310, 313; grant to Jas. Rogers, 340; petition from John Tinker, 347; packer appointed, 347; provisions for courts there, 352, 374; orders respecting bounds, 366, 374, 393, 397, 411, 413, 419, 429; ordnance loaned to them, 352; list makers fined for errors in rating, 392, 405.
See Pequot, and Nameag.
Newtown; name changed to *Hartford*, 7.
Newtown, (L. Island); deputy sent from, 406; comm'r for, 428; freemen admitted, 430.
New York, committee appointed to visit,—and settle bounds, 435.
Niantic; (Nianticut) land there granted to Capt. Mason's soldiers, 208, 228, 230; meadow granted to Pequot, 209, 221; right of ferry, to Gov. Winthrop, 357.
Niantic Indians; see Ninigret and Narragansetts.
Ninigret; payment for E. Pomry's mare, demanded from, 227; war with, declared, 261.
Norwottuck; 14, 294, 302.

Norwalk, provision respecting settlement of, 210 ; made a town, 224 ; subject to rule of rating, 228, 355 ; difference with Fairfield, 242 ; with the Indians, 353 ; bounds of, 414, 418 ; orders respecting, 235, 277, 357 ; fined for neglect to return lists, 279, 360.

Norwich, committee to be sent from, about its admission as a town, 374 ; grant to, from Uncas, to be recorded, 393 ; freemen accepted, 406. See Mohegan.

Oaths, forms of, 25, 26, 54, 62, 545 ; of fidelity, to whom administered, 139, 293 ; of allegiance, to be taken, by householders, 439.

Orders ; see Laws.

Ordinaries ; keepers of, to be appointed in each town, 103 ; orders respecting, 154, 338, 533.

Overseers of towns ; see Townsmen.

Oyster Bay ; commissioner for, appointed, 428.

Packers, to be appointed, 391 ; at N. London, 347.

Pacomtuck(et) ; 14, 294, 302.

Particular Court ; see Court, Particular.

Patent : enlargement of, sought, 126 ; Mr. Fenwick requested to go to England, to attend, 128 ; measures for procuring a new, (see Charter) ; the old, never transferred to the colony, 268, 568, 586.

Pawcatuck ; liberty for a trading house there, to Tho. Stanton, 204 ; grant to Mr. Haynes, 234, 250, 298. See Mystick and Pawcatuck.

Peage ; not to be received unless well strung, 179, 546 ; price of fixed, 61, 79.
See Wampum.

Penal laws, to be published &c. 39.

Pequannock ; proceedings of Mr. Ludlow, 35 ; court to be erected there, 36 ; difference with Mr. Prudden, 36 ; to send deputies, 36 ; bounds of, to be settled, 47, 62, 68 ; oath for freemen there, 54. See Stratford.

Indians ; 28, 348 ; see Golden Hill.

Pequot Indians ; war declared against, 9 ; provisions for prosecution of, 9, 10, 11 ; payment of expenses of, 12 ; expedition against, 32.

country ; committee appointed to view, 60 ; grant to Capt. Mason and his soldiers, 70 ; lands to be disposed of by Part. Court, 71 ; controversy with Massachusetts, respecting, 311, 335, 570.

plantation of ; Mr. Winthrop commissioned a magistrate, 164, 179 ; freed from public charges, 185 ; boundaries of, 185, 208, 221; court erected there, 186 ; name of *Fair Harbor* recommended, 186 ; orders respecting, 233, 251, 256, 265 ; proceedings in relation to M. and Pawcatuck, 293, 299, 300 ; ordinary, licensed there, 276, 285, 292 ; support of ministry at, 292 ; dispute with Uncas about lands, 434 ; named *New London*, 310, 313 ; list of estates, 311.

See New London ; Nameage ; Mystick and Pawcatuck.

Petitions to Gen. Court ; fee on entry of. 38.

Pewter-pot brook ; north bound of Wethersfield, 7, 8.

Physicians and surgeons ; Jasper Gunn, exempted from watching &c. 298 ; Tho. Lord, allowed a compensation, 234 ; Dan. Porter's salary stated, 279, 290, 377.

Pipe staves ; size and price, regulated, 69, 79 ; inspection of, 67 ; exportation of, 200.

Pitch and tar, manufacture of, 91, 114, 248 ; first made by J. Griffin, 410.

Pleas, to be filed with Secretary, before trial, 85.

Plymouth ; letter to be sent to, about Warwick, 220 ; sale by, to Windsor, 53.

Podunk Indians ; their quarrel with Sequassen, 304 ; orders respecting them, 307, 344, 371 ; lands to be laid out, 344 ; agreement with Tho. Burnam, 345, 346, 364.

Poisoning, punishable with death, 77.

Pomakuck ; farm granted Maj. Mason there, 432.

Poquannock ; see Pequannock.

Pounds and pound breach ; orders respecting, 379, 546.

Powder ; see Military Stores.

Prison ; repairs of. 230 ; addition to be made to 430. See House of Correction.

Provisions, not to be exported, 236, 258, 383 ; to be reserved for public use, 240, 383.

Public debts ; see Debts.

Pyquag ; name of Wethersfield, 19.

Quakers, orders respecting, 283, 303, 308, 324.

Quinnabaug, proposed settlement there, by Gov. Winthrop, 337 ; inhabitants of, admitted to jurisdiction, 337.

Quinnipiac ; 28, 31, 32, 35, 58.
See New Haven.

Quorum, of Gen. Court, how formed, 24, 119 ; of Comm'rs of U. Colonies, 157.

Rape, punishable with death, 77.

Rates ; levy of, 12, 30, 32, 48, 79, &c.
to be collected by treasurer, 12 ; apportionment of, 25 ; for repair of fort, 95, 139 ; in what articles payable, 13, 61, 69, 79, 550 ; collection of, 113, 213, 215, 284, 357, 362, 391, 393, 547 ; assessment of, 59, 380, 390, 548.

Real Estate ; see Lands.

Rebellion ; how punished, 78.

Recognizances, fees on, 196.

Recorders, to be chosen in each town, 37, 552 ; to record lands, 37 ; marriages and births, 48, 105 ; deeds and mortgages, 38, 83 ; wills and inventories, 38.

Records, of penal laws &c., to be made in each town, 39 ; of marriages &c. 48, 105 ; copies, how authenticated, 38 ; to have force in other colonies, 179 ; orders respecting, 551–554.

Registers ; see Recorders.

Replevin ; bond to prosecute, to be given, 105.

Retailers ; see Licenses.

Rhode Island ; fugitives harbored by, 220 ; commission to Tho. Baxter, 253 ; bounds with, to be settled, 435.

River, purchase of ; see Saybrook ; and Fenwick, George.

Robin Cassasinamon ; allowed to retain the Mohegan (or Pequot) tributaries, 292 ; note respecting him, 292 ; Mohegans to remain with, (Seano,) 340 ; land to be set out for, 440.

Rum ; see Spirituous Liquors.

Sales, at excessive rates, prohibited,
of land, to be recorded, 37, 152, 552 ; by officer, on execution, 152 ; after caveat entered, void, 152.

GENERAL INDEX. 603

Salt, proposed manufacture of, on L. Island, 68.
Saybrook; tax for repairs of fort, 95, 139, 161; orders respecting, 128, 161; dwelling house to be erected, 187, 188, 200, 206; lay out of lands, 188; fencing of common fields, 232; grant to, from Mr. Fenwick, 282; provisions for defence of, 237, 238; order respecting farm at 6 mile island, 333; proposed settlement of Mohegan, 336; ferry authorized, 391; enforcement of town orders, 353; proposed plantation east of river, 419; orders respecting, 418, 429.
purchase of; see Fenwick, George.
Seal, of the colony; order respecting, 386.
Sealers; see Weights and Measures; and Leather.
Seamen, exempted from training, 316.
Secretary; election of Mr. Hopkins, 27; to record grants of land &c. 38; to cause laws to be published, 39, 555; fees on entry of civil actions &c. 196, 277; for recording, 277, 331; on licenses to retailers, 333; compensation for recording code of 1650, 216; increase of fees, 277.
Secrets, of the Court; penalty for disclosing, 39, 520.
Select men; see Townsmen.
Sequassen; reference to treaty with, 28; Rich. Lyman complains against, 33; a friend of the English, 56; lived at Mattanag, 56; charged with plotting against the English, 73; allied with Uncas, against the Podunks, 304; Major Mason's testimony respecting his defeat by Uncas, 434.
Sequin; see Sowheag.
Servants; see Apprentices.
Setauk(et;) petition from, 341; admitted to jurisdiction, 365; committee to settle matters there, 406; called *Ashford*, 421; commissioner appointed, 428.
Sheep; at what value rated, 349.
Sickness; intercourse with New Netherlands suspended, during prevalence of, 398; among the Indians, 398.
Sodomy, punishable with death, 77.
Soldiers; see Military Force.
Southampton; admitted to jurisdiction, 129; copy of combination with, 566; complaint of Jonas Wood, 281; difference with the Indians, 295, 316; letter to be sent to, 307; powers of magistrates, 336; orders respecting, 134, 348, 368, 402; acts of court there approved, 414.
Southold; admitted to jurisdiction, 386; letter from, 386; freemen accepted, 388; magistrates appointed, 390, 402, 428; privileges confirmed, 406.
Sowheag (Sequin;) Wethersfield purchase from, 5; murderers harbored by, 31; accounted an enemy, 58; implicated in Indian plot, 73; preparations for war against, 74; difficulties with Wethersfield, 19; land reserved for his posterity, at Wonggum, 434.
Spirituous Liquors; sale of ,prohibited, 100; regulated, 154, 263, 283, 331, 332, 533; sale to Indians prohibited, 255, 263; not to be imported, 255, 322; duty on, 255, 332.
Springfield; declaration of the Court, respecting the payment of fort rate by, 189.
See Agawam.
Stamford, admitted to jurisdiction, 388; order respecting, 403; account of constables there, (for pursuit of regicides,) disallowed, 393; declared to belong to Connecticut, 410, 411.
Stanton, Thomas; sent to Warranoke, 17; appointed interpreter, 19; allowed to make a voyage to L. Island, 72; quarrel with Rich. Lord, 94; controversy with Math. Allyn, 123; his salary discontinued, 139; restored, 175, 200; liberty to erect trading house at Pawcatuck, 204; sent to Narragansett, 227; proceedings against, 303; fined, 306; comm'r at Mystick and Pawcatuck, 435.
Staves; see Pipe Staves.
Stonington; 570. See Mystick and Pawcatuck; and Pequot.
Stratford; magistrates sent there, 86; letter to be sent to, 105; ferry, 163; complaint about mode of rating, 201; assistants appointed, 233, 252; constables fined for neglect, 278; bounds of, 281, 367, 402; troop raised, 351; difference with Lt. Seely, 403.
See Cupheage and Pequannock.
Stubbornness, of children; law to be provided against, 80, 138; how punished, 78, 515.
Sumptuary law;, relating to excess in dress, 64.
Surveyors of highways; see Highways.
Swine: orders respecting, 1, 64, 83, 118, 131, 188, 214, 291, 557.

Tanners and Curriers; see Leather.
Tantonimo; his quarrel with Sequassen, 304; agreement with Tho. Burnam, 346, 347.
See Podunk Indians.
Tar; see Pitch and Tar.
Taverns; see Ordinaries.
Taxes; see Rates.
Thanksgiving, days of, appointed, 33, 113, 201, 209, 212, 225, 235, 262, 266, 279, 285, 307, 325, 343, 357, 373, 412, 435; to be appointed by magistrates, in recess, 277.
Theft; punished, 110, 115; by Indians, how punishable, 52.
Timber; orders for presentation of, 60, 67.
Tobacco; use of, regulated, 53, 146, 153, 558; duty on imported, 380.
Toll, on exports, payable to Mr. Fenwick, 119–122; of millers, regulated, 393.
Towns, powers of, 36–39; clerks of, 37, 38, 105, 151; bounds of, 512.
Townsmen, how appointed,—and their duties, 37, 101, 118, 214.
Trade; right of, at Waranocoe, granted to Mr. Hopkins, 57; at Pawcatuck, to Tho. Stanton, 204; at Mohegan, by Jon. Brewster, 209; with the Dutch, prohibited, 114, 197; restrictions on, removed, 261, 391, 402.
Treasurer; appointed, 12, 27; orders respecting, 26, 30, 31, 68; allowance of salary to, 307.
See Rates.
Trespasses, by Indians, to be paid by the Sachems, 19; by cattle, law to be provided concerning, 60; damages, how assessed, 558.
Tribute, of the seaside Indians, called for, 52; Sequassen exonerates himself from, 56; due from L. Island Indians, 79, 164.
Tunxis; (Unxus ʃSepus;) committee to view, 42; orders respecting planting of, 52; hostile meeting of Indians there, apprehended, 133; plantation there, named *Farmington*, 133.

GENERAL INDEX.

Uncas; treaty with proposed, 28, 32; men sent to abide with, 65; permitted to enter the plantations, 106; proposed war, for the defence of, 130; order respecting, 186; difference with Pequot, 251, 256; beleaguered by the Narragansetts, 301; provision for his defence, 302; allied with Sequassen, against the Podunks, 304, 306; agreement with Rich. Haughton, 309; refuses to pay a fine, 355; his grant to Norwich to be recorded, 393.

Uncoa; (Uncoway;) Mr. Ludlow's proceedings there, 35, 41; bounds with Pequannock, 47; tribute from Indians there, 52; bounds with Cupheage, 53; court established, 53; magistrates sent there, 86; letter to be sent to, about rating, 105.

Union with New Haven. See New Haven.

United Colonies; acts of, respecting maintenance of ministers, 112; poor scholars, at Cambridge, 112; force of verdicts, in other colonies, 113; sale of ammunition &c. to foreigners, 113; wampum, 179.

Unxus Sepus; 42, 52. See Tunxis.

Verdicts, may be given by a majority of the jury, 84; to be of force in the other colonies, 113; may be varied by the court, when, 118, 138; may be given by jury of 6 or 12, 118; *special*, when to be given, 85.

Wages: orders regulating, 52, 61, 65, 205; may be paid in corn, 61.

Wampum; value of stated, 13, 61, 79; to be well strung, 179, 546.

War; with the Pequots, 9–12; with Stamford Indians, 197, 198; with the Dutch, 241, 244, 259; with Ninigret and the Niantics, 130; against Sowheag, proposed, 58, 74.

Warranoke(-ocoe); exclusive trade with, granted Mr. Hopkins, 57; *Indians*, 14, 17.

Warrants, for collection of fines, 151; in civil actions, 196; for election, 23.

Warwick; reference of question of jurisdiction, to the Comm'rs of U. Colonies, 220.

Watch and Ward, to be maintained in all the towns, 1, 28, 560; who exempt from, 15, 48, 62, 99, 234, 298, 349, 350; orders respecting, 74, 196, 350; constable to give charge to, 403.

Watertown; breadth of, to be surveyed, 3; church covenant approved, 2; controversy with Lieut. Seely, about lands, 4, 49; name changed to *Wethersfield*, 7.

Weights and Measures; standards of, how regulated, 16, 85, 99, 104, 159, 541.

Westchester; included in charter limits, 387; committee to report about settlement of, 403;

to settle differences there, 406; accepted as a town, 411; officers appointed, 412, 426.

Wethersfield; named, 7; boundaries, 7; purchase from Sowheag, 2; treaty with Sequassen, 28; desire a plantation at Tunxis, 42; ask an answer respecting Uncoa, 41; constable sworn, 43; difference with Mr. Smith, 45, 87, 90; agreement with the adventurers, 4, 49, 63; number of the guard, decreased, 162; ship, owned there, 200; first settled, of the River towns, 513.

See Watertown; and Ecclesiastical Affairs.

Wickford, named, and officers appointed, 407.

Wills and Inventories; orders respecting, 34, 179; to be proved and recorded, 38, 553; fees for recording, 105, 277, 556.

record of; of Wm. Butler, 482; Ed. Chalkwell, 492; Rob. Day, 487; John Elsen, 480; Wm. Frost, 465; Giles Gibbs, 504; Tho. Hooker, 498; John Horskins, 483; Eph. Huit, 458; Blaynch Hunt, 457; Wm. Lotham, 474; Rich. Lyman, 81, 442; Tho. Nowell, 506; Jas. Olmstead, 446; Henry Packs(?) 56; John Porter, 475; John Purkas, 466; Tho. Scott, 453; Henry Smith, 502; Wm. Spencer, 449; Joyce Ward, 451; Wm. Whiting, 493; Geo. Willis, 468; Ed. Veir, 463.

For Inventories &c. of intestate estates,' see Estates.

Windsor; named, 7; bounded, 7, 8, 72; bridge and meeting house built, 42; constable sworn, 43; purchase from Plymouth, 53; ferry established, 71,—and granted, 174, 281, 298, 310, 394; families living remote from neighbors, 196; petition of inhabitants of, 312; church; see Ecclesiastical Affairs.

See Dorchester.

Wine; see Spirituous Liquors.

Winthrop, John; commissioned to execute justice, at Pequot, 157; a magistrate, there, 164; nominated magistrate, 179; made free, 207; letter from, respecting mines &c., 222; resided at Nameag, 224; chosen governor, 297; requested to reside at Hartford, 298, 301, 306; grant to, at Quinnabaug, 337; ferry at Niantic cut, 357; prepares the address to the King, 367; agent to procure charter, 368, 579'; allowance to, 369; acknowledgment of his services to the colony, 416.

Witchcraft, punishable with death, 77; suspicions of, at Saybrook, 338; case of Jos. Garlick, from L. Island, 573.

Wolves; bounty for killing, 149, 561; to be paid by the towns, 377; penalty for taking from the pit of another person, 283; repeal of order granting a bounty to Indians for killing, 367.

ERRATA.

Page   9, 12th line from bottom, for *only*, read *any*.
"   12, 15th line from top, for *John*, read *Jehu*.
"   67, in list of deputies, for *John* Burr, read *Jehu* Burr.
"   75, 7th line from bottom, for [49] read [91].
"   144, 17th line from bottom, for *Fiske*, read *Fishe*.
"   151, 16th line from bottom, for [169] read [164].
"   207, in list of deputies, for *Nath:* Griswold read *Math:* Griswold.
"   280, in list of magistrates, *John* Clarke ; the first name is partially *erased*, in the original.
"   343, 3d line from top, for 50, read 59.
"   472, 2d line from bottom, (in note,) for page 122, read page 136.
"   487, 19th line from top, for 1848, read 1648.

www.ingramcontent.com/pod-product-compliance
Lightning Source LLC
Chambersburg PA
CBHW071429300426
44114CB00013B/1363